SPORT IN SOCIETY

ISSUES AND CONTROVERSIES

SPORT IN SOCIETY

ISSUES AND CONTROVERSIES

Jay J. Coakley, Ph.D.
Center for the Study of Sport and Leisure
University of Colorado
Colorado Springs

FIFTH EDITION

with 120 *illustrations*

 Mosby

St. Louis Baltimore Boston Chicago London Madrid Philadelphia Sydney Toronto

Dedicated to Publishing Excellence

Publisher: James M. Smith
Editor: Vicki Malinee
Developmental Editors: Cheryl Gelfand-Grant, Amy Winston
Designer: David Zielinski

FIFTH EDITION

Printed in the United States of America

Mosby–Year Book, Inc
11830 Westline Industrial Drive
St. Louis, Missouri 63146

Library of Congress Cataloging in Publication Data

Coakley, Jay J.
    Sport in society : issues and controversies / Jay J. Coakley. —
5th ed.
        p.   cm
    Includes bibliographical references and index.
    ISBN 0-8016-7557-X
    1. Sports—Social aspects.   2. Sports—Psychological aspects.
I. Title.
GV706.5.C63   1994
306.4'83—dc20   93-32720
                                                            CIP

96 97 98 C/D 9 8 7 6 5 4 3

PREFACE

PURPOSE OF THE TEXT

The fifth edition of *Sport in Society: Issues and Controversies* has a twofold purpose: *first*, it is designed to provide a sound introduction to the sociology of sport; and *second*, it is written to encourage students to ask questions and think critically about sports as parts of social life.

I have organized the chapters to focus on curiosity-arousing issues. These issues are discussed in terms of recent research and theory in the sociology of sport. Although the concepts and source materials are not exclusively taken from sociology, discussions throughout the book are grounded in a sociological approach. Therefore, the emphasis is clearly on sports and sport-related behaviors as they occur in social and cultural contexts.

FOR WHOM IS IT WRITTEN?

Sport in Society is written for students taking their first look at sports from a sociological perspective. The content of each chapter is presented so it can be understood by beginning college students in either physical education or sociology. The discussion of issues does not presume prior courses in social science or in-depth experiences in sports. However, I have tried to present materials in ways that push students to think more critically about sports and how sports are related to their social lives.

Since the book is organized in term of an "issues approach" the content of many chapters is useful for those concerned with sport policies and program administration. My emphasis throughout the book is on making sports more democratic and sport participation more accessible to all people.

CHANGES IN THE FIFTH EDITION

Nearly 35% of the fifth edition of *Sport in Society* has been rewritten. Updated material has been added to all chapters, and half the chapters have been reorganized in response to new research findings and new theoretical developments in the field. More than 175 new references are cited in this edition, and most highlight work published since 1989.

New Theory Chapter

Recent developments in theory have raised serious questions about the scope and goals of social theory. These developments are reflected in this revised chapter. There is an extended discussion of critical theory coupled with examples of research based on critical theory. There is a new section on symbolic interactionism that contains examples of research based on interactionist frameworks. The goal of this chapter is to show students how research is informed by theory.

Revision Themes

New materials in this edition generally reflect recent work done on gender and gender relations, the connection between sports and cultural ideology, and the globalization of sports. The inclusion of these materials has led to a reworking of the chapters on gender relations, race and ethnicity, and class relations (Chapters 9-11); it has also led to major new sections in other chapters.

New Topics

New information in this edition highlights idiocultures created by little league baseball players (Ch. 5), the Sport Ethic and deviance in sports (Ch. 6), coaching education programs (Ch. 8), Latinos and Asian Americans in sports (Ch. 10), retirement from sports (Ch. 11), images and messages in mediated sports (Ch. 13), politics in sports (Ch. 14), budget crises and athletes' rights in varsity sports (Ch. 15), problems encountered by Christian athletes and organizations (Ch. 16), and strategies for changing sports (Ch. 17).

New boxed sections highlight special topics including the body and the sociology of sport (Ch. 1), feminist theory (Ch. 2), the history of Native American sports (Ch. 3), the Military Model and the Partnership Model of sports (Ch. 7), women bodybuilders (Ch. 9), comparison of employment contracts for two basketball coaches—a man and a woman (Ch. 11), sports and religions around the world (Ch. 16), and the use of rituals in sports (Ch. 16).

New Photographs

There are 35 new photos in this edition. The use of photos, cartoons, tables, and figures have been carefully planned to visually break up the text and make reading more interesting for students (and instructors!). I spent many days taking and selecting photos directly related to the content of each of the chapters.

INSTRUCTOR'S MANUAL AND TEST BANK

An Instructor's Manual has been developed to assist those using *Sport in Society* in classroom settings. It includes the following:

Chapter outlines. These can be used to get a quick overall view of the topics covered in each chapter. They are useful for organizing lectures, and they can be reproduced and given to students as study guides.

Test questions (multiple choice). These questions have been designed to test the student's awareness of central points made in each chapter. The focus is on ideas and concepts rather than single, isolated facts. For the instructor with large classes these questions are useful for chapter quizzes, midterm tests, or final examinations.

Discussion/essay questions. These questions can be used for tests or to generate classroom discussions. They are designed to encourage the student to synthesize and apply materials in one or more of the sections in each chapter. None of the questions asks the students to simply list points or give definitions.

Class projects. Projects are to be used in conjunction with standard classroom materials. Although the projects are usually quite simple, they are meant to be starting points for discussion leading to an understanding of chapter content.

ACKNOWLEDGMENTS

This book has evolved out of ideas coming from a variety of sources. Thanks must first be extended to students in my sociology of sport courses. They have provided constructive critiques of my ideas and opened my eyes to new ways of looking at sports as social phenomena. Special thanks is also deserved by Robert Hughes and Cheryl Cole, two of my colleagues at the University of Colorado in Colorado Springs. Each in their own way has inspired my own critical thinking about sports in society.

My appreciation goes to the publisher's reviewers. Their suggestions were crucial in the planning and writing of this edition. They include the following:
Dana Brooks, West Virginia University
Don Chu, California State University, Chico
Steve Houseworth, Illinois State University
Peter Kasson, University of Wisconsin, Stevens Point
James LaPointe, University of Kansas
Jan Rintala, Northern Illinois University
Many of the photographs in this edition were selected from the files of the *Colorado Springs Gazette Telegraph*. Thanks go to sports editor Ralph Routon and the fine photographers who cover sports in this area. Other photos were provided by friend and photographer, Tini Campbell, and by the Sports Information office at the University of Colorado in Boulder.

Jay Coakley

TO NANCY, DENNIS, AND DANIELLE
FOR REASONS HAVING NOTHING TO
DO WITH THIS BOOK

CONTENTS

1 The Sociology of Sport: What is it and Why Study it? 1

About This Book, 2
About This Chapter, 2
What is the Sociology of Sport? 3
Why Study Sports as Social
    Phenomena? 5
What is the Current Status of the Sociology
    of Sport? 9
What are Sports? 12
Sports: A Definition, 21
Summary: Why Study Sports? 23

2 Using Social Theories: What can They Tell Us about Sports in Society? 25

Theories in Sociology, 26
General Theories about Sports
    and Society, 27
Alternative Theoretical Approaches, 34
Using Sociological Theories:
    A Comparison, 47
Summary and Conclusions: Is There a Best
    Theoretical Approach to Use when
    Studying Sports? 49

3 A Look at the Past: How have Sports Changed Throughout History? 52

An Opening Note on History, 53
Sports Vary by Time and Place, 54
Games in Ancient Greece: Beyond the
    Myths (1000 BC to 100 BC), 55
Roman Sport Events: Spectacles and
    Gladiators (100 BC to 500 AD), 57
Tournaments and Games during the Middle
    Ages: Separation of the Masters and the
    Masses (500 to 1300), 58
The Renaissance, Reformation, and
    Enlightenment: Games and Diversions
    (1300 to 1800), 60

The Industrial Revolution: The Emergence
    of Standardized Sport Forms (1780 to
    Present), 61
Summary and Conclusion: Looking at Sport
    at Different Times and Different
    Places, 74

4 Competition in Sports: Does it Prepare People for Life? 77

The Concept of Competition, 78
Reward Structures and Competition in
    Sports, 81
Competition and Character, 92
Sport Competition as Preparation
    for Life, 98
Summary and Conclusions, 102

5 Organized Sport Programs for Children: Are They Worth the Effort? 104

Formal vs. Informal Games:
    A Comparison, 106
What Happens in Organized Programs? 114
Recommendations for Changing Organized
    Sport Programs for Children, 126
Prospects for Change, 129
Conclusion: Are Organized Youth Sport
    Programs Worth the Effort? 132

6 Deviance in Sports: Is it Getting Out of Control? 134

Problems Faced when Studying Deviance in
    Sports, 135
Defining and Studying Deviance in Sports:
    Three Approaches, 136
Research on Deviance among Athletes, 144
Performance-Enhancing Substances: A Case
    Study of Deviance in Sports, 150
Summary and Conclusion: Is Deviance in
    Sports Out of Control? 159

7 Aggression in Society: Are Sports a Cure or a Cause? 162

What is Aggression? 163
Sports as a "Cure" for Aggression in Society, 163
Sports as a "Cause" of Aggression in Society, 170
Sports and Aggression among Spectators, 179
Summary and Conclusion: Cure or Cause? 186

8 Coaches: How do They Fit into Sport Experiences? 189

The Coach in Recent History, 190
Coaches as Individuals: What are Their Personal Characteristics? 191
The Role of Coach and the Behavior of Coaches, 193
Role Conflict: How Do Off-the-Field Roles Affect Coaches? 198
Coaching as a Subculture: How are the Behavior Patterns of Coaches Perpetuated and Passed on to New Coaches? 201
Coaches as Significant Others": Do They Influence Athletes? 202
Summary and Conclusions: How to Coaches Fit in? 206

9 Gender: Is Equity the Only Issue? 208

Participation and Equity Issues, 209
Ideological and Structural Issues, 225
Summary and Conclusions: Is Equity the Only Issue? 236

10 Race and Ethnicity: Are Skin Color and Cultural Heritage Important in Sports? 239

Culture, Sports, and the Meaning of Race, 240
Racial Ideology and Sports: A Critical Analysis, 242
Sport Participation Patterns: Group by Group, 255
The Racial Desegregation of Certain American Sports, 262
Sports and Intergroup Relations, 266

Summary and Conclusion: Are Skin Color and Cultural Heritage Important? 271

11 Class Relations and Social Mobility: Is Sport Participation a Path to Success? 274

Sports and Class Relations, 275
Opportunities in Sports: Myth and Reality, 281
Sport Participation and Occupational Careers Among Former Athletes, 294
Summary and Conclusion: Is Sport Participation a Path to Success? 300

12 Sports and the Economy: What are the Characteristics of Commercial Sports? 302

Emergence and Growth of Commercial Sports, 303
Commercialization and Changes in Sports, 307
Owners, Sponsors, and Promoters in Commercial Sports, 311
Legal Status and Incomes of Athletes in Commercial Sports, 317
Summary and Conclusions: The Characteristics of Commercial Sports, 327

13 Sports and the Media: Could They Survive Without Each Other? 330

Unique Features of the Media, 331
Sports and the Media: A Two-Way Relationship, 333
Images and Messages in Media Sports, 342
The Professional of Sports Journalism, 350
Summary and Conclusion: Could Sports and the Media Live Without Each Other? 356

14 Sports and Politics: Can They be Kept Separate? 358

The Sports-Government Connection, 359
Government Involvement and "The Common Good," 368
Political Consequences of International Sports, 368
The Globalization of Sports, 378

Politics in Sports, 379
Summary and Conclusions: Can Sports and
    Politics be Kept Separate? 383

**15 Sports in High School and College: Do
Varsity Sports Programs Contribute to
Education? 386**

Arguments For and Against Interscholastic
    Sports, 387
Interscholastic Sports and the Experiences of
    High School Students, 387
Intercollegiate Sports and the Experiences of
    College Students, 394
Do Schools Benefit From Varsity Sports
    Programs? 405
Varsity High School Sports: Problems and
    Recommendations, 409
Intercollegiate Sports: Problems and
    Recommendations, 413
Summary and Conclusions: Are Varsity
    Sports Educational? 417

**16 Sports and Religion: Is it a Promising
Combination? 420**

How Do Sociologists Define and Study
    Religion? 421
What are the Similarities and Differences
    Between Sports and Religion? 422
Sports and Christian Organizations and
    Beliefs, 428
The Consequences of Combining Sports and
    Religious Beliefs, 437
Summary and Conclusion: Is it a Promising
    Combination? 441

**17 Sports in the Twenty-First Century: What
can we Expect? 444**

Models of Sports for the 21st Century, 445
Continuing Trends and Expected Changes in
    Sports, 451
Conclusion: The Challenge of Making the
    Future, 457

Bibliography, B-1

CHAPTER 1

(Colorado Springs Gazette Telegraph and Jerilee Bennett)

The more I learned . . . studying various cultures and countries . . . [the] more apparent it became that all societies in all periods of history have needed some kind of public entertainment, and that it has usually been provided by sports.

James Michener, Author (1976)

. . . sports is an element of American life so pervasive that virtually no individual is untouched by it . . . [The] United States is a nation made up of sports fans . . . [and] sports participants.

Miller Lite Report on American Attitudes Toward Sports (1984)

If sociology seeks to understand human behavior it is difficult to ignore the extent to which sport-related activities and organizations serve as the settings for behavior across a wide range of different societies.

Sociology of Sport Journal (1984)

THE
SOCIOLOGY OF
SPORT

What is it and why study it?

ABOUT THIS BOOK

Most of you reading this book have personally experienced sports, as athletes or spectators or both. But many of you have probably not spent much time thinking about issues that go beyond the physical and emotional experiences of sport participation, the performances of others, and the competitive outcomes of events. This book focuses on these issues. It deals with what might be called the deeper game associated with sports, a game through which sports are connected to the social and cultural worlds in which we live. For example, when students in American high schools participate on a varsity basketball team, their participation may effect their status within the school and have implications for how they are treated by teachers and fellow students; it may have implications for their honor and prestige in the surrounding community, for their self-images and self-esteem; it may even affect future relationships and opportunities. The sociology of sport tries to understanding this deeper game associated with sports and sport participation.

Sociology provides concepts, theoretical approaches, and research methods for describing and understanding social relations, that is, the ways human beings feel about, think about, and relate to each other. Sociology focuses on the connection between behavior and the social and cultural context in which behavior occurs. The social and cultural context encompasses political and economic relationships as well as the meanings and understandings that underlie the ways people make sense out of their own lives and the world around them. In this book we will use sociology to describe and understand issues related to sport as a social and cultural phenomenon.

Culture consists of the ways of life created by people in a particular society as they struggle over the meanings of objects, relationships, and events that make up their experience, as they struggle over how they will organize their relationships with one another, and as they struggle to meet their own needs and achieve some sense of personal significance in the process. Sport itself is part of culture. Like other cultural practices, sports are the creations of groups of people. In other words, they are what we might call social constructions. As social constructions sports can be studied in terms of how they are connected to the interests and resources of the people in particular societies, communities, organizations, and groups. This is why sociologists want to know why certain physical activities have been selected and designated as sports in particular societies, why sports are organized in certain ways, and why certain meanings are associated with sports and sport participation in different social groups, communities, and societies.

Sports differ from one culture to the next, and people create and use sports for a variety of purposes. The types of sports played in a group, how they are organized, the resources dedicated to sports and sport programs, who gets to play sports, the conditions under which sport participation occurs, who sponsors and controls sports, the rewards that go to athletes, and the meanings associated with participation are all connected to social relations. This is the "stuff" of the sociology of sport, and this book presents discussions of 16 major issues related to sport in society.

ABOUT THIS CHAPTER

The purpose of this chapter is to describe the sociology of sport as a subfield of physical education and sociology and explain what is meant by the term **sport** as it is used in the following chapters.

This chapter focuses on four questions:

1. What is the sociology of sport?
2. Why study sports as social phenomena?
3. What is the current status of the sociology of sport as a field of study?
4. What are sport and how are they related to similar activities, such as play, recreation, games, and dramatic spectacle?

The answers to these questions will serve as guides for understanding the materials in Chapters 2 to 17.

WHAT IS THE SOCIOLOGY OF SPORT?

This question would be best answered at the end of the book instead of the beginning. However, you should have at least a brief preview of what you will be reading for the next sixteen chapters.

Most people in the field agree that the sociology of sport is a subdiscipline of sociology that focuses on the relationship between sports and social relations. Its major goals are to understand the following:

1. How and why sport in general and certain sports in particular have been created and organized in certain ways
2. The connection between sports and other spheres of social life, such as family, education, politics, the economy, the media, and religion
3. How sports and sport participation inform the way people think about their own bodies and about gender, social class, race and ethnicity, disability, and so on
4. The social organization, group behavior, and social interaction patterns that exist within sport settings
5. The cultural, structural, and situational factors affecting sports and sport experiences
6. The social processes that occur in conjunction with sports, processes such as socialization, competition, cooperation, conflict, social stratification, and social change.

The Sociology of Sport: What Is It and How Does It Differ from the Psychology of Sport?

Psychologists study behavior in terms of things that occur inside individuals; sociologists study behavior in terms of the social and cultural settings in which individuals make choices, form relationships with others, and create the social organization needed to survive and exert control over they way they live their lives.

Psychologists focus on motivation, perception, cognition, self-esteem, self-confidence, attitudes, and personality; they also deal with interpersonal dynamics including communication, leadership, and social influence. Sociologists, on the other hand, focus on culture, social organization, power relations, social inequality, socialization, and social change. Sociologists are concerned with how behavior, relationships, and group dynamics are related to the social meanings associated with age, gender, race, ethnicity, disability, and social class and with the power relations that occur in connection with these and other characteristics that people may define as socially relevant.

Whereas psychologists deal with what we might call the "personal troubles" of individuals, sociologists are concerned with "social issues" affecting entire categories or groups of people. For example, when dealing with burnout among young athletes a psychologist would focus on stress in the lives of individual athletes and initiate clinical intervention in an effort to help them manage stress through goal-setting, personal skills development, and the use of relaxation and concentration techniques. A sociologist, on the other hand, would focus on the social organization of sport programs and athletes' social relationships with parents, peers, and coaches. Since burnout is usually related to a lack of power, sociological intervention would emphasize the need for changes in the way sport programs are organized. These changes would give athletes more control over the issues that affect their lives. This is one of the reasons why sociology has not been used much by those who have power and control in sport organizations. These people are hesitant to use any approach that would lead to conclusions calling for shifts in the way their power and control are exercised within those organizations.

When it comes to sport, a psychologist would help individual athletes manage stress and develop imagery and concentration skills for the purpose of maximizing athletes' personal growth and development and their performance potential. A sociologist, on the other hand, would help people in sport develop policies, programs, and organizational structures that would meet the developmental needs and interests of sport participants, reduce tensions between groups and organizations, and extend sport participation opportunities to a wider range of people.

Like any science, sociology can be used in either of two ways: (1) to assist people in positions of power as they relate to others and strive to achieve organizational goals and maintain their power in the process, or (2) to assist those who lack power to make choices and create social worlds in which they have autonomy and opportunities to pursue their interests. In other words, sociologists must decide how they are going to "do" sociology and what they want the consequences of their work to be. Sociologists cannot escape the fact that the interests of different groups of people are not always the same, that group interests often are in conflict. In light of this, I am interested in achieving four goals as you read this book. I hope to help you use sociology to (1) identify and understand social problems and social issues, (2) learn about the social consequences of different forms of social organization, and (3) understand, manage, and change those parts of your lives related to sports and sport participation, and (4) think about how sports might be transformed to provide those who lack power in the social world opportunities to exercise more control over their lives.

Controversies Created by the Sociology of Sport

Research in the sociology of sport sometimes creates controversy. This is because sociologists often call attention to the need for changes in the organization of sports and the structure of social relations in society as a whole. This often threatens certain people, especially those in positions of power and control in sport organizations, and those who benefit from the way sports are currently organized. These people are the ones with the most to lose if changes are made in social relations and social organization. After all, their power and control have been achieved within existing social structures, and changes in those structures could jeopardize their positions. This leads them to favor approaches to sports

that explain problems in terms of the characteristics of individuals rather than in terms of social conditions. If problems are blamed on individuals, solutions will emphasize better ways of controlling people and teaching them how to adjust to the world as it is, rather than emphasizing changes in the way that world is organized.

The potential for controversy in the sociology of sport can be illustrated by looking at some of the research findings on sport participation among women in many countries around the world. Research shows that married women with children have lower rates of participation than other categories of people. The reason for this is that these women don't have the resources or the opportunities to become involved in sports. They are short of free time; they don't have money for child care; they often lack transportation; there are few sport programs related to their interests and needs; and their husbands often expect them to nurture and provide for the emotional needs of the family.

It is easy to see the potential for controversy when a sociologist would say that changes should be made in the ways women and men relate to each other so that sport participation rates among girls and women might increase. Sociological recommendations for change **would not** focus on giving motivational talks to the women themselves. Instead, the recommendations would focus on the need for child care, affordable opportunities to participate, equal access to opportunities, changes in how husbands and wives relate with each other, legal changes affecting gender equity in sports, and even changes in the way sports are defined and organized.

As you can see, these sociological recommendations would create controversies. They call for community resources to be reallocated on the basis of new priorities, for men to share the resources they use for their sport programs, for husbands to share in child care and homemaking, for the development of job opportunities for women so they will have the resources needed to make choices, for political representatives to pass laws that redefine the rights of women, and for people in sports to engage in critical self-reflection about the meaning and organization of sports and sport competition.

Such changes threaten those who benefit from the way things are organized now. This is why the sociology of sport is sometimes seen as too critical and negative. Studying sports as social phenomena certainly can help us understand more about the world in which we live, but it also forces us to take a critical look at the social conditions that affect our lives on and off playing fields.

In summary, the sociology of sport is concerned with the relationship between sports and society. It focuses on behavior patterns and social processes that occur in sports and explains them in terms of the structure of sports and the social structures in which sport activities exist. It also focuses on the connection between sports and the way people see, evaluate, and participate in their own social worlds. It does not ignore individuals, but its purpose is to highlight the ways people are affected by the world around them and the ways people can and do change that world.

WHY STUDY SPORTS AS SOCIAL PHENOMENA?

Sports Are a Part of People's Lives

The most obvious answer to this question is that sports cannot be ignored because they are such a pervasive part of life in contemporary society. It does not take a sociologist to call our attention to the fact that during the twentieth century the popularity and visibility of sports have grown dramatically in many countries around the world. A survey of the mass media shows that newspapers in most cities devote entire sections of their daily editions to the coverage of sports. This is especially true in North America, where space given to sports coverage frequently surpasses the space given to the economy, politics, or any other single topic of interest. Radio and television stations bring numerous hours of live and taped sporting events to people all around the world. Sport personalities

are objects of attention—as heroes and antiheroes. Young people in many countries are apt to be more familiar with the names of top-level athletes than with the names of their national religious, economic, and political leaders. For a large segment of people of all ages in industrialized countries, sports are likely to be included in their everyday lives through their involvement as participants or spectators, through their reading, or through their conversations with friends and acquaintances.

Sports Are Connected to Major Social Institutions

In most industrial countries sports are clearly connected to events and relationships in each of the major spheres of social life, such as the family, education, politics, economics, and religion. These connections are the topics of various chapters in this book, but it is useful to highlight them at this point.

SPORTS AND FAMILY In North America, for example, millions of children are involved in a variety of organized sport activities throughout the year. It is primarily their parents who organize leagues, coach teams, and attend games. Family schedules are altered to accommodate practices and games. These schedules are also affected by the patterns of sport involvement among adult family members. Watching televised sport events sometimes disrupts family life and at other times provides a collective focus for family attention. In some cases relationships between family members are nurtured and played out during sport activities or in conversations about these activities.

SPORTS AND EDUCATION At all levels of education sports have become integral parts of the experiences of North American students. Most schools in the United States and Canada sponsor interscholastic sport teams, and it is not uncommon for these teams to attract more attention than academic programs do among students and community residents. At the university level some schools even use their teams to promote the quality of their academic programs,

Family schedules are often altered to accommodate sports involvement. *A*, Sometimes participation disrupts family life; *B*, sometimes it provides a collective focus for family activities.

making or losing large amounts of money in the process. In the United States some large universities have public relations profiles built on (or seriously damaged by) the reputations of their sport programs.

SPORTS AND POLITICS Sports are often linked to feelings of national pride. Despite frequent complaints about mixing sports and politics, most North Americans have no second thoughts about displaying national flags and playing national anthems at sporting events. Political leaders at various levels of government promote themselves by associating with sports as both participants and spectators. In fact, it has become a tradition for U.S. presidents to make congratulatory postgame phone calls to the locker rooms of championship teams. International sports have become hotbeds of political controversy in recent years. And both the United States and Canada, as well as most other countries around the world, have used sports to enhance their reputations in international political relationships.

SPORTS AND THE ECONOMY The economies of most Western industrial countries have been affected by the billions of dollars spent every year for game tickets, sports equipment, participation fees, athletic club membership dues, and bets placed on favorite teams and athletes. The economies of many local communities have been affected by the existence of major sport teams. In some countries tax dollars partially support those teams. In the United States some universities gross millions of dollars per week at their football games and pay their athletes the equivalent of minimum wages. Television networks and cable stations in the United States pay hundreds of millions of dollars for the rights to televise games and events. Many professional athletes and a few amateurs make impressive sums of money from various combinations of salaries, appearance fees, and endorsements. Advertisers have paid well over $1 million for a single minute of commercial television time during the Super Bowl, and they have paid well over a million dollars to have their corporate names associated with national teams and major events such as the Olympics.

SPORTS AND RELIGION There is even a relationship between sports and religion. For example, local churches and church groups in both the United States and Canada are some of the most active sponsors of athletic teams and leagues. Parishes and congregations have been known to revise their Sunday service schedules to accommodate their members who would not miss an opening kickoff in an NFL game for anything—not even their religious beliefs. Religious rituals are increasingly used in conjunction with sport participation, and there are a few large nondenominational religious organizations that have been created for the sole purpose of attracting and converting athletes to Christian beliefs. Other religious organizations have used athletes as spokespersons for their belief systems in the hope of converting people who strongly identify with sports.

Sports Inform Cultural Ideology

In addition to being linked to the major spheres of social life in many societies, sports and sport participation inform the way people think about themselves and about the world they experience on a day-to-day basis. On a very basic level, sports and sport experiences also affect our "common sense explanations" of the world and our ideas about what is "natural" and what is not. For example, sport experiences may inform things such as:

- How we think about our own bodies (as performance machines; what is "attractive" and what is "healthy." See "The body and the sociology of sport" in the box on p. 8)
- How we define pleasure (achieving performance goals; being "in shape")
- How we define pain ("no pain, no gain")
- How we define excellence (setting records and outperforming others in competitive activities)
- How we think about sexuality (meanings and behaviors associated with "heterosexual" and "homosexual")
- How we think about masculinity and femininity (are men hard, strong, and forceful and women are soft, vulnerable, and graceful?)
- How we think about what is important in our lives (are hard work and sacrifice signs of moral worth?)

These are just a few of the examples that we will deal with in the following chapters.

In most countries sports have been given ideological support through the formation of be-

lief systems that outline the positive consequences of sports for individuals and society. For example, it is popularly believed that sports build character, provide outlets for aggressive energy, and serve as the basis for group unity and solidarity. In capitalist countries many people believe that sport involvement leads to the development of competitive traits; in socialist countries many people believe it leads to cooperation and commitment to the group. Regardless of differences in political or economic systems, people in most countries tend to believe that sports are positively linked to their ways of life. This is especially true in industrialized societies, although many developing nations have promoted sports and sport involvement as means to develop individual character and enhance their reputations in the international political arena. These issues will also be discussed in the following chapters.

Sports and Social Relations

Now let's get back to our original question: Why study sports as social phenomena? It could be said that studying sports is important because it will help us learn more about human behavior and the settings in which that behavior occurs. Furthermore, sports offer unique contexts for the study of social relations and social processes. Sport teams provide ideal settings for studying group interaction and the inner workings of large organizations (Ball, 1975). The public nature of sport activities and events allows easy access to information on a variety of questions related to the sociological understanding of behavior.

Studying sports also enables us to describe and understand how people relate to each other. For example, we can use sports to understand more about gender relations and various forms of intergroup relations such those related to social class, race and ethnicity, and nation-states. These are all good reasons for sociologists to be interested in sports. After all, sociology is concerned with understanding everyday life, learning how behavior is influenced by the settings

REFLECT ON **SPORT**

The Body and The Sociology of Sport

Most people have until recently viewed the body as a fixed, unchanging fact of nature. In other words, they have seen the body as a "natural" phenomenon rather than a social or cultural phenomenon. But an increasing number of people in different academic fields now recognize that the body cannot be fully understood unless it is considered in cultural context (Heller, 1991). For example, medical historians have recently shown that the body and body parts have been socially defined in different ways through history and from one cultural group to another; and they have shown that these definitions are important because they affect government policies, social theories, and the everyday experiences of human beings (Laqueur, 1990).

Changes in the ways bodies have been socially defined (or "constructed") over the years have had implications for how people think about sex, sex differences, sexuality, ideals of beauty, self-image, fashion, hygiene, health, nutrition, eating disorders, fitness, body-building, racial classification systems, AIDS, drugs and drug testing, violence and power, and many other things that affect our lives. In fact, body-related ideas have even affected the way people in some countries view desire, pleasure, pain, and the quality of life. For example, "getting your life together" for many Canadians and Americans often means getting "in shape" physically (Cole, 1991). But the meaning of "in shape" has undergone significant changes in con-

nection with cultural changes, changes in social relations in the society at large, as well as medical beliefs.

The body remains a biological organism, but it is also a part of culture in the sense that it can be "socially constructed" in a variety of different ways. Social definitions of the body are grounded in social relations and heavily influenced by those with the power to promote agreement about what should be considered "natural" when it comes to the body.

This new way of thinking about the body has challenged the traditional mind-body split that has characterized Western thought since the time of Plato. It has also opened up new questions and issues in the sociology of sport. Some people in the sociology of sport are now working with colleagues in other disciplines who share interests in the body. In their work they are asking critical questions about how the body is trained, disciplined, and manipulated in sports and how some sport scientists are using technology to probe, invade, monitor, measure, test, evaluate, and rehabilitate the body as a performance machine. These are crucial questions to ask although asking them tends to make many people associated with sports uncomfortable because the questions often challenge the way many sports itself have been organized and played, the way excellence has been defined, and the way rewards have been allocated to people who participate in sports and administer sport organizations.

in which it occurs, and learning how people can change those settings through their own actions.

Sport Sociology As a Specific Interest

Not everyone who studies sports as social phenomena is primarily interested in learning about human behavior, social relations, culture, and ideology. Some people have more specific interests. They are concerned more directly with learning about sports. Their involvement in the sociology of sport focuses on understanding how sports are organized and learning how changes in organization lead to changes in sport experiences for both athletes and spectators. In many cases they are concerned with discovering the forms of sport organization that are most likely to benefit those involved.

The ultimate goal of people with these interests is often to improve sport experiences for current participants and to make sport participation a more attractive and accessible activity for those who do not currently participate. They may also want to help athletes improve their performances, help coaches be more supportive of athletes and more successful in competition, and help sport organizations grow and operate more efficiently.

People with these interests, whether they were trained in physical education or in sociology, generally refer to themselves as **sport sociologists.** They tend to see themselves as part of a subdiscipline in the larger field of **sport sciences;** they are more concerned with sport science issues than with general sociological issues.

In summary, the sociology of sport deserves attention because sports affect many people's lives, because sports are connected with major social institutions, cultural ideology, and social relations. Furthermore, sports serve as contexts for important everyday experiences, and they are related to every major sphere of social life within a society. They offer research opportunities for those interested in understanding social phenomena on a general level and for those interested in understanding the organization of

sports for the sake of using their knowledge to change sports and maximize the benefits of sport experiences.

WHAT IS THE CURRENT STATUS OF THE SOCIOLOGY OF SPORT?
The Sociology of Sport Is a New Field of Study

Only since 1970 have physical educators and sociologists given serious attention to sports as social phenomena. The reasons for this include the following:

1. *Recent increases in the social significance of sports.* Organized sports as we know them today have only recently become such a pervasive part of social life. It took the invention of television and increasing amounts of affluence in industrial societies to make organized sports such a popular and visible part of contemporary life. Now that sports have become fixtures on the social landscape, both physical educators and sociologists pay more attention to them as social phenomena.

2. *Intellectual biases in Western culture.* In Western cultures clear-cut distinctions have traditionally been made between play and work and between physical and intellectual activities. Because of the strong influence of the work ethic, all forms of play activities have been traditionally defined as nonserious. Therefore they were not given the attention customarily received by serious, productive activities. Additionally, because sport was a physical rather than an intellectual activity it was traditionally viewed as a lower form of culture, and for that reason it was not seen as worthy of serious scholarly attention. Although attitudes on these issues have changed, these orientations still affect the status of the sociology of sport.

3. *Intellectual traditions in physical education and sociology.* The study of sports as social phenomena has seldom been defined as an ac-

tivity that would benefit the professional careers of scholars. In physical education, research has traditionally focused on performance and motor learning. The social dimensions of sport experiences were usually taken for granted and not seen as worthy of serious attention. This meant that until recently sport sociology was considered irrelevant to the central concerns of physical educators. Among sociologists, a concern with sports was usually seen as more of a hobby than a serious career interest. These feelings among sociologists have begun to change, but they still exist in some departments in both Europe and North America.

One of the indicators of increasing acceptance of the sociology of sport is the number of journals that accept and publish the research of those who study sports using sociological perspectives. These journals are identified in the box on p. 11.

Organizational Support for the Sociology of Sport

Professional associations in both sociology and physical education now sponsor regular sessions in the sociology of sport at their annual conferences. The North American Society for the Sociology of Sport, organized in 1978, is a professional association that has held annual conferences since 1980 and has sponsored the *Sociology of Sport Journal* since 1984. The Sport Sociology Academy, one of 10 disciplinary academies in the National Association for Sport and Physical Education, conducts business and organizes sessions included in the annual conferences of the American Alliance for Health, Physical Education, Recreation and Dance. The International Committee for Sociology of Sport (ICSS) holds conferences in connection with the International Sociological Association, and it co-sponsors the *International Review for the Sociology of Sport* and the *ICSS Bulletin*. With this type of organizational endorsement and support, it

seems that the sociology of sport will continue to grow as sports continue to become increasingly significant in society.

Future growth will also depend on whether the sociology of sport can prove itself useful as a means of better understanding social life and as a means of making the world a better place. This is important for those of us in the field to remember and it is also a topic that can be controversial, as we will see in the next section.

Disagreements within the Sociology of Sport

Not everyone associated with the sociology of sport sees the field in the same way. People disagree about what they prefer to study, how they want to do their research, what types of research questions they ask, what theoretical perspectives they use to guide their research, and what goals they identify for their research. For example, some people in the field see themselves as "scientific experts" who serve as consultants to those who can afford to buy their expertise. Others dislike this approach because it aligns the sociology of sport with people who have the power and money to hire experts- and people with power and money seldom want to ask tough critical questions about sports and the way sports are organized.

Those who favor the "scientific expert" model argue that the future of the sociology of sport depends on people in the field establishing reputations as researchers, getting large research grants, using research money to fund graduate assistants and recruit young scholars into the field, and using the knowledge produced in their research to maintain a professional image that can be marketed and sold to sport organizations. Those who favor what might be called a "critical approach" argue that if research in the sociology of sport serves only to reproduce what already exists in sports, then people in our field simply become "efficiency experts" who pander to the specialized interests of those who can afford to hire them. Critical sociologists also argue that when research and scientific knowledge are directed at providing

REFLECT ON SPORT

Publication Sources for Sociology of Sport Research

JOURNALS DEVOTED PRIMARILY TO SOCIOLOGY OF SPORT ARTICLES

Sociology of Sport Journal (quarterly)
International Review for the Sociology of Sport (quarterly)
Journal of Sport and Social Issues (3 issues per year)

SOCIOLOGY JOURNALS THAT SOMETIMES INCLUDE ARTICLES ON OR RELATED TO SPORTS

British Journal of Sociology
Sociological Review
Sociology
Sociology of Education
Theory, Culture and Society

SPORT SCIENCE AND PHYSICAL EDUCATION JOURNALS THAT SOMETIMES INCLUDE ARTICLES ON OR RELATED TO SOCIOLOGY OF SPORT TOPICS

Canadian Journal of Applied Sport Sciences
Exercise and Sport Science Reviews
Journal of Physical Education, Recreation and Dance
Journal of Sport Behavior
Journal of Sport Sciences
Physical Education Review
Quest
Research Quarterly for Exercise and Sport

JOURNALS IN RELATED FIELDS THAT SOMETIMES INCLUDE ARTICLES ON OR RELATED TO SOCIOLOGY OF SPORT TOPICS

Adolescence
Aethlon: The Journal of Sport Literature
International Journal of the History of Sport
Journal of Human Movement Studies
Journal of Leisure Research
Journal of Popular Culture
Journal of Sport and Exercise Psychology
Journal of Sport History
Journal of the Philosophy of Sport
Leisure Sciences
Play and Culture
The British Journal of Sport History
Youth & Society

useful information to people in positions of power, scientists may unwittingly ignore those who lack power and resources. When this occurs there is a danger that science and scientists can become agents of control and oppression rather than agents of human freedom and emancipation.

This debate about the "applications" of the sociology of sport is not unique to our field. It occurs in other fields as well. In general, it is a debate about science and how scientific knowledge is produced and used. These debates often occur in sociology before they occur in other social sciences because sociology is less closely tied to and supported by powerful interests in society. For example, political scientists often work for and are supported by governments; economists often work for and are supported by business and large public agencies; and psychologists are often supported by their ties to personal testing and clinical practice. These external sources of support may keep people in these fields "in business" but they also focus the work of these people on the interests of "the state," on "production and profit," and on helping people cope with and adjust to the status quo.

Sociologists, on the other hand, are more likely than many other social scientists to be in positions where they have little to lose by asking critical questions about sports. This is important because it enables them to explore alternative ways of looking at and organizing sports, and it enables them to consider projects that challenge the status quo and deal directly with problems and issues affecting the lives of people who lack power or who have been socially marginalized in particular cultures. Of course, the downside of not having established sources of external support is that sociologists are not as likely to get big research grants or consulting jobs. Those whose interests would be served by asking critical questions about sports usually do not have the money to fund big grants or hire consultants.

Each of us in the sociology of sport has to make choices about how we will do our work and what we want the consequences of our work to be. Science is not as neutral and value free as we have been led to believe. The entire notion of being a "scientific expert" is tied to issues of power and control. This is because knowledge is a source of power in our complex world, and because power has an impact on how knowledge is produced. In other words, doing research to "build knowledge" in the sociology of sport has political implications because it has an impact on how people see sports and how they think about their own lives and the world around them. Unless people in the sociology of sport think about these things when they do their work, they will limit their understanding about why sports have come to mean certain things in our lives and how sports have an impact on our lives.

WHAT ARE SPORTS?

For anyone reading this book, the question "What are sports?" may seem elementary. We have a good enough grasp of the meaning of sports to talk about them with others. However, to study sports in a systematic way, it is necessary to develop something more than just a general definition of the term.

Most people realize that no scientific discipline could go very far without developing precise definitions of the things it studies. However, developing scientific definitions of terms widely used in everyday language presents problems. To precisely define a commonly used word like *sports* means that many of its connotations must be eliminated, and its meaning must be limited in ways that restrict its use. This offers critics of the social sciences an ideal opportunity to say that sociologists do nothing more than redefine words we already know so that the words become confusing to everybody except sociologists. To avoid this criticism sociologists sometimes invent new terms. But critics then say the new terms are unnecessary jargon used to mystify what everyone already knows.

When it comes to defining sports, my intent is not to confuse or to mystify; it is only to define sports in a way that will help us understand sports as parts of social life. Some of the questions initially raised in a course about the sociology of sport point to the need for a good definition. For example, can we say that a group of eight children in a sandlot game of baseball or backyard football is engaging in a sport? Their activity is quite different from what goes on in Yankee Stadium or the Rose Bowl or even in Williamsport, Pennsylvania, at the Little League World Series. These differences become significant when parents ask how participation in sports may affect their children.
participation in sport may affect their children.

Some of my students have wondered if jogging is a sport. How about weight lifting? Hunting? Skin diving? Table tennis? Automobile racing? Some people have even referred to camping and chess as sports. Are they? In the face of such questions, it becomes obvious that we need to specify *what kinds of activities* we want to include in our discussions of sports. It may be helpful to differentiate sports from informal games, physical recreation, aesthetic activities, and conditioning activities.

There is also the possibility that some activities may be classified as sports when engaged in under certain circumstances—but not when the circumstances change. For example, do we want to include activities such as skiing, surfing, mountain climbing, and biking in our definition of sports regardless of the *conditions* under which people engage in them?

Finally, should we distinguish sports from other activities, such as play or work, by taking into account the *subjective orientations* and *motivations* of the participants in our definition? For example, when a person's only goal in an activity is spontaneous personal expression, do we want to say that person is involved in a sport or in something else, like play? How about when a person's only goal is to entertain an audience for the purpose of earning a salary—do we want to call that a sport or something else, like drama or spectacle?

From these questions there seem to be three major issues to consider in developing a definition of sports:

1. Do we want our definition of sports to refer to specific types of activities?
2. Do we want our definition of sports to depend on the conditions under which the activities take place?
3. Do we want our definition of sports to depend on the subjective orientations of the participants involved in the activities?

Sport Activities

Most definitions of sports include the notion that they are *physical* activities. In other words, sports involve the use of physical skill, physical prowess, or physical exertion. This simple distinction narrows things down, but different physical activities clearly vary in the extent to which they are characterized by physical skill, prowess, or exertion. For example, the physical factors in playing chess are minimal. The physical skill does not go beyond being able to move chess pieces without knocking over everything on the board. Except for long, involved matches that may be emotionally and physically exhausting, concentration and other cognitive skills are the dominant factors in this game. Therefore we could say that because chess does not involve the use of any *relatively complex* physical skills or *vigorous* physical exertion, it is not a sport, according to our definition. The same thing could be concluded about card games or checkers. Although they require complex cognitive strategies, none involves vigorous physical exertion, and although they involve physical movement, the skill required is limited to a single action with only simple variations.

A more difficult activity to classify is automobile racing. Auto racing combines person and machine. It demands intense mental concentration, an extensive knowledge of the mechanical limitations of the car, and physical skills such as quick reactions and highly coordinated, fine motor movements. Which of these three elements is most important is difficult to say. The physical activity in racing does not necessitate a physical training program such as those used by participants in more vigorous activities, but it does require considerable practice to achieve the reaction speed and fine motor skills necessary to handle a racing machine. Thus we could argue that automobile racing is a sport because it *does* involve the use of relatively complex physical skills.

These two examples, chess and automobile racing, illustrate that the determination of what is a complex physical activity and what is not may be difficult. Where the line is drawn between physical and nonphysical, between complex and simple, and between vigorous and nonvigorous is largely an arbitrary decision. The reason we try to draw this line is that the social meanings that develop around intellectual or physically passive activities are different from

Chess and other board games, along with card games, are competitive, but because they do not involve complex physical skills, or vigorous physical exertion, they are not considered sports according to the definition used in this book. (Tini Campbell)

the meanings developed around physically active and rigorous activities in most countries.

In addition to differences in how *physical* an activity is, there are also differences in the various body movements used in sport participation. Complex physical skills may refer to coordination, balance, quickness, or accuracy; physical prowess and exertion imply the use of speed, strength, endurance, or a combination of all three. The activities encompassed by these terms are numerous. They include everything from a short routine on a balance beam to lifting weights, or from taking an opponent to the mat in a wrestling meet to maneuvering a motorcycle into a hairpin turn in a motocross race.

Of course, most of us would argue that our definition of sports should not include all activities involving complex physical skills or vigor-

ous physical exertion. Such a definition would not be very useful because it would include everything from sex to changing the oil in your car! In light of this, it could be argued that our definition should also take into account the conditions under which people engage in physical activities.

Sport Conditions

Participation in physical activities can take place in situations ranging from informal and unstructured to formal and organized. For example, two friends can spontaneously decide to shoot baskets on a makeshift driveway court. As a social event, this is very different from a scheduled game between the Boston Celtics and the Los Angeles Lakers during which the score and statistics are recorded and specific rules are en-

These two boys are engaged in *play*; their behavior is free, spontaneous, and expressive. There are no formal rules governing their wrestling behavior. (Jen Cembalisty)

forced by trained officials. But both situations involve a physical activity commonly described as basketball. Should they both be included in our definition of sports?

If our definition does not distinguish between what occurs on the driveway and what occurs in the Boston Garden, we will have a difficult time talking about sports and their connections to social relations. The social dynamics and consequences of these two activities are very different, and it would be useful for a sociological definition of sports to take into account those differences.

In light of this we might want to say that sports are characterized by some form of competition occurring under formal and organized conditions. This means that the Celtics and Lakers playing a scheduled NBA game are engaged in what we might call a sport, but two friends shooting baskets on a driveway are not. In other words, we could argue that *sports involve competitive physical activities that are institutionalized.*

Institutionalization is a sociological concept referring to a patterned or standardized set of behaviors maintained over time and from one situation to another. When we say that sports are institutionalized, competitive, physical activities, the elements of institutionalization generally include the following:

1. *The rules of the activity are standardized.* This means that the rules are not simply the products of a single group getting together on an informal basis; they are based on more than spontaneous expressions of individual interests and concerns. In sports, the rules of the game define an official set of behavioral and procedural guidelines and restrictions.

2. *Rule enforcement is taken over by official regu-*

latory agencies. Whenever the performances of teams or individuals are compared from one competitive event to another, it becomes necessary for some regulatory agency to sanction games and meets and to ensure that standardized conditions exist and rules are enforced. Regulatory agencies could include everything from a local community rules committee for a children's softball league to the highly organized central office of the National Collegiate Athletic Association (NCAA).

3. *The organizational and technical aspects of the activity become important.* Competition combined with external rule enforcement leads the activity to become increasingly *rationalized.* This means that players and coaches come to develop strategies and training schedules to improve their chances for success. Additionally, shoes, uniforms, and other types of equipment are developed and manufactured to enhance performance and maximize the range of experiences available through participation.

4. *The learning of game skills becomes formalized.* This occurs for two major reasons. First, as the organization and the rules of the activity become more complex they must be systematically learned. Second, as the concern with being successful grows, participants at various skill levels begin to seek guidance from experts. Teaching experts or coaches are often supplemented by others such as trainers, managers, and team physicians.

In summary, it is useful for a sociological definition of sports to include those physical activities that involve the standardization and enforcement of rules, an emphasis on organization, and formalized skill development. In other words, sports are activities that are patterned and regularized. In sociological terms, sports are activities that have undergone the process of institutionalization. It is through this process that

an unstructured, informal physical activity such as throwing (or balancing) a Frisbee becomes an activity that would fit our sociological definition of sports. This is because we are saying that sports involve competition and organization. The recent histories of Frisbee competitions, judo, bodybuilding, and motorcycle racing are all classic examples of how the sociological aspects of activities change as they become institutionalized. The institutionalization of basketball is described in the box on pp. 17–18.

Subjective Orientations of Participants

Do we want to use the subjective orientations of those involved in an activity to identify sports? Some definitions of sports assume that the subjective orientations of participants are irrelevant (Meier, 1981). Others assume that participation in sports is necessarily characterized by a "spirit of play" (Keating, 1964), that participants must be primarily motivated by the intrinsic satisfaction of involvement for an activity to be considered a sport. Still others assume that the highly organized structure of sports stifles the existence of a "play spirit" and that participants in sports are motivated only by external factors such as money, medals, and fame.

All of these approaches can be useful. In thinking about my own involvement in sports (that is, organized, competitive, physical activities), I can remember times when the play spirit was the primary force underlying my participation. However, I can also remember times in college when the only reason I showed up in the gym was because my scholarship required showing up. Sometimes my motives were intrinsic, sometimes they were extrinsic. For this reason, many people would argue that it is useful to say that sports should include activities in which participants combine internal and external motivations.

This approach was taken by the late Gregory Stone in a classic article on sports. Stone (1955) said that sports are composed of two types of behaviors: play and dis-play. "Play" refers to behavior growing out of a participant's personal

REFLECT ON SPORT

Basketball
*A Case History of Institutionalization**

Before the invention of basketball, few people used gyms; gyms were not exciting places to visit. This presented a problem to the supervisors of athletic clubs. During the winter months their members were bored by indoor exercises such as push-ups, sit-ups, and chin-ups (hardly a surprising fact). Without exciting indoor activities, club memberships began to dwindle. There was a definite need for a competitive game that could be played inside a gym; the game had to be simple, easily learned, and as interesting as the popular outdoor sports of football and baseball. To create such a game was the task assigned to 29-year-old Jim Naismith, a student at the International YMCA Training School in Springfield, Massachusetts.

Naismith was an unordained Presbyterian minister who left his religious studies to work in the newly developing field of athletics. In the summer of 1891, he signed up for a seminar on the psychology of play. One of the concerns of his instructor was the absence of any competitive game to fill the winter months between the end of football season and the start of the track and baseball seasons. The seminar continued through the fall with each student trying to invent an indoor activity to meet the program needs of the training school and other YMCAs in North America.

One day, during the fall term, young Naismith went to a faculty meeting and offered suggestions on what physical education instructors might do to improve their courses. His seminar instructor responded by giving him the responsibility of teaching a gym class for a 2-week period. So in late November, Naismith found himself with the job of de-

veloping a set of activities or a game that would hold the interest of a bunch of bored football players concerned with staying in shape through the winter and having fun at the same time.

For nearly the entire 2 weeks, Naismith tried various adaptations of grade school games and outdoor adult games. All of his attempts failed; the grade school games were boring and the adult games became so rough that his students experienced more injuries than fun. In a desperate, all-night session before his last day of class, Naismith outlined a description of what was to later be named basketball. The morning of the class he typed up a set of rules and took them to his skeptical students. After a little pep talk he was able to convince them to choose sides and try the new game. Although there were no out-of-bounds lines, and they had only an old soccer ball and some peach baskets for goals, the students were intrigued by the game.

Information about the game spread rapidly, and what began as an assignment for Naismith's seminar soon developed into an enjoyable competitive activity; out of the competitive activity emerged the sport of basketball. This is what occurred as basketball went through process of institutionalization:

- *The rules became standardized.* Through the established communication system of the YMCA, copies of Naismith's original rules for basketball were distributed around the United States. YMCA staff members and athletes throughout looked to Springfield YMCA for new developments and changes in the game rules.
- *Clubs and organizations began to sponsor teams.* Although basketball was first played by informal groups, the establishment of permanent teams representing various clubs and organizations came quickly. At first, the games between these

*Much of the material in this section is derived from Loy (1968a), Vanderzwaag (1972), and Webb (1973).

Continued.

Basketball—cont'd
A Case History of Institutionalization

teams were arranged by local YMCAs. Then some colleges started playing one another on an informal basis, and in 1896, Yale organized the first regular college team to play an official schedule. The next year, the Amateur Athletic Union (AAU) sponsored the first basketball tournament, followed in 1898 by the first game in the professional National Basketball League headquartered in New Jersey.

- *Rule enforcement was taken over by official regulatory agencies.* Rules and regulations for basketball were first handled by the staff at the Springfield YMCA Training School. But they were quickly taken over by the AAU, followed by the National Collegiate Athletic Association (NCAA) in 1908, and by a combination of the AAU and the NCAA in 1915. These governing organizations formalized the boundaries of the playing area, the size and height of the basket, the size of the backboard, the size and weight of the ball, the role of officials, and many other aspects of the game.

- *The organizational and technical aspects of the game became important.* Once it became an official game, basketball took on additional characteristics. It became more rationalized. Offensive and defensive strategies were developed, equipment became crucial to performance efficiency, and the roles of players and coaches became specialized and well defined.

- *The learning of game skills became formalized.* After the game of basketball was invented by Naismith, it took only 13 years for the first book on

technique to be published (*How to Play Basketball* by George Hepbron). Instructions on how to play were given by YMCA athletic clubs and schools around the country. Teaching experts were soon joined by other experts including coaches, trainers, managers, and more recently, team physicians.

- *Spectators became characteristic at games.* Spectators appeared in the first year of basketball's existence. Soon they became so common that gyms built after the turn of the century contained seating for those interested in watching basketball games.

Basketball was quickly transformed from an informal game into a sport through the process of institutionalization. The reasons for this rapid institutionalization were many. At first, basketball was an activity fitting the needs and interests of athletes and the organizations to which they belonged. When the potential for capturing the interests of players and spectators was seen, the agencies sponsoring teams had additional reasons for promoting a formalized version of the game. Some were interested in financial profits; others, such as high schools and colleges, were interested in promoting their prestige and public images. Basketball was also seen as a mechanism through which students or the members of athletic clubs could be brought together and given something to do during the winter months. All of these things contributed to the motivation needed for basketball to be converted from a game to a sport.

The wrestlers in this high school meet are engaged in *sport*. The match is a form of institutionalized competition in which the participants are motivated by a combination of internal and external factors. (Colorado Springs Gazette Telegraph and Bob Jackson: Chuck Miller)

concerns with the dynamics of the activity itself. "Dis-play" refers to behavior that symbolically represents the action of the activity for the purpose of making it more amusing to spectators. Stone (1955) further explained the meaning of these two elements in the following way:

> Play and dis-play are precariously balanced in sport, and, once that balance is upset, the whole character of sport in society may be affected. Furthermore, the spectacular element of sport may, as in the case of American professional wrestling, destroy the game. The rules cease to apply, and the "cheat" and the "spoilsport" replace the players.

What Stone has suggested is that it might be useful to distinguish sports from play since sports are not characterized by complete freedom and spontaneity. However, it is useful to include a reference to the spirit of play in a definition of sports because this distinguishes sports from activities "acted out" according to a preplanned script. Stone wanted to acknowledge that sports include activities that socially unfold from one moment to the next according to the choices and actions of those involved. This happens when organization and structure coexist with freedom and spontaneity.

We can use Stone's ideas to make distinctions between play, sports, and what we might call **spectacle**. To do this we would say that sports involve a combination of motivation based on the intrinsic satisfaction of involvement and motivation based on the concern for external rewards. If this balance were tipped so that intrinsic motivation *replaced* all concerns for external rewards, the organization and structure of the sport activity itself would change into what we might define as play. If the balance were tipped in the other direction so external rewards *replaced* all the intrinsic satisfaction associated with involvement, the activity would change from a sport to what we might refer to as *spectacle*.

In contemporary industrialized societies, the likelihood of intrinsic motivation replacing extrinsic motives and rewards is slim. The reverse is more likely. External motivating factors such as money, medals, and fame have become in-creasingly prevalent in sports over the past few decades. If these ever replaced all intrinsic motivation, our definition of sports would lead us to conclude that the activities in question would be spectacles rather than sports. Cases in which this has happened have been described by James Michener in *Sports in America* (1976):

In 1946, boxing and wrestling and roller derbies were still taken seriously, but when they began to grab for the nearest dollar, the quickest laugh, the most grotesque parody of violence, their credibility was destroyed. When enough people begin laughing at the exaggerations of any sport, it is doomed.

American professional wrestling is an example of a *spectacle*. Behavior is dominated by "display," and the emergent quality of the activity is replaced by the drama needed to foster spectator interest. External factors take precedence over intrinsic satisfaction.

Stone (1955) also warned of this possibility. He pointed out that when a sport becomes commercialized "spectators begin to outnumber participants in overwhelming proportions, and the spectator, as the name implies, encourages the spectacular—the dis-play."

When participants begin to lose the play spirit and when external rewards and audience satisfaction become prevalent, any sport is in danger of being transformed into a form of spectacle. This has occurred to such an extent with sports in the United States that 55% of the respondents in a national survey indicated that many sport events have become too much like spectacles (Miller Lite Report, 1983). According to our definition, the existence of sports depends on maintaining a balance between intrinsic and extrinsic motivations. It does not have to be a 50:50 balance, but when either of these sources of motivation starts to become insignificant, we would say the activity becomes something else—something with a different structure, different social dynamics, and different consequences for those involved.

It should also be pointed out that during a single sport event it is possible for the participants to shift back and forth from intrinsic to extrinsic sources of motivation (Harris, 1980). This means that at one point the play spirit may be the major source of motivation for participants and that at other times the participants may be primarily motivated by external factors such as money, a trophy, or approval from the coach, a parent, or a group of spectators.

Most people who have participated in sports can give examples of when they became so absorbed in the activity itself that it seemed to "flow" or "carry" them along with it (Csikszentmihalyi, 1990). The so-called runner's high may be an example of this phenomenon. However, "flow states" do not last indefinitely. When they fade, intrinsic sources of motivation must then be supplemented by extrinsic motivation. In this manner, the play spirit gives way or is *temporarily* replaced by a concern with external rewards.

SPORTS: A DEFINITION

In light of each of the three issues just discussed, we can define sports in the following way:

> Sports are institutionalized competitive activities that involve vigorous physical exertion or the use of relatively complex physical skills by individuals whose participation is motivated by a combination of intrinsic and extrinsic factors.

In evaluating this or any other definition, it should be remembered that a definition is only a tool. It serves to specify at some level of precision the meaning implied by a certain word. The definition just given offers a relatively precise characterization of the term *sports* as used throughout this book. However, before leaving this topic a few clarifications and warnings should be given.

Clarifications

There may still be some confusion regarding the precise application of the term **sports** as just defined. Our definition refers to what are popularly described as **organized sports.** This is done to distinguish what happens on the beginners' slope at Vail, Colorado, from what occurs during the Winter Olympics. The official skiing events at the Olympics clearly meet the criteria of our definition, but such is not the case for the Sunday afternoon skier at Vail. The activity engaged in by the individual at Vail certainly involves complex physical skills and may involve vigorous exertion, but it is not a form of institutionalized competition. Instead of describing such an activity as a sport, it might be more appropriate to call it **recreation.** In this sense, recreation is more closely related to play than to sport, but, unlike play, it is generally a response to the concerns of ordinary life rather than a free, spontaneous activity. We engage in recreation for refreshment or release; it is a "recreation" of the individual in terms of health or personal enjoyment or growth.

If our skier found someone of similar ability and decided to challenge that person to a race

SIDELINES

MY MISTAKE WAS TEACHING HIM THAT IT'S MORE IMPORTANT TO HAVE FUN THAN TO WIN

Sport involves a combination of intrinsic and extrinsic motivation. When intrinsic motivation exists to the exclusion of extrinsic motivation, sport is converted into pure play.

from the start of a ski run to some point further down the slope, we might say that skiing in that instance becomes a form of a **contest** or **match.** It has become competitive, but it proceeds in a more or less informal manner. Only when those two skiers follow formalized rules and confront one another under standardized conditions can we say that they are engaged in a sport according to our definition. If you find this difficult to accept, think of what confusion would exist if we called driving our car a sport just because automobile racing at the Indianapolis Speedway is a sport. Taking a Sunday drive is to automobile racing as recreational skiing is to the Olympic Alpine events.

It should be pointed out that most students in my sociology of sport classes find this definition of sports overly restrictive. They argue that it excludes too much of what they have traditionally referred to as *sports*. This objection is legitimate; it is not necessary to alter your conceptualization of sports when you talk to your friends or read *Sports Illustrated*. However, when you discuss things such as how sport participa-

tion affects young people, how sports are related to masculinity or aggression, if sports should be sponsored by the elementary school in your neighborhood, or if race and ethnic relations are related to sports and sport participation, it is necessary to be able to explain what you mean by *sports*. Accurate descriptions and explanations require precise definitions. This is true for questions having either practical or theoretical relevance. And it is true for the social sciences just as it is in medicine and the physical sciences.

Warnings

Our definition of sports is not sacred. It simply identifies three characteristics that enable us to focus our attention on a limited range of social activities. However, it is important to remember that when we focus our attention too much we sometimes ignore important things that fall outside of the definitions and conceptual frameworks we use as sociologists.

For example, when we focus our attention on institutionalized, competitive activities (as our definition specifies) we may overlook physical activities that affect the lives of many people who do not have the resources to formally organize their physical activities or the desire to make their activities competitive. In other words we may spend all our time considering the physical activities of elite groups in society because those groups have the power to formally organize physical activities that fit their interests. If this happens then we are in danger of unintentionally leading people to believe that the activities of elite groups are more important in society than the activities of other groups. This can lead us to further marginalize people who already have been pushed to the outer boundaries of society, and do it in the name of science! But if we are aware of this tendency we can control it and still ask critical questions about how sports have come to be what they are in particular societies and what social purposes they serve in those societies. And we can also raise questions about how sports are connected to power, privilege, social marginalization, and what changes are needed to increase access to sport participation.

CONCLUSION:

WHY STUDY SPORTS?

Sociology studies the social arrangements created by people as they live together and make sense out of their lives. Sociologists are concerned with social issues, social relationships, social organization, and social change. Their overall goal is to enable people to understand, control, and change their lives so human needs are met at both individual and group levels.

When sociologists turn their attention to sports, they study sports as parts of culture. They look at sports in terms of their importance in people's lives, how they are organized, and their connections to major social institutions, cultural ideology, and social relations. Research in the sociology of sport helps us understand sports as social phenomena, but beyond that, it often leads to the discovery of problems based in the structure of sports or society itself. When this happens, the recommendations made by sociologists tend to threaten those who would like sport activities and programs to remain as they are now. Therefore sociology is sometimes controversial.

The sociology of sport is a new field with roots in both sociology and physical education. It is likely to grow in the future because it is supported by professional organizations and a body of literature in academic journals. However, growth also depends on whether those of us in the field are able to make meaningful contributions to the way people live their lives.

Complicating the issue of future growth is the fact that not everyone in the field agrees on how to "do" sociology of sport. Some use a "scientific expert" model to guide their work, while others use what might be called a "critical approach". Those using the scientific expert model emphasize questions of organization and efficiency, while those using a critical approach emphasize social transformation and empowerment of powerless and marginalized peoples. Differences between these two approaches raise important questions about the way scientific knowledge is produced and used. These questions are currently being debated by many of us in the field.

For the purpose of this book, sports have been defined as activities involving the following: (1) the use of physical skill, prowess, or exertion, (2) institutionalized competition, and (3) the combination of intrinsic and extrinsic motivation among participants. When assessing this definition it should be remembered that it is only a tool that enables us to focus on the social organization, dynamics, and consequences of a particular set of highly visible and popular physical activities in many countries around the globe. Our definition enables us to distinguish sports from play, recreation, contests, and spectacle. However, in using this definition it is important to realize that it directs our attention to the lives of people who have the resources and the desire to formally organize physical activities in competitive ways. If we realize this, we are still able to ask critical questions about the relationship between sports and power and privilege in society; and we can be concerned about how sports might be transformed so more people have access to the positive things that organized physical activities have to offer.

SUGGESTED READINGS

Callois R. 1979. Man, play, and games. Schocken Books, New York (*a translation of a classic 1958 book in which a French sociologist outlines the nature of games in society*).

Edwards, H. 1973. Sociology of sport. The Dorsey Press, Homewood, Ill. (*especially Ch. 3: Definitions and clarifications*).

Guttmann, A. 1978. From ritual to record. Columbia University Press, New York (*especially Ch. 1: Play, games, contests, sports*).

Heinemann, K., ed. 1987. Special topical issue on the sociology of sport in various countries. *International Review for the Sociology of Sport 22, 1 (five articles on the sociology of sport — in Finland, France, the German Democratic Republic, Japan, and the United States*).

Huizinga, J. 1955. Homo ludens. Beacon Press, Boston (*a translation of a classic 1944 book in which a Swiss philosopher outlines the nature of play in culture*).

Loy, J.W., G.S. Kenyon, and B.D. McPherson, eds. 1981. Sport, culture, and society. Lea & Febiger,

Philadelphia (*especially the four articles in Part One: The sociological analysis of sport*).

Morgan, W.J., and K.V. Meier, eds. 1988. Philosophic inquiry in sport. Human Kinetics Publishers, Inc., Champaign, Ill. (*especially the eight articles and bibliography in Part I, The nature of sport, play, and game*).

CHAPTER 2

USING SOCIAL THEORIES

What can they tell us about sports in society?

. . . it is legitimate to ask ourselves how sports can truly contribute to the improvement of modern society. We are all concerned on this account because sports can degenerate into manifestations which dishonor the noble ideals which they can promote. . . .

Pope John Paul II (1989)

Sports are a tremendous force for the status quo. . . . They do distract millions from more serious thoughts—as do . . . all other "escape" entertainments. As mass entertainment, they are definitely antirevolutionary.

Leonard Koppett, Sports Reporter and Columnist (1981)

Games and athletic contests offer a dramatic commentary on reality rather than an escape from it. [They are] a heightened reenactment of communal traditions, not a repudiation of them.

Christopher Lasch, Author and Social Critic (1979)

Sports, and football in particular, may have many virtues, but one of its more undesirable and unintended consequences is to promote or reproduce various forms of social inequality.

Doug Foley, Anthropologist (1990)

When sociologists talk theory they sometimes bore or confuse students. Social theories are often explained in ways that make them seem unrelated to people's lives. I don't want this to happen in this chapter, so I will talk about theory in a down to earth, practical, and personal way.

The goals of this chapter are to do the following:

1. Explain what is involved in theorizing about social life.
2. Describe and critique the major theories and theoretical approaches used in the sociology of sport.
3. Provide examples of research inspired by these theories and theoretical approaches.
4. Compare the policy implications associated with major theories and theoretical approaches.

THEORIES IN SOCIOLOGY

Whenever we ask why our social world is the way it is and then imagine how it might be changed, we are "theorizing" (hooks, 1992). Theorizing involves both reflection and analysis. We don't have to use big words, complex sentences, and long paragraphs to develop theories. In fact, the best theories are those we can understand and then use to make sense out of the world and empower ourselves as we deal with that world.

Most of the theorizing done by sociologists over the past 150 years has been motivated by a desire to pull together as much information as possible about the social world and develop an overall explanation for how and why social life is organized in particular ways. Underlying this motivation has been the belief that if we could only identify the key forces that drive and shape social life, then we humans could become masters of our own destiny. In other words, if we developed a valid and reliable theory, we could outline rational strategies for organizing social life in progressively efficient and satisfying ways.

This hope that humans could make the world better by controlling it through science was the foundation of the Enlightenment period in history and it marked the beginning of what we call "modernism" in Western societies. Modernism in the social sciences involves the idea that progress based on rationality, science, technology, and organization would eventually lead to utopia in the form of efficient, just, and harmonious societies.

Most sociologists have traditionally wanted to be a part of this process of collecting information, testing theories, and eventually discovering "the truth" about how the social world works and how it might be controlled. Many have searched for "social laws" and "cause-effect relationships" that would explain all social life—regardless of time, place, and culture. These sociologists have tried to find the building blocks of social life by identifying the types of relationships and organizational structures that enable people to live together in groups and societies. This search for foundations and building blocks has taken different people in different directions, as you will see when I describe functionalist theory and conflict theory in the next section of the chapter.

But not all sociologists have joined in this search for a general theory of social life. Some have argued that the search for an overall explanation for what drives and shapes social life has led to the development of deterministic theories that ignore important parts of everyday life. Others argue that the whole idea of building a general theory is worthless because it keeps sociologists from focusing on specific problems and helping exploited and oppressed people gain more control over their lives and over the conditions shaping their lives. In recent years an increasing number of sociologists have argued that social life is so complex, diversified, contradictory, and rapidly changing that it is impossible to develop any theory that transcends a particular time, place, and culture. Finally, some sociologists have become discouraged because they often see sociological theories used to manage and control people rather than to empower and emancipate people.

My point in this section is that sociologists in the 1990s use many different theoretical approaches as they ask questions and think about social life and about sport as a part of social life. This means that people in the sociology of sport go in many different directions when it comes to asking questions and doing research on sports as social phenomena. But before I discuss social theories and sports, I want to explain *why* there are so many different theoretical approaches used in sociology and the sociology of sport.

The diversity of approaches used in sociology is due to some very important changes in our world. *First*, feminist scholars and women around the world have raised important questions about the validity of any science or scientific theories that have largely ignored the everyday experiences of half the world's population; they have also developed new and challenging ideas about how science and social life have been affected by gender and changing definitions of masculinity and femininity. *Second*, global changes have forced Western social scientists to recognize that they have looked at the world from a Eurocentric viewpoint for over 2000 years; as the people of the world have become more interconnected, and as people from Asia, Latin America, and Africa become more powerful players in these connections, many social scientists in "western" countries have come to realize there are many different ways to look at and explain the social world. *Third*, new communications technology have created such a rapid and infinitely diverse stream of media-generated images and simulations of reality that our sense of what is real has changed or become fuzzy; this change has led some sociologists to use new approaches that enable them to consider dimensions of social life that are outside traditional boundaries and fixed structures. *Fourth*, more sociologists have begun to realize that science itself is a part of culture and that it is often

used to maintain the power and privilege of an elite few rather than enabling those who lack resources to control their lives; this realization has led these sociologists to choose new theoretical approaches as they ask research questions and collect information about social life.

GENERAL THEORIES ABOUT SPORTS AND SOCIETY

Until the 1970s most sociologists used one of two general theories of social life to guide their questions about relationship between sports and society—some used functionalist theory, others used conflict theory. Each of these theoretical approaches is based on different assumptions about the foundation of social order in society and each leads to different questions about social life and the role of sports in social life. Not surprisingly, each also leads to different conclusions about the importance and consequences of sports in societies and communities. The differences between functionalist theory and conflict theory are outlined in Table 2-1 on p. 35 and explained in the next two sections.

Functionalist Theory: Sports Are an Inspiration

Functionalist theory is based on the idea that society is best studied by using a **systems model.** Sociologists who use functionalist theory to study sports assume that society is an organized system of interrelated parts. They also assume that all societies are held together because the people in them share the same basic values and because the major parts of societies (family, education, the economy, government, religion, leisure, and sport) all fit together in mutually supportive and constructive ways.

According to functionalist theory, the driving force underlying all social life is the tendency for any social system to maintain itself in a state of balance so it continues to operate efficiently. In other words, all social systems "naturally" tend to seek balance through an emphasis on consensus, common values, and coordinated organization. When certain behaviors or forms of organization upset this balance, they are **dysfunctional.** This means they have negative effects on the "natural" order that exists in the system. On the other hand, when behaviors or forms of organization contribute to the maintenance of the social order, they are **functional.** This means they have positive effects. Functionalist theory also assumes that social change is dysfunctional unless it occurs in a gradual evolutionary manner—much like the evolutionary changes in the biological world. When sociologists use functionalist theory they emphasize research questions related to social stability, social structure, and social organization.

When functionalist theory is used to explain how a society, community, school, family, or any other social system works, attention is focused on how each part in the system contributes to the system's overall operation. For example, if Canadian society is the system being studied, a person using functionalist theory would be concerned with how the Canadian family, economy, government, education, religion, and sport are related to each other and how they all work together in contributing to the smooth operation of the society as a whole. The analysis would focus on the ways in which each of these different spheres of social life helps to keep the larger social system operating efficiently.

According to functionalist theory, the following four things must happen if a social system is to operate efficiently:

1. There must be methods for teaching people in the system the basic values and rules they are supposed to live by; and since frustration and tension are often created when values and rules are taught, there must also be ways for people within the system to release tension and frustration in harmless behaviors.
2. The system must contain social mechanisms for bringing people together and es-

tablishing cohesive and integrated social relationships.
3. There must be methods for teaching people in the system the goals that are supposed to be important in their lives and also for teaching the socially approved ways of achieving those goals.
4. The social system must contain built-in mechanisms for handling social and environmental changes occurring outside the system while preserving order inside the system.

According to functionalist theory these four things represent the building blocks of social order in any society. And when functionalist theory is used to study sports as a part of the social system, attention is focused on how sports function to help meet these system needs.

FUNCTIONALIST THEORY AND RESEARCH ON SPORT Theories always influence the kinds of questions we ask in our research. Sociologists using functionalist theory have usually asked questions about how sports "fit" into social life and contribute to stability and social progress in communities and societies. Their questions have led them to search for the ways that sports contribute to the four basic needs of social systems. The types of studies most often done by those using functionalist theory generally fall into the following four categories:

1. *Studies of the relationship between sport participation and good character.* These studies are concerned with whether sports provide socialization experiences through which people learn the values and rules of society, and whether sports provide settings in which tension and frustration can be released in safe ways so that order and stability in society are preserved.
2. *Studies of sports and social integration in groups, communities, and societies.* These studies are concerned with whether sports bring people together and create the unity

The functionalist approach leads to the conclusion that sport unites people who otherwise have little in common, such as these two men from different generations. In other words, sport serves "integration functions." (Paul Joyce and Notre Dame Magazine)

and integration needed to maintain order and efficiency in society.

3. *Studies of sport participation and achievement motivation.* These studies are concerned with whether sports teach people to be committed to social progress as it is defined in their society, and whether sport participation teaches the importance of working hard to achieve social progress.

4. *Studies of sports participation and the development of abilities needed to defend society against external threats.* These studies are concerned with whether sport participation creates survival skills and prepares people to help their societies survive in the face of external social and environmental changes.

In conclusion, functionalist theory focuses attention on how sports satisfy the needs of social systems. Because of this emphasis, those who use functionalist theory often study the ways in which sports contribute to personal growth and the preservation of social order at all levels of social organization. This is why a functionalist approach is often popular among people who have a vested interest preserving order and stability in society. These people want sociology to tell them how sports contribute to the communities in which they live. They are interested in seeing how sports can provide valuable lessons for young people and opportunities for people of all ages to let off steam in harmless ways. They want to see how sports strengthen "social togetherness" by giving everyone in their group or society something to share. They also want to know how sports can provide models for setting and achieving goals in their group or society. And finally, they tend to see sports as activities that improve health and fitness and keep their country prepared to defend itself economically and militarily. These people like functionalist theory because it leads to the conclusion that *sports are an inspiration for both individuals and societies.*

Throughout the world a functionalist approach has been used to make numerous decisions about sports and sport programs at both the national and local levels. Those using it have encouraged the development and growth of organized youth sports, the continued funding of interscholastic sports in high schools and colleges, the growth of sport opportunities for girls and women, the use of sports in military training, and the promotion of the Olympic Games to maintain international goodwill. This widespread use of functionalist theory makes it important for us to be aware of its limitations.

LIMITATIONS OF FUNCTIONALIST THEORY
The *first* problem with functionalist theory is that it usually leads to exaggerated statements about the positive effects of sports. This is because it is based on the assumption that social systems tend to reject any of its parts that do not contribute to order and efficiency. Therefore if sports had negative consequences, they would not have existed for so many years in many societies. Unfortunately, this conclusion ignores the possibility that sports might create negative consequences in a society and that sports might highlight the need for significant changes in the society itself. Those using functionalist theory tend to overlook possibilities that sports could distort values and norms and destroy motivation, create frustration and tensions, and disrupt social integration. They also overlook possibilities that sports could interfere with setting and achieving important goals and could also divert people's attention away from crucial social problems in the system.

The *second* major problem with functionalist theory is that it is based on the assumption that the needs of all the individuals and groups within a society are the same as the needs of the society as a whole. The existence of real conflicts of interest within a social system is inconsistent with the functionalist assumption that all groups, communities, and societies are naturally held together in a state of balance. This means that when functionalist theory is used to study sports, there is a tendency to overlook the possibility that sports may benefit some groups more than others within a community or society. The existence of conflict between groups in society is ignored when it is assumed that if something is good for one group—especially the dominant group in society—it must be good for all other groups. This not only limits an understanding of social life, but it discourages a detailed discussion of social change and the ways that sports are related to processes of change in society.

The *third* major problem is that functionalist theory does not recognize that sports in any society are "social constructions." Those who use this theory are so concerned with how sports promote basic system needs that they disregard the possibility that sports are created and defined by members of society to promote their own interests and the interests of the groups to which they belong. This means that functionalist theory leads people to overlook the ways in which the development of different sports is connected to historical processes and a wide range of cultural factors in particular groups, communities, and societies.

The weaknesses of functionalist theory are summarized in this way:

> Clearly the trouble with functionalism is that it is committed to the present society, with all its dilemmas, contradictions, tensions, and indeed, with all its immorality. The trouble with functionalism is, in a way, that it is not really committed to social order in general, but only to preserving its own social order. It is committed to making things work despite wars, inequities, scarcity, and degrading work, rather than finding a way out (Gouldner, 1970).

In sociology, the general theory that calls attention to the dilemmas, contradictions, and tensions in society is **conflict theory.**

Conflict Theory: Sports Are an Opiate

Many people living in societies that have market economies don't like conflict theory because it doesn't fit with their ideas about how society works. Those who use conflict theory do not view society as a relatively stable system of interrelated parts held together by common values and consensus; instead, they view it as an ever-changing set of relationships characterized by inherent differences of economic interests. Social order, according to conflict theory, results from the fact that some groups of people are able to use their resources to coerce and subtly manipulate others to accept their view of the world as the correct view. This means that anyone using conflict theory is concerned with identifying who has economic power and how economic power is used; they are not concerned with identifying general system needs. Their analysis of society focuses on processes of change and the consequences of social inequality rather than on what is required to keep society stable and orderly.

Conflict theory is based on an updated version of the ideas of Karl Marx. Although it can be used to describe and understand any situation in which masses of people lack resources and have little control over their lives, it has generally been used to explain events and social life in countries with market economies—that is, all countries that have capitalist economic systems. According to conflict theory, sports are determined or shaped by the structure of the economic system in society. Here's an example of a conflict theory explanation of sports in any country with a market economy (such as the United States, Canada, England, Germany, etc.):

1. All market (or capitalist) economies require the development of highly efficient work processes through which an ever-increasing amount of consumer goods can be mass-produced.
2. To meet this need for efficiency, it is necessary to create large industrial bureaucracies.
3. Within industrial bureaucracies, the vast majority of workers end up performing highly specialized and alienating jobs.
4. Because of the lack of control and lack of excitement on the job, workers are constantly searching for activities offering a combination of escape and tension-producing excitement.
5. Within societies with market economies these workers are subtly coerced and manipulated (through advertising in the media) to seek the satisfaction they need through consumerism and mass entertainment spectacles.
6. Under these social conditions, sports emerge as especially popular forms of entertainment spectacle for two reasons: First, sports can be tied to consumption through the promotion and sale of equipment, tickets, and items linked to teams and players (for example, the sale of official NFL clothing, Air Jordan athletic shoes, and University of Miami Hurricane coffee cups). Second, sports can be organized on the same basic principles as work in a market economy (for example, people can use sports to emphasize efficiency, rationality, production, obedience, discipline, and competitive success through the achievement of goals).

According to conflict theory, sports in societies with market economies ultimately promote the interests of people with economic power. This is because sports keep workers emotionally focused on escapist activities that distract them from the need to make changes in the way social life is organized. In other words, sports are distorted forms of physical exercise shaped by those possessing power and resources in capitalist societies. This means that those using conflict theory see sports as an opiate, not an inspiration.

CONFLICT THEORY AND RESEARCH ON SPORTS The sociologists who use conflict theory usually ask questions about how sports serve to perpetuate the power and privilege of elite groups in society, and how sports serve as tools of economic exploitation and oppression. Research inspired by conflict theory generally involves the following:

Conflict theorists conclude that sports generate forms of nationalism and militarism that justify violence initiated by the state to maintain the status quo and protect the interests of economically powerful groups in society. (Colorado Springs Gazette Telegraph)

1. *Studies of how athletes become alienated from their own bodies.* These studies are concerned with whether sport participation in certain societies leads athletes to define and experience their own bodies as tools of production, as machines designed to produce entertainment and profits for others rather than feelings of pleasure for self (Brohm, 1978); these studies are also concerned with whether athletes might use performance enhancing drugs because they are victims of profit making sport systems.

2. *Studies of how sports can be used to coerce and control people so they will not question the way social life is organized.* These studies are concerned with whether sports distort people's thoughts about social life and divert attention away from finding solutions to social, economic, and political problems in society.

3. *Studies of the relationship between sports and the development of commercialism in society.* These studies are concerned with whether sports are used to promote capitalist expansion by creating profits or by serving as an advertising medium to encourage people in society to use consumption as an indicator of self-worth and quality of life; these studies are also concerned with issues of social inequality in society and how sport reflects and perpetuates inequality.

4. *Studies of the relationship between sports and various forms of nationalism and militarism.* These studies are concerned with whether sports create superficial, irrational, and potentially harmful feelings of nationalistic pride and whether sports could be used to justify violence in society, especially violence initiated by the state for the purpose of maintaining the status quo and

protecting the interests of economically powerful groups.

5. *Studies of the relationship between sports and racism and sexism.* These studies are concerned with whether sports serve to divide people by race and gender, perpetuate racial stereotypes and distorted definitions of masculinity and femininity, and create racial and gender inequities in society.

In conclusion, conflict theory focuses attention on how sports are used by powerful people to promote attitudes and relationships enabling them to maintain their power and privilege. Like functionalist theory it is based on the assumption that society is driven and shaped by specific "needs," although conflict theory emphasizes "market needs" as the driving force determining social organization and social relationships in society. Unlike functionalist theory, conflict theory focuses attention on how sports reflect the unequal distribution of power and economic resources in capitalist societies and how they perpetuate those inequalities. This leads to an emphasis on the negative consequences of sports and to the need for radical changes in sports and society as a whole. In fact, the goal of most conflict theorists in the sociology of sport is to bring about the development of a humane and creative society so that sports can become sources of expression, creative energy, and physical well-being. But until society is changed they will continue to conclude that *sports are an opiate.*

Most beginning students in the sociology of sport don't feel comfortable with conflict theory. They say it is too negative and too critical of sports and their societies. They usually prefer functionalist theory because it fits closely with what they have always believed about sports and because it does not lead to conclusions that threaten the structure of either sports or society. However, conflict theory has been very useful in calling attention to the problems in sports and the need for changes in sports and society as a whole.

Limitations of Conflict Theory

Conflict theory, like functionalist theory, has weaknesses. *First*, it assumes that all social life is driven and shaped only by economic factors. Conflict theory focuses on the relationship between the economic "have's" and "have-nots" in society. It assumes that since the "have's" own the means of production in market economies, they possess economic power and use that power to control the "have-not's." It also assumes that the "have-nots" are destined to be the victims of economic exploitation and live lives characterized by powerlessness and alienation. These assumptions lead people who use conflict theory to focus exclusively on class relations when they study sports. Although economic factors and class relations are important, sports cannot be totally explained in terms of class relations or the interests of economically powerful people in society. This is especially true when considering recreational and mass participation sports.

Second, conflict theory ignores the possibility that gender, race, ethnicity, age, sexual orientation, and other factors can be used as a basis for the ways people think about themselves, the ways they relate to others, and the ways they organize social life. Conflict theory is based on the Marxist assumption that all history and social organization revolves around class relations and does not acknowledge that other forms of social relations may also drive and shape social life. Therefore those who use conflict theory to study sports do not acknowledge that inequalities in society might be related to something other than struggles between social classes. The fact that struggles related to gender, race, ethnicity, age, religion, sexual orientation, physical ability (abled and disabled) might also drive history and social life is not considered by conflict theory.

Third, conflict theory ignores the possibility that sport participation, even in a market economy, can be an empowering experience on both a personal and group level. For example, numerous testimonials from athletes indicate that sports do more than alienate people from their own bodies, despite the fact that some athletes do take harmful drugs and use their bodies as tools of production. In fact, sport participation can be a personally creative and liberating experience. Furthermore, sports can also serve as sites for challenging and resisting the interests of economically powerful groups; in some cases they could even be sites for transforming the way power is distributed in an organization or community (Birrell and Richter, 1987; Donnelly, 1988; Willis, 1981).

Therefore, the major problem with conflict theory is that it leads people to see sports simply as reflections of the economic forces operating in society. As sociologist Mike Messner points out, this type of deterministic framework leaves "no room for seeing people as anything but passive objects who are duped into meeting the 'needs' of capital" (1984). Furthermore, conflict theory contributes little to our understanding of the dynamics of gender and intergroup relations apart from their connection with class relations. Even though sports are sometimes used as instruments of economic control and expansion in society, it must also be recognized that sports can be personally empowering activities and sites for resisting and even transforming the way social life is organized in groups and communities. This recognition is consistent with the theoretical approaches discussed in the next section.

ALTERNATIVE THEORETICAL APPROACHES

Most people in the sociology of sport do not spend much time debating the relative merits of functionalist and conflict theories. These theories have not been completely abandoned, but sociologists are now using other theoretical approaches thought to be more helpful in describing and understanding the everyday realities of sports in the lives of individuals, groups, and societies. These alternative approaches take many different forms, but they have one thing in common: they avoid the assumption that all social life is somehow driven and shaped by a unified set of factors that exist outside of people's relationships with each other. This means that even though sociologists all agree that behavior and social life are limited by historical and social conditions, many do not believe sociology can come up with an overall explanation of how society works that can be applied to all societies regardless of time, place, and culture.

Sociologists today are using theoretical approaches that are flexible enough to take into account the complexity and diversity of social life. They want these approaches to help them ask critical research questions and do studies that critically examine social life; and they want these approaches to help them make the world better—not more rational and efficient, but more fair and open to diversity. In other words, they want theoretical approaches that focus on particular problems and situations and sensitize people to the need for practical programs of human emancipation. The quest for a "universal, grand theory of society" is no longer an important goal for many sociologists.

There are many theoretical approaches that try to do some or all of these things, but I will focus on two that are more widely used in the sociology of sport—critical theory and symbolic interactionism.

Critical Theory: Sports Are More Than Reflections of Society

Critical theory is about *power* in social relations; it consists of various approaches designed to understand where power comes from, how power works in different situations and in different aspects of people's lives, and how power shifts as people struggle over the many issues that affect their lives.

Critical theory is also about *action and political involvement*; it has grown out of efforts to make social life more fair and open to diversity, and it has been designed to inform future efforts to develop practical programs that promote equity, fairness, and openness. Most people who use critical theory are interested in explaining that all human relationships are grounded in political struggles over how social life should be de-

Table 2-1 Functionalism, conflict theory, and critical theory: a summary and comparison

Functionalism	Conflict theory	Critical theory
I. ASSUMPTIONS ABOUT THE SOCIAL ORDER		
Social order is based on consensus, common values, and interrelated subsystems.	Social order is based on coercion, exploitation, and subtle manipulation of individuals.	Social order is created by people within the constraints imposed by historical forces and social conditions.
II. MAJOR CONCERNS IN THE STUDY OF SOCIETY		
What are the essential parts in the structure of social systems? How do social systems continue to operate smoothly?	How is power distributed and used in society? How do societies change, and what can be done to promote change?	How is society created and maintained through ideas and cultural practices, and how can people become agents for making society into what it could and should be?
III. MAJOR CONCERNS IN THE STUDY OF SPORT		
How does sport contribute to basic social system needs, such as pattern maintenance and tension management, integration, goal attainment, and adaptation?	How is sport related to alienation, coercion and social control, commercialism, nationalism and militarism, sexism, and racism? How is sport used to maintain the interests of the power elite?	How have sports come to be defined and organized the way they are? What roles do sports play in the development and change of society?
IV. MAJOR CONCLUSIONS ABOUT THE SPORT-SOCIETY RELATIONSHIP		
Sport is a valuable social institution benefiting society as well as individual members of society. Sport is basically a *source of inspiration* on personal and social levels.	Sport is a distorted form of physical exercise shaped by the needs of capitalist economic systems. Sport lacks the creative and expressive elements of play; *it is an opiate.*	Sports can reaffirm the status quo or oppose it. Sports can repress or liberate.
V. GOALS OF THE SOCIOLOGY OF SPORT		
To discover ways in which sport's contribution to personal growth and the maintenance of social order can be maximized at all levels	To promote development of a humane and creative society so that sport can be a source of expression, creative experiences, and physical well-being	To discover (1) what sports could be, (2) how they are influenced by social conditions, and (3) how they could be changed to represent the interests of more people and serve as catalysts for change in society
VI. MAJOR WEAKNESSES		
Exaggerates positive consequences of sport; assumes the existence of sport proves it serves positive functions. Ignores internal differences and conflicts in society; assumes sport serves equally the needs of all groups in society. Ignores historical and economic factors in the creation of sport by people within society	Deals with historical and economic factors in a deterministic manner; ignores factors other than capitalism in analyzing the development of sport in society. Focuses too much attention on top-level spectator sport; overemphasizes extent to which sport involvement is controlled by power elite	Does not provide a tight, clearly understood framework. Provides no explicit guidelines for determining when sports either reaffirm or oppose the status quo. Has seldom led to a consideration of the experiences of actual people in everyday life settings

fined and organized. These struggles occur in all aspects of people's lives. For example, they involve economic struggles over labor law, rights of workers, property ownership, and power structures in organizations; and they involve personal and legal struggles over family violence, child and spouse abuse, and women's control over their own bodies. In the case of sports they involve struggles over basic questions such as: What activities get to count as "sport"? How is it that sports have come to involve aggression, competition, and the rational pursuit of goals through the use of performance technology? Why is excellence in sports defined in terms of measurable achievements in highly specialized activities that have little to do with general fitness or life off the playing field?

Those using critical theory realize that dominant forms of sport in most societies have been socially constructed in ways that privilege some people over others, and they want to expose this fact and examine it in ways that will open the door for thinking about alternative ways of defining and "doing" sports.

Critical theory has existed for quite some time. It encompasses a variety of approaches to understanding social life, including those used by neo-Marxists, feminists, and people in cultural studies.* (Feminist theory is discussed in the box on pp. 37-39). Most of these approaches have grown out of a desire to avoid the economic determinism of conflict theory and the pretentious quest of functionalist theory to explain all social life by discovering universal "social laws." Critical theory is used in the sociology of sport because more and more people recognize that sports cannot be explained simply in terms of the needs of the social system or the production needs of a market economy. These people want a theoretical approach that allows them to rec-

ognize that sports are created and organized by people using their power and resources as they struggle to develop and establish cultural practices that promote their interests and concerns.

Critical theory is unique because it is based on the idea that agreement and conflict exist simultaneously in social life. Critical theory assumes that agreement and shared values are never permanent because they depend on never-ending processes of negotiation, compromise, and coercion between various groups in society. And it assumes that the basis for conflicts of interest in any society changes from one location to another as historical circumstances and economic forces change. This means that according to critical theory the relationship between sports and society is never set once and for all time: sports change as historical conditions and economic forces change; sports change with new developments in government, education, the media, the family; and sports change with new ideas about masculinity and femininity and about race, ethnicity, age, sexual orientation, and physical ability. Therefore, critical theory helps us ask questions about why women were not allowed to play certain sports in the past, why there were Negro leagues in baseball, why the Gay Games and the Disabled Games have been developed, and why the Senior Olympics and Special Olympics exist in many communities around the world.

Critical theory is based on the notion that sports cannot be understood or analyzed apart from the specific historical and cultural circumstances in which they exist. Therefore the definition and organization of sports vary over time and from one group to another. Usually that definition and organization will reflect things in the rest of society, but it is also possible for sports to become sites for challenging, resisting, and even transforming the way social life is organized. This is why critical theorists say it is an oversimplification to describe sports simply as a reflection of society (see box, "Sports are more than reflections of society" on p. 40). They

Text continued on p. 41.

---

*People in cultural studies are concerned with the processes through which cultural practices and the ideologies and beliefs underlying those practices are created, reproduced, and changed through people's actions and interactions.

Feminist Theory
A Critical Look at Gender and Sports

Feminist theory is a unique form of critical theory. It is based on clear evidence that women have been systematically devalued, exploited, and often oppressed in society; it is also tied to a strong commitment to develop programs of social action that will improve conditions for women (Acker et al., 1983). Feminist theory grew out of a general dissatisfaction with intellectual traditions that ignored women and failed to recognize the extent to which men's values and experiences had shaped science and the production of scientific knowledge.

Although feminists are all committed to changing the way social life is organized, they don't all agree on the changes needed. *Liberal feminists* identify discrimination and unequal opportunities as the issues in most need of attention. Their goal is to promote "full and equal participation for girls and women" in all spheres of social life including employment, education, politics, and sports (Lenskyj, 1992b). In the case of sports, liberal feminists focus on the issue of fair and equal access for women to participate as athletes and share in the rewards available to athletes, to coach at all levels of competition, and to gain positions in the power structures of sport organizations. According to Helen Lenskyj, "Liberal feminists would probably agree with the statement, 'If it's good for males, it's good for females, too.' " (1992b, p. 1).

Radical feminists, on the other hand, believe that problems go much deeper than issues of discrimination and equal opportunity. They argue that if fairness and equity are the only issues addressed and if success is measured only in terms of participating in activities and organizations created by and for men, feminists will end up reproducing the very orientations toward social life and social relationships that led them to be devalued and exploited in the first place. Radical feminists say that since many activities and organizations have been

shaped to represent and promote the power and privilege of men, there must be goals that go beyond equal participation opportunities; they would *not* agree with the idea that if it's good for men, it must also be good for women (Vertinsky, 1992). In the case of sports, radical feminists would question the merits of wanting to play and work in sport activities and organizations where aggression, competition, goal-orientation, and rational efficiency are used as the most important standards for evaluating organizational success and individual qualifications.

Most radical feminists do not dismiss the approach or the goals of liberal feminists. They do not claim that liberal feminists are going in the wrong direction, but they do argue that liberal feminists do not go far enough in their analysis of sports or social life. Radical feminists contend that to fully understand the history and social significance of organized sports in our lives we must understand how sports have been and continue to be ordered along gender lines. They would support this contention by reminding us that organized sports were developed at a time in British history when many people feared that home life was controlled by women and that boys raised by women would not learn to be tough enough to control colonized peoples around the world, fight wars, and expand capitalist economies. Overall, men in England feared what might be called the "feminization of social life."

It was in connection with this fear that organized sports came into being. Organized, competitive sports not only became the activities used to toughen up boys and create men who fit dominant definitions of masculinity at that time but were also used to demonstrate that men's bodies could endure and engage in violence in ways that made them superior to women's bodies. Boxing, rugby, football,

Continued.

Feminist Theory—cont'd
A Critical Look at Gender and Sports

and other contact sports were not only widely used in military training but also seen as proof that men were naturally superior to women and that maleness, power, and the ability to physically dominate others were uniquely male qualities grounded in biology itself (Messner, 1992). Women were systematically excluded from contact sports and discouraged from participating in most strenuous physical activities because women's bodies were seen as incapable of aggression, physical power, and stamina. Of course, the more important implication of this exclusion and discouragement was that women's bodies were defined as naturally inferior to men's bodies, and that women's biological destiny was to be controlled by men (Bryson, 1991). This ideological rationale for the development of organized sports also existed in other western cultures, including the United States and Canada.

Feminists also note that when physical strength has practical utility in employment and when force and violence are widely used in society, the balance of power between men and women is likely to favor men. And in a society where physical strength is not needed in the economy and displays of force and violence are controlled, men will seek other means of maintaining a rationale for their superiority. This rationale is at least partially provided by football, boxing, ice hockey, and other sports defined as "manly" or "aggressive." These sports are promoted and popularized partly because they perpetuate the belief that force and aggression are important parts of life and that men are fundamentally and naturally superior to women because they are more forceful and aggressive (Bryson, 1991).

Feminists describe sports as "gendered" activities. The fact that organized sports were developed to emphasize competition, efficiency, and performance ranking systems and to devalue supportiveness, kindness, responsiveness, and caring contributed to their "gendered" character. To say that sports are "gendered" activities and to say that

sport organizations are "gendered" structures means that they have been socially constructed out of the values and experiences of men. It also means that certain "masculine values and experiences" are highly regarded and used as standards for evaluating everything from organizational success to the qualifications of everyone from athletes to athletic directors: when you are aggressive, forceful, and committed to efficiently achieving competitive success, you are seen to be "qualified" as an athlete, coach, or administrator; but when you are supportive and focused on being responsive to others, you are only qualified to be a cheerleader, host the next booster club luncheon, or work in public relations. In the gendered world of sports, being supportive, kind, caring, and responsive to others doesn't count for much, and it certainly doesn't make you qualified to do anything important, unless it's to be a volunteer on the hospitality committee.

In light of this analysis of sport, critical feminist theory leads people in the sociology of sport to ask the following questions when they do their research:*

- To what extent have the character and structure of dominant sport forms in most societies been formed by the ways people think about gender and about masculinity and femininity?

- Would sports *as we know them today* in North America even exist if gender were not used as an organizing principle for sport activities and organizations?

- How are certain forms of masculinity and the power and privilege of men in society connected

---

*Most of these questions are paraphrased versions of general questions listed in Joan Acker's (1992) discussion of "Gendered Institutions" in today's society.

REFLECT ON SPORT

with the packaging, promotion, and playing of today's most popular sports?

- How have the images, symbols, and ideologies associated with dominant sport forms in North America led to a "gendering" of sport participants, activities, and organizations?

- How has the devaluation and exclusion of women been built into the structures and operational dynamics of sports and sport organizations?

- How have athletes and coaches constructed gendered personas or personal images that enable them to "fit" into sports and sport organizations without being defined as deviant or threatening?

These are "boat rocking" questions, and it is easy to see why many people, both men and women, feel threatened by the feminists who ask them. This is why there has been such a concerted effort over the past 10 to 15 years to portray feminists as social demons. These efforts have been so successful that many college students today would forfeit an A in a sociology class before they would ever describe themselves as feminists much less radical feminists!

But despite popular opinions about feminism, these are crucial questions. They have made me aware of many important issues and other questions that must be addressed in the sociology of sport and in my own thoughts and research. For example, why have many men in American sports resisted the spirit of Title IX for over 20 years? Why have strong and powerful women athletes been accused of being lesbians unless they design athletic fashions, wear long fingernails, and travel with their husbands? Why are men's locker rooms full of homophobia, gay-bashing vocabulary, and comments that demean women? Why do we constantly read about doctors warning women that vigorous exercise might not be good for their health while 40,000 young men get carried off football fields every year with serious knee injuries? Why are sexual harassment and sexual assault low priority issues in most sport organizations? Would an openly gay football player ever be pictured on the cover of *Sports Illustrated* for any reason except his sexual identity? And why are so many women's intercollegiate teams called "Lady this" and "Lady that"?

Many of these questions are explored in different chapters in this book, but others are left for you to consider on your own, if you don't mind using critical feminist theory to guide your thoughts.

REFLECT ON SPORT

Sports Are More Than Reflections of Society
A Clarification

In the sociology of sport it is often said that sports are reflections of society. This way of looking at sports is a helpful starting point when someone is just beginning to study sports as a part of social life. But it is not very helpful for someone who really wants to take an in-depth sociological look at sports. The problem with saying that sports are reflections of society can be demonstrated by shifting our attention away from sports onto another sphere of social life: the *family*. Like sports, families are reflections of society. But our personal experience tells us that everyday family life is more than that. Real families are the creations of people interacting with one another in a variety of ways depending on their abilities, resources, power, and their definitions of family life. Of course, the opportunities and choices available to the members of any particular family are influenced by factors in the larger social setting—including laws, economic conditions, government policies, and general beliefs about how husbands and wives and parents and children should relate to one another. This means that there will be patterns of similarities from one family to the next in any society. However, it does not mean that families are predestined to be mere reflections of society.

Society serves only as the context within which specific family practices are defined, developed, and maintained by individuals. Within that context, it is possible for changes to be initiated by family members, individually or together. In this way, families each take on their own unique "way of life." Furthermore, families can become sites for raising questions about and resisting dominant values and attitudes about how families and family life should be organized (as former Vice President Dan Quayle, a spokesperson for dominant family values, discovered when the fictional TV character Murphy Brown opted for an "alternative" family structure in her sitcom life). In other words, human beings can become agents for social change—not just in their immediate family lives but in the larger social settings in which they live.

So it is with sports. On one hand, the entire sphere of sport—its structure and dynamics—is a reflection of the society in which it exists. But that tells only part of the story. Sports are the creations of people interacting with one another. No voice comes out of the sky and says, "I am society, and this is the way sports should be." Of course, this is not to deny the powerful influence of social conditions on the structure and dynamics of sports. Social conditions are important, but within some limitations set by those conditions it is possible for people themselves to change sports or to keep them the way they are. In fact, it is even possible for people to define and create sports in ways that are uniquely different from dominant forms of social life in a particular society.

This is a helpful way of thinking about sports as parts of social life. It not only recognizes that sports can have both positive and negative effects on participants but also calls attention to the possibility that people define and create sports in their own lives and that sports can be defined and created in ways that actually stand in opposition to dominant forms of social relations that are unfair and geared to the interests of those with power and resources in society (Donnelly, 1988).

say that sports are socially constructed by people as they cope with the realities of everyday life in their own changing families, groups, communities, and societies. Since this process of "social construction" never stops, the relationship between sports and society is a dynamic one—sports take different forms and exist for different reasons for different people at different times. To understand this, the critical theorists say, we must carefully outline how sports are connected to various forms of social relations as well as the overall processes of social development in societies.

CRITICAL THEORY AND RESEARCH ON SPORTS Critical theory inspires research that focuses on *why* sports have taken certain forms and been organized in certain ways in particular groups, communities, and societies. For example, when studying a country like the United States, critical theorists would be interested in the way *excellence* has been defined in dominant forms of sport. If excellence was defined in terms of setting records and winning championships instead of general abilities across a wide variety of sports, they would want to know how and why such a definition came into existence. They would also want to know about alternative definitions of excellence and how those definitions might be viewed and evaluated by people. Finally, they would try to explain how and why one definition of excellence came to be accepted over others, and in their explanations they would note who benefits most from the dominant definition of excellence, and who benefits least. They would outline the consequences of that definition, and compare them to the possible consequences of other definitions.

Critical theory is designed to be a tool for the critical examination of society and the way it operates. However, the ultimate goal of critical theory is to be more than simply an analytical tool. Anderson and Gibson (1978) explain this goal in the following way:

> A critical perspective [also] seeks to cultivate an understanding of what the *potential* of society is and what the society *ought* to be, given its level of

social and material resources. It [focuses on] the tension between actuality and potentiality and seeks to liberate human thought and action for the purpose of potentiality.

In other words, the ultimate goal of research based on critical theory is *change*. In the sociology of sport this means that critical theorists focus on (1) what sports *could be* in society, (2) how sport opportunities vary from one group to another, (3) how sports could be changed to reflect the interests of participants, and (4) when and how sports could become sites for promoting changes in social relations in particular situations. It is best to illustrate these points through some examples of research based on various forms of critical theory.*

Example 1: Creating alternatives to dominant forms of sport. Susan Birrell and Diana Richter (1987) combined two forms of critical theory (feminist theory and cultural studies) to study how a specific sport experience was socially constructed by a group of women playing on certain teams in slow-pitch softball leagues in 2 communities. For 4 years the researchers did intensive interviews and observations that focused on how the feminist consciousness of these women might inform and structure their sport experiences, their interpretation of those experiences, and the integration of sport experiences into their lives.

Birrell and Richter reported that the women in their study were concerned with developing and expressing skills, playing hard, and challenging opponents, but that they wanted to do these things without adopting orientations characterized by an overemphasis on winning, power relationships between players and coaches, social exclusion and skill-based elitism, an ethic of risk and endangerment, or the derogation of opponents. In other words, the women attempted to create alternative sport experiences that were "process oriented, collective, supportive, inclusive, and infused with an ethic of

---

*These three examples are adapted from Coakley (1993a,b).

care" (p. 408). Transformations in the way teams were organized and the way games were played came slowly over the 4-year research period; even many women found it difficult to try an alternative to the sport forms that had been created out of men's values and experiences. But as changes occurred the women experienced a sense of satisfaction, enjoyment as softball players, and a reaffirmation of their collective feminist consciousness and feelings of political empowerment.

Birrell and Richter's study shows that sports are not so much "reflections of society" as they are "social inventions" of people themselves. The definition and organization of sports are grounded in the consciousness and collective reflection of the participants themselves, and this means that people can alter sports through their own efforts. In other words, not only are sports social constructions, but so too are the consequences of participation. This research finding makes a significant contribution to our overall understanding of sports in society.

Example 2: the social construction of masculinity in sports. Michael Messner (1992) used a form of critical feminism to study the ways in which masculinities were socially constructed in connection with men's athletic careers. Open-ended, in-depth interviews were conducted with 30 former athletes from different racial and social class backgrounds to discover how gender identities developed and changed as men interacted with the socially constructed world of elite sports. Messner noted that the men in his study began their first sport experiences with already gendered identities; in other words, when they started playing sports they already had certain ideas about masculinity. They had not entered sports as "blank slates" ready to be "filled in" with culturally approved masculine orientations and behaviors.

As their athletic careers progressed, these men constructed orientations, relationships, and experiences consistent with dominant ideas about manhood in American society. Overall,

their masculinity was based on (a) trying to make a public name for themselves and make money in the process, (b) relationships with men in which bonds were shaped by homophobia and misogyny (a disdain for women), and (c) a willingness to use their bodies as tools of domination regardless of consequences for health or general well-being. This socially constructed masculinity not only influenced how these men presented themselves in public but it also influenced their relationships with women and generated a continuing sense of insecurity about their "manhood."

Messner also found that the consequences of sport participation in the lives of the men he interviewed were complex and sometimes confusing. For example, sport participation brought many of the men in his study temporary public recognition, but it also discouraged the formation of needed intimate relationships with other men and with women. Sport participation enabled the men to develop physical competence, but it also led to many chronic health problems. Sport participation opened some doors to job opportunities for these men, but opportunities also varied depending on the sexual preferences and the racial and class backgrounds of the men. Sport participation provided these men guidelines on how to be a man, but the involvement and success of women in sport also raised serious questions for those who had learned that becoming a man necessarily involved detaching themselves from all things female. Overall, sport participation for the men was a process through which they enhanced their public status, created nonintimate bonds of loyalty with each other, perpetuated patriarchal relationships with women, and constructed masculinity in a way that privileged some men over others. Even though this process was sometimes challenged by the men, transformations of sports and sport experiences were difficult to initiate because dominant forms of sport have been constructed to perpetuate the notion that male privilege is grounded in nature and biological destiny.

Messner's work calls attention to the fact that gender is a social construction and that sport offers a fruitful site for studying the formation of gender identities.

Example 3: sport rituals and social life in a small town. Anthropologist Doug Foley (1990a) studied the connection between sport events and community socialization processes in a small Texas town by using field methods (observation, participant observation, and informal and formal interviews) over a 2-year period. His analysis was guided by a form of critical theory (he calls it "performance theory"), and one of his goals was to examine the extent to which sports might be used by certain community members as sites for challenging and making changes in the capitalist, racial, and patriarchal order that defined social life in their town.

Although Foley was looking for progressive practices challenging the dominance of a small elite group who controlled the town's economy, he found few examples connected with sports. There were a handful of athletes, cheerleaders, and local townspeople who challenged certain traditions and ways of doing things, but they produced no real changes in the social life of the town. This led Foley to conclude that high school sports in general and high school football in particular were important community rituals in the town he studied, but that they ultimately reproduced existing inequities related to gender, race, ethnicity, and income.

Foley's study shows that sports are tied to the economic, political, and cultural systems in a community, and that it is difficult to use sports as sites for challenging and changing the way social life is organized.

In conclusion, critical theory emphasizes that *sports are more than reflections of society.* Of course, like other spheres of social life, sports share things in common with the social settings in which they exist. But according to critical theory, sports have never been developed in a neatly ordered and rational manner, and there are no simple rules for explaining sports as social phenomena. Instead, the structure and or-

ganization of sports in any society varies with the complex and constantly changing relationships within and between groups possessing varying amounts of power and resources. In addition to being concerned with how sports come to be what they are in society, critical theorists are concerned with how sports affect the processes through which people develop the orientations and beliefs used to explain what happens in their lives. They want to know how and when sports become sites for encouraging changes in the way people see and interpret the social world around them.

LIMITATIONS OF CRITICAL THEORY Critical theory comes in many different forms so it is much more flexible and much less pretentious than either functionalist or conflict theory. Its major limitation is that none of its variations provide many guidelines for determining when sports reproduce dominant forms of social relations in society and when they become sites for resistance and the transformation of social relations (Critcher, 1986). Although some recent work has focused on the ways in which sports become sites for oppositional forces in society, research using critical theory provides few examples of when this has ever occurred in the past and little information on the circumstances under which it might occur in the future. Furthermore, the work of some critical theorists has focused so much on class relations and the reproduction of economic power, that other issues have been ignored.

Symbolic Interactionism: Meaning and Identity in Sports

Symbolic interactionism is a widely used theoretical approach in sociology. It assumes that human behavior involves choices and that choices are based on meanings or definitions of the situation that people create as they interact with others. According to a symbolic interactionist approach we don't simply respond in an automatic fashion to the world around us; instead, we choose to behave in certain ways in anticipation of the impact we think our behavior will have on ourselves, the people around us, and the social world in which we live.

As we behave and as we see the impact of our behavior on ourselves and the world we develop a sense of who we are and how we are connected to the rest of the social world. This sense of who we are is the *self*. The self is a very important concept in symbolic interactionism. The self forms as we interpret the connections between our lives and the social world, and then the self mediates our choices as we participate in social interaction and "construct" our social worlds. In other words, the self is a basis for *self*-direction and *self*-control. The self is never formed once and for all time because it emerges out of our relationships with other people, and those relationships are constantly changing as we meet new people, as people change, and as we face new situations.

Those who use a symbolic interactionist approach to behavior are concerned with understanding how people themselves define and give meaning to their social worlds. The term *symbolic interaction* comes from the idea that human beings develop and use symbols to represent and understand the world. These symbols are created as people interact with each other and give meaning to what happens in their lives. These meanings then become the "reality" that people use as contexts for making decisions about who they are and for understanding the implications of their own behaviors and the behaviors of others.

Symbolic interactionists see "meaning" and interaction as "social creations." They see behavior in terms of an emerging process, not in terms of cause-effect relationships. They define human beings as choice makers, not as "responders" to stimuli. This is why symbolic interactionists study real life situations and processes as they are created by people interacting with each other. Symbolic interactionists do not do experiments designed to discover cause-effect relationships because they don't believe that human behavior can be explained by using cause-effect models.

Symbolic interactionists are interested in the meanings and identities associated with sport participation. Meanings associated with youth sports vary from one culture to another. (Jay Coakley)

When they study human behavior and social events, symbolic interactionists believe that behavior is contingent, not determined. This means they are open to the possibility that human beings can behave in surprising and unconventional ways (McCall and Becker, 1990); as they study behavior they assume that:

> Nothing has to happen. Nothing is fully determined. At every step of every unfolding event, something else might happen.

However, symbolic interactionists also recognize that behavior reflects individual resources and situational constraints and opportunities. They realize that under certain circumstances the behaviors of many different people are likely to be similar; but they also realize it doesn't have to be that way because human beings have minds of their own.

SYMBOLIC INTERACTIONISM AND RESEARCH ON SPORTS When symbolic interactionists study sports they usually focus on how people develop meanings and identities associated with sport participation, and how those meanings and identities inform their behavior and relationships with others. The goal of this research is to reconstruct and describe the reality that exists in the minds of the people being studied. The research methodology used by symbolic interactionists is designed to gather information on how people see their social worlds and their connections to those worlds. This is why symbolic interactionists do studies that involve participant observation and in-depth interviews. These are the best methods for understanding how people define situations and use those definitions as a basis for identifying themselves and making choices about their behavior. The best way to explain research done by symbolic interactionists is to give some examples. I could choose many, but I will highlight three of my favorites.*

Example 1: the complex process of becoming an athlete. Sociologists Peter Donnelly and Kevin Young (1988) used symbolic in-

teractionism to guide their collection and analysis of ethnographic, observational, and interview data on mountain climbers and rugby players. Their analysis enabled them to develop a model showing that becoming a serious athlete involves a problematic, long-term process of identity construction and confirmation. According to their model, becoming a mountain climber or rugby player involved more than simply receiving encouragement and rewards from other people and being exposed to opportunities to climb mountains or play rugby. Instead, it involved long-term processes through which individuals (1) acquired knowledge about their sport, (2) became associated with a group of recognized athletes in their sport, (3) learned the norms and expectations shared by group members, (4) earned the acceptance of group members, and (5) experienced repeated confirmation and reconfirmation of their identities as climbers or rugby players as they interacted with group members.

Donnelly and Young's study shows that becoming a serious athlete involves more than a single decision or event, and it involves more than the influence of a particular person or set of persons. Instead, it involves an extended interactive process through which people come to identify themselves as athletes as they become knowledgeable and accepted members of particular sport groups or subcultures.

Example 2: the meaning of Little League baseball. Sociologist Gary Alan Fine (1987) used a symbolic interactionist approach in his study of the sport experiences of 10- to 12-year-old boys on 10 teams in five different youth baseball leagues. Over a 3-year period he collected data through a combination of participant observations, informal conversations, and interviews. Fine's analysis showed that the boys on each team developed their own systems of meanings and understandings to assess their baseball experiences and guide their interaction with teammates through the season. Fine called these systems of meanings and understandings **idiocultures.** These idiocultures were important be-

---

*These three examples are adapted from Coakley (1993a,b).

cause they served as the contexts in which the boys interpreted and made sense out of their little league experiences. For example, Fine found that idiocultures were used by the boys as "experience filters" through which they redefined and transformed the idealized rules and moral lessons presented to them by coaches and parents during the season. Instead of taking the rules and lessons at face value the boys changed them in ways that fit their own immediate needs, primarily needs for acceptance among peers. These changes were not noticed by coaches and parents because the boys were so good at presenting themselves in ways that led the adults to think that the boys understood and internalized everything they said.

The boys didn't completely ignore the moral talk offered by adults or see it as useless, but they did transform it to fit their own definitions of the situation. For example, Fine found that while parents and coaches talked about the importance of effort and sportsmanship, the boys were primarily concerned with being socially accepted by their peers. And according to team idiocultures, social acceptance among the boys' peers generally depended on being able to present themselves to others as "men" in a traditional moral sense. This led many of the boys to choose behaviors that expressed autonomy and established distance between themselves and anyone defined as weak and submissive, such as girls and younger children. To avoid being identified with girls or younger children the boys often mimicked stereotypical models of traditional masculinity. This tendency was encouraged by some coaches because it could be used to motivate the boys to play in aggressive ways; the coaches saw aggressive behavior as proof of "effort" and "hustle." Therefore, little league experiences perpetuated definitions of masculinity that valued toughness, risk-taking, and dominance, and systematically devalued girls as weak and unable to physically stand up to boys. This was not something that the adults wanted to happen, but it occurred as the boys defined their experiences in their own terms.

Example 3: the meaning of pain in an athlete's life. Sociologist Tim Curry (1992) examined biographical data on the sport career of an amateur wrestler. Case study data were collected through three 2-hour interviews over a 2-month period. These interviews followed several years of observing the college wrestling team on which this young man (in his early 20s) participated. Curry's analysis clearly outlines the social processes through which many athletes come to define pain and injury as normal parts of their sport experiences.

Curry's report shows that this young wrestler initially learned to define pain and injury as a routine part of sport participation simply by observing other wrestlers and interacting with people connected to the sport. As he progressed to higher levels of competition he became increasingly aware of how the endurance of pain and injury are commonplace among fellow athletes and former athletes who are now coaches. Over time this young man learned the following in connection with his wrestling career: to "shake off" minor injuries, to see special treatment for minor injuries as a form of coddling, to express desire and motivation by playing while injured or in pain, to avoid using injury or pain as excuses for not practicing or competing, to use physicians and trainers as experts whose roles were to keep him competing when not healthy, to see pain-killing anti-inflammatory drugs as necessary performance enhancing aids, to commit himself to the idea that all athletes must pay a price as they strive for excellence, and to define any athlete (including himself) unwilling to pay the price or to strive for excellence as morally deficient. Finally, a combination of spine and knees injuries, and repeated injuries that disfigured his ears ("cauliflower ear" is common among longtime wrestlers), led him to stop wrestling. But because he was defined as a model of dedication and commitment, he became a role model for younger wrestlers.

The experiences associated with this young man's wrestling career clearly illustrate the way in which painful and self-destructive experiences can be defined as positive in the life of an athlete, especially a male athlete. Athletes in many sport groups may even come to use these experiences as proof of self-worth and evidence of a special form of character that separates them from others who are less dedicated and committed. But the important thing about this study is that it shows how meanings associated with sport experiences are grounded in social interaction processes.

LIMITATIONS OF SYMBOLIC INTERACTIONISM The strength of symbolic interactionism is that it has generated many empirical studies of meaning, identity, and interaction. However, one of its weaknesses is that many of these studies focus almost exclusively on personal definitions of the situation and interaction dynamics without identifying the ways in which meanings and interaction processes are related to the social structure of society as a whole. Therefore symbolic interactionism does a poor job of explaining how structured forms of inequality operate in sports and societies.

Another weakness of symbolic interactionism is that it does a poor job of explaining behaviors grounded in processes other than rational problem solving and choice making. Furthermore, because it focuses on meanings and interaction as a basis for the development of the self, it leads people to ignore the importance of the body and physical experiences in social life (Glassner, 1990; McCall and Becker, 1990). This is important to note as we think about the usefulness of a symbolic interactionist approach in the sociology of sport. Those using this approach should note this weakness and incorporate the body and physical experience into their future studies of meanings, identities, and interaction in sports.

USING SOCIOLOGICAL THEORIES: A COMPARISON

Many people think that theories don't have practical applications. However, this is not true. Many of our own actions are based on our predictions of their consequences for ourselves and those around us, and our predictions are based on our personal theories about social life. Our theories about social life may be incomplete, poorly developed, based on limited information, and biased to fit our own needs, but we still use them to guide our behavior. The better our theories, the more accurate our predictions, and the more effective we become in managing our relationships with others and controlling the situations in which we live our lives. None of the theories and theoretical approaches discussed in this chapter is perfect, but each can be useful as we attempt to move beyond our own limited personal perspectives when we try to understand the social world.

When people make decisions about sports, when they make policies, and when they fund or cut money from sport programs, they usually base their decisions on personal theories about sports and their connections to social life. Even when people are not familiar with theories in the sociology of sport, they still base their decisions on personal ideas about how sports and social life work. Since many people use a systems model to understand how the social world works, their view of sports fits with a view guided by functionalist theory. In other words, they assume that society is held together by shared values, and they see sports as contributing to the order and stability of society.

The use of **functionalist theory** leads people to promote changes in sports that emphasize traditional societal values. If individualism, competition, and success are important values in society, a person using functionalist theory would call for changes leading to increases in individual achievement, winning records, and overall participation in sports. Since functionalist theory generally leads to the conclusion that sports build the kind of character valued in the society as a whole, it also leads to policy recommendations calling for more organized competitive programs, more structured sport experiences, more supervision of athletes, more coaching education programs, the development of more training centers for top-level athletes, and increased drug testing to control the behavior of

Critical theorists are interested in why certain decisions about sport are made and how these decisions affect different groups of people, especially groups with different amounts of power and economic resources. For example, who determines policies about who may or may not use sport facilities at certain times of the day or week, and whose interests are best served by these policies? (Suzanne Tregarthen/Educational Photo Stock)

athletes. In the case of youth sports, recommendations generally call for more developmental programs, coaching certification requirements, and a sport system that builds skills leading to success at elite levels of competition.

Conflict theory, on the other hand, leads to concerns with different questions and issues, and it certainly leads to different policy decisions about sports. Conflict theorists are interested in bringing about major changes in the structure of sports by making athletes and spectators aware of how they are manipulated and oppressed for the profit and personal gains of the economic elite in society. This approach is based on the assumption that problems in sports exist because power does not rest in the hands of athletes themselves. Conflict theorists argue that if the profit motive were eliminated in sports and if athletes controlled sports, many of the most serious problems in sports would disappear. Sports would be reorganized in more play-like forms that would offer liberating and empowering experiences to participants. In the realm of

policy making, conflict theorists endorse players' unions and any athlete organizations that could serve as vehicles for making reforms in sports. Their policies would ultimately discourage the development and growth of spectator sports, and promote the idea of games for the players themselves.

Critical theorists, like conflict theorists, are interested in how sports are related to transforming the way social life is organized in society as a whole. However, their policy position is that changes depend on more than simply shifting the control of sport to the participants themselves. Critical theorists emphasize that most athletes and spectators are aware of who controls sport in their societies and have learned not only to accept those systems of control but to define them as correct. Therefore their policy recommendations emphasize changes leading to increased choices and opportunities for current and future participants and spectators. Critical theorists call for increases in the number and the diversity of sport participation alternatives available in society and increases in the choices available to participants in any sport. Their goal is to provide as many people as possible with the opportunities to create and maintain forms of sport participation that enhance personal development and create critical abilities leading to transformations in sports and society as a whole.

Symbolic interactionists are interested in understanding the meanings and interaction dynamics associated with sports and sport participation. They emphasize the complexity of human behavior and the need to understand behavior in terms of how people themselves define situations through their relationships with others. This suggests that changes in sports must take into account the perspectives and identities of sport participants. Of course, the best way of doing this is to restructure sport organizations so that everyone involved, especially athletes, have opportunities to raise issues about the purpose and conditions of sport participation. This means that sport organizations need to become more democratic and abandon the rigid vertical hierarchies that are so prevalent today.

CONCLUSION:

IS THERE A BEST THEORETICAL APPROACH TO USE WHEN STUDYING SPORTS?

As someone who studies sports in society I'd like to think that knowledge in the sociology of sport is cumulative and progressive, and that we can build on what we know today so we can know more tomorrow. This is a reasonable goal, but it needs to be qualified because sports are cultural practices subject to redefinition and transformation as social relations change and as other changes occur in the social world. Thus our knowledge about sports is always in danger of being irrelevant or obsolete. Furthermore, as sociologists we have discovered that there are always new ways of looking at and analyzing any social phenomenon, including sports.

Sociology provides a number of theoretical frameworks that can be used to understand the relationship between sports and society, and each takes us in a different direction. In this chapter we focused on four of those frameworks: *functionalism, conflict theory, critical theory*, and *symbolic interactionism*. The purpose of the chapter was to show that each framework has something to offer in helping us understand sports as social phenomena. For example, *functionalist theory* offers an explanation for positive consequences associated with sport involvement in the lives of both athletes and spectators. *Conflict theory* identifies serious problems in sports and offers explanations of how and why players and spectators are oppressed and exploited for economic purposes. *Critical theory* suggests that sports are connected with social relations in complex and diverse ways, and that sports change as power and resources shift and as there are changes in social, political, and economic relations in society. *Symbolic interactionism* suggests that an understanding of sports requires an understanding of the meanings, identities, and interaction associated with sport involvement.

It is also useful to realize that each theoretical perspective has its weaknesses. *Functionalist theory* leads to exaggerated accounts of the positive consequences of sports and sport participation; it mistakenly assumes there are no conflicts of interests between groups within society; and it ignores powerful historical and economic factors that have influenced social events and social relationships. *Conflict theory* is deterministic, it overemphasizes the importance of economic factors in society, and it focuses most of its attention on top-level spectator sports, which make up only a part of sports in any society. *Critical theory* provides no explicit guidelines for determining when sports are sources of opposition to the interests of powerful groups within society, and it is only beginning to generate research on the everyday experiences of people involved in struggles to define and organize sports in particular ways. *Symbolic interactionism* does a poor job of relating what goes on in sports with general patterns of social inequality in society as a whole, and it generally ignores the body and physical experiences when it considers the self and issues of identity. Furthermore, none of these theoretical approaches, apart from critical feminist theory, has encouraged a systematic consideration of gender relations in the study of sports. However, this will change in the future as feminist theory continues to raise issues that encourage people to rethink the way they use these and other theoretical frameworks in their study of social life.

Which theory or theoretical framework will lead us to the truth about sports? This depends on the goal of the person asking the question. If the goal is simply to understand more about sports as social phenomena, it would be wise to use many different approaches. However, if the goal is to use an understanding of sports as a basis for becoming involved and making changes in sports and social life, then more care must be taken in choosing a theoretical framework. As we have just seen, each framework has different implications for action and change.

In my experience I have found all the frameworks discussed in this chapter useful. I have used symbolic interactionism to guide much of my own research, but I also think that a combination of critical theory and feminist theory offers the best framework for understanding sports and engaging in political action. I am much more interested in increasing choices and alternatives for people in sports than I am in dismantling sports or trying to make sports a more efficient means of teaching traditional values in society. Creating alternatives requires an awareness of the values underlying dominant forms of sport in society today, and a vocabulary for thinking about creative possibilities for the future; a combination of critical and feminist theory is especially helpful in exposing those values and providing the vocabulary needed to critique sports and develop new sport forms.

SUGGESTED READINGS

It is difficult to classify books and articles strictly in terms of the theoretical frameworks they represent. Many use a combination of perspectives. However, in the list below each reference is classified according to the major framework used to draw conclusions about the relationship between sport and society.

FUNCTIONALISM

Guttmann, A. 1978. From ritual to record. Columbia University Press, New York (*especially Ch. 3: Capitalism, Protestantism, and modern sport; Ch. 4: Why baseball was our national game; Ch. 5: The fascination of football; and Ch. 6: Individualism reconsidered*).

Lengyel, P., and A. Kazancigil, eds. 1982. Sporting life. Special issue of the International Social Science Journal 34(2) (*each article focuses on sport in a different country and most use functionalist theory to guide their analyses*).

Lever, J. 1983. Soccer madness. University of Chicago Press, Chicago (*analysis of the relationship between soccer and Brazilian society*).

Luschen, G. 1981. The interdependence of sport and culture. In J.W. Loy et al., eds., Sport, culture, and society (pp. 287-295). Lea & Febiger, Philadelphia (*classic functionalist explanation for how sports are connected with cultural values and how they serve system needs in society*).

Ponomaryov, N.I. 1981. Sport and society (translated by James Riordan). Progress Publishers, Moscow (*a functionalist analysis of sport and physical culture in the former Soviet Union*).

Wohl, A. 1979. Sport and social development. International Review of Sport Sociology 14(3-4):5-18 (*classic discussion of the relationship between sport and "system needs"*).

CONFLICT THEORY

Brohm, J-M. 1978. Sport: a prison of measured time. Ink Links, Ltd., London (*essays on how sport is distorted by economic and political forces in contemporary society*).

Goodman, C. 1979. Choosing sides. Schocken Books, New York (*analysis of how street life and games in a New York City neighborhood were shaped and eventually destroyed by the political and economic forces in American capitalism*).

Hoch, P. 1972. Rip off the big game. Doubleday & Co., Inc., New York (*analysis of how sport is distorted by capitalism*).

Rigauer, B. 1981. Sport and work (translated by A. Guttmann). Columbia University Press, New York (*analysis of how sport is turned into work in contemporary society, especially in capitalist societies*).

CRITICAL THEORY

Cole, C., and S. Birrell, eds. (In press.) Women, sport, and culture. Human Kinetics Books, Champaign, Ill. (*collection of papers dealing with sports and sport-related topics from different feminist perspectives*).

Donnelly, P., ed. 1992. British cultural studies and sport. Special issue of the Sociology of Sport Journal 9(2) (*presents an explanation, a critique, and a series of examples of cultural studies approaches to sports*).

Foley, D.E. 1990. Learning capitalist culture. University of Pennsylvania Press, Philadelphia (*insightful use of a form of critical theory to analyze a field study of social life in a small town; sport rituals are central in the analysis*).

Gruneau, R. 1983. Class, sports, and social development. University of Massachusetts Press, Amherst, Mass. (*major theoretical contribution to the sociology of sport; uses critical theory to explain relationship between sport and social development*).

Hargreaves, J. 1986. Sport, power, and culture. St. Martin's Press, New York (*historical analysis of the link between sport and power in Britain*).

Harvey, J., and H. Cantalon, eds. 1988. Not just a game. University of Ottawa Press, Ottawa (*15 papers in which critical theory is used in the analysis of sport in Canada*).

Hollands, R. 1985. The role of cultural studies and social criticism in the sociological study of sport. Quest 36(1):66-79 (*explanation of "cultural studies" and how it can be used to understand the sport-society relationship*).

Messner, M. 1992. Power at play: sports and the problem of masculinity. Beacon Press, Boston (*critical feminist theory is used to guide a study of men's sport experiences; this is the best critical analysis of masculinity I have found*).

Messner, M., and D. Sabo, eds. 1992. Sport, men, and the gender order: critical feminist perspectives. Human Kinetics Books, Champaign, Ill. (*the 18 papers in this anthology use a combination of critical and feminist theory to understand different aspects of sports*).

Sage, G.H. 1990. Power and ideology in American sport: a critical perspective. Human Kinetics Books, Champaign, Ill. (*a clearly written, informative critical analysis of dominant sport forms in the United States; excellent book to use as an introduction to critical theory*).

Sage, G.H. ed. 1993. Sociocultural aspects of sport and physical activity: a critical perspective. Quest 45(2):Special Issue (*8 papers that critically assess sports and offer suggestions for making sports more democratic, just, and humane*).

SYMBOLIC INTERACTIONISM

Adler, P.A., and P. Adler. 1991. Backboards & blackboards: college athletes and role engulfment. Columbia University Press, New York (*insightful study uses an interactionist framework to explain identity formation processes among intercollegiate male athletes in a big-time sport program*).

Coakley, J., and A. White. 1992. Making decisions: Gender and sport participation among British adolescents. Sociology of Sport Journal 9(1):20-35 (*study shows how sport participation decisions among working class adolescents are mediated by a combination of meanings attached to past experiences, current resources, self-definitions, and cultural forces*).

Glassner, B. 1990. Fit for postmodern selfhood. In H.S. Becker and M.M. McCall, eds., Symbolic interaction and cultural studies (pp. 215-243). University of Chicago Press, Chicago (*this article presents an insightful analysis of fitness by combining a symbolic interactionist and a postmodern approach*).

Stevenson, C.L. 1990. The early careers of international athletes. Sociology of Sport Journal 7(3):238-253 (*this informative interactionist analysis explains the complex process through which people go as they make decisions leading to involvement in elite amateur sports*).

Schmitt, R.L., and W.M. Leonard. 1986. Immortalizing the self through sport. American Journal of Sociology 91(March):1088-1111 (*study shows how the collective memory of athletic accomplishments is created through interaction among sport fans and then used to socially construct the identities of individual athletes*).

REFERENCES ON FIGURATIONAL THEORY

Dunning, E., and C. Rojek, eds. 1992. Sport and leisure in the civilizing process: critique and counter-critique. University of Toronto Press, Toronto, Ontario (*although not discussed in this chapter, figurational theory is increasingly used in the sociology of sport; this book focuses on the strengths and weaknesses of this theoretical approach*).

Dunning, E., J.A. Maguire, and R.E. Pearton, eds. 1993. The sports process: a comparative and developmental approach. Human Kinetics Publishers, Champaign, Ill. (*the editors favor a figurational approach, but they pull together 12 pages using various perspectives to view comparative and developmental issues in sports*).

Elias, N., and E. Dunning. 1986. Quest for excitement. Basil Blackwell, Inc., New York (*uses figurational theory to guide discussions of sport as a form of pleasurable excitement that counterbalances the stress-tensions in the rest of people's lives*).

(H. Armstrong Roberts)

A LOOK AT THE PAST

How have sports changed throughout history?

To understand sports as social phenomena in today's world it helps to try to get a sense of what sport activities have been like in past times and different places. Therefore the purpose of this chapter is to briefly and selectively summarize the organization of sport activities in different cultural and historical settings. The material I present will focus on (1) the ancient Greeks, (2) the Romans, (3) the Middle Ages in parts of Europe, (4) the Renaissance and the Enlightenment in parts of Europe, and (5) the Industrial Revolution through recent times, with special emphasis on the United States.

This material is presented to illustrate that in each of these times and places, our understanding of how sport activities have been defined, organized, and played depends on what we know about the social lives of the people who created, played, and integrated those activities into their everyday experiences. In particular, it is especially important to know how people used their power and resources as they struggled with each other to shape physical activities that fit their needs and interests.

When sports are viewed in this way, we don't get bogged down with sequences of dates and events. Instead, we focus on the ways in which sport activities reflect relationships between various groups of people at particular times and places. This will be the focus throughout the chapter.

AN OPENING NOTE ON HISTORY

When we think about history, most of us think about a chronological sequence of events that build on each other and gradually lead to a better, or more "modern," society. Even the terminology used in many discussions of history leads us to think this way (as noted by Gruneau, 1988). For example, historical accounts are often full of references to societies that are traditional or modern, primitive or civilized, underdeveloped or developed, preindustrial or industrial. This terminology leads people to think that history is moving in a particular direction, and as it moves in that direction, things are improving and getting more modern and developed. In other words, history is frequently presented as linear and progressive.

Although this approach enables some people to feel superior because it allows them to conclude that they are the most modern, civilized, and developed people in history, it does not lead to an accurate analysis of what history is all about. For example, in the case of sports there are literally thousands of "histories" related to the development and organization of physical activities among thousands of groups of people in different places around the world. These histories involve patterns of changes that many people would not call progress. And it is important to remember that the definitions of progress used by different people are themselves products of their cultural experiences.

Evidence collected by many people suggests that physical activities of one sort or another have existed in all cultures. But the forms of these activities and the meanings people gave to them were the results of people interacting with each other and determining what sports should be, who should play them, and how various sport activities should be integrated in the culture as a whole. To say that sport activities over the years have evolved to fit a pattern of progress or modernization is to distort the life experiences of people all over the world (Gruneau, 1988). People around the world may be playing more and more of the same kinds of physical games today, but this is not because sports are being formed in various societies to fit some grand scheme for how physical activities should be organized. Nor does it mean that sports mean the same thing in different societies and cultural groups. Instead, similarities around the globe are due to who has power in the international arena and how that power is used to sponsor and promote particular sports and sport forms.

The importance of power relations in sports is clearly illustrated through the Olympic Games. For example, when new events are added to the Olympic Games, they usually reflect the interests of countries who can influence

SIDELINES

©1982 M.T.F.-T.W.S.-Lakewood, CO   Bill Whitehead 1982

"HOW CAN YOU STOP TO SHOOT POOL ON THE WAY HOME WHEN IT WON'T BE INVENTED FOR ANOTHER TEN MILLION YEARS?"

In prehistoric times there were no sports as we know them today. People hunted for food and used their physical abilities to defend themselves and establish their status and power among others.

the decisions made by the International Olympic Committee. This is why games from Africa, Latin American, and vast parts of Asia are not included in the Olympics. It is also why golf is being considered as a demonstration sport in the 1996 Summer Games in Atlanta—golf represents the interests of countries with large gross national products (GNPs) and high per capita income rates. To call this progress is to make a political statement, not an historical one.

So as you read this chapter don't conclude that it is a story of progress. Instead it is a series of stories about people at different times and places struggling over what they wanted their physical activities to be and how they wanted to include them in their lives. Certainly there is some continuity in many of these struggles in particular cultures, but continuity does not always mean that things are getting better. It would be encouraging to think that sports are somehow better today than they were in the past and that they will be better yet in the future. But human history does not follow some grand plan of progress. When progressive things do

happen it is because people have made them happen at a particular time, and those people usually realize that unless they keep an eye on things progress is often only temporary.

Therefore this analysis of sports at different times and places is *not* meant to be a history of sports. A history of sports would look at the development and organization of physical activities across each of the continents and from one cultural group to another over time. This would be an ambitious and worthy project, but it is not one I am prepared to undertake. The times and places I have chosen to review in this chapter are limited to "the Western world," so we must be careful not to conclude that they somehow represent the entire world *or* the most important part of the world. This chapter is just one look at a few past times and places.

SPORTS VARY BY TIME AND PLACE

People in all cultures have engaged in playful physical activities or used human movement as a part of their ritual life. As we look at cultural variations, it is necessary to remember that few cultures have organized their physical activities into sports as we have defined them in this book. This shows that even people's definitions of sports—and the meanings people attach to physical activities—are influenced by social and cultural factors. Furthermore, definitions and meanings change over time, and from group to group and place to place.

In prehistoric times there were no sports as we know them today. Physical activities were tied directly to the challenge of survival and the expression of religious beliefs. People hunted for food and sometimes used their physical abilities to defend themselves or establish status and power among others. Archaeological evidence suggests that people on each continent of the globe created unique organized forms of physical challenges—for the purpose of appeasing their gods—by acting out events having important symbolic or real meaning in their everyday lives. These challenges, even though they may have taken the form of games, were inseparable from sacred rituals and ceremonies. In fact, they were usually played as forms of religious worship, and sometimes their outcomes were determined by religious necessity rather than the physical abilities of the people involved (Guttmann, 1978).

The first forms of organized games around the world probably emerged from this combination of physical exercises and religious rituals. From what we can tell, these games not only reflected the social structures and the belief systems of the cultures in which they existed but they usually re-created and reaffirmed dominant cultural practices. But this was not always the case. Sometimes they served as sources of protest or opposition against dominant ways of doing things and thinking about things in a particular group or society.

Variations in the forms and dynamics of physical activities from time to time and place to place remind us that any cultural practice, even sports, can serve a variety of social purposes. This raises the question of how the definition and organization of sports in any society promotes the interests of various groups within that society. Since sport activities are created by people who operate within the constraints of the social world in which they live, not everyone has an equal say in the way activities are defined and organized. Those with the strongest vested interests and the most *power* in a group or society will generally have the most impact on the way sports are defined, organized, and played in that group or society. Of course, sport activities will not totally reflect the desires of powerful people, but the activities will represent their interests more heavily than the interests of other groups within society.

This approach to studying sports calls attention to the existence and consequences of social inequality in society. Social inequalities have always had a significant impact on how sport activities are organized and played in any situation. And the most influential forms of social inequality are those related to wealth, political power, social status, gender, age, and race

and ethnicity. We will pay special attention to these in the following discussions of times and places.

GAMES IN ANCIENT GREECE: BEYOND THE MYTHS (1000 BC TO 100 BC)

The games played by the early Greeks (circa 900 BC) were grounded in mythology and religious beliefs. They were usually held in conjunction with festivals involving a combination of prayer, sacrifices, and religious services, along with music, dancing, and ritual feasts. Competitors in these early games were from wealthy, respected Greek families. They were the only ones who had the resources to hire trainers and coaches and had the time needed to travel to the various games. Events were clearly based on the interests of young males. They consisted primarily of warrior sports, such as chariot racing, wrestling and boxing, javelin and discus throwing, foot racing, archery, and long jumping. Violence and serious injuries were commonplace compared with today's sport events (Elias, 1986; Kidd, 1984). The sport activities engaged in by Greek women, children, and older people were occasionally included in the festivals, but they were never incorporated into the games held at Olympia.

The locations and dates of the Greek festivals were also linked to religious beliefs. For example, Olympia was chosen as one of the festival sites because it was associated with the achievements and activities of celebrated Greek gods and mythological characters. In fact, Olympia was dedicated as a shrine to the god Zeus about 1000 BC. Although permanent buildings and playing fields were not constructed until about 550 BC, the games at Olympia were held every 4 years. Additional festivals involving athletic contests were also held at other locations throughout Greece (Corinth, Delphi, and Nemea), but the Olympic Games became the most prestigious of all athletic events.

Women were traditionally prohibited from participating in the Olympic Games. They could not even enter the playing areas or the stadium as spectators. However, women held their own games at Olympia. Dedicated to the goddess Hera, the sister-wife of Zeus, these games grew out of traditional Greek fertility rites. And according to some estimates, the Heraean Games even predated the exclusively male Olympic Games. Unfortunately, serious women athletes often risked their heterosexual reputations in the eyes of males when they engaged in sports. Physical prowess did not fit with popular definitions of femininity among the Greeks. Therefore participation in the major Greek games led to questions about sexuality and sexual orientation (Kidd, 1984). For example, the sexuality of the goddesses who possessed physical strength and skills in Greek mythology was questioned by many. The discrimination against women who participated in sports was grounded in a patriarchal family structure in which females had no legal rights and only limited opportunities for experiences outside their households. Although some women from well-to-do Greek families did become regular participants in the games at certain locations, their involvement was limited to only a few events and their achievements were not promoted and publicized like the achievements of male athletes.

As the visibility and popularity of the games at Olympia grew, they took on political significance. Opponents began to compete for the glory of their city-states. When this happened, slaves were often recruited as athletes, and physically skilled young men from lower-class backgrounds were hired by wealthy patrons or funded by the tax revenues of city-states to train especially for the Olympics and other games. Victories brought these hired athletes cash prizes in addition to their living expenses. Victories also earned them reputations that could be converted into cash rewards when competing in the other popular Greek games. In fact, rewards were attractive enough to create a group of professional male athletes in Greece. During the second century BC, these professionals organized athletic guilds similar to the players' associations and unions in today's North American

sports. Through these guilds they bargained for athletes' rights and "to have a say in the scheduling of games, travel arrangements, personal amenities, pensions, and old-age security in the form of serving as trainers and managers" (Baker, 1982).

Greek athletes specialized to such an extent that they made poor soldiers. They engaged in warrior sports, but they lacked the generalized skills of warriors. Furthermore, they concentrated so much of their time on athletic training that they ignored intellectual development. This evoked widespread criticism from Greek philosophers. According to many philosophers, Greek games were brutal and dehumanizing, and athletes were useless and ignorant citizens—people with limited physical skills and dull minds. It seems that the "dumb athlete" stereotype emerged long before the days of college scholarships.

Sports in Greek culture influenced art, philosophy, and the everyday lives of a number of people, especially those wealthy enough to train themselves, hire professionals, or travel to games. However, Greek games and contests were different from the organized, competitive games that we call sports today (see box on pp. 66-67). First, they were grounded in religion; second, they lacked complex administrative structures; and third, they did not involve the measurements and record keeping that characterize what we defined as sport in Chapter 1 (Guttmann, 1978). However, there is one major similarity: they reflected and re-created dominant structural characteristics and patterns of social relations in the society as a whole. The power and advantages that went along with being wealthy, male, and young in Greek society served to shape games and contests in ways that limited the participation of women, older people, and those without many economic resources. In fact, the definitions of excellence used to evaluate performance even reflected the abilities of young males. This meant that the abilities of others were by definition substandard (Kidd, 1984). We can see the same things in many organized sports today.

ROMAN SPORT EVENTS: SPECTACLES AND GLADIATORS (100 BC TO 500 AD)

Roman leaders used sport activities to train soldiers and provide entertainment spectacles for the general population. They borrowed events from Greek games and contests, but they geared athletic training to the preparation of obedient military men. They were critical of the Greek emphasis on individualism and the development of specialized physical skills that were useless in battle. Furthermore, they packaged their sport activities in ways that would appeal to spectators.

Through the first century AD, Roman sport events increasingly took the form of circuses and gladiatorial contests. Chariot races were the most popular events during the spectacles. Wealthy Romans recruited their slaves as charioteers. Spectators bet heavily on the races, and when they became bored or unruly, the emperors passed around fruit and bread to keep them from getting too hostile. In some cases, free raffle tickets for attractive prizes were distributed through the crowd to keep riots from starting when people became overexcited. This tactic not only pacified the crowds but it allowed the emperors to use sport events as occasions to celebrate themselves and their positions of power. Government officials outside of Rome did the same thing during local events to maintain control in their communities.

As the power and influence of the Roman Empire grew, sport events and spectacles became increasingly important as a source of diversion for the masses. By 300 AD, half of the days on the Roman calendar were public holidays. Many workers held only part-time jobs, and unemployment was extremely high. Something else was needed to spice up the chariot races, boxing matches, and other athletic events. Bearbaiting and bullbaiting along with animal fights were added to keep the game days more interesting for spectators. Another addition involved men and women being forced into the arena to engage in mortal combat with lions, tigers, and panthers. And sometimes condemned criminals were dressed in sheepskin and thrown in with partially starved wild animals. Gladiators, armed with a variety of weapons, were pitted against one another in gory fights to the death. According to Baker (1982), these spectacles achieved two purposes for the Romans: they provided "entertainment for an idle populace while at the same time disposing of the socially undesirable." "Undesirable" people included thieves, murderers, and Christians.

Some Romans criticized these spectacles as tasteless activities, devoid of any cultural value. However, criticisms were not based on concerns for slaves, troublemakers, or Christians. They were based on the idea that no good could come out of events during which people from different social classes mixed and fraternized with one another while watching "common people" being maimed and killed. In other words, the objections were based on prejudice against the lower classes. Other than some outspoken Christians, few people objected to the spectacles on moral or humanitarian grounds.

The objections coming from the Christians had little effect on the fate of the events. In fact, the demise of Roman sport spectacles went hand in hand with the fall of the Roman Empire. As the Roman economy went deeper and deeper into depression, there were not enough resources to support sport spectacles. Sport historian, William Baker (1982) explains this process in the following way:

> Taxes and prices rose disastrously, trade declined, and prominent families left the cities for the simpler security of country life. Thus the [sport] spectacles, dependent on abundant wealth and a large urban population, declined in popularity.

Women were seldom involved in Roman sport events. They were allowed in the arenas to watch and cheer male athletes, but few of them had any opportunities to develop their own athletic skills. Within the Roman family, women were legally subservient to and rigidly controlled by men. As with Greek women, the pursuit of interests beyond the confines of the household was restricted.

Although folk games and local sport activities existed throughout the Roman Empire, there is little information on how they were organized and played and what they meant in people's lives. The spectacles did not capture the interests of everyone, but they certainly evoked considerable attention in major population centers. Roman sport events differed from organized sports today in that they were sometimes connected with religious rituals, and they seldom involved the quantification of athletic achievements or the recording of outstanding accomplishments (see box on pp. 66-67).

TOURNAMENTS AND GAMES DURING THE MIDDLE AGES: SEPARATION OF THE MASTERS AND THE MASSES (500 TO 1300)

During the Middle Ages, the Greek festivals and the Roman spectacles were replaced by local games and tournaments. The games played by the peasants emerged from the combined influence of local customs and the Roman Catholic Church. The tournaments of the feudal aristocracy, however, emerged from the demands of military training and the desire for entertainment among the nobles and those who served them.

Local games of this period have an interesting history. As Roman soldiers and government officials moved throughout parts of Europe during the fourth and fifth centuries, they built bathing facilities to use during their leisure time. To loosen up before their baths they engaged in various forms of ball play. Local peasants picked up on the Roman activities and gradually developed their own forms of ball games. These games were often integrated into local religious ceremonies. For example, tossing a ball back and forth was sometimes defined as a representation of the conflict between good and evil, light and darkness, or life and death. As the influence of the Roman Catholic Church spread over the continent during the early years of the Middle Ages, these symbolic rituals were redefined in terms of Roman Catholic beliefs.

During most of the medieval period, the Roman Catholic Church accepted peasant ball games. In fact, local priests encouraged games by opening up church grounds on holidays and Sunday afternoons to groups of participants. In this way the games simply became a part of village life. They were played whenever there were festive community gatherings. They were included with the music, dancing, and religious services held in conjunction with seasonal ceremonies and saints' feast days. These local ball games contained the roots for many contemporary games, such as soccer, field hockey, football, rugby, bowling, curling, baseball, and cricket.

The games played in peasant villages had little structure and few rules. Play was guided by local traditions, and traditions varied from one community to the next. Baker (1982) provides an interesting description of a thirteenth century "futball" game played in England on Shrove Tuesday, the day before the start of Lent:

> At Derby . . . teams from the two parishes of St. Peter's and All Saints squared off. The three miles of countryside separating the parishes constituted the "field" of play. The size of the teams was not fixed; anyone living in the parishes played. There were no written rules. The purpose of the game was simply to kick, carry, or throw the ball against the opponents goal—a prominent gate in the parish of St. Peter's, an old waterwheel in All Saints' parish. Inspired by local pride and Shrovetide ale, villagers kicked, bit, and mauled each other. Some took the opportunity to even old scores.*

The games of the upper classes were distinctively different from the games of the peasants during the Middle Ages. Access to equipment and facilities allowed the nobility to develop

---

*Material reprinted from *Sports in the Western World* by permission of the author and the publisher, Rowman and Littlefield Co., Totowa, N.J., 1982.

early versions of billiards, shuffleboard, tennis, handball, and jai alai. Ownership of horses allowed them to develop various forms of horse racing (while their stable hands developed a version of horseshoes). From horseback they also participated in hunting and hawking. With some exceptions, women seldom engaged in any of these active pursuits. Gender relations were patterned so that roles were clearly differentiated and upper-class women did little outside the walls of their dwellings. And their activities seldom involved physical exertion.

Through a good part of the medieval period, the most popular sporting events among the upper classes were tournaments consisting of a series of war games, designed to keep knights and nobles ready for battle. Early versions of tournaments differed very little from actual battlefield confrontations. Deaths and serious injuries occurred, victors carried off their opponents' possessions, and losers were often taken as prisoners and used to demand ransoms from opposing camps. Later versions of tournaments were not quite so serious, but they still involved injuries and occasional deaths. Gradually, the warlike nature of tournament confrontations was softened by colorful ceremonies and pageantry. Entertainment and chivalry took priority over the issues of military preparation and reaping the fruits of victory.

The upper classes paid little attention to and seldom interfered with the leisure activities of the peasants because they perceived games and other expressive activities among peasants as safety valves against social discontent (Baker, 1982). However, things began to change in the fourteenth and fifteenth centuries. Wars throughout Europe convinced monarchs, government officials, and church authorities of the need for increased military strength. In response to this need they enacted new rules prohibiting popular peasant pastimes. The time peasants spent playing games was seen as time that could be spent learning to defend the lands and lives of their masters. But despite the pronouncements of bishops and kings, the peasants did not readily give up their games. In fact, the games sometimes became rallying points for opposition to government and church authority.

Throughout the medieval period women were less apt to be involved in physically active games and sport activities than were their male counterparts. Restricted opportunities were grounded in a combination of religious dogma (the Roman Catholic Church taught that women had inferior status) and a male-centered family structure. A woman's duty was to be obedient and submissive. This orientation did not change much through the Middle Ages. However, peasant women were involved in some of the games and physical activities associated with the regular rounds of village events during the year. Women in the upper classes sometimes engaged in "ladylike" games and activities, but because they were subject to the control of men and often viewed as sex objects and models of beauty, their involvement in active pursuits was limited. Feminine beauty during this time was defined in passive terms—the less active a woman was, the more she was likely to be perceived as beautiful. Therefore meeting the expectations for beauty precluded all but very limited involvement in physical exercise (this sounds familiar to anyone over 40 years old in North America!).

Medieval tournaments and games were not much like today's organized sports, even though they contained the roots for many of today's sport activities in Europe and North America. They lacked the specialization and organization of today's competitive sports. They never involved the measurement and recording of athletic achievements, and they were not based on a commitment to equal and open competition among athletes from diverse backgrounds (see box on pp. 66-67). This latter point has been vividly described by Guttmann (1978):

> In medieval times, jousts and tournaments were limited to the nobility. Knights who sullied their honor by inferior marriages—to peasant girls, for instance—were disbarred. If they were bold enough to enter a tournament despite the loss of status, and were discovered, they were beaten

and their weapons were broken. Peasants reckless enough to emulate the sport of their masters were punished by death.*

Many of the characteristics of medieval sport activities were carried over through the Renaissance and Enlightenment periods.

THE RENAISSANCE, REFORMATION, AND ENLIGHTENMENT: GAMES AS DIVERSIONS (1300 TO 1800)

The Renaissance began during the fourteenth century and lasted through the early sixteenth century. During the first half of this period, the scholar-athlete became the ideal among the aristocrats and the affluent. In fact, the "Renaissance man" was someone who was "socially adept, sensitive to aesthetic values, skilled in weaponry, strong of body, and learned in letters" (Baker, 1982). While this ideal was being pursued by the wealthy, the peasants continued their own local versions of folk games and sport activities. Although the authorities during the fifteenth century did not support or promote the sport activities of the peasants, they did little to interfere with them.

Throughout the Renaissance period, women had relatively few opportunities to be involved in sport activities. Although peasant women sometimes played physical games, their lives were restricted by the demands of work both inside and out of the home. They often did hard physical labor, but they were not encouraged to be competitive or to engage in public activities that called special attention to their abilities and accomplishments. Upper-class women sometimes participated in activities like bowling, croquet, archery, and tennis, but because women were seen as being "naturally" weak and passive, their involvement was limited. These women may have been pampered and occasionally put on proverbial pedestals, but their lives were tightly controlled by men who maintained their positions of power partially by promoting the idea that women were too fragile to leave the home and do things on their own.

During the Protestant Reformation a growth in negative attitudes regarding games and sport activities adversely affected the participation of both men and women, especially in locations where either Calvinism or Puritanism was popular. For example, between the early 1500s and the late 1600s the English Puritans worked hard to eliminate or control leisure activities, including games and sports, in everyday life in England. The Puritans were devoted to the work ethic and, according to one social historian (Malcolmson, 1984), this is how they viewed sports:

> . . . [Sports] were thought to be profane and licentious—they were occasions of worldly indulgence that tempted men from a godly life; being rooted in pagan and popish practices, they were rich in the sort of ceremony and ritual that poorly suited the Protestant conscience; they frequently involved a desecration of the Sabbath and an interference with the worship of the true believers; they disrupted the peaceable order of society, distracting men from their basic social duties—hard work, thrift, personal restraint, devotion to family, [and] a sober carriage.

The primary targets of the Puritans were the games and sports of the peasants. Peasants didn't own their own property, so their festivities occurred in public settings and attracted large crowds; thus they were easy for the Puritans to attack and criticize. And the Puritans did their best to eliminate them—especially festivities scheduled on Sunday afternoons. It was not that the Puritans objected so much to the games themselves, but they disapproved of the drinking and partying that accompanied the games and did not like the idea of holding games on the Sabbath. The sport activities of the affluent were less subject to Puritan interference. Activities like horse racing, hunting, tennis, and bowling took place on the private property of the wealthy, making it difficult for the Puritans to enforce their prohibitions. As in other times and places, power relations have much to do with who plays what activities under what conditions.

Despite the Puritans and despite social changes affecting the stability and economic structure of English village life, many peasant people maintained their participation in games and sports. However, some of their traditional public activities had to be adapted so they could be played in less public settings. During the early 1600s the Puritan influence in England was challenged by King James I, who issued *The King's Book of Sports.* This book, reissued in 1633 by Charles I, emphasized that lawful recreational pursuits among the English people should not be discouraged by Puritan ministers or officials. Charles I and his successors ushered in a new day for English sporting life. Traditional festivals were revived, and public games and sport activities were actively promoted and supported. A few sports, including cricket, horse racing, yachting, fencing, golf, and boxing, became highly organized during the late 1600s and the 1700s.

In colonial America, Puritan influence lasted into the eighteenth century. The Pilgrims were not playful people—hard work was necessary for survival. However, as the life-styles of the colonists became established and as free time became available, Puritan beliefs ceased to be as important as making old games a part of life in new communities. Town laws prohibiting games and sports were gradually abandoned, and traditional leisure activities, including sports, grew in popularity.

During this time, the games of Native Americans were not affected by the influence of the Puritans. Native peoples in the East and Northeast continued to play games that had been a part of their cultures for centuries. In fact, sport and sport participation has many histories across North America. The material in the box on pp. 62-63 explains how and why the history of sports among Native Americans has been distorted.

During the Enlightenment period (1700 to 1800), many games and sport activities in parts of Europe and North America started to resemble sport forms that we are familiar with today.

With some exceptions they were no longer grounded in religious ritual and ceremony; they involved some specialization and some degree of organization, achievements were sometimes measured, and records were occasionally kept. Furthermore, the idea that events should be open to all competitors, regardless of background, became increasingly popular. This same commitment to equality and open participation gave rise to world-changing revolutions in France and the United States.

However, sport activities during the Enlightenment period were different from high profile sport forms of today in at least one important respect: they were defined strictly as diversions, that is, as interesting and often challenging ways to pass free time. They were not seen as having any utility for athletes in particular or society in general. No one seriously entertained the idea that sport and sport participation could change the way people thought or behaved or the way social life was organized. Therefore there were no reasons for people to organize sport activities for others or to build sport organizations to oversee the activities of large networks of participants. People formed a few sport clubs, and they occasionally scheduled competitive events with other groups, but they did not feel compelled to form leagues or national and international associations. This all began to change during the Industrial Revolution.

THE INDUSTRIAL REVOLUTION: THE EMERGENCE OF STANDARDIZED SPORT FORMS (1780 TO PRESENT)

It would be an oversimplification to say that the organized, competitive sports of today are simply a product of the Industrial Revolution (Gruneau, 1988). They clearly emerged during the process of industrialization, but they were actually the "social constructions" of people themselves—people who were simply trying to play their games and maintain their sport activities while they coped with the realities of everyday life in their own changing families and communities. The fact that sports are con-

REFLECT ON **SPORT**

Lessons from History: Distorted Views of Indian Sports

The history of sports is noteworthy as much for what it does not tell us as for what it does tell us. This is especially true when it comes to the physical activities, games, and sports of native Americans. In the Prologue of his book, *American Indian Sports Heritage*, educator Joseph Oxendine explains why this is so. Here's what he says:[*]

Several major difficulties accompany the task of presenting American Indian sports in historical perspective. Foremost among these is the lack of adequate recorded history. Of course, there is no written history of the American Indian prior to the arrival of Columbus in 1492. It was another two to three centuries before significant cultural information was recorded about the Indian. Consequently, most of the relevant literature has been produced within the past two centuries, a period during which Indian culture was being greatly influenced by non-Indians. Nevertheless, Indian oral history and mythology have contributed importantly to the body of information about sports and games. In addition, archaeologists and anthropologists have been able to establish hypotheses about traditional Indian culture, including sports, on the basis of playing implements, ball courts, eyewitness reports, and other evidence that has become available during recent years.

Over the past two centuries, reporting on Indians and Indian sports has been seriously distorted. The 19th century, for example, was a very atypical period for Indians, given the almost constant rash of "Indian wars." In addition, the nonIndian population of this country increased rapidly and constantly pushed westward into traditional Indian lands. Along with the general mistreatment of Indians, this caused Native American lifestyles to bear less and less resemblance to traditional patterns.

It became practically impossible, furthermore, for nonIndians to observe Indian games and ceremonies in the Indians' traditional form and significance. When they did enter the Indians' midst, it was usually as an oddity, either not able or not wishing to participate fully in the activities. [Furthermore, being watched by nonIndians certainly]. . . tended to restrain the behavior of Indians who were aware that they were being watched and studied. By the time sizable numbers of Indians had acquired a facility with the English language, their rituals, games, and ceremonies had been appreciably altered.

Several Indian games were essentially religious rites; they were more religion than *play* in today's meaning of the term. . . . As such, nonIndians

[*]From *American Indian Sports Heritage* (pp. xxi-xxiii) by J.B. Oxendine, 1988, Champaign, IL: Human Kinetics. Copyright 1988 by Joseph B. Oxendine. Reprinted by permission.

REFLECT ON SPORT

were not usually allowed to view these activities in their traditional form. Consequently, complete and accurate descriptions of these activities have not been reported in the literature.

Despite the many diversities among the tribes and in addition to the communications problems, there were commonalities that transcended most traditional Indian cultures. . . . [M]any games and practices tended to be universal and were found in most tribes. These games and customs were transmitted through normal communication and interaction that took place among tribes during their centuries of residence in this hemisphere.

In recent years, a major problem in reporting on Indian sports performers has been the lack of a systematic way of identifying persons as Indians. During the last two decades, Indians have participated in practically all sports in all parts of the country, both as amateurs and as professionals. Although some have been identified or recognized as Indians, others have not. The lack of a uniform identification system, as well as a central record-keeping mechanism, makes the task of highlighting Indian athletic performance particularly difficult. In former years it was relatively easy to identify a Native American. Today's increasing interaction among races, including assimilation and other social developments, makes such identification less clear. Some Indians, both full-blood and mixed-blood, have welcomed such identification, whereas others have not (pp. xxi-xxiii).

Oxendine's analysis tells us things about history that are important to know when we do the sociology of sport. He clearly shows that people's ideas about what they want sport to be and how they include it in their lives are often influenced by social, political, and economic forces that are far beyond the control of individuals in particular groups or societies. Oxendine's analysis reminds us that if we want to understand the social importance of an historical event such as the establishment in 1983 of the Iroquois National Lacrosse Team (see Ch. 14 in Oxendine), we need to know about Native American cultures in general, about the history and organization of the six nations of the Iroquois Confederation, about the relations between Native Americans and the U.S. government, and about the experiences of Native American men and women as they have struggled to honor their cultural heritage and survive in a society where powerful others have consistently tried to strip them of their dignity, language, religion, and customs.

History is much more than a chronological series of events, and it can be viewed from many different perspectives. Therefore when we study the history of sports we must be aware of whose perspectives are being represented and whose are being ignored or described by "outsiders."

structed in connection with social relations is one of the reasons why sport activities and organizations have always differed from one country to another and from one group to another within countries. This point is further explained in the next section.

It is difficult to pinpoint the beginning of the Industrial Revolution. It is not marked by a single event, but it started with the development of factories and the mass production of consumer goods. It was associated with the development of cities and an increased dependence on technology. It involved changes in the organization and control of work and community life and was generally accompanied by an increase in the number of middle-class people in the societies in which it occurred. The Industrial Revolution first began in England around 1780. Shortly after that time it became a part of life in other European countries; in the United States and Canada it started around 1820.

The Early Years: Limited Time and Space

During the early years of the Industrial Revolution it was difficult for most people, except the very wealthy, to maintain their involvement in games and sport activities. For those who worked on farms and in factories, free time was a scarce commodity; the workday was 12 to 15 hours long for everyone, including many children. For those who lived in cities, there were few open spaces for sport activities. Production took priority over play and sport activities in the plans of city leaders. Parks did not exist. Furthermore, working people were discouraged from getting together in large groups outside the workplace. Industrialists perceived such gatherings as dangerous because they wasted time that could be used for work and because they provided opportunities for workers to organize themselves into groups that might threaten the production process and the interests of the wealthy.

This orientation was strongly endorsed by the clergy in most industrializing countries. They preached about the moral value of work

and the immorality of play and idleness. In fact, they generally banned sports on Sundays and accused anyone who was not totally committed to work as being lazy. Work was a sign of goodness. Not everyone agreed with this way of looking at things, but working people had few choices. For them, survival depended on working long hours, regardless of what they thought about work, and they had little power to change these definitions of work or what it took for them to survive.

In most countries, games and sport activities existed during this period despite the Industrial Revolution, not because of it. People in small towns and farm communities still had opportunities to participate in games and sport activities during their seasonal festivities, holidays, and public ceremonies. But most city people had few opportunities to organize their own games and sports. The only exceptions to this were those few people who were able to use newly acquired family fortunes to maintain lives of leisure. For the working classes, sport involvement seldom went beyond the role of spectator at a commercialized event. Although there were variations from one country to the next, urban workers watched a combination of cricket, horse racing, boxing and wrestling, footraces, rowing and yachting races, cockfighting, bullbaiting, and circus acts, among other things. It seems that the rules against getting together in large crowds were suspended when people were participating in a controlled commercialized spectator event. A fear of riots led to restrictions on many neighborhood events that might have attracted crowds, but organized commercial events were seldom objected to in most industrial societies, even when they attracted large groups.

Active sport participation among urban workers existed, but it was relatively rare during the early days of the Industrial Revolution. For example, in the United States it was usually limited to activities like bowling and billiards, and these were played mostly by males. The constraints of work and the lack of material resources made it difficult to engage in any-thing but informal games and sport activities. There were some exceptions, but they were rare.

Around the middle of the nineteenth century, things began to change. Through the first part of the century, people had become worried about the physical health of workers in industrial countries. Weak and sickly workers could not be productive workers. There were calls for open spaces and "healthy" leisure pursuits. Fitness became highly publicized, and there was an emphasis on calisthenics, gymnastics, and outdoor exercises. These fitness activities did not necessarily include sports, but they definitely excluded hanging around in pool halls, bowling alleys, and bars. The emergence of formally organized, competitive sports required more than calls for healthy leisure activities, but this was the time during which their foundations were established. In discussing more recent issues related to sport in society, the next section will focus heavily on events in the United States.

The Later Years: Changing Interests, Values, and Opportunities

Through the late-nineteenth and twentieth century there has been a growing emphasis on rationality and control in American society as a whole. For example, common interests in sport activities led to the establishment of organized clubs through which sport participation was sponsored and controlled. Club membership was usually limited to the wealthier people in urban areas and to college students at the exclusive Eastern schools. However, the clubs did sponsor competitions that often attracted spectators from all social classes. The games and sport activities of the people in lower income groups did not occur under the sponsorship of clubs or organizations, and they seldom received any publicity. The major exception to this pattern occurred in connection with baseball. Middle- and working-class male participation in baseball was relatively widespread, and after the

Civil War, baseball games were organized, sponsored, and publicized in many communities throughout the East and Midwest. Leagues were established at various levels of competition, and professional baseball became increasingly popular. Professional women's teams existed, but they seldom received the sponsorship needed to grow in popularity.

As sport activities became more organized and controlled, they generally reinforced existing class distinctions in society. Upper-class clubs emphasized achievement and "gentlemanly" involvement—an orientation that ultimately provided the basis for later definitions of amateurism. These definitions of amateur then became tools for excluding working-class people in the sport events organized to fit the interests of upper-class participants (Eitzen, 1988). The activities of the working classes, however, were much more likely to emphasize folk games and commercialized sports—a combination that ultimately led to professionalization. This two-phased process related to amateurism and professionalization was not unique to the United States; in different ways it also occurred in Canada and a number of European countries, especially England.

Underlying the increasing organization of sport activities was a growing emphasis on the seriousness of sports. Instead of being defined simply as enjoyable diversions, organized sports came to be seen as tools for achieving economic progress and social development. Many people linked sport participation with economic productivity, national loyalty, and the development of admirable character traits, especially among males. This new way of looking at organized sports started to become popular during the middle of the nineteenth century in England and toward the latter part of the nineteenth century in the United States and Canada. It was grounded in a wide array of changes in every segment of industrial society—changes tied to the economy, politics, family life, religion, education, science, philosophy, and technology.

The Characteristics of High Profile, Organized, Competitive Sports

A comparison with sport forms from the past shows that the organized, competitive sports of today have unique characteristics. When Allen Guttmann (1978) made such a comparison he found that dominant sport forms today are very different from the games and sport activities played before the Industrial Revolution. According to Guttmann, the dominant form of today's sports has seven interrelated characteristics that have never appeared together in sport forms of the past. These seven characteristics are:

1. *Secularism*. Today's sports are not directly linked to religious beliefs or religious rituals. They are a means of entertainment rather than worship; they are played for personal gains rather than the appeasement of gods. Today's sports are not intended to transcend the material world; instead, they embody the immediacy and values of the material world. They are not part of the sacred even though many people may define them as important parts of life.

2. *Equality*. Today's sports are based on the ideas that participation should not be regulated by birthrights or social backgrounds and that every contestant in a sport event should face the same set of competitive conditions; that is, everyone begins competing as an equal, regardless of who they are or where they come from. Of course, perfect equality never exists, but today's sports are based on the assumption that the quest for equality should guide the playing of competitive events.

3. *Specialization*. Today's sports are dominated by the participation of specialists and the spectators who watch them. Athletes often dedicate themselves exclusively to participation in a single event or position within an event. Positions in sports are often defined and distinguished from one another by skills and responsibilities. Equipment, such as shoes and clothing, is specialized to fit the demands of particular activities.

Organized, competitive sports today are characterized by an emphasis on quantification, among other things. Everything that can be defined in terms of time, distance, or scores is measured and recorded. (Colorado Springs Gazette Telegraph and Bob Jackson)

REFLECT ON SPORT

4. *Rationalization*. Today's sports consist of complex sets of rules and strategies. Rules specify goals and how goals are to be pursued; they also regulate equipment, playing techniques, and the conditions of participation. Strategies inspire rationally controlled training methods that affect the experience of sport participation and the evaluation of athletes.

5. *Bureaucratization*. Today's sports are controlled through the establishment of complex organizations on the international, national, and local levels. The people in these organizations oversee and sanction athletes, teams, and events. They make up and enforce rules, organize events, and certify records.

6. *Quantification*. Today's sports feature an abundance of measurements and statistics. Everything that can be reduced to a time, distance, or score is measured and recorded. Standards of achievement are discussed in clearly measurable terms, and statistics are used as proof of achievements.

7. *Records*. Today's sports involve an emphasis on setting and breaking records. Performances are compared from one event to another, and records are published for individuals, teams,

leagues, events, communities, states, provinces, and continents. Most important, of course, are world records.

One or more of these traits have characterized the sport forms of previous historical periods, but until the 19th century never have all seven appeared together in a single sport form. This does not mean that today's organized, competitive sports are somehow superior to the games and activities of the past. It means only that they are different in the way they are organized. We are concerned with those differences because they have implications for who participates and how participation is experienced.

Table 3-1 summarizes Guttmann's historical analysis of sports in terms of these characteristics. It illustrates that today's organized competitive sports are indeed different from the sports played by people in times past. However, it does not explain why the differences exist.

Finally, it should be remembered that these seven characteristics are not found in all sports today. Sports are social constructions, and many people seek alternatives to the organized, competitive sports in which these seven characteristics exist.

Table 3-1 Historical comparison of organized games, contests, and sport activities*

Characteristic	Greek games and contests (1000 BC to 100 BC)	Roman sports events (100 BC to 500 AD)	Medieval games and tournaments (500 to 1300)	Renaissance and Enlightenment games and sport activities (1300 to 1800)	Modern sports
Secularism	Yes & no	Yes & no	Yes & no	Yes & no	Yes
Equality	Yes & no	Yes & no	No	Yes & no	Yes
Specialization	Yes	Yes	No	Yes & no	Yes
Rationalization	Yes	Yes	No	No	Yes
Bureaucratization	Yes & no	Yes	No	No	Yes
Quantification	No	Yes	No	Yes & no	Yes
Records	No	No	No	Yes & no	Yes

*This is a modified version of a table developed by Guttmann (1978). Guttmann's information on primitive sports has been dropped; information on sports during the Renaissance and Enlightenment has been added; and column titles have been changed.

This 1906 drawing of "The Hockey Girl" illustrates that sports at the turn of the century were included in the leisure activities of the wealthy. It also suggests that wealthy women at that time were not excluded from playing hockey on a competitive level. It took a while for systems of gender exclusion and discrimination to develop in certain sports. (Sally Fox)

THE GROWTH OF ELITE, COMPETITIVE SPORTS IN THE UNITED STATES: 1880 TO 1920

Power and wealth in action. The years between 1880 and 1920 were crucial for the development of elite, competitive sport forms in the United States (Cavallo, 1981; Mrozek, 1983). Very wealthy people during this time developed lives of leisure in which sport activities played a major role. In fact, the rich used participation in certain sports to prove to the world that they were successful enough to be able to "waste" time engaging in frivolous, nonproductive activities (Veblen, 1899). Although the wealthy often used sports to reinforce status distinctions between themselves and the rest of the population, they also influenced the ways in which sports were played and organized by others, especially those in the middle class who aspired to enter the ranks of the "rich and famous."

The influence of the wealthy affected the development of norms for both players and spectators, the development of standards for facilities and equipment, and the ways in which sports were defined and integrated into the leisure patterns of people in other social classes. Specifically, people with economic power were able to use their resources to encourage others to define sport as a consumer activity to be played in *proper* attire, using the *proper* equipment in a *proper* facility, and preceded or followed by *proper* social occasions having little or nothing to do with employment and the workplace. Through this process of "encouragement" (referred to as hegemony by many sociologists; see Chapter 4, p. 88), sports became tied to the economy because they involved consumption, but they were also separate from the economy in that they were defined by people as "nonwork."

The emergence of these ideas about how sports "should be played" was important because it enabled people with power to reproduce their power without coercively forcing workers to do certain things and think in certain ways. Instead of maintaining their power by being nasty, people with economic power promoted sport forms that were entertaining and fun at the same time that they reinforced the values and orientations that were good for capitalist business expansion. This is how sports are both "political" and "economic" activities even though most people just see them as fun physical activities and events.

During the period from 1880 to 1920, opportunities for sport involvement among middle and working class people grew. Labor unions, progressive government legislation, and economic expansion combined to improve working and living conditions. The efforts of unions and social reformers gradually led to increases in the free time and the material resources available to working-class people. This process was complemented by the expansion of the middle class, a collection of people with at least some leisure resources. The spirit of reform around the turn of the century was also associated with the development of parks, recreation programs, and organized playground activities for city people, especially children.

Ideas about sport participation and "character development." Early in this century opportunities for sport involvement increased, but the kinds of opportunities available to most people were shaped by factors beyond the interests of the participants themselves. Important changes in the ways people thought about human behavior, individual development, and social life led to an emphasis on organized, competitive sports as "character-building" activities.

Until the latter part of the nineteenth century, most people believed human behavior was unrelated to environmental factors. They believed that individual development was dictated by fate or supernatural forces and that social life was patterned by necessity and coincidence. However, these ideas began to change as people became aware of the links between the environment and behavior and of the possibility to intentionally change the way social life was organized. This new perspective was a crucial catalyst in the growth of modern sports; it made sports into something more than just enjoyable pastimes. Gradually, sports were defined as sources for potential educational experiences—experiences with important consequences for both individuals and society as a whole. This change provided a new basis for organizing and promoting sport participation. For the first time in history, people saw sports as tools for changing behavior, shaping character, building unity and cohesion within a diversified population, and creating national loyalty.

The seriousness of organized sports became widely recognized throughout the United States. For example, some members of religious groups suggested there was a link between physical strength and the ability to do good works; they promoted sport involvement as an avenue for spiritual reform. Others saw sports as tools for teaching immigrant children lessons to help them become contributing members of a corporate-bureaucratic-democratic society; they promoted organized playground programs in which team sports were used to undermine traditional ethnic values and replace them with an Americanized version of looking at the world. People interested in economic expansion tended to see organized sports as means of generating profits and introducing untrained workers to activities emphasizing teamwork, obedience to rules, planning, organization, and production; they promoted sports for the purpose of creating good workers who could tolerate poor working conditions. In summary, organized sports became important because they were seen as useful in training loyal and hardworking bodies dedicated to achievement and production for the glory of God and country. Sport activities took forms that people believed would promote this type of character development.

Organized sports, masculinity and femininity. This new emphasis on the character-building effects of sport participation was applied primarily to males. Those who organized and sponsored new programs thought organized sports, especially team sports, could be used to tame what they perceived as the savage and undisciplined character of young, lower-class males. The intent was to create orderly citizens and cooperative workers. Sport programs for young males from middle-class backgrounds, on the other hand, were used to counteract the influence of female-dominated home lives. Participation was intended to turn what many feared to be "overfeminized males" into assertive, competitive, achievement-oriented young men who would make good leaders in business, politics, and the military.

Although an increasing number of women participated in sport activities between 1880 and 1920, females were often ignored when opportunities for involvement were provided. Participation in organized sports was not seen as an important factor in their character development. Young girls were sometimes included with boys in the organized games in playground programs, but sex-integrated sport activities were discouraged for children nearing the age of puberty. There were strong fears that if boys and girls played with one another they might become good friends, and that if they were friends, their relationships would lose the mystery that led people to be interested in getting married. (We may laugh at such a "theory" today, but I've recently heard people say things that are just as laughable when they talk about women who want to try out for football and wrestling teams).

While boys were taught to play a number of different sports on the playgrounds after the turn of the century, girls were often given shady places where they could rest and preserve their complexions. These were the days when fair skin was seen as a mark of beauty and dark tans were indicators of lower-class or immigrant background. Therefore girls were encouraged to avoid activities that took them outside and exposed their bodies to the sun.

Organized activities for girls often consisted of domestic science classes designed to make them good homemakers and mothers. When opportunities were provided for girls to play games and sports, the playground organizers designed activities that would cultivate "ladylike" traits, such as poise and body control. This why so many girls participated in gymnastics, figure skating, and other "grace and beauty" sports (Hart, 1981). Another goal of the activities was to make young women healthy for bearing children. Competition was eliminated or controlled, and the activities emphasized personal health, the dignity of beauty, and good form (much like some exercise classes in the 1990s). In some cases, one of the reasons games and sports were included in girls' activities was to provide the knowledge they would need to introduce their own children, especially their sons, to active games when they became mothers.

Limited opportunities and a lack of encouragement did not stop women from participating in sports, but it certainly restricted the extent of their involvement. Some middle- and upper-class women engaged in popular physical exercises and recreational sport activities, but apart from a limited number of intercollegiate games and private tournaments, they had few opportunities to engage in formal competitive events.

During the 1920's the women's suffrage movement was strong, there was widespread emphasis on women's rights, and some women played what were defined as "men's sports." In some cases, these women's games drew significant crowds, even though many people thought such sports were inappropriate for women. (Sally Fox)

The participation of girls and women from lower income groups was restricted to informal street games, a few supervised exercise classes, and field days in public schools. Ideas about femininity were changing between 1880 and 1920, but Victorian attitudes and numerous misconceptions about the physical and mental effects of strenuous activities on females prevented the "new woman" of the early twentieth century from enjoying the same participation opportunities and encouragement as those received by her male counterpart (Lenskyj, 1986). In fact, medical beliefs did more to subvert the health of women during these years than to improve it (Vertinsky, 1987).

Sport and ideas about age and disability. Aging involves biological changes, but the connection between aging and sport participation depends on the social meanings given to those changes. Because developmental theory around the turn of the century emphasized that development occurred during childhood and adolescence, sport programs were created and sponsored for young people, not for older people. The theories suggested that older people were already developed: they were "grown up" and their characters could no longer be expected to develop any further. Furthermore, medical knowledge at the time discouraged older people from engaging in strenuous activities that might put too many demands on the heart and other muscles. This did not stop older people from participating in certain forms of sport activities, but those activities were seldom sponsored by public or private groups. Furthermore, when participation did occur among older people it

SIDELINES

WHY DON'T WE SETTLE THIS IN A CIVILIZED WAY?
WE'LL CHARGE ADMISSION TO WATCH!

Dominant forms of sports in many societies are created by and for men. Usually, they celebrate a particular form of masculinity emphasizing aggression, conquest, and domination.

was in age segregated settings.

People with most forms of physical or mental disability during this time were either denied
the opportunity to participate or actively discouraged from engaging in most physical activities, especially sports. People were unsure
about the effects of strenuous exercise on their
behavior or physical well-being.

1890 to 1920 — a summary. Although opportunities for participation in organized, competitive sports were not equally distributed by
social class, gender, age, or ability during these
years, participation increased dramatically. This
was the case in all Western industrial societies.
Furthermore, the organizational attributes we
associate with today's high profile organized
sports became clearly established during this
time. The games people played featured a combination of secularism, a growing commitment
to participation among competitors from all
socio-economic backgrounds, increased specialization, rationalization, bureaucratization, quantification, and the quest for records. As explained in the box on pp. 66-67, these are some
of the sociologically relevant characteristics that
have become the foundation for what many people define as sports in the 1990s.

Since 1920, the resources devoted to physical activities organized along these lines have increased in many societies around the world.
Technology has been used to change sport experiences for both participants and spectators,
and there has been a tremendous growth in the
number of sport-related industries and in government sponsorship of sports. But many of today's struggles about what sports are and how
they should be integrated into people's lives
were visible in some form 70 years ago.

**SINCE THE 1920s: THE STRUGGLES CON-
TINUE** Major cultural links between sports and
American society had been established by the
1920s. The desire to make or raise money had
led to the creation and marketing of spectator
sports on the professional and intercollegiate levels. Entertainment had become at least as important as the development of moral character in the
sponsorship of sports. The most heavily promoted sports were football, baseball, and basketball—each native to the United States, each
celebrating a particular form of masculinity (emphasizing aggression, domination, and emotional control), and each used to generate profits, patriotism, and national loyalties. An emphasis on competition, winning, and record set-

ting had been promoted in connection with commercial interests.

Basic organizational structures for professional sports had been established, and on the college level there were a number of athletic conferences along with a national association governing intercollegiate sports. There were numerous other national associations connected with a wide variety of amateur and professional sports, and the Olympics had been revived and held on six different occasions, once in Greece, 4 times in western Europe, and once in the United States.

By the 1920s there had already been investigations of problems in intercollegiate sport programs, and college football in particular had been accused of being too violent, too professionalized, and unrelated to educational goals. Major league baseball was controlled by powerful economic and political interests. It had already had serious problems with player-management relations, and it had faced a highly publicized gambling scandal in the 1919 World Series.

Lavish stadiums and field houses had been constructed by universities and local governments for the purpose of showcasing their men's team. Newspapers promoted and sensationalized sport events to boost their circulations; radio broadcasts brought sports into people's homes and maintained spectator interest in both urban and rural areas.

High school and college athletes had become a primary focus of attention within many schools, and the "dumb athlete" stereotype had become popular in many colleges and universities. The organization of interscholastic programs continued the elitist and sexist traditions in sports. Schools generally ignored the participation interests of female students and provided them only limited participation opportunities; some women struggled to make changes in these "traditions." With rare exceptions, sports at all levels of participation were racially segregated; However, blacks had formed and sponsored their own teams in many communities (Ruck,

1987). Black athletes received widespread attention only when it was in the financial interests of whites to provide coverage.

Coaching had emerged as a specialized, technical profession, and coaches were hired to supervise teams and maintain winning records. The control of teams had shifted from the players to coaches, managers, owners, and top administrative staff. Principles of scientific management were used to teach strategies and train athletes. Some athletes even took substances they thought would enhance their performances. There was a heavy emphasis on obedience to authority both on and off the field. Control over the lives of athletes had become an important issue because of the commercial and reputational consequences of events; it was easier to sell "clean" events and "clean" athletes than it was to sell "tarnished" events and athletes. Rules had become standardized on a national level so that commercially attractive intersectional competitions could be held. Records and statistics were kept by sponsoring organizations and were frequently published in newspapers and discussed in radio news broadcasts. The broadcasters used dramatic flair and exaggeration to dramatize events and enhance their own images and reputations.

In summary, sports in the 1920s looked much like the sports of today. There were fewer teams and leagues, there was no television, no instant replays, no domed stadiums or artificial turf, no corporate ownership of professional teams, and no agents bargaining for bigger player contracts. But these are minor differences. Things have gotten bigger over the past 70 years, but sport itself continues to be socially constructed through the struggles of various groups to integrate organized, competitive physical activities into their lives in ways that meet their interests. Therefore sports remain integrally linked to commercial interests. The importance of winning and the character-building consequences of involvement are still emphasized.

In other words, people continue to struggle

over the following things:

- The purpose and organization of sports
- Who should participate in what sports under what circumstances
- Who should sponsor and control sports and sport events
- The meanings associated with sports, sport sponsorship, and sport participation.

For example, people change rules in their sport leagues so they can have more fun; others form groups that have no formal rules and organization. Some people push to expand women's opportunities in sports; others call for women to develop alternative sport forms emphasizing partnership rather than domination (Nelson, 1991). Professional athletes organize themselves into unions and even call strikes to gain more control of the conditions of their own sport involvement; owners lock players out and collude with each other to maintain their power. These things all happen in social, political, and economic contexts that limit alternatives and influence the choices made by individuals and groups. The sociology of sport is concerned with these struggles and these contexts.

CONCLUSION:

LOOKING AT SPORT AT DIFFERENT TIMES AND DIFFERENT PLACES

Throughout human history games and sport activities have always been integrally related to the social, political, and economic relationships between people in any given society. As these relationships have changed and as power has shifted, there have been changes in the organization and meanings of games and sport activities.

In ancient Greece, games and contests were grounded in mythology and religious beliefs. They focused on the interests of young males from the wealthier segments of society. As the outcomes of organized games took on political implications beyond the events themselves, athletes were recruited from the lower classes and

paid for their participation. This process of professionalization was accompanied by developments similar to those associated with certain professional sports in the 1990s.

Roman sport events emphasized mass entertainment. They were designed to celebrate and preserve the power of political leaders and pacify masses of unemployed and underemployed workers in Roman cities and towns. Athletes in Roman events were often slaves recruited for the events or "troublemakers" who were coerced into jeopardizing their lives in battle with one another or with wild animals. This type of sport spectacle faded with the demise of the Roman Empire.

Sport activities in Europe during the Middle Ages clearly reflected gender and status differences in medieval societies. The peasants played highly localized versions of folk games in connection with seasonal events in village life. The knights and nobles engaged in tournaments and jousts. Other members of the upper classes, often including the clergy, used their resources to develop numerous games and sport activities to occupy their leisure time.

This pattern continued through the Renaissance in parts of Europe, although the Protestant Reformation tended to generate negative attitudes about any activities interfering with work and religious worship. The impact of these attitudes was felt most sharply by peasants, who seldom had the resources to avoid the restrictive controls imposed by government officials inspired by Puritan orientations. The games and sports of the wealthy continued within the safe confines of their private grounds.

During the early days of the Industrial Revolution, the influence of the Puritans faded in both Europe and North America, but the demands of work and the absence of spaces for play generally limited sport involvement to the wealthy and people in rural areas. This pattern began to change in the United States during the middle to late nineteenth century, when the combined influence of labor unions, progressive legislation, and economic expansion led to the creation of new ideas about the consequences of sport participation and new opportunities for involvement. However, opportunities for involvement were primarily shaped by the needs of an economy emphasizing mass production and mass consumption. It was in this context that people shaped what we now refer to as organized, competitive sports.

Sports have never been so pervasive and influential in the lives of people as they are in many societies today; never before have people had so much leisure time, and never before have physical activities in any form been so closely linked to profit making, character building, patriotism, and personal health. Organized sports in the United States have become a combination of business, entertainment, education, moral training, masculinity rituals, technology transfer, and declarations of political allegiance. However, sports are also contests in which people seek physical challenges and exciting expressive experiences seldom available in the rest of their lives. All these things have made organized, competitive sports important social phenomena, in the past and today.

SUGGESTED READINGS

Baker, W.J. 1982. Sports in the Western world. Rowman & Littlefield, Totowa, N.J. (*survey and analysis of European and North American sports starting with the ancient Greeks and ending with contemporary commercial sports*).

Blanchard, K., and A. Cheska. 1985. The anthropology of sport. Bergin & Garvey Publishers, Inc., South Hadley, Mass. (*survey of cross-cultural material on games and sport; discussion of games of native peoples in North America*).

British Journal of Sports History. 1984 to present (*contains papers on all aspects of sports history, especially those related to England*).

Cavallo, D. 1981. Muscles and morals: organized playgrounds and urban reform, 1880-1920. University of Pennsylvania Press, Philadelphia (*excellent discussion of how sports became connected with American values around the turn of the century*).

Dunning, E., and K. Sheard. 1979. Barbarians, gentlemen and players: a sociological study of the development of rugby football. University Press, New York (*uses sociological concepts to explain the development of one of Britain's most popular sports*).

Elias, N., and E. Dunning. 1986. Quest for excitement. Basil Blackwell, Inc., New York (*an historical overview of how sport and leisure are linked to the civilizing process in Western societies*).

Goodman, C. 1979. Choosing sides: playground and street life on the Lower East Side. Shocken Books, New York (*critique of the efforts of playground organizers who used organized recreation programs to subvert the street games of immigrants in New York City around the turn of the century*).

Gruneau, R. 1983. Class, sports, and social development. University of Massachusetts Press, Amherst (*Ch. 3 contains a social history of sport and social development in Canada*).

Gruneau, R. 1988. Modernization or hegemony: two views of sport and social development. In J. Harvey and H. Cantelon, eds., Not just a game. University of Ottawa Press, Ottawa (*concise critique of conceptual approaches to the history of sport; read this article before reading any of the "historical accounts of sport events" in this list*).

Guttmann, A. 1978. From ritual to record: the nature of modern sports. Columbia University Press, New York (*comparative analysis of the characteristics of sports in different historical periods*).

Guttmann, A. 1988. A whole new ball game: an interpretation of American sports. University of North Carolina Press, Chapel Hill, N.C. (*a readable interpretation of sports within the social context of U.S. history; includes chapters on sports and Native Americans, Puritans, and Southerners, among other topics*).

Hargreaves, J. 1986. Sport, power and culture: a social and historical analysis of popular sports in Britain. St. Martin's Press, New York (*focusing on power, class, sex, and race, the analysis discusses the role of sport in education and modern consumer culture*).

Higgs, R.H. 1982. Sports: a reference guide. Greenwood Press, Westport, Conn. (*contains two reference chapters on the history of sport plus a 40-page appendix by Jack Berryman entitled "Important events in the history of American sports: a chronology"*).

Howell, R. 1982. Her story in sport: a historical anthology of women in sports. Leisure Press, West Point, N.Y. (*42 papers on special topics related to the history of women's sports, especially sports in North America from the eighteenth century through the 1970s*).

Journal of Sport History. 1974 to present (*contains numerous good papers on the history of sport, especially in North America*).

Lucas, J.A., and R.A. Smith. 1978. Saga of American sport. Lea & Febiger, Philadelphia (*looks at the history of American sports as they reflect dominant value themes in the rest of society*).

Mandell, R. 1984. Sport: a cultural history. Columbia University Press, New York (*discussion of the cultural importance of sport through history in Western Europe and North America; analysis is generally grounded in a functionalist approach to the sport-society relationship*).

Mrozek, D.J. 1983. Sport and American mentality, 1880-1920. The University of Tennessee Press, Knoxville (*excellent social historical analysis of the origins of modern sports in the United States*).

Rader, B.G. 1983. American sports: from the age of folk games to the age of spectators. Prentice-Hall, Inc., Englewood Cliffs, N.J. (*explanation of how and why the informal games of colonial Americans evolved into modern, spectator-centered sports*).

Riess, S.A. 1984. The American sporting experience: a historical anthology of sport in America. Leisure Press, West Point, N.Y. (*24 papers on sports from colonial times until the present*).

Ruck, R. Sandlot seasons: sport in black Pittsburgh. 1987. University of Illinois Press, Urbana (*unique look at the sporting life and the meanings of sport in the community life of blacks in Pittsburgh in the early twentieth century*).

Spears, B., and R.A. Swanson. 1988. History of sport and physical education in the United States. W.C. Brown Co., Publishers, Dubuque, Iowa (*an introductory text that traces the development of sport and physical education in the United States*).

(Chuck Miller)

COMPETITION IN SPORTS

Does it prepare people for life?

We have elevated our faith in competition to fanatical . . . levels. But. . .the evidence [shows] that it is not the main-spring of achievement . . . as we have been brought up to believe.

Dr. Benjamin Spock (1986)

. . . the professional [athlete] . . . is for all practical purposes terminally adolescent . . . [T]he longer the exposure to the profes-sional [sport] environment . . . the further athletes will drift from an ability to understand and cope with the demands of the real world.

Tom House, Psychologist, former major league pitcher (1989)

I [always] knew I didn't want a regular job. If I couldn't play sports and had to work for a liv-ing, I'd be in trouble . . . I worked one week in my life and hated it . . . After a week I just quit and walked home. I didn't even wait for my ride.

Michael Jordan, Professional basketball player (1989)

Competition in sports can be a controversial topic for discussion. Some people claim that sport competition builds character and prepares participants for life in today's society. Others say it destroys confidence, leads to an overemphasis on winning, and subverts the spirit we need to live peacefully together without destroying the earth. In light of these differences, four questions will be considered in this chapter:

1. What is "competition" and how is it different from other social processes?

2. How is competition incorporated into sports and sport behavior?

3. What is the connection between competition and the development of character?

4. Does competition in sports provide people with experiences that will make them more successful in the rest of their lives?

THE CONCEPT OF COMPETITION

The term **competition** is used in many different ways. People say that they compete against others, against themselves, against the clock or the record book, against objects or the elements (as in mountain climbing or in white water kayaking), and even against animals (as in hunting). Although it would be worthwhile to analyze "competition" in each of these forms, this chapter focuses on *competition as a social process that occurs when rewards are given to people on the basis of how their performances compare with the performances of others doing the same task or participating in the same event.* When competition is defined in this way—as a social process—it can be distinguished from other social arrangements that involve facing challenges and achieving goals. According to this definition, competition is a process through which "winners" and "losers" are identified and all people are hierarchically ranked on the basis of who does better than others in a particular task. Although individual participants may bring different personal goals to competitive events, the competitive process itself is focused on outperforming or defeating opponents.

Competitive Reward Structures

Competition involves the use of a distinctive **reward structure.** This means that any competitive event has rules for distributing rewards among participants. These rules indicate that the success of one participant (individual or team) automatically "causes" the failure of others. Rewards are distributed on the basis of how each competitor compares with the others. *Competition always involves a direct comparison of participants.* Sociologists are interested in competition because it influences how people relate to one another.

A classic example of a competitive reward structure is a classroom in which the traditional grading curve is used. Teachers who use a grading curve assume they have a certain number of As, Bs, Cs, Ds, and Fs to give to their students and that these grades should be given out to fit a statistical distribution—usually a "normal" or "bell-shaped" distribution. When these assumptions are made, each of the relatively few students receiving an A will be matched with an equal number of students receiving Fs. The number of Bs and Ds given out would be greater than the number of As and Fs, but for every B there would be an accompanying D. Finally, the most frequently given grade would be a C. Each grade is assigned on the basis of how the score of a student compares to the statistical average of scores in the class as a whole.

Using a competitive reward structure in a classroom guarantees that student evaluations range from above average to below average, regardless of how much students learn and regardless of how students perform in terms of their own expectations or the expectations of the teacher. For example, everyone might learn little and there would still be a certain number of As, even if all scores were generally low. Or everyone might learn much and there would still be a certain number of Fs, even if all scores were generally high. This means that "success" for students graded on a curve simply depends on how they perform in comparison with others in the class. Within a competitive reward structure like this, the goals of the students are mutually exclusive—in other words, the students are "in competition" with one another.

Of course, using a competitive reward structure is not the only way to evaluate students and award grades in a classroom. It is just one of many reward structures teachers could use, and most avoid using it because it does not promote learning among all students. In fact, it often undermines relationships through which students help each other learn. Students who live with grading curves in their schooling often learn to thrive on the failure of their classmates. They literally want classmates to do poorly because the worse their classmates do on a test, the better their grade will be. Most teachers realize that this orientation undermines learning by encouraging students to focus on beating classmates rather than on helping each other learn. Other teachers still use it because it is an easy way to award grades, or because they do not understand how competitive reward structures negatively affect relationships and learning patterns among students.

Cooperative and Individualized Reward Structures

Competition is not the only process through which performance can be evaluated and rewarded. *Cooperation* or *individualized approaches* are two alternatives to competition.

Cooperation is a social process through which performance is evaluated and rewarded in terms of the collective achievements of a group of people working together to reach a goal. In a cooperative reward structure, everyone shares rewards equally, depending on group achievement. An example of this is a classroom in which students participate together in a group project or try to help each other do well on a test so the whole class will look good. Although individual grades could be used to reward students who helped others in the class, the emphasis would be on an overall group grade.

When *individualized approaches* are used to evaluate performances and give out rewards, there is no direct dependence on other people. The quality of a person's performance does not depend on any comparison with others nor does it necessarily depend on any cooperation. Instead, rewards depend on reaching a prearranged personal goal or level of achievement. Individualized reward structures are found in classrooms in which grades are given on the basis of how each student meets a predetermined set of individualized expectations. Those who surpass maximum expectations receive As; those who fail to meet minimum expectations receive Fs. Students in an individualized reward structure can help each other learn without worrying if their classmates might "raise the curve;" success does not depend on everyone else doing poorly nor does it depend on everyone doing well.

Competition As an Individual Orientation

In addition to being a social process and a reward structure, competition can be viewed as personal orientation. Again, it is necessary to distinguish between a competitive orientation and cooperative and individualized orientations.

A *competitive orientation* is characterized by the tendency for people to evaluate their own and others' performances strictly in comparative terms. People with competitive orientations view achievement in terms of outperforming others. Success for them means being superior to others, and they do not feel comfortable working cooperatively or judging themselves apart from how they or their teams measure up against others. People with competitive orientations are often concerned with dominating others.

A *cooperative orientation* is characterized by a tendency to promote group accomplishment and define rewards in group terms. People with a cooperative orientation view achievement in terms of maximizing rewards for all participants through coordinated action. Suc-

In North America competitive reward structures are heavily emphasized. Lip service is given to cooperation and individual development, but most of the formal rewards go to the winners rather than to the "best sports" or to those who develop their own potential. (Colorado Springs Sun and Chuck Bigger)

cess for them means getting others involved in an activity so the group's potential will be maximized.

An *individualized orientation* is characterized by a tendency to see rewards in independent terms, as unrelated to the behavior of others. People with an individualized orientation evaluate their behavior by using personal standards based on their past experiences or future goals.

Success for these people has nothing to do with how they compare to or work with others.

CONFUSION ABOUT COMPETITION AND ACHIEVEMENT Many Americans and some people from other capitalist countries have a tendency to think that competitive reward structures automatically make people work hard, and that people who work hard always have competitive orientations. Although it is true that some hard workers have competitive orientations, many people with cooperative and individualized orientations work just as hard—but they use noncompetitive strategies to achieve their goals, and they evaluate their accomplishments differently than people with competitive orientations.

Successful, achievement-oriented, hard-working people are not necessarily competitive people. They may simply combine strong achievement orientations with cooperative or individualistic orientations. People who are cooperative or who judge themselves without making comparisons with others are just as likely to be successful, even in a capitalist economy, as those who always try to outdo and establish superiority over others.

In fact, it is a myth that competitive reward structures are necessary for productivity and that people must be cut-throat competitors to survive in today's world. Productivity in today's complex organizations is more often the result of cooperation than competition, and international economic and political cooperation is absolutely necessary if we are to avoid destroying the earth on which we depend for survival. Competitive reward structures may be useful in situations in which people perform relatively simple, physical tasks over short periods of time; but whenever a task is complex and involves coming up with solutions for difficult problems, cooperative reward structures are clearly superior (Kohn, 1986, pp. 45-78). For example, David and Roger Johnson (1983) reviewed 122 studies on reward structures and productivity and concluded the following:

> Currently there is no type of task on which cooperative efforts are less effective than are competitive or individualistic efforts, and on most tasks cooperative efforts are more effective in promoting achievement (1983, p. 146).

This is why people who are effective cooperators are usually well-rewarded in all aspects of their lives. Furthermore, they are usually happier than their peers who have competitive orientations, and they are certainly more pleasant to play sports with (Kohn, 1986).

Competitive reward structures can create drama and excitement, and they can present people with challenges that lead to self-discovery and the extension of personal skills. However, competitive reward structures also have a downside. For example, they tend to do the following:

- *Discourage participation* among those who do not see themselves as having chances to qualify for rewards. Research shows that only those who expect to succeed in a particular task will be highly motivated when faced with competition.
- *Encourage specialization* to the point that diverse experiences and overall social development are restricted. In the face of competition many people will simply find one thing they are good at and then focus all their energy and attention on that one thing.
- *Promote standardization* requiring all competitors in the reward structure to do the same thing under the same conditions and rules in order for performance comparisons to be meaningful. This means that over time, competitors will come to resemble one another in many ways and creativity may be stifled.

Despite this downside, many people believe that competitive reward structures inspire motivation and hard work.

REWARD STRUCTURES AND COMPETITION IN SPORTS

According to our definition in Chapter 1, sport always involves some form of competition. However, sport also offers opportunities for combining competitive with cooperative and individualized reward structures. For example, a sport activity could be organized so that competitive outcomes are not the only ways to define success and failure. Formal recognition or rewards could be given to participants who initiate or maintain cooperative relationships or achieve personal goals.

The use of competitive reward structures varies from one culture to another. For example, competing and identifying "winners" and "losers" is more important in the United States than in most other countries. For this reason we will take a closer look at this aspect of American culture.

Competitive Reward Structures and Sports in the United States

People who visit the United States from other countries are often amazed at the extent to which competition is used to distribute rewards and evaluate the worth of human beings. Most Americans do not realize this until they leave the United States and see life in other parts of the world. This point was recently made by Dean Smith, the men's basketball coach at the University of North Carolina. After returning from an extended trip outside the United States, he observed that "Our American culture is far more competitive than any other culture I have observed." He went on to say that Americans "tend to toast 'winners'—whether it is in business or athletics—regardless of the methods used to become a winner" (Quoted in Pritchard, 1984).

Statements by other coaches and athletes clearly support Smith's observations. They all point to the same conclusion: competition is heavily emphasized in U.S. sports. The formal and valued rewards are given to the victors, and victory depends solely on overcoming opponents. Cooperation and individual development may be mentioned in speeches, but the real focus is on being "Number One." This emphasis is so strong that even silver medals and second place trophies are sometimes defined as reminders that someone else was better. This is graphically illustrated by the photo on p. 83. Another illustration is found in media interviews with American athletes who win silver and bronze medals in the Olympics—these athletes are often consoled as "losers" by media interviewers.

To suggest that sports should use and emphasize cooperative or individualized reward structures would be considered by many Americans as a distortion of what they think is the "natural essence" of sport. This is why there is such a strong emphasis on win-loss records, league standings, play-offs, and championships. In some cases, sports in the United States are even organized to take coaches and athletes beyond the philosophy that "winning is the only thing." For example, one successful basketball coach in a Pennsylvania high school explains how this happened to him:

> Through the years I've developed my own philosophy about high school basketball. Winning isn't all that matters. I don't care how many games you win, it's how many championships you win that counts (Quoted in Michener, 1976).

Such an approach to sports reflects a reward structure in which winning is important only when the first-place tournament trophy is brought to your sponsor's display case.

There may be rewards for individual accomplishments or for special displays of cooperative behavior in some American sports, but these are often viewed as consolation prizes. Many American athletes would even say that victory is preferred to a good individual performance or a game in which everyone worked well with teammates. In fact, if members of a losing team take visible pleasure in their own accomplishments or in their good feelings about cooperating with teammates, they may be subject to the criticism of fans, coaches, and other players. Therefore athletes are quick to learn that personal accomplishments and good feelings about cooperation are meaningless unless they lead to victories, and they are quick to point this out in their public statements.

Americans may make many references to "sportsmanship" but it is generally understood that this simply refers to following rules and shaking hands after an event. If "being a good sport" really meant that cooperative behavior occurred *at the expense* of competitive success, ath-

The emphasis on being "number 1" is so strong in the United States that second place trophies are often perceived as reminders that someone else was better. Second place may even be defined as a "loser's spot" in some situations. It is not like this in all cultures. (Colorado Springs Gazette Telegraph and Bob Jackson)

letes might be accused of not taking the game seriously or lacking the "killer instinct." The locker room slogan "Show me a good loser and I'll show you a loser" may not be endorsed by all Americans, but it certainly serves as a warning to those who might carry a cooperative orientation in sports too far.

In the United States, much lip service is given to the idea that winning means doing your best. However, most sports are not organized to emphasize individualized reward structures. Many coaches have taken the idea that "winning means doing the best we can" and turned it into the statement, "We can beat this team if we only do our best." This gives lip service to doing your best but it clearly establishes that performance will be evaluated in terms of competitive success rather than individual development.

These comments on dominant sport forms in the Unites States should not be taken to mean

that only competitive behavior exists in all U.S. sports. My point is simply that formal rewards are given *primarily* to those who are successful within sport's competitive reward structure. From Little Leaguers to professionals, the emphasis on being "Number One" permeates U.S. sports. Individuals, teams, and coaches are evaluated and remembered by their win-loss records. Other qualities may be mentioned and described in books, but books are written about winners. If players and coaches are not winners, their personal qualities will gain them friends and good memories but no sport trophies. This shows that little has been done to control the heavy emphasis on winning in American sports. Competitive behavior is taken for granted, and competitive success is seen as a means to fame and fortune by many. Cooperation and individualized approaches rarely receive the emphasis put on competition, nor do the people who use them receive the publicity given to those with outspoken competitive orientations.

THE U.S. CASE: A QUALIFICATION AND EXPLANATION Competitive reward structures are emphasized in the dominant sport forms in the United States, but there are notable exceptions to this pattern. In fact, different reward structures are emphasized in different sports and at different levels of competition. For example, the account of a Special Olympics event on pp. 86-87 illustrates a case in which competition is balanced with reward structures emphasizing cooperation and individualized reward structures and orientations. Other examples are found in certain youth sport programs and in what are called "recreational sport programs" in many communities; groups of women athletes and gay athletes have also tried to develop alternatives to highly competitive sports (Birrell and Richter, 1987; McDonald, 1992). However, when the rewards for competitive success increase in most American sport programs, it is likely that competitive behavior will be given a higher priority by most participants, coaches, and spectators. It is not inevitable that this will occur but it is likely.

This raises a sociological question: Why are competitive reward structures emphasized in the dominant sport forms of certain countries, especially the United States? This is a tough question, and we can answer it only if we understand something about *power relations* in society. Since sports are parts of culture, sport forms are created by people as they live their lives and interact with others. In most cases, the people with the most power and resources in a cultural group want sports to be "constructed" in ways that promote or "reproduce" relationships and orientations that help them maintain their privileged positions in the group or society. Let me explain this process further.

Powerful and wealthy people in society maintain their power and wealth through a variety of means. For example, they might use the military to control those who would challenge them, or they might try to get most people in the society to believe that large amounts of power and wealth rightfully belong to them. If they choose the latter strategy, they would use a variety of means to develop widespread agreement among people throughout the society that their privileged position in society is legitimate, that they really deserve the power and wealth they possess.

In countries where there are monarchies, it is widely believed that power and wealth come with a person's birthright, so there is a need to convince people that birthrights are grounded in a powerful external force such as a God or gods. But in democratic countries most people use "merit" to judge whether power and wealth is legitimate. This means that in a democracy, power and wealth can be maintained only if most people believe that rewards in the society as a whole go to those who have earned them. When there is widespread inequality in a democratic society, those who have power and wealth must find ways to promote the idea that their privileged position was earned through ingenuity or hard work, and that those who are poor and powerless must lack the character needed to improve their condition.

One way to promote the idea that rewards in a society are based on merit alone is to emphasize competition and get people to accept that competitive reward structures are not only fair but that they are a "natural" part of social life. This strategy is explained by Edgar Friedenberg:

> The classic device for legitimating the unequal distribution of rewards in a democratic society is, of course, competition in which the same rules are applied to all the contestants and the status system of the society is protected by the nature of the rules rather than by their inequitable application. The people in society thus learn to divide themselves into winners and losers and to blame themselves for being among the losers if they are (1974, p. 96).

This connection between power relations and an emphasis on competition helps us understand why certain sport forms are so widely promoted and supported in the United States and some other countries. It is in the interests of powerful and privileged people in democratic societies to emphasize competitive sports so that people in society as a whole will see competitive reward structures as fair and "natural" ways to distribute rewards. When people think this way they are also likely to conclude that rich and powerful people deserve their privilege and power.

This means that competitive reward structures will be heavily emphasized in the dominant sport forms of any democratic society in which there are extensive inequalities between people. It is in the interests of privileged people in these societies to support these sport forms because they want everyone to think that competition is not just the best way to distribute rewards in society, but that it is the only way. Be-

In the Special Olympics, competition is controlled so the emphasis is on friendship and participation. Competitive success is important but is given lower priority than cooperation and personal development. Exceptions to this are rare.

REFLECT ON SPORT

The Special Olympics
A Case for Controlled Competition

When competitive orientations are pervasive in a society people often forget that sports can be organized to emphasize cooperative and individualized reward structures. The Special Olympics serves as a good reminder that alternatives to highly competitive sports have many advantages. When I went to my first Special Olympics event a number of years ago I became aware of how competitive reward structures and orientations had influenced the way I thought about sports.

When I entered the stadium where a local Special Olympics meet was being held there were few spectators in the stands. However, the track and the grassy infield were teeming with activity. Everyone was milling about, and there was much laughter and joking. It certainly didn't look like any track meet I had ever seen, and I naively wondered when the people were going to get serious and when the events were going to begin.

To my surprise, some of the events were already under way, and the people on the infield were the eager participants accompanied by dozens of volunteer coaches, organizers, and officials. After a few minutes of watching, I identified people with a wide range of different skills participating in the standing long jump, the high jump, the softball throw, and the Frisbee toss. I later discovered that many of the athletes were also involved in the swimming and gymnastics events taking place inside the facilities next to the stadium. The running events began shortly after I arrived. They included the 50-, 100-, and 220-yard dashes; the 440-yard and mile runs; and the 440-yard relay.

The athletes received unconditional support from spectators, coaches, and peers. Everyone in attendance seemed to be overjoyed whenever a finish line was crossed—no matter who won. Even the athletes cheered for each other and hugged their fellow competitors after an event was completed—no matter what the outcome. And the coaches and other volunteers congratulated the athletes and gave them words of praise whenever they participated—no matter how well they performed. I had never seen anything like it.

The athletes knew who won and who lost; they tried hard; and they cherished their first-, second-, and third-place ribbons *and* the ribbons they received for each event they entered. Their warmth and enthusiasm were contagious. Their coaches gave them advice on technique mixed with encouragement, but the advice seemed to always focus on the individual's effort, not on competitive reward structures. The competitive outcomes were important to the athletes, but they took a back seat to the sheer pleasure and camaraderie of personal involvement. I was repeatedly amazed to see athletes so excited when they or their peers finished an event. The excitement of the person coming in last was just as intense and spontaneous as the excitement of the winner. And those watching cheered everyone.

About halfway through the meet, I watched a 220-yard race in which three 12-year-olds were participating. They were evenly matched, and when the starter's gun fired, they ran shoulder to shoulder into the curve on the track. As they came out of the turn, one of the runners had taken a two-step lead, but about 25 yards from the finish line he tripped and fell on the cinder track. Instead of racing past him to victory, his two opponents simultaneously stopped, turned around, and helped him up. Together they brushed him off, and then, each holding one of his hands, jogged together across the finish line. It was a three-way tie for first place.

In all my years of playing and watching sport, I had never seen anything like it. I later discovered that the response of the two runners was made without prior advice from the coaches or anyone else. They did it on their own, and they did it so matter-of-factly that it looked like they never gave it a second thought. Unlike "normal" athletes, their compassion was not overwhelmed by a focus on competitive rewards.

That evening I wondered how many other athletes would have responded in the same manner. Most of us would have displayed compassion for our fellow competitor, but it would have been displayed *after* we crossed the finish line and checked to see if our times had been properly recorded. Our competitive orientations would have led us to focus our attention on the race and the finish line; to do otherwise would have been defined as a "break in concentration."

There are lessons to be learned from athletes in the Special Olympics. Watching them compete on the local, state, and international level has shown me that a competitive event can evoke joy and compassion when it emphasizes cooperation and individual development. The purpose of the Special Olympics program is to provide positive, successful experiences in sport to people with mental re-

tardation. Through those experiences, it is hoped that they can build confidence, physical skills, and healthy self-images.

The parents of the participants judge their sons and daughters on the basis of effort and personal progress—not on the basis of wins, losses, ribbons, trophies, or championships. Pride in their children exists, and, to an extent, they vicariously experience their children's accomplishments. But they are careful not to compare their child with other participants. They remember that each special athlete is a unique individual and that he or she should be judged on the basis of past personal performances coupled with realistic goals for the future.

Special Olympics coaches are not concerned with victories and championships; their jobs do not depend on winning or producing top performers. Instead, they are concerned with the feelings and the overall social and psychological development of their athletes.

What exists in the Special Olympics is carefully controlled competition. Competition exists, but it is controlled to the point that participants focus on fellowship and pride in their own physical skills in addition to outcomes. After working with a local Special Olympics program for over 10 years, I am convinced that if coaches and organizers ever forget the spirit of the Special Olympics, the participants themselves will continue to keep it alive. Their humanity will remind those who work with them that sports can involve more than competition and that success in sports can be measured in terms of cooperation and human development in addition to competitive outcomes. Most of us who have grown up playing organized, competitive sports need these reminders.

cause American society is characterized by extreme inequality when it comes to power and wealth, competitive sport forms are heavily emphasized and other forms are often discounted or discredited.

Popular beliefs about competition are part of what sociologists refer to as cultural ideology. **Cultural ideology** in any society consists of the sets of ideas that people use to "figure out how the social world works, what their place is in it and what they ought to do" (Hall, 1985). Ideology is the basis for determining what is important and unimportant in a particular culture. And if the dominant ideology in a culture leads people to conclude that success is based on hard work and that hard work leads to success, the privileged and successful people in that culture will find it easy to maintain their power and wealth. In fact, they will be respected within the society as a whole and will even be used as "culturally correct" models for doing things; some people will even try to imitate them and will want to read about them and watch television programs about them.

This complex process of producing ideologies that enable people with power to maintain their positions of privilege in society is called **hegemony.** Another way of saying this is that hegemony is the process through which the influence of an already privileged group is extended by promoting the idea that inequities are "natural," that inequities are just meant to be and should be accepted the way they are. When sports are constructed to emphasize competitive reward structures and promote an ideology of success geared to the interests of privileged people in society, they contribute to hegemony. They become social "sites" where the interests of dominant groups become institutionalized and accepted as "natural" parts of life. This is why people with wealth and power are so interested in sponsoring and promoting elite, competitive sport forms in the United States and all over the world. In fact, the global expansion of elite, competitive sport forms is a very high priority

among the very wealthy and powerful. This is why it is legal to deduct the cost of luxury boxes and season sport tickets as business expenses in the United States, why civic and university leaders often argue that public funds ought to be used to support professional and intercollegiate sports, and why multinational corporations such as General Motors and Coca-Cola sponsor the Olympics and other competitive sport forms in the United States and around the world.

The importance of competitive sports for powerful individuals and corporations goes far beyond ticket sales and financial profits from T.V. rights. Competitive sports are important because they are tied to how people think about what the goals of society should be, how society should be organized, and how rewards in society ought to be distributed. These are crucial social issues, and sport is related to each of them (as will be explained in other chapters in this book).

Competitive Reward Structures and Sports in Socialist Societies

It is interesting that sports in socialist societies have been defined differently than they have been in capitalist societies. This is because it is not in the interests of the powerful in socialist countries to emphasize the competitive dimension of sports to the same degree or in the same way it is emphasized in capitalist countries.

In China, for example, there is a heavy emphasis on cooperation and "collective spirit" in sport. Chinese leaders talk about using sport to gain strength for the cause of socialism. Even though sport is heavily tied to militarism, and even though there has been a recent emphasis on winning medals in international sport events, cooperative reward structures remain widely used in Chinese sport programs. In fact, sport itself is seen as a part of the larger sphere of "physical culture" in socialist society. Success is defined in terms of a person's or group's contribution to the larger community. Sport is seen

Youth sports are heavily promoted in Japan because adults believe that they build good Japanese character. (Jay Coakley)

as a tool for physically strengthening people and developing in them the kind of collectivist spirit needed to make socialism a success.

People in positions of power in China and other socialist societies must be careful to balance their support for elite sport with their support for physical culture as a whole. The general population must believe that its participation in physical culture is valued or else they will raise critical questions about socialist ideology. The preservation of a collectivist spirit requires a popular belief in the state's commitment to social progress and responsiveness to social needs despite the existence of differences between people within society. Individual achievements can be highlighted, but they must be highlighted to show how they contribute to the group rather than what advantages they bring to individuals.

My purpose in this section is to show that

there are important differences in the way competitive reward structures are incorporated into sports in socialist and capitalist societies. As a country leans more toward socialism, it will place less emphasis on competitive reward structures in sports and more emphasis on cooperative reward structures; as a country leans more toward capitalism, it will place more emphasis on competitive reward structures in sports and less emphasis on cooperative reward structures.

Cultural Variations and Reward Structures

It is often difficult for many of my students to understand that competitive sport forms simply do not fit into certain cultures. Studies in anthropology provide many examples of cultures in which competitive rewards structures are controlled or eliminated in physical activities, games, and life in general (Kohn, 1986).

Competitive behaviors in certain cultures may even be defined as deviant, and in some cultures the very idea of competition is inconceivable—in fact, the languages used by some cultural groups do not even have a word for competition. Here's a few examples to illustrate cultural variation.

Anthropologist Ruth Benedict (1961) has reported that Zuni Indian culture (in Northern New Mexico) stresses cooperative orientations to the point that competition is defined as deviant. Even Zuni games stress cooperation. Winning is not celebrated, winners are not given special recognition, and may even be prevented from participating in future games. Benedict notes the special cultural characteristics of Zuni sport forms when she explains that

> Even in contests of skill like their foot races, if a man wins habitually he is debarred from running. [The Zuni] are interested in a game that a number can play with even chances, and an outstanding runner spoils the game: they will have none of him.

Like the Zuni, the Hopi, the Acoma, and the Sioux all define competitive reward structures as incompatible with important dimensions of their cultural ideologies.

A summary of Burridge's (1957) study of the Tangu people in New Guinea provides another interesting example:

> . . . the Tangu . . . play a popular game known as *taketak*, which involves throwing a spinning top into massed lots of stakes driven into the ground. There are two teams. Players of each team try to touch as many stakes with their tops as possible. In the end, however, the participants play not to win but to draw. The game must go on until an exact draw is reached. This requires great skill, since players sometimes must throw their tops into the massed stakes without touching a single one. Taketak expresses a prime value in Tangu culture, that is, the concept of moral equivalency, which is reflected in the precise sharing of foodstuffs among the people (Leonard, 1973, p. 45).

The necessity of maintaining cooperative forms of social relations seems to discourage the use of competitive reward structures in many cultures. The emphasis in these cultures is on cooperation, sharing, and mutual identification. This creates a situation in which competition is not only discouraged but defined as deviant. Other examples of cultures in which this occurs are summarized by Alfie Kohn (1986) in *No Contest*, a book that reviews research findings on competition. Kohn points out that many peoples around the globe do not incorporate competitive reward structures into their lives or even into their physical activities and games.

What Happens When Reward Structures and Personal Orientations Don't Match?

In cultures in which dominant ideology emphasizes the importance of competition, those who accept that ideology and use it to interpret the world around them may feel uncomfortable when they encounter situations calling for cooperative or individualized orientations and behaviors. For example, research shows that Anglo children from middle class families in the United States often have such strong competitive orientations that they sometimes engage in competitive behavior even when it is in their best interests to cooperate. These children insist on defining success in terms of establishing superiority over others even when greater personal rewards are available through cooperation with equals (Pepitone, 1980).

It has also been found that rural Mexican children consistently outperform Mexican-Americans and Anglo-Americans in tasks where problems are best solved through cooperative solutions. The rural Mexican children quickly devise solutions, Mexican-Americans take longer to devise solutions and discover them less frequently, and Anglo-American children miss cooperative solutions most often because they see things in terms of competitive reward structures even when the structures don't exist (Nelson and Kagen, 1972).

People with competitive orientations are not the only ones to resist situational pressures to behave in different ways. For example, among some native American peoples, cooperative orientations are so strong that tribal members either avoid competition or redefine competitive situations to emphasize cooperative relationships (Allison, 1979; Allison and Luschen, 1979; Benedict, 1961; Duda, 1981). In the case of Navajo high school athletes in the 1970s, Maria Allison has reported that cooperative orientations influenced their perceptions of opponents, their definitions of opponents during games, and their responses to rewards for competitive success. When compared with Anglo athletes, the Navajo students were more likely to use sport as a means of reaffirming their relationships with others. Group solidarity was more important to them than winning. They were also more concerned with using sport to extend their personal qualities; they used individualized instead of competitive approaches to evaluate their own performances. They were less likely to try to dominate opponents, and they felt uncomfortable using their bodies as tools of domination. Finally, they were embarrassed by the status and rewards that accompanied competitive success because they had always been taught not to raise their heads above others (Allison, 1979).

Of course, there are exceptions to Allison's findings. In cases where traditional Navajo culture has been weakened, some young Navajos have learned Anglo orientations toward competition. This has also occurred among other native peoples in the United States and Canada and among some immigrant groups in both countries. Even when people come from cultural backgrounds in which cooperative orientations have been emphasized, many of them gradually take on competitive orientations as they face the challenges of attending schools and living in U.S. communities where competitive orientations and competitive reward structures are highly valued. In some cases, teachers and coaches who work with native American students on reservations have even used systematic strategies to encourage them to abandon their cultural ideologies that emphasize cooperation and to accept dominant Anglo cultural ideology that emphasizes competition. For example, coaches sometimes try to instill a so-called killer instinct in their football and basketball players even though native American athletes do not feel comfortable with the notion of seeking personal rewards by dominating other human beings. A high school football coach in Arizona recently complained that students at Hopi High School "aren't used to our win-at-all-costs, beat-the-other-man mentality. Their understanding of what it means to be a good Hopi goes against what it takes to be a good football player" (in Garrity, 1989). The coach then admitted that to get his team to win he had to do "exactly what the missionaries tried to do—de-Indianize the Indians" (Garrity, 1989).

These examples illustrate that ideology is a part of culture, not genetics or "human nature." It is through human relationships and social experiences that people gradually form explanations for how the social world works. I realized this a number of years ago when my daughter came to me crying because she had just beaten her best friend in a game of 2-square (a variation of 4-square, which is a type of floor handball that uses a playground ball). She told me that winning made her sad because her friend was sad about losing. I concluded that she had not yet started to use dominant American ideology to inform her feelings and her interpretations of social relations; she had not put winning ahead of friendship and cooperation. As she has finished school and entered the world of work she is still attuned to alternative ways of looking at the world and has continued to resist dominant American ideology about competition and winning. She does not see an emphasis on winning to be a "natural" part of life in society.

This example shows that even dominant ideologies are not automatically accepted by individuals and groups. People can resist, challenge, and even transform dominant cultural practices. But resistance can be painful, and transformations of culture are difficult to produce. Significant social change does not come easily or without careful planning because people who have resources are often threatened by changes in the dominant meanings associated with sports. Therefore they often try to "de-program," discredit, buy off, or even criminalize those who resist or challenge dominant cultural ideology.

People who participate in elite competitive sports usually don't have to be de-programmed, discredited, or bought off when it comes to accepting competitive reward structures. They usually have strong competitive orientations and they often see competition as a "natural" part of human life. However, when athletes raise questions about competition or begin to doubt their need to outperform others in competitive reward structures, they may be regarded as needing psychological help. This is especially likely to happen in the United States. In fact, some American sport psychologists have even suggested that athletes who have weak competitive orientations that interfere with competitive success in sport might be suffering from "success phobia" (Ogilvie and Tutko, 1966). Strong competitive orientations are defined as normal in North American sport, so when people deviate from "normal" they are thought to need help until they correct their problem and become "normal" again. This is a clear example of how "normalcy" and "sickness" are defined in terms of cultural ideology.

When reward structures and personal orientations do not match, people may try to transform the reward structures or they may gradually come to accept them as appropriate. Efforts to transform reward structures depend on being aware of alternatives. This is where sociologists and sport scientists can be helpful. They can encourage people to think about and experiment with alternatives to dominant sport forms in society, and they can use their research to discover the alternatives that already exist in various groups that have traditionally resisted competitive reward structures in their sports and physical activities. For example, Ken Kageyama (1988), a sport sociologist in Japan, has introduced the notion of TROPS ("sport" spelled backwards) to encourage people to think about alternatives to competitive sports and to revive contemporary forms of traditional folk games within family and community activities. The "New Games" movement in the United States was based on similar concerns about the need to make available many sport forms that people can use to meet their own needs and challenge the ideologies and systems of meaning associated with dominant sport forms. If this is done successfully, sports will contain more "spaces" for people to participate and they will be more democratic and inclusive activities.

COMPETITION AND CHARACTER

"Sports build character." This is said so often that it has become a cliche in some societies. It is so widely accepted that it has been used as a basis for encouraging children to play competitive sports, for funding sports programs, for building new sport stadiums, and for promoting sport leagues and events such as the Olympic Games.

The widespread belief that sports build character raises interesting sociological questions: When did this belief originate? How has it been maintained? Why do so many people accept it without question? Is it true?

Although the material in Chapter 3 explained the origins of the belief that competition, and especially competitive sports, builds character, it is important to repeat that this belief has existed for over a century in many Western societies. In fact, it was during the middle nineteenth century that exclusive British schools incorporated competitive sports into their programs. School administrators at that time were convinced that rule-governed competitive games produced loyal, disciplined, moral, and patriotic young men fit for leadership in civil and military life. Others have since believed that competitive sports could be used to reshape the cultural ideologies of new immigrants and colonized peoples around the globe. It was also thought that competitive sports could teach working class people in industrial societies the value of organization, productivity, and goal achievement. Certain religious groups even tied participation in competitive sports to the formation of good moral character.

More recently, participation in highly competitive sports, has been connected to physical toughness, aggressiveness, and a willingness to make personal sacrifices in the name of achievement. Today, many parents often expect sport programs to provide their children with character-building experiences. And top-level players reinforce these expectations with testimonials about how sport has saved them from lives of delinquency and crime.

The belief that competitive sports build character has inspired social and behavioral scientists to do many studies of athletes. Researchers have been eager to see if there were really differences between athletes and other people, and if any differences could be attributed to character building dimensions of sport participation. However, the studies have produced inconsistent findings and have not been able to prove that participating in competitive sports has any character building effects (see Coakley, 1993a, 1993b, 1993 [in press]).

Unfortunately, most of the research on this topic has been based on three faulty assumptions (McCormack and Chalip, 1988). *First*, researchers have mistakenly assumed that participation in competitive sports involves a unique set of human experiences that are equally shared by all athletes, and that these experiences have a powerful character-shaping potential. *Second*, the researchers have mistakenly assumed that athletes passively internalize all the "character-shaping lessons" they are exposed to when they participate in competitive sports. And *third*, researchers have mistakenly assumed that competitive sports involve certain character-shaping experiences that are not available to people in other activities and other settings.

In other words, the researchers have generally ignored that: (a) sports can be constructed in different ways in different situations, (b) people who participate in sports can have a variety of different experiences, and (c) sport experiences take on different meanings, depending on the circumstances and relationships associated with participation. Furthermore, researchers have ignored the fact that competitiveness and achievement values can be learned in everything from video games to junior high math classes in the United States and many other countries. Therefore comparing the character traits of people who participate in sports with the traits of those who do not participate in sports is not a very fruitful research approach. This is why the research findings have been so confusing and offer no proof that competitive sports provide special character building experiences.

In fact, a survey of numerous studies in the sociology of sport led to the following conclusion back in 1978:

> There is little, if any, valid evidence that participation in [organized] sport is an important or essential element in the socialization process, or that involvement in sport teaches or results in . . . character building, moral development, a competitive and/or cooperative orientation, good citizenship, or certain valued personality traits. (Loy et al., 1978)

Since this conclusion was made, there have been no studies that would contradict it (Coakley, 1993 a, b; Frey and Eitzen, 1991; Kohn, 1986; McCormack and Chalip, 1988; McPherson, 1985; Sage, 1988). However, it needs to be emphasized that just because we have found no automatic connection between participation in competitive sports and character development, we should not conclude that sport participation has no effect on people's lives. Sports do affect the lives of many people in many different ways, but sport participation itself does not automatically lead to the development of particular character traits. Although research has not supported the belief that sports competition builds character, many people accept this belief in some form. I think that their acceptance is related to one or more of the following five factors.

1. When we watch highly skilled athletes display their physical abilities on the playing field, we often conclude that their success must also be related to admirable

character traits. This is called the "halo effect" and it is related to our desire to believe that people who do great things must be great people. It is much easier for us to see skilled athletes as heroes when we think this way, and we tend to ignore information that would tarnish or defame our heroes.

2. Highly competitive sports are organized to attract and select people with high levels of self-confidence and other attributes valued by coaches. Those with low self-confidence usually do not try out for teams (McGuire and Cook, 1983; Medrich et al., 1982; Orlick and Botterill, 1975; Roberts et al., 1981), and those with traits not valued by coaches are cut from teams. This means that athletes at higher levels of competition often possess unique character traits, but this does not happen because sport competition builds those character traits. Instead, those with certain traits become successful in sport and use sport as a setting to nurture and display those traits. The effect of this selection process in sport can be illustrated by discussing physical traits rather than character traits. For example, if participants in youth sport programs were stronger, faster, and more coordinated than nonparticipants, would it be reasonable to conclude that strength, speed, and coordination among athletes were solely a *result* of their involvement in sport? Obviously, it would not. It is rather clear that children with certain physical attributes will be attracted to sport, and, once involved, they will be continually encouraged by peers, parents, and coaches. Furthermore, children who lack strength, speed, and coordination would be less likely to try out for competitive teams, or if they did try out, they would be less likely to make teams. In older age groups the competition for team membership becomes tougher, and those who are physi-

cally deficient in some respect are more likely to be excluded from participation or to drop out voluntarily. Those possessing the desired attributes will probably stay involved and further develop those attributes through continued participation. This does not mean that sport participation has no effect on the development of physical attributes, but it does mean that the effects of sport participation are often limited to those who are physically predisposed to that development. Therefore children who are already strong may become stronger through participation, and those who are coordinated may further develop coordination. However, it should be pointed out that fast or coordinated young people may improve their skills even without participation in competitive sports. The same is true for young people with certain character traits.

3. People tend to use visible and articulate athletes as examples of the character they think is developed through sport participation. Of course, using such a limited "sample" of sport participants is biased and leads to faulty conclusions. This is like making conclusions about the effect of the American school system on students by gathering data only from Ph.D.s, or making conclusions about market economies by listening only to corporation presidents and millionaires. Such "research methods" would reveal a few things worth knowing, but they certainly would not give us a total picture of the effects of our educational and economic systems on human beings. They focus strictly on success stories and ignore all those people who have not risen to the top. This guarantees that "conclusions" will emphasize the positive things happening to people and overlook most of the negative things. This is especially true in the case of sports.

4. Sport events provide a public stage on

which we see athletes cope with significant challenges. We seldom see how other people might deal with such clearcut challenges and we often assume that athletes must have special characters to do what they do and that these characters must have been built through sport participation. This conclusion is sometimes made by parents and other adults who see young people publicly display their abilities in sport events. Because adults seldom have opportunities to see their children perform in nonsport situations they often conclude that the "character" displayed in sports is the product of sport participation itself. However, what usually happens is that sport gives adults opportunities to see young people display traits that have been developed over a number of years and across a variety of different experiences.

5. Our exposure to top level athletes is usually through media coverage and interviews. Since the media deal almost exclusively with topics related to athletes' lives in sports, the athletes often appear and sound knowledgeable and self-confident. We often conclude that this knowledge and self-confidence extend to other areas of life, even though we have no evidence that these athletes know anything about life outside the sport arena.

If people would be more critical as they thought about sports they would not be as likely to accept the belief that sports builds character. But this belief persists, and it has an effect on what they expect from athletes and how they view gender relations in society; these are the topics of the next two sections.

Sports As Character Builders and Athletes As Role Models

When people believe that sports build character, they tend to expect athletes to be role models in organizations, communities, and societies. This expectation often leaves them disappointed and angry when athletes fail to exhibit model behavior. And the disappointment and anger often lead them to condemn individual athletes who have "let everyone down."

The unfounded and naive belief that sports are unique sources of character-building experiences leads people to ignore the situational and cultural factors influencing athletes' behaviors. This is not meant to provide excuses for athletes who have failed to live up to expectations. However, it is meant to provide a more realistic perspective from which to understand the behavior of athletes. For example, when athletes take pain-killing drugs administered by team physicians, many people say they are exhibiting character. When athletes take street drugs to maintain motivation in the face of long road trips and extended seasons, the same people say they are letting everyone in the society down. When athletes generate thousands of dollars for their colleges while they play for what often amounts to minimum wages, people say they have character. When they strike to improve working conditions and salaries in professional sports, people say they are letting everyone down. This is a strange way of assessing character. It conveniently ignores all the dimensions of sports and sport experiences that do not fit with the belief that sports build character.

Sometimes it is necessary to take a critical look at the way sports are organized to understand why some athletes fail to live up to expectations. But when sports are believed to be special settings in which character is created, few people are motivated to take a critical look at sports themselves. Instead they simply see sports as essentially good social phenomena and they condemn the individual athletes whose behaviors do not confirm the myth they continue to believe. Unfortunately, many athletes do not realize the implications of this myth. They, too, perpetuate the idea that sports build character and in the process set themselves up for condemnation if their behavior does not measure up to others' expectations.

"So this is what Harold meant when he said that sport builds character."

Gender Relations and Sports As Character Builders

The belief that sports build character generally leads people to think of character in ways that emphasize attributes traditionally defined as manly (Messner, 1992). Traditionally, it has been the character of male athletes and male coaches that have come to be defined as ideal when sports are seen as unique sources of character-building experiences. This puts women at a serious disadvantage. It not only perpetuates the power and privilege of men in society as a whole, but it subtly encourages girls and women to buy into the very same attitudes that have limited their sport opportunities in the past and limited the extent to which they are taken seriously as athletes in the present. Let me explain further.

According to dominant definitions of character associated with participation in most highly competitive sports, women would have to be aggressive, unemotional, willing to play in pain, and willing to sacrifice their bodies for the sake of a victory so as to be seen as having character. In other words, to show they have "character" they must exhibit behaviors consistent with dominant definitions of masculinity. However, if they do not strive to dominate opponents, if they are sensitive to others, if they show emotion, if they are sensitive to the risk of injury, and if they prize their health over competitive success, then they are seen as lacking character as it has been defined in dominant sport forms.

The definition of what character means in many sports is tied to a long history of male participation and female exclusion (see Chapter 3). This way of thinking has created serious problems in and out of sports. For example, women have constantly been told that to get ahead in the occupational world, they must demonstrate they are qualified. The problem is that men have defined qualifications to fit the way they have done things for years. This means that a woman is qualified only to the extent that she does her job like a man. The problems this has caused for women outside of sports should alert us to the negative implications of saying that sports build character when sports have reflected the interests of males throughout history.

Can Participation in Competitive Sports Interfere with Character Development?

This is a controversial question because it challenges popular beliefs about sports and competition. However, it is worth considering in light of the experiences of some athletes. For example, Tracy Sundlum, a former coach of middle-distance runner Mary Decker Slaney, pointed out that because Slaney used her accomplishments on the track as the sole measure of her worth as a person, she created problems for herself. Sundlum also said that most people

overlook the fact that "the competitive nature we so admire in [Slaney] is actually a huge personality flaw." But when people identify with a successful athlete, they are hesitant to admit the existence of these flaws.

According to both players and behavioral scientists, competitive sports are seldom structured to promote character building. For example, former NFL player Merlin Olsen (1981) has observed from his experience in football that "the athlete doesn't have to grow up because the coach lives his life for him." He goes on to say that "the sad thing is [that] it actually benefits the team to keep the player naive and dependent." Chris Evert (Mill) has reached a similar conclusion about her experiences in tennis: "You know, I think it takes tennis players longer to grow up than other people. We're so pampered . . . so protected from the real world. I'm still trying to grow up, and, I believe I'm getting there" (in Collins, 1984).

Dorcas Susan Butt (1976), a former top-ranked tennis player in Canada and now a clinical psychologist, agrees with Olsen and Evert. She explains that the "social behavior expected of an athlete resembles in many ways that expected of a young, ill, or irresponsible person. Athletes are rewarded to an extreme for good behavior (winning) and punished (often inconsistently) for misbehavior." She goes on to say that athletes are not expected to understand why rules exist, but only to be aware of the fines and penalties that force them, like children, to behave. This, she concludes, is *not* the way to build character. The rigid rules enforced by many coaches give outside observers the impression that character is being built, but in reality these rules deprive the athletes of the very experiences needed to become responsible and mature people.

The notion that participation in highly competitive sports can discourage the development of certain positive character traits and the expression of prosocial behavior such as sharing, altruism, and a concern for others has been noted by a number of social scientists (Bredemeier, 1984, 1985, 1987; Bredemeier and Shields, 1986, 1993; Dubois, 1986; Kleiber and Roberts, 1981; Lee, 1986). Furthermore, the lives of many athletes in competitive sports are often controlled so tightly that it is difficult for them to make moral choices and act according to those choices. This means that athletes are sometimes denied opportunities to become socially responsible human beings through their sport participation. When sport teams are organized autocratically, with coaches calling all the shots, athletes have few chances to make independent choices except to decide which rules they will follow and which ones they will discretely ignore. This is *not* the way to build responsibility (Hellison, 1990, 1993; Williamson and Georgiadis, 1992).

In summary, we can say that some athletes may have their characters shaped through their experiences in sport competition, but sports in general are not organized in ways that encourage character development. However, people cling to their beliefs about the benefits of competition for five reasons:

1. Their belief is promoted by a "halo effect" that leads them to assume that if athletes do great things on the playing field, they must be great people.
2. They are unaware of the selection processes in sport that lead people with certain character traits to become athletes and to remain on teams.
3. They have a biased perspective because they focus their attention on successful top-level athletes and then generalize about what happens in sports as a whole.
4. They overlook the possibility that athletes may be perceived as different from others only because sports provide them with a stage to display the traits they have developed in the course of normal maturation.
5. They focus their attention on limited media portrayals of athletes in which athletes tend to look and sound knowledgeable and self-confident.

The belief that sports build character leads people to expect athletes to be role models, to con-

demn athletes when they fail to exhibit model behavior, and to ignore problems related to the structure and organization of most sports. The idea that sports build character also leads people to define character in terms of traditional male attributes. This creates a definition of the ideal person that works to the disadvantage of the female half of the world's population.

Finally, there is reason to believe that when sport participation is rigidly controlled it can restrict the experiences of athletes in ways that can limit the development of certain character traits, especially those related to interpersonal awareness and social responsibility.

SPORT COMPETITION AS PREPARATION FOR LIFE

Because many people in capitalist societies believe that life is a relentless competitive struggle, they assume that sport participation is good preparation for handling everyday events. They believe that because sports involve both victory and defeat, they provide people with opportunities to experience success and failure. And the lessons of these experiences are believed to be unique and valuable.

This approach to sport competition is illustrated through the words of Chuck Neidel, who, as a 12-year-old, played first base on a New York team that won the Little League World Series. After thinking about the kinds of experiences that would be good for his own young son, he made the following statement:

> Robbie, he's a little shy; he needs a little of the Mike Maietta [the coach of Neidel's team] treatment. You know, Mike, he used to purposely try to break kids; he would scream and yell at us and put the pressure on, to see which of us would break down and cry. If you broke down and cried in practice, he figured you'd break down and cry in a game. I don't think it hurt me a bit because that's what life is all about anyway, pressure and competition. Yeah, I'd like my son to go through what I went through. . . it would be good for him. You know, a lot of what I learned . . . carried through in work. Competition, hard work; I don't outhustle the other guy or beat him, I out-

Many Americans believe that pressure, competition, and adversity prepare young people for adult life. However, this belief is not supported by research evidence. (Colorado Springs Gazette Telegraph and Travis Spradling)

sell him now . . . . You might say I learned the importance of winning when I was real young. I'd like my son to learn it, too.

Now, I'm 31 years old, and I spend all my time working because I'm a successful salesman and I like it. It's like winning in life, instead of winning in baseball . . . . You know, when I was playing in Little League, it was like putting on a uniform and going to work, right? . . . I guess you might even go so far as to say that I learned what life was all about when I was in Little League. That's why I'd encourage my son to play; that's why I'll probably be there as a coach or a manager when he does, to make sure he learns the right way.*

---

*From *Destiny's Darlings* by M. Ralbovsky (p. 209). Copyright 1974. Reprinted by permission of Hawthorne Books, Inc. All rights reserved.

Although few fathers have had a chance to play on a world championship team, many of them would voice an approach to sport competition similar to the one expressed by Neidel.

We can certainly draw some parallels between sports and our everyday lives, but it is doubtful that the similarities are as great as Chuck Neidel claims. In fact, competition may interfere with the "efficient use of resources that cooperation allows" (Kohn, 1986). For example, many managers have discovered that using competitive reward structures among employees often subverts the relationships the employees need to have with one another to perform their jobs efficiently. Success in today's world often depends much more on a person's ability to cooperate and to maintain intrinsic sources of motivation than on the ability to compete and the desire to dominate others. Those who are motivated only to outdo others often cut themselves off from the allies they need to become successful.

Outside of sports, most of us try to avoid, minimize, or eliminate competition in our lives. For example, my teaching colleagues often react negatively when told to formally compete with one another for promotions, tenure, salary increases, and student enrollment. Similarly, lawyers, doctors, and other professionals often form organizations that restrict competition in their work lives. Leaders in the business world may proclaim the merits of competition in speeches and then get together to devise ways of concealing trusts, monopolies, and other anticompetitive practices so they can increase profits while avoiding government sanctions. In less powerful and prestigious occupations, workers sometimes form unions to restrict competition in their jobs. Students respond in similar ways when they are forced to compete against fellow students in the classroom. They develop anti-achievement norms, and they sometimes give the most competitively successful students a hard time by referring to them as nerds, curve breakers, brownnosers, or rate busters. The terms vary from one school to another, but they are almost always negative. This simply reaffirms that we are not naturally competitive. In fact, when we have the power to do so, we restrict competition in the most important spheres of our lives.

Differences Between Sports and Everyday Life

One of the reasons many people enjoy sport competition is that organized competitive sports are different from the rest of our lives in important ways. Table 4-1 outlines these differences. The purpose of this comparison is not to say that all sports are the same or that organized competitive sports are worthless sources of learning. It is obvious that sports are a part of many people's experiences and, like other experiences, they can serve as contexts for learning. But it is likely that the overall value of organized, competitive sports as sites for learning is distorted when people think that everything learned in sport competition contributes to success in the rest of life. It is when the differences between sports and everyday life are recognized that people are able to open themselves up to new experiences in sports.

When these differences are recognized, one of the most beneficial consequences of sport competition is that it can provide opportunities for experiencing success and failure in an activity unrelated to careers, family life, and friendships. In other words, striking out in a baseball game can be a valuable experience when the game is seen as separate from everyday life. And playing a tennis match after school or work can be a valuable experience simply because the outcome of the game does not have any impact on grades in class, job evaluations, the love of family members, and the quality of friendships.

Making these distinctions between sports and everyday life is especially important in the lives of children. Children need activities that allow them the freedom to experiment with their physical skills. This is because their self-conceptions are in the formative stages, and their experiences in sports can enhance their body images and boost confidence in their physical capabilities—two crucial dimensions in their developing self-concepts. According to sport psychologist Doug Kleiber this freedom to test oneself through competition is valuable because it "can provide opportunities for establishing identity and a sense of significance" (1980).

However, when people get carried away with the importance of competition and the lessons it supposedly teaches, sport participation can lead to negative consequences. For example, equating competition in sports with everyday life could lead people to form a limited definition of success in life. If they learn that success depends strictly on establishing superiority over others, they could set themselves up for a succession of defeats in their lives and cut themselves off from other people. Kleiber emphasizes this when he points out that competition has the potential to restrict the range of a person's experiences and

Table 4-1 Organized, competitive sports versus everyday life: A comparison.

Organized, competitive sports	Everyday life
• *Sports* have artificial boundaries in time and space, and participation is not universal.	• *Life* encompasses much more than competitive games and its boundaries are natural and universal (birth and death).
• *Competition* is part of sport experiences; it is often taken for granted.	• *Competition* is incidental in everyday life experiences; it is often avoided.

• *Sports* are simplistic and intentionally clearcut.*
    Meanings are predefined and explicit.
    Events are distinctly delimited in time and space and have definite beginnings and ends.
    Evaluation is based on objective scores, and outcomes are clearcut and easy to understand.
    Opponents are known and confronted directly; their goals are explicit and their progress toward goals is observable.
	• *Life* is complex and essentially ambiguous.*
	    Meanings are emergent and open to question.
	    Events occur in a continuous series, each growing out of the past and leading into the future.
	    Evaluation is generally subjective, and outcomes are often difficult to define and understand.
	    Opponents may be unknown or confronted only indirectly; their goals and progress toward achieving goals may be indeterminable or intentionally hidden.

• *Rules* are clearcut and formally agreed upon; they are enforced by formal agents of control (referees, umpires, etc.) who directly observe the actions of those involved.	• *Rules* are often ambiguous and may not be based on consensus; enforcement usually depends on self-control, since formal agents of control have little or no opportunity to make direct observations.
• *Success* depends primarily on physical skills; only a minimum of interpersonal skills is required for participation.	• *Success* depends primarily on interpersonal skills and is generally unrelated to physical skills.
• *Individuals* usually seek out competitors who will test their abilities.	• *Individuals* try to avoid or eliminate the influence of competitors.
• *Events* are organized so all participants face standardized sets of conditions; everyone starts out as equals within the competitive structure of sports.	• *Events* are not organized, and everyone faces different conditions; some people have advantages over others because of inequalities.
• *Action* involves ethical choices related to immediate issues that seldom have significance beyond the event itself.	• *Action* involves ethical choices related to ultimate issues and these ethical choices sometimes have pervasive implications.

*This point has been discussed in detail by John Valentine (1980).

relationships and "replace caring and cooperation with the pursuit of personal gain" (1980).

Bob Cousy, a former standout player for the Boston Celtics (NBA) and a former college coach, has vividly explained that when competitive orientations are taken too seriously they can "kill [a person's] moral sense, the happiness of a family, even the [person] himself" (1975). Cousy's personal statement is supported by a study of 57 ice hockey players trying out for the 1980 U.S. Olympic team. It was found that players with cooperative orientations measured higher on psychological adjustment and health than players with strong competitive orientations (Johnson et al., 1987).

A former NFL player has raised additional questions about the consequences of participating in highly competitive professional sports when he noted that

[Athletes are] in one of the most highly stressed jobs in the country, and there's no assistance, so its gonna continue to turn out guys who are mentally unstable, bankrupt, divorced, alcohol and substance abusers. Athletes are set up to be very high-risk people in terms of being abusers of things—money, substances, everything. These problems have to be dealt with by attacking the problem, and not just the symptom. *And the problem is being ill-prepared for life* (taken from an interview done by Michael Messner, 1992, p. 127; emphasis added).

In other words, competition in sports does not automatically prepare people for anything but competition in sports (Sadler, 1977).

In summary, organized competitive sports and everyday life are different. Sports can provide a combination of pleasure and excitement that is different from what is experienced in serious, everyday life situations (Elias and Dunning, 1986). Sports may mimic the rest of life and arouse emotions similar to those experienced in other activities, but the emotional arousal occurs in controlled settings. According to Elias and Dunning, this means that the emotions created by sports "are transposed into a different key. They lose their sting. They are blended with 'a kind of delight'" (1986). People may wish that life could be more like sports, but when sports and life are equated, people expect too much of sports and misunderstand what is involved in everyday life. When sports are viewed as preparation for life, the emotions aroused by sports do not lose their sting, and much of what sports have to offer as a source of learning is lost.

CONCLUSION:

Is sport competition valuable?

The purpose of this chapter has been to clarify the concept of sport competition and to show how it is related to culture, society, and behavior. *Sport competition* was defined as a *process through which success is measured by directly comparing the achievements of those who are performing the same physical activity under standardized conditions and rules.* It was distinguished from *cooperation*

and the use of *individualized standards*, both of which are alternative processes through which behavior may be evaluated and rewards distributed. Competition was also described as an orientation people use to evaluate themselves and approach their relationships with others. Most important, it was shown how a competitive orientation is not to be confused with an achievement orientation; achievement-oriented people may not always be competitive people. Achievement may also be emphasized in conjunction with cooperative and individualized orientations.

The ways in which competitive reward structures and competitive orientations are included in sports are connected to the culture and social structure in which sports exist. An emphasis on the competitive dimensions of sports in capitalist societies is used to strengthen a popular belief in the existence of a meritocracy. This belief reaffirms the legitimacy of inequality and promotes the interests of the wealthy and powerful. In socialist societies, an emphasis on the cooperative and developmental dimensions of sports is used to promote a collectivist spirit and maintain widespread participation in physical culture. In both capitalist and socialist societies, sports are officially defined and promoted in ways that re-create dominant political and economic ideologies. Similarly, there are cultures in which competition does not exist or in which competitive behavior is defined as deviant. Generally, these are cultures in which cooperation is widely recognized as being necessary for survival.

Although sports in any society often perpetuate interpretations of the world that work to the advantage of people in privileged positions, some people may ignore or reject dominant sport forms in a society and participate in alternative sport forms grounded in new and different ways of viewing themselves and the world around them. In this way they offer challenges to dominant cultural ideology and, in some cases, they might even promote changes in that ideology.

In the section on competition and character, it was noted that participation in competitive sport does not involve any unique experiences that lead to the development of special character traits. Furthermore, the belief that participation in sports builds character leads to distorted expectations for athletes and it promotes definitions of character that serve to disadvantage women and encourage methods of evaluating behavior that privilege men.

Finally, sport competition was viewed in terms of whether it prepares people for life. It was concluded that people are most likely to learn valuable lessons from their experiences in sport competition when sports are *not* used as a metaphor for life. An emphasis on sports as preparation for life often interferes with experiencing competition in sports in ways that lead to learning and self-discovery.

SUGGESTED READINGS

Allison, M., and G. Luschen. 1979. A comparative analysis of Navajo Indian and Anglo basketball sport systems. International Review of Sport Sociology 14(3-4):75-85 (*outlines how athletes' perceptions of the sport experience vary by culture*).

Coakley, J. 1993a. Socialization and sport. In R.N. Singer, M. Murphey, and L.K. Tennant, eds., Handbook on research in sport psychology (pp. 571-586). Macmillan Publishing Company, New York (*a general overview of sport socialization research including research on socialization through sports*).

Coakley, J. 1993b. Sport and socialization. Exercise and Sport Sciences Reviews 21 (169-200) (*a critical review of sport socialization research with an emphasis on the need for interactionist models and qualitative methodologies*).

Eitzen, D.S., and G.H. Sage. Sociology of North American Sport (ed. 5). Brown and Benchmark Publishers. Dubuque, Iowa (*Chapter 3 on "Sport and societal values" provides a general discussion of how competition is related to the American value system*).

Gilbert, B. 1988. Competition: is it what life's all about? Sports Illustrated 68(20):88-100 (*journalistic discussion of competition; incorporates both psychological and sociological perspectives in a critique of the American emphasis on competition*).

Kohn, A. 1986. No contest: the case against competition. Houghton Mifflin Company, Boston (*readable, thorough review of research on competition; critique of the role of competition in society*).

Le Clair, J. 1992. Sport and physical activity in the 1990s. Thompson Educational Publishing, Inc., Toronto (*Chapter 3, "Culture and competition" is a readable discussion of Canadian cultural ideology and sport competition*).

Miner, V., and H.E. Longino, eds. 1987. Competition: a feminist taboo? The Feminist Press, New York (*20 papers on dimensions of the relationship between competition and gender relations in society*).

Orlick, T. 1978. Winning through cooperation. Acropolis Books, Ltd., Washington, D.C. (*discussions on how to incorporate cooperation into sport experiences*).

Pepitone, E. 1980. Children in cooperation and competition. Lexington Books, Lexington, Mass. (*thorough review and discussion of research*).

Sage, G.H. 1988. Sports participation as a builder of character? The World and I 3(10):629-641 (*excellent discussion and critique of the popular conception of sport participation as a character builder*).

Sherif, C. 1981. The social context of competition (pp. 132-149) *and* Females in the competitive process (pp. 461-486). In M. Hart and S. Birrell, eds., Sport in the socio-cultural process. Wm. C. Brown Company Publishers, Dubuque, Iowa (*a review of social psychological information related to the dynamics of competition and the performance of girls and women in competitive reward structures*).

Tutko, T., and W. Bruns. 1976. Winning is everything and other American myths. Macmillan, Inc., New York (*easy-to-read review of the role and consequences of competition in sport*).

(Suzanne Tregarthen/Educational Photo Stock)

CHAPTER 5

ORGANIZED SPORT PROGRAMS FOR CHILDREN

Are they worth the effort?

Kids want the opportunity to do things for themselves. I think they're just sick and tired of having adults organize things for them.

Joe Paterno, Football Coach, Penn State University (1971)

The most important part of play is learning how to set up the game, choose sides, agree with your peers, make compromises, figure out answers, submit to self-directed rulings so that the game can continue. . . . These important civilizing functions are bypassed by adult-run leagues.

Leonard Koppett, Sports Reporter and Columnist (1981)

Sometimes the preparation is so hard, so intense . . . The crying, the screaming . . . We are not in the gym to be having fun. The fun comes at the end, with the winning and the medals.

Bela Karolyi, Gymnastics coach (1992)

If there were no sports, life would be easier because you wouldn't have to go play games every other day. . . .

Fifth grade student, Colorado Springs (1991)

Adult organization of children's play is nothing new. As soon as it was realized that the behavior and character of children were shaped by the social environments in which they lived, adults in industrialized countries took it upon themselves to control those environments so their children could grow up in the "correct" ways. In North America and in parts of Europe, young boys were provided with organized sport activities. It was hoped that sports, especially team sports, would teach boys from lower-class backgrounds how to cooperate and work together peacefully. In the case of middle-class boys it was hoped that strenuous sport activities would turn them into strong, assertive, competitive men by providing them with an alternative to home lives dominated by women. Girls were provided with quiet games and other activities to train them to become able mothers and homemakers; the teaching of domestic skills took priority over the teaching of sport skills to girls.

Of course, there were exceptions to these patterns, but this was the general framework out of which most organized youth sport programs developed after World War II in North America. Through the 1950s and 1960s those programs grew dramatically with the help of powerful public, private, and commercial sponsors (Berryman, 1982).* In addition, parents entered the scene. Fathers eagerly became coaches, managers, and league administrators. Mothers became chauffeurs and short-order cooks to meet the demands of practice and game schedules.

The vast majority of these sport programs were for boys between the ages of 8 and 14. They emphasized competition as a means of building the achievement orientations that would hopefully lead to personal success and community growth. Until the 1970s, girls' interests in sports were largely ignored in most countries. Girls were relegated to the bleachers during their brothers' games and given the hope of growing up to be high school cheerleaders. Then the women's movement, the fitness movement, and government legislation prohibiting sex discrimination (Title IX in the United States) all came together to provide an impetus for the development of new programs. During the 1970s and early 1980s these programs grew to the point that girls in North America have almost as many opportunities as boys. However, their participation rates remain lower than those for boys—for reasons discussed later in this chapter (and in Chapter 9).

Participation in organized youth sport programs has now become an accepted part of growing up in most industrialized societies, especially among the middle and upper classes, where resources enable adults to sponsor, organize, and administer many programs for their children. National surveys show that Americans strongly support the sport involvement of both boys and girls; 90% of parents say they encourage their children to participate in sports, and 62% indicate their children participate in some type of organized sport activity (the Miller Lite Report, 1983). However, not all people surveyed accept organized sport programs for children without question. In fact, about 85% of the general public in the United States say that coaches in organized programs take games too seriously and that too much emphasis is placed on winning and not enough on the physical and psychological development of the participants.

Why are there mixed feelings about organized youth sport programs? Why are the programs so widely supported while, at the same time, so widely criticized? Are they really worth all the effort, time, and money that adults put into them? The purpose of this chapter is to explore what happens to the children in those programs and how the programs can be changed to meet more effectively the interests of the children.

*In Canada, Australia, New Zealand, and the United States, the growth of these programs was also fueled by the large numbers of baby-boom children who were 5 to 15 years old between the late 1950s and the late 1970s.

FORMAL VS. INFORMAL GAMES: A COMPARISON

One of the ways to learn about what happens in organized youth sport programs is to compare the games in those programs with the games children play on their own. The students in my sociology of sport classes and I have used this approach on a number of occasions. One of the things we have learned is that the individual players in each of these game settings define and interpret their personal experiences in many different ways (see also Harris, 1983). However, despite this diversity we also discovered that there were consistent patterns of differences between what happens in organized, adult-controlled games and in informal, player-controlled games. These findings are summarized in the following sections.*

Informal, Player-Controlled Games

Our observations of informally organized, player-controlled games were made over a 12-month period. We observed 84 games in backyards, parks, vacant lots, and school playgrounds. In each game, interviews were conducted with at least two of the players. The observations and interviews indicated that when children get together and play on their own, they are interested in four things:

1. *Action*, especially action leading to scoring
2. *Personal involvement* in the action
3. A *close score* (that is, a challenging or exciting contest)
4. *Opportunities to reaffirm friendships* during the game

In the majority of games observed, the number of players ranged from 2 to 12. Usually the players knew one another from games played on previous occasions. In most cases, teams were formed quickly. Skill differences and *friendship* patterns were the criteria used to choose teams.

A process of systematically choosing players one-by-one seldom occurred. However, it was clear that getting an informal game started and keeping it going was a complex operation. The amount of *action* in the game depended on how good the players were at managing interpersonal relationships and making effective decisions.

The games and game rules resembled those used in organized programs, but they contained many modifications to maximize *action*, scoring, and *personal involvement* while *keeping the scores close* at the same time. For the sake of *action*, free throws were eliminated in basketball, throw-ins were kept to a minimum in soccer, yardage penalties were dropped from football, and the pitcher's mound in baseball and softball was moved closer to the batter when someone was having a hard time hitting the ball. Similar types of rules were found in kickball, team 4-square, individual 4-square, 2-square, 1-wall handball, street hockey, tennis, Frisbee, and other games. Further proof for the importance of *action* were the extremely high scores in the vast majority of the games.

Personal involvement was maximized through a number of clever rule qualifications and handicap systems. Restrictive handicaps were used to keep the highly skilled players from dominating the action in the games. Other forms of handicaps allowed advantages to the less skilled players. Furthermore, the less skilled players seemed to have unstated permission to use special rules in their own favor; they were the ones most likely to use "do-over" or "interference" calls to get another chance or to compensate for the effect of their mistakes on the outcomes of games. This tactic seemed to save them personal embarrassment and preserve their integrity as "contributing" members of their teams. It also served to *keep the game scores close*. The overuse of these special rules was not usually a problem, but when it was, it was controlled informally through jests or teasing.

The *personal involvement* of each of the players was also promoted by unique game rules. In baseball there was a rule against called strikes;

---

*For a detailed description of the methods used in this project, see Coakley, 1980, 1982, or 1983a.

this allowed most everyone a chance to hit (and catch the ball in the field). In football there was usually a rule that made everyone on the team eligible to receive a pass on any play. When the interviewers asked the players what the biggest source of fun was in their games, answers almost always referred to hitting, catching, kicking, scoring, or some other form of *action* in which they were personally involved. All the young people liked to be a crucial part of what was going on in the game.

Keeping order in the games depended on the extent to which players were committed to the *action*. Usually, the more they were personally involved, the more committed they were. Tactics (sanctions) used to control behavior were most often used to keep players from disrupting the *action* of the games. The players did joke around, and sometimes even ignored the rules, but these forms of deviance were ignored as long as they did not interfere with the flow of *action*. The observers noted that many different performance styles, such as batting opposite-handed, throwing around-the-back passes, running unplanned pass patterns, and moving out of position, were all accepted as long as *action* in the games was not destroyed. The players with the greatest skill were the ones who had the most freedom to use these styles because they could do it without upsetting game *action* or interfering with the *personal involvement* of the other players.

Prestige and social status among the players was important because it usually determined the extent to which individuals became involved in decision-making processes during the games. The older players or those with the greatest skills usually had the most status, although status was sometimes given to other players when they were especially good at solving arguments.

Surprisingly, arguments among the players were not major problems. Over 50% of the observed games did not contain any arguments lasting long enough to slow down the normal flow of *action*. In the remaining games, arguments occurred, but they were solved in all but

The informal games of young people usually emphasize action, personal involvement, close scores, and the reaffirmation of friendships. (Tini Campbell)

eight cases. It seemed as if the players had played together enough times to work things out so that games were seldom stopped because of fighting.

A WORD OF CAUTION The informal games of children should not be romanticized. Problems sometimes do get out of hand. Bigger and stronger children may exploit smaller and weaker ones. Girls are often treated in sexist ways when they try to become a part of groups of boys. And those who are chosen last or ignored during team selection processes often feel rejected by their peers (Evans, 1988). Additionally, the dynamics of games usually vary depending on the availability of play spaces and equipment. For example, when a large group is using the only basketball court in the neighborhood, the games will exclude many who want to play, the team that wins will take on challengers rather than giving up the court to others, and those with less-developed skills will not be given special concessions when it comes to participation. But when there are many courts and only a few players, the goal is often to accommodate everyone's interests so nobody will leave and end the game. This is a major reason why the informal games of children in low-income areas with few facilities and resources are often different from the games played by children in higher-income areas where facilities are more plentiful than children to use them (Carlston, 1986). External conditions in the society as a whole have important effects on the way informal games are played. The majority of children in our research were from middle- and upper-middle income neighborhoods.

Formal, Adult-Controlled Games

We also observed 121 formally organized, adult-controlled games and interviewed at least two of the players in each game. We found a strong interest in action and personal involvement, but, unlike the participants in informal games, those in the organized games were more likely to be serious and concerned with performance quality and game outcomes. The most apparent aspect of these games was that the action, the personal involvement, and the behavior of the players were strictly regulated by specialized *rules*. These *rules* were enforced by adults.

Also important to the players were the formal *positions* they played on their teams. In fact, they often referred to themselves in terms of those *positions*. They seemed to take pride in describing themselves as "defensive halfbacks" or "offensive ends" or as "center forwards," "left wingers," "catchers," or whatever. This was the case for substitutes as well as first-string players. The importance of *positions* was further emphasized by coaches and spectators, who often encouraged players to "*stay in position*" during the games (this happened regularly in basket-

ball, soccer, and hockey—and sometimes in softball).

The actual play of the game was governed by time schedules, the weather, and the setting of the sun. Individual playing time for the participants varied according to skill levels. Most often it was the smaller, visibly timid and less skilled children who sat on the sidelines. Although everyone usually got into the game for at least a short period of time, those whose action time was low often maintained only a token interest in the game. While these substitutes were on the sidelines, they were usually bored with the whole situation or interested in things unrelated to the games. Highly skilled players were most likely to exhibit strong interest in the games and express disappointment when taken out of the lineup. When taken out, they stayed close to the coach and waited or sometimes asked to be put back into the games.

An additional consequence of adult control and the high degree of organization was the visible absence of arguments and overt displays of hostility between players from opposing teams. The few arguments noted by observers were between members of the same team and the cause was usually a player's inability to remember game *rules*, stay in *position*, play the *position* efficiently, or carry out team strategy. Adult control and the formal organization (*rules* plus *positions*) not only held the group together but also restricted the visible display of affection and friendship during the play of the game. Exceptions to this were observed during the scheduled breaks in the game (halftime or the half of the inning during which a team came to bat in baseball and softball), but apart from these breaks, it was difficult to determine who was friends with whom. And the nature of interpersonal relationships seemed to have little relevance to what happened in the game itself.

The major purpose of game *rules* seemed to be the standardization of competition and the control of player behavior. The impact of the *rules* on the extent of action and involvement was most apt to take the form of an interruption, but there were few visible indications from the players that they resented these breaks in the action. The only signs of displeasure came when the delay was caused by a penalty called against their team. *Rule enforcement (social control)* was based on the self-control and obedience of players, but it ultimately rested in the hands of adults— coaches and referees. The applications of *rules* by adults were based on universalistic criteria. In other words, no visible exceptions were made taking into consideration individual abilities or characteristics; individual freedom was restricted by *rules* and the expectations of coaches.

Compliance with *rules* and with the expectations of coaches was extremely high. Deviance resulted more often from a player forgetting or not knowing what to do than from attempts to gain an unfair advantage over opponents. On the playing field, the observed cases of deviance were usually accompanied by formal sanctions regardless of whether the deviance had an effect on game action or on the success of the team. Off the field, *rules* varied from one team to another. When deviance occurred, it usually took the form of "joking around" or exhibiting a lack of interest in the game or the team. Responses to these behaviors also varied. Coaches and parents used both verbal and nonverbal sanctions. The game *rules*, team *rules*, and sanctions were all used to control behavior and to preserve the organization of the game and the values underlying the authority of referees and coaches.

The observations and the interviews indicated that the players were usually serious about

In organized sport programs for children, the involvement of adults is overwhelming. It is the adults who: *A*, determine the rules; *B*, plan strategy and call plays; *C*, debate questionable calls and settle disputes; and *D*, wait anxiously for results (*A* and *D*, Ken Willis; *B* and *C*, James Bryant).

A, determine the rules;

Continued.

B, plan strategy and call plays;

C, debate questionable calls and settle disputes; and

D, wait anxiously for results.

the games. But excessive concerns about playing well and winning games were *not* characteristic. Interestingly, those most likely to be over-concerned with these things were the highly skilled players and members of the most successful teams. In other words, the outward emphasis on performance and victory was highest for those who performed best and won most frequently. Among the majority of others, participation was typically described in terms of intrinsic rewards. Similarly, the disappointment associated with a game or an entire season was usually related to personal opportunities to play. Of course, a desire to play more is not related only to intrinsic rewards. Playing for the better part of a game or making a starting team is also a means for gaining extrinsic rewards from peers and parents. Lastly, players were usually able to provide a statement of their team record and what the record meant in the league standings.

Status on the organized teams seemed to depend largely on the coaches' assessments of the relative physical abilities among players and the potential of those players for contributing to a team's success. It was also observed that the better players were sometimes given more responsibility on teams and more latitude in determining what they would do during the game. Physical skill and acknowledgment by coaches were usually the basis of status and autonomy among the players. And acknowledgment by coaches usually depended on following team *rules*.

Finally, the stability of the group was extremely high in organized, competitive sports. Games did not end until the "final whistle" and players never walked away from the games without permission from a coach or referee. The games always continued regardless of the quality of play or the satisfaction of the players. The *rules* and the adults who enforced them controlled the time when the games were over.

Summary and Analysis of Differences

The personal experiences of the players in each of these game settings were considerably different. The informal games were generally *action-centered* whereas the formal games were *rule-centered*. The experiences in the informal games revolved around the maintenance of action; and action was maintained through making decisions and managing relationships between players (the box on pp. 120-121 discusses some of the complex management problems faced by the players in informal games). The experiences in the formal games revolved around learning and following rules, as well as obeying the adults who made and enforced the rules.

Which of these experiences is more valuable in the development of children? The answer to this question is not only important to the children involved but also to the adults who have invested so much of their time and resources into organized programs. After doing quite a bit of research on this issue, my belief is that each experience makes different contributions to the development of young people. However, the contributions made by participation in organized programs have traditionally been overrated by the general public, and the contributions made by participation in informal games have often been forgotten or taken for granted.

But things are starting to change—especially in the way people look at organized programs. Research and media coverage have helped people realize that organized programs are not all they are cracked up to be. The most frequent targets of popular criticism have been insensitive coaches and the win-at-all-costs philosophy that seems to underlie certain programs. But what many people don't realize is that the origins of problems in organized programs are not so easily identified. Eliminating a few insensitive coaches and preaching about how fun is more important than winning will not do much to change the experiences of the children in those programs. Many more changes are needed. However, it is difficult to make those changes because many adults who administer and support the programs have a vested interest in keeping them the way they are. They know the programs are not perfect, but they are afraid that changing them will eliminate many of the good things they have accomplished in the past.

Differences in Play Activities and Informal Games of Boys and Girls

Patterns of informally organized activities are not the same for all children. There are differences between geographical regions, urban and rural areas, inner-city and suburban areas, upper-income areas and lower-income areas, various age groups, and boys and girls. A study designed by sociologist Janet Lever (1976, 1978, 1980) focused attention on the differences between the informal games played by boys and those played by girls. She studied the after-school activity patterns of 181 fifth graders (10 to 11 years old) from three schools in Connecticut. She used four different methods to collect information: (1) observations on school playgrounds, (2) semistructured interviews, (3) written questionnaires, and (4) activity diaries kept by the children themselves.

Her findings revealed these seven differences between the games of boys and girls:
• Boys played outdoors more than girls.
• When with friends, boys played in larger groups than girls.
• The play groups of boys were more age-mixed than those of girls.
• Boys played competitive games more frequently than girls.
• The games played by boys had more explicit goals and involved teams and team formation processes more often than girls' games.
• The games played by boys were more complex; they had more rules, a greater number of different positions (roles), and more player interdependence (teamwork).
• Girls played games with predominantly male groups more often than boys played games in predominantly female groups.

Lever summarizes the characteristics of girls' play and games in the following way (1978):

Girls' (activities) are very different. They are mostly spontaneous, imaginative, and free of structure or rules. Turn-taking activities like jumprope may be played without setting explicit goals. Girls have far less experience with interpersonal competition. The style of their competition is indirect rather than face to face, individual rather than team affiliated. Leadership roles are either missing or randomly filled.

Perhaps more important, girls' play occurs in small groups. These girls report preferring the company of a single best friend to a group of four or more. Often girls mimic primary human relationships instead of playing formal games, or they engage in conversation rather than play anything at all.

It is important to know about the causes and consequences of these activity differences between boys and girls. Despite the growth of organized sport programs for girls, traditional gender differences in informal activities continue to be perpetuated through socialization experiences. The importance of gender in the minds of many people shapes how men and women define and set expectations for themselves and how they relate to the rest of the world. Childhood experiences have an effect in this process.

Research clearly shows that immediately following birth, girls are treated differently than boys. This differential treatment is grounded in the male-oriented nature of contemporary society. But it is real, and until it is changed people must be aware of its implications. In this discussion, one of its implications is that girls under the age of 12 are less likely than boys to have experiences that encourage participation in a wide range of competitive physical activities—either in informal games or organized programs. The following list summarizes the research findings that outline these differences:
• Newborn baby girls are perceived by their parents as softer, cuter, smaller, and less attentive than newborn baby boys are perceived by their parents—despite the absence of any measurable physical differences between the girls and boys (Chafetz, 1978).
• The parents of newborn baby girls spend more time teaching them to smile and less time discouraging them from crying than is done by the parents of newborn baby boys (Chafetz, 1978).

- The parents of daughters worry more about the physical safety of their children than do the parents of sons; for example, in comparison with boys, baby girls are not allowed to crawl as far away from their parents before being picked up and carried back to where their parents are located; and when they face barriers or obstacles, the girls receive assistance more rapidly and more completely than the boys (Lewis, 1972a, b).
- The parents of baby girls allow their daughters to cling to them more readily than baby boys are allowed to cling to their parents (Lewis, 1972b).
- In comparison to baby boys, baby girls are talked to more often by their parents, but they are handled less actively and jostled less; boys are thrown into the air more and handled in a rougher manner than girls are handled (Lewis, 1972a).
- Parents of girls spend more time managing the physical appearance of their daughters (bows in hair, dresses, tights, fancy underwear, dress shoes, etc.) than the parents of boys spend on their sons; and girls are taught to be more aware of maintaining the neatness of their appearance (Chafetz, 1978).
- The parents of daughters put more emphasis on the importance of affiliation (getting along with others) and less on the development of problem-solving abilities than do the parents of sons (Chafetz, 1978).
- Compared with boys, girls are taught to be more sensitive and responsive to the opinions and needs of others very early in their childhood (Caplan, 1981), and boys are encouraged to manipulate physical objects and engage in physical play (Langlois and Downs, 1980).
- Compared with boys, girls are given gifts that are more likely to be physically passive, nonmechanical, emotionally expressive, related to household settings, and played with inside the house (Chafetz, 1978).
- Compared with boys, girls have more parental restrictions placed on their activities and relationships (Caplan, 1981), and boys are given more encouragement to explore and utilize the environment to meet their own interests (Langlois and Downs, 1980; Lewis, 1972b).

- Fathers spend more time with their sons than with their daughters, and when they do spend time with their daughters, they are less likely to do physical things like playing catch or running (Ross and Pate, 1987).

Although people have revised some of their ideas about gender over the past 2 decades, these differences still exist in the 1990s. Of course, some girls experience them more strongly than others. But even though there are differences from one family to the next, it is easy to see how the experiences of girls may make them less likely than boys to become involved in competitive physical activities. After reviewing these research findings, it is easy to see why the girls in Janet Lever's study had patterns of game playing that were different from the patterns among boys. It is difficult to play complex, competitive games involving large, age-mixed groups when faced with so many subtle, "protective" restrictions. (See Chapter 9, p. 233, for more information on this topic.)

When boys and girls have such different experiences in connection with play and games during childhood, additional questions are raised. Because play and games are often viewed as training grounds for developing skills that carry over into adulthood, there is speculation about how boys and girls are being prepared to meet future challenges. Do males have an advantage in the occupational world because they played more complex competitive games while they were growing up? Are females more sensitive to the needs of others because their play activities were more cooperative and personal? Research will help us answer these questions, but in the meantime, it would be wise to encourage a wide variety of play activities and games among both boys and girls. All children benefit from involvement in spontaneous and cooperative activities as well as activities that are structured and competitive. In industrial societies children need to learn a combination of expressive, interpersonal, and organizational skills. Success requires the abilities to form and maintain personal relationships with family members and close friends and the ability to deal with the complexity of career challenges and large-scale organizations without being overwhelmed. Playing games during childhood may be related to all these abilities.

Good things *have* happened in organized programs. Anyone connected with them realizes this. But changes are needed. Most people realize this as well. This is why people have mixed feelings about the programs. On one hand, they do not want their own children missing out on the good things the programs have to offer. But on the other hand, they have heard the horror stories about what has happened to others, and they don't want their children to become the victims of uncaring coaches or of the philosophy that winning is more important than personal development and a concern for others. Therefore they support the programs, but they are also critical of them.

As these people learn more about how and why certain things happen to the participants in organized programs, they will become more sensitive to the types of changes needed to improve them. Existing research already provides a useful basis for understanding children's experiences and suggesting changes. In the two major sections that follow, we will look at (1) some of the important questions about what happens to the players in organized programs and (2) the ways in which organized programs might be changed to meet the needs and interests of young people.

WHAT HAPPENS IN ORGANIZED PROGRAMS?

To deal with this broad area of inquiry, our discussion will focus on six questions frequently asked by students, parents, and people connected with organized sport programs.

Do Parents and Coaches Expect Too Much from Children in Organized Sport Programs?

We have all heard horror stories about the extreme behaviors of some "little league parents" and insensitive, win-oriented coaches. Fortunately, these stories describe only a minority of the adults connected with organized teams and leagues (Fine, 1987). Most parents and coaches have good intentions. They do not try to make children unhappy and miserable. However,

they do make mistakes. And one of the most frequent mistakes is to expect their children and their teams to act like miniature versions of adults and adult teams.

Parents and coaches often forget or they do not realize that most children under the age of 12 do not have the cognitive abilities to fully grasp the meaning of strategy in team sports. Anyone who has ever watched two teams of 8-year-old soccer players probably understands what this statement means. Many children under the age of 12 play what might be called "beehive soccer"; after the opening kick there are 20 bodies and 40 legs within 10 yards of the ball. And they follow the ball like a swarm of bees following its queen. In other words, everyone is out of position and they usually stay that way for the majority of the game. Meanwhile, many of the adults on the sidelines are loudly pleading with their children to "Stay in position!" or to "Get back where you belong!" But one of the problems in many team sports is that positions change depending on where the ball and the other players are. Therefore the only way players can really determine where they belong is to mentally visualize the relationships between teammates and opponents over the entire field. But the ability to visualize all these relationships and think in terms of an overall social system is not often developed before the age of 12. (This is the same reason that some 8-year-olds have a difficult time grasping the idea that their uncles are the sons of their grandmothers while they are also the brothers of one of their parents.)

This inability of children frustrates parents and coaches. Without understanding why children have such a difficult time conforming to team strategy, adults accuse them of not trying hard enough, not thinking, or having a bad attitude. This, in turn, frustrates the young players who are trying and thinking as best they can. Like their parents and coaches, they do not realize that their inabilities are related to normal developmental processes.

The only way to avoid "beehive soccer" and its equivalents in other sports is to carefully and

"I know this is too soon to get him into sport, but I can't let him get too far behind the rest of the kids in the neighborhood if he is ever going to play on a team in high school."

tediously condition young players to respond in certain ways to certain situations during games. This means that during practices, the coaches must create various game situations and then have each player rehearse the correct individual responses to each of the situations. Doing this with every player for even a few basic situations makes practices very tedious and boring. When coaches use this tactic, they may be able to get their players to do the right things more often, and they may win a few more games, but they destroy much of the action and personal involvement that children value in their sport experiences. And then the coaches wonder why their players don't like to come to practices or why they "horse around" while they are there.

Although the inability to mentally visualize complex sets of social relationships has an obvious effect on what can be expected from children in most team sports, it also has implications for what can be expected of children under the age of 12 in any competitive sport activity. According to theories and research in social psychology, children are not born with the ability to compete or cooperate with others. They must learn how to handle these relationships. This learning is based on experience, but it is also governed by the gradual development of abstract thinking abilities. As these thinking abilities develop, children move from a stage in which they can see the world only from their own limited viewpoint to a stage in which they can see the world from an objective "third-party perspective"—one that is not simply limited to their own view or the view of any single other person they know (Coakley, 1984, 1985b; Mead, 1934; Selman, 1971, 1976). This third-party perspective is needed to fully engage in any complex group interaction. Since it usually is not developed before age 12, a child's view of involvement in competitive relationships is different than an adult's view (Roberts, 1983).

As it is now, most adults do not appreciate the differences between their views of competition and the views of children. For this reason, too many parents and coaches have unrealistic expectations for their children in sport programs. Developmental theory and research suggest that we need to think more seriously about restructuring organized leagues and teams to fit the cognitive and conceptual abilities of young participants.

Do Organized Sport Programs Affect Relationships Between Parents and Children?

The *informal* games of children do not usually have an effect on family life as a whole. Children get together on their own and use makeshift equipment and unofficial playing fields. They have no uniforms, lineups, scoreboards, or after-game treats. But the games in organized sports are different; participation is often a family affair. Sociologist Gai Berlage (1982) provides an explanation of what this means:

> Certainly children don't participate in these programs separate from the family. Their commitment means a family commitment of time, money and often parent participation. . . . The commitment on the part of the parents is both physical and emotional. Family schedules must be adjusted to children's practice and game schedules. Parents must adjust their schedules, so that they can watch their children compete.

It is clear that family schedules are affected when a child participates in an organized sport program—any parent with young children in

those programs can attest to this (Snyder and Purdy, 1982). But surprisingly, few sport sociologists have done research on how family *relationships* are affected by involvement in those programs, even though it has been said that "it is quite possible that organized children's athletics has had as large an impact on family structure and behavior as any other societal event in the past three decades" (Ash, 1978). This may be an overstatement, but data from a national study in the United States indicate that over 80% of parents with children in sport programs attend their children's games on a frequent basis (Miller Lite Report, 1983). This may not indicate that involvement is actually influencing the *nature* of family relationships, but it emphasizes that at a time when so many activities in industrial societies are age-segregated, organized sport programs provide activities that often involve both parents and children (Berlage, 1982).

However, we must be careful not to jump to the conclusion that whenever parents and children are involved in something together, they get along in positive ways. According to two sociologists who studied organized youth baseball leagues in California, some parents act in ways that can damage their relationships with their children (Yablonsky and Brower, 1979). Another study in Michigan indicated that when parents become too emotionally involved in organized youth sports, their behavior often overwhelms and creates anxiety for their children (State of Michigan, 1978).

The most potentially destructive situation occurs when children believe that their relationship with one or both parents depends on continued involvement in sport or on the quality of their performances as athletes. Young people sometimes find themselves in a double bind: if they do not perform well, they get negative feedback; if they do perform well, they are treated like "little pros" instead of children. Mike Messner, a sociologist from the University of Southern California, discovered examples of this double bind in his interviews with men who had been elite athletes. Many of the men in

Messner's (1992) study remembered their first experiences in sport because those experiences brought them together with their fathers who were otherwise away from home and emotionally distant from them. The boys wanted to please their fathers and maintain their attachment to them, but they generally discovered that the types of togetherness that accompanied sports did not involve sharing information about fears and weaknesses. This prevented the boys from using participation in organized sports to develop emotional bonds with their fathers that would carry over into other settings and connect to issues other than just sports. Therefore they felt they had to stay in sports and become good athletes to maintain basic, nonemotional connections with their fathers.

Many parents are becoming more aware of the necessity to eliminate pressure on their children to win games and perform without mistakes. However, they may unintentionally create destructive pressures through other means. To illustrate how this can happen, you have to put yourself in the shoes ($110.00 top-of-the-line athletic shoes) of an 11-year-old participant in an organized sport program:

> As an 11-year-old you clearly remember that before you became a skater, a football player, a soccer player, etc., your parents were good to you and told you they loved you, but now things are somehow different. In the past, they always let you know how hard they worked for the $5 they gave you to go to a movie and that money did not grow on trees. But now that you are an athlete, they do not hesitate to spend from $150 to $400+ per season to outfit you in the best sport gear and to pay entry fees and instructional fees. After years of hearing how busy your parents were and how they needed a vacation, they are now giving up weekends to drive you to games, meets, and practices. They even changed the family vacation schedule to accommodate your playoff games. And they fix special dinners five nights a week so you can get to practice on time. They try to come home from work a little early to catch the last part of your practice or get to your game on time. They

make it a point to ask how things are going at practice and they give pep talks on the merits of sport involvement. At the same time they did not make a special effort to attend the quarterly PTA meeting at which your latest art project was displayed and they complained about how it was impossible for them to leave work to get to a parent-teacher conference at which your academic progress was to be discussed. Of course, they continue to tell you that your education is important, but their behavior indicates that what happens at school is not nearly as crucial as what happens in the game next Saturday morning.

Under these conditions, most 11-year-olds conclude that their involvement in sports is much more important than their parents say it is. If parents are not careful about the content of these unspoken messages, they can lead their children to think that being an athlete is a prerequisite for continued parental interest and concern. And such a thought is potentially upsetting for most 11-year-olds.

In summary, we need to know more about how the participation of children in organized sport programs affects family relationships. There are cases in which participation has brought families together, and there are cases in which participation has caused problems. Research is needed to discover when and why each of these things happen. But researchers must also be open to discovering that participation makes no systematic impact on family relationships. It may be that sport programs simply provide families with an additional setting to play out their relationships in ways that would have occurred in other settings.

Does Participation in Adult-Controlled, Organized Programs Have an Effect on the Abilities of Children to Create and Maintain Informal Games?

In a study of childhood activity patterns, two social psychologists have noted that the television viewing time of middle-class North American children increases "in direct proportion to the efforts adults make to involve them in organized activities" (Sherif and Rattray, 1976). The inference underlying this observation is that adults may be wasting their time and money organizing sport programs for children because the programs interfere with learning how to actively organize informal games and activities.

This case has been made by others as well. Devereux (1976) suggests that organized programs create a negative condition he calls "little leaguism." This condition robs children of valuable learning experiences because it undermines informal games and the abilities to play those games. Historical surveys of informal games have led researchers in both the United States and Great Britain to similar conclusions (Goodman, 1979; Opie and Opie, 1969). In fact, two British researchers have issued the following warning about organized games to their colleagues in physical education and recreation:

> In the long run, nothing extinguishes self-organized play more effectively than does action to promote it. It is not only natural but beneficial that there should be a gulf between the generations in their choice of recreation. . . . If children's games are tamed and made part of school curricula, if wastelands are turned into playing-fields for the benefit of those who conform and ape their elders, if children are given the idea that they cannot enjoy themselves without being provided with the "proper" equipment, we need blame only ourselves when we produce a generation who have lost their dignity, who are ever dissatisfied, and who descend for their sport to the easy excitement of rioting, or pilfering, or vandalism (Opie and Opie, 1969).

I think of this warning whenever I hear young people complain that they have "nothing to do." Could it be that the well-meaning attempts to give children ready-made activities to fill their leisure time have backfired? Are the children who live in leisure-rich industrial countries growing up without learning how to organize their own games? Can't these children play games in which they don't have the assistance of referees, uniforms, coaches, and time clocks?

Research does show that participation in informal games is less characteristic among middle- and upper-income children than it is among children from lower socioeconomic backgrounds (Medrich et al., 1982). And organized sport programs are much more common in middle- and upper-income neighborhoods than in low-income neighborhoods.

However, research by sports psychologists Doug Kleiber and Glyn Roberts (1983) suggests that the existence of organized sport programs is not always associated with low rates of participation in informal games. Interviews with 160 9- to 11-year-old boys and girls from middle-class neighborhoods in a midwestern city led them to conclude that informal games are not disappearing and that children who have participated the longest in organized sport programs have the highest rates of participation in informal games. Data collected from low-income children in Oakland, California, have led other researchers to similar conclusions (Medrich et al., 1982).

One explanation for these findings is that participation in both informal games and organized sports is related to the same factors; another explanation is that participation in organized programs could actually provide some children with incentives and models for their own informal games (Lever, 1976, 1978; Wohl, 1970, 1979). In fact, Coakley and Westkott (1984) have argued that organized programs are especially important for girls because they provide a working knowledge of game models that can be carried over into play groups, and organized programs encourage girls to include active and competitive games in their lives.

In my own work on this topic I have observed that some children can use their experiences in organized sport programs as starting points for getting together with friends and making up their own games. But other children who have had the same experiences do not seem to have the faintest idea about how to create games on their own. For them, the experiences in organized sports seem to have led them to define informal games as second-rate because they are different from "real" games. Without uniforms, referees, coaches, nine players on each team, and a nicely lined field they can't play baseball.

In summary, the idea that organized sports undermine the informal games of children needs to be explored further. Current research findings are confusing. Until future studies help us understand the relationship between organized programs and informal games, adults need to realize that each offers different experiences and that children benefit from the combination of those experiences.

Does Participation in Organized Sport Programs Lead Children to Value Winning More Than Playing Fair or Having Fun?

Some research has led people to conclude that children who participate in organized sport programs develop a "professional attitude" about games (Blair, 1985; Kidd and Woodman, 1975; Mantel and Vander Velden, 1974; Webb, 1969). In other words, children in organized programs become more concerned about playing well and winning than they do about fairness and fun. But a closer examination of the studies reporting these findings shows that this conclusion requires qualification (Coakley, 1985a; Greer and Stewart, 1989; Knoppers, 1985; Knoppers et al., 1989).

First of all, organized sports probably attract children who enjoy the challenges of goal-oriented activities. Therefore these children would be expected to score higher than others on any scale that measured so-called professional attitudes—not because of their experiences in the organized programs but because of the orientations they brought to the programs. Secondly, organized sport programs are intentionally set up to emphasize winning and playing well. Children realize this. And when they become a part of organized programs they give a high priority to these things. After all, they don't have to worry about fairness because coaches and referees take care of rules and rule enforcement. And winning and playing well are

two of the criteria children use for defining fun (Scanlon and Passer, 1978, 1979a).

The important issue is whether this professional attitude carries over into informal games and interferes with the way these games are played. Carryover may occur (Podilchak, 1982), but there is nothing to indicate that children who participate in organized programs become so obsessed with winning and playing well that they cannot keep informal games going on their own.

In summary, when children participate in organized sport programs, they will define winning and playing well as important. This orientation may carry over into informal games, but there is no reason to believe that it upsets those games. It is likely that extreme concerns with winning and playing well are most often the result of situational pressures imposed by adults. Children demonstrating these attitudes are usually responding to these pressures rather than displaying deep-seated personality traits created by their experiences in organized sports.

Do Organized Sport Programs Create "Dropouts" from Healthy Forms of Lifetime Sport Involvement?

One of the criticisms of organized sport programs is that they expose children to an overly serious sport experience before they develop an awareness of all the good things sports and physical activities have to offer. The critics claim that when this happens, many children are intimidated and turned off to the point of dropping out of all sport activities at an early age. The extent to which this happens to the children in organized programs is not known. But according to those working in youth sports in North America, the question of why children drop out of organized programs has been identified as the most important research topic in their field (Gould, 1982).

Doing research on dropouts is tricky. It is easy to show that a certain percentage of children who play in a league at age 11 do not return to play again at age 12. But what does this mean? Have they dropped out of sports alto-

Street Ball
Where Foul Is Fair and Fair Is Foul
*by M. Bloom**

When the baseball season marks its slow pace through the summer, broadcasters will remind us about "key plays" that may ultimately be responsible for the fall playoff matchups. We will be nursed through the season with the well-placed hit, the improbable stolen base, the rarely applied ground rule, the miraculous stab at third base. To paraphrase my mother, "They don't know what good is."

You want exciting, first-class baseball? Go to almost any neighborhood in New York City and find a bunch of 14-year-old kids with torn jeans, worn Converse sneakers, and a few hours to kill. It's free, too.

The neighborhoods of New York are a potpourri of makeshift baseball. Without the sterile accoutrements of organized ball, their games depend less on rain or shine than on an abandoned car at second base or the erratic moods of local residents.

Whether it is hardball, softball, punchball, or stickball, the city kids have taken the basics of baseball and molded them like skilled craftsmen. From Tottenville to Riverdale, Flatbush to Forest Hills,

the local "pros" have produced their own brand of the national pastime.

Let us go to the streets of New York to the daily after-school stickball game, played on a typical tree-lined block in a residential neighborhood.

It is three against three. One kid plays first base, marked by a sewer. Another kid is at third, marked by a crack in the curb pavement. The other plays the outfield and also handles any action at second base, marked by the sweatshirt of the youngest kid in the game.

Because seven kids showed up—and the seventh one owns the bat—one kid is the "official" pitcher. His chore is to lob the ball in and "just let the guy hit it" so the game can unfold with all of its mighty prowess. He is neutral. He must field and make pickoff attempts equally. He also covers home plate when necessary. However, he is not allowed to bat.

Although first and third base are inside the curbs, that is, in the gutter, the foul lines extend to matchbox lawns that continue to the end of the block. The pitcher, a left-hander, is using a right-hander's glove. There are chips on the ball, a 50-cent Spaldeen.

They will play five innings, or until the men

REFLECT ON SPORT

come home from work and park their cars on the court. Whoever is ahead at that time wins. Each side gets two outs, not three. There are no balls and strikes. Each batter gets two swings.

You think you know baseball? O.K., you're the umpire. How do you rule on these plays:

1. The batter stubbornly refuses to swing. He says he does not like the pitches. He is waiting him out.
2. A ball is hit into the trees in fair territory—but falls to the ground in foul territory.
3. A ball is hit way over the outfielder's head and rolls into the congested traffic of the intersecting street. While the fielder waits for the traffic to abate so he can retrieve the ball, the batter runs all the way home.
4. A line drive hits a bird in flight over second base. The bird is dead. Is the ball dead?
5. A nibbler is hit past third and rolls smack into the spot just vacated by a St. Bernard. The outfielder, who has charged the ball, will not pick it up. The batter scores, laughing all the way.
6. A batter singles and stands on first base, knowing he cannot move until the ball is hit. His mother calls him from across the street. He does not call time and steps off first. He is picked off.
7. A batter misses the ball by a mile on both swings. In a rage, he slams the bat to the ground. The bat cracks. What happens?
8. There is a play at the plate. The ball and runner reach home simultaneously. The runner cannot step on the plate, marked by the side of a cardboard box, which has blown away.
9. Runners are on first and second. The batter hits a single. The bases are loaded. But the runner at second base is scheduled to be the next batter.
10. (*Extra Credit*) It is raining lightly. The score is 2-2, last of the fifth. A runner is on first, and there is one out. The batter gets a base hit. The run scores. The onlooking neighbors say the runner never touched third base. The runner tells the neighbors what they can do with third base. The neighbors kick the kids off the court.

NOTE: Bloom raises these ten intriguing questions for a reason. He is very aware that when young people must confront and solve the problems characteristic of competitive play situations, they gain valuable learning experiences. However, when the young people participate in activities organized and structured for them, they miss many of those experiences. This means that in addition to sponsoring and administering organized youth programs, adults should encourage and promote involvement in informal games. Girls often need extra encouragement, too, because they do not receive as much indirect support as boys receive through the media and general social feedback.

gether, or have they switched their participation to a different program or to a different sport? And did they leave a particular program because of the way the program was organized or because of factors unrelated to their experiences in organized sports?

Research shows that there is usually a combination of factors that influence a child's decision not to return to a particular sport program.* Young people usually say they drop out because they have other things to do, but this does not explain why these other things have become more important in their lives than continuing their participation in a particular program. It is known that dropping out of sport does not occur in a social vacuum. Peers, family members, boyfriends or girlfriends, and teammates may all exert influence on the way young people set their priorities and choose their activities (Coakley and White, 1992). Personal growth requires that people, young and old, occasionally revise their activity patterns so they can experience new things and form new relationships (Patriksson, 1987).

This means that dropping out of a particular sport program should not always be defined as a problem (McPherson, 1984). Most so-called dropouts continue participating in other sport programs. They simply switch from one type of program to another in the same sport, or they switch to another sport. Others may temporarily discontinue their participation in organized sports because they have become involved in other satisfying leisure activities. In each of these cases, the choices made by young people indicate normal changes in priorities rather than a dropout problem; these children are "switchers," not quitters.

Real dropouts do exist, however, and sometimes children revise their participation priorities because of negative experiences caused by

---

*Brown, 1985; Gould, 1982, 1987; Gould et al., 1982; McGuire and Cook, 1983; Passer, 1982; Roberts, 1983; Roberts et al., 1981; Robinson and Carron, 1982; Watson and Collis, 1982; Coakley and White, 1992.

things associated with particular organized programs. It is in reference to these cases that we can talk about a dropout *problem*. The adults connected with organized programs realize that particular programs do not appeal to all children. But most of those adults do not want their programs to scare children away or serve as the scenes for negative experiences. Studies of dropouts indicate that negative experiences are often associated with programs in which competitive abilities and competitive outcomes are emphasized at the expense of concerns with the mastery of sport skills and the improvement of individual performances. This idea has been explored in detail by Glyn Roberts (1983). He explains that children are concerned with demonstrating their own abilities while at the same time contributing to the success of the group in which they are playing. When they feel that they do not have the skills to meet the demands of the situation, they drop out. On the other hand, when they feel they *can* demonstrate their abilities and contribute to the success of the activity and the group, they are likely to stay involved.

BURNOUT: A SPECIAL CASE OF DROPOUT Related to questions about dropouts are questions about *burnout*. The term *burnout* is often used by people in sport to refer to someone who drops out of a particular sport after being an age-group champion or after demonstrating considerable promise for future success. This phenomenon is getting to be a serious problem in many high performance sport programs, and when burnout occurs it is often upsetting to the parents and coaches who have "invested" considerable time, energy, and money in the training of the young athlete. This investment can involve years of work for coaches and, among other things, thousands of dollars for parents.

What happens to young skiers (ages 13 to 17), for example, who drop out when they are close to becoming world-class competitors? Why would they quit when they are on the verge of reaching their potential? Why quit when they are about ready to reap the rewards of their hard

Children are concerned with learning and demonstrating abilities in situations in which they are accepted by their peers and other important people in their lives. When sport programs help build competence and acceptance and provide participants with opportunities to be spontaneous and expressive, they are generally worth the effort needed to organize them. (Chuck Miller)

work and intense training? According to the athletes I've talked to informally, the reasons are boredom, fatigue, nagging injuries, a loss of motivation, and a growing desire to find other activities and new challenges. According to coaches and parents, the reasons young people quit sports are more likely to refer to some form of character weakness such as laziness, a lack of courage, a fear of hard work, or a distorted sense of priorities.

Actually, the explanation for burnout may be more complex than those given by athletes, coaches, or parents. It is possible that some successful teenage athletes have received so many external rewards for their performances since they were 7 or 8 years old that they are no longer interested in such feedback; they have become *satiated*. But in addition to satiation, there may be another explanation (Coakley, 1992). Be-

tween the ages of 14 and 17, identity questions become crucial and young people often become engrossed in searches for their own uniqueness. At this point in their lives, establishing personal autonomy is an important developmental task. And since autonomy is based on a combination of a *sense of competence* (feelings of mastery) and *independence*, a young person may reject activities or social settings that provide few opportunities for making choices and exploring new dimensions of themselves.

If a young person's involvement in sport has been sustained through encouragement (and pressure) from others and characterized by a high degree of specialization, one of the most obvious ways to achieve autonomy is to make the decision to quit their sport and search for other activities. Many young athletes come to the conclusion that if their sport involvement is no longer under their own control, the only way they can gain control over their lives is to choose something different from sport. They realize that to stay in a sport at their level means that they make no choices; they simply follow the orders of their coaches and the advice of their parents—none of whom want them to be burdened with any choices, not even when or where they play next (Coakley, 1992; McDermott, 1982). Young children may not be negatively affected by such a situation. But once adolescence begins, many young people become much more sensitive to the often restrictive nature of high performance sport competition. This sets the stage for potential burnout among young people.

In summary, dropping out of sport usually involves a complex process influenced by the social environment and the self-assessments of athletic skills by the young people involved. In many cases, dropping out of a particular organized sport program should be considered part of normal childhood development. Children choose to change their involvement patterns as they become aware of new alternatives and as they change their views of themselves. Dropping out only becomes a real problem when it occurs because of negative experiences in an organized program and when it leads to a general withdrawal from sport and other physical activities for an extended period of time. This is most likely to happen when programs ignore issues related to individual development among young people. In a similar manner, burnout occurs when young people become more concerned with personal autonomy than with their continued success in programs that allow them few opportunities to make choices and little time to explore new dimensions of themselves.

Do Girls and Boys Have the Same Kinds of Experiences in Organized Sport Programs?

Research indicates that girls and boys often have different types of experiences when it comes to early involvement in physical activities (White et al., 1992). Parents, especially fathers, play with their sons differently and more often than they play with their daughters. In general, the physical activity messages received by young boys often differ from the messages received by girls, both inside and outside family settings. One of the results of this difference is that before most children take their first physical education class or play in their first organized sport program they have clear ideas about their physical skills and potential. And boys are likely to see themselves as being more physically skilled than girls see themselves, even though gender differences in actual skill levels are small or nonexistent (see JOPHERD, October, 1990, p. 9). Boys are more likely than girls to think they are better than they actually are when it comes to their sport-related skills. This has an effect on their self-confidence and their willingness to use and test their bodies in active ways and voluntarily participate in physical activities.

Gender-related patterns of differences in physical self-concepts are grounded in the fact that many people expect different levels of sport-related skills from girls than they do from boys. And when these patterns are exhibited in the actual behavior of girls and boys, they encourage people to continue various forms of differential treatment. This may be one of the reasons why some physical education teachers have relatively low expectations for girls' performances in sports, and why they have relatively high expectations for boys. These expectations, combined with other factors, may account for the fact that boys' ball games often dominate the space on elementary school playgrounds "while girls play less vigorous games in smaller groups" (White et al., 1992). Of course, there are some teachers who actively discourage such gender-based patterns.

At this point there are no studies that compare the structures of boys' and girls' sport programs. However, it is likely that many parents and coaches have orientations and expectations that are different for boys than for girls who play in these programs. In explaining these differences, it is difficult to tell when they are based on (a) realistic assessments of the actual experiences girls bring to the programs, (b) well-intentioned but paternalistic concerns about protecting girls from "too much" stress and "too many" challenges, or (c) sexist beliefs about the supposed physical inferiority of girls.

Some people would argue that motives for differential treatment are irrelevant—that differential treatment is always wrong because it perpetuates inequalities and subverts the potential of girls and women. However, this argument is often based on the assumption that the way things are done for boys is always the right way—and this is a debatable assumption. Undoubtedly, if girls are provided with fewer opportunities and fewer challenges to become physically competent through sport, they are being short-changed. And if girls are "protected" in ways that keep them from developing a sense of physical self-empowerment, they are being cheated. But on the other hand, if adults are more sensitive to the feelings and physical well-being of girls than of boys, then boys are being short-changed. Similarly, if adults take more care to provide a wider range of sport participation alternatives for girls than they do for boys, then boys are being cheated.

When it comes to the actual experiences of boys and girls in organized sport programs, research suggests that there are important differences. For example, when Gary Alan Fine (1987) did his creative study of 10- to 12-year-old middle-class white boys on 10 Little League teams in the eastern United States, he found that each team developed its own idioculture and that there were interesting similarities in the idiocultures for each of the teams. Fine defines an *idioculture* as the collection of orientations, norms, behaviors, and shared meanings created by the members of a group who share experiences over an extended period. He points out that over the course of a season, the members of any youth sport team are likely to develop their own team idioculture. This occurs because team members gradually create in-group jokes, make up special nicknames for one another, use special words and phrases in their interaction, encourage or tease each other in special ways, and develop their own unique way of responding to games and practices, winning and losing, and the decisions of coaches, umpires, referees, and so on.

On the basis of his observations and interviews, Fine reports that the boys on the teams he studied developed idiocultures that supported or encouraged the use of obscene language, involvement in pranks, risk-taking behaviors, displays of aggression in personal behavior and relationships, telling obscene and racist jokes, dealing with girls as sex objects, and describing blacks and Hispanics in racist terms. Overall, the teams provided social settings in which boys tried to present themselves as "men" in terms of how they defined "manly" in their preadolescent social worlds. Their definitions of manly were based on macho models and a general caricature of traditional masculinity. And their desire to be "manly" led them to carefully separate themselves from anyone who was female or younger and weaker than they were. However, their connections with other males were often regulated and limited by their prejudices and by the status hierarchy they used to compare themselves with peers. Other research has also found that boys in sports often regulate and limit their connections with one another because of the homophobic fear of being labeled a "fag" or "gay" (Messner, 1992).

At this point, nobody has done a study of girls' teams to see what their idiocultures are like. However, according to the women in my classes who have read Fine's book (*With the Boys*), the content of idiocultures on girls' teams is probably very different from the content of idiocultures on boys' teams. Obscene language and jokes are not so important, nor are pulling pranks, taking risks, and being aggressive. The girls are not so likely to use racist slurs, nor do they deal with boys as sex objects. What the girls incorporate into their idiocultures is open to debate, but according to Sheila Scraton (1987), a teacher in England who has studied the subcultures of young people, girls' groups develop different patterns of norms, orientations, behaviors, and shared meanings because girls' lives are restricted more than boys' lives. Girls' lives are more closely watched by parents, teachers, coaches, and other adults. Adults often use a "boys will be boys" attitude when they interpret and respond to boys' behaviors, but they are much more critical when they interpret girls' behavior, especially when the behaviors push limits of social or moral acceptance.

In summary, research on the actual everyday experiences of boys and girls in youth sport programs is scarce. We need to know more about how sport experiences are integrated into the lives of young people, and how the meanings associated with those experiences overlap or vary for girls and boys. At this point it is clear that youth sport experiences help perpetuate popular ideas about gender, and that success in sports is much more important for the popularity of boys than it is for girls (Adler, Kless, and Adler, 1992; Chase and Drummer, 1992).

RECOMMENDATIONS FOR CHANGING ORGANIZED SPORT PROGRAMS FOR CHILDREN

There is a wide variety of organized sport programs for children. This is especially true in the United States where there is no centralized state authority through which programs are funded, controlled, and administered. Programs vary from one sport to another, from community to community, and from league to league. However, conditions could be improved in most programs. Efforts are needed to maximize posi-

tive experiences and minimize negative experiences for participants. This is true in other countries as well as the United States.

In making recommendations for changes, most people agree that organized programs should be set up to meet the needs of the children who participate in them. This means that children themselves are a valuable source of information about how programs should be restructured. Since children have fun by emphasizing action, involvement, close scores, and friendships in the games they create for themselves, it makes sense that organized programs should be restructured to emphasize these things. If this were done, children would have more fun and the programs would do a better job of meeting their interests. The following discussion gives examples of how the informal games of children can be used as sources of information for recommending changes in organized sport programs.

Increasing Action

In their own games, children create, modify, and eliminate rules to increase action. Much activity occurs around the "scoring area," and scoring is usually so frequent that it is difficult to keep track of any personal performance statistics. However, organized sports are not often the scenes of such free-flowing action. Games in organized, competitive programs are divided into periods and stopped for time-outs and strategy sessions. Numerous delays are brought about by the action-killing whistles of the referees. Game rules are designed to promote order, standardized conditions, and predictability rather than action. And the strategy of many organized teams is to *prevent* action rather than stimulate it. Parents and coaches sometimes even describe high-scoring games as undisciplined "free-for-alls" caused by poor defensive play. The desired defensive strategy in the minds of many adults is to avert action; to strike out the batter, to stop the runner at the line, to stall the game when you are in the lead. The desired offensive strategy often aims to control and limit action: a sacrifice bunt, a safe running play for a 3-yard gain, and waiting for just the right shot.

These may be good tactics for getting into the play-offs, but they limit the most exciting aspects of any game: action and scoring. But coaches still dream of the game when their team shuts out the opposition. And they try to convince their players that being able to limit and contain action is really more exciting than being involved in it. The players learn that if the ball is never hit, they will never make an error; and if the other team never gets the ball, their team will never lose.

RECOMMENDATIONS* Increasing action and scoring opportunities is easy in any organized program, as long as adults do not view game models as sacred and unchangeable. Bigger goals, smaller playing areas, and fewer rules are the best means to increase action. Why not double the width of soccer and hockey goals? Why not shorten the field and make all players eligible to receive a pass in football? Why not give a batter four strikes and a team five outs per inning in baseball? Why not limit the speed of pitching in baseball or use softer balls in soccer and football? Why not use a larger, lightweight puck in hockey or a fatter bat in softball, or a 6-foot basket in a half-court basketball game?

It is unfortunate that many adults hesitate to make changes in the way youth sports are organized and played. Adults will often make changes in the interests of safety, but they are not so quick to make changes that would promote the things children see as fun. This ultimately leads organized games to be less exciting and interesting than they could be—at least for the children playing them.

Increasing Personal Involvement

There is no sitting on the bench in informal games. Smaller or less-skilled players may not

contribute to the action as much as others, but they play the whole game. If they are treated badly and do not receive the opportunities they expect, they do not show up the next day. And when they stay home, they are not branded as quitters by their parents or given long lectures on responsibility and commitment.

Rule qualifications and handicap systems are often developed to maximize the involvement of all participants and to sustain action in informal games. "Do-overs," "interference" calls, and other special rules are used by the less skilled to compensate for a lack of ability and to stay involved at a personally satisfying level. The better players may have to bat opposite-handed, shoot from outside the free throw line, play goalie, or be tagged instead of tackled in the games.

In organized games, the range and extent of personal involvement is often seriously limited for all but the most skilled players. Specialization by position restricts the range of involvement. For example, when 10-year-olds describe themselves as left defensive tackles or center fielders or left wingers or center halfbacks, it is a sure sign that the range of personal involvement has been unnecessarily limited in their sport experiences. It is sad when a 12-year-old has played 3 years of organized football and never touched the ball or never played on the defensive line. It is sad when a Bobby Sox softball player goes an entire season without ever starting a game or playing a position other than right field.

In organized games, sitting on the bench is an all-too-frequent experience—especially for those who need playing time most. Even when everyone is required to play, the substitution process is a constant source of problems for the coach and a source of pressure for the players.

RECOMMENDATIONS Personal involvement in organized sport programs can be extended in a number of ways. For example, players could be rotated from position to position or limited to a single position for no longer than a quarter of the game. The top players from each

---

*A number of these recommendations have been made by Orlick and Botterill (1975).

team could be taken out of the game at the same time, or playing time for starters could be restricted to the first and third quarters.*

It is also possible to alter the number of players on the field. Players could be added to the game, or, if necessary, roster size could be cut with fewer players in the game at any one time. Why should a game ever be forfeited because one team is a player or two short? The other team could simply play with fewer players or players could be loaned to the team needing them.

Batting lineups for baseball and softball should include all team members regardless of who is playing the 9 or 10 positions in the field. In ice hockey, the games could be played across the width of the rink allowing three times as many teams to compete at the same time. Portable dividers and lightweight goals could be used and "lifting" the puck could be made illegal. In basketball, the first-string teams could play a half-court game at one basket while the second-string teams play one another at the other basket. A combined score could be used to determine the winner. These are just some of the many changes that could be made to open up possibilities for involvement.

Creating Close Scores

The term "good game" is generally used when the outcome of a contest is in doubt until the last play; double overtime games are the best. Lopsided scores make games uninteresting unless there are other reasons for the involvement.† Children realize this and set up their games accordingly. Children like competition or, more precisely, they like the *uncertainty* associated with a close contest. Winning is important in informal games, but more important is keeping the game close and the players happy. Since motivation partially depends on how peo-

ple perceive chances for success, a close game usually keeps players motivated and satisfied.

In informal games, teams are modified and rules are developed to generate the uncertainty necessary to make the game interesting for everyone involved. If this does not occur, the game ceases to exist; most children learn this early in their game-playing experiences. When they become adults, they will do like most of us do and seek out sports with ability ratings or handicap systems so they can preserve uncertainty and keep involvement interesting. Children are like adults in that they will avoid sport activities in which their perceived chances for success are low.

In organized games, uncertainty occurs only when teams are evenly matched. An analysis of game scores and team records in most organized leagues over an entire season will show that lopsided scores are common and team records are quite uneven. Keeping players motivated under these circumstances has always been difficult. The coaches of losing teams talk about "pride" to keep their players motivated, and coaches of winning teams use scoring as a measure of hustle and a method of intimidating future opponents. In organized sport programs, coaches and parents often urge their teams and players to take an early lead during games. They forget that an early lead destroys uncertainty and motivation unless, of course, the players can be taught that winning is more desirable than the fun of a challenging contest.

RECOMMENDATIONS People connected with organized programs are usually hesitant to make any changes affecting the outcomes of games. However, if game scores were not published, and if league standings and play-offs were abolished, they might be willing to discuss some of the possibilities. For example, close scores could be encouraged by altering team rosters or by using handicap systems during a game. The underdog could be given an advantage such as using extra players or being given five downs or five outs or a bigger goal. The team in the lead could be required to move the

---

*Eitzen (1979) made a similar suggestion for high school teams.

†Close scores may be sacrificed when close friends want to be on the same team; playing with friends is sometimes more important than having evenly balanced teams.

player scoring its last goal to a less strategic position. In baseball and softball, the team in the lead could be required to switch pitchers every inning. Numerous other possibilities can be developed as long as the game model is not viewed as sacred by the adults who organize and control the programs.

Maintaining Relationships

The reaffirmation of friendships is important in informal games. It influences how teams are chosen, as well as the dynamics of problem-solving processes during games. Organized sport programs sometimes provide a useful context for the development and maintenance of relationships between players, but more could be done to facilitate and improve relationships and to give players opportunities to handle relationships with one another in a wider variety of situations.

RECOMMENDATIONS Groups of players in organized sport programs could be encouraged to plan game strategies or coach practice sessions. Some players could be given the responsibility of teaching skills to low-ability teammates. Players could be encouraged to talk with opponents, help them when they are knocked down, and congratulate them when they do something commendable. Too often, relationships between opposing players are cold and impersonal. Players should be given the opportunity to learn that even formal competition can occur between friends, and that games have a human component that can be recognized during play.

Most importantly, players should be expected to enforce most of the rules themselves during games. Through self-enforcement they would learn why rules are necessary and how any collective action depends on taking other people and the expectations of others into consideration. Self-enforcement of rules would also help to control the largest financial expense and administrative headache in most organized programs—the hiring and training of officials. Many people argue that self-enforcement would

never work, but if organized programs do not teach young people how to control themselves so that playing a game without referees is possible, then those programs are not worth our time and effort. Too many coaches and players blame officials for anything that goes wrong during a game. They see rules (norms) as coercive restrictions rather than necessary guidelines. And remember, many youth and high school tennis competitions involve self-enforcement.

PROSPECTS FOR CHANGE

Some important changes have been made in many organized youth sport programs over the past decade. Most often these changes reflect recommendations based on a functionalist approach to sport (see Chapter 2). In other words, they have involved efforts to increase efficiency and organization in youth sports. This means there are now more training programs for coaches, more formal rules regulating the behavior of parents and spectators, more rules for what is expected from players and from coaches, more promotional brochures and advertising in the local media, more of an emphasis on performance and skills development, and more contacts with other organized programs in the same sport so there can be state and regional play-offs.

This increase in organization is more common in private programs than in public, tax-supported programs. Tax cuts and funding cutbacks in some communities have led park and recreation departments to limit or drop their support of organized sport leagues for young people. In response to this turn of events, concerned parents have often organized private leagues for their children. These private leagues offer many of the same kinds of sport participation opportunities that have existed in public programs. However, they are expensive, and they tend to attract children from middle- and upper-middle-income families. Even when there is a willingness to waive fees for young people from low income families, few of these young people participate. In some cases, this also means that most of these private programs exclude young people from minority families and neighborhoods.

The emphasis in these private leagues is on the development of skills in a specific sport. Leagues for younger children feed into leagues for older children and then into high school programs. Parents sometimes define fees and equipment expenses (which are often quite high) as investments in their children's future. They are concerned with development, and as their children get older, they use the private programs as sources of information about college sport programs, about scholarship opportunities, and about how to contact coaches and athletic departments in ways that will benefit their sons and daughters. They approach their children's involvement in a rational manner, and they see clear connections between childhood sport participation and future development, educational opportunities, and adult life.

The people who take the time, money, and trouble to organize these private programs are likely to recognize the importance of qualified coaches for their children. Coaches can have a major impact on the way young people develop skills and define their experiences in sport (Fine, 1987). Therefore the adults connected with these programs stress coaching education and coaching certification programs along with coaches' responsibilities. The people who coach in these programs are concerned with the welfare of young athletes, but they are unlikely to follow many of the recommendations made in this chapter. Some of the recommendations may be considered at the league level, but leagues are not likely to make changes in official game models. Such changes would threaten their relationships with the influential state and national organizations that many of the players' parents have paid to join.

One factor that could produce significant changes in many of these private youth programs is *burnout*. Burnout is a dreaded phenomenon among parents who have given long-term support to the participation of one or more of their children. They do not want their children to drop out or burn out after years of successful

participation. If burnout becomes common, or if more than a few parents expect it to be a problem, program organizers and coaches may be willing to consider structural changes that would alter the experiences their young people have in sport.

In the absence of any studies of this shift to privately organized youth sport programs, my observations take the form of hunches rather than conclusions. It is difficult to make generalizations about things that will happen as we move through the 1990s, but my hunches are these:

1. Public programs, such as those sponsored by local park and recreation departments, will decrease.
2. Private programs will increase.
3. Local opportunities for participation will decrease for children from low-income and minority families.
4. Private programs will be designed primarily to enhance sport skills among children.
5. Changes in these programs will emphasize more and more organization, unless parents collectively perceive burnout as a probable outcome for their children.

I hope there will be many exceptions to these hunches. Organization and efficiency are not always the means for improving the experiences of children in youth sport programs.

Coaching Education As a Means of Producing Changes

Coaching education programs will continue to grow in popularity during the 1990s. Most of the existing programs in North America and England are designed to give coaches the information and training they need to (1) deal with young people responsively and safely and (2) enhance the performance of young people as athletes. Most coaching education materials emphasize applications of sport science knowledge so coaches can be safer and more effective in the way they organize their practices, control their athletes, and teach the skills needed for athletes and teams to be successful.

As publicly funded youth sports are cut back or eliminated, an increasing number of youth sports will be offered through private clubs that have membership fees beyond the means of many families. For example, gymnastics has traditionally been offered through private clubs. (Colorado Springs Gazette Telegraph and Travis Spradling)

Although most coaching education programs emphasize putting the needs of athletes ahead of winning, none of the programs I have seen provide coaches with information on how to critically assess the sport programs in which they work with young people. None has information on how to make structural changes in the programs themselves and none has information on creating alternatives to existing programs. Coaching education materials are generally based on the assumption that existing sport programs are pretty good, but they could be better if coaches only knew more about applied sport science. In some cases these materials focus more on enhancing performance and controlling the behavior of young people as athletes than they do on understanding young people as human beings who are involved in competitive sports as a part of their overall lives.

Although I am a strong proponent of coaching education, I worry that some coaching education programs will ultimately foster what might be called a "technoscience approach" to youth sports. Such an approach would emphasize the control of young people rather than an overall understanding of young people as human beings. If this happens coaches will become "sports efficiency experts" rather than teachers who provide young people opportunities to become autonomous and responsible decision-makers able to control their own lives. At this point, most coaching education programs have contributed to the overall improvement of responsible coaching in youth sport programs. But as we assess coaching education programs and take a good critical look at their place at all levels of sport it would be good to remember that the former East Germany had one of the most efficient and highly respected coaching education programs in the world—before everyone realized that their extreme "technoscience approach" to coaching did not always contribute to the overall development of young people as human beings. The East German experience reminds us that without critical self-reflection, the application of sport science knowledge to coaching will not necessarily make sports or the world any better. But with critical self-reflection, coaching education could lead to many positive changes in sports programs for people of all ages.

CONCLUSION:

ARE ORGANIZED YOUTH SPORT PROGRAMS WORTH THE EFFORT?

According to the official policy handbooks of organized youth leagues, all participants should come out of organized programs as models of virtue and good character. However, this does not happen. The consequences of participation are mixed—some positive, some negative. This is because every sport participation environment is different in terms of the experiences offered to young people (McCormack and Chalip, 1988).

Organized programs obviously serve a vast number of young people, especially those coming from all but the lowest socioeconomic groups in industrialized countries. For some of those young people, the programs provide opportunities to develop physical skills, self-confidence, and status among peers. And in areas where play groups are scarce for one reason or another, they assist children in making friends and getting together in group activities. On the other hand, there are problems associated with organized sport programs. Some parents use bribes and pressure to push their children to achieve; some coaches interfere with the development of young people by being authoritarian and abusive; for some players sport becomes a crutch that prevents them from devel-

oping other dimensions of themselves; for others sport is boring and tedious. And there are also cases of parents arguing with coaches; referees being attacked by parents, coaches, or spectators; children being injured by the violent tactics of opponents; and adults being more concerned with game scores than the interests of children.

However, changes are possible. Of course, no program can guarantee that it will make children into models of virtue, but programs can be changed to cut down the number of problems. What this means is that organized sport programs for children are worth the effort when the adults controlling them put the interests of children ahead of the organizational needs of the programs, and ahead of their own needs to experience success as defined in adult sport programs.

SUGGESTED READINGS

Albinson, J.G., and G.M. Andrews, eds. 1976. Child in sport and physical activity. University Park Press, Baltimore (*12 papers on various dimensions of youth sports*).

Coakley, J. 1992. Burnout among adolescent athletes: a personal failure or social problem? Sociology of Sport Journal 9(3): 271-285 (*reports findings from in-depth interviews of 15 adolescents identified as "sport burnouts"; presents a model of burnout that is an alternative to psychological, stress-based models*).

DeKoven, B. 1978. The well-played game. Anchor Books, Garden City, N.Y. (*past director of the New Games Foundation gives a philosophy for game involvement for people of all ages*).

Fine, G.A. 1987. With the boys: Little League baseball and preadolescent culture. University of Chicago Press, Chicago (*in-depth study of 10 teams showing how boys create their own ways of experiencing organized sport*).

Gould, D., and M. Weiss, eds. 1987. Advances in pediatric sport sciences: behavioral issues. Human Kinetics Publishers, Inc., Champaign, Ill. (*12 articles on practical issues related to children's involvement in youth sports*).

Martens, R., ed. 1978. Joy and sadness in children's sports. Human Kinetics Publishers, Inc., Champaign, Ill. (*38 articles from popular and journal sources;*

articles accompanied by practical applications drawn by the editor).

McCormack, J.B., and L. Chalip. 1988. Sport as socialization: a critique of methodological premises. The Social Science Journal 25(1):83-92 (*excellent discussion showing why research results on socialization through sport have been inconsistent*).

Morris, G.S.D. 1980. How to change the games children play. 2nd ed. Burgess Publishing Co., Minneapolis (*describes a model that can be used to analyze, change, and create games for children; contains useful guidelines for teachers, parents, and some youth league coaches*).

Orlick, T., and C. Botterill. 1975. Every kid can win. Nelson-Hall, Chicago (*written for adults who want to change the structure of organized games played by children; contains many practical suggestions*).

Ralbovsky, M. 1974. Destiny's darlings, Hawthorn Books, Inc., New York (*a journalist looks at what happened to the nine starters and the coach on the 1954 Little League World Series team during the 20 years after their victory*).

Smoll, F.L., R. A. Magill, and M. Ash, eds. 1988. Children in sport. 3rd ed. Human Kinetics Publishers, Inc., Champaign, Ill. (*22 papers by leading researchers; good papers on the history and development of youth sports in North America and good papers on psychological issues and social processes related to youth sports*).

Tutko, T., and W. Bruns. 1976. Winning is everything and other American myths. Macmillan, Inc., New York (*a practical and easy-to-read critique of sport programs in the United States; special emphasis is given to problems in youth sports*).

Weiss, M.R., and D. Gould, eds. 1986. Sport for children and youths. Human Kinetics Publishers, Inc., Champaign, Ill. (*37 papers from the Olympic Scientific Congress sessions on youth sports; six papers on youth sport in different countries*).

Yablonsky, L., and J. Brower. 1979. The Little League game. Times Books, New York (*a journalistic summary of a season-long study of a Little League program in California*).

(Colorado Springs Gazette Telegraph)

DEVIANCE IN SPORTS

*Is it getting out of control?**

Simply, I had grown tired of losing. I didn't cheat because the Joneses did or because it made me a big man, I did it because I didn't want to get beat anymore. That's all.

Tates Locke, College Basketball Coach (1985)

[As] high school athletes . . . we were told to give up sex, partying and alcohol. I often felt I was playing for the coach and not for myself. I found myself trying to get away with as much as I could. . . . Stay up as late as you could. Drink and use drugs if you could get away with it. I got away with it.

Tony Elliott, NFL Player (1986)

When I got hurt it was simply my option to get shot up and play. . . . coaches left it up to me. I learned after playing 14 years you play with pain. There was nothing secretive about getting the shots. My dad knew, and he didn't object.

Football player, Colorado State University (1992)

Athletes don't use drugs to escape reality—they use them to enforce the reality that surrounds them.

Mauro G. Di Pasquale, M.D., Editor, *Drugs in Sports, vol. 1, no. 1, p. 2* (1992)

*This chapter is co-authored with Robert Hughes.

Cases of on-the-field and off-the-field deviance among athletes, coaches, agents, and others connected with sports have attracted much attention since the late 1970s. Seldom was anything said about deviance in sports before the middle 1970s. Media coverage of what seems to be an unending list of rule violations in sports has led some people to conclude that deviance in sport is getting out of control.

Because popular beliefs have always emphasized positive aspects of sport participation, widely publicized cases of deviance have shocked and disappointed many people. In their disappointment, some of them have concluded that deviance among athletes and others involved in sports simply proves that the moral basis of society is eroding. In light of this extreme conclusion, the purpose of this chapter is to look at the following issues:

1. What problems are faced when we study deviance in sports?
2. What is deviance, and how can we identify deviant behavior in sports?
3. How often does deviance occur in sports, and is it a serious problem?
4. Why do athletes use performance-enhancing drugs, and is it possible to control the use of drugs in sports?

These questions direct attention to important questions about society and social behavior.

PROBLEMS FACED WHEN STUDYING DEVIANCE IN SPORTS

Studying deviance in sports presents special problems because athletes are allowed and even encouraged to behave in ways that are prohibited or defined as criminal in other settings. Much of the behavior of athletes in contact sports would be classified as felony assault if it occurred on the streets; boxers would be criminals. Race car drivers would be arrested for speeding and careless driving according to the definitions of deviance used off the track. Athletes in high-risk sports such as speed skiing and motocross racing are encouraged to engage in

dangerous behaviors that would be discouraged and defined as deviant in other settings. However, even when serious injuries or deaths occur in sports, criminal charges are not filed, and civil lawsuits are generally unsuccessful.

Even in noncontact sports the use of hate as a source of motivation contradicts norms used by most people to guide their behavior in families, religious congregations, classrooms, and work settings. The emphasis outside of sport is on getting along with and being supportive of others. Within many sports, the emphasis is often on being hostile toward and overcoming others. This emphasis is so widely encouraged that when athletes cause injuries to others, they are not sued for damages. The reason for this is that people believe that sport participation is entered with an assumption of risk and that the experience of risk is often central to involvement in sports.

Another thing making sports unique is that athletes, especially elite athletes, often devote so much time and energy to developing their physical skills that the development of other parts of their lives suffers. They practice, work out with weights, attend camps and clinics, play in year-round leagues, and do off-season training in the quest of skills having little or no practical utility or instrumental value outside of sport. Their training prevents these athletes from being involved in other things such as social activities and part-time jobs, things that many believe are necessary for full social development. This extreme form of commitment would be defined as deviant in the case of other activities, but in the case of sports it is usually praised and rewarded, even when it causes serious inconvenience and hardship for close friends and family members (Retton, 1992).

These examples show that when it comes to studying deviance, sports are "different." Extremely compulsive or self-destructive behavior, the use of drugs, ignoring the physical well-being of others to the point of causing injuries, and using the ends (winning) to justify the means (violating rules), are not so quickly condemned in sport as they are in other activities. The motives of people in sports, especially athletes, are often seen as positive because their behavior, even when it clearly oversteps accepted limits, is directed toward the achievement of success for their team, school, community, or country. Therefore it may be ignored or even praised rather than condemned.

Much of the deviance in sports does *not* involve a *rejection* of commonly accepted norms and expectations for behavior. Instead, it involves *overconformity*, or *overacceptance* of norms and expectations. For example, participation in sports is strongly encouraged among young people in North America; it is defined as right and good. Young men in certain sports such as football are encouraged to increase their weight and strength so they can continue to participate and make valued contributions to the reputations of their schools and communities. When young men go too far in their acceptance of these expectations for getting bigger and stronger, when they become so committed to continued participation in sport and the success of their teams that they use certain drugs, they become deviant. This type of deviance is dangerous, but it is grounded in a completely different set of social dynamics from the deviance of a young person who gives up all hope for the future, rejects commonly accepted rules and expectations, and uses heroin to deaden awareness of the world. This difference between what has been called **positive deviance** and **negative deviance** must be taken into account when studying behavior in sports.

This is not to say that positive deviance should be accepted or condoned; it should not. But it does present special problems in the analysis of deviant behavior. Unfortunately, many discussions of deviance in sports don't take these special problems into account. Analyses of deviance are often based on theories and conceptual frameworks focusing only on negative deviance. As we will argue in the next section, these analyses add little to our understanding of deviance in sports or to our understanding of sports as a part of culture.

DEFINING AND STUDYING DEVIANCE IN SPORTS: THREE APPROACHES

Most sociologists agree that deviance involves behavior that violates social norms or rules, but they don't agree on how to identify rules and violations of rules. Some sociologists search for an absolute set of rules or ideals and then use them to evaluate behaviors as either right or wrong. Others say that rules reflect the interests of whoever has the most power in a group and that deviance is any behavior labeled wrong or bad by those people; they say the determination of deviance is strictly relative and arbitrary. Because these approaches are widely used in sociology and the sociology of sport, each will be examined more closely. Then we will offer an alternative approach for defining and studying deviance. This alternative is based on the idea that deviance can involve overconformity as well as underconformity and that deviants are not always morally bankrupt failures or pitiful victims of the system.

The Absolutist Approach: "It's Either Right or Wrong"

When sociologists use certain theoretical frameworks they define deviance in terms of how actual behavior compares with a designated norm or ideal. The greater the difference between the actual behavior and the norm, the greater the deviance. The problem with this approach is that definitions of ideals in any social setting often reflect biases related to gender, social class, race, and other factors, or they are based on some arbitrary distinction between right and wrong. Because different people have different conceptions of ideals in sports, this approach creates considerable confusion. For example, if I say the ideal in sports is fair play and you say it is winning, then I see any violation of the rules as deviant, while you see some violations as "good fouls" that contribute to winning. If I see sports as a form of play in which intrinsic satisfaction is the primary reason for participation and you see sports as "war without weapons" fought for external rewards such

It is difficult to study the deviance in sport with commonly used theoretical frameworks. This is because athletes are often encouraged and rewarded for behaviors prohibited or defined as criminal in other settings. For example, this behavior would get you arrested or sued if it happened outside the boxing ring. (Colorado Springs Gazette Telegraph)

as trophies and cash prizes, then I see aggressive behavior as deviant, while you see it as a sign of courage and commitment. Because we don't see eye to eye on the ideals of sports, we don't identify deviance in the same way.

Despite the fact that the absolutist approach creates confusing analyses, most people use it in their discussions of deviance in sports. This means that when the behaviors of athletes, coaches, management, or spectators do not fit with what these people see as the ideals of sports, those behaviors are identified as deviant. In other words, "it's either right or wrong." And when it's wrong, the behavior and the person who engages in it are seen as problems.

This is the traditional structural-functionalist approach to deviance, and it has usually been ineffective in producing an understanding of deviant behavior or in formulating programs to control deviance. Part of the reason for this ineffectiveness is that this approach is based on the assumption that existing value systems and rules are absolutely right and should be accepted the way they are. This leads to a "law-and-order orientation" in which it is believed that the only way to establish social control is through four strategies: establishing more rules, making rules more strict and inflexible, developing a more comprehensive system of detecting and punishing rule violators, and making everyone more aware of the rules and what happens to those who don't follow them. This approach also leads to the idea that people violate rules only because they lack moral character, intelligence, or sanity, and that good, normal, healthy people wouldn't be so foolish as to violate rules. Therefore people who reject rules and don't live up to expectations are deviants, and all deviant behavior involves the rejection of rules and norms or a refusal to comply with them. However, this approach does little to help us understand much of the deviance in sport, and it provides a poor basis for developing programs to control deviance in sport. More will be said about this throughout the chapter.

The Relativist Approach: "It All Depends on Who Makes the Rules"

According to this approach, no behavior and no person is inherently deviant. Instead, deviance is defined through a labeling process in which some behaviors (or people) are identified as bad, undesirable, or unacceptable on the basis of rules made by people in positions of power. Those who use this approach assume that all people act in their own interests, and that people in power use their position and influence to make sure *their* definitions of good and bad become the *official* definitions of good and bad in the society as a whole. Of course, it is also assumed that those who lack power in society are at a real disadvantage because they don't have anything to say about the content or enforcement of rules. Therefore the behavior of people who lack power is labeled as deviant more often than is the case for people with power. To make matters worse, people who lack power don't have the resources to resist being labeled as deviant when their behavior does not conform to the standards of the rule makers.

This approach is usually used by conflict theorists when they study deviance in sports. They assume that rules in sports organizations reflect the interests of owners and sponsors and ignore the interests of athletes. Therefore deviance among athletes is seen as a result of rules that not only discriminate against them but also force them to deny their own interests and follow the expectations of those in power, even though their health and well-being may be harmed in the process. This approach views athletes as victims whose only hope is tied to either disagreeing with the rules or rebelling against them.

The relativists have a problem because their approach leads to the conclusion that all deviance in sports is simply the result of labeling processes influenced by who has power and who doesn't. This conclusion is difficult to defend when many forms of deviance that exist in big-time intercollegiate and professional sports are also found in less formal sport settings, where athletes themselves are often in positions of power and control. For example, to say that violent behavior in pro football is the result of norms and rules through which athletes are forced to sacrifice their bodies for coaches and team owners does not hold up when similar forms of violence exist in games between rugby clubs in which players themselves control much of what goes on. In other words, it is unlikely that all bad things in sports would disappear if athletes were in charge. This, however, does not mean that athletes should not have more control over the conditions of their sport participation; they should. But our point here is that since much of the deviance in sports involves overconformity and overacceptance of existing rules among athletes, it is unrealistic to expect that most athletes would have the critical insights needed to change how sports are played. Athletes certainly need to play a crucial role in making changes in sports, but the relativists are hoping for too much to think that all the reasons for deviance in sports would automatically disappear if athletes made all the rules.

The relativists also have a problem because they do not identify any behavior as objectively deviant. To them, nothing is bad or wrong in itself. But without an objective definition of deviance, behaviors such as the use of violence or taking performance-enhancing drugs are simply seen as outgrowths of alternative definitions of right and wrong accepted as normal among people in certain groups where violence and drug use are valued and seen as positive. When deviance is defined in this way, efforts to control or change deviant behaviors are often dismissed as biased or oppressive. Therefore the relativists emphasize two ways to control deviance in sport:

1. Change the distribution of power in sports so athletes are no longer victims of the labeling processes used by those who currently have power in sports.
2. Change the political and economic systems that create tendencies among athletes to engage in destructive and dehumanizing behaviors when they play sports.

The relativists argue that when social systems become more humane, so will the behaviors of those within the systems. This is why those who use this approach often talk about the need to change society as a whole to control deviance in sports. But they don't talk much about the everyday problems faced by people who manage sport organizations or facilities, or coach school teams, or have sons or daughters who must make decisions about what they should do to gain skills and make their teams in high school. For this reason, many people disagree with the approach of the relativists.

An Alternative Approach: "Deviance Can Be Negative or Positive"

The absolutist and relativist approaches provide some insights about deviance, but neither is very useful in helping us understand much of the deviance in sports. The absolutists define deviance as a failure to conform, and they see rule violators as disruptive and morally bankrupt. Relativists define deviance as behavior that violates the interests of people with power, and they see rule violators as exploited victims. One of the main flaws in these approaches is that both ignore deviance that involves an overconformity to rules and expectations.

It is clear that most people who violate rules in sports can't be classified as morally bankrupt or as victims. For example, it is not accurate to say that young people lack moral character when they go overboard in accepting and overconforming to ideas about what it means to be an athlete. Nor is it accurate to define all athletes who engage in deviance as victims of the system. Of course athletes don't control many things about sports, but they do play an important part in the creation and maintenance of the norms that guide their own decisions and behaviors in sports.

Therefore our understanding of deviance in sports could be expanded if we assumed that actual behavior in any setting varies along a continuum in a way that resembles the statistical distribution of cases in a normal bell-shaped curve (Figure 6-1). When this "normal distribution approach" is used, we see that most behavior falls into a normal range of acceptance. Cases of deviance occur when behavior falls outside this range of acceptance. Therefore deviance exists on *either side* of what might be defined as "normal," and it can involve either underconformity or overconformity.

Underconformity is behavior that doesn't measure up to commonly accepted rules or standards of behavior; it is behavior grounded in a rejection or lack of awareness of rules. Underconforming behavior is described as **negative deviance.** Overconformity is behavior that goes so far in following commonly accepted rules or standards that it interferes with the well-being of self or others; it is behavior grounded in an uncritical acceptance of rules. This overconforming behavior is described as **positive deviance.** But remember, positive deviance is still deviance; it is often as dangerous and disruptive as negative deviance and it can be more difficult to control than negative deviance. The differences between these two types of deviance can be further understood by noting that in their most extreme forms negative deviance leads to anarchy and positive deviance leads to fascism.

Keith Ewald and Robert Jiobu (1985) illustrated the usefulness of this approach to deviance in sport. They collected information from a sample of adult men seriously involved in one of two sport activities—bodybuilding or competitive distance running. After studying both

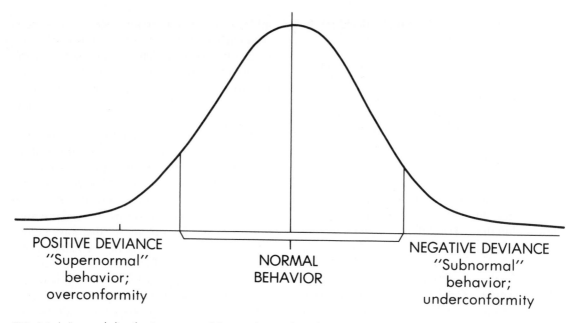

POSITIVE DEVIANCE
"Supernormal"
behavior;
overconformity

NORMAL
BEHAVIOR

NEGATIVE DEVIANCE
"Subnormal"
behavior;
underconformity

FIG. 6-1 A "normal distribution approach" to understanding deviance.

groups, they concluded that members of each displayed classic characteristics of deviance in the form of addiction. Many of the bodybuilders and distance runners pursued goals in their sports to such an extent that family relationships, work responsibilities, and/or physical health were negatively affected. Other studies have identified similar forms of positive deviance: self-injurious overtraining among distance runners (Nash, 1987); pathogenic eating behaviors and unhealthy weight control strategies among women athletes in intercollegiate and other amateur sports (Donnelly, 1993; Johns, 1992; Rosen et al., 1986); extremely rigid and exclusive dedication to training and competition among ultramarathon bicyclists (Wasielewski, 1991) and triathletes (Hilliard and Hilliard, 1990); and uncritical commitment to playing sports with pain and injury (Curry, 1992; Nixon, 1991, 1993).

When we use the normal distribution approach to define and study deviance in sports, we are forced to distinguish behavior showing a lack of concern for or a rejection of norms and rules from behavior showing an uncritical commitment to and overacceptance of norms and rules. Using this approach also forces us to critically examine the value system that exists in sports, especially high performance sports. This value system often operates in a way that encourages overconformity to a set of norms or guidelines that athletes use to evaluate themselves and others as they participate in sports. Because of this, much of the deviance among athletes (and coaches) involves unquestioned and unqualified acceptance of and conformity to the value system embodied in what might be called the "sport ethic."

THE "SPORT ETHIC" AND DEVIANCE IN SPORTS* The "sport ethic" refers to what many people in sports have come to use as the dominant criteria for defining what it really means,

---

*This section is adapted from Hughes and Coakley (1991).

in their minds, to be an athlete. Information about athletes and coaches has led us to tentatively conclude that the following four beliefs make up the core of this ethic:

1. *An athlete makes sacrifices for "the game."* The idea underlying this dimension of the sport ethic is that "real athletes" must love "the game" above all else and prove it by subordinating other interests for the sake of their sport. To prove they care about their sport, athletes must have the proper attitude, be committed to their sport, live up to the expectations of fellow athletes, and make sacrifices to continue participating. In other words, being an athlete involves meeting the demands of others in the sport and the demands of competition without question. This is the spirit underlying the notion that athletes must make sacrifices, that they must be willing to "pay the price" to stay involved in their sport. Coaches' pep talks and locker room slogans are full of references to this guideline.

2. *An athlete strives for distinction.* The Olympic motto of "Citius, Altius, Fortius" (swifter, higher, stronger) captures the meaning of this dimension of the sport ethic. "True athletes" seek to improve, to get better, to come closer to perfection. Winning symbolizes improvement and establishes distinction; losing is tolerated only because it's part of the experience of learning how to win. Breaking records is the ultimate standard of achievement in sports. This is because "real athletes" are a special group dedicated to climbing the pyramid, reaching for the top, pushing limits, excelling, exceeding or dominating others, and trying to become Number One.

3. *An athlete accepts risks and plays through pain.* According to the sport ethic, an athlete does not give in to pressure, pain, or fear. The voluntary acceptance of risks to health and well-being is a sign of physical courage and dedication among athletes. This guideline also emphasizes moral courage as being able to sustain physical performance under pressure even when the risk of injury is low. The idea is that an athlete doesn't back down from any challenge, that standing up to challenges involves moral and physical courage. Being an athlete means that one willingly confronts and overcomes the fear and the challenge of competition, and accepts the increasing risk of failure and injury as one moves to higher levels of performance.

4. *An athlete accepts no limits in the pursuit of possibilities.* Finally, the sport ethic stresses the openness of possibilities for achievement, and the imperative to pursue them without question. An athlete doesn't accept a situation without trying to change it, to overcome it, to turn the scales. "Real athletes" believe that sport is a sphere of life in which anything is possible, *if* a person is dedicated enough. They feel obligated to pursue dreams without reservation; they ignore external limits as they focus on the attempt to achieve success.

At first these guidelines that make up the sport ethic don't sound dangerous; in fact, they sound like slogans hanging on locker room walls or written in self-help and motivation books. People who play sports, especially at elite levels, use these guidelines to evaluate themselves as athletes, and they even use them to evaluate others who claim to be athletes. But when the sport ethic is considered more carefully and critically, it is seen that it can be dangerous if people come to accept it without qualification and decide to follow it regardless of *all* the consequences.

Unfortunately, many people in sports do not draw lines to determine how far they will go in conforming to the sport ethic. In fact, sport heroes are usually those who unquestioningly follow the ethic to the point of risking their own safety and well-being. Media commentators glo-

When young people become seriously involved in sport, they learn to accept injuries as a part of being athletes. Unless they are prepared to take risks, they may be cut from teams or they may jeopardize their chances of being involved at higher levels of competition. (Chuck Miller)

rify athletes who overconform to the sport ethic; they praise athletes who play with broken bones and sprained muscles, and who have surgery after surgery to come back and play "the game." Many spectators have even defined drama and excitement in terms of whether athletes are willing to go overboard in conforming to the sport ethic. Therefore it is not surprising that many athletes accept the sport ethic without qualifications. In fact, many athletes may overconform to the ethic even though it creates problems, causes pain, jeopardizes their health and safety, or even shortens life itself.

WHY DO SO MANY ATHLETES OVERCONFORM TO THE SPORT ETHIC? Not all athletes overconform to the sport ethic, but many do. There are two reasons why overconformity to the sport ethic occurs so frequently in sports:

1. Athletes find their experiences in sports so exhilarating and thrilling that they want to continue participating as long as possible.
2. The likelihood of being chosen or sponsored for continued participation in sports increases when athletes overconform to the sport ethic. After all, coaches praise athletes who overconform, and make them models, and when coaches accuse athletes of lacking "desire" and "hustle," athletes can use overconformity to the sport ethic to prove they have desire and that they are hustling.

Thus, overconformity to the sport ethic is so widespread that many athletes use it to define and evaluate their sport experiences. Athletes don't see their overconformity as deviance. Instead, they see it as confirming and reconfirming their identities as athletes and as members of select sport groups. Following the guidelines of the sport ethic to an extreme degree is just what they do as athletes, especially when continued participation and success in sports take on significant personal and social meanings.

Special bonds between athletes are often created when they demonstrate their unqualified commitment to the sport ethic under conditions of stress and challenge. These bonds not only reaffirm their unqualified commitment to the sport ethic on a day-to-day basis but they also create special feelings of fraternity, especially in groups of athletes in the same sports. These special feelings separate athletes from other people because most athletes don't think that "outsiders" really know what it's like to be an athlete. When this sense of separateness and uniqueness is combined with the fact that athletes are often held in awe by "outsiders," athletes often develop superiority complexes. These feelings of superiority can lead them to look down on "normal" members of the community, who live their lives without sacrificing for a team, seeking distinction, taking risks, or pushing limits. And it can also lead them to think they live their lives in a special zone that exempts them from following community rules. This may account for certain forms of negative deviance among various athlete groups.

These special feelings that come with overconforming to the sport ethic also lead many athletes to extend their playing careers even when their health is endangered, and why some even mourn the passing of those careers. These feelings may also lead some athletes to have knee surgery after knee surgery so they can play for "just one more year." And they may lead others to inject unbelievable amounts of hormones into their bodies on a regular basis without even thinking twice. After all, being a "real athlete" means taking risks, making sacrifices, and paying the price to be all you can be.

The point is that much of the deviance of athletes is not motivated primarily by a desire to win or by the rewards that come with winning. Instead, it is motivated by the desire simply *to play, to be an athlete,* and to *maintain membership in the special and elite athletic fraternity.* We can't forget that many athletes who clearly realize they will never win championships, or make money from their athletic accomplishments still engage in forms of positive deviance including violence and taking performance-enhancing drugs. This is not to say that a desire to win or make money is irrelevant to athletes; both are important parts of the overall context in which many forms of deviance occur. But much deviance among athletes clearly rests in overconforming to the values promoted through the sport ethic itself. When this occurs, deviance is especially difficult to control.

CONTROLLING POSITIVE DEVIANCE IN SPORTS Positive deviance presents special social control problems in sports. Owners, managers, sponsors, and coaches—all of whom exercise control within sports—often benefit when athletes overaccept and overconform to the sport ethic. Having athletes who overzealously pursue the ideals framed by the ethic is seen by most of these people as a blessing. The fact that athletes often use overconformity to the sport ethic as a gauge of personal commitment and courage for themselves and fellow athletes works to the advantage of those concerned with victories or entertainment. This is why there is a certain unwillingness among the controllers of sports to discourage athletes who engage in forms of positive deviance.

The issue of social control is even further complicated by the tendency to promote extreme overconformers into positions of power and influence in sports. Overconformers have already proved they're willing to "pay the price" and to live the sport ethic without reservations. So they often become coaches and then expect athletes to be like them.

This means that athletes often get strong encouragement to overconform to the guidelines of the sport ethic. This means also that a powerful source of deviance and ethical problems among athletes lies in the way sports are organized, within athletes' relationships with one another, and within their relationships with coaches and managers. Paradoxically, the "sport ethic," when taken to an extreme, actually promotes the corruption of sports. Controlling this form of "inside" corruption may be the biggest challenge facing those concerned with deviance in sports today.

Effectively controlling positive deviance depends on constantly raising questions about the meaning and organization of sports. Athletes must be encouraged to raise questions about playing with pain and injury and to develop definitions of courage that don't involve ignoring health and well-being. Controlling deviance in sports depends as much on participants working together to set limits for conformity as it does setting up detection programs and increasing punishment for rule violators. Unless limits are set to discourage overconformity to the sport ethic, detection programs and penalties won't affect many major forms of deviance among athletes and coaches.

The continuation of any social activity or organization depends on awareness of the consequences of both underconformity and overconformity. In the case of sport, this means that athletes, coaches, administrators, and spectators must all work to strike a balance between accepting rules and questioning rules. This balance will never be achieved once and for all time, but it is a goal that must be continually sought and struggled over. The more everyone in sports is involved in questioning and qualifying norms and rules, the closer they will come to controlling forms of positive deviance, even though the control will never be perfect or permanent.

RESEARCH ON DEVIANCE AMONG ATHLETES

Systematic studies of deviance among athletes are rare. Instead of doing systematic studies, people often take lists of alleged cases of athletes' misconduct from newspaper accounts, pick the behaviors they dislike the most, and then try to come up with explanations for those behaviors. This approach makes for interesting reading, but it doesn't tell us much about whether deviance is out of control in sports, whether there is more deviance today than in the past, whether deviance is due to overconformity or underconformity, or whether deviance is caused by the profit motive, power hungry coaches and administrators, or societal pressures to be Number One.

In reviewing accounts of deviant behavior among athletes, it is important to distinguish on-the-field deviance from off-the-field deviance. Each is connected to different types of rules, and their causes and consequences differ in important ways.

On-the-Field Deviance

On-the-field deviance includes violations of norms that occur while preparing for or participating in sport events. Commonly reported examples are things like using the spitball and brushback pitches in baseball, using intimidation and violence in contact sports, taking performance-enhancing drugs, engaging in unsportsmanlike conduct, and generally finding ways of getting around the rules to achieve victories or other honors. Some people say this type of deviance has become a serious problem at all levels of competition in many sports because young athletes learn them by watching their "heroes" in televised events (Smith, 1983). Others argue that the real cause of this deviance is the pressure to win created by a combination of commercialization, television, and political goals (as in the Olympics).

However, none of these explanations has been consistently supported by research. For example, no study has found that cheating, or dirty play, or shaving points, or any other sport-related deviance except the use of performance-enhancing drugs is more common today than it was in the past. (An explanation of the increased use of performance-enhancing drugs is discussed in the next section of the chapter.) In fact, some historical reviews suggest that many forms of deviance are *less* common today and that the behavior of athletes during recent years is more "civilized" and rule-governed than the behavior of athletes in the past (Elias and Dunning, 1986; Maguire, 1986).

When people blame money and television for

today's sport-related deviance among athletes, they overlook the fact that dirty play, cheating, and violence were serious problems in a number of popular North American sports long before games were televised and winners earned big money. Even today certain forms of deviance continue to be problems in nontelevised, noncommercialized sports. For example, the administrators of many community-based adult leagues complain that deviant behavior is a major problem during games. Even Little League officials complain about deviance among athletes and coaches. These examples of deviance are not caused by the profit motive or television.

Research suggests that athletes in most sports interpret rules very loosely during games, and they may even create alternative norms that stretch official rules (Bredemeier and Shields, 1984a, 1986; Donnelly and Young, 1985, 1988). The players themselves usually understand and respect these "revisions" of the rules. For example, some of the official rules in contact sports have been "revised" by players to allow them to present tests of courage to their opponents during competitions and even to their own teammates during practices and preseason tryouts. These tests are designed to see what other players can take. This is an example of overconformity to the sport ethic and it is the way violence sometimes comes to be used by athletes to prove they are tough enough to be respected by opponents and accepted as teammates (Faulkner, 1974a, 1974b; Surface, 1977). Proving your worth as an opponent or teammate and earning respect by using aggressive behaviors is a factor underlying many rule violations on the field. When this happens, deviance is due to the dynamics of participation itself rather than money, television coverage, or a desire among players to cheat in their games.

More research is needed before any conclusions can be made about on-the-field deviance among athletes. At this time evidence suggests that deviant behavior is not out of control. Problems do exist in certain sports, but the major reason for these problems seems to be grounded in

In cases in which winning is the sole measure of achievement, and when the rewards for winning are great, people may *sometimes* use deviant behavior to improve their chances for success.

the unquestioned acceptance of norms related to what it means to be an athlete. And if rates of deviance are really higher than they have been in the past, the reason for the difference may be that there are simply more rules to violate today than ever before. A look at the rules of various amateur sport organizations (the International Olympic Committee, NOCs, and sport federations) and the rules of the National Collegiate Athletic Association (NCAA) clearly illustrates that there are literally thousands of rules today that did not exist 50 years ago in sports. There are simply many more ways of becoming deviant in today's sports!

Off-the-Field Deviance

Cases of off-the-field deviance among athletes often receive widespread attention. When athletes are arrested, involved in fights, accused of using "recreational" drugs, accused of taking certain courses to stay eligible in high school or college sports, or linked to shady business deals, it makes big headlines. But there has been little research on how athletes behave off the field. The only exceptions to this are a handful of studies of delinquency and sport participation among high school students and studies of academic deviance among high school and college athletes.

The results of these studies generally contradict attention-grabbing headlines about athletes. For example, when rates of off-the-field delinquent and deviant behavior among varsity athletes and other students have been compared, the rates for athletes have never been higher than the rates for other students from similar backgrounds. This general finding seems to hold up for athletes in different sports, athletes in different societies, and both boys and girls from different racial and social class backgrounds.* Of course, the reasons for these findings may be that students with histories of deviant behavior do not try out for sport teams, or that coaches cut them when they do try out, or that athletes receive preferential treatment that keeps them out of the courts when they get into trouble. But until more is known about off-the-field behaviors, it is difficult to argue that athletes are any more deviant in their everyday lives than other people from comparable backgrounds.

Even the charge that college athletes stay eligible by cheating and avoiding substantive academic courses has never been examined thoroughly enough to make any conclusions about off-the-field patterns of deviance. It is true that many athletes do not graduate from college in 5 years or less, but this is true of many students, and comparisons suggest that intercollegiate athletes as a group are not much different from other students when it comes to completing degrees (Henschen and Fry, 1984; Shapiro, 1984; Walter et al., 1988).

The idea that athletes take more academic short-cuts than other students also needs further study. If compared with members of many fraternities and sororities, athletes would probably be found to choose courses and complete coursework in much the same way as do some other

groups of students. Fraternity and sorority members, who have never had their academic career patterns critically studied, tend to come from upper-income backgrounds, and they are often able to use their advantaged positions, family and peer connections, and experience to succeed in school and in their careers. Athletes from lower-income and minority backgrounds are often the object of studies, and they are routinely criticized for failing to live up to the academic ideal of attending college to pursue intellectual truth. Whether they are unique in their failure to live up to this ideal has not yet been documented through systematic research. Documentation would require comparisons with other special groups of students.

We also need research on why men in certain sports, military units, and other rigidly controlled fraternal groups in which physical dominance is emphasized have exceptionally high rates of physical and sexual assault, especially rape and gang rape. Rape rates among athletes are reportedly high (Lenskyj, 1992b; Loy, 1992; Melnick, 1992; Moore, 1991), but systematic research on why rape rates are high is scarce. Tim Curry (1991) has reported that locker room talk among men on intercollegiate sport teams "generally treated women as objects, encouraged sexist attitudes toward women and, in its extreme, promoted rape culture" (p. 119). Others have made a convincing case that many sports consist of cultural practices that perpetuate a gender order that not only privileges men but leads to the systematic subordination and degradation of women in society (cf., Messner and Sabo, 1992). But the link between certain sport forms, male bonding, and rape needs to be further explored and explained through research.

In conclusion, most forms of off-the-field deviant behavior among athletes do not seem to be out of control. Research suggests that athletes aren't much different from peers who come from similar social backgrounds. An exception to this is that physical and sexual assault rates among athletes seem to be relatively high. Interestingly, while some people claim off-the-field de-

---

*(Buhrmann, 1977; Landers and Landers, 1978; Rankin, 1981; Schafer, 1969; Segrave, 1986; Segrave and Chu, 1978; Segrave and Hastad, 1982; Segrave et al., 1985; Thorlindsson, 1989).

viance among athletes is getting out of control, others claim sport can be used to control delinquent behavior among young people. Although this idea also needs further testing, it is worth discussing (see "Sport participation as a 'cure' for deviant behavior" in box on pp. 148-149).

Why Focus Only on Deviance among Athletes?

This chapter focuses almost exclusively on deviance among athletes. This is an important issue and we wanted to cover it in some detail. However, it should be remembered that athletes are not the only people in sports who engage in behavior that violates norms. A few other examples of deviance include:

• Coaches who hit players, treat players inhumanely, use male players' insecurities about masculinity as a basis for motivating them, sexually harass women in and out of

Off-the-field deviance among athletes may decrease if they are explicitly taught a philosophy of nonviolence, respect for self and opponents, the importance of control, confidence in physical skills apart from winning, and a sense of responsibility. As explained in the box on pp. 148-149, this has occurred among young people in Tae Kwon Do even though it is a contact sport. (Mark Reis)

REFLECT ON SPORT

Sport Participation As a "Cure" for Deviant Behavior

It is widely believed that sports keep kids off the streets and out of trouble and that being an athlete somehow teaches character and discourages deviant behavior. Studies generally report lower rates of deviance among student athletes than among nonathletes in U.S. and Canadian schools, but they provide no data on why these differences exist. In most cases, differences are probably due to selection factors leading young people with records of misbehavior to avoid extracurricular activities controlled by adults or to get cut by coaches when they do try out for teams. But could other factors be at work?

There is one study that provides some clues about the connection between sports and the treatment of juvenile delinquents. Michael Trulson* took 34 young men, aged 13 to 17, who had been classified as delinquents and gave them a series of tests on aggression and personality adjustment. After matching the young men as closely as possible for age, scores on the personality tests, and their socioeconomic backgrounds, Trulson got their parents' permission to put them into a sport-based treatment program. In the program the subjects

were assigned to one of three treatment groups: group 1 received traditional Tae Kwon Do training; group 2 received nontraditional, or so-called modern, martial arts training, in which only fighting and self-defense techniques were taught; and group 3 received no martial arts training but served as a control group for maturation, increased physical activity, and the influence of being with the instructor.

For 6 months each group met three times a week for 1-hour training sessions with the same instructor. During the 6 months, information on a variety of measures were collected from the young men. The training sessions were organized so that those assigned to group 1 began with a period of meditation, designed to focus their attention on practice sessions, as well as to reflect upon their position, aspirations, and goals in life. This was followed by a sequence of calisthenics and stretching exercises, and then a brief lecture concerning Tae Kwon Do philosophy about life. This philosophy, which is an integral part of traditional Tae Kwon Do training, emphasizes respect for others, building confidence and self-esteem, the importance of physical fitness, patience, perseverance, and honor. There is also a heavy emphasis on always maintaining a sense of responsibility. The brief lecture was followed by practice on basic Tae Kwon Do techniques (blocks, punches, kicks), forms, free spar-

*Trulson, M.E. 1986. Martial arts training: a novel "cure" for juvenile delinquency. *Human Relations* 39(12):1131-1140.

REFLECT ON SPORT

ring, self-defense techniques, and ending with another period of meditation.

The young men assigned to group 2 practiced a "modern" version of the martial art in which only free-sparring and self-defense techniques, in addition to calisthenics and stretching exercises, were taught; there was no mediation or lectures on philosophy. The young men in group 3 participated in a number of other activities with the instructor, including basketball, jogging, and football.

The findings indicated clear-cut changes among the young men in group 1. After 6 months they were classified as normal instead of delinquent on a major psychological test (the MMPI); their scores on aggressiveness were below normal; and they exhibited less anxiety, increased self-esteem and social skills, and more agreement with commonly held values. The young men in Group 2 didn't fare so well. Their scores on delinquency were higher, and according to other measures, they were more aggressive and less well-adjusted than when the study began. Young men in Group 3, the ones who ran and played basketball and football, showed no change on delinquency scores or most personality measures, but their scores on self-esteem and social skills improved over the 6 months.

These results suggest that certain types of sport participation might be useful in working with young people. However, positive results can be expected *only if* sport participation occurs in conjunction with the explicit teaching of (1) a philosophy of nonviolence, (2) respect for self and others, (3)

the importance of fitness and control over self, (4) confidence in physical skills, and (5) a sense of responsibility. The experiences of the young men in groups 2 and 3 indicate that these five things don't automatically occur during sport participation. In fact, athletes sometimes learn the exact opposite in most sports: they may come to value violence as a strategy for success, to be hostile to opponents, to jeopardize their health in trying to dominate others, to be insecure about their abilities, and to follow the orders of coaches regardless of what they say. If participation in sports follows the models found in groups 2 and 3 rather than in group 1, it could create more harm than good when it comes to behavior changes among young people.

This is important to remember when evaluating various sport programs designed simply to get young people off the streets. These programs can be useful in the sense that they may communicate to young people that some people in their communities care about them. The programs may also be useful in the sense that they can put young people in touch with adults who might serve as advocates in their lives (see Chapter 8 for a discussion of "advocates"). But simply opening a gym and establishing a late night basketball league is not going to work wonders in the form of changing general behavior patterns. Changing behavior is a complex process, and to do it in connection with sport participation requires a clear-cut program of intervention into the lives of young people. Simply getting young people to play sports will *not* keep them from engaging in deviant behavior.

sports, and subvert efforts to provide women with equal participation opportunities in sport.

- Program administrators who ignore Title IX legislation in the United States, other administrators who treat women's sport programs as second class, and who operate sport programs that do not cover athletes with proper health and accident insurance.
- Sport team owners and others who use racist criteria for evaluating athletes and hiring staff and coaches.
- Media promoters and programmers who deliberately misrepresent sport events so they can generate good television ratings or newspaper sales.
- Wealthy race horse owners who have horses killed to collect on life insurance policies (Nack and Munson, 1992).

Most of these and other examples of deviant behaviors will be discussed in other chapters.

PERFORMANCE-ENHANCING SUBSTANCES: A CASE STUDY OF DEVIANCE IN SPORTS

The use of anabolic steroids by well-known athletes has focused worldwide attention on drugs in sports. But history clearly shows that drug use in sports is not new. Athletes have taken a variety of substances over the years, and substance usage has never been limited just to elite athletes (Todd, 1983, 1987). These points raise the following important questions about this form of deviance in sports:

1. If the use of performance-enhancing substances is not new, how can we now say it is caused by money, television coverage, an overemphasis on winning, or deterioration of values among today's athletes?
2. What are performance-enhancing drugs, who identifies them, and on what basis are they banned in different sports?
3. Why are athletes tested for drug usage, and what are the dangers associated with the testing of athletes?

4. What theoretical approach to deviance is most helpful in developing programs for controlling this serious problem?

History and Causes of Substance Use Among Athletes

Evidence indicates that athletes have sought and used performance-enhancing drugs for many centuries.* Athletes in Greece and Rome used a variety of potions and substances, including hallucinogenic mushrooms, believed to improve physical performance. Strychnine and brandy was the potion of choice among European distance skaters in the 1700s and distance runners during the 1800s. Heroin was used as a painkiller by boxers before 1900, and as early as 1886 a cyclist died from using a mixture of heroin and cocaine. This mixture was called a *speedball*, and many athletes in different sports used it in the late 1800s. Other drugs, including opium, alcohol, caffeine, strychnine, ethyl ether, and nitroglycerine, were also used during this period. Cyclists in the 1930s and British soccer players in the 1950s used amphetamines in combination with cocaine (see Todd, 1987, for a detailed historical account of substance use in sports).

This brief review is not intended to give the impression that all athletes through history have been heavy drug users. The majority of athletes have not used performance-enhancing drugs, although many at elite levels of competition have experimented with and used a wide variety of different substances believed to enhance performance (Hoberman, 1992; Voy, 1991). But the use of these substances is not new, and this is an important point to remember when we try to explain why athletes use them today.

Historical evidence also shows an increase in the use of performance-enhancing drugs in the 1950s (Hoberman, 1992; Todd, 1987; Voy, 1991). This was due to two factors: (1) the de-

*See Donohoe and Johnson, 1986; Goldman, 1984; Goldman, Bush, and Klatz, 1992; Hoberman, 1992; Todd, 1983, 1987; Voy, 1991.

velopment and official use of amphetamines in the military during World War II, and (2) advances in biology and medicine that led to the laboratory isolation of human hormones and the development of synthetic hormones, especially hormones fostering physical growth and development. Experiences with amphetamine use during the war alerted many young people to the possible use of these drugs in other settings, including sports. Athletes in the 1950s fondly referred to amphetamines as "bennies." Research on the use of synthetic hormones in sport had been done as early as the 1920s, but it wasn't until the 1950s that testosterone, steroids, and growth hormones from both humans and animals became more widely available. They didn't become very widely used, however, until weight training and strength conditioning programs began to be emphasized among athletes in certain sports. When athletes realized that muscle growth and lean body mass could be significantly extended, they became increasingly interested in specialized weight training programs, planned diets, vitamin supplements, and a variety of newly developed chemical substances. As might be expected, the growth of bodybuilding has also been closely connected with substance use, especially the use of hormones and hormone derivatives.

When Harold Connelly, the 1956 Olympic hammer-throw champion, testified before a U.S. Senate committee in 1973 that the majority of athletes he had known "would do anything, and take anything, short of killing themselves to improve athletic performance," he was probably describing what many athletes through history would have done. Other evidence suggests that this willingness to do anything and take anything exists among both men and women in capitalist and socialist, industrial, and preindustrial societies. The reason drug use has increased so much since the 1950s is not that sports or athletes have changed but that drugs believed to enhance physical performance have become so widely available. If today's drugs had been available in the year 300, 1600, or 1800, they would have probably been used to the same extent they are used by athletes in the 1990s (Hoberman, 1992; Todd, 1987). This makes it difficult to totally blame drug use on the profit motive, commercial interests, television, or the erosion of traditional values.

This "substance availability hypothesis" must be examined more closely, but it clearly fits with the model of positive deviance presented in this chapter. The use of drugs and other substances by athletes is generally not the result of defective socialization or lack of moral character. After all, users are often the most dedicated and committed athletes in sports! Nor are the users helpless victims of coaches and trainers who lack moral character, although coaches and trainers who push the sport ethic without question may indirectly encourage the use of performance-enhancing substances. Instead, most substance use and abuse is clearly tied to an overcommitment to the sport ethic itself; it is grounded in overconformity—the same type of overconformity that leads injured distance runners to continue training even when training may cause serious physical problems, and the same type of overconformity that leads American football players to risk their bodies through excessively violent physical contact week after painful week in the NFL.

Apparently, many athletes will use whatever means available to continue participating in their sport. They enjoy playing their sport and are dedicated to doing whatever it takes to stay involved. Usually they must be winners to avoid cuts or elimination, but winning is secondary to just playing. And as long as even a few athletes are willing to take performance-enhancing substances to gain the edge they need to continue playing at their level of participation, many others will conclude they must use similar substances to stay competitive, even if it is against their better judgment. These dynamics, all connected with overconformity to the sport ethic, seem to operate at various levels of sports from bodybuilding in local gyms to the locker rooms of professional sport teams and among both women and men across a wide variety of sport events from the shot put to the 100-meter sprint.

The implications of the drug availability hypothesis and the positive deviance model become especially clear when we examine efforts to define, test for, and control the use of performance-enhancing substances and other forms of deviance.

Defining, Identifying, and Banning Performance-Enhancing Drugs

Defining what constitutes a drug is tougher than it seems (Goode, 1988). Drugs can include anything from aspirin to heroin; they may be legal or illegal, harmless or dangerous, socially acceptable or unacceptable, commonly used or exotic. Furthermore, they may produce real physical changes, psychological changes, or both.

The International Olympic Committee defines drugs in terms of its general definition of "doping." IOC policy describes doping as:

> . . . the administration of or use by a competing athlete of any substance foreign to the body or any physiological substance taken in abnormal quantity or taken by an abnormal route of entry into the body with the sole intention of increasing in an artificial and unfair manner his/her performance in competition. When necessity demands medical treatment with any substance which, because of its nature, dosage, or application, is able to boost the athlete's performance in competition in an artificial and unfair manner, this too is regarded by the IOC as doping (USOC, 1992).

This definition may sound good, but it leaves many questions unanswered. What is a substance "foreign" to the body, and why are the "foreign" substances of aspirin and Tylenol not banned while the "natural" hormone testosterone is banned? What is an "abnormal" quantity and an "abnormal" route of entry? Why are megadoses of vitamins not banned, but small amounts of many decongestants are banned? Why can athletes be stripped of medals when they take medications without intending to enhance performance? And with new scientific discoveries being made every day and applied to

sports, what is artificial and what is unfair? Why isn't the electronic stimulation of muscles banned? Isn't it artificial? Why is the use of biofeedback and other psychological technologies defined as "natural" and "fair" while drinking certain forms of herbal tea are defined as "unnatural" and "unfair"? Are vitamins natural? Amino acids? Caffeine? Human growth hormone? Gatorade? How about other artificial foods designed to enhance performance? And is it "natural" to deprive yourself of food to make weight or meet the demands of a gymnastics coach who measures body fat every week and punishes athletes who eat "normal" diets?

Outside amateur sports, the questions are just as complicated. Was John McEnroe being deviant when he had rehydration fluids dripped into his veins to help him recover from an exhausting tennis match in the heat? How about football players who take 20 (200 mg) ibuprofen pills every day as NFL player Kenny Easley did in the mid 1980s? Why do we call people who get shot up with pain killers heroes, and then condemn the same players for taking other drugs to help them build muscle or relax and recover after they have pushed their bodies too far? Why do many athletes see the use of drugs as a noble act of commitment and dedication while many spectators see it as a reprehensible act of deviance even though they love to watch people whose behavior is drug-aided?

These and hundreds of other questions about what is artificial, natural, foreign, fair, and abnormal show that any definition of doping will lead to endless debates about the technical and legal meaning of terms (Hoberman, 1992, p. 261). While these debates occur in offices and courtrooms, there are physicians, pharmacists, chemists, inventors, and athletes who will continue to come up with new and different aids to performance, chemical and otherwise. And this "endless game of scientific hide and seek" shows no sign of letting up (Hoberman, 1992, p. 101). This is why Wildor Hollman, president of the World Federation of Sports Medicine, said in 1984, "Never again, not even in the distant fu-

SIDELINES

"Is this what steroids and those other drugs are supposed to do, Carl?" Steroids have numerous negative side effects when they are taken in heavy dosages and combined with a variety of other drugs. In fact, not all the side effects are yet known.

ture, will we see a type of high performance sport without doping" (cited in Hoberman, 1992, p. 262).

Even more thought provoking than Wildor's statement are the words of Heinz Liessen, a German sport physician, who recently explained his own approach to research on performance enhancement in the following way: "Every adaptation to training occurs in the brain, in the nervous system. It is there, through hormonal regulation of the body, that we must do our regulating." This raises another tough question: is it "unnatural" to stimulate the "natural" production of "natural" hormones in the athlete's body? It does not involve any "abnormal" swallowing or injecting, just the use of a little brain-related technology. And finally, as you read this book the Human Genome Project is discovering new things about genes and DNA that will make possible numerous forms of genetic engineering that could be used for performance-enhancing purposes among athletes. How will we define, identify, and deal with deviance in light of all these possibilities? According to Australian sport sociologist Jim

McKay, "The argument that drugs are 'unnatural' pales in comparison to the array of biological, biochemical, social, biomechanical, psychological, environmental, and technological regimens which manipulate athletes bodies" (1990, p. 7). Drug use among athletes seems to be only one of many issues related to technology and athletes' bodies; sooner or later we will have to deal with all these issues.

Further complicating decisions about which drugs to ban is the confusion about their effects on athletic performance. It is often impossible to do laboratory studies on the effects of certain drugs because of the ethical and legal constraints in administering drugs to experimental subjects. For example, when medical researchers study the effects of anabolic steroids using 10 mg dosages, while athletes use 10 to 50 times that amount up to five times per week in the locker room, there is bound to be some disagreement about what the drugs actually do for performance! Furthermore, some athletes mix a wide variety of various substances and even use specially designed forms of anabolic steroids or testosterone unknown to most researchers. This is why the official position in medical circles has been so different from what athletes have consistently claimed about the effects of steroids. And this is why "official statements" about the negative effects of these drugs have been discredited and ignored among many athletes.

Official information about drugs and other substances has often excluded information that could be used by athletes looking for things to enhance their performance in sport. For this reason, many athletes, even the ones not looking for new substances, don't see these sources as totally credible. The athletes know that the official sources deliberately exclude information. Sport organizations defend this approach by saying they don't want athletes to know too much about drugs because many would discover how effective performance-enhancing drugs can be and how difficult they are to detect in certain cases. However, since the late 1980s there have been a number of publications that make the latest information from a variety of scientific and nonscientific sources available to athletes and anyone else who wants to read them (Di Pasquale, 1992a). The authors of these publications argue that athletes need to have the best information available so they can make informed choices about substance use rather than choices based on rumors and ignorance.

Most arguments for banning the use of performance-enhancing substances are at least partially based on the belief that these substances are dangerous to the health of athletes. This is true in some cases, but it is tough to make this case when athletes are encouraged to take so many other risks and give up so much to dedicate themselves to their sports. For example, telling young athletes who have just given 4 to 8 years of their youth to make a national team that taking certain hormones could shorten their lives by 5 years is not very convincing. Why would athletes be frightened, especially if the hormones could help them make the national team and go to the Olympics? And most athletes don't respond well to scare messages. They know that being an athlete means taking risks and often suffering injuries in the process. For example, Kim Zmeskal, the 15-year-old who was the best U.S. gymnast in 1991, explained that she feared little because she had already lived through painful injuries. In an interview before the 1991 World Championships she calmly explained that she had competed with "the same stress fracture for six years." And then she said, "It's nothing unusual for a gymnast. Our trainer told us that if they took a bone scan, they'd find stress fractures all over our bodies" (Woodward, 1991). This approach to sports makes it very difficult to convince athletes that hundreds of substances should be banned because they might lead to health problems. Sport participation itself often leads to health problems!

Finally, some people even challenge the policy of banning drugs in sports. They argue that because drugs are widely used in society as a whole for the purpose of improving performance or treating conditions that interfere with performance at home or on the job, athletes ought to be allowed to do the same. They say that tranquilizers, pain controllers, mood controllers, anti-depressants, decongestants, diet pills, birth control pills, caffeine, nicotine (and "the patch" to kick nicotine dependence), or alcohol are used by the majority of adults in North America. Most of these "users" say they are against drugs, but they generally do not see anything wrong with their own usage of various "life-enhancing" substances. If people really did say no to drugs, life in industrial societies would change drastically. Coffee breaks would disappear, life habits would change, and medical treatment would be forced to return to the distant past. Therefore why bother to control athletes in ways that other college students and other adults are not controlled? After all, do colleges have a policy against drinking coffee to aid late night studying for a test? Do teachers make students sign an oath against having a beer when they want to relax on weekends? If not, why should athletes have to do these things? This is an important question to be considered.

In the meantime, it remains very difficult to even begin to define, identify, and ban drugs and doping procedures used in sports. This brings us to the issue of drug testing.

Drug Testing in Sports

BACKGROUND AND HISTORY The creation and enforcement of rules regulating drug use among athletes has always been the responsibility of individual sport associations, federations, leagues, and conferences. The IOC has taken the lead in banning substances and testing for use. Other organizations have generally followed their lead, although there are differences in the drugs banned by various sport organizations in different countries.

The IOC first defined and banned doping in 1967. The first drug tests in international sport were administered at the 1968 Olympic Games in Mexico City, but they were done for research purposes only and no punishments were given to those testing positive. In 1968 there was no technology for detecting anabolic steroids, few administrators in sports were aware of how many athletes were using steroids, and most medical experts claimed steroids had no significant effect on performance (Todd, 1987). These first regulatory drug tests were prompted because of suspicions about drug-related deaths among cyclists and soccer players and because of rumors about widespread drug use among athletes in Western Europe.

The absence of tests for steroids opened the door for rapid increases in the number of athletes using them. According to an unofficial poll taken by Jay Sylvester, a member of the U.S. track team in 1972, 68% of all track and field athletes used some form of anabolic steroid in preparing for the 1972 Games in Munich (Todd, 1987). Accurate tests to detect steroid use were developed in 1973, and they were first administered on an experimental basis at the 1974 Commonwealth Games. No athletes were punished even though about 20% of the competitors in the sample tested positive.

During the 1976 Olympic Games in Montreal, eight out of 275 athletes tested positive for steroids, but at that time many had already switched to pure testosterone instead of synthetic steroids. This was ironic because anabolic steroids were originally developed and used in medical treatment because they were safer than testosterone. However, because testosterone is a natural substance in the human body, it created detection problems for the testers. The policy used in Olympic sports was that a positive test for testosterone meant that an athlete's urine contained more than a 6:1 ratio of testosterone and epitestosterone (T/E ratio), both of which are naturally occurring hormones in both men and women (normal T/E ratios are about 2:1 or less). Drug tests done in 1980 indicated that over 20% of the U.S. athletes who would have competed in the Moscow Olympic Games (if there had been no boycott) tested positive for the use of exogenous (not "naturally" produced) testosterone, according to the T/E ratio definition of doping.

In 1982 the IOC added testosterone to its list of banned substances. The next year 15 male athletes from the United States tested positive for steroids at the Pan American Games in Caracas, and a dozen others packed up and returned home before competing in their events when they heard about the testing. This created considerable attention and led to numerous investigations of drugs in sport by sport organizations, journalists, and others. The popular press was full of drug reports. The investigations suggested that drug use existed among many athletes, both amateur and professional, in a wide range of sports. Ironically, many of the European countries in which the use of steroids had first been widespread had already begun to institute strong antidrug programs for their athletes at the time when the United States and Canada were only just discovering there was a problem.

The USOC stepped up its testing efforts during the Olympic trials in 1984. There were no punishments for 86 athletes who tested positive, but the athletes got the message that testing procedures were accurately detecting steroid use. According to some reports, this turn of events led many steroid users to take unbanned masking drugs, switch to the use of human Growth Hormone (hGH), or control their testosterone use more carefully (Todd, 1987). The reason for the switch to hGH was that growth hormone could not be detected through the standard testing methods, and testosterone was allowed as long as the T/E ratio was not beyond 6:1. However, both hGH and testosterone are more dangerous and more powerful than anabolic steroids (Donohoe and Johnson, 1986). Additional rumors in the mid 1980s suggested a few athletes may have even experimented with "monkey juice," the growth hormones of monkeys and apes (Todd, 1987).

The outcome of the drug-testing program for the 1988 and 1992 Summer Olympic Games in Seoul and Barcelona appears to be very similar to the outcomes of testing at other events since 1968: only a few athletes testing positive amidst continuing rumors of widespread use. However, there is much evidence to suggest that various forms of anabolic steroids and other hormones are being used by many athletes in a wider range of events. Usage is no longer limited to weight lifting and other so-called strength sports. Many people believe the relatively small number of positive tests in the 1988 Olympic Games was due to the use of masking drugs, a more careful and knowledgeable determination of usage cycles and dosages among athletes, and the use of hGH and other substances not detected in the tests. For example, some athletes have now become so experienced in the use of testosterone that they are able to take it in dosages that keep the detectable amount below allowable limits, which have in some cases been raised to a 9:1 T/E ratio.

The histories of drug testing in other sport organizations are different from the history in the IOC. Every organization has its own policies, procedures, and banned substance list. And each organization's policy is influenced by unique sets of internal political issues and external factors such as the policy positions of players' associations, the availability of money to conduct tests, and the legal limits of testing in certain situations.

TESTING AS A DETERRENT Drug testing is a controversial issue in sports, and there are a number of arguments against it. One of the main arguments is that it simply doesn't prevent athletes from using drugs. In the face of testing, athletes have engaged in a series of evasive tactics, including the use of masking drugs (diuretics and others), the use of undetectable drugs (hGH and others), adjustment of their own usage patterns, and hiring of their own "chemists" to show them new performance-enhancing substances and new ways of avoiding detection. Critics of the ban on steroids argue that it not only criminalizes the use of a helpful drug but it also forces athletes to obtain drug supplies in the black market and isolates users from the supervision and guidance of physicians (Courson, 1988; Bender, 1988). According to Mauro Di Pasquale, editor of the journal, *Drugs in Sports*, the policy of banning substances and testing athletes has failed. He claims that instead of "decreasing the use of drugs in sports and protecting the health of athletes, legislation against drug use and extensive drug testing have increased drug use and subsequently led to the use of more dangerous drugs" (Di Pasquale, 1992b, p. 5).

Another practical argument against testing is that it cannot detect all the substances athletes use to enhance their performance. Athletes are often one step ahead of the rule makers and testers when it comes to new forms of performance-enhancing substances and new means of masking substance use. By the time sport organizations ban substances and the testers calibrate their tests to detect new banned substances, the athletes have moved on to something else, or they are using new ways of masking the presence of banned substances in their systems. Meanwhile, the list of banned substances is growing to catalog length and athletes are being overwhelmed with rules.

Other arguments against drug testing are based on legal issues and social considerations. Mandatory testing or testing without cause not only violates a person's right to privacy but also sets precedents that could lead people to see testing as permissible in other spheres of life. Privacy issues apply primarily to amateur athletes because the rights of professionals in most team sports are negotiated in agreements between players' associations and team owners. But privacy issues are very important in light of the fact that future tests may call for blood and DNA as well as urine samples. Because athletes are used as models, the testing of athletes could lead many people to consent to testing in their own lives. This would not only open the door to oppressive forms of social control in everyday life but it also would encourage the use of social stigma to mark people whose bodies have been labeled as "impure" or "contaminated" (Cole, Denny, and Coakley, 1993).

Arguments in favor of drug testing also reveal interesting dimensions of the drug use problem in sports. Many people agree that performance-enhancing drugs should be banned from sports because they allow athletes to perform beyond their "natural" abilities and give them an unfair advantage over opponents. They say that this destroys the basis for competition and threatens the health and well-being of athletes even to the point of causing permanent physical damage or death (Bender, 1988). Others favor testing because they have simply decided drug use is morally wrong and should be stopped in whatever way possible.

When these people are told that current testing programs are not effective they call for more comprehensive testing programs. Some of those who think testing should be a part of an overall drug-control program say that the only way tests will be effective is if they are widely and regularly administered—without warning—mandatory for everyone (no excuses), and 100% effective and accurate (so athletes have faith in them). If some athletes are taking drugs because "everyone else is doing it," nothing short of this type of program will have a very good chance of being effective as a means of control. All athletes must be convinced that the testing program is designed so *no* performance-enhancing drugs are allowed, and *all* users will be identified and punished. If the program falls short of this standard, its effectiveness will be seriously limited. But even if it meets this standard, it will still not deter experimentation with new substances and procedures among many athletes (Di Pasquale, 1992 c, d; Hoberman, 1992; Todd, 1987).

As they are now administered, drug testing policies and programs are not trusted by many experienced athletes. Most athletes realize that international sports are heavily influenced by political interests that cloud the validity and reliability of tests. Furthermore, they know how bureaucratically complicated the drug testing process is, and they are aware that mistakes could be made at any one of a number of points in that process. This has been illustrated through court cases in which the accuracy and fairness of drug testing procedures has been called into question.

In 1992 Butch Reynolds was awarded (but hasn't collected) $27.3 million in a suit against the international track federation (IAAF) for a wrongful drug suspension. A federal judge in the U.S. determined that Reynolds was innocent after allegedly testing positive for steroid use in 1990. The politics and accuracy of drug testing is a cause for concern among many athletes. (Wide World Photos, Inc.)

Controlling Substance Use in Sports

Today's athletes, like their counterparts in the past, seek continued participation and excellence in sports. And when they push the sport ethic too far and overconform to norms promoting risk taking, striving for improvement, and "paying the price," they are unlikely to see the use of performance-enhancing substances as deviant.

In the face of contemporary drug use among athletes, the explanations for deviance offered by the absolutists and the relativists are not very helpful. Most athletes do not use performance-enhancing substances because they lack character, intelligence, or sanity. Nor do they use them because they are victims of biased and coercive rules. The solutions offered by the absolutists and relativists are also unsatisfactory. Tougher rules and increased testing have not and will not control the problem, nor will it be controlled by simply letting athletes make the rules.

As long as athletes are encouraged to accept without qualification norms emphasizing the value of taking risks, reaching beyond their potential, playing with pain, and "paying the price," they will continue to be willing to try anything or take anything to continue to participate. Overreactions to drug use and oversimplified solutions will not make athletes decide to stop using substances they see as important tools of their sports. Such decisions will be made only if the norms of sport are questioned in ways that lead to qualifications and the setting of limits on conformity.

In light of this approach, recommendations for controlling substance use in sport should begin with the following changes:

- To avoid hypocrisy in our efforts to make changes, we need to eliminate the use of so-called "legal" performance-enhancing drugs and procedures, which may harm the health of athletes. Pain killers, massive injections of vitamin B-12, blood boosting and the use of EPO, playing with pins in broken bones or with high tech "casts" to hold broken bones in place during competition, and playing with special harnesses to restrict the movement of injured joints seem to be no more harmful to health than taking anabolic steroids, and they must be regulated and controlled to begin to limit the use of performance-enhancing drugs.
- Rules must be put into place that clearly indicate that risks to health are undesirable and unnecessary in sports.

- No athlete should be allowed to play while hurt or injured until certified as "well," not simply "able to compete," by a physician chosen by someone outside the athletic program in which the athlete is involved. Outsiders are necessary to avoid medical opinions mediated by overconformity to the sport ethic.
- Norms emphasizing an awareness of one's limits must be developed so that courage would come to mean being able to accept the discipline necessary to become well, instead of being able to disregard the consequences of injuries.
- The goals of sport science must be reframed to emphasize the growth and development of athletes through the expansion and continuation of the sport experience for participants at all levels of involvement. The emphasis on the enhancement of performance must be informed by this goal or sport scientists become high tech panders. For example, sport psychology should help athletes understand the consequences of their choices to participate in sports, and to reduce the extent to which guilt, shame, and pathology influence participation and training decisions; this is the alternative to the increasingly popular technique of "psycho-doping," which encourages overconforming deviance by making athletes more likely to give body and soul to their sport without ever raising questions about why they are doing what they are doing.
- The process of questioning and qualifying the sport ethic must be made formal in sports and sport organizations, and it should involve all sport participants. Unless this happens, deviance grounded in overconformity will continue to occur. What we need is for athletes *and coaches* themselves to come up with new guidelines that discourage overconformity to the sport ethic, guidelines that emphasize health and development as well as performance.

In connection with these recommendations there is a need to make drug education part of a general program of "deviance education" for coaches, managers, administrators, and athletic directors, not just athletes. Education will be successful in controlling substance use among athletes if it involves critical reflection on the following issues:

- Creating norms regulating the use of new and extremely powerful forms of technology and medical knowledge.
- Questioning and critically examining the value systems and the norms that guide behavior in sport, and then setting limits on conformity while controlling underconformity.
- Redefining the meaning of sport experiences (unless this is done, what would stop athletes from using an undetectable, easily obtained, nondangerous drug that would enhance performance?).
- Becoming more aware that the behavior of athletes is based on choices and that the avoidance of self-destructive and meaningless choices depends on athletes having valid and reliable information and being full participants in rule making in sports.

Therefore "deviance education" in sports calls for a critical examination of the way sports are defined, organized, promoted, and played. This approach to social control is based on critical theory rather than functionalism or conflict theory (see Chapter 2). It assumes that rules and relationships are the creations of people and that changes are possible when people critically examine the values, norms, and social conditions affecting the way they make choices and live their lives.

As it is right now, we face a future without any clearly defined ideas about what achievement in sports means in light of recent changes in the rewards associated with participation, the new importance of participation in the lives of many young athletes, and the new technologies that can be used to enhance performance. We need to establish new guidelines instead of trying to reestablish those that worked in the past. There are new issues now and they call for new responses.

Controlling positive deviance in sports demands that athletes, coaches, and others critically question the widely accepted norm that athletes must be willing to take risks, ignore pain, and "pay the price" to show they have what it takes. As long as athletes overconform to the norm inferred by this t-shirt (many athletes from different sports wore shirts with this logo prior to the 1992 Summer Olympic Games), positive deviance will be a problem in sports. (Tini Campbell)

CONCLUSION:

IS DEVIANCE IN SPORTS OUT OF CONTROL?

Studying deviant behavior in sports presents an interesting challenge. This is because deviance in sports, especially among athletes, often involves overconformity with norms rather than underconformity or a rejection of norms. Therefore rule violations frequently take the form of positive deviance.

Some of the conceptual frameworks used by sociologists ignore the existence of positive deviance, and they don't offer many helpful recommendations about controlling deviant behavior in sports. When deviance is defined in terms of how behavior measures up to a set of ideals and deviants are described as lacking moral character (the absolutist approach), an analysis of deviance in sport runs into problems. Ideals are difficult to identify, and athletes may violate norms because they go overboard in their acceptance of them, not because they lack character.

It also doesn't help much when deviance is defined as a result of a labeling process in which definitions of good and bad held by the powerful are forced on those without power (the relativist approach). Describing rule violators as victims is seldom accurate, and changing the rules and the rule makers is not likely to decrease positive deviance in sports.

A normal distribution approach seems to be most useful when explaining deviance in sports. Such an approach distinguishes negative deviance, or extreme underconformity, from positive deviance, or extreme overconformity. This distinction is essential because the most serious forms of deviance in sports are created by behaviors in which athletes, coaches, and others go overboard in their acceptance of norms. For example, when being an athlete is defined in terms of taking risks, striving to be the best, playing with pain, and "paying the price" through sacrifice and commitment, extreme overconformity is bound to be a problem if no limits are set on expectations. It is the unqualified acceptance of these norms in sport that accounts for much of the deviance among athletes.

Research strongly supports this explanation. Most on-the-field behavior among athletes falls within a normal range of acceptability, and when it falls outside this range, it often consists of overconformity with the norms of many sports. This overconformity is grounded in an unqualified acceptance of what is expected of athletes. Off-the-field deviance among athletes often makes the headlines, but most evidence indicates rates of deviance among athletes are not higher than they are among comparable people who don't participate in sport. A likely exception to this are rates of physical and sexual assault. However, in general, it does not seem that deviance in sports is out of control.

There are certain forms of deviance among athletes that do constitute serious problems. The use of performance-enhancing substances is a case in point. According to many reports, the use of these substances is becoming increasingly widespread despite new rules, testing programs, educational and treatment programs, and strong punishments for violators. Historical evidence suggests that recent increases in rates of use are primarily due to the increased availability of substances rather than to changes in the values or character of athletes or changes in sports. Most athletes throughout history have sought ways to continue to participate and to improve their skills, but today the search is more likely to involve drugs because more performance-enhancing drugs are available. Unfortunately, science and medicine have been used to control athletes' bodies rather than to enable athletes to control themselves and their lives and critically assess the impact of science and medicine on their lives (McKay, 1990).

Even though lists of banned substances have expanded every year since 1967, athletes have generally stayed one jump ahead of the rule makers and testers. When one drug is banned, athletes tend to use another, even if it is more dangerous. If a new detection test is developed for a drug, athletes switch to an undetectable drug, or they use masking drugs to confuse the testers. Until valid and reliable tests are developed, the use of hGH, blood doping, and other new procedures will be the focus of much attention among athletes and rule makers. When performance enhancement is tied to "natural" chemicals and processes, testing is a problem. Testing is also a problem because it often violates privacy rights valued in many cultures.

Dealing with the problem of positive deviance requires a serious reexamination of norms in many sports. A balance must be struck between accepting and questioning norms and rules; people in sports must be able to make qualifications of norms and rules, and limits must be set on conformity so that athletes who engage in self-destructive behaviors are not defined as heroes. Everyone in sports must not only question existing norms but also create new norms related to the use of medical science and technology. The meaning of sport experiences must be redefined if positive deviance is to be controlled. After all, what would happen if someone discovered a cheap, nondetectable, nondangerous performance-enhancing drug that would work wonders if athletes took it?

Effective change also requires that all participants in sports be involved in this continual process of questioning, examining, and redefining. For example, athletes must be empowered within sport organizations so they can make informed decisions about their behavior. Solutions require a critical examination of the values and norms in sports as well as a restructuring of the organizations controlling and sponsoring sports so that all participants are included in the examination process. Without these changes, positive deviance will continue to be a significant problem in sports.

SUGGESTED READINGS

Di Pasquale, M.G. 1992. Drugs in Sports (*this new journal contains no sociological analysis, but it is an invaluable source of information about performance-enhancing substances and technologies; it is not an underground publication, but it is not endorsed by most sport organizations*).

Donohoe, T., and N. Johnson. 1986. Foul play: drug abuse in sports. Basil Blackwell, Inc., N.Y. (*clearly written overview of the history of drug use by athletes; thorough discussion of major drugs currently being used; focus is primarily on world-class amateur sport*).

Eitzen, D.S. 1981. Sport and deviance. In G. Luschen and G.H. Sage, eds. Handbook of social science of sport. Stipes Publishing Company, Champaign, Ill. (*makes the case that current structure and organization of sport promote deviance and that patterns of deviant behavior in sport reflect patterns in society at large*).

Ewald, K., and R.M. Jiobu. 1985. Explaining positive deviance: Becker's model and the case of runners and bodybuilders. Sociology of Sport Journal 2(2):144-156 (*research dealing directly with the issue of positive deviance in sport; conceptually, the article covers material that ties in with some of the work on positive addiction in the psychology of sport*).

Goldman, B., and R. Klatz. 1992. Death in the locker room, II. Elite Sports Medicine Publications Inc.

Chicago, IL (*written from a medical and personal point of view; thorough discussion of drug use in sports and various substances and doping procedures used by athletes; lists 345 up-to-date references along with other reference information*).

Hoberman, J. 1992. Mortal engines: (*this is an insightful analysis of the use of sport science in the quest of extending human limits; reading this book will leave you wondering about the benefits and dangers of science*).

Hughes, R., and J. Coakley. 1991. Positive deviance among athletes: The implications of overconformity to the sport ethic. Sociology of Sport Journal 8(4):307-325 (*this article provides a detailed explanation of the concept of positive deviance and the usefulness of that concept in explaining deviance in sports*).

McIntosh, P. 1979. Fair play: ethics in sport and education. Heinemann Educational Books, London (*philosophers discuss deviance in terms of ethics; this is an excellent overview of issues related to the development of norms in and about sport*).

Messner, Michael A. 1992. Power at play. Beacon Press, Boston (*this book is not directly on deviance, but it does a good job of showing how positive deviance in sport is also linked to certain definitions of masculinity*).

Morgan, W.J., and K.V. Meier, eds. 1988. Philosophic inquiry in sport. Human Kinetics Publishers, Inc., Champaign, Ill. ("*Competition, sportsmanship, cheating, and failure*" and "*Drugs and sport*" *contain 14 articles dealing with deviance in sport from a philosophical point of view*).

Stuck, M.F., ed. 1988. Drugs and sport. ARENA Review 12(1) (*six papers reflecting different theoretical and methodological themes*).

Todd, T. 1987. Anabolic steroids: the gremlins of sport. Journal of Sport History 14(1):87-107 (*historical analysis of the use of drugs by athletes with special reference to the recent use of steroids and efforts to control their use*).

Trulson, M.E. 1986. Martial arts training: a novel "cure" for juvenile delinquency. Human Relations 39(12):1131-1140 (*a unique study raising questions about how certain sports under certain circumstances might be used to decrease deviant behavior among young people*).

Voy, R. 1991. Drugs, sport, and politics. Leisure Press, Champaign, Ill. (*overview of drug usage in sports, critique of doping control policies in amateur sports, and recommendations for drug control policies; highly critical of current efforts to control performance-enhancing substances among athletes*).

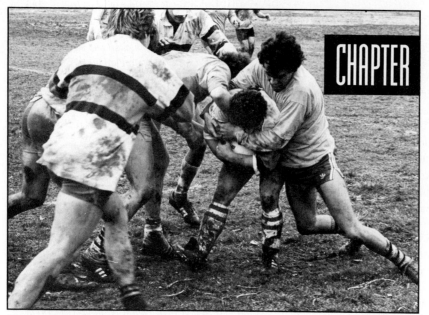

(Patrick Watson)

AGGRESSION IN SOCIETY

Are sports a cure or a cause?

CHAPTER 7

Serious sport has nothing to do with fair play. It is bound up with hatred, jealousy, boastfulness, disregard of all rules and sadistic pleasure in witnessing violence. In other words, it is war minus the shooting.

George Orwell (1950)

I developed a style the coaches loved. . . . From an early age, I had learned to endure violence and brutality as simply a part of my life. But in football, the brutality became legitimate, a way of being accepted on the football field and off.

David Meggyesy, former NFL player (1970)

Three out of every five Americans believe that violence is a serious problem in sports today, while half say fights between players lessen their enjoyment of the game. Seventy percent believe that sports violence is harmful to young viewers.

Miller Lite Report on American Attitudes Toward Sports (1983)

I get a charge out of pounding a guy. All the guys do. Hey, if you can't get a goal, get a hit. You can always hit somebody out there.

Eric Lindros, Philadelphia Flyers (Hockey team), (1992)

Some people say sports provide players and spectators opportunities to let off steam, release feelings of aggression, and learn to cope with stressful and highly emotional situations without resorting to overt aggression. They conclude that sport participation holds down rates of aggression and violent crime in society at large. Others reach the opposite conclusion. They say sports arouse the aggressive tendencies of players and spectators, teach people that success often requires aggressive tactics, and promote the idea that human beings, especially men, have an aggressive nature that will always be expressed in some form of violence.

The purpose of this chapter is to examine each of these conclusions in light of available research evidence. After defining aggression and violence we will look at the relationship between aggression and (1) instincts, (2) frustration, and (3) learning self-control through sport participation. Then we will examine the possibility that sports promote aggression as a legitimate way to achieve goals and as an inevitable expression of "human nature." Human aggression has long been a popular research topic in the social and behavioral sciences, so I will refer to a variety of studies in this chapter.

WHAT IS AGGRESSION?

People sometimes come to different conclusions about the relationship between sports and aggression because they do not define important terms in their discussions. Words such as *physical, assertive, rough, competitive, intimidating, aggressive, violent,* and *destructive* are often used interchangeably. Players are not always distinguished from spectators. Sports are usually lumped together without differentiating between those involving heavy physical contact, incidental contact, or no physical contact; and sport forms are seldom distinguished in terms of the goals and orientations of participants. Finally, the short-term effects of playing or watching are seldom distinguished from the long-term effects.

In this chapter I will use the term *aggression* to refer to all behavior intended to destroy another person's property or to injure another person, psychologically or physically. This definition allows me to distinguish aggressive behavior from other behaviors that might be described as assertive, competitive, or achievement-oriented. The term *violence* will be used to refer to all acts of physical aggression. In other words, *violence* is a form of physical assault based on an intent to injure another person or destroy the property of others. The term *intimidation* will be used to refer to verbal or physical behaviors that threaten violence. *Intimidation* does not cause physical harm, although it is often designed to produce psychological consequences, enabling a person to physically overpower or dominate another.

SPORTS AS A "CURE" FOR AGGRESSION IN SOCIETY

Those who see sports as a cure for aggressive behavior generally base their arguments on assumptions about human instincts, the connection between frustration and behavior, and the learning that occurs during sport participation.

Human Instincts and Aggression

It is widely believed that all forms of aggressive behavior are grounded in instincts. Theoretical support for this idea is usually based on the work of Sigmund Freud. According to Freudian theory, all humans possess a *death instinct*, sometimes referred to as the death wish. This death instinct takes the form of destructive energy within a person's psyche. If this energy is not released intentionally, it will eventually build up and be involuntarily released in the form of aggression against self (the extreme form of which is suicide) or against others (the extreme forms of which are murder and warfare). The only way this potentially destructive energy can be controlled is by finding an activity through which it can be released safely. This safe form of release is called a *catharsis*. Even though Freud's theory leaves many unanswered questions about the nature and operation of the death instinct, many people have applied it to sports. Their conclusion is that sport participation allows both players and spectators to safely release, or "drain off," innate aggressive energy.

Many ethologists have also advanced the idea that aggression is based on instincts (Ardrey, 1961 and 1966; Lorenz, 1966; Morris, 1967, 1981). Ethologists are scientists who are concerned with the biological foundations of animal behavior, and they usually study the behavior patterns of fish, birds, or animals in their natural habitats. Some have used this research as a basis for explaining human behavior. They argue that aggression is a product of evolution and that without aggressive instincts no species (including humans) would be able to survive. Like Freud, some of the ethologists assume that aggressive energy can safely be released through sports by both players and spectators. The spectators experience this release vicariously through watching and identifying with the actions of the players (Lorenz, 1966).

SIDELINES

"NOW THAT WE'VE INVENTED VIOLENCE, WE NEED A SPORT TO USE IT IN."

The connection between sport and violence has existed for a long time. The purpose of this chapter is to review material that will help us to understand this connection.

Peter Marsh (1978, 1982), a British social psychologist, has expanded the ideas of both Freud and the ethologists to argue that sport events serve as occasions for "ritual confrontations" between fans. In analyzing the behavior of young, male soccer fans in England, he concludes that these confrontations are relatively harmless, symbolic displays of aggressive energy. They are highly structured and predictable, and they serve to control the extent to which aggression is expressed in other spheres of life. In fact, Marsh argues that if the aggressive behaviors associated with soccer were suppressed, the rates of violent crime and fighting behavior in nonsport settings would increase.

The assumption underlying all three of these approaches is that humans are instinctively aggressive and that sports, especially contact sports, provide a safe "outlet" for aggressive behaviors that must be expressed in some form. This assumption is widely accepted by people in sports. For example, Vince Lombardi, the legendary American football coach, once explained that "the nature of man is to be aggressive and football is a violent game." For Lombardi, contact sports were basic expressions of human nature.

Mike Ditka, a former pro football player and former NFL coach, went beyond Lombardi's idea when he declared:

> There's no question about it. I feel a lot of football players build up a lot of anxieties in the off-season because they have no outlets for them. . . . I'm an overactive person anyway and if I don't get rid of this energy, it just builds up in me and then I blow it off in some other way which is not really the proper way (cited in Fisher, 1976).

For Ditka, participation in heavy contact sports was not only an expression of human nature, but it protected the rest of society from the violent expression of his aggressive energy.

Using instinct theory to argue that sports are a cure for aggression in society suffers from four weaknesses. These include the following:

First, there is no research support for the notion that aggressive behavior in humans is the product of biologically based destructive energy. Studies of the behavior of fish, birds, and mammals have suggested that some aggression may be natural, but these studies are of little help in developing a theory of *human* aggression. Human behavior is much more complex than the behavior of other species. Furthermore, the existence of instincts in humans has been questioned and debated for many years. And even if someone could make a convincing case that humans do have aggressive instincts, it would tell us little about human behavior. We would still have to explain why the rates of aggression vary from one group to another, why they vary over time in any single group, why aggression is highly correlated with certain social conditions, and why most human beings have to be coerced or socialized to do harm to others.

A *second* weakness in the instinct argument is that it assumes all sports are effective outlets for the aggressive energies of both players and spectators. However, it is quite certain that all sport activities do not provide the same opportunities for the release of aggression. For example, some sports do not even involve direct physical contact between opponents. Even in contact sports opportunities for players to engage in actual aggressive behavior may be few. Most of what occurs in a sport event would be a poor substitute for actual violent behavior. If it is a poor cathartic substitute for the players, there is little chance for spectators to vicariously release "innate aggressive energy" through merely watching and identifying with the action in a game. Furthermore, some athletes take care to minimize aggression in certain sport forms. This is illustrated in the box on pp. 168-169.

A *third* weakness is that there are no research findings supporting the idea that sport participation provides a catharsis for the supposed aggressive instincts of players or spectators. Numerous studies show that the existence and popularity of contact sports goes hand in hand with aggression and violence in societies around the world. Instead of allowing people to release the pent-up energy that instinct theorists say is the foundation of all aggression, contact sports seem to be expressions of the same orientations that underlie warfare and high rates of murder, domestic violence, and assault. For example, in a carefully designed comparison of 10 peaceful societies and 10 societies with long traditions of fighting many wars, anthropologist Richard Sipes (1975, 1976) found that contact sports were popular in 90% of the warlike societies and in only 20% of the peaceful societies. He would have found the exact opposite if contact sports actually helped people drain off aggressive energy. Other studies have shown that homicide rates in the United States increase immediately after television broadcasts of highly publicized boxing matches (Phillips, 1983) and that military activity is positively related to the popularity of contact sports in countries participating in the Olympic Games (Keefer et al., 1983).

The *fourth* weakness in the instinct argument is that it constantly refers to the aggressive behavior of men, and it ignores women and the ways through which so-called aggressive instincts and impulses might be released in the behavior of women. Since women are not usually involved in warfare or other forms of group violence or heavy contact sports to the same extent as men, what are their outlets for their supposed aggressive instincts? If women turn aggressive energy inward, their suicide rates should be much higher than the suicide rates for men; however, this is not the case. If women are releasing their aggressive impulses in other ways, they should be used as role models for men around the world.

In summary, the instinct argument provides no valid support for the notion that sport participation can serve as a cure for violent behavior among athletes or spectators. However, this argument remains popular because many people still use what I call the "language of catharsis" in their everyday conversations about human behavior. References to "releasing pent-up feelings of aggression" are continually made without thinking about the theoretical model implied by such statements.

Frustration and Aggression

Some people argue that aggression is always the result of frustration and that playing or watching sports can help people release frustrations and make them less likely to engage in aggressive behaviors. It would certainly be convenient if all of our feelings of frustration could be dealt with in such a way. But there is no evidence that direct involvement in sports does much beyond making us physically tired. Being physically tired can be a welcome feeling for a frustrated individual, but we should not equate being tired with being nonaggressive.

Playing racquetball, soccer, or any other sport for an hour does not guarantee that a person is going to be less aggressive when the game is over, nor does it do anything to eliminate the sources of frustration in a person's life. No matter how hard someone plays, the person or the situation that was the source of frustration today will still be there tomorrow. Playing or watching sports is not going to change the behavior of other people or the realities of life.

How about the possibility that vigorous physical exercise in sports makes people less violent by producing physiological or biochemical changes in the body? This is an interesting possibility. People frequently say they "feel better"—more relaxed and less stressed—after vigorous physical exercise. And research shows that vigorous exercise is associated with reductions in (1) muscular tension, (2) certain forms of anxiety, and (3) depression among some people (Morgan, 1984). However, it is not known if these changes are direct outgrowths of the *physiological and biochemical* consequences of exercise, or if exercise simply serves as a "time out" in the daily schedules of people who are temporarily bored, busy, or mildly depressed about how things are going in their lives (Mihevic, 1981; Morgan, 1984). Furthermore, none of the research on this topic has dealt with the possible links between sport participation and violent behavior.

If there is a decrease in the intent to do harm or inflict injury on others after sport participation, it probably results from the fact that intense involvement in any activity can put *time* between the individual and the frustrating conditions in the rest of life. Time can be used to calm down or to outline rational, nonaggressive ways of coping with the source of frustration. But playing a game of chess, meditating, or reading a good book could do the same thing *if* one became intensely involved in that activity. Playing sports with friends, however, may give people opportunities to get advice from others on how to define and deal with sources of frustration in their lives. In other words, in addition to a "time out," playing sports could provide an occasion for getting good advice on why not to do something aggressive in response to frustration.

Sport participation is often seen as a way to relieve frustration mainly because it involves intense concentration and often produces physical exhaustion. For most of us, participation in sports puts us in a setting separate from the more serious concerns of our daily existence. This, along with the heavy focus on physical movement and the social interaction occurring while we participate, makes sport refreshingly unique in most of our lives. However, those who use sports as a means of *proving* themselves rather than *expressing* themselves often create frustration in their lives. When these people lose or play poorly, they may leave the gym or playing field with more aggressive feelings than they had when they began their sport participation.

Just as there is nothing magic or automatic about playing sports and relieving frustrations, there is no evidence that watching sports serves to eliminate the frustrations of spectators (Smith, 1983). Watching sports may temporarily distract people from things causing them to be frustrated, but this does not necessarily make spectators more mellow and less aggressive in the rest of their lives.

In summary, arguments that link frustration and aggression provide only qualified support

There is no evidence supporting the widespread popular belief that players in heavy contact sports experience a catharsis, or draining off, of aggressive energy, making them less aggressive in other settings.

for the idea that sports can serve as a cure for aggression and violent crime.

Learning to Control Aggressive Behavior through Sports

It is popularly believed that sport participation teaches people to control aggressive responses in the face of defeat, hardship, and pain. In making this case, people often assume that learning to endure such negative conditions in sports will carry over into the rest of life and enable people to behave nonaggressively despite any adversity they might encounter.

There is some research support for this idea. For example, Zillmann et al. (1974) found that when male athletes were verbally insulted during a laboratory game they were less likely than nonathletes to respond by inflicting punishment on their opponents. Of course, this was a labo-

ratory situation and it is difficult to say whether similar results would occur in everyday life. Thirer (1978) found that after viewing a violent film on the activities of a street gang, scores on an aggression scale decreased slightly for female intercollegiate athletes and increased slightly for nonathletes. But these were scores on a paper-and-pencil test and they tell us little about what types of behavioral controls athletes learn during sport participation. Nosanchuk (1981) interviewed 42 students in three traditional karate dojos (studios) and found that training in karate was negatively associated with scores on an aggressive fantasy test. However, the training emphasized nonviolence, the individual mastery of skills, and self-defense (a standard philosophy in traditional karate and quite unlike the philosophies characteristic in Western contact sports).

In a study summarized in Chapter 6 (pp. 148-

The Military Model vs the Partnership Model:
Two Approaches to Sport

Not everyone sees sports in the same way, and there are many different ways to organize and define sports and physical activities. This is the theme underlying Mariah Burton Nelson's book, *Are we winning yet? How women are changing sports and sports are changing women*. Nelson's research and personal experiences as an intercollegiate and professional basketball player led her to conclude that there are two contrasting models people use to organize and guide their involvement in sports. Of course, most people don't use these models in pure forms; instead, they lean toward one or the other.

The most visible and highly publicized approach to sports in North America is embodied in what Nelson calls the *Military Model*. This approach to sports is characterized by an emphasis on the following:

- Obsessive ranking of teams and individuals according to playing statistics or earnings;
- Authoritarian, derisive relationships between coaches and players;
- Antagonism between opponents; and
- The inevitable question, "Who won?" (1991, p. 9).

Nelson says that the language used in connection with the Military Model emphasizes the use of bodies as tools or weapons and the need to destroy or dominate the opposition. Those who use this model to organize and guide their sport experiences see pain and injury as an inherent part of sport participation, and they emphasize the ability to play through pain and injury regardless of personal cost. They view opponents as enemies. They define power in terms of intimidation and physical domination. They form sport organizations characterized by autocratic leadership and a hierarchical ranking of members, and these organizations emphasize obedience to rules made up by people who are not directly involved in playing the sport.

In contrast to the Military Model is what Nelson calls the *Partnership Model*. The Partnership Model emphasizes that:

> teammates, coaches, and even opposing players view each other as comrades rather than enemies. Players with disparate ability levels are respected as peers rather than ranked in a hierarchy, and athletes care for each other and their own bodies. "To compete" is understood from its Latin source, *competere*: "to seek together" (Nelson, 1991, p. 9).

People who use the Partnership Model to organize and guide their sport experiences are motivated by their connection to others along with a love for their sport. They define power in terms of competence and believe that athletes should emphasize safe and open participation.

REFLECT ON   SPORT

The Partnership Model is not anticompetitive, but it is based on the assumptions that (a) athletes do not have to see opponents as enemies, (b) hate is not required for motivation, (c) coaches can be democratic, (d) violence has no place in sports, (e) facing challenges is more important than outscoring opponents, and (f) teams and players do not have to use scores and rankings to be motivated to seek excellence or evaluate sport experiences.

Nelson sees women as more likely to use the Partnership Model to organize and guide their sport experiences, and men as more likely to use the Military Model. But this pattern is related to cultural factors rather than to biological ones, and there are many exceptions to it. For example, a growing number of men use some variation of the Partnership Model in their sport participation. These men have recognized that the Military Model often leads to behaviors that destroy fitness and health. But in high-profile sports, men use the Military Model almost exclusively; for example, American football in high school, college, and the pros is clearly based on this model.

A growing number of women are confused about the relative merits of each model. Most don't like the Military Model and most don't want to use it to organize and guide their own sport experiences. However, many women are not ready to forfeit the rewards that come with playing and working in sport programs and organizations where the Military Model is used. Though more women are realizing that these programs and organizations have been developed by and for men over the years, they also know that if they want some of the external rewards that are available to men in sports, they have to participate in programs in which the Partnership Model is seen as inferior. Furthermore, some women use men as models of achievement and excellence and they accept the Military Model that men have used to guide and evaluate their sport experiences.

To the extent that the Military Model is used to organize sports and guide sport participation, aggression will be an institutionalized part of sport experiences—aggression will be defined as "natural." To the extent that the Partnership Model is used, aggression will be controlled and defined as a form of deviance among athletes, coaches, and spectators. At present, there is no evidence to suggest that the Military Model will be abandoned or even changed in the vast majority of organized sport programs in North America; the men who control major sport programs and organizations have long used that model to evaluate athletes and the qualifications of employees. They say that to be "qualified" as an athlete or an employee in a sport organization a person must be competitive and aggressive, and that being supportive and caring are nice but they don't really count as qualifications. This is how sports have become "gendered" and how aggression has come to be defined as a part of the actual structure of many sports.

149) Trulson (1986) found a decrease in aggressive tendencies among male juvenile delinquents given training in the philosophy and techniques of Tae Kwon Do. The philosophy emphasized "respect for others, building confidence and self-esteem, the importance of physical fitness, patience, perseverance, . . . honor, . . . [and] a sense of responsibility." Aggressive tendencies increased among similar young men who received training in Tae Kwon Do *without* the philosophy, and they remained unchanged in a group participating in running, basketball, and football with standard adult supervision.

Therefore it seems that participation in sports, even in the martial arts, can encourage the control of aggressive behaviors *if* sports promote an orientation that emphasizes a clear-cut philosophy of nonviolence. However, a philosophy of nonviolence is not regularly taught in conjunction with most sports in Western societies. Instead there is usually an emphasis on hostility and physical domination and willingness to sacrifice physical well-being and endure pain for the sake of competitive success. In connection with this type of "military model" many sports announcers refer to these forms of positive deviance as "courage," and this generally undermines a philosophy of nonviolence.

It is likely that much of the control learned in dominant sport forms in many societies, including the United States and Canada, is related to doing an effective job within the legal limits of game rules. Therefore certain forms of aggression are discouraged simply because they often bring penalties. But control is not based on any real concerns for the safety and well-being of other people. Players are seldom told to be careful not to hurt opponents. This means athletes may be learning only a limited form of control aimed at winning games rather than at controlling violence in life in general (Russell, 1983).

In a similar fashion, the nonviolence of athletes in noncontact sports probably has little to do with any controls learned through sport participation. Noncontact sports provide few opportunities to be aggressive or violent. For example, it is difficult to say that swimmers or marathoners are learning to control the expression of aggression just because they don't physically attack other swimmers or runners. Instead, violence is absent because it is totally inappropriate and there are no opportunities to be violent.

Even if it could be shown that athletes do learn to control aggressive behaviors during a game or contest, it would be another thing to say that this control carries over into the rest of life. Just because a football player does not attack a referee after being called for a penalty does not mean he has learned to control himself when dealing with authority figures. And just because a player does not fight during a game does not mean the same restraint will be used on the street after a game.

In summary, there is little evidence suggesting that athletes learn to control the expression of aggressive behaviors through their involvement in sports. There is no evidence that this occurs for spectators. When control is shown on the field by athletes, it is more likely to be based on concerns for winning games than on concerns for the physical well-being of others. Of course, any reason for controlling aggression is good. But if motivation is solely based on a concern for winning games it is very doubtful that it will carry over into nonsport situations.

SPORTS AS A "CAUSE" OF AGGRESSION IN SOCIETY

The argument that many sport forms increase rates of aggression and violent crime in society is based on three beliefs: (1) that participating in or watching sports creates frustrations leading to violence, (2) that people involved with certain sports learn to define violence as a useful tool for achieving success, and (3) that dominant sport forms in many societies perpetuate ideas about masculinity that lead people to think that men are naturally superior to women because of men's ability to do violence.

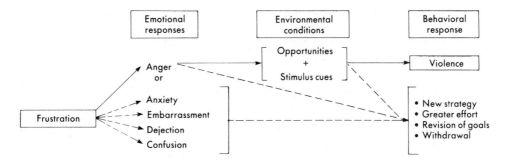

FIG. 7-1 The link between frustration in the sport experience and the aggressive behavior of athletes.

Sport Experiences, Frustration, and Aggression

Some athletes may love to play their sports so much that they never get frustrated at how they play or if they lose, and some spectators may be so taken in by the beauty of a performance or the efforts of the performers that they feel no frustration when they watch sports. However, few people fit into these categories. Usually, athletes and spectators *are* concerned with outcomes, and they *do* see sports as means of proving something to themselves or others. This means that frustration often accompanies sports participation.

Two things are necessary for frustration to lead to aggression: (1) the frustration must give rise to an emotional response of *anger*, and (2) the situation must contain *opportunities* and *stimulus cues* for aggressive behavior (Berkowitz, 1969). Figure 7-1 illustrates this chain of events. Just follow the solid line in the figure to see when aggression is likely to be a result of the frustration experienced in sports. Each of the broken lines indicates all of the possible nonaggressive responses to frustration. The broken lines indicate the following:

1. Anger is not the only emotional response to frustration; athletes may experience other emotional responses that would lead to nonaggressive behaviors.

2. Anger, even when it does occur, can be channeled into nonaggressive behavioral alternatives.

3. The combination of anger, opportunities to be aggressive, and the existence of stimulus cues (that is, things that can be used as tools for violence) increase the likelihood of aggressive behaviors, but players may still choose alternative behaviors for many reasons.

Anger is most likely when players feel they are victims of unfair calls by referees or unfair tactics by opponents (Mark et al., 1983). Opportunities to be aggressive are most frequent in heavy contact sports, and stimulus cues are strongest in sports in which athletes use equipment that can be associated with violence and transformed into weapons. Therefore violence is most likely to be a problem in a sport such as ice hockey, in which physical contact affords opportunities and hockey sticks can be used as weapons. Football provides opportunities to be violent, but stimulus cues are less apparent—except when the helmet is seen as a weapon. Baseball, even though it involves little physical contact, provides pitchers with opportunities for violence, and baseballs in the hands of pitchers have occasionally been seen as weapons. However, it must be remembered that anger plus opportunities and stimulus cues do not automatically lead to violence; they only increase the likelihood that violent forms of aggression will occur. Figure 7-1 is also helpful in explaining displays of aggressive behaviors among *spectators*. For frustration among fans to lead to aggression, the following three things must happen:

1. There must be enough of an identification with one of the players or teams to provide the basis for frustration.
2. Anger must be the dominant emotional response among the fans.
3. Opportunities for aggression and/or stimulus cues must be present.

In many cases, individual spectators may not identify with players or teams to the extent necessary to produce frustration. However, when identification is strong enough and when frustration is followed by anger, the threat of aggression is prevented only by the absence of opportunities or the lack of stimulus cues. This is the reason why spectators from opposing sides are sometimes separated from one another during and after a game and why there are rules prohibiting them from bringing bottles and cans into the stands. Contact between angered losers and exuberant winners creates an obvious opportunity for violence, and objects such as bottles and cans are easily seen as stimulus cues for violent behavior when an official makes a "bad call" or when players and coaches do not live up to expectations.

Sport Experiences and Learning to Use Aggression As a Strategy

NONCONTACT SPORTS In certain forms of noncontact sports, participants may psychologically intimidate their opponents, but the actual use of violence is rare. When violence does occur it is usually outside the normal action of the sport, and it is generally punished with fines or other severe sanctions. Players in noncontact sports are seldom, if ever, rewarded for violent behavior. Therefore it is doubtful that playing or watching these sports teaches people to use

violence as a strategy on or off the field. If athletes in these sports act violently off the field, their actions may be related to frustrations caused by their sport careers, the repressive control systems used by their coaches (or parents), or many other factors. But the violence is not likely to be a carryover from the actual behavior patterns learned in their sport experiences.

Intimidation is used in some noncontact sports. However, little has been written about the forms this intimidation might take or how it might be related to general forms of aggression outside sport settings. Usually, research focuses on violence, not intimidation.

CONTACT SPORTS: MALE ATHLETES Violent behavior and intimidation are often learned as strategies in dominant sport forms in many societies. Both can be used to win games and build rewarding reputations. Evidence shows that rule-violating behaviors and certain forms of violence are readily accepted by players in contact sports, and as the amount of contact increases in a sport, so does this acceptance (Silva, 1983; Bredemeier and Shields, 1983, 1984b, 1985). Intimidation and violent behavior are often seen as permissible, as long as they do not disrupt the flow of action in the games or lead to injuries that affect players after games are over. Athletes in certain contact sports sometimes talk about wanting to injure opponents enough to take them out of games, but not enough to negatively affect their lives apart from sports (see the cartoon on p. 175).

In heavy contact sports (such as football, ice hockey, and rugby), intimidation and violence have become widely used as strategies for winning games, promoting individual careers, and increasing profits for sponsors. For example, a professional hockey player explains that "sometimes when you're losing or your team is flat, you need to rough it up a bit to give the other team a message . . . [Y]ou have to fight . . . [and] I'd like to think I helped our team to win some games because I did rough it up . . ." (cited in Swift, 1986). As long as this orientation exists among players, and as long as rules

The connection between violence and masculinity runs deep in many cultures. This connection often carries over into sports at both behavioral and symbolic levels. This is shown in the uniforms of an amateur baseball team in Japan and the jacket of a student-organized rugby club in an American high school. Among certain groups of men the willingness and ability to engage in violence is a basis for status among peers. (Jay Coakley)

permit its expression in a sport, violence and intimidation will be used.

Jack Tatum, the NFL defensive player whose tackle in 1979 broke Darryl Stingley's neck, also provides telling insights into the use of violence and intimidation as strategies. First, he proudly states that he would like to believe that his "best hits border on felonious assault" (1979). Then after discovering that one of his assaults left Stingley paralyzed from the shoulders down for life he explained that, "It was one of those pass plays where I could not possibly have intercepted, *so because of what the owners expect of me when they give me my paycheck* I automatically reacted to the situation by going for an intimidating hit" (1979, emphasis added). After Tatum made the hit on Stingley, a loud cheer came from the stands. And later, while Stingley sat in his wheelchair, Tatum wrote and published a money-making book entitled *They Call Me Assassin*. Violence sometimes pays off in contact sports.

Of course, few players in contact sports would say they want to seriously injure their opponents; but some admit they try to hurt their opponents enough to dominate them during a game. For example, Dick Butkus, a former NFL linebacker, explained his use of physical tactics this way: "You want to hurt, but not to injure. . . . I want to flatten and intimidate my opponents. I want to absolutely destroy them. But I still want them ready to go the next day" (1972). Such an attitude certainly suggests violence. And it would certainly encourage violent behaviors among some opponents.

The use of violence in contact sports is no secret. In fact, in some sports it has become a serious problem. Journalists have described it, sociologists and psychologists have tried to explain it, and athletes have bragged, complained, and testified in court about it (Goldstein, 1983; Horrow, 1980; Smith, 1983). And whenever an athlete dies or is paralyzed the media run a series

SIDELINES

WHEN ARE YOU GONNA LEARN WHEN IT'S NECESSARY TO USE UNNECESSARY ROUGHNESS?

In heavy contact sports, violent behavior and intimidation are often learned as strategies. Both can be used to win games and build reputations.

of stories on violence in sports. Although all players do not feel comfortable with the amount of violence in their sports, they have generally come to accept it. Even those who don't like it may reluctantly use it as a way of improving or maintaining their positions on teams and their popularity with spectators. Those who don't use it may find their positions on teams in jeopardy—as happened to an NHL player when he refused to obey his coach's order to join a fight in progress during a game; the player was quickly demoted to the minor leagues as punishment (Schaap, 1982).

Athletes in contact sports learn very early in their sport careers that they will be evaluated on their ability to use violence in combination with physical skills (Vaz, 1982). During this learning process, they are encouraged to be violent by peers and teammates and sometimes by coaches and parents (Smith, 1983). By the time they reach top levels of competition, they don't even give violence a second thought during a game (Faulkner, 1974a, b; Pilz, 1979). For example, after seriously injuring another player in an

NFL game, a defensive lineman explained that, "I just got a little too rough. It was just a reaction. I just took him down. I wasn't thinking of a shoulder injury or a knee injury or anything. We just go for live meat" (cited in Bock, 1986). However, before the game this lineman came on to the field with what he called his "hit list" written on a towel tucked in his waist. The first name on the list belonged to the player he injured. This violence may have been the result of a thoughtless reaction during the game itself, but the scene was knowingly set to ignore the consequences of violence.

Sports do not have to be played this way, but there is little effort to discourage such scenes. Owners, television announcers, and sponsors seldom say a discouraging word. In fact, violent incidents are often replayed in numerous slow-motion shots during the game and after the game and may even be put in special videotapes to be sold to fans who want to see dozens of such scenes one after another. The players in these scenes are often praised for what are violent acts.

To make matters even worse, some players act as designated "enforcers" or "goons" or "hit men" on heavy-contact sport teams. These team members are expected to intimidate, provoke, or injure opponents. They are paid to be violent. As one enforcer explains, "Nobody thought I'd ever amount to anything as a hockey player. I never skated well. . . . But I started making teams because I could fight. That's how I made it this far" (cited in Swift, 1986). A general manager of an NHL team explains why players like this make it to the top: "Intimidation is . . . a big factor in hockey. In fact it's probably the major factor. Every team likes to have one or two enforcers or designated hit men so that the rest of the team feels comfortable" (cited in Swift, 1986). And just how do enforcers make their teammates feel comfortable? According to a legendary hockey goon, "It makes sense to try and take out a guy who's more important to his team than I am to mine" (cited in Kennedy, 1975). Questions are now being raised about this strategy because some of hockey's most skillful and popular players have been sidelined for serious back injuries resulting from constantly being hit from behind by goons and goon-like opponents.

The role of enforcer has nothing to do with frustration or anger generated during a game, so it is hard to explain this type of violence with frustration-aggression theory. Another hockey player, known for his fighting and violent behavior, explains this very clearly: "I don't know if I ever really get all that mad. You have to have a clear head when you fight. You don't want to be swinging wildly. You try to aim at the nose or the chin, someplace where . . . it'll cause damage. Broken nose, broken jaw. . . . There's no sense getting into a fight if you're not trying to hurt them" (cited in Swift, 1986).

Because of the visibility and popularity of professional sports, the violent behavior of top-level athletes is often imitated by players at lower levels of competition. Michael Smith (1974) found that Canadian high school hockey players who identified with violent professional players were more assaultive in their own games than high school players who identified with less violent professional players. Unless something is done to break this cycle, the problem of violence in sport will continue to grow.

Do violent strategies learned in sports carry over to the rest of life? Research clearly shows that many male athletes in heavy contact sports learn to accept and use violence and intimidation as strategies during competition. But does this learning carry over into the rest of their lives? This important question remains unanswered. It would seem that most athletes are capable of distinguishing between the playing field and other types of interaction settings. And most should realize that the aggressive strategies

"How many times do I have to tell you, ref, I'm not a violent player! I didn't want to injure him, I only wanted to hurt him enough to make him afraid of me for the rest of the game."

used in their sports are not appropriate in the classroom, in a bar, or on the streets. However, the violent off-the-field reputations of some athletes indicate that research is needed on this question.

Research on the carryover issue must be carefully designed. If data show a high rate of off-the-field aggression among athletes, this does not mean that their aggressive behavior patterns were learned in sports. It is possible that people who choose to play heavy contact sports are more likely than others to see aggression as an appropriate way to deal with life events. Playing contact sports may not be making them any more aggressive than they would have been without sport involvement. Furthermore, athletes with reputations for being aggressive on the playing field might receive extra encouragement from people outside of sports to be violent on the streets. They may even be challenged to get involved in fights because of their reputations in sports. If this does happen, researchers must be careful in deciding whether off-the-field behavior patterns of athletes are learned in sports and then carried over into other situations or whether they are grounded in other factors.

How is violence connected to masculinity and race? The carryover question cannot be separated from issues related to the social construction of gender and the social construction of sports. For example, according to many social scientists (cf. Bryson, 1987; Connell, 1987a,b; Messner, 1992; Messner and Sabo, 1992; Sabo, 1986), dominant sport forms in most societies have been socially constructed in ways that not only ritualize aggression but tie the expression of aggression to certain forms of masculinity. Being able to "do" violence has become a part of gaining respect "as a man" within many male groups (Loy, 1992; Messner, 1992). This is especially true in certain sports. Sociologist Mike Messner explains:

> Young males come to sport with identities that lead them to define their athletic experience differently than females do. Despite the fact that few

males truly enjoy hitting and being hit, and that one has to be socialized into participating in much of the violence commonplace in sport, males often view aggression, within the rule-bound structure of sport, as legitimate and "natural" (p. 67).

In fact, Messner explains that many male athletes learn not to see injurious acts as violence, even when they are done with intent to hurt, as long as they are within the rules of the game and as long as they are not motivated by anger.

This orientation makes contact sports especially dangerous places to be, but many men choose to be there because they have learned to define masculinity in terms of being tough enough to participate in the give and take of violent confrontations. And when the give and take of violence leads to injury and pain, men learn to "suck it up" and stay in the game, not just because of what it means to be an athlete, but because of what it means to be a man in their world. As long as men do not question this self-destructive orientation, contact sports will continue to be the sites for aggressive and self-destructive behaviors.

Issues of masculinity often overlap with racial issues when it comes to aggression in sport. For example, Messner's study of male athletes led him to conclude that some black male athletes capitalize on the racist stereotypes held by whites by presenting a "bad-assed" image to intimidate competitors. This is explained by a quote from one of the men he interviewed:

> I'm tall, I'm thin, I'm a black person with a shaved head, and I'm fearful. You have to intimidate mentally . . . you've got to talk shit in this game, you have to say, . . . "If you come close to me, I'm gonna hurt you!"

This statement illustrates how gender and race get tied together for some athletes, and it also shows that the connection between these two can provide the basis for increased violence in sports.

CONTACT SPORTS: FEMALE ATHLETES
There is very little information on violence among girls and women in sports. One study of

a small sample of U.S. intercollegiate athletes found that women who participated in contact sports had lower scores on an "attitude toward violence scale" than men who participated in either contact or noncontact sports (Brown and Davies, 1978). The women were less likely to see violence as an acceptable method of solving problems. But the study did not address the question of actual behavioral differences between men and women. Nor did it explain how attitudes toward violence might be related to things other than gender.

Other research has also reported lower tolerance of violence and intimidation among women than men in both North America (Bredemeier, 1982, 1984; Bredemeier and Shields, 1984a; and Silva, 1983) and Europe (Pilz, 1979). But as the level of competition gets higher, both male and female players are increasingly tolerant of rule

violations and violent acts on the playing field. But this pattern is less clear among women than among men. According to Brenda Bredemeier (1984) and others (Duquin, 1984; Nelson, 1991) this may be due to one or more of the following factors: (a) the ways girls and women are socialized, (b) the ways many women prefer play sports (see box on pp. 168-169), and (c) the fact that dominant conceptions of femininity have never been linked to aggression.

After a thorough review of the issue of women, sports, and violence, sociologist Michael Smith (1983) concluded that since the early 1970s, women's participation rates increased in contact sports, and that violence among women in those sports does occur. However, the studies did not enable him to make conclusions about whether violence among women athletes is increasing or about the causes of violence among women.

Although many women are tough competitors in sports they are less likely than men to use the "Military Model" and therefore less likely to incorporate violence into their games and matches to the same extent that some men have done. (Colorado Springs Gazette Telegraph and John Russell)

Whether violence among girls and women will ever match the violence in sports played by boys and men is unlikely. However, it could be hypothesized that as the rewards for winning continue to increase for women in certain sports, women will increasingly use aggressive tactics. And as girls are taught to define sports in the same way as boys, they may develop similar strategies for success. In the terms explained by Mariah Burton Nelson (1991), some women may be willing to use the Military Model rather than the Partnership Model if the external rewards are high enough. But women may never accept debilitating injuries to the same extent that men do because they will not use injuries as "femininity badges" like men use injuries as "masculinity badges." In other words, violence will not be seen by women as a means of reaffirming their womanhood. In most women's lives "daring" will remain less important than "caring" when it comes to the way they define what is important to them (Lenskyj, 1986). Therefore the production of violence in women's sports will continue to be different in at least one respect from the production of violence in men's sports.

Sports, Violence, and the Gender Order

"Men are naturally superior to women." This statement will arouse anger among many people today. But many others still believe it, and when the believers defend their position they often turn to sports to get "proof" of so-called male superiority. For example, J. Carroll, a physical educator in England, argues that women are naturally tender, nurturant, and compassionate, and that when women participate in sports they destroy the political and military values that define what he thinks sports and masculinity are all about (Carroll, 1986). For this reason, Carroll even argues that women ought to be excluded from playing sports.

The irony in Carroll's position is that if gender differences were really grounded in biology, there would be no need for them to be taught and preserved through sports; they would just

come "naturally." But gender differences are not grounded in biology and they don't come naturally, so those who have an interest in promoting so-called "natural" differences often promote certain forms of sports that emphasize the physical power and strength of men. For example, when Michael Messner asked a 32-year-old white man in a professional job what he thought about the recent promotion of a woman to a high position in his organization, the man replied,

> A woman can do the same job I do—maybe even be my boss. But I'll be *damned* if she can go out on the [football] field and take a hit from Ronnie Lott (1992, p. 168).

Messner argues that even though this man could not "take a hit" from the San Francisco 49ers defensive back (Lott) either, he identified with Lott as a man, and then he used that identification to explain that men are superior to women because of men's ability to do violence.

This way of thinking about men and gender relations is strongly related to child abuse, spouse abuse, rape, gang rape, assault, and murder in the United States, Canada, and other societies. The idea that power and strength are the basis for superiority is now being challenged by many people, but sports have been used to "naturalize" this idea in the minds of many men and women. This is why some people promote sports in which aggression is commonplace. And these are usually the same people who reject rules against fighting and other forms of violence by saying that "we can't turn our sport into a girls' game"! For example, when recent rules were passed to partially limit fighting in hockey, Tie Domi, a hockey player with a reputation for being aggressive complained:

> If you take out fighting, what comes next? Do we eliminate checking? Pretty soon, we will all be out there in dresses and skirts (1992).

Domi's point is that unless men can do violence in hockey there will be nothing that makes them different from women, and nothing is worse than being like women—unless men are homophobic, and then the only thing as bad as being a woman is being gay.

In fact, when athletes fail to make plays, some coaches will refer to them as girls or question their manhood in some other way (such as calling them "fags"). A respected intercollegiate men's basketball coach has been known to grab his players between the legs when they make mistakes and tell them he's checking to see if they are really men (what would happen to a college teacher who did that?!). These threats to masculinity have been known to motivate young men to do extremely violent things on the playing field in an effort to demonstrate they are really men. And the coaches who motivate them in this way are often held in high esteem by others who want to preserve the notion that men are indeed superior to women. Meanwhile, violence gets built right in to certain sports and it stays because it is tied to the way some people define manhood. This makes violence very difficult to control, and those who do try may even be called "pussies" by those who define masculinity in terms of an ability to be violent and physically dominate others (which makes my point about violence and the gender order better than I ever could!).

Summary and Analysis

Aggression in the forms of violence and intimidation occurs in certain sports, especially those involving physical contact. The origins of aggression are related to a combination of (1) frustration coupled with anger and stimulus cues, (2) strategies used by athletes and encouraged by coaches, spectators, and sponsors, and (3) definitions of masculinity emphasizing violence as a basis for manhood and for the superiority of men over women. However, there is no research showing that athletes themselves are more likely to use violence in nonsport settings *because of* their experiences in sport. This is not to say carryover never happens, but we have no proof that it occurs regularly or in an identifiable pattern.

Another fact that could be related to aggres-

sion in sports is the great insecurity associated with being an athlete on a highly competitive sport team. The idea that "you're only as good as your last game" is widespread. This means personal feelings of worth along with each player's status as a team member are constantly threatened within many sport settings. Under these circumstances, athletes are often willing to take extreme measures to "prove" themselves, even if they involve violence. Therefore violence becomes a means for athletes to prove their worth and establish membership on their teams. In the case of men it also becomes a way to reaffirm their manhood. This is how injuries often become defined as indications of personal failure, if they force a player to quit during a game. But if the player remains in the game, injuries become "badges of courage" after the game is over. And for men they also become badges of "manhood."

Within the social context of the team, the willingness to face and use violence and to endure its consequences creates an intense form of drama and excitement that can facilitate strong emotions among the members of a team. The sharing of these emotional experiences sometimes leads to relationships that athletes perceive as special. In fact, some ex-athletes talk about their sport experiences and relationships with old teammates in the same way that war veterans talk about old military buddies and battlefield relationships. Despite the pain and injuries they may still carry with them, they claim that the risks and relationships associated with sport participation made them feel alive and aware in ways that nonathletes simply cannot understand. As long as athletes feel this way, they will continue to define violence as behavior that extends their lives rather than as behavior that restricts, limits, and sometimes ends their lives.

SPORTS AND AGGRESSION AMONG SPECTATORS

Does violence in sports increase rates of violence in the personal lives of spectators? This question is important because so many spectators around the world seem to be attracted to sports that emphasize action and physical contact.

In considering this question it is important to note that most spectating takes the form of quiet watching and orderly behavior. Spectators watching noncontact sports such as golf, tennis, swimming, gymnastics, bowling, track and field, figure skating, and so on are generally well-behaved. They have killed no officials, maimed no athletes (until 1993), and they have not disrupted games, matches, meets, or races. Those who watch contact sports are more vocal and emotional, but are not usually violent.

After carefully reviewing the social psychological research on violence among sport spectators, Dolf Zillmann and his colleagues (1983) concluded that "the typical sports fan manages his or her emotions admirably. He or she may yell and stomp the ground, but, after the game, he or she will usually be no more vicious than after an exciting movie or a stimulating concert." Allen Guttmann (1986) reached a similar conclusion in his historical analysis of *Sports Spectators*.

Norms for behavior are different at sport events than they are in other settings, but norms do exist, and spectators generally follow them. People may feel free to be more animated and vocal while expressing their emotions at a football game than at a sale in a shopping mall, but that does not mean there are no rules for behavior at the game. When rowdy fans interfere with the enjoyment of others, most people realize that norms have been broken and something should be done to control the behavior of the offending person or group.

Expressive behavior is accepted and encouraged at sport events, but most fans manage to control their behavior so it falls within acceptable limits. Exceptions to this do occur, but they are amazingly rare at most events. (Jen Cembalisty)

The Effects of Watching Sports at Home

It is well known that people who watch sports on television enjoy action, conflict, and highly motivated performances by athletes (Coakley, 1989), but care should be taken before using this fact to conclude that media audiences want to see violence or that watching violence in sports makes them more violent in their personal lives. It is doubtful that more than a small number of media spectators would be entertained by regularly watching random or blatantly irrational displays of violence in sports. The shock value of such incidents may be high, and people may talk about them in their accounts of games, but most do not see them as entertaining in themselves.

In dealing with this issue, Michael Smith, the author of *Violence and Sport* (1983), asked young hockey fans in Canada what they thought about the fighting in professional hockey games. Of the 756 young people interviewed, 60% of those who played hockey and 87% of those who were not hockey players wanted *less* fighting in professional games. Only 2% of the entire sample wanted more fighting. Of course, when fights do occur, they attract attention, but this does not mean that people watching these sports are ready to incorporate violence into their own lives, or that they approve of violence in a moral sense, or that they even look forward to seeing violence in future sports coverage.

Spectators usually define roughness in sports as enjoyable when the roughness is seen as an outgrowth of an athlete's motivation and efforts to achieve a legitimate goal. When roughness and violent acts are seen to interfere with goal achievement or disrupt action, spectators do not define them as entertaining. Therefore when a player on a fan's favorite football team makes a bone-breaking legal tackle that stops the opposition from scoring the winning touchdown, the fan cheers; but when the same player starts a fight that leads to a penalty, the fan calls the player a fool. The average fan is looking for highly motivated, goal-directed action, not violence.

Finally, research shows that watching violence in sports does not have any short- or intermediate-term effects on the way people play sports (Smith, 1983). There may be long-term effects, but these have not been pinpointed in research. Furthermore, there have been no studies indicating that "exposure to the media coverage of sports has any effect on general attitudes or everyday life behaviors" (Coakley, 1989). This does not mean that watching certain sports has no effect on aggressive behavior in society, but this issue requires more investigation, preferably through interviews and observations rather than experiments and questionnaires.

The Effects of Going to an Event

Media reports of violent behavior at sport events around the world have led many people to conclude that spectator violence is quite common and very serious. There is no doubt that when deaths, injuries, and property damage occurs, the actions of spectators take on serious implications. But considering the number of events held every week, the record of behavior among sport fans is surprisingly nonviolent.

When spectators do engage in violence, their behavior is related to three sets of factors:

1. The action in the sport event itself.
2. Crowd dynamics and the situation in which the event is watched.
3. The historical, social, economic, and political context in which the event is planned and played.

VIOLENCE AND ACTION IN THE EVENT Research indicates that spectator violence is related to the actions of players during an event. If players' actions are perceived as violent, spectators are more likely to engage in violent acts during and after games (Berkowitz, 1972a; Smith, 1983). This point is important because the perceptions of spectators are often influenced by the ways in which events are promoted. If an event is promoted for its potentially violent content, spectators are more likely to perceive violence during the event itself and, when they perceive

"HEY WATCH IT, PAL! YOU STEPPED ON MY FOOT!"

The language used in association with sports often refers to violent behavior, but it is not known if that language is actually associated with violence among spectators.

violence, they are more likely to be violent themselves. Because of this, some people argue that promoters and the media have a responsibility to advertise events in terms of the action and drama expected, not the blood and violence. I agree.

Another important factor in the event is the action of the officials. If referees or umpires make calls perceived as unfair by spectators, the likelihood of violence increases (Mark et al., 1983). Research on this issue is needed, but it seems that when fans believe a crucial goal or a victory has been "stolen" by a clearly incompetent or unfair call by an official, they are more likely to engage in violent acts during or following the event. This is why it is important to have competent officials at crucial games and matches, and why it is important for them to control game events so actions that may be perceived as violent are held to a minimum. Knowing that a riot may be precipitated by a crucial call late in a close, important contest puts heavy responsibility on the shoulders of the officials.

VIOLENCE, CROWD DYNAMICS, AND SITUATIONAL FACTORS The characteristics of a crowd and the immediate situation associated

with a sport event also influence behavior patterns among spectators. Spectator violence is likely to vary with one or more of the following factors:*

- The size of the crowd and the standing or seating patterns among spectators
- The social composition of the crowd (age, sex, socioeconomic characteristics, and the racial/ethnic mix of people are often important)
- The importance of a victory or the meaning of the event for one or both opponents
- The history of the relationship between the teams and groups of spectators attending the event
- The system of crowd control used at the event (police, attack dogs, or other security measures)
- The amount of alcohol consumed by the spectators
- The location of the event (that is, is it in a neutral location or at the home site of one of the opponents?)
- The motivations among spectators for attending the event

Each of these factors will not be discussed in detail, but here's an example that explains how many of them might be related to the incidence of spectator violence: The *location of an event* is important because it has implications for the form of transportation used by spectators. This means a football game played in Los Angeles between the Rams and the New York Giants is very different from a soccer game played in Manchester between Manchester United and Liverpool. Few New York fans can attend the game in Los Angeles, and those who do make the trip are likely to keep a low profile because they don't have many fellow New Yorkers around them. Furthermore, the Los Angeles

---

*See Edwards and Rackages, 1977; Gilbert and Twyman, 1983; Goldstein, 1989; Guttmann, 1986; Lewis, 1982; Maguire, 1986; Murphy et al., 1990; Smith, 1983; Taylor, 1982, 1987; White, 1982; Williams et al., 1984.

Coliseum is best reached by car, which means that spectators go to the game in small groups and, in most cases, they will not be drinking heavily during the drive. Game tickets cost $30, so those going to the game are middle class or upper middle class and have much to lose if they are arrested.

On the other hand, in England it is only a 20-mile train ride from Liverpool to Manchester. The soccer teams in both these cities have existed for nearly 100 years, and the rivalry between them has a long tradition. When they play each other, thousands of fans for the visiting team fill dozens of train cars to make the trip to the game. Game tickets are reasonably priced, so many spectators are young working class men (soccer itself has always been defined as a "working class men's game"). These fans arrive at the host city in large groups at the same train station. Drinking may be heavy; scarves are worn to identify team loyalties; and many fans, especially young males who are looking for action, want to make their presence known when they arrive at the stadium. This sets up a completely different set of crowd dynamics from those in Los Angeles. The crowd dynamics at the soccer game in England are more likely to foster violence than are the crowd dynamics at the NFL game in Los Angeles.

The *system of crowd control* used during events may also be an important factor influencing spectators' behavior. For example, British soccer stadiums have generally been fortified to look like and feel like prison camps rather than sport facilities. The security systems often include 12-foot fences, barbed wire barriers around the stadium and between sections within the stadium, tightly segregated seating that restricts movement, one-way turnstiles and gates often guarded or locked, police patrols around the field and through the stands, and few amenities to meet the needs and interests of the spectators. As Allen Guttmann has noted, this approach to crowd control not only makes the spectators, most of whom are working-class males, feel like outsiders, but it also fosters a siege mentality that encourages defensiveness if

not violent confrontations. After all, "Build a cage to hold a person and that person is likely to act like a caged animal" (Guttmann, 1986).*

Crowd dynamics may also be influenced by *crowd size and composition.* This is not to say that big, homogeneous crowds are especially prone to violence. However, when a crowd is made up almost exclusively of working class young men, many of whom are looking for action and memorable experiences, and when the stadium is packed with people representing opposing teams, it would be reasonable to be prepared for violent incidents. These incidents can take numerous forms. They might be celebratory riots among the fans of the winning team, fights between fans of opposing teams, random attacks on property perpetrated by fans of the losing team as they leave town, panics incited by some perceived threat unrelated to the event itself, isolated attacks on a referee who makes an unpopular call, or planned confrontations between groups using the event as a convenient place to face off with each other.

Whenever thousands of people get together for an occasion intended to generate collective emotions, crowd dynamics and circumstances become important forces influencing the behavior of individuals and groups. This is especially true at sport events, and sometimes violence among spectators is the result. After it starts, this violence can be especially destructive because it is fueled by what some social psychologists call *emotional contagion.* In other words, when circumstances are confusing, people look to each other for cues as to how to feel and how to behave. As they see others acting in extreme ways, they often follow suit, if they think extreme behavior is warranted.

---

*The causes of violence at British soccer games are much more complex than I can explain in a short example. Many books have been written about the behavior of soccer fans in general and English soccer fans in particular (Murphy et al., 1990; Taylor, 1982, 1987; Williams et al., 1984). And there remain a number of debatable issues about the causes of spectator violence at soccer games.

VIOLENCE AND THE OVERALL CONTEXT IN WHICH THE EVENT OCCURS Sport events are not held in social vacuums. When spectators attend events, they bring with them the histories, issues, controversies, and ideologies that exist in the communities and societies in which they live. They may be racists who want to harass others. They may resent negative things in their lives and want to express their bitterness. They may be powerless and alienated and looking for ways to be noticed and defined as socially important. They may be young men who believe that manhood is achieved through violence and dominance over others. Or they may be living lives so devoid of significance and excitement that they want to create a memorable occasion they can proudly discuss with friends for weeks to come. In other words, when thousands of spectators attend a sport event, their behavior is grounded in factors going far beyond the event and the stadium.

When conflict and violence are widespread in a community or society, sport events are likely to be characterized by related forms of conflict and violence. For example, some of the worst spectator violence in the United States has been grounded in racial tensions aggravated by highly publicized rivalries between high schools whose students come from different racial or ethnic backgrounds (Guttmann, 1986). When housing segregation leads to heavily segregated schools, the racial conflicts within communities may lead to confrontations—between whites and blacks, Anglos and Hispanics, blacks and Hispanics—before, during, and after games. When gangs stake out territories around a sport stadium and when gang members have weapons, sport events may become scenes for displays of gang power. Similarly, when the members of the National Front, a neo-Nazi organization popular among some young people in Europe, attend soccer games in England, they often taunt black players and directly confront black spectators. Violence sometimes occurs in connection with these confrontations. Through the 1990s there may be similar confrontations between various right-wing groups of young people and identifiable immigrants in some European countries.

In his classic book, *Power and Innocence: A Search for the Causes of Violence* (1972), Rollo May observes that all human beings need some means of achieving a sense of personal significance. Significance, he says, is best achieved when people can make their own decisions and when they have the resources to shape their own lives. But when people are powerless and without resources, "violence may be the only way individuals or groups can achieve a sense of significance." This may be a crucial factor explaining the sometimes violent behavior of young, male soccer fans in England. These fans, commonly referred to as "soccer hooligans," are predominantly young working-class males in England who lack power and believe the soccer teams they identify with have been taken over by wealthy industrialists with no ties to the local community, to the players, or to the longtime fans of the teams. It is to be expected that at least some of these young spectators perceive violence as a means of temporarily achieving feelings of significance. After all, violence forces others to take notice and respond to your existence, even if they look down on you. These are not the only factors underlying the behavior of young male soccer fans in England, but they are part of an historical, social, political, and economic context that must be understood if violence is to be explained.

Controlling Spectator Violence

Effective efforts to control spectator violence must be based on an awareness of each of the three sets of factors discussed above.

First, the notion that violence gives birth to violence indicates a need to limit violence among athletes during events. If fans do not define the actions of players as violent, crowd violence will decrease. Furthermore, perceptions of violence are likely to decrease if events are not hyped as violent confrontations between hostile opponents. Players and coaches could be used to make public announcements that defuse hostil-

Crowd violence has not been a major problem at most sport events, but when it occurs there is a need for controlled intervention so serious injuries can be prevented. (The Denver Post and John Leyba)

ity and emphasize the skills of the athletes involved in the event. High-profile fans for each team could make similar announcements. The use of competent and professionally trained officials is also important. Competent officials who can maintain control of a game and make calls the spectators see as fair decrease the possibility of spectator violence grounded in anger and perceived injustice (Mark et al., 1983). These referees could meet with both teams before the event and calmly explain the need to leave hostilities in the locker rooms. Teams officials could organize pregame unity rituals involving an exchange of team symbols and displays of respect between opponents. These rituals could be given media coverage so that fans could see that athletes do not view opponents with hostility.

Second, controlling violence among spectators depends on awareness of crowd dynamics and the conditions that can precipitate violence. Preventive measures are important. The needs and rights of spectators must be known and respected. Crowd control officials must be properly trained to intervene in potentially disruptive situations without increasing the chances for violence. The consumption of alcohol must be realistically regulated. Facilities should be safe and allow for spectators to move around. But there must also be ways of limiting contact between hostile fans of opposing teams. Exits should be accessible and clearly marked, and spectators should not be herded like animals before or after games.

Third, there must be awareness of the historical, social, economic, and political issues that often underlie spectator violence. Calls for restrictive law-and-order responses to crowd violence will not get at the real causes of many forms of violent behavior. Needed are policies dealing with issues of inequality, economic difficulties, unemployment, a lack of political representation, racism, and distorted definitions of masculinity in the community and in society as a whole. These are the factors often at the root of conflict and violence. Also needed are real efforts to establish connections between teams and the communities in which they are located. These connections can be used to defuse potentially dangerous feelings or plans among groups of spectators or community residents. This does not mean that teams merely need better public relations. There must be actual connections between the teams, the facilities, and the communities in which they exist. Players and coaches need to be engaged in community service. Owners must be visible supporters of community events and programs. Teams must develop special programs to assist in the development of local neighborhoods, especially those around the stadium or arena.

Summary

There is no clear indication that watching sports on television makes people more violent or more accepting of violence in their own lives. This issue is difficult to study because watching television sports is only a small part of people's lives, and violence is usually only a small part of what occurs in a televised sport event. However, there is a need to study how people actually interpret the action they see in televised sport events and how they relate those interpretations to situations and relationships in their own lives. The fact that people respond to and talk about violence in an event does not mean they accept or morally permit violence in everyday life. More research is needed on this issue.

The effects of going to a sport event are also difficult to pinpoint. Although spectator violence is relatively rare, it does occur. When it occurs, it seems to be related to (1) what happens on the playing field, (2) crowd dynamics

and the situation at the event itself, and (3) the overall historical, social, economic, and political context in the community and society. When spectators regularly become violent in a particular community or society, it is probably related to issues going far beyond the sport event and the stadium. Regular violence signals other serious problems calling for responsive social policies affecting opportunities and relationships within the society. Other ways of controlling spectators' violence include limiting violence on the playing field and managing crowd dynamics in constructive ways.

Because cultural context is so important when trying to understand spectator violence, it is very difficult to compare violence from one country to another. We need more comparative research, but comparative research cannot be done without good information on the history, structure, and dynamics of spectator violence in the societies being compared (Murphy et al., 1990).

CONCLUSION:

CURE OR CAUSE?

The relationship between sports and aggression has been widely discussed. Those who argue that sports are a cure for violence in society have little research evidence to support their case. Neither playing nor watching sports seems to "drain off" the energy that might lead to violent behavior. But under certain circumstances, sport participation may help people separate themselves from sources of frustration in the rest of their lives. If this separation gives them the time they need to redefine and cope effectively with these sources of frustration, then they may become less violent. But this possibility needs to be explored in research. Athletes may also learn to control violent behavior during games, especially the types of violence leading to penalties. But it is doubtful that this learning has any long-term effects on behavior off the field unless it has been intentionally linked to a philosophy of nonviolence and respect for oneself and one's opponents.

Those who argue that sports are a cause of violence have more research to support their case, but they cannot show that what happens in sports has a *direct* impact on violent behavior in the rest of society. Sport experiences sometimes create the frustration that leads to violence among both players and spectators; but for this to happen, frustration must be followed by anger, combined with opportunities and stimulus cues for violence. Athletes in contact sports learn to use violence and intimidation as strategic tools, but it is not known if these strategies are carried over into nonsport settings. Among males, learning to use violence as a tool within their sport is frequently tied to the reaffirmation of a form of masculinity that emphasizes a willingness to risk personal safety and a desire to intimidate others. If males who participate in certain sports learn to define this orientation as natural or appropriate, then sports may intensify serious forms of nonsport violence, including violence against women and children and other forms of physical assault (Theberge, 1989). Furthermore, ideas about the so-called "natural superiority of men" are often grounded in beliefs that the ability to engage in violence is part of the essence of being a man; references to sports violence are often used to make this argument.

Violence among spectators is influenced by violence on the field of play, by crowd dynamics, by the situation at the event itself, and by the overall historical and cultural context in which spectators live. Isolated cases of violence are probably best controlled by improved crowd management, but chronic violence among spectators usually signals that something needs to be changed in the way certain sports are defined and played or in the actual social, economic, or political structure of the community or society.

SUGGESTED READINGS

Bredemeier, B., and D. Shields. 1986. Athletic aggression: an issue of contextual morality. Sociology of Sport Journal 3(1):15-28 (*a clearly written conceptual discussion of how athletes define aggression in their own sports*).

Dunning, E.P., P. Murphy, and J. Williams. 1988. The roots of football hooliganism. University of Leicester Press, Leicester, England (*in-depth analysis of the behavior of British soccer fans, based on many years of research*).

Eitzen, D.S., ed. 1984. Sport in contemporary society. St. Martin's Press, New York (*see Section III: Violence and sport*).

Goldstein, J.H., ed. 1983. Sport violence. Springer-Verlag, New York (*contains 12 articles, most of which are written from a social psychological perspective*).

Goldstein, J.H., ed. 1988-1989. Violence in sport. Special issues of Current Psychology: Research & Reviews 7(4); 8(1) (*ten papers and two book reviews devoted to deviance, the media, boxing, and recent incidents involving British soccer fans—all with a focus on violent behavior*).

Guttmann, A. 1986. Sports spectators. Columbia University Press, New York (*good overview of the behavior of spectators; includes an examination of the history of sports spectators and an in-depth analysis of important sociological, psychological, and economic dimensions of spectatorship*).

Horrow, R.B. 1980. Sports violence. Carollton Press, Arlington, Va. (*written by a lawyer, it provides a legal perspective on violence in sport*).

Horrow, R.B., ed. 1980. Violence in sport. ARENA Review 5(1):special issue (*contains 9 papers, each representing a different disciplinary approach*).

Marsh, P. 1978. Aggro: the illusion of violence. J.M. Dent & Sons, Ltd., London (*a social psychological analysis of hooliganism in England*).

Murphy, P., J. Williams, and E. Dunning. 1990. Football on trial. Routledge, London (*a policy-based overview of spectator violence associated with soccer around the world; special emphasis is given to British spectators, and there is an interesting section on why there has been no equivalent of British soccer hooliganism in the United States*).

Sipes, R.G. 1984. Sports as a control for aggression. In D.S. Eitzen, ed., Sport in contemporary society. St. Martin's Press, New York (*useful review of Sipes's work on the relationship between the existence of combative sports and rates of violence in different societies*).

Smith, M.D. 1983. Violence and sport. Butterworths, Toronto (*this is the best survey of the literature on this topic*).

Telander, R. 1989. The hundred yard lie. Simon and Schuster, New York (*a critique of American college football; shows what happens when the Military Model is taken to an extreme in organizing sports and evaluating sport experiences*).

Williams, J., E. Dunning, and P. Murphy. 1984. Hooligans abroad. Routledge & Kegan Paul, Boston (*sociological analysis of the behavior of English soccer fans attending games through Europe; contains recommendations for controlling violence*).

(Colorado Springs Gazette Telegraph)

COACHES

How do they fit into sport experiences?

As people grow and face new situations they are influenced by others. Those who exert a strong influence in someone's life are described by sociologists as *significant others*. Because of their position in sports it is possible for coaches to become significant others in the lives of athletes. How do coaches define and respond to this situation? Are they primarily concerned with the well-being of their athletes or with win-loss records and building their own reputations?

The purpose of this chapter is to examine the factors that shape the orientations and behaviors of coaches. Our discussion begins with a brief description of the coach in recent history, followed by information on the coach as an individual, the role of coach, coaching as a subculture, and finally, the impact of coaches on athletes.

THE COACH IN RECENT HISTORY

Coaches were never supposed to be like traditional teachers. When people have participated in physical activities simply for reasons of health, enjoyment, and personal development they have looked to physical educators for guidance. The specialized roles of coach, trainer, and sport physician did not exist until physical activities took the form of competitive sport. In other words, the job of a coach has always been to help athletes get ready for competition. The profession of coaching, unlike physical education, is directly related to competition and competitive success.

In the United States, for example, the word *coach* was not even used in connection with games or athletic competition before the Civil War. Up until that time *coach* was an English term used to describe a private tutor responsible for teaching manners or academic subjects. It was not until the 1870s that the coaching of sports emerged as a specialized profession. The values underlying this new profession were shaped by the growth of organized competitive sports rather than by the field of physical education (Mrozek, 1983).

The first real coaches in the United States were associated with established schools and wealthy private athletic clubs in New England. Although coaches were not regarded as teachers, they were sometimes given academic status in universities and preparatory schools. This was done so the faculty and administration in those schools could officially keep the athletic programs of the students under their control. But coaches had no direct ties to academic programs.

Historian Donald Mrozek (1983) concludes that coaches, along with the trainers who assisted them, became the new management experts in the field of sports and sport competition. As team records and the achievements of individual athletes became more important for the reputations of the sponsoring schools and clubs, the importance of coaches increased. This development was greeted with mixed feelings by physical educators. On the one hand, physical educators felt sports could be used to scientifically develop the human body. But on the other hand, they were disappointed that sports were generally not being used for that purpose. This split between coaching and physical education still exists today.

Although some people complain about how the coaches of today put too much emphasis on winning, this orientation is not new to the profession of coaching. In 1904, an internationally known rowing coach from Syracuse University talked about winning in the following terms:

> Who is it that gets "a hand" . . . at the finish line? No thought is given to the losers, it is all for the victors. . . . It is human nature, and things will not change. . . . There is no getting behind the fact that races are entered to be won. (James A. Ten Eyck, cited in Mrozek, 1983).

This sounds much like the "winning is the only thing" philosophy popular with some coaches today. The point is that the profession of coaching has grown out of a commitment to competitive success. And as the rewards for success have grown, so has the pressure for coaches to win. Even volunteer coaches in organized youth programs sometimes feel pressure. But it is greatest at the intercollegiate and professional levels where millions of dollars often depend on win-loss records. This has created a situation in which winning coaches are hailed as the symbols of schools and the saviors of cities, and losing coaches are ridiculed and fired. Regardless of their success, coaches must learn to live with pressures to win, and they must learn to handle the expectations of the many different people they deal with while they are doing their jobs. More will be said about this through the chapter.

COACHES AS INDIVIDUALS: WHAT ARE THEIR PERSONAL CHARACTERISTICS?

Efforts to understand the behavior of coaches have often been based on the assumption that coaches do what they do because they possess certain character traits. Therefore when the behaviors of coaches are questioned, so too are the personal characters of coaches themselves. Coaches who act in inflexible and traditional ways are often believed to be inflexible and traditional people. But is this the case? Research suggests that it is not.

Studies indicate that the personality traits of coaches are not much different than the traits of other people of the same age and sex.* In other words, coaches are no more or less inflexible, manipulative, traditional, or conservative than their peers in the rest of the community. They may have characteristics that make them somewhat different from the faculty in most American high schools and colleges, but this does not mean they are a completely unique group in society as a whole.

Few studies of the personalities and orientations of coaches have included women in their samples. In fact, we know little about the personalities or behavior patterns of women who are coaches. Some studies have reported that the

---

*See Bain, 1978; Gould and Martens, 1979; Locke, 1962; Rejeski et al, 1979; Sage, 1974a, b; Stillwell, 1979; Walsh and Carron, 1977.

personal character traits and orientations of female coaches are generally similar to those of their male counterparts (Bain, 1978; Eitzen and Pratt, 1989; Kidd, 1979; Loy, 1969a, b). But other studies identify some differences. For example, Bain (1978) found that when compared with their male counterparts, female high school coaches were more interested in providing general learning experiences for all students and were more sensitive to student-athletes' rights to privacy. Eitzen and Pratt (1989) found that female high school basketball coaches were slightly more likely than their male counterparts to emphasize traditional ideas, such as requiring athletes to maintain good grades, display good sportsmanship, and avoid using obscenities. But we don't know if these differences between female and male coaches are due to gender differences in relational skills or leadership styles, or whether they are due to what athletic directors might look for when they recruit, hire, and evaluate coaches.

It is important to remember that personal leadership styles are grounded in personal experiences and histories. If female coaches have different styles than male coaches and it appears that this occurs regularly, it is because women have different experiences and histories than men have. Because leadership (as opposed to management) involves relational skills, differences sometimes exist between the leadership styles of men and women, primarily because relational skills are often emphasized in women's experiences. This could account for some differences between female and male coaches, but it is likely that the range of those differences would also depend on recruitment, selection, and promotion processes in athletic departments and sport organizations.

If the people who recruit, hire, and promote coaches tend to evaluate female applicants and female coaches in terms of whether they have the same approaches to coaching and the same leadership styles as male coaches have, there will be few differences between female and male coaches (as the data suggest). In other words, if women who think and act differently than male coaches are deemed as unqualified, too sensitive, not tough enough, or lacking the "killer instinct," they will not be hired or promoted. Because men have always set the standards for evaluating "quality" among coaches, it is likely that women must become like men to be deemed qualified. Some people say this is a form of institutionalized discrimination, whereas others say it is objective and fair. I agree with the former, but I have found it difficult to argue my case with the men who administer athletic departments. This is another example of how gender relations are tied to issues of power and privilege in sport, and it is another reason why female coaches are often more frustrated and less satisfied in their jobs than men are (Pastore and Judd, 1992). Chapter 11 contains more information on this topic.

In summary, coaches as a group do not seem to have manipulative personalities, nor do they have ultraconservative political and social values. However, they may have other traits in common because they do share similar social backgrounds and athletic experiences and interact with one another in ways that would reinforce similarities in how they view themselves and how they handle their jobs (Sage, 1975a, 1980b). It is probably for these reasons that some researchers have concluded that coaches are generally assertive, organized, traditional, and highly achievement-oriented (Ogilvie and Tutko, 1966; Sage, 1980b). But it must be remembered that people can act assertively *without* being insensitive; they can be organized *without* being manipulative; they can be traditional *without* being reactionary; and they can strive for success *without* being corrupt. This suggests that *the behavior of coaches is influenced by much more than personality.* Behavior is also influenced by relationships and social situations. This is especially true for coaches because they occupy visible positions in important organizations and the roles they play consist of a unique set of expectations and demands.

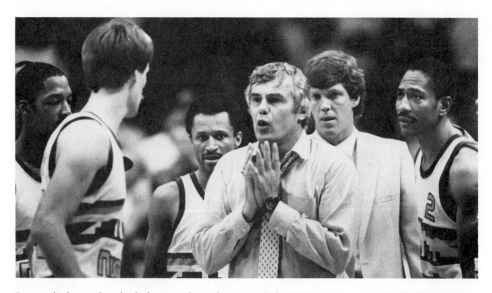

Research shows that the behavior of coaches, even when it is extreme, is influenced by much more than personality factors. More important are the demands and expectations associated with the job of being a coach. (Colorado Springs Gazette Telegraph and Chuck Bigger)

THE ROLE OF COACH AND THE BEHAVIOR OF COACHES

In sociology, a **role** is a more-or-less consistent pattern of behavior associated with a person's position in a set of social relationships. These patterns of behavior always emerge from interaction with others. For example, a parent's role emerges from interaction with his or her children, and a student's role emerges from interaction with a teacher. Although roles reflect the characteristics and wishes of the people who play them, they are also influenced by the expectations of others and by general social and cultural factors.

This description of a role means that the behavior of coaches reflects three sets of factors: (a) the personality traits and ideas of coaches themselves, (b) what occurs in the organizational settings in which coaches work, and (c) general cultural beliefs about what coaches should do and how they should act. In sociology we focus on the second and third of these factors.

General Cultural Beliefs about Coaches and Coaching Behaviors

Little research has been done on cultural variations in coaching behaviors. But it is likely that cultural beliefs about the importance of coaches and about the appropriateness of certain leadership styles would set general limits for coaching behaviors from one society to another.

My experiences lead me to think that Americans generally approve of the use of autocratic, command styles of leadership by coaches, especially coaches in elite sports. For example, when I've asked students in my sociology of sport classes to assess the feasibility of organizing sport teams along democratic lines many of them argue that being a coach and being democratic are incompatible. They say that coaches alone should make decisions on sport teams, that athletes should not be included in decision-making processes. Their reasons include the following:

- Coaches have more experience and know more about sports than athletes do

- Athletes cannot be trusted to make responsible decisions
- Coaches must make decisions if they are to be respected
- If athletes made decisions it would destroy the basis for discipline and authority on teams
- Athletes look to coaches for decisions and answers, and would be lost if they had to make decisions for themselves
- Coaches have the right to make all the decisions because their jobs are on the line when athletes and teams do not meet performance expectations

I would question each of these reasons, but more importantly, I find it strange that so many students would say that democracy is not appropriate in sports, especially in a society in which it is widely believed that sport participation prepares people to live as democratic citizens.

These beliefs about coaches as autocratic leaders could create problems in any society because they make it easy for coaches to invade the privacy of athletes and to get away with verbal, psychological, and physical mistreatment. For example, would parents be more likely to file a complaint if a teacher slapped their 12-year old daughter for dropping a piece of chalk during class or if a gymnastics coach slapped their daughter for making a mistake during a practice? Would parents be more likely to file a complaint if a teacher dragged their teenage son by the hair to the principal's office because he failed a homework assignment or if a football coach pulled him by the face mask on his helmet around a football field for missing a block? I would guess that parents are much more likely to see the coaches' behaviors in these examples as appropriate, or at least excusable, whereas the teachers' behaviors would be seen as cause for complaints, if not lawsuits.

These examples are **not** meant to imply that coaches regularly do these things; they are simply meant to indicate that we know little about general cultural beliefs about the role and behavior of coaches in the United States or any other country. We need studies of popular beliefs about coaching in different cultures to identify and explain cultural variations and their implications for how and why coaches become important in the lives of athletes.

Organizational Settings and Pressure

In comparison with other positions, such as teacher, student, parent, husband, or social worker, the position of coach is often unique. This is especially true in the United States, where coaches often face a form of pressure that others can avoid (see the comparison of coach and classroom teacher in the box on p. 195). Unlike people in other occupations, American coaches are held totally accountable for the results of competitive activities that are highly spontaneous and unpredictable (Edwards, 1973). What makes the position of coach even more unique is the fact that these competitive activities are highly visible, and the results of the competitions are publicly reported and discussed. This means that the behavior of coaches can be viewed by spectators—sometimes numbering in the millions—and that the success rates of coaches can be objectively measured by wins and losses.

When coaches are held accountable for results, it means that they are given credit for wins and they are blamed for losses. In many organizational settings, winning is the most important—if not the only—criterion used to determine if coaches are successful.

This combination of accountability, unpredictability, visibility, and the objective measurement of success creates exceptional pressures for coaches. This pressure is illustrated in the following quote from Ara Parseghian, a former football coach for the University of Notre Dame:

> My doctor ordered me to quit. . . . I found myself taking blood pressure pills, tranquilizers, and sleeping pills, and that's not right. So I backed off and said, "What the hell is happening?" It's not a twelve-month job; it's more than that. You can't understand the demands of this job until you walk

SIDELINES

©1982 M.T.F.-T.W.S.-Lakewood, CO

"I CAN GUARANTEE YOU WE WON'T LOSE TOMORROW... MAINLY BECAUSE WE DON'T PLAY TOMORROW!"

Coaches are held totally accountable for the results of the events which are by their very nature unpredictable. In most cases the only time coaches can predict their teams will not lose is when they don't play.

in the shoes of the man who has it (quoted in Yeager, 1979).

Of course, not all coaches face the same degree of pressure. Those at top levels of competition feel it most, but it is also experienced by many coaches in highly competitive youth leagues and varsity high school programs.

Relationships and Role Strain

In addition to facing unique forms of pressure, coaches are also subject to what some sociologists describe as **role strain.** The role strain they experience is the result of being in a job in which it is necessary to interact with people in many different positions. Because these people occupy different positions, they tend to have different ideas about how coaches should do their jobs. Whenever coaches try to live up to the expectations of all these different people, they are bound to experience strain. They simply cannot please everyone.

Figure 8-1 illustrates the different relationships that may have an effect on the role behav-

The Classroom Teacher and the Interscholastic Coach
A Comparison of Two Roles

Some people have compared the role of coach to the role of the classroom teacher and argued that coaches should deal with interscholastic athletes in the same open-ended ways that many teachers deal with students (Scott, 1971). This is a good suggestion, but it overlooks crucial differences between the two roles. James Michener (1976) has outlined some of these differences as they sometimes exist at the college level in the United States:

> No other member of any faculty is subjected to the close and constant scrutiny which the coach experiences. He [sic] is written about in the papers, criticized on radio and television, and reviewed constantly by the alumni who pay the bills. . . . Nor is any other faculty member subjected to the rigorous performance-evaluation which a coach must undergo. If he is deficient, a crowded stadium witnesses his failure, and he is not allowed to remain deficient very long. An ordinary faculty member can get away with murder for decades without detection (pp. 254-255).

Michener refers to *male* coaches in high-profile, big-time college sports in the United States, but his analysis indicates that the pressures faced by these coaches are greater and more clear-cut than the pressures faced by teachers. When coaches fail to meet expectations, their failures are publicly observed and discussed. Teachers, on the other hand, can fail in relative privacy. Their students in particular classes may be aware of failures but nobody televises them, analyzes them in newspapers, or uses them as direct measures of on-the-job achievements. Therefore teachers can afford to deal with students in less dogmatic ways than coaches deal with athletes. Teachers can afford to make more exceptions to rules and be less concerned about discipline. And they do not have to be as concerned about what their students do outside of class.

To understand this point more clearly, try to imagine what a college teacher might be like if the teacher role was patterned after the role of coach. If teachers were hired, evaluated, and promoted on the basis of how their students performed in scheduled competitions with students from other schools, they would probably act differently in their classrooms. If these competitions were used to determine conference standings and national championships and as a basis for their universities' reputations, they might be more authoritarian with their students.

If the contests between their students and the students from other schools were televised, attended by the press, and watched by school administrators, important alumni, fellow teachers, and thousands of other students, the teachers might even become concerned with discipline and what their students did on the night before the weekly contest. If teachers' careers and the economic status of their families depended on how a group of 18- to 22-year-old students responded to a set of unpredictable academic challenges, they might even develop ulcers to go along with the traditional and rigid training methods they would use more frequently in their classrooms.

This example should not be used to justify the behavior of coaches. In fact, the behavior of some coaches is impossible to justify no matter how much pressure they face. Instead, the example is intended to help understand why the attitudes and methods used by most coaches tend to differ from the attitudes and methods used by most classroom teachers. Personality is *not* the major reason for behavior differences between teachers and coaches. When coaches are more concerned with rules, discipline, and traditional approaches to their jobs, it is likely that many of their attitudes and methods are grounded in the pressures and relationships that characterize their social environments. This does not mean that coaches cannot change. But it does suggest that the likelihood of change is greatest when organizational settings for sport programs are restructured and when coaches realize how those settings influence their behavior.

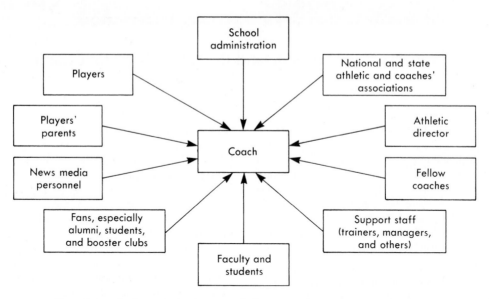

FIG 8-1 The origins of role strain for the interscholastic coach. Because coaches have so many different relationships, they have trouble meeting everyone's expectations. The behavior of coaches often takes the form of tactics used to reduce the strain associated with their jobs.

ior of high school or college coaches. Because the relationships are so diversified and because the people in each of these different positions expect different things from coaches, few coaches are able to escape strain in their jobs. It's not easy to meet the expectations of everyone from presidents to sportswriters and from principals to students. Coaches will often have to ignore the expectations of some people if they are to meet the expectations of others. When this happens, coaches must be tactful and diplomatic, or they will end up making enemies who can threaten their jobs and make their lives miserable.

Handling Pressure and Strain

So how do coaches cope with the pressure and role strain that come with their jobs? The most effective strategy is simply to win all their games, meets, or matches. Winning makes everyone happy. However, perfect records are rare, and nobody remains undefeated forever, so coaches must use other tactics. Usually, coaches use these tactics:

1. *Generating support* for their programs and coaching methods
2. *Gaining control* over their programs and the people connected with them
3. *Being expedient* (that is, using a combination of cleverness and wisdom) when dealing with other people

GENERATING SUPPORT Coaches often try to cut down pressure and strain by convincing others that their ways of doing things are the right ways. To do this coaches must be able to describe their programs and coaching methods in simple terms and then explain why these programs will be successful. Although coaches can admit there are other ways of doing things, they must convince those around them that their methods are the best methods.

This strategy generally fails if coaches show a lack of confidence in their own methods. Any display of uncertainty invites criticism and advice from numerous people. Unfortunately, this need to appear confident often locks coaches into methods that cannot be changed without leading people to question their abilities. If they admitted that their methods might be weak, the pressures and strains would increase. Therefore they may continue to do things the same way even though they are not always successful. This is why some coaches are perceived to be egotistical, stubborn, and dogmatic. However, this image of the coach as rigid and inflexible is tied more to the unique social environment in which coaches work than to their individual personalities.

GAINING CONTROL According to Penn State University football coach Joe Paterno, coaches cannot do the jobs expected of them unless they have control over their programs and the people connected with them. Coaches often think that without the freedom to make decisions and formulate rules and policies, the success of their teams will be affected by too many unexpected factors. As long as the outcomes of competition remain unpredictable, they often feel a need to control as many of the factors related to those outcomes as possible. Paul Brown explains how this need determined his approach to players when he was a coach in the NFL:

> I never left anything to the players' imagination: I laid out exactly what I expected from them, how I expected them to act on and off the field and what we expected to accomplish. . . . Our team had training rules, too, and we enforced them even though they were grown men.

In further efforts to gain control, coaches often ask for guarantees of autonomy from team owners, school administrators, or athletic directors. This frees them from the expectations of at least one of the important people in their social environments. Control can also be maximized by using a strategy of "strategic withdrawal" (Massengale, 1975). This involves avoiding contact with people and thereby avoiding their expectations.

When coaches try to gain control over all the events and people connected with their jobs, they are often seen as power hungry and manipulative. When control is maintained through strategic withdrawal, coaches isolate themselves

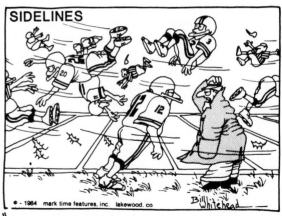

"REMEMBER, THE WIND COULD BE A FACTOR TODAY."

The outcomes of the games are often affected by factors not subject to the control of coaches. This is one of the reasons why coaches become so concerned with control-related issues with their players.

from everyone except other coaches. This makes them prime targets for negative stereotypes; and again, the personalities of coaches rather than the role of coach are mistakenly seen as the causes of coaching behavior.

BEING EXPEDIENT Even if they are good at generating support and gaining control, coaches still experience role strain because they cannot avoid all situations in which they must decide whose expectations to meet and whose to ignore. In handling these situations many coaches quickly become aware of who can help or hurt them and then make decisions to protect themselves. This is not a unique way of handling role strain. Most of us use cost-reward calculations to assign priorities to the conflicting expectations of others. And when we face serious pressures to be successful, we are even more likely to use expedience in responding to these priorities. The same is true for coaches. When they are in high-pressure situations, they are much more likely to respond to conflicting expectations only after carefully assessing costs and rewards (Carron, 1978; Sage, 1975b).

The problem with the strategy of being expedient is that coaches risk getting reputations for being manipulative and insensitive. But not using this tactic may lead coaches to be overwhelmed by people who think they could take over the coaches' jobs and win more games and run programs more efficiently.

ALTERNATIVE STRATEGIES If coaches let others know that coaching involves more than being concerned with wins and losses, they can control some of the pressure and role strain they face. Instead of launching a quest for undefeated seasons or using only the strategies listed above, coaches might use some of the following tactics:

- Make sure others understand your commitment to the growth and development of young people; emphasize that success can be measured in terms other than wins and losses; talk about the importance of developmental goals, and discuss those goals as central to your program; make sure players, parents, boosters, the press, and others in the organization become aware of the broad range of goals you are working toward as a coach.
- Discourage people from developing unrealistic expectations for the competitive success of your athletes or teams; in your discussions of games, meets, or matches emphasize that commitment and hard work are only part of what it takes to produce wins, and that there are factors outside the control of coaches and athletes that influence competitive outcomes.
- Emphasize respect for the quality and potential of opponents; never hesitate to praise opponents who are good or who play better than expected. Remind others, including your players, that facing the challenge of competition is more important than dominating opponents.
- Take advantage of your visibility and talk about achievements highlighting growth and development among the young people you coach. When your athletes do something that makes you proud of them, make sure you tell others about it (if athletes don't mind going public), even if it is not directly related to

sports. Additionally, prepare your athletes for the responsibility of talking about themselves and their achievements, and make sure they have opportunities to express themselves in controlled situations.
- Don't let other people, including parents, the press, or spectators, treat the young people you coach only as athletes. Emphasize that there is more to those young people than what they do on the playing field, and make sure others know about positive qualities and achievements unrelated to sports.
- Demand that athletic directors, principals, presidents, school district officials, and other leaders take strong public stands emphasizing the developmental and educational goals of interscholastic sport programs.

In summary, much coaching behavior is shaped by the pressures and strains associated with the social settings in which coaches do their jobs. Coaches must deal with the *pressure* of being held totally accountable for results in unpredictable and highly visible events. *Role strain* often occurs because coaches are frequently expected to please many different people all at once. Coaches often deal with this pressure and strain by gaining support for their methods, gaining control over their programs and the people connected with them, and being expedient when dealing with other people. These tactics may cause coaches to appear traditional, authoritarian, manipulative, and power hungry, despite the fact that these traits may not be parts of their own personalities. This suggests that there may be a need for other types of tactics, tactics that would change the way people think about sports and the role of a coach.

ROLE CONFLICT: HOW DO OFF-THE-FIELD ROLES AFFECT COACHES?

In addition to pressure and role strain coaches often face another set of problems created by conflict *between* their coaching role and the other roles they play. The roles most likely to conflict with coaching are those related to teaching and family.

Coaches do more than simply coach. In most American high schools, for example, they are expected to teach a full load of courses. Additionally, most coaches have families. Roles may conflict when coaches try to meet the expectations associated with all of their positions.* For many coaches, the day does not contain enough hours for them to do everything.

Teacher-Coach Role Conflict

Research has clearly documented the existence of teacher-coach role conflict in U.S. schools (Chu, 1981; Massengale, 1981; Sage, 1987). Many of those who play both roles indicate they do not have enough time to meet the expectations in the classroom and on the playing field—even though they work over 60 hours per week trying to do both things. The consequences of teacher-coach role conflict are vividly explained in the following statements of three high school coaches interviewed by sport sociologist George Sage (1987):

> *Coach A:* "There just aren't enough hours in a day to do everything that you want. I know I want to be as innovative and creative as I can as a teacher but my role . . . as a coach really prohibits me from achieving what I want in the classroom. . . . My role as a teacher definitely does suffer because of my dual role as a coach."
>
> *Coach B:* "You can get so wrapped up in your coaching that you don't do any teaching . . . you may be so wrapped up in preparing for this next team that you give the kids the shaft in your class."
>
> *Coach C:* "Anytime a coach is teaching a full load he has to make decisions [about] which [job

he's] going to do well. . . . I know why they hired me, [the school board] probably won't say [this] but . . . you know why you've been hired. . . . If you do a halfway good teaching [job] they're not going to fire you, and if you don't do a good job coaching they probably are."

When teacher-coaches are faced with conflicting demands, they do not always give priority to their coaching jobs. Some may cut back on the time they spend coaching so they can do a better job in the classroom. Others drop out of coaching to make time for teaching. Unfortunately, this form of role conflict is becoming more intense in the lives of many teacher-coaches. Parents and students now expect more from teachers than they have in the past, and people involved with sports expect more from coaches than they have in the past. Teacher-coaches are expected to be experts not only in their teaching areas but also in everything from nutrition to drugs, from weight training to biomechanics, and from exercise physiology to eligibility rules in high school and college.

As expectations for both teaching and coaching roles have increased, the number of teachers who coach has decreased. This means many schools must now depend on "walk-on coaches" from the local community—people who are not certified teachers but who are thought to know something about a particular sport. People interested in education and the sociology of sport should study the implications of this development. At the moment, we know very little about it except that it has caused many schools and school districts to think more seriously about the merits of making coaching education programs mandatory for some or all of the people who coach in schools.

Coach-Family Role Conflict

Many coaches also deal with what might be called coach-family role conflict. Giving up nights and weekends for practices and games can be a significant problem for coaches who are spouses and parents. The words of three more

---

*Sociologists often *distinguish* between role conflict and role strain. *Role strain* is related to the problems a person faces while playing a single role. *Role conflict* is related to the problems a person faces while playing more than one role at a time. For example, trying to be a college student and a college athlete at the same time often causes *role conflict* because there is not enough time to meet the expectations associated with both roles. But *role strain* occurs when an athlete tries to meet the different expectations of the head coach, the assistant coach, teammates, and sport reporters about how the role of center on a basketball team should be played.

coaches from George Sage's study (1987) provide clear statements of this problem:

Coach A: "If it's not [time] away from home doing things in your football program, it's time at home when your mind is somewhere else and you're not really relating to your wife or children like you would if you were not . . . involved in coaching."

Coach B: "When I first got into coaching/teaching, coaching was everything, I mean it was everything. . . . I didn't approach it right, I didn't take time for my family and I lost my wife; I was divorced, and to this day I look back on it and I should have done things differently, but I didn't realize it at the time."

Coach C: "Coaching has taken a tremendous toll on my family because there were times when I should have been there when I wasn't. . . . I cheated my family . . . and to be very honest, any success my children will have I credit my wife rather than myself because of the fact that I just wasn't there."

Marriage partners may think that coaching interferes with maintaining a satisfying husband-wife relationship, and children may feel ignored when one parent is always at school or with a sport team. Although this form of conflict affects both men and women who coach, it is likely that married women with children feel it most. Unless a married couple has negotiated their relationship in a way that frees the wife from most child care and housekeeping tasks, the woman will have a difficult time maintaining the necessary time commitments to her role as a coach. It is tough to supervise practices every night, plan game strategies, prepare and teach classes, go to games on weekends, and still have dinner on the table every night, take care of the kids, and clean the house.

Coach-family role conflict is probably one of the reasons why female high school coaches drop out of coaching more frequently than males (Mathes, 1982). Of course, males experience this conflict as well. But they are more likely to be able to negotiate their marriage relationships in ways that free them from all but a few home-making tasks. When a husband-father is not home in time for dinner, he simply has to eat warmed-up food; when a wife-mother is not home in time, she has to listen to her family complain about how tough it is without her, and how they had to order pizza for the third night in a row.

Being a successful coach in a highly competitive interscholastic program requires extreme dedication and time commitments. This, in turn, requires exceptional support from family members. Men with long coaching careers have often had spouses who would do everything from washing team uniforms to hosting team picnics and attending countless games as loyal fans (Sabock, 1979). Women coaches seldom have such support, and when they do their husbands are likely to be treated as local heroes. Without spouse support, coaches may become frustrated and leave coaching.

HELPING COACHES CONTROL ROLE CONFLICT It is difficult for teacher-coaches to control role conflict by themselves. Organizations should provide assistance. This assistance may be initiated by athletic directors, principals, department chairpersons, school district administrators, and others who can effect changes in the lives of teacher-coaches. But teacher-coaches can lobby for action and encourage their superiors to do the following:

- Make explicit statements about priorities related to the goals of academic and athletic programs.
- Develop procedures for integrating coaches into the faculty; emphasize the importance of the teacher/coach role within the overall learning and teaching process, and utilize coaches as important sources of information about young people and they way young people learn.
- Relieve teacher-coaches from many of the trivial and mundane matters that consume their coaching time. Role conflict would decrease if coaches did not have to do janitorial work, drive buses, schedule competitive events, raise funds, launder uniforms and practice gear,

make travel arrangements, fill out insurance forms, maintain equipment and facilities, and so on. Athletic directors should handle some of these tasks, support staff should handle others, and "student-assistants" could be assigned tasks that would provide them useful experiences.

- Institute evaluation procedures emphasizing coaching as teaching. And when teacher-coaches are evaluated, the evaluation process should include indicators of role conflict (and role strain) so administrators will become sensitive to its existence and severity. Administrators should develop indicators of successful coaching (apart from win-loss records) and include them in the evaluation process for teacher-coaches.
- Limit the number of sports any one person can coach during an academic year (2 per year should be the maximum), or reduce teaching responsibilities during sport seasons so teaching demands are more in line with time resources.

Role conflict cannot be handled simply by taking courses on team management, time management, and stress management; actual changes must occur in the organizations that sponsor sports if conflict is to be controlled over the long run.

In summary, the conflict between coaching and other roles frequently affects coaches. Teacher-coaches often have a difficult time handling the work loads associated with both their roles. Often, coaches may respond to this conflict by decreasing their commitment to teaching or by dropping out of coaching. Coach-family role conflict may also be a problem. The expectations of spouses and children can seldom be met by the family member who is dedicated to meeting expectations in his or her coaching role. This sometimes forces coaches to choose between their families and their careers. However, it is possible for athletic directors to develop strategies for helping coaches avoid some aspects of role conflict.

COACHING AS A SUBCULTURE: HOW ARE THE BEHAVIOR PATTERNS OF COACHES PERPETUATED AND PASSED ON TO NEW COACHES?

It has already been explained that the pressures and strains associated with being a coach often lead to "strategic withdrawal." This response provides the basis for the development of a coaching subculture. In sociology, a *subculture* is defined as a way of thinking and behaving that sets a group apart and makes it unique. A subculture consists of values, beliefs, and customs maintained through relationships among a group of people who interact with one another because of shared interests. These relationships provide the social contexts in which identities are shaped, experiences shared, and common interests and values reaffirmed. The relationships also provide group members with social and emotional support, guidelines on how to handle everyday life situations, and feedback to increase attachment to the group itself.

Any subculture is able to perpetuate commonly accepted methods of doing things within a group. This is especially true among coaches (Massengale, 1974, 1975). Their occupational subculture provides behavioral guidelines that reflect traditional coaching methods. Older, successful coaches are often used as role models within the subculture. Those who do not follow the accepted coaching methods risk rejection from others in the profession. Rejection can be a serious problem for young coaches because their futures usually depend on the sponsorship of established coaches (Loy and Sage, 1973).

While the coaching subculture provides needed support for coaches, it also tends to discourage change within the profession. When a coach uses a new method, success may have to be demonstrated repeatedly before it is accepted within the subculture. This perpetuates the use of traditional tactics and discourages innovations.

The influence of the coaching subculture also extends to those who want to be coaches. This influence often begins in adolescence when

The occupational subculture that exists among coaches is characterized by shared values, beliefs, and customs that are passed on from one generation of coaches to the next. This tends to perpetuate traditional coaching methods and discourage change within the profession. (University of Colorado and Eddie Kosmicki)

young people try out the coaching role in youth leagues or as assistant coaches in school programs. These experiences, along with the influence of popular role models within the coaching subculture, encourage new coaches to use traditionally accepted methods. After they become coaches, their relationships with others in the subculture simply further their commitment to those methods.

Although there is no research on the existence of separate coaching subcultures for men and women, the long-time organizational separation between men's and women's sport programs and physical education programs suggests that separate subcultures might exist. This should be studied if we want to understand how gender and gender relations affect coaching behavior. It is possible that combining women's and men's sport programs under a single male-dominated administrative structure has led to a

general emphasis on values, beliefs, and customs grounded in the coaching subculture of men. But we need to know more about this process and how it might vary from one situation to another.

In summary, the coaching subculture exerts considerable influence on the behavior of coaches. It is a mechanism through which new coaches learn traditionally accepted coaching methods and established coaches become more committed to those methods. Because any subculture represents a relatively *stable* pattern of thinking and behaving, the existence of a subculture among coaches tends to discourage changes in their methods and attitudes, even when pressures and strains are decreased through changes in organizational settings and interaction networks.

COACHES AS "SIGNIFICANT OTHERS": DO THEY INFLUENCE ATHLETES?

The idea that coaches are "character builders" has existed for many years and it has been supported by many athletes who claim that coaches have made a significant impact on their lives. When this claim is made, it generally means that coaches did one or more of the following things for athletes:

1. Coaches may use such rigid and pervasive control tactics that athletes become dependent on them. When this happens, coaches become important in the lives of athletes in the same way dictators become important in the histories of the countries they rule. Their influence is great, but it does not lead to positive developmental outcomes unless athletes rebel or unless the coach eventually provides them opportunities to make their own decisions.

2. Coaches may share with athletes information about themselves to the point that athletes are able to use them as role models. When coaches become role models, athletes attempt to pattern their lives to resemble what they perceive to be the lives of their coaches.

3. Coaches may serve as advisers or advocates for athletes. This involves helping athletes ex-

The image of coaches as character builders has been supported by many athletes who claim coaches influenced their lives. However, this may be true only in cases in which coaches have developed unique relationships with athletes. (Colorado Springs Gazette Telegraph and Mark Reis)

plore alternatives, meet challenges, make choices, and deal with the consequences of successes and failures. When this is done, coaches become adult allies for athletes. As allies or advocates, coaches can use their position and influence to keep young people out of serious trouble and in control of their lives and their immediate futures.

Unfortunately, we know little about the actual ways in which coaches have become important in the lives of athletes. Judging from the love-hate terms used by some athletes to de-

scribe their coaches, I suspect that some coaches are important because they made athletes dependent on them. People in dependent relationships often use love-hate terms to describe those who have power over them.

It is my guess that few coaches ever become real role models for athletes. Most athletes never get to know enough about their coaches' lives to use them as models, and few coaches feel comfortable with the idea of presenting their lives as models for young people to follow. In light of this, expectations for coaches to be role models are usually unrealistic. Social development does not occur by simply modeling one's life after the life of another person. Instead, it occurs through a long process of making decisions based on information from a variety of sources.

I would hypothesize that coaches most often become important in the lives of athletes by simply providing good advice and useful assistance at key points in athletes' lives. Coaches can be invaluable adult allies when they give tangible forms of advice and assistance to athletes who must make choices or cope with crises in their lives (Snyder, 1972). All young people need adults in key positions looking out for them and for their interests. Without this it would be difficult for them to recover from their mistakes or take advantage of the opportunities occurring during adolescence and young adulthood.

Research suggests that the vast majority of coaches want to exert a positive influence in the lives of their athletes (Stewart and Sweet, 1992; Stillwell, 1979). In fact, the primary reason many people become coaches is their desire to work with young people. This fits with the idea of coaches as "significant others." It also fits with what most interscholastic athletes expect from coaches—they want them to be understanding, patient, and sensitive to their personal needs (Steinbrecher et al., 1978; Messing, 1978).

Despite what coaches say and athletes want, the actual behavior of coaches often emphasizes the development of physical skills and overlooks the general social and psychological needs of young people. For example, youth league coaches say that they are concerned with the social and psychological needs of their young players (Weiss and Sisley, 1984); but out on the playing fields, their interaction with players is almost focused totally on improving physical skills for the purpose of winning games (Dubois, 1982; Lombardo, 1982). Unfortunately, it is likely that the pressures and strains associated with coaching lead many coaches to be more concerned about controlling the lives of athletes than about responding to the overall developmental needs of the young people they coach.

The Need for Coaching Education Programs

Coaching education programs are increasingly seen as effective tools for helping coaches work more responsibly with athletes, especially young athletes. Most of the major North American programs* emphasize the need for coaches to focus on the overall development of young people. For example, the motto of the American Coaching Effectiveness Program is "Athletes First, Winning Second." However, care should be taken before concluding that coaching education turns coaches into more effective "significant others." The reason for this is that some coaching education courses and programs are designed to help coaches use sport science to become technical performance experts rather than to understand young people and work with them as human beings. As stated in Chapter 5, we should remember that East Germany had one of the so-called best coaching education programs in the world before the Berlin wall was taken down. But their program emphasized performance rather than the overall social development of young athletes. This wins medals but it does not really put "athletes first."

An increasing number of youth sport programs in North America and some European countries now sponsor some form of coaching education. Some programs even require that coaches become certified by taking approved educational courses or workshops. This also occurs at the high school level in the United States and in many sport federations in various countries. The coaching education programs endorsed by youth leagues and high school athletic departments generally emphasize the role of the coach in the overall development of young people. The

---

*American Coaching Effectiveness Program (ACEP), Coalition of Americans to Protect Sport (CAPS), National Youth Sports Coaches Association (NYSCA), Program for Athletic Coaches Education (PACE), Canadian National Coaching Certification Program (CNCCP) are the most frequently mentioned programs. For a description of each and examples of programs in operation, see Sawyer (1992).

programs endorsed by sport federations are more likely to emphasize performance enhancement through the use of sport science rather than knowledge about overall personal and social development.

Those who argue for coaching education and certification point out that coaches are seldom required to have any training or any credential certifying them as qualified even though they often spend more time with young people than many other adults (Stewart and Sweet, 1992). Public school teachers, for example, are required to have college degrees and teaching credentials. But many sport programs, especially those that depend on volunteer coaches, do not have coaching education requirements because the requirements might discourage adults who do not think a volunteer should be forced to take a course or earn a license. The shortage of coaches in youth leagues and high schools is becoming so severe that many administrators in these programs are very hesitant to establish coaching education requirements. But school administrators also know that it is difficult to argue that varsity teams are part of educational programs when an increasing number of varsity teams are coached by adults who are not certified teachers. This could lead some school boards to think more seriously about cutting interscholastic sport programs.

The tradition in coaching is that people learn to coach by playing the sport and by watching or working with other coaches. This is how the top coaches in most sports learned to coach and this is how many youth team and high school coaches think they should learn. However, this "learning by doing" process seldom includes a systematic introduction to the information a person needs to be responsible for the safety and well-being of athletes and to promote the overall physical, psychological, and social development of athletes. College and professional coaches may *sometimes* be able to live without this information because they work with doctors, trainers, and psychologists who can advise them and work with athletes on their behalf. But

it is clearly dangerous for youth league and high school coaches not to be trained to deal with young people safely and responsibly and not to know something about overall human development (physical, psychological, and social). It is also foolish in light of the legal liability that comes with assigning adults to work with young people. One lawsuit can destroy an entire sport program! But if programs are indeed dangerous, they *should be* legally challenged.

Finally, this notion that you learn to coach by playing and working with an established coach clearly creates what many people call an "old boy network" in coaching. In other words, it cuts out most women and many minorities who don't have either certain types of playing experiences or the close contacts needed to get coaches to "mentor" them. This is partly why there is a coaching shortage in many programs: many women and minorities who are potential coaches either do not think they are qualified or they lack sponsorship to enter the ranks of coaching. Coaching education programs can be designed to tap into this pool of potential coaches and link them up with sport leagues, athletic departments, and even private sport organizations. For example, there is no reason why coaching education programs cannot be set up to recruit women into coaching. Women could coach both boys' and girls' teams in youth leagues and high schools just as men do. Other programs could be set up in neighborhoods and communities with heavy minority populations so as to create a credentialed group of people ready to coach young people in a variety of settings, including high schools.

If they are carefully organized, coaching education programs can help coaches exert positive influence in the lives of young people and increase the number of coaches in youth leagues and high schools. I would hope that education and certification programs could also help coaches build the professional image they need to be respected and rewarded for their work with young people. This would be appropriate in any society in which people claim to care for children.

In summary, our understanding of the extent to which coaches serve as socializing agents for players is weak. The influence of coaches may be based on dependency, role modeling, or advocating for the interests of their athletes. When the pressure to win is great, coaches are less likely to be concerned about the overall development of their athletes. The extent to which coaches actually influence the lives of athletes could be increased through quality coaching education programs. These programs could help coaches understand more about the people they coach and they could be used to recruit additional people into sport programs suffering a shortage of good coaches.

CONCLUSION:

HOW DO COACHES FIT IN?

The profession of coaching emerged as sport activities became institutionalized during the late nineteenth century. Although efforts to make sports seem educationally relevant have led coaches to become thought of as builders of character, their major purpose has always been to train athletes to compete in sports.

Research on the personalities of coaches indicates that, as a group, they are not insensitive and manipulative people—at least no more so than other adults. Coaching behavior, though it certainly reflects the traits and wishes of coaches themselves, is influenced by a combination of cultural beliefs about coaching and coaches, the organizational settings in which coaches work, and coaches' social relationships. The fact that coaches are held totally accountable for unpredictable outcomes of sport events creates pressure in their lives. This pressure is intensified by the public nature of sports and by the ease with which the competitive successes and failures of coaches can be measured. Coaches also have to contend with the strains created by dealing with so many different relationships while performing their jobs. The fact that expectations vary from one relationship to the next makes it difficult to keep everyone happy.

The behavior of coaches often reflects their efforts to deal with pressure and role strain. Strategies used by many coaches include *generating support* for their coaching methods, *gaining control* over factors that could influence the outcomes of competitions, and *being expedient* in managing relationships. These strategies may enable coaches to handle the pressure and role strain in their jobs, but they also lead coaches to appear insensitive, manipulative, and authoritarian. This contributes to their reputations as tough disciplinarians, but according to research, their actions "would appear to be a result of the requirements of the situation and not a product of underlying, generalizable traits" (Carron, 1978). This image of coaches could be changed if new tactics were used to deal with pressure and role strain. These tactics involve efforts to change priorities related to the goals and purposes of sport programs.

Coaches are also affected by conflicts between their coaching roles and the other roles they play. Teacher-coach role conflict is caused by a combination of the heavy work load associated with performing both roles at once. This conflict often leads to a response involving a redefinition of career priorities. Coach-family role conflict is often an issue for those with spouses and children. Although this conflict affects both men and women who coach, it is probably felt more acutely by women. The most common responses to this form of conflict involve a redefinition of priorities related to family and career. New approaches to controlling role conflict involve management and administrative changes in the organizations in which coaches work.

The traditional behavior patterns of coaches are perpetuated and passed on to new coaches through the coaching subculture, especially for men. This subculture discourages changes in commonly accepted methods and orientations. Consequently, coaches continue to engage in the behavior patterns that lead them to be stereotyped as traditional and conservative.

Research on the extent to which coaches actually influence the lives of their athletes is scarce, and we do not know if influence occurs because coaches make athletes dependent on them, become role models for athletes, or serve as advocates. Coaches want to influence the lives of athletes in positive ways, but as long as pressures and role strains are strong they may focus more of their attention on building winners than on creatively responding to the developmental needs of athletes.

Coaching education programs could help coaches exert a positive influence in the lives of athletes, but programs are sometimes difficult to put into operation. It is likely that coaching education would improve the quality of coaching and that strategically designed programs could increase the number of qualified coaches and enhance the image of coaching as a career.

SUGGESTED READINGS

Hastings, D.W. 1987. College swimming coach: social issues, roles, and worlds. University Press of America, New York (*an in-depth look at the job of a swimming coach in an American university; highlights the demands of the job from a practitioner's viewpoint; eye-opening for anyone thinking of becoming a coach*).

Locke, L., and J. Massengale. 1978. Role conflict in teacher-coaches. Res. Q. 49(2):162-174 (*a review of how teaching and coaching often present conflicting demands in the lives of people who try to do both*).

Massengale, J. 1974. Coaching as an occupational subculture. Phi Delta Kappan 56(2):140-142 (*an insightful look at the origins and dynamics of the coaching subculture, especially as it exists in educational settings*).

Pastore, D.L., and M.R. Judd. 1992. Burnout in coaches of women's team sports. JOPERD 63(5):74-79 (*a study of community college coaches that deals with similarities and differences in the experiences of female and male coaches*).

Ralbovsky, M. 1974. Lords of the locker room. Wyden Books, New York (*journalist takes a critical look at coaching behavior and the effect of coaches on players, especially players in youth leagues*).

Sabock, R.J. 1979. The coach. W.B. Saunders, Philadelphia (*description of coaches' lives; interesting discussion about how the success of male coaches has depended on support and assistance from spouses*).

Sage, G.H. 1980. Sociology of physical educator/coaches: the personal attributes controversy. Research Quarterly for Exercise and Sport 51(1):110-121 (*review of the literature by the sport sociologist who has done much of the research on the personal attributes of coaches*).

Sage, G.H. 1987. The social world of high school athletic coaches: multiple role demands and their consequences. Sociology of Sport Journal 4(3):213-228 (*use of observation and in-depth interviews to provide an insightful look at the everyday lives of male high school coaches*).

Sawyer, T. 1992. Coaching education in North America. JOPERD 63(7):34-64 (*this special section contains 10 articles on coaching education; the articles provide discussions of the need for coaching education and certification programs, and they provide examples of how real programs have been put into operation*).

Stewart, C.C., and L. Sweet. 1992. Professional preparation of high school coaches—the problem continues. JOPERD 63(6):75-79 (*an excellent overview of arguments for coaching education programs; the overview is presented in light of data collected in a study of coaches in Montana*).

Weiss, M.R., and B.L. Sisley. 1984. Where have all the coaches gone? Sociology of Sport Journal 1(4):332-347 (*good review of research on youth sport coaches and useful analysis of the orientations and motivations of a sample of those coaches*).

(Colorado Springs Gazette Telegraph and Bob Jackson)

CHAPTER 9

GENDER

Is equity the only issue?

We have never had total equality in women's athletics, and I don't know that we ever will have. . . . There is no women's baseball or women's wrestling. I have heard of women's mud wrestling.

Henry Bellmon, Governor of Oklahoma, as he justified cutting women's basketball at OU (1990)

They call her "toughie," but it's hard to imagine that someone so beautiful could be tough.

Verne Lundquist, CBS announcer, as he described a woman skater during the 1992 Winter Olympic Games

On a superficial level, some women want the muscled look because it's being depicted by the media as very trendy. . . . On a deeper level . . . muscles give women a sense of empowerment and self esteem . . . It says to others, "I will not accept or tolerate sexual abuse or harassment.

Barbara McDowell, University Women's Center Director (1992)

[While watching women athletes in] old film clips from . . . the 1930s and 1940s, I was shocked to see how friendly the athletes seemed with each other, holding hands, tossing arms around each other, giggling together. Such spontaneous affection has been squelched by modern-day homophobia. . . .

Mariah Burton Nelson, Author and former pro basketball player (1991)

Gender has become the most popular topic in the sociology of sport during the 1990s. This is because more sociologists have begun to realize that it is important to explain why sports have traditionally been defined as men's activities, why half the world's population has traditionally been excluded or discouraged from participating in many sports, how sports influence peoples' ideas about masculinity and femininity, and why the topic of sexual orientation and sports is so controversial. Although gender issues underlie many topics discussed in this book, a separate chapter is needed to identify the full range of gender issues in sports and the political implications of those issues.

When gender is discussed in the sociology of sport people deal with (1) participation and equity issues, and (2) ideological and structural issues. When they deal with participation and equity issues they focus attention on:

- Sport participation patterns among women
- Gender inequities related to participation opportunities, support for athletes, and jobs in coaching and administration
- Changes needed to achieve equal opportunities for girls and women in the future

When they deal with ideological and structural issues they focus attention on:

- How sports are connected with ideas about masculinity and femininity
- The need for alternative definitions of masculinity and femininity if real and lasting gender equity is to be achieved
- The need for changing the way sports are organized, promoted, played, and portrayed if real and lasting gender equity is to be achieved

My goal in this chapter is to discuss these two major issues and to show that even though many people deal with them separately, participation and equity issues go hand-in-hand with ideological and structural issues in real life.

PARTICIPATION AND EQUITY ISSUES
Participation Patterns among Women

Since the early 1970s, the single most dramatic change in the world of sport has been the increase in participation rates among girls and women. This has occurred in many countries around the world, especially those with reasonably strong economies. Girls and women participate in a variety of school, community, and club programs that didn't even exist 25 years ago.

Why Participation Has Increased

Five major factors account for recent increases in sport participation among girls and women in North America and other countries around the world:

1. New opportunities
2. Government legislation demanding equal treatment for women in public programs
3. The women's movement
4. The health and fitness movement
5. Increased media coverage of women in sports

NEW OPPORTUNITIES The primary reason more girls and women participate in sports today is that there are more participation opportunities than ever before. Before the mid-1970s, many girls and women did not participate in sports for one simple reason: teams and programs didn't exist. The young women of today may not realize it, but few of their mothers had the opportunities they now enjoy in their schools and communities. Teams and programs developed over the past two decades have uncovered and cultivated interests ignored in the past. Girls and women still do not receive an equal share of resources in most programs (as I will explain in this chapter), but increased participation has clearly accompanied the development of new opportunities.

GOVERNMENT LEGISLATION Although people often complain about government regulations, many sport participation opportunities available to girls and women today have been created in response to local and federal policies and legislation. These policies and rules were passed as a result of concerted efforts to raise legal issues and apply pressure on political representatives. For example, in the United States it took years of lobbying before Congress passed Title IX of the Educational Amendments in 1972. Title IX declared, "No person in the United States shall, on the basis of sex, be excluded from participation in, be denied the benefits of, or be subjected to discrimination under any educational program or activity receiving federal financial assistance." The men who controlled athletic programs in high schools and colleges objected to this "radical" idea and delayed the enforcement of Title IX for 5 years after it was passed into law. Many men claimed that equity was impractical and burdensome. They wanted to continue benefiting from being more equal than women!

In 1984 the U.S. Supreme Court ruled in *Grove City v. Bell* that Title IX did not apply to school athletic programs because they did not directly receive money from the federal government. Consequently, 800 cases of alleged discrimination under investigation at the U.S. Department of Education's Office for Civil Rights were dropped or narrowed (Sabo, 1988). It then took Congress another 4 years to pass the Civil Rights Restoration Act (over President Reagan's veto in March, 1988), which again mandated equal opportunity in *all* programs in any organization receiving federal money. This was helpful, but this act did not contain enough incentives for schools and other sport organizations to try to achieve equity, nor did it encourage people to challenge inequities. Then in 1992 the U.S. Supreme Court ruled that if schools intentionally violated Title IX, women athletes and coaches could sue for financial damages. This ruling is likely to make a positive impact on efforts to establish gender equity in sports, although it will come only through court cases.

The Canadian experience has been similar. After a Royal Commission on the Status of Women was established in 1970, studies to doc-

ument the existence of inequality were done. Then the Fitness and Amateur Sport Women's Program was established in 1980. It provided a combination of government-funded programs, training, and policy development opportunities for women (Lenskyj, 1988). This, along with other federal and provincial programs, led to the 1986 publication of *Women in Sport: A Sport Canada Policy*, which outlined national policy on women in sports. It not only set the official goal of equality of opportunity for women at all levels of sport but it also called for a specific action-oriented program to achieve this goal. Thus Canada became the only Western country to have an official policy on women in sports.

THE WOMEN'S MOVEMENT In connection with a worldwide women's movement over the past 25 years it has been emphasized that females are enhanced as human beings when they have opportunities to become competent and able, intellectually and physically. This has encouraged many women of all ages to pursue interests in sports, and it has led to the creation of new interests among those who, in the past, would never have thought of participating in sports. The women's movement has also helped redefine occupational and family roles for women. This has provided more women with the time and resources they need to participate in sports. As the ideals of the women's movement have become more widely accepted and as male control over the lives and the bodies of women has weakened, more women have chosen to be involved in sports. More change is needed, especially in poor countries and among low income women, but the choices now available to women are less restricted than in the past.

THE HEALTH AND FITNESS MOVEMENT Since the mid-1970s increased health awareness and the fitness boom have combined to encourage women to become involved in many physical activities, including sports. Although much of the emphasis in this movement has been tied to the traditional female ideal of preserving youth and being thin, there has also been an emphasis on the actual *development* of physical strength and competence. Muscles have become more widely accepted as desirable attributes among women of all ages. Traditional standards still exist, as illustrated by many clothing fashions and marketing methods associated with women's fitness, but some female athletes have moved beyond those standards to emphasize development of their bodies rather than the enhancement of their "looks." More women are now giving a higher priority to enjoying their bodies and physical competence than to trying to resemble anoretic models out of the pages of fashion magazines.

INCREASED MEDIA COVERAGE OF WOMEN IN SPORTS Increased participation rates have increased the visibility of female athletes. Even though women's sports are not covered as often or in the same detail as men's sports (see chapter 13), girls and women are now able to see and read about the achievements of women athletes in a wider range of sports than ever before. This has promoted the idea that all sports should be human activities rather than merely male activities. Seeing women athletes on television, attending women's sport events, and talking to female friends who participate in sports are especially important in encouraging girls and women to be active as athletes themselves. As girls grow up, they need to see what is possible before they will experiment with and develop athletic skills. This is especially important because girls may not receive the same kind of verbal and emotional support to be athletes as boys receive from parents, teachers, and peers (Greendorfer et al., 1986; Knoppers, 1988; Ross and Pate, 1987).

In summary, it is clear that increased opportunities, government legislation, the women's movement, the health and fitness movement, and increased coverage and publicity given to women athletes have all combined to encourage sport participation among girls and women. These changes are part of the growing worldwide awareness that equal participation opportunities cannot be systematically denied to half the human population.

Although some women use sport for cosmetic fitness and preserving youthful appearances, others now use it to strengthen and develop their bodies. (Randall J. Strossen, Ph.D.)

Reasons to be Cautious when Predicting Future Participation Increases

If opportunities and encouragement continue to expand, participation rates among girls and women will continue to increase, or will they? There are at least five reasons to be cautious when predicting future increases: (1) budget cutbacks and budget priorities, (2) resistance to government policies and legislation, (3) a decline in the number and proportion of women coaches and administrators, (4) a growing emphasis on "cosmetic fitness" and thinness among women, and (5) continued trivialization of women's sports.

BUDGET CUTBACKS AND BUDGET PRIORITIES Many public programs in schools and communities are threatened by budget cutbacks. If cutbacks are required, the programs for girls and women are often the most vulnerable. They are newer than the programs for males, they often don't have the same kind of administrative and community support, and they are not usually seen to be as important for the overall future of the sponsoring organizations. As one woman said, "It seems like the only time women's pro-

"All that we're asking is that you *each* lose ten pounds. Is that too much to ask?"

grams are treated equally is when cuts must be made." According to Christine Grant, women's athletic director at the University of Iowa, this creates problems because "women's sports were never equal in the first place, so when you cut equally, you're cutting women disproportionately" (quoted in Muscatine, 1991). Furthermore, programs for girls and women are often new programs, and they generally require *greater* financial support than long-established programs for boys and men. This is widely recognized in the business world—new businesses always have higher start-up costs, and if this is not recognized by investors, the new businesses are especially likely to fail. Therefore when

women's programs are new and underfunded, they may fail at a faster pace in the face of cuts than men's programs fail. Boy's and men's programs are less vulnerable because they have enjoyed years of support and development—even when few boys and men tried out for teams. But women are not getting the same breaks men got in the past.

RESISTANCE TO GOVERNMENT POLICIES AND LEGISLATION When new policies or rules are passed by governments, people often debate what they mean for the actual operation of programs. For example, people have been debating the implications of Canada's national policy on women in sport ever since it was established in

1986, and gender equality and fairness still do not exist. Changes have been contested by those with vested interests in doing things according to old ways, so progress has come only after continued struggle over resources and power. The same is true in the United States. Finally, there is legal support for the principle of equal participation opportunities for women, but the fight over equity continues in most organizations that sponsor sport programs for men and women. It will take time and effort to establish legal precedents and to see that the spirit of policies and rules actually becomes a part of the everyday operation of sport programs.

A DECLINE IN THE NUMBER AND PROPORTION OF WOMEN COACHES AND ADMINISTRATORS Despite a phenomenal increase in the number of sport programs for girls and women since the mid-1970s, there has been a significant decline of women coaches and administrators in those programs. This is the case in both the United States and Canada. Of course, it is possible for men to do a good job coaching and administering these programs, but without seeing women in positions of authority and power within their own programs, younger females may not define sport participation as an important part of their own futures. If women are not visible throughout the entire structure of sport programs, people tend to conclude that women's involvement is not appropriate or valued. This conclusion can reduce participation. (The issue of power and control over women's programs is discussed in the next section of the chapter.)

GROWING EMPHASIS ON "COSMETIC FITNESS" AND THINNESS AMONG WOMEN Since the early 1980s, there has been a move away from promoting sport as a means for women to experience personal freedom, independence, and power and a move toward the use of sport to lose weight and increase sexual attractiveness (MacNeill, 1988; Cole, 1993). The emphasis is now on displaying "heterosexualized hard bodies" through the latest fashions in body suits, leotards, and other sport gear. This emphasis is related to participation in two ways: (1) many

women of all ages don't want to begin participating in physical activities and sports until they are thin enough to look "right" and to wear the "right" clothes, and (2) many women who do participate combine their physical activity with pathogenic weight-control behavior that lowers body fat but produces amenorrhea and deprives them of necessary nutrients and increases the likelihood of injuries. Studies show that an alarming number of women athletes use laxatives, diet pills, diuretics, self-induced vomiting, binges, and starvation diets in conjunction with their training.* This increases the probability of injuries, jeopardizes health, and keeps alive the idea that women must conform to the latest definitions of heterosexual attractiveness or else they will be rejected by men and by women who also buy into those definitions. Furthermore, when the goal of participation is cosmetic fitness rather than physical competence, women have a tendency to drop out of sport programs when appearance meets expectations. Of course, it is possible for those seeking cosmetic fitness to discover that sports are fun, but this result is not assured; too many women seem to be on an impossible quest to look like Barbie dolls.

CONTINUED TRIVIALIZATION OF WOMEN'S SPORTS Female athletes sometimes have it tough—when they're not physically skilled, some people make fun of their inability; yet when they're very skilled, some people raise questions about whether they are "real women" (meaning heterosexual women who are attractive enough to be desired by men). In either case, women athletes and what they do are trivialized. The trivialization of women's sports is also driven by homophobia, or the irrational fear of homosexuality. In response to homophobia many women athletes will go to great lengths to "prove" they are "real women" by emphasizing that being an athlete is not nearly as important as eventually getting married, settling down,

---

*Barr, 1987; Brownell et al., 1987; Clark, 1988; Clark et al., 1988; Rosen et al., 1986; Smith, 1980.

having children, and becoming a nurturing homemaker. These issues are often more important in the media coverage of women athletes than their athletic accomplishments—remember, reporters can be homophobic, too.

Women's sports may also be trivialized through the use of team nicknames or mascots inconsistent with physical competence. Colleges and universities in the United States still do this. For example, the Mercer University (Georgia) men's teams are called the Bears, and the women's teams are called the Teddy Bears. Other examples are the Blue Hawks and the Blue Chicks,

The tradition of using "Lady" to describe women's athletic teams was initiated earlier this century when people would only allow women to play sports if it was clear that they would not renounce the idea that they should be soft and "feminine." (Colorado Springs Gazette Telegraph and Tom Kimmell)

the Wildcats and the Wild Kittens, the Boll Weevils and the Cotton Blossoms, the Rams and the Rambelles, and so on (Eitzen and Zinn, 1989, 1993; Fuller and Manning, 1987). Women took these names or used "Lady" or "-ettes" or "-elles" to describe their teams (Lady Longhorns, Lady Tigers, Buc-ettes, Rambelles, etc.) because it was important in the early years of women's sports to make sure that men understood that playing sports would not lead women to renounce their softness and femininity. The women would never have been funded if anyone thought that sports would make them like men. But if you were an athletic director would you give the same amount of money to the Wild Kittens as you would to the Wildcats? How would it sound if a TV announcer kept referring to the Gentlemen Longhorns and the Gentlemen Hurricanes? The use of cute nicknames may arouse some interest among some people, but it is hardly a tool for achieving real gender equity in sports. In fact, it trivializes women's sports.

In summary, sport participation rates among girls and women will not continue to increase automatically. Just as the participation of men has for years been nurtured and developed through consistent support and supplying of resources, so it must also be for women. Without continued support and encouragement, some of the progress of the past could be jeopardized. However, it is not likely that we will ever backslide to the extreme inequality that existed before 1970.

Gender Inequities in Sports

PARTICIPATION OPPORTUNITIES The availability of sport participation opportunities for women has often reflected traditional definitions of femininity. When femininity emphasized grace, heterosexual attractiveness, petiteness, flexibility, and balance, there were opportunities in figure skating, ice dancing, gymnastics, swimming, tennis, golf, and other sports that people believed were unrelated to strength, power, and other "manly" traits (this was before

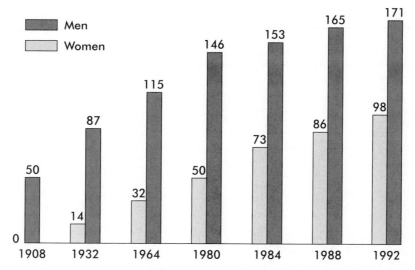

FIG. 9-1 Number of Summer Olympic events open to women and men.

Chris Evert decided that lifting weights could improve her tennis game). But even when girls and women were encouraged to play these sports, there was never anything even close to gender equity in the availability of participation opportunities. This pattern still exists in many sport organizations and communities today, especially in situations in which resources are in short supply.

The unique thing about the 1990s is that the vast majority of people in the United States and many other countries agree that women should have the same participation opportunities as men, but few are willing to make the changes needed to bring about equity. They say that equity is great as long as long as women don't want to wrestle or do other "unladylike" sports, as long as women don't want to play on men's teams, as long as we won't need to make any changes in opportunities available for men, as long as we won't have to cut football programs in any way (for example, down to 45 players instead of 145!), as long as women don't want tee times on weekends, as long as women don't want equal prize money or scholarships, and as long as men won't have to share too much of their power in sports organizations and athletic departments. As long as people say these things, boys and men will continue to outnumber girls and women by a 2-to-1 or 3-to-1 margin in most youth programs, varsity sports in high schools and universities, and community sport programs.

Inequities also exist outside of school and local community programs. In international sports, for example, it is more difficult to promote equity through government legislation. Therefore fewer events for women exist in the Olympic Games and other international competitions. Although changes have occurred over the past decade, women athletes remain underrepresented in international sports. Information on the modern Summer Olympic Games illustrates this point (Table 9-1 and Figure 9-1); through the years women have always had fewer events, and there have always been fewer women participants. The male-dominated International Olympic Committee (IOC) did not approve a women's 1500 m run until the 1972 Games in Munich. It was not until the 1984 Games in Los Angeles that women had the opportunity to run the 3000 m and marathon. The IOC has still not approved the 5000 m and 10,000 m runs for women, despite the fact that

Table 9-1   Male and female athletes in the modern Summer Olympic Games

Year	Place	Countries represented	Male athletes	Female athletes	Percent female
1896	Athens	13	311	0	0%
1900	Paris	22	1,319	11	0.01
1904	St. Louis	12	617	8	1.3
1908	London	22	1,999	36	1.8
1912	Stockholm	28	2,490	57	2.2
1916 No Olympics due to war–scheduled to be held in Berlin					
1920	Antwerp	29	2,543	64	2.5
1924	Paris	44	2,956	136	4.4
1928	Amsterdam	46	2,724	290	9.6
1932	Los Angeles	47	1,281	127	9.0
1936	Berlin	49	3,738	328	8.1
1940 Olympics (scheduled for Tokyo) cancelled due to World War II					
1944 Olympics cancelled due to World War II					
1948	London	59	3,714	385	9.4
1952	Helsinki	69	4,407	518	10.5
1956	Melbourne	71	2,958	384	11.5
1960	Rome	83	4,738	610	11.4
1964	Tokyo	93	4,457	683	13.3
1968	Mexico City	112	4,750	781	14.1
1972	Munich	122	6,077	1,070	17.6
1976	Montreal	88	4,915	1,274	20.6
1980	Moscow	81	4,238	1,088	20.4
1984	Los Angeles	140	5,458	1,620	22.8
1988	Seoul	160	7,105	2,476	25.8
1992	Barcelona	170	7,555	3,008	28.5

Modified from Boutilier and SanGiovanni (1983).

women have been running those distances for years in other events.

One reason why equity is difficult to attain on the international level is that some countries have fundamentalist religious beliefs that define sport participation for women as immoral. For example, Islamic countries seldom have women on their national teams because women are not permitted to expose any parts of their bodies in public. In many Catholic countries, women have traditionally had few legal rights to pursue activities not approved by the men who control the resources in society, including the resources related to sport participation. Similar patterns exist in connection with some other religious belief systems.

Women have few participation opportunities at the professional level. North American women must go to Europe to play professionally in sports such as volleyball and basketball. It seems that many North Americans believe that unless women play basketball in Spandex shorts and wear make-up, people won't pay to see them play. This topic will be discussed in Chapter 11, but here it is important to note that women have many fewer sport participation opportunities than men have because most women have to retire from competition when they leave college.

SUPPORT FOR ATHLETES There has never been equity in the support received by women athletes in the vast majority of North American high schools and colleges or other sport sponsoring organizations around the world. Take American schools as an example. Historically, there have been serious inequities in the realm of facilities and equipment. Women were often given the old gym when the new gym was completed for the men. Along with the inferior gym came inferior locker rooms, shower facilities, and heating and cooling systems. Other hand-me-downs included the old swimming pool, old uniforms from the men's teams, and used equipment. When hand-me-downs were not available, the women either had nothing or had to share facilities and equipment with the men. When things were shared, the women usually had their practices and game times scheduled at the most inconvenient times of the day or week.

Women athletes have never had the coaching and training support that was available in men's programs. Full-time women's coaches were rare, and assistant coaches were unheard of at most schools. Trainers, team physicians, and access to training room facilities were also rare for women's teams. Furthermore, when the men's teams took planes to away games, women's teams took buses; when men's teams took buses, women's teams drove their own cars or requested rides from their parents or friends. Media coverage of women's games was minimal or nonexistent at most schools, whereas men's games were always reported in the newspapers, often heard on the radio, and sometimes even seen on television.

Eliminating these overt inequities has been a major goal among some people, but the development of the guidelines to accomplish this goal has been a complex and politically controversial task. The enforcement of equity guidelines has been even more complicated. Nevertheless, changes have occurred and a few women athletes now have support similar to the support men have. But major inequities remain. These often appear in areas such as:

- Availability of scholarships*
- Program operating expenses*
- Provision and maintenance of equipment and supplies*
- Recruiting budgets*
- Scheduling of games and practice times
- Travel and per diem expenses
- Opportunity to receive coaching and academic tutoring
- Numbers of coaches assigned to teams
- Salaries for administrators, coaches, trainers, tutors, etc.
- Provision of medical and training services and facilities
- Publicity for individuals, teams, and events

Serious inequities are widespread in many of these areas across many programs in the United States and other countries. This is true even in programs in which Title IX has called for equity since 1972. These and other inequities led Donna Lopiano, the executive director of the Women's Sports Foundation, to say in 1992 that "we are so far from gender equity [in intercollegiate athletics] that it is laughable."

Inequities also exist in many community programs, but they often go undocumented unless some local resident digs through data from Park and Recreation Departments and other local groups. Access to facilities, the number of available programs, and the staff assigned to programs are the most likely areas in which differences would be found. This is a worthwhile project for anyone concerned with gender equity issues.

Most people now realize that a lack of support for athletes leads to a lack of interest, and a lack of interest leads to less participation. So it can no longer be claimed that real equity isn't necessary because girls and women are simply not interested in participating in sports.

---

*See Chapter 15 pp. for data documenting inequities in these areas.

JOBS FOR WOMEN IN COACHING AND AD-MINISTRATION The athletic lives of most women are controlled by men. Whereas women's sport programs have increased in number and importance all over North America, there has been a significant decline in the number and proportion of women coaches and administrators in many sport organizations, especially the athletic departments of high schools and colleges. This clearly indicates that equity does not exist in these organizations.

Data at all levels of competition show that women do not have equal opportunities when it comes to jobs in coaching and administration; the higher and more powerful the job, the fewer the women. For example, here's some information on American intercollegiate sports (taken from Acosta and Carpenter, 1992a):

- In 1972 when Title IX became law, 90% of the coaches of women's teams were women; in 1992 only 48.3% of the coaches of women's teams were women. Table 9-2 highlights these changes in 10 NCAA Division I women's sports.
- Between 1982 and 1992 there was an increase of 812 head coaching jobs for women's teams; women head coaches increased by 181 during the same period while men head coaches increased by 631.
- In 1972 over 90% of women's athletic programs had a woman director; in 1992 only 17% had a woman director, and 28% of all women's programs had no women administrators, and less than one female per school has a job as an administrator in women's sport programs.
- The decline in the proportion of women coaches and administrators has been most dramatic at the highest levels of competition and in the highest-paying jobs.
- Only 1.3% of the coaches in men's programs are women.

What would men say if over 50% of the coaches and 83% of the administrators in men's pro-

Table 9-2 Percentage of women coaches for the 10 most popular women's intercollegiate sports, 1977 and 1992

Sport	1977	1992	Percentage point decline
Basketball (BB)	79.4%	63.5	−15.9
Volleyball (VB)	86.6%	65.7	−20.9
Tennis (TE)	72.9%	48.0	−24.9
Softball (SB)	83.5%	63.7	−19.8
Cross country (CC)	35.2%	20.1	−15.1
Track (TR)	52.3%	20.4	−31.9
Swim/dive (SD)	53.6%	28.2	−25.4
Field hockey (FH)	99.1%	47.0	−52.1
Golf (GO)	54.6%	45.7	−8.9
Soccer (SO)	29.4%	25.8	−3.6

Modified from Acosta and Carpenter (1992a).

grams were women and they had only 1% of the jobs in women's programs? They would be outraged! And they would certainly call for major affirmative action programs.

The situation is much the same in Canada and England as well (Theberge, 1980, 1984; Whitson and Macintosh, 1989; White and Brackenridge, 1985). Vested interests among males in coaching and administrative jobs in amateur sports are strong, and men are unwilling to make changes favoring the interests of women. Systematic data on coaches are not easy to collect from country to country, but there are relatively few female coaches at the world-class amateur level; Olympic teams are almost never coached by women (Theberge, 1990, 1993).

Reasons for the underrepresentation of women in coaching and administrative positions in women's sports have been widely debated and studied. According to women working in the athletic programs of U.S. colleges and universities, the major reasons for this underrepresentation are (see Acosta and Carpenter, 1985, 1992b):

- Men's use of an efficient "old boy" network to get jobs
- The failure of women to use their own network to help female friends and associates
- Unconscious discrimination in the selection process
- Lack of qualified women coaches and administrators

According to men the reasons are:

- Lack of qualified women applicants
- Unwillingness among women to travel and recruit athletes
- Failure of women to apply for jobs
- Time constraints on women with families

Regardless of the real reasons for the underrepresentation of women in coaching and administration, these perceptions are very important. Because men are in positions of power in most women's sport programs, their perceptions shape whom they recruit, interview, hire, and promote. Perceptions among women are important because they are used as a basis for making career decisions related to coaching and administration.

Need for Changes to Achieve Gender Equity

Equity is about who gets what. Gender equity in sports is important because access to valued opportunities and rewards is crucial when it comes to controlling what happens in your life and making changes in the world around you. But achieving gender equity in sports continues to be difficult. Appeals to fairness sound good but they haven't been very effective. Everyone supports fairness, but many don't want to give up anything to achieve it. This has certainly been the pattern in sport programs in which men control most of the power and resources. Most men support the idea of gender equity, but few of them are willing to sacrifice men's participation, support, or jobs to achieve it.

This resistance has forced those interested in equity to ask government and the courts for as-

SIDELINES

©1982 M.T.F.-T.W.S.-Lakewood. CO

Women have traditionally been expected to play support roles in sports, while men have done the important things on the field and in administrative positions. This is illustrated in the box on pp. 220-222.

sistance. However, the government has been slow to respond, especially in the United States. In fact, between 1972 and 1988 there were over 1025 official complaints about gender inequities filed with the U.S. Department of Education's Office for Civil Rights, and not one of them resulted in any cuts of federal funds at any of the schools. Some court decisions have been supportive of gender equity in sports, but court cases often involve costly legal fees and long-term commitments for complainants. So far, few girls or women have been interested in going into debt and giving up years of their lives to see if they can force a sports programs to change (especially because they would usually be too old to benefit from the change even if they did win the case after a number of years). However, the courts may become more valuable in the future since women in the United States can now sue schools and sport programs for personal damages in equity cases.

According to Donna Lopiano, former director of women athletics at the University of Texas and now executive director of the Women's Sport Foundation, equity can be achieved

Text Continued on page 223.

Cheerleaders:
The "Sideshow" of American Sport?

Cheerleaders in the 1990s. They fit a variety of images—vocal pep leaders, tumblers, stunt performers, entertainers, dancers, sex objects, sideshows for men's power sports. But images change and they depend on historical and cultural factors. For example, in the late 1800s the very first cheerleaders were men. Women weren't allowed because cheerleading was part of sports, and sports were manly activities separate from the world of the feminine, as it was defined back then.

The first women who became cheerleaders were defined as rebels or deviants, invaders of male space. Up through the 1940s they received warnings from educators that cheerleading was bad for their health and overall development as women. Laurel Davis (1988) tells of an educator who wrote in 1938 that he found women cheerleaders "frequently became too masculine for their own good," that they developed "loud and raucous voices," and they often took to using "slang and profanity" because they hung out with rough and tough male cheerleaders.

But many women didn't listen to these warnings, and social definitions of both femininity and cheerleading continued to change. By the 1950s cheerleading was dominated by women, and most men dropped out because they didn't like being associated with what was becoming "a girls' activity" (Davis, 1988). By the 1970s many people thought cheerleading was "naturally" suited for females and females were "naturally" suited for cheerleading. In fact, some people even thought cheerleading was an activity in which girls could learn about real femininity and through which young women could show they were socially accepted in the highly gendered world of junior and senior high schools. Re-

cently in Texas, it was even alleged that a mother put a murder contract out on a girl who might beat her daughter out of a spot on a junior high cheerleading squad. This mother, similar to many other parents in recent years, thought that being a cheerleader was a basis for popularity and that being especially popular among males was the most important thing in a female's life.

It is difficult to make generalizations about cheerleading today. But whenever I see the "honey shots" of the made-up young women smiling and posing (for men?) on the sidelines of NFL games, and when I go to Denver Nuggets games and hear fans make demeaning remarks about the bodies and overall looks of the dance team/cheerleader squad, I am reminded that many Americans still evaluate men in terms of what they do and women in terms of how they look. In the most popular team sports in American society, men are the doers; they make the decisions, play the games, and get credit for their skills. Women are spectators; they become part of sport by standing on the sidelines as showpieces for the teams they represent or by entertaining fans when the men on the field need a rest. Their role is to provide emotional support for men or simply to fill in breaks in the men's game that everyone came to see. Men must be aggressive and able to dominate others to be athletes, but according to Nancy Collins (writing in *Esquire*) the two most important characteristics needed to be a cheerleader are "blondness, congenital or acquired, and a compulsively cute, nonstop bottom." She adds that "it also helps to date the quarterback." (That reminds me—most cheerleaders are white even when the majority of athletes is black. Why is that?)

Of course, this depiction of cheerleaders is not universally true. High schools and universities select female cheerleaders on the basis of many attributes, including character, grades, popularity, spirit, voice, and gymnastic abilities. But physical attractiveness is seldom overlooked. In fact, those who have many of the attributes needed to become a cheerleader but lack "looks" are encouraged to join the pep club and sit in the bleachers with the band. There they can provide support for the team without being individually seen and evaluated. What if coaches used "looks" as a criterion for selecting members of the football team? They would be laughed out of school or fired for being deviants. But when cheerleaders are chosen, "looks" is a definite qualification.

Cheerleaders like to think they contribute to the success of their teams, and they like to be noticed by the men they support. But most male athletes quickly learn to ignore cheerleaders and not take them seriously as part of sport itself (although they may date them after the games are over). Male athletes are the show; cheerleaders are the sideshow.

This pattern can be observed even in youth sports. For example, when my daughter was 7 years old, some of the 11- and 12-year-old girls in our neighborhood wanted her as the mascot of their cheerleader squad. They were eager (with their mothers' encouragement) to inspire and cheer the 12-year-old boys on one of the local football teams. And Danielle wanted to be a cheerleader. After much hesitation I gave Danielle approval to join the squad. I talked to the girls and told them they could practice in our yard. At first I was impressed with their dedication and creativity in developing complex routines. For 3 weeks they taught each other cartwheels, walkovers, and handsprings, and formed themselves into a proud, coordinated group. Then things changed. The girls knew that their ultimate reason for being cheerleaders was to provide support for their brothers and male friends. They decided that if they were to do this effectively they should go to the park where the team practiced and let the boys "notice" them and get accustomed to their cheers. They set off proudly to show the boys their routines. Two hours later a discouraged group of girls returned. The boys had not even looked at them. Even after practice, the boys ignored them on the way home.

But the girls didn't quit. They went back to the practice field hoping the boys would notice and approve of them. Their mothers made them uniforms, drove them to games, and told them to keep cheering even though the boys continued to ignore them. Meanwhile I wondered if the girls were learning that it was their duty to provide emotional support for ungrateful others and that their self-esteem ultimately depended on feedback and approval from males who didn't take them seriously (at least as part of sport). Fortunately, Danielle quit when the older girls focused more on being noticed by boys than doing their tumbling routines. Instead of cheering football players she continued to focus on what her body could do and how good it made her feel to be an athlete.

Continued.

Cheerleaders—cont'd:
The "Sideshow" of American Sport?

Unfortunately, some girls don't change their priorities. In many schools being a cheerleader is still a more important basis of popularity than being an athlete. Traditional definitions of femininity are still alive. Wriggling female centerfolds still capture the attention of cameramen and leering spectators between plays and during time-outs. These women are showpieces. They are expected to be alluring and sensuous, but they are also expected to be pure, wholesome, and dedicated to the teams they support. In fact, if they use their bodies to make money for themselves (by posing for certain magazines), the male administrators of the teams will dismiss them without thinking twice—being alluring and sensuous at a football game is wholesome, doing it for your own financial gain is immoral. Now, those are strange rules! I wonder who made them up? Not everyone agrees with my analysis of cheerleading. Lawrence Herkimer, past president of the National Cheerleaders Association, claims that cheerleading builds qualities leading to success in life. This may be true because many other parts of life are gendered in the same way sports are. But is that the way things should be? What do you think?

Young girls are often encouraged to be cheerleaders, and in some schools, being a cheerleader is still more likely to lead to popularity than being an athlete. (Colorado Springs Gazette Telegraph)

only through strategic political organization and pressure (1992). She has called for the development of grass roots organizations to systematically support and publicize girls' and women's sports programs. As these organizations publicly recognize the achievements of female athletes and their sponsors, other people will begin to see the value of women's sports and join efforts to achieve equity.

Lopiano (1991) has also urged people in sport sponsoring organizations to use the following strategies to promote gender equity:

- Confront discriminatory practices in your organizations and become advocates for women athletes and women coaches and administrators.
- Learn about and educate others about the history of discrimination in sports and how to recognize the subtle forms of discrimination that operate in sports today.
- Object to any policies that would result in a decrease in women's sport participation or participation opportunities.
- Package and promote women's sports as revenue producers so there will be financial incentives to increase participation opportunities for women.
- Recruit women athletes into coaching, and establish internships and other programs to recruit and train women to enter jobs at all levels in your organizations.
- Be an advocate and a watchdog and insist on fair and open employment practices in your organization.
- Keep track of data in your organization and publish a "gender equity score card" every year.
- Use women's hiring networks when looking for coaches and administrators in all sport programs.
- Create a supportive work climate for women in your organization, and establish policies to eliminate sexual harassment.

These are useful suggestions. They emphasize a combination of public relations, political lobbying, pressure, education, and advocacy. They

are based on the assumption that increased participation and opportunities for women will not come without struggle, and that favorable outcomes depend on organization and persistence.

However, it is very important for those who struggle for gender equity in sports to understand the origins of inequities and critically assess the ideology that has shaped the structure and organization of dominant forms of sport. If women become participants in existing sports and sport organizations without understanding the connections between sports and dominant definitions of masculinity in society, they will end up contributing to and recreating a set of ideas about social life that not only work to the advantage of men but guarantee that there will always be gender inequities in sports. Striving for equity in activities and organizations that have been shaped over the years by the values and experiences of men *will not* eliminate problems for many women as they play and work in sports.

Equity is an important goal, but participating in sports based on what Nelson has described as the "Military Model" (see Chapter 7, pp. 168-169) must be critically assessed. Many people in the sociology of sport have argued that real gender equity can never be achieved in sports activities and organizations exclusively shaped by the values and experiences of men. They say that real equity requires the development of new models of sport participation, models shaped by the values and experiences of women and of men who do not see themselves in terms of dominant definitions of masculinity.[3]*

SPORT PARTICIPATION, PERSONAL EMPOWERMENT, AND STRIVING FOR GENDER EQUITY Research in the sociology of sport suggests that playing sports can be a personally empowering experience for girls and women (Blinde, Taub, and Han, 1993). Being an athlete, especially a skilled athlete, can change the way women see themselves. It can make them

---

*This case is made in the following sources: Birrell, 1988; Bryson, 1990; Cole, 1993; Hall, 1990; Messner, 1992; Whitson and Macintosh, 1989.

Sport participation often enables girls and women to establish identities based on skills respected by peers and the community. (Tini Campbell)

feel physically stronger, more competent, and more in control of their lives as independent individuals (Coakley and Westkott, 1984). This is important because social life is often organized in ways that lead girls and women to see themselves as weak, dependent, and powerless (Cantor and Bernay, 1992).

Sport participation also provides girls and women with opportunities to reconnect with the power of their own bodies. Many images of women in society present the female body as an object to be looked at, evaluated, and consumed. Girls and women even learn to objectify their own bodies as they apply these images to themselves. Because identity and a sense of power are grounded in a person's body and body image, sport participation can help women overcome the perception that their bodies are objects. Developing physical skills can give women a distinct feeling of physical power (Deem, 1986). Furthermore, the physical strength often gained through sport participation goes beyond simply helping a woman feel fit; it can also make her feel less vulnerable, more independent, and

more in control of her physical safety and psychological well-being.*

Sport participation can also change the way a girl or woman relates to males. For example, a young woman who began working out with weights and training to be a power lifter explains (cited in Richmond, 1986):

> I haven't been the same since. I love it. All of a sudden I find I'm stronger than anyone else in the place—all the girls and practically all of the guys. . . . The guys respected me right away, and that's important. They all act like they're so tough, then you go in and lift more than they can. They can't ignore that there's a girl over in the corner doing more than them, and they hang their heads.

A 17-year-old working-class woman in England expressed similar feelings about her own weight training (Coakley and White, 1991):

> I think mainly I want to be . . . equal with the blokes because I think too many girls get pushed around by blokes. They get called names and things. I think that's wrong. They say "a girl can't do this, a girl can't do that," and I don't like it at all. I'd rather be, you know, equal.

Although feelings of personal empowerment are not always associated with sport participation, they occur frequently enough to raise the question of how they might be related to the achievement of gender equity in sports.

The answer is that feelings of empowerment can lead women to be more assertive in their efforts to gain leadership positions in sports and sport organizations. However, feeling personally empowered and being in leadership positions does not guarantee that women will critically assess sports and figure out how to change them so they will not automatically work to the advantage of men. Sometimes the women promoted into leadership positions in sports are those who have demonstrated their commitment to doing things exactly how men have done them for years, even though those things have not worked to the advantage of anyone other than men who thrive on aggression and competition and constantly evaluate success in terms of dominating others. When women become cheerleaders for this type of approach to sports,

*For an explanation of this point, see Birrell, 1983, 1988; Brown et al., 1982; Bryson, 1990; Coakley and White, 1991; Deem, 1986; Ho and Walker, 1982; Kleiber and Hemmer, 1981; Lopiano, 1984; Nelson, 1991; Snyder and Spreitzer, 1983; Theberge, 1987; and Trujillo, 1983.

and to life in general, they do little to further the cause of equity over the long run. But when women combine personal empowerment and leadership positions with a critical analysis of sports and then use their power to actually change the structure and organization of sports, real and lasting gender equity can be achieved.

MEN AND THE NEED FOR CHANGES TO ACHIEVE GENDER EQUITY Gender equity is not just a women's issue; equity also involves opening up spaces for men to participate in forms of sports that are not based on dominant definitions of masculinity. When sports emphasize aggression and domination they often lead to self-destructive orientations in the forms of chronic injuries, an inability to relate to women, fears of intimacy with other men, homophobia, and a compulsive concern with comparing oneself to other men in terms of what might be called "life success scores" (Messner, 1992).

It is important for men to understand that seeking status and rewards in sport activities and organizations, in which success is defined in terms of dominating other men, ultimately constrains and distorts their relationships with each other and with women. For example, Bruce Kidd, a former Olympic runner and now a physical educator-social scientist, has pointed out that:

> Through sports, men learn to cooperate with, care for, and love other men, in [many] ways, but they rarely learn to be intimate with each other or emotionally honest. On the contrary, the only way many of us express fondness for other men is by teasing or mock fighting (1987, p. 259).

For men who want to get beyond the expression of fondness through teasing and mock fighting there is good reason to join with those women concerned with critically assessing the structure and organization of dominant sport forms in their society.

In summary, gender equity is an important issue, but efforts to achieve equity must be grounded in a clear understanding of how gender is related to ideological and structural issues in sports.

IDEOLOGICAL AND STRUCTURAL ISSUES
The "Gender Logic" of Sports

Dominant forms of sport in most cultures are played and organized in ways that work to the advantage of most men and to the disadvantage of women. When people participate in sports they often learn a form of "common sense" that leads to the conclusion that women are "naturally" inferior to men. For example, when someone throws a ball correctly, people often say that she or he "throws like a boy"; and when someone throws a ball incorrectly, people say he or she "throws like a girl." The same is true when running or other sport skills are assessed. In sports, if something is done right, it's done as a boy or man would do it, and if something is done wrong, it's done as a girl or woman would do it. This **gender logic** is used by coaches when they criticize male team members by telling them they are "playing like a bunch of girls" when they make mistakes or do not play aggressively enough. In other words, being female, according to the *gender logic* of sports, means being a failure. This is *not* a way of thinking that works to the advantage of girls and women; in fact, it clearly privileges boys and men and gives them power over girls and women both in and out of sports.

SIDELINES

• - 1984 mark time features, inc. lakewood, co

The "gender logic" used by many people leads them to exclude women from certain sports or simply to ignore women's athletic abilities.

Another aspect of the *gender logic* used in many sports is the belief that men and women are naturally different, and that the natural characteristics of men are superior to the natural characteristics of women when it comes to anything except giving birth and nursing babies. For many years this "logic" led women to be excluded from sports. Women were told by male doctors that if they played sports they would damage their uteruses and experience other physical problems endangering their abilities to have children. Today's college students may laugh at these myths because they have information to refute them. But their mothers and grandmothers didn't have this information and neither do many of today's women in countries where literacy rates are low. For these women, myths about the physiology of women have kept them out of sports.

The gender logic of "natural" male/female difference has also led many people to approve of the exclusion of women from some or all sports. Since this logic led to the conclusion that women could never equal or surpass men's achievements, and since many people believed that sports were primarily about setting records and dominating others, they saw no reason to even let women get involved. Unfortunately, this way of thinking about gender and sports still exists. Many people continue to compare women and men in terms of performance *differences* and then go on to say that differences will never disappear because men are simply physically superior to women. Of course, most of these people never wonder what kinds of physical skills would be needed by athletes if sports had been shaped by the values and experiences of women instead of men. It is certain that if sports had been created by and for women, the Olympic Games motto would not be *Citius, Altius, Fortius* (faster, higher, stronger); instead it might be "balance, flexibility, and ultraendurance"!

The "logic of difference" continues to be used to the disadvantage of women. For example, the men on the International Olympic Committee still "protect" women by not allowing them to participate in certain distance events in running and swimming. Millions of other women have been "protected" over the years by people who would not let them play certain sports considered to be too rough or demanding. It takes time to change these gendered forms of "common sense" based on the *logic of difference*.

The *logic of difference* also leads many people to conclude that even when women play sports they are not exciting to watch because they can't match standards set by men. When gender logic leads to the conclusion that women are, by definition, inferior to men, women will never achieve equity in any sports or sport programs that evaluate success in terms of abilities to physically dominate others in entertaining ways.

From "Gender Logic" to Ideology: Sports As a Celebration of Masculinity

In chapter 4 it was explained that ideology consists of the ideas people use to explain (1) how the social world works, (2) how they are connected to that world, and (3) what they should do as they live their lives in that world. But ideology is so much a part of our lives that we seldom think about it, and we almost never raise questions about it; we just take it for granted. As physical educator-social scientist Bruce Kidd bluntly reminds us, "Ideology is like B.O.; you never smell your own." I would add that when you do smell it, you spray something on it so you can continue to ignore it.

This tendency to ignore our own ideology is especially true for many of us who have been involved with sports for most of our lives. Many men see sports as one of the most exciting and satisfying activities in their lives, and it is difficult for them to critically examine something they like and enjoy so much. Some women also find it difficult to critically examine sports. This is especially true for women who have watched sports, participated in them, and wished they could share some of the rewards enjoyed by male athletes. When sports have been important in one's life it is difficult to raise critical questions about how they are structured and organized.

When we take a critical look at dominant sport forms in many societies around the world, we see that they often involve "an acting out of masculine virility and power" (Birke and Vines, 1987). Sports are usually structured and organized to emphasize values and experiences associated with dominant ideas about masculinity in society. Sport spectacles in most societies celebrate an interpretation of the world that privileges men and perpetuates the power they have to organize social life in ways that fit their interests. This is why Kidd (1987) has described sports stadiums and domed arenas as "men's cultural centers." These multimillion dollar facilities built with tax monies cater to the interests of men and host sports in which men "kill," "whip," "roll over," "punish," and "annihilate" other men while people cheer them on. The images associated with these sports are images of a manhood based on aggression, physical power, the ability to dominate others, and a concern with ranking people in terms of their ability to dominate. This is why sports tend to reinforce and perpetuate ideologies (interpretations of social life) that favor the interests of men over the interests of women.

Ideology in Action: the Social Construction of "Sissies" and "Tomboys"

Sports emphasizing aggression and competition "fit" with the dominant definition of masculinity in Western cultures, especially American culture; they do not fit with any ideas about femininity or alternative definitions of masculinity. This has presented problems for many boys and men who don't have the interest or ability to be competitive in sports requiring physically aggressive behaviors. It has also presented problems for many women who aren't comfortable trying to aggressively dominate others or who are such tough competitors that they don't fit with dominant definitions of femininity. The boys who avoid sports during childhood, especially sports involving physical toughness, are

often called "sissies." The girls who excel in those sports are called "tomboys."

Boys labeled "sissies" often get teased and excluded from peer group relationships and activities; they are *socially marginalized* because of their characteristics. They may even be defined as "abnormal" because they don't fit the dominant definition of masculinity in society, a definition that many people think is based in "nature" or the "will of God." As they get older these boys often continue to be marginalized because they are seen as threats to the ideology that many people use to define "nature" and interpret how the social world works. This is when questions may be raised about the boy's sexual orientation and when terms such as "fag," "gay," and "queer" are used to describe them, regardless of their sexual orientation.

When the dominant definition of masculinity in society is based on the assumption that in addition to being aggressive and competitive, all "real men" must be heterosexuals, "gay" becomes defined as a derogatory identity label and an abnormal lifestyle. This, of course, leads gay men to hide their identities and feelings when they play sports and it encourages all men to idealize extra-aggressive behavior so they won't be seen as gay. It also leads to frequent gay-bashing comments in locker rooms and on playing fields. In fact, men's coaches may question a player's heterosexuality when he makes a mistake or is not as aggressive as he is expected to be; the assumption is that when players are called "girls" or "fags" they will try extra hard to be aggressive and dominate the other "real men" they are playing against. This is one of the ways that a combination of misogyny (a disdain for women) and homophobia (a fear of homosexuality) gets built into the structure and organization of dominant forms of sport in a society. If you have doubts about this, go to the locker room of a major college football or men's basketball team and listen to what is said by the athletes over the course of a season (Curry, 1991).

Gay male athletes have responded to homophobia in a variety of ways (Pronger, 1990).

Some simply put up with feelings of estrangement and aloneness as they enjoy participating in sports, some laugh inside at the irony of participating in activities that glorify a combination of domination and heterosexuality, some use sports as a hiding place where they can "prove" masculinity to themselves or others, and some have organized the Gay Games or local teams and events that bring together gay athletes to compete in sports.

When girls are labeled "tomboys," they don't experience the same social disapproval experienced by boys labeled "sissies." Tomboys often receive praise. This is because behaviors associated with boys and men are highly valued and rewarded in society, even when they are exhibited by girls. But as girls get older and their bodies become sexualized in terms of dominant gender ideology, they get messages that being physically tough is not nearly as important as being physically attractive and sexually desirable in the eyes of men. They also hear that sport turns boys into men, and they wonder what it does to girls. Sometimes their boyfriends encourage them to drop out of sports that are too rough or that interfere with their availability for the young men (Coakley and White, 1992).

Different young women deal with these "femininity messages" in different ways, but those who continue to play certain sports sometimes discover that unless they are careful to act in "ladylike" ways, the label of tomboy might change to "lesbian." Women who aren't "soft" and "graceful" don't fit the dominant definition of femininity. But these women can lower their chances of being socially marginalized if they present themselves to others in ways that give "proof" that they are really "normal" (meaning *heterosexual*) women. This can be done with bows, ribbons, ponytails, make-up, dresses, hose, heels, boyfriends or husbands, engagement or wedding rings, and statements about wanting to eventually settle down and have children. If women athletes in "power sports" don't do these things, some people will define them as threats to the dominant definition of femininity and even threats to their ideas about "nature" and morality. This happens regardless of the sexual orientation of the women themselves. This is how homophobia gets built into sports and then serves to control all women, gay and straight (Nelson, 1991). This is illustrated in the box on pp. 229-231.

Homophobia has worked in strange ways over the years. Women who grew up between 1910 and 1950 heard from doctors and other "scientific experts" that playing certain sports would turn them into physiological monsters and cause their genital organs to decay and their bodies to change into men's bodies (see some of these warnings listed in Birke and Vines, 1987; Lenskyj, 1986; Vertinsky, 1987). Women who grew up during the 1950s and 1960s heard that most women athletes were "dykes" and that vigorous exercise could damage their uteruses and cause them to have childbirth problems. They were also warned that playing sports would lead to the development of bulging muscles and other characteristics that men would not find sexually attractive. Today's women who dedicate themselves to success in "manly" sports may be called lesbians or they may simply be viewed as abnormal by certain people. For example, when women athletes are heavily muscled or very big and strong, people may say, "They don't look like women!" or "How ugly! They look like men!" or "They must be on steroids!" or "Change the channel! Let's watch gymnastics or figure skating where the athletes look like women!" Of course, some people simply say, "Hey, this is how athletes look in certain sports," or "These people are great athletes," or "How impressive! What great bodies!" In the 1990s these latter comments are seldom heard; the former comments are heard regularly. This is because dominant gender ideology in society, including homophobia, runs deep.

To make matters even worse for women, some people believe it is necessary to discriminate against lesbian athletes because gender equity will never be achieved if people think some women athletes are lesbians. People holding this

Text continued on p. 231.

REFLECT ON | SPORT

Women Bodybuilders:
The "Sideshow" of American Sport?

Women bodybuilders in the 1990s. They fit a variety of images—powerful women, unfeminine freaks, the ultimate hard bodies, new women, "gender benders," entertainers, sideshows for real sports. But images depend on historical and cultural factors (Bolin, 1992). For example, before the late 1970s there was no such thing as competitive women's bodybuilding. It didn't exist because it so totally contradicted dominant definitions of femininity and what people saw as natural muscular development for women. But women bodybuilders have consistently challenged those definitions of femininity, pushed boundaries of social acceptance, and raised questions about what is "natural" when it comes to the bodies of women.

Most people have seen women bodybuilders as rebels or deviants, freaks of nature. This is because most people in Western cultures see gender in terms of differences that divide all humans into two distinct and mutually exclusive categories: females and males. According to this classification system, females are defined as "the weaker sex" and femininity is associated with being soft, petite, emotional, and in need of protection. In fact, the dominant definition of feminine beauty over the past century has been associated with vulnerability and weakness. Males, on the other hand, are defined as the stronger sex and masculinity is associated with being hard, strong, rational, and the defender of women. In fact, masculine attractiveness has traditionally been associated with invulnerability and strength, and many people simply assume that "nature" intended it that way.

Women bodybuilders have challenged this gender ideology, and in the process they have threatened people's ideas about how the world works.

According to dominant gender ideology, women-bodybuilders are unfeminine because they are "too muscular," and ugly because their bodies aren't soft and petite. But not everyone accepts this ideology. For those seeking alternative definitions of femininity, women's bodybuilding has provided new images that some young people, especially some young women, find attractive. They like the idea of challenging traditional notions of female frailty and raising questions about the biology of gender difference. Women's bodybuilding has encouraged this process by showing that hardness and strength are not exclusively the attributes of males.

Despite the fact that women bodybuilders, similar to women athletes in other power sports, are what might be called "gender benders," they are not able to completely escape the constraints of dominant definitions of femininity. The first women bodybuilders were careful not to be too good at building muscles. They emphasized a toned, symmetrical body displayed through carefully choreographed graceful moves. Their goal was to somehow stay within the boundaries of "femininity" as determined by contest judges. But this presented problems because definitions of femininity have never been set once and for all time. Definitions constantly change and that made it impossible for judges to spell out what was "too muscular" or what body symmetry was supposed to look like for women. As judges tried to devise a bodybuilding ideal that balanced muscularity and body symmetry, women bodybuilders tried to anticipate judges' standards and often challenged the standards used from contest to contest. The controversy surrounding this issue of defining standards was the central theme in *Pumping Iron II: The*

Continued.

Women Bodybuilders—cont'd:
The "Sideshow" of American Sport?

Women, a movie about women's bodybuilding in the early 1980s.

This issue of trying to define "femininity" was frustrating to bodybuilders who were into muscularity during the early 1980s. For example, one woman stated that:

> When you compete, your muscularity is all, but the judges insist on [us] looking womanly. They try to fudge the issue with garbage about symmetry, proportion, and definition. What they really want is tits and ass (Cammie Lusko, cited in Bolin, 1992b).

According to Anne Bolin (1992), a bodybuilder and an anthropologist who has studied bodybuilding, the constraints presented by dominant definitions of femininity have led women bodybuilders to make clear distinctions between what they do and how they present themselves during competitive posing on the one hand, and in their workout gyms on the other hand. In other words, the women carefully separate their lives into frontstage and backstage regions (see Goffman, 1959).

In the backstage region of the gym women bodybuilders focus on bodywork and building muscles; serious training overrides concerns about how gender is defined outside the gym. Femininity is irrelevant, and gym workouts are not "gendered" in any way—all bodybuilders, women and men, train the same way. But when the women get ready for the frontstage they try to neutralize the stigma of having too many muscles. They do this by using what might be called "femininity insignias." In other words, they carefully construct a presentation of self that highlights the "looks" of dominant femininity. They may dye their hair blond, wear it in a long, fluffy style and adorn it with a ribbon. Finger and toe nails are manicured and polished, or false fingernails may be glued on. Make-up is professionally applied, posing bikinis are carefully chosen for color and material, earring studs are worn, an engagement or wedding ring may be worn, all body hair is shaved, and plastic surgery may be used to soften the contours of their faces. When they pose, they walk on their toes, use graceful dance moves, and smile incessantly. If possible they try to be seen with husbands or male friends, and they cautiously flirt with male judges. All this is done to appear "natural" according to dominant definitions of femininity (this process is described in Bolin, 1992b).

Women bodybuilders are not unique when it comes to their presentation of self. Any women in a power sport has two choices if she wants to avoid being socially rejected by most people:

> (1) change dominant definitions of femininity, or (2) neutralize the stigma associated with being muscular by creating an image that fits dominant definitions of femininity.

However, when women bodybuilders walk on stage, these femininity insignias contrast with their muscularity to such an extent that it is difficult for anyone who sees them not to realize that "femininity" is a social construction rather than a biological fact. The contestants in women's bodybuilding events today are clearly more muscled than 98% of the men in the world, and they make it difficult to maintain the notions that women are the weaker sex or that femininity implies frailty.

REFLECT ON SPORT

Of course, another thing to consider is the fact that the popularity of women's bodybuilding has not gone unnoticed by people who benefit from dominant definitions of femininity. These people have tried to appropriate the image of the "hard body" and redefine it as a sexy body, a body desired by men, a body dependent on men for sexual satisfaction if not protection. They use air brushed photos of hard bodies in sensual poses on exercise machines (or using thigh masters) to emphasize that staying in shape really does mean staying more physically attractive than other women (Cole, 1993). Women bodybuilders often go along with this sexualized image of their bodies so they can get publicity, endorsement contracts, and appearance fees. They are photographed leaning on or looking up to even more muscular men. But in the gym they train in ways that clearly show that conventional femininity is grounded in culture.

I would argue that despite the use of femininity insignias and the fact that the hard body image has been commercially manipulated to get women to view each other as competitors in a heterosexual mating marketplace, women bodybuilders have opened up possibilities for some women to view the development of muscles and strength as a source of personal empowerment. These possibilities focus on personal change rather than the development of a progressive politics among women collectively, but those personal changes encourage raising questions about the limiting consequences of dominant definitions of femininity. Isn't this one of the things that sports should do? What do you think?

belief have seldom thought about ideological issues or the full social implications of homophobia. For example, when coaches of women's teams adopt "no lesbian" policies, they cause "all athletes to live in fear that their clothes, women friends or hairstyle might cause suspicion" (Griffin, 1992). After all, what do lesbians really look like?!

Homophobic fears are expressed in a variety of ways in connection with women's sports, and they can cause serious harm. At Northwestern State University in Louisiana it was a combination of homophobia and gender ideology that led to the production of a media guide featuring the members of the women's basketball team in their uniforms with *Playboy*-like bunny ears and fluffy tails. Homophobia leads many young women to be confused and ashamed as they deal with real questions about their own sexuality, and it leads lesbian women to hide their identities as they interact with teammates who fear lesbian labels (Blinde and Taub, 1992a, b). Homophobia has also led some universities to put "no sexual harassment" clauses in contracts for women coaches of women's teams, whereas they have no such clauses in the contracts for any of the men coaches, even though nearly all sexual harassment allegations name men as the harassers. If heterosexual men had public behavior records similar to the records of homosexual women, harassment, sexual abuse, and rape would not even be problems in society. So where is "heterophobia" in society and sports?

Need for Ideological and Structural Changes

The major point of this section is that real gender equity in sports requires a complete rethinking of our definitions of masculinity and femininity and our ideas about the purposes and goals of sports and sport organizations. This is a challenging task, but I will outline some of the ways it might be approached.

ALTERNATIVE DEFINITIONS OF MASCULINITY We need new definitions of masculinity in society. As things are now, dominant sport forms naturalize the idea that masculinity involves aggressiveness and a desire to outdo or outperform others. Strong and aggressive men are lionized and made into heroes in sports, whereas nonaggressive men are marginalized and emasculated (Jansen and Sabo, 1993). As boys and men apply this ideology to their own lives they tend to view manhood in terms of things that jeopardize the safety and well-being of themselves and others. They may ride the tops of elevators, drive cars at breakneck speeds, play various forms of "chicken," drink each other "under the table," fight, keep sexual scores in heterosexual relationships, and, sometimes, rough up girlfriends and wives, rape, kill "unfaithful" women, and go to war. Or they may conclude that what you can get away with in life depends on how big and tough you are, and how much you can get others to fear or depend on you. If they take this ideology far enough they may get in the habit of "forcing their way" on others through physical intimidation, coercion, or assaultive behavior.

Even though this ideology of masculinity can be dangerous, athletes are seldom criticized for using it to guide their behavior in sports. For example, I've never heard coaches scold athletes for hitting someone too hard or showing no feeling when they blow out someone's knee or knock someone unconscious. Is it dangerous to teach young men to not express remorse when they hurt people? Does this destroy their ability to empathize with others and feel their pain? If boys are taught to be tough and to dominate others, will they be able to develop intimate and supportive relationships with other men or with women? How will they handle their relationships with women? Will their rates of assault and sexual assault be high? These are all things

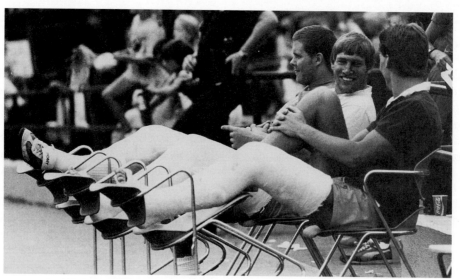

When dominant definitions of masculinity are combined with overconformity to "the sport ethic" (see Ch. 6), athletes put their bodies at risk. But even when serious injuries are common, few people raise questions about gender ideology or the meaning of being an athlete. (University of Colorado and Bobette Brecker)

that must be studied in the sociology of sport.

The frightening record of men's violent and destructive behavior suggests that there is definitely a need to develop alternative definitions of masculinity. The dominant definition of masculinity is closely associated with serious problem behaviors in many societies around the world—in sports as well as in other spheres of everyday life. However, dominant forms of sport in today's society seem to blind people to the need to raise questions about gender ideology. The sociology of sport is one of the tools for raising these questions.

ALTERNATIVE DEFINITIONS OF FEMININITY The experiences of many women athletes also suggest a need for alternatives to the dominant definition of femininity. This need was highlighted in 1990 when the fathers of two girls in an under-12 soccer league in Texas demanded proof that the goalie on the opposing team was really a girl. They said she was too skilled as an athlete to be a girl, and they wanted her to prove her sex by disrobing in front of a woman observer in the locker room. If this sounds bizarre, remember that women athletes in major international sport competitions still (as of 1993) must submit to genetic tests to "prove" they are really women.

Until there is widespread acceptance of alternative definitions of femininity, women will continue to face problems in connection with playing sports. These problems can take many different forms. For example, some girls still do not receive the same kind of encouragement as their brothers to be socially independent and physically active in play activities and sports. As infants, they are handled more gently and protectively than boys. Boys are thrown into the air more often, given more toys requiring active play and the use of motor skills, and allowed to explore more of their physical environments before being "cautioned" and constrained by their parents. Girls are watched over more closely, even before they start to walk. This pattern of "protectiveness" and constraint continues through childhood (see

Chapter 5) and limits girls' participation in sport activities (Coser, 1986).

In most North American families young girls are not discouraged from playing sports but may be treated differently than their brothers in at least three respects. *First*, they are less likely to learn that physical activities and achievements in sport can or should be uniquely important sources of rewards in their lives. *Second*, fathers spend considerably *less* time in shared physical exercises and activities with daughters than they do with sons (Ross and Pate, 1987). *Third*, the play time of girls is more likely to be regulated and controlled by parents. For example, when a young girl asks one of her parents for permission to go and play, she often hears something such as this: "It's okay for you to go play *as long as you* . . . :

- Stay in the house"
- Don't leave the yard"
- Don't go far away from the house"
- Go with a friend"
- Play with children whom I know"
- Get back home at exactly 4 o'clock—no later!"
- Don't do anything dangerous"
- Keep your clothes clean"
- Don't play rough or get hurt"
- Don't get into fights or arguments with your friends"
- Get back in time to set the table"
- Take your little brother (or sister) with you"

This *conditional permission* is an outgrowth of the dominant definition of femininity, and it often destroys the chance for girls to play or organize complex competitive games involving physical skills. Such games require going outside the house, leaving the family yard, playing with large groups (including some children unknown to parents), getting dirty, having arguments and fights now and then, playing rough, and sometimes getting hurt. Furthermore, it is impossible to do these things when curfews are inflexible and younger brothers or sisters have to be watched.

It is no wonder that girls end up playing different kinds of games than their brothers (Lever, 1976, 1978). Boys do not have nearly as many parental constraints limiting their activities. This enables them to quickly move beyond their sisters in the development of sport skills, even before they reach the age of puberty.

Fathers reinforce these "femininity restrictions" when they treat their daughters as "Daddy's little girls." This protectiveness is well-intentioned, but it serves to constrain the play activities of girls, and it focuses girls' attention on catering to the needs of their fathers—an orientation that precludes the development of social independence. Mothers reinforce these femininity restrictions when they treat their daughters as "Mommy's little helpers." Of course, there is nothing wrong with girls helping their mothers, unless they get locked into caretaking and nurturing roles and locked into overly dependent relationships with their mothers. When this happens, girls seldom have opportunities to develop competence in physical activities and sports. Alternative definitions of femininity would alert parents and others to the problems that now exist because of femininity restrictions.

The need for alternative definitions of femininity is also illustrated through the following story told by a young lesbian as she described her gym class in school:

Gym classes were segregated . . . I would play with the girls and they always said that I played "too rough." They said I could play with the girls with my left hand only, or play with the boys. So, of course, I decided to play with the boys. . . . So we were in the gym one day and all the girls were lined up against the wall and there I was along with the boys playing [dodge ball]. The girls were really cheering for me and I had this really mixed thing that has stayed with me ever since. I wanted to wipe out every boy in that group and I did, by the way, I won. I was the last person standing. I wanted to win for them, for the girls, for them to see that it could be done. At the same time, what was mixed up with this was this incredible contempt for the girls because they were all in their little dresses and little shoes sitting pas-

sively on the side, cheering for me, and I didn't want to be one of them and yet I knew I was one of them (Whitfield, cited in Lenskyj, 1992a).

This story portrays the feelings experienced by a lesbian who was lost between mutually exclusive definitions of femininity and masculinity that didn't leave any space for her. Interestingly, her sense of herself was more "natural" than the definition of femininity that held the girls in the class on the sidelines. If girls and women are going to feel good about being involved in all types of sports there is a need for new femininities that recognize diversity as natural.

CHANGING THE WAY WE "DO" SPORTS Gender equity also calls for changes in the ways sports are organized, promoted, played, and portrayed. There is a need for new types of programs, new vocabularies to describe those programs, new images that people can associate with sports, and new ways to evaluate success and the enjoyment of sport experiences. But at the same time, there is a need to become a part of existing programs and work to change them from the inside.

The creation of new programs can be guided by many different goals. Some of the possibilities include the following:

1. New programs promoting lifetime sport participation among women, and emphasizing combinations of competition and partnership, individual expression and teamwork (see Nelson, 1991).
2. Programs reflecting the values and experiences of women and promoting the interests of women in society as a whole.
3. New programs providing coaching and administrative opportunities for women, thereby creating more experiences that generate feelings of empowerment and opportunities to put those feelings into action.

But the creation of new programs should not be the only strategy used in changing sports. Those interested in equity and change should be aware that new programs sometimes present political

If girls and women are going to feel good about being involved in all types of sports, there is a need for definitions of femininity that recognize diversity as normal and appropriate. (Colorado Springs Gazette Telegraph and Bob Jackson)

problems when it comes to gender equity issues. For example:

1. When women's sport programs are structured differently from men's programs, it can be difficult to determine if there are equal opportunities for girls and women.
2. New sports programs that differ from existing programs risk being perceived as "second class," thereby perpetuating the gender logic of female inferiority.
3. New sports programs are more difficult to promote than programs based on existing models, and it is much easier to apply pressure for equal resources within schools and other organizations when you are asking for comparable programs.

The point is that efforts to participate in domi-

nant sport forms run the risk of compromising ideals, whereas efforts to create new sports run the risk of inadequate funding and the loss of some community support. This suggests that in the long run it may be most effective for those interested in promoting gender equity to maintain both approaches simultaneously (Coakley and Westkott, 1984). This means that those who strive to participate in existing sports and sport organizations should continue to be aware of alternatives for the future. Then as they gain power in sports they will have a vision of what is possible for improving opportunities for both women and men. In the same fashion, those who envision new sport forms should recognize that participation in existing sports and sport organizations can be used to establish credibility and gain access to power and resources.

Ideological and structural changes in sports can also be encouraged by changing the way we talk about sports. The goal is to eliminate what might be called the "language of difference and domination" associated with sports and sport participation (Kidd, 1987). For example, using "jock" to refer to athletes perpetuates the idea that sports are for men. Using labels such as sissy, tomboy, fag, wimp, etc. serves to inscribe gender into sports in ways that interfere with gender equity. Motivating young men by telling them to go out and prove their masculinity on the playing field has similar consequences. Calling young adult intercollegiate athletes "kids" perpetuates a hierarchical organizational structure in which coaches control and possess the men and women on sport teams; this type of structure works against the interests of women. Using locker room language that bashes gays and demeans women also subverts the achievement of gender equity; standing by and saying nothing in response to this language perpetuates inequities. Using military metaphors to describe what happens in sports is another way that sports are masculinized: "throwing long bombs" and "killing the opposition" are just two examples of metaphors that are based on the experiences of men, not women.

Structural and ideological changes promoting gender equity could also be encouraged through rule changes in sports. For example, there is a need for rules to eliminate violence in sports such as hockey, football, rugby, and soccer. Men will object to such rules by saying they make sports into "girls' games," but this proves the rules are necessary. Rules promoting safety are needed in many sports, and there is a need for policies about not playing in pain or when injured. Sports also need more rituals that bring opponents together in ways that emphasize partnership rather than hostility and rivalry. An example of how people can get together and change the ideology and structure of sports is summarized in Chapter 2 (pp. 41-42)—it was the case in which women used a form of partnership model to alter the way softball was

played by teams in two leagues (Birrell and Richter, 1987).

Gender equity depends on sports being redesigned from the outside and the inside and the development of new sports reflecting the values and experiences of women and men who don't identify themselves in terms of the dominant definition of masculinity.

CONCLUSION:

IS EQUITY THE ONLY ISSUE?

Through the 1970s and 1980s sport participation among females increased significantly. This was primarily the result of a growth in opportunities combined with government legislation, the women's movement, the health and fitness movement, and increased publicity given to women athletes.

Despite past increases, future increases in sport participation among girls and women will not be automatic. In fact, there are good reasons for being cautious when predicting increases. These reasons include budget inequities and threatened budget cuts affecting women's programs, resistance to government policies and legislation, declines in the number and proportion of women coaches and administrators, a growing emphasis on cosmetic fitness and thinness among women, and continued trivialization of women athletes through ridicule and the use of sexist nicknames for women's teams.

More women than ever are playing sports and working in sport organizations, but gender inequities continue to exist in participation opportunities, support for athletes, and jobs for women in coaching and administration. Even when sport participation leads to feelings of personal empowerment among women, the achievement of complete and lasting gender equity is impossible without a critical analysis of gender ideology and the structure of sport itself. This critical analysis is important because it not only gives direction to women's efforts to achieve equity but it shows there are reasons for men to join women who are trying to achieve equity.

The major point of this chapter is that gender equity in sports is integrally tied to issues related to gender ideology and the structure of sport itself. Gender equity will never be complete or lasting unless there are changes in the way people think about masculinity and femininity and unless there are changes in the way sports are organized and played. Dominant sport forms in society are currently based on a "gender logic" that leads to the conclusion that girls and women are, by definition, physically inferior to boys and men. This gender logic is associated with a "logic of difference" that "naturalizes" the superiority of men over women. This means that sports celebrate a form of masculinity that leads to the social marginalization of many men and women. When this form of masculinity is celebrated through sports, homophobia and misogyny get built into the structure of sports and sport organizations.

Because of "gender logic" and the shaping of sports by the values and experiences of men, real and lasting gender equity depends on changing dominant definitions of masculinity and femininity and changing the way we "do" sports in our own experience. New sports and sport organizations must be created, and existing ones must be changed from the inside. Changing sports from the inside can be accomplished through a combination of strategies. These strategies include new ways to "talk sports"; new rules to control violence and injuries and to foster safety for all players; and new rituals and orientations based on partnership models (as opposed to military models; see Chapter 7, pp. 168-169) of sports. Unless ideology changes, gender equity will never be completely achieved.

SUGGESTED READINGS

Birrell, S., and C.L. Cole, eds. (In press). Women, sport, and culture. Human Kinetics Publishers, Champaign, Ill. (*this is the most up-to-date set of readings in which sports are viewed from the perspective of feminist theory; 19 articles written by people from a variety of academic backgrounds*).

Birrell, S. 1988. Discourses on the gender/sport relationship: from women in sport to gender relations. Exercise and Sport Science Review, vol. 16, Macmillan, New York (*a thorough overview of recent literature on women and sport, combined with an evaluation of the current status of knowledge on this topic*).

Boutilier, M.A., and L. SanGiovanni. 1993. The sporting woman. Human Kinetics Publishers, Inc., Champaign, Ill. (*a comprehensive discussion of women and sport*).

Deem, R. 1986. All work and no play: the sociology of women and leisure. Open University Press, Philadelphia (*a unique study focused on how women integrate leisure and sport into their lives; how patterns of leisure behavior vary by race, age, and class; and how men influence women's participation patterns*).

Dyer, K., ed. 1989. Sportswomen towards 2000. Hyde Park Press, Richmond, South Australia (*40 conference papers presented during Women's Week in Australia in 1988; papers deal with politics, law, medicine, participation, training, coaching, and promoting women's sports*).

Green, T.S., et al., eds. 1981. Black women in sport. AAHPERD Publications, Reston, Va. (*brief discussion and review of the literature on black women in sport*).

Janis, L. 1985. Annotated bibliography on minority women in athletics. Sociology of Sport Journal 2(3):266-274 (*useful list of references in a variety of sources*).

Journal of the National Association for Women Deans, Administrators, & Counselors. 1984. Women and sports. Special issue. 47(2) (*six articles on issues having policy implications for school administrators and teachers*).

Lenskyj, H. 1986. Out of bounds: women, sport and sexuality. Women's Press, Toronto (*a brief but insightful analysis of gender relations in sport; excellent information on sport and the body*).

Lenskyj, H. 1991. Women, sport and physical activity: research and bibliography. Minister of State, Fitness and Amateur Sports, Ottawa, Canada (*a thorough and useful overview of literature on feminist theory and sociological, psychological, and physiological research on women and sport; future work on this topic should use this source as a starting point*).

Messner, M.A. Power at play. Beacon Press, Boston (*insightful, in-depth analysis of the connection between masculinity and sports*).

Messner, M.A., and D.F. Sabo, eds. 1990. (*19 papers dealing with sports, masculinity, sexuality, and the gender order from feminist perspectives*).

Nelson, M.B. 1991. Are we winning yet? How women are changing sports and sports are changing women. Random House, New York (*selected as winner of the 1992 Amateur Athletic Foundation's Book Award; readable description and analysis of the everyday experiences of a diverse collection of women athletes*).

Pronger, B. 1989. The arena of masculinity: Sports, homosexuality, and the meaning of sex. St. Martin's Press, New York (*examines the experiences of gay athletes in straight sports and sports in gay communities in North American cities; this is an interpretation of the gay and athletic experience combined*).

CHAPTER 10

RACE AND ETHNICITY

Are skin color and cultural heritage important in sports?

I truly believe [African Americans] may not have some of the necessities to be . . . a field manager or perhaps a general manager. . . . They are gifted with great musculature. . . . They are fleet of foot. . . . [But] as far as having the background to become club presidents or president of a bank . . . I don't know.

Al Campanis, former Vice President for Player Personnel, Los Angeles Dodgers (1987)

. . . the crazy theories of black intellectual inferiority are alive and well. . . . [Coaches and] managers have to think, and the conventional wisdom among sports' ruling elite is that . . . blacks don't think as well as whites.

Arthur Ashe (1992)

Right in the square block area it was definitely rough, it was dog-eat-dog. I had to be a mean dog . . . young guys wan'ed to take yer money and beat ya up an' you jus' had to fight or move out the neighbo'hood. I couldn't move, so I had to start fightin'.

Professional Boxer in Chicago (1992, cited in Wacquant)

During Patrick Ewing's years [in college], students threw bananas onto the court [and] nothing was done about it. This year . . . I watched as students . . . chanted "Black boy, Black boy," at a light skinned black point guard . . . The only thing missing was a cheerleader with a sheet over his head."

Steve Kelley, Sportswriter, Seattle Times (1987)

Popular beliefs about race and ethnicity have a major impact on what happens in sports; and sports have become social activities in which people either challenge or accept dominant forms of racial and ethnic relations in a society. For example, I recently invited five, athletic 10 to 12 year olds to be on a "children in sports" panel in my sociology of sport course. Each of the young people was white. During the discussion with students in my course, a 6th grade boy, known in his elementary school for his sprinting and basketball skills, was asked if he was going to try out for those sports in junior high next year. Surprisingly, he said no. When asked to explain, he said, "I won't have a chance because all the black kids who go there will beat me out." He went on to point out that he wasn't upset by this since he was a good soccer player and distance runner, too. He said he would try out for those sports instead of sprinting and basketball. He also said he had never played with black kids while in elementary school.

About the same time this 6th grader was making these decisions, a local high school graduate, student body president, class valedictorian, and equally talented football and basketball player was asked by a sports writer which sport he would play the following year as a student recruited by the football and basketball coaches at a top ranked Division I university. He answered this way: "I guess, right now, I'd take football because its more unique to be a 6-6 quarterback . . . than a 6-6 *white* forward" (emphasis added). This young man was trying to anticipate his odds for succeeding as a college athlete.

Both of these student-athletes had watched sports on television, had listened to people talk about the abilities of athletes, and had developed their own ideas about race, physical abilities, and chances for success in various sports. Their "whiteness" had a major influence on their decisions about their athletic futures. In fact, they voluntarily limited their options because of their skin color. Not surprisingly, the social meanings associated with skin color and cultural heritage

also influence the decisions of people from other racial and ethnic groups as they watch and play sports. At an even deeper level, sports are parts of culture through which people formulate and put into action ideas about skin color and cultural heritage that are then carried over into the rest of society.

In light of these factors, the goal of this chapter is to look in depth at race and ethnicity in sports. Specifically, I will deal with the following topics:

1. The meanings of race and ethnicity.
2. How racial ideology affects racial and ethnic relations in sports.
3. Sport participation patterns for different racial and ethnic groups in the United States.
4. Why certain American sports have been racially desegregated.
5. The dynamics of intergroup relations in sports, and how sports might be used as sites for improving racial and ethnic relations.

CULTURE, SPORTS, AND THE MEANING OF RACE
Definition of Terms

Discussions about race and ethnicity can be very confusing when people don't use clearly defined terms. In this chapter, **"race"** refers to a category of people regarded as socially distinct because they share genetically transmitted traits believed to be important in a group or society. When people talk about "races" they assume the existence of a classification system used to categorize all the people of the world into distinct groups on the basis of certain biological traits or dispositions present *at birth*.

"Ethnicity" refers to the cultural heritage of a particular group. Ethnicity is *not* based on genetically determined physical traits or dispositions; instead, it is based on characteristics related to culture and cultural background. An **"ethnic group"** is a category of people regarded as socially distinct because they share a way of life associated with a common cultural background.

Confusion is created when people use "race" and "ethnicity" interchangeably as they deal with issues related to human behavior. One reason some people use these terms interchangeably is that most racial and ethnic groups are assumed to be **"minority groups."** However, this is not always true. **"Minority group"** specifically refers to a socially identified group that is a target of discrimination, that suffers social disadvantages because of discrimination, and that has a strong self-consciousness based on their shared social experiences.

It is important to remember as you read this chapter that the definition of race focuses on biologically based traits and characteristics, the definition of ethnicity focuses on culturally based orientations and behaviors, and the definition of minority group focuses on discrimination directed at a collection of people because they share traits or ways of life that other people define as socially unworthy. **"Bigotry,"** as used in this chapter, refers to a set of interrelated attitudes and beliefs that leads a person to define an entire category of people as different and treat those who fit into the category as inferior in some way.

Origins and Implications of the Concept of Race

The classification systems used to divide all human beings into various racial categories are grounded in social meanings and social definitions; they are *not* based on objective biological factors. In a biological sense, the concept of race is so confusing that it is meaningless. Over the past three centuries no one has ever developed an objective biological classification system that can be used to divide humans into distinct racial groups. Scientists in Europe and the United States have tried since the early 1700s to develop such a system. They've used classifications based on mental characteristics, brain size, skin color, and various combinations of head shape, hair form, skin color, stature, and nose shape. These systems have led scientists to "discover"

dozens of races, subraces, collateral races, and collateral subraces (these are actual terms used in their racial classification systems). There were so many different groupings of people with so much overlap in characteristics that it was impossible to fit them into a few categories; instead, dozens of categories were needed and even then there were other collections of people that fell between or around categories. This meant that racial classification systems were useless; they remain useless today.

Here's the problem people confront when they try to develop a scheme for dividing the world into separate racial groups on the basis of biological factors. Usually they pick a physical characteristic such as skin color or some other "continuous trait" possessed by humans. A **continuous trait** is one that exists to some degree in everyone. In other words, everyone has more or less of it. Take height, for example. It's not that some people have height and others don't; people simply vary from short to tall. Height falls along a continuum with the shortest person in the world on one end of the continuum, the tallest person on the other, and everyone else in between. The same is true for skin color. Skin color varies from *snow white* to *midnight black*, with an infinite array of color shades in between. When you use a continuous trait such as skin color to identify so-called races, the trick is determining where you should draw the lines to distinguish one racial group from another. Lines can be drawn anywhere and everywhere. You can draw two lines or 2000 lines; there are no absolute biological rules. Once lines are drawn in particular places along the continuum, someone else can decide to draw them in other places! The decisions on where to draw the lines and how many lines to draw are social ones, not biological ones. This is why nearly all scientists have abandoned the search for a biology-based racial classification system.

However, people on the street have not given up. They continue to use either their own racial classification systems or someone else's. Widely used systems in the United States are based on more or less shared social meanings associated with skin color. If someone cannot be identified as "all white," they are classified as "black," unless they have an identifiable cultural background that leads them to be classified in a particular ethnic group rather than a racial group. For example, the record breaking American decathlete, Dan O'Brien, has a black father, a white mother, and he was adopted by a family in which his brothers and sisters were Mexican, Native American, and Korean. O'Brien says, "I feel black when I want to, I feel white the rest of the time. . . . [and] when I hang out with my friends, I'm just Dan" (in Patrick, 1991). But where does he fit in a racial classification system? It's all very confusing. To make matters even worse, race is defined in different ways in different cultures. People socially defined as "blacks" in the United States would sometimes be defined as "whites" in other cultures or they would be put into some racial category not even used in the United States. Furthermore, not everybody depends on skin color alone for his or her classification systems. This makes race biologically meaningless and race theories useless. However, race and race theories are appropriate topics for sociological analysis because they reflect racial ideologies that were popular at different points in history over the past 400 years. At this point, it is best to assume there is one race—the human race; it contains combinations of changing physical similarities and differences, and the meanings given to those similarities and differences are developed by all of us as we interact with one another.

This discussion about the biological meaninglessness of race is important in sports. Many people, including some scientists, have tried to explain the physical abilities and achievements of athletes in racial terms even though race is socially determined. They have used social definitions to divide people into blacks and whites to do their studies and measurements. Usually, the exact genetic backgrounds of these people are never outlined, and it is assumed that everyone in the black group is alike genetically, and everyone in the white group is alike genetically. This is a risky and foolish assumption to make. Furthermore, the studies seldom make any connections between specific physical characteris-

tics and what it takes to be successful in a certain sport. For example, no researcher has even come close to being able to identify a set of traits that would together explain Magic Johnson's ability to see the floor and make great passes, Michael Jordan's ability to make jump shots at the buzzer, Dominique Wilkens' ability to jump, Kevin Johnson's ability to dribble, Scotty Pippin's ability to steal the ball, Charles Barkley's ability to rebound, Patrick Ewing's ability to block shots, and Lenny Wilkens' ability to coach and develop strategies. To say that these different individuals, each possessing different physical and mental skills, are great athletes or coaches because of something related to skin color makes little sense. It denies the uniqueness of each person and the complexity of the physical and mental skills involved in basketball. Using skin color to explain performance records across many different sports makes even less sense.

Interestingly, most people use their racial theories to explain the success of people with black skin in certain sports and the failures of people with white skin: for example, "blacks are 'natural leapers' and whites have 'white man's disease.'" This is odd because people with white skin have dominated most sports for many years even though people of color have long outnumbered white skinned people in the world. When people with white skin consistently do well in a sport event, why do people talk about their character, dedication, work ethic, dependability, and intelligence rather than their "natural physical abilities"? Answers to this question are given in the next section, and in the box on pp. 245-247.

RACIAL IDEOLOGY AND SPORTS: A CRITICAL ANALYSIS

People never even used the term "race" until the 1700s when white Europeans began to look for a system to explain why everyone in the world didn't look and act as they did. Since then there have been countless attempts to discover relationships between physique and character, between external physical characteristics and internal characteristics such as temperament, personality, intelligence, moral standards, criminal tendencies, and overall cultural vitality. These attempts have turned up empty, but they have resulted in a wide range of "pseudoscientific folklore and stereotypes" about the characteristics of people with certain shades of skin color (Hoberman, 1992).

White observers in colonial times were convinced that people of color were primitive physical types who were driven by brawn rather than brains. This belief was used to explain why whites were able to conquer darker skinned peoples around the globe and to justify the colonization and subsequent exploitation of those peoples. White Europeans and Americans developed racial theories that enabled them to convert the apparent physical superiority of people with dark skin into a sign of their intellectual inferiority. Such theories fit neatly with Charles Darwin's model of human evolution in which mental traits were seen to be superior to physical traits in the human animal. They also fit neatly with the idea that white skinned people really were superior and they deserved to be in positions of power and control around the world (this belief is called Social Darwinism). I will refer to this way of thinking as *race logic*."

This **race logic** that white skinned people were intellectually superior and that people of color were "animal-like savages" was very convenient to white colonial powers (Hoberman, 1992). It enabled them to kill without guilt and to subjugate dark skinned natives for the purpose of making them "civilized." For these reasons, this race logic eventually became institutionalized in the form of a complex racial ideology about skin color, intelligence, character, and physical skills. This ideology has been revised over the years to fit new circumstances and to continually justify new forms of racial discrimination. For example, just after the Civil War a surgeon in New Orleans who treated "colored" soldiers wounded in the war noted that "at present, [my colored patients are] too animal to have moral courage or endurance" (in Hoberman, 1992, p. 44). His conclusions suggested that maybe "colored people" would eventually evolve into something less animal. But when Af-

ricans and other people of color engaged in courageous behavior, whites quickly pointed out that the courage of dark skinned people was based in ignorance rather than real character. In fact, some white people went so far as to say that people of color did not feel pain in the same way whites did and that this permitted dark skinned people to engage in superhuman feats. But those feats were seen as meaningless because whites explained them as acts of desperation rather than civilization. Expectedly, when whites did extraordinary physical things, other whites claimed it was due to fortitude and moral character.

Whites in the United States and other Western countries used this racial ideology to justify the physical mistreatment of African slaves. Then they used it to explain the success of African American boxers in the early part of this century. According to the ideology of race, black males were believed to have unique physical stamina and skills; but it was also believed that those physical attributes were grounded in an absence of feelings and intellectual awareness. In fact, many whites even believed that the skulls of black people were so thick that they could not be bruised or broken by a white man's fist (Hoberman, 1992). When black boxers were successful, the ideology of race was used to explain their success. For example, after Joe Louis, the legendary black heavyweight boxing champion, defeated Italian Primo Carnera in a heavily publicized fight before 60,000 people in Yankee Stadium in 1935, sportswriters in the United States described him as "savage and animalistic." A major news service story sent all over the country began this way:

> Something sly and sinister and perhaps not quite human came out of the African jungle last night to strike down and utterly demolish . . . Primo Carnera. . . . (cited in Mead, 1985).

Noted sportswriter Grantland Rice referred to Louis's quickness as "the speed of the jungle, the instinctive speed of the wild." Before another Louis fight, *New York Times* sports editor Paul

Gallico wrote a nationwide syndicated column in which he described Louis as:

> the magnificent animal. . . . He eats. He sleeps. He fights. . . . Is he all instinct, all animal? Or have a hundred million years left a fold upon his brain? I see in this colored man something so cold, so hard, so cruel that I wonder as to his bravery. Courage in the animal is desperation. Courage in the human is something incalculable and divine.

Despite hundreds of these stories, Joe Louis remained dedicated to representing black Americans as an ambassador of goodwill to whites. Although he trained hard and presented himself as a gentleman, he was still described as "a natural athlete . . . born to listen to jazz . . . eat a lot of fried chicken, play ball with the gang on the corner and never do a lick of heavy work he could escape" (from a story in a New York paper, cited in Mead, 1985). Race logic is powerful; it shapes what people see and how they interpret the world in black and white.

These descriptions of Joe Louis capture race logic as it was applied to sports in the United States earlier this century. But what they don't tell us is that over the past two centuries many whites in Western countries have had difficulty accepting the idea that they might be physically inferior to people of color. Contrary to Darwin's notion that brains were always superior to muscle, many whites have believed the ancient Greek idea that strong minds and strong bodies came together in the same package. This led them to wonder: Could it be that dark skinned peoples were superior in some way to light skinned people? Many whites worried about this. In fact, they worried so much that they accepted a number of myths designed to restore faith in their own racial superiority.

A classic example of these myths is "Tarzan, King of the Jungle"—the black African jungle. In 1914, Edgar Rice Burroughs wrote *Tarzan of the Apes*, his first of 24 Tarzan novels. His stories then found their way into comic books, which were read by millions of people. Tarzan stories were very popular through much of this century for many reasons. One reason was that

white people in Western industrial societies found it very comforting and exciting to read about a white man with British ancestry who used a combination of physical strength and intelligence to become "king of the jungle" and ruler of the "noble black savages" and other physically imposing beasts living in "uncivilized" colonized territories (Hoberman, 1992). This white man was a real role model. His appearance resembled a combination of a Roman gladiator and a Greek god, and even though the fictional Tarzan was raised and socialized by apes, he eventually exhibited inner, in-born qualities that enabled him to not only survive but rise above the "primitive" conditions in Africa. Therefore those who read Tarzan could conclude that whites really were superior to all people of color.

Burrough's purpose in writing Tarzan novels was not to contribute to the formation of racial ideology; he mainly wanted to convince all the sedentary Englishmen living off the fruits of imperialism to change their ways and take their physical condition more seriously before they became weak and vulnerable. But his stories were popular because his readers lived in countries built through combinations of slavery and colonialization, where people had many fears and insecurities about people of color. Although the Tarzan myth has faded in recent years, it has been replaced by "Rocky," "Rambo," and other myths that focus on new interests and new fears in new political times (Hoberman, 1992). It seems that many Americans, men in particular, still like to fantasize that they are tough and have an inner spirit and character that enables them to eventually rise above their adversaries.

But fears about racial differences are not dead; race logic and racial ideology are still with us. In fact, it has been suggested that the increasing importance of sport in North America has reawakened people's curiosity about racial differences (Hoberman, 1992). Just as some white people in the 1920s and 1930s were looking for Tarzan, some white people today seem

Text continued on p. 248.

REFLECT ON | SPORT

Preserving Racial Ideology Through Sports

Skiers from Switzerland, a country half the size of South Carolina with a population 1/30th the size of the United States, win 10 times as many World Cup Championships as U.S. skiers. Even though this happens year after year, no scientists study Swiss people to discover why they are such good skiers. Everyone already knows why: the Swiss live in the Alps, they learn to ski before they go to pre-school, they grow up in a culture in which skiing is highly valued, they have many opportunities to ski, and they see fellow Swiss skiers being rewarded for success in highly publicized (in Switzerland) competitions. A search for a "ski gene" has not occurred.

Similarly, there have been no studies looking for a weight-lifting gene among Bulgarian men, or a swimming gene among East German women, or a cross-country skiing gene among Scandinavians, or a volleyball jumping gene among Californians who hang out on beaches. There have been no claims that Canadians owe their success in hockey to naturally strong ankle joints, or instinctive eye-hand-foot coordination, or an innate tendency not to sweat so they can retain body heat in cold weather. Nobody has looked for or used genetic explanations for the successes of athletes packaged in white skin.

But as soon as athletes with black skin excel or fail at a certain sport, regardless of where they

"THAT'S ANOTHER DOWNHILL MEDAL WON BY THE SWISS! THOSE WHITE PEOPLE FROM SWITZERLAND MUST HAVE A SKIING GENE, OR THEY MUST HAVE NATURAL ABILITIES TO TWIST THEIR BODIES AROUND SLALOM GATES."

This explanation for the success of Swiss skiers is just as faulty as the explanation often given for the success of athletes from other racial groups in other sports.

Preserving Racial Ideology Through Sports—cont'd

come from in the world, many people start looking for "race-based" genetic explanations. They want to explain the successes and failures of black athletes in terms of "natural" or "instinctive" qualities or weaknesses. They assume white skinned athletes succeed because of tradition, training opportunities, dedication, and personal sacrifice, not the genetic heritage of the entire white population of a region, a country, or the world.

The tendency for some white people to explain the achievements of athletes by skin color is firmly grounded in Western racial ideology. This ideology emphasizes racial difference, and some people do studies and distort history to give them reasons to continue believing it. It seems strange to think a single genetic trait or even a combination of traits could explain the successes or failures of a genetically diversified group of athletes from many areas around the world across a range of different sports requiring different physical abilities and characteristics. But racial ideology has set some people out on a quest for such a trait.

Success in many different sports depends on combinations of different psychological and experiential factors in addition to many different physical factors. How could the color of a person's skin have anything to do with sport skills? Why should skin color be related to other physical traits that have performance implications in certain sports? And why do dark skinned and light skinned athletes come in many different sizes and shapes, even in the same sports? For example, great sprinters have been tall and short, slender and muscular, highly emotional and unemotional, highly intelligent or not, and until the 1960s, almost all have been white. Just because recently successful sprinters have dark skins is no more strange than the Swiss winning so many World Cup skiing events, light skinned Californians dominating men's volley-

ball around the world, and 71 minor and major league shortstops coming from the Dominican Republic.

Some people, including Jimmy "the Greek" Snyder, a former sports analyst for CBS, have combined genetic and experiential factors to seek explanations for the success of African American athletes in certain sports. In 1988 Snyder suggested that African Americans make good ball carriers in football because they were bred to have big, strong thighs when they lived as slaves. Snyder conveniently ignored millions of African Americans with skinny thighs, and he was ignorant of the historical fact that the control of white slavemasters over the sexual behavior of black slaves was never extensive enough to shape the genetic traits of even a small portion of the U.S. African American population.

Snyder's explanation of the achievements of African American football players is as ridiculous as saying that Californians are great volleyball players because their ancestors migrated west in covered wagons and all those who were not strong enough or couldn't jump up on the wagons died during the tedious journey! Is this why the U.S. men's volleyball team has been dominated by white Californians who have great vertical jumps and amazing "hang times"? Their ancestors survived by jumping on covered wagons? This sounds funny until you listen to similar explanations about slavery being related to success in sprinting and basketball. Did Africans survive the long journey chained on shelves on slave ships because they could run fast and jump high? Did slave owners breed slaves to be fast runners and high jumpers? And wouldn't the fastest runners and best jumpers have escaped the slave traders in West Africa? And why do one-third of all U.S. Olympians, both black and white, come from California?

REFLECT ON SPORT

Is it possible that dominant racial ideology also influences how African Americans interpret their own physical abilities and their potential as athletes? This is a controversial idea, but some young black men in the United States may grow up believing that the black body is special and superior when it comes to physical abilities in sports. This belief could lead them to think that playing certain sports and playing them better than anyone else in the world is part of their destiny. This belief is encouraged in the United States as young black men look around and see employment discrimination and dead-end jobs in the traditional world of work, while at the same time they see the possibility of big money, respect, slam dunks, end-zone catches, and Olympic sprint victories in sports. Even boxing would look better than a minimum wage dead-end job.

So what would happen if many African American males grew up with (1) a belief in black athletic superiority, (2) a sense of destiny about becoming great athletes, (3) an awareness that the traditional economy offered little hope, (4) a perception that fantastic opportunities awaited them in certain sports if they had the desire and skills, and (5) opportunities to develop those skills on playgrounds and in public school sports programs? If all these things came together they would form a powerful force. This force could drive young black men to dedicate the very fabric of their beings to achieving greatness in certain sports.

Is this what has led to the notable achievements of African Americans in basketball, football, track, and boxing? Is this why African Americans have a longer and more impressive list of accomplishments in sports than all blacks living in Africa, even though black Africans outnumber black Americans by over 20 to 1? I don't know, but this explanation of the accomplishments of male African American athletes makes much more sense to me than an explanation based on mystical biological factors somehow associated with skin color. After all, when a group of people feel destined to greatness in an activity, when their feelings are grounded in an ideology emphasizing the "naturalness" of their achievements, and when their social worlds are structured so those feelings make sense in their lives, *it shouldn't be surprising when they achieve notable things.*

Ideology can be powerful, especially when it is combined with other factors that lead it to be used as a framework for self-evaluation and self-motivation.

Unfortunately, race logic and race ideology will continue to blind people to the fact that people of color around the world have diverse genetic traits, diverse cultural and experiential backgrounds, and diverse records of achievement in a diverse range of sports. Unless this ideology is critically analyzed, skin color will continue to be used by many people as an indicator of how people's minds and bodies perform. But sooner or later we humans may come to realize how this ideology fuels hatred and ignorance around the world, and we will drop our silly concerns about skin color and stop asking racist questions about sport performance. Until then many people will continue to use sports to preserve racial ideology. What do you think?

to be looking for the great white male athlete. In fact, some of the articles being written today about sport performance differences between so-called races leads me to think that I'm back in the nineteenth century with a bunch of white people waiting for Tarzan to swing from his vine into the world of sports.

Race Logic in Sports: Recent Examples

Race logic is still manifested as bigotry against blacks in the United States and other countries. Even in the 1980s, former tennis star Arthur Ashe could name places in the United States where he would not be allowed to play tennis because of his color. Ashe pointed out that a college tennis team coached by one of his friends was denied practice time at certain clubs because one of the team members was black (Bock, 1981). And when the Downtown Athletic Club in New York awarded the Heisman Trophy to black running back Marcus Allen in 1981, the club had no black members and no black person had ever spent the night in its guest rooms (Ballinger, 1981).

In 1991, when the PGA scheduled its annual championship at the Shoal Creek Golf Club in Birmingham, Alabama, the club founder proudly noted that there were no blacks in the club because they would make his fellow white members uncomfortable. He explained that club policy was basically a matter of preference, not prejudice or discrimination (!). When the PGA looked into the matter it found that such "preferences" existed all over the United States, not just in the South. In 1993, major league baseball investigated one of its owners for antisemitism and racial bigotry. Among many other things, the owner referred to one of her players on the Cincinnati Reds as her "million dollar nigger." The white owners had a difficult time conducting the investigation because she made many bigoted remarks in their presence on many different occasions and they never corrected or reprimanded her. So when they found her guilty they had to indirectly admit that they had long allowed blatant racism to exist in their midst.

The expressions of race logic are usually more subtle in the 1990s than when Joe Louis was being described in the 1930s. For example, when a *Sports Illustrated* writer tried to explain why so many great distance runners came from the mountains of East Africa, where kids regularly run 4 miles to and from school every day, he said, "Sports is a pale shadow of the competitive life that has gone on forever across this high, fierce, first continent. Is it any wonder that frail European varieties feel threatened?" (Moore, 1990, p. 79).

These examples raise the issue discussed in the last chapter: Sometimes ideology is like B.O.; you never smell your own—but when you do, you spray something on it so you can ignore it.

Race Logic and Gender

Race logic is interconnected with gender logic in complex ways in the social world of sports. Sociologists are just now beginning to explain some of those interconnections (Birrell, 1989; Messner, 1992; Majors, 1991). What we think we know at present is that the implications of race logic are different for black men than for black women. This is partly because the bodies of black men have been socially constructed and perceived differently from the bodies of black women. For example, whites have traditionally grown up fearing the power of black male bodies, anxious about their sexual capacities, and fascinated with their movements. This has created a situation in which black male athletes can become valuable entertainment commodities. Black female bodies, on the other hand, have undergone different social constructions. They've been sexualized, but not feared, and they haven't been defined in ways that make black women athletes valuable entertainment commodities, especially in sports that emphasize power and domination.

Sociologist Richard Majors (1986, 1991) has suggested that black male bodies have been socially constructed to emphasize what he calls "cool pose." He argues that black men in the

United States have accepted the dominant definition of masculinity in American culture. They have bought into the idea that men should be strong breadwinners and protectors in their families and dominant in their relationships with women. But the race logic used by many whites has closed off many avenues in school, work, or politics for them to prove their masculinity and meet the expectations they have for themselves as men. This has produced a combination of frustration, alienation, anger, and even emotional withdrawal from families. Black men in the United States have coped with these things "by channeling their creative energies into the construction of unique, expressive, and conspicuous styles of demeanor, speech, gesture, clothing, hairstyle, walk, stance, and handshake" (Majors, 1991, p. 111). These styles are what Majors describes as "cool pose." Cool pose is all about being "bad," about being in control, tough, and detached. Cool pose says different things to different people. To the white man it says, "Although you may have tried to hurt me time and time again, I can take it (and if I am hurting or weak, I'll never let you know)." It also says, "See me, touch me, hear me, but, white man, you can't copy me" (1986, pp. 184-185).

Majors suggests that cool pose has become institutionalized among many black males in the United States and has also become an integral part of the sports in which many athletes are black men. Is this how "style" got to be such a big part of basketball (George, 1992)? Is this why some black athletes are known for their "talk" as much as their action on the playing field? Do black men use cool pose to intimidate white opponents? Does cool pose sell tickets and create spectator interest in college basketball, the NBA, and football? Do people come to see dunks and other moves inscribed with the personas of the men who perform them? Is this what Deion Sanders has brought to baseball? Is cool pose the result of what happens when black men face a combination of race logic, gender logic, and the realities of class relations in the American economy? Majors says yes, and I think he may be on to something worth considering.

When sociologists consider these questions, they should work with historians to discover if in the past there were other variations of cool pose exhibited by men in ethnic minority groups who were depicted as less than human. For example, in the nineteenth century, cartoons depicted Irish immigrants in the United States as apes. People used the ethnic slur that "God invented the wheelbarrow to teach the Irish to walk upright." Red hair, a quick temper, and a fighting temperament were thought to be genetic traits of the Irish. The Irish faced job discrimination. Most of the boxers of the time were Irish. And there were the "Fighting Irish" from Notre Dame. Did Irish men exhibit "cool pose"? This is an interesting question in need of research.

Race Logic and Stacking Patterns in Team Sports

The persistence and pervasiveness of racial ideology is also apparent in the fact that black athletes seldom occupy the so-called thinking positions in major team sports in the United States and in other countries where sport has been racially desegregated. It seems that for many years the white people who controlled sport teams (recruiters, coaches, administrators, and owners) believed that blacks were especially good at running and catching footballs, but they could not be expected to quarterback the team or be leaders on defense. Blacks were thought to be good at running after and catching fly balls in the outfield, but they were not thought to be suited for strategy positions such as pitcher and catcher. Blacks were thought to be strong inside rebounders and outstanding scorers in basketball, but it was the white guards who brought the ball up the floor, called the plays, and set the defensive strategy.

Remnants of these patterns still exist in professional baseball and football, although they have shifted to reflect changes in coaching strat-

As college football teams in the U.S. changed their offensive strategies so quarterbacks became more like running backs, more blacks were recruited for the position. On the one hand, this represents a favorable change; on the other hand, it is simply a modified version of traditional racial stacking patterns in football. (University of Colorado)

egies and associated changes in responsibilities for players in different positions. For example, quarterbacks in college often run the ball more now than in the past, and they seldom call their own plays in the huddle; shortstops in baseball rarely make decisions about where outfielders should play for certain hitters; guards in basketball no longer call plays when they dribble the ball up the court. In recent years, coaches have taken over many of the thinking tasks in all team sports, such as calling plays and setting defensive formations. This has affected the extent to which racial ideology can be seen in sports.

Sociologists have long been interested in player position patterns in team sports and how those patterns conform to the race logic in particular cultures. Since the early 1970s these patterns have been identified in numerous studies.* When players from a certain racial or ethnic group are either over- or underrepresented at certain positions in team sports, we say that "racial stacking" exists.

Because discussions of stacking can be confusing for anyone unfamiliar with positions on certain sport teams, I've provided summary information and illustrations for three major spectator sports in Table 10-1 and Figures 10-1, 10-2, and 10-3. Research on stacking patterns can be summarized as follows:

- Black players on major league baseball teams are most heavily concentrated in the outfield positions; white players are concentrated in the positions of pitcher, catcher, and all the infield positions except first base.
- Black players on college and professional football teams are most likely to play safety, cornerback, and end on defense and running back and pass receiver on offense; whites are overrepresented at quarterback and guard on offense and, in the past, at one of the middle linebacker positions on defense.
- During the 1950s and 1960s, blacks in basketball were clearly overrepresented at forward; whites were overrepresented at guard and center. This pattern was less evident in the 1970s and generally disappeared in the 1980s as basketball itself changed dramatically.
- In women's intercollegiate volleyball in the United States, blacks are overrepresented

*For documentation of the existence of stacking, see Berghorn et al. (1988), Best (1987), Curtis and Loy (1978a, b), Hallinan (1988), Jones et al. (1988), Lapchick (1984, 1988, 1989), Lavoie (1989), Leonard (1977a, b; 1987), Maguire (1988), Williams and Youssef (1972, 1975, 1979), and Yetman and Eitzen (1984).

Table 10-1   Percentage of blacks, whites, and other players in positions on NFL, Major League Baseball, and NBA teams.

Sport	Positions	Black (%)	White (%)	Other* (%)
NFL (1992)				
	TOTAL PLAYERS	**68**	**30**	**2**
	Offense			
	Quarterback	6	94	0
	Running back	92	7	1
	Wide receiver	88	11	1
	Center	19	76	5
	Guard	35	62	3
	Tight end	59	39	2
	Tackle	46	50	4
	Kicker	7	83	10
	Defense			
	Cornerback	98	2	0
	Safety	88	12	0
	Linebacker	71	28	1
	Defensive end	73	26	1
	Defensive tackle	67	30	3
	Defensive back	92	7	1
	Nose tackle	60	35	5
	Punter	10	85	5
Major League Baseball (1993)				
	TOTAL PLAYERS	**16**	**67**	**17**
	Pitcher	5	82	13
	Catcher	1	87	12
	First base	19	69	11
	Second base	13	58	26
	Third base	12	75	12
	Shortstop	8	42	50
	Outfield	50	33	17
NBA (1993)				
	TOTAL PLAYERS	**77**	**23**	**0**
	Center	55	45	0
	Forward	80	20	0
	Guard	83	17	0

Source: Center for the Study of Sport in Society (*1993 Racial Report Card* compiled by RE Lapchick and JR Benedict.)
*In baseball this includes Latinos from many different national and cultural backgrounds. In football it includes a combination of Latinos, Pacific Islanders, and Asian Americans from diverse cultural backgrounds.

at spiker and whites at setter and bumper (Eitzen and Furst, 1988).

- In Canadian hockey, French Canadians are overrepresented at goalie, and English Canadians are overrepresented in defensive positions (Lavoie, 1989).

- Black West Indians and black Africans in British soccer are clearly overrepresented in the wide forward positions, whereas whites are disproportionately found at goalie and midfielder (Maguire, 1988; Melnick, 1988).
- Aborigines in Australian rugby are over-

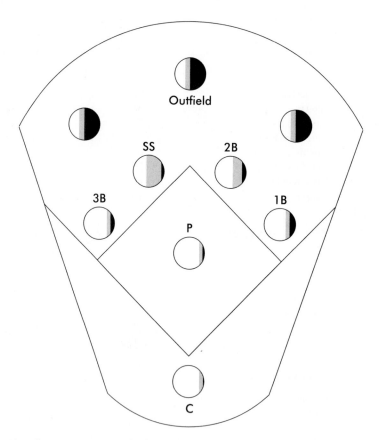

FIG. 10-1 This illustration portrays the baseball data from Table 10-1. The percentage of black players in each baseball position during the 1993 season is represented by the shaded areas; the percentage of Hispanics is represented by the grey areas. Blacks remain concentrated in the outfield positions; whites are overrepresented in the positions of pitcher and catcher; Hispanics are slightly overrepresented at second base and strongly overrepresented at shortstop.

represented in the wide positions, whereas nonaborigines are overrepresented in the central team positions (Hallinan, 1988).

Why do stacking patterns exist? This question often leads to discussions that get tied up with the race logic that is widely accepted in the society as a whole. Racial stacking patterns in American football, baseball, and women's volleyball correspond closely with racist beliefs about skin color and intelligence, leadership and decision making, dependability, motivation and emotion, running and jumping, and what many people call instincts. The thinking and dependability positions are stacked with white athletes; the speed and physical reaction positions are stacked with black athletes. Even when white athletes are in the speed positions, they are often described by coaches and announcers as dependable and smart, and when black athletes are

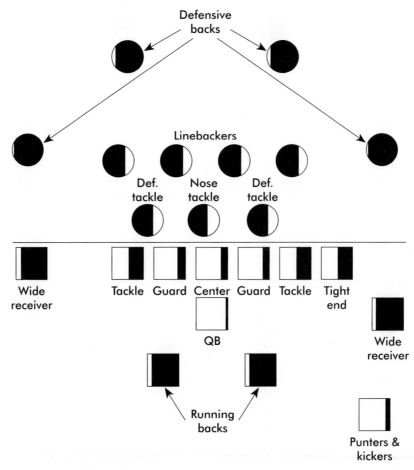

FIG. 10-2 This illustration portrays the football data from Table 10-1. The percentage of black players in each of the offensive and defensive positions during the 1992 season is represented by the shaded areas. As in baseball, blacks are overrepresented in the positions defined as requiring speed, quickness, and quick physical reactions. Whites are overrepresented in the positions that require leadership, decision-making skills, and dependability.

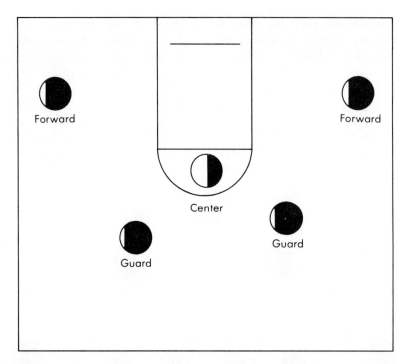

FIG. 10-3 This illustration portrays the professional basketball data from Table 10-1. Positions are shaded to represent the proportion of black players during the 92-93 season. Stacking patterns are no longer clear or well defined in professional basketball. Note: Because of recent changes in ideas about the skills and characteristics needed to play various positions, basketball is unique when it comes to the issue of stacking.

in the thinking and dependability positions they are sometimes described in terms of their "natural" physical attributes. Of course, this is not always the case, but the patterns exist.

Stacking patterns in Canadian hockey correspond with dominant ethnic ideology and ideas about the characteristics of French Canadians (Lavoie, 1989); in British soccer they correspond with prevailing ideas about black West Indians and Africans (Melnick, 1988; Maguire, 1987); and in Australian rugby they correspond with prevailing ideas about Aborigines (Hallinan, 1988).

Of course, when people from a particular racial or ethnic group become the majority of players in a certain sport, and especially when they

start to be hired as coaches, there is a decrease in stacking patterns based on dominant racial ideology. However, stacking patterns can be maintained and sometimes even intensified when the members of a racial or ethnic group become aware of how their futures in sport may be improved or hindered if they play certain positions. For example, young black athletes playing the thinking and dependability positions on all-black football teams in high schools have sometimes chosen to try out for the speed and physical reaction positions in college so they will not be overlooked by the scouts and coaches of professional teams, who might be using race logic as they evaluate them. These players choose to conform to stacking patterns, but they do so to cope with the consequences of racial ideology, not because they want to switch positions. This is how racial ideology is perpetuated in sport and in many other spheres of life.

Race Logic and Jobs in Coaching and Administration

While dominant racial ideology has worked to turn black men into entertainment commodities in sports, it has nearly kept them completely out of management positions in sport organizations. This has been clearly noted by Arthur Ashe in a 1992 Newsweek article when he said, ". . . the crazy theories of black intellectual inferiority are alive and well. . . . [Coaches and] managers have to think, and the conventional wisdom among sports' ruling elite is that . . . blacks don't think as well as whites." As Table 10-2 shows, the proportion of black men in coaching positions is not even close to the proportion of black athletes in the major professional team sports in the United States. This is also the case in college sports

Apart from general racial issues in sports, the underrepresentation of blacks and other minorities in coaching and administration jobs has been one of the most widely publicized topics in sports during the last decade. This issue will be explored further in Chapter 11, but at this point it is important to see how this pattern fits with a combination of race logic and stacking patterns in team sports. For example, coaches and managers are frequently former athletes who played the thinking and dependability positions in their sports (Kjeldsen, 1980; Loy et al., 1978). Athletes who played the speed and physical reaction positions don't get picked as coaches because they never showed how bright and dependable they were when they were players. Unfortunately, this works against many black athletes who want to move into coaching positions. But race logic still leads many people to believe that skin color signifies character and thinking abilities. If there had been a football team in the jungle, you can bet that Tarzan

Table 10-2 Percentages of black athletes and black coaches in the NFL, NBA, Major League Baseball, NCAA Football (Div I-A), and Basketball (Div I).

	Black athletes (%)	Black head coaches (%)
NFL (1992)	68	7
NBA (1992)	77	26
MLB (1993)	16	14
NCAA FB (1992)	40	3
NCAA BB (1992)	60	19

Source: Center for the study of sport in society.

would have been the quarterback and then he would have been hired as the coach.

SPORT PARTICIPATION PATTERNS: GROUP BY GROUP

Sports in North America have long histories of racial and ethnic exclusion. This has led to underrepresentation of all minorities in most competitive sports at all levels of competition, even in high schools and community programs. Before the 1950s, the organizations sponsoring sport teams and events seldom opened their doors to blacks, Native Americans, or Hispanics. When members of minority groups played sports, they usually played with each other in segregated games and events.

Blacks and Sport Participation

Before the early 1950s, most whites in North America systematically avoided playing with and against blacks; blacks were systematically excluded from participation in white-controlled sport programs and organizations. But blacks had their own baseball and basketball leagues. Occasional games with white teams were held behind closed doors, they were not considered official, and did not affect the records of white teams. Because black teams sometimes beat even the best white teams and because the exclusion of blacks in white leagues was rationalized by the notion that blacks didn't have the character or fortitude to compete with whites, these games received no publicity in the white press.

Since the 1950s the sport participation of blacks has been concentrated in just a handful of sports. Even in the 1990s black athletes are underrepresented or nonexistent in most North American sports at many levels of participation. This is often overlooked because those who watch college and professional football and basketball and major league baseball see many black athletes on teams. But these are just three of the 44 men's and women's sports played in college, only two of the dozens of sports played at the international amateur level, and three of the many professional sports in North America. Many people forget there is a virtual absence of black athletes—male or female—in hockey, figure skating, swimming, diving, soccer, golf, tennis, gymnastics, bicycling, rodeo, auto racing, motocross, bowling, softball, archery, shooting, badminton, alpine and nordic skiing, kayaking, table tennis, equestrian events, sailing, men's volleyball, many field events in track and field, and other sports. The exceptions to this pattern stand out because they *are* exceptions. In fact, the underrepresentation of blacks in these sports is much greater than the underrepresentation of whites in sports such as basketball and football—many more whites play basketball and football in high school than there are blacks who play high school tennis or golf.

Throughout American sports history the participation of black women has been severely limited and has received little attention apart from occasional Olympic medal winners in track events. Black women suffer the consequences of dominant forms of gender logic and race logic.

Overall, sport participation rates in middle- and upper-middle-income white communities in the United States is much higher than in the vast majority of predominantly black communities. This, and the information above, is often ignored by many people; all they seem to see are black male athletes making high salaries in high profile sports. This exemplifies how dominant racial ideology influences what people "see" in their social worlds.

Native Americans and Sport Participation

There are nearly 2 million Native Americans in the United States. Although they are officially classified as one minority group, Native Americans comprise nearly 200 diverse cultural groups. To native peoples, the differences between these groups are important; however, most Anglos (whites who are neither Hispanic nor Native American) tend to think of them all as "Indians" and use stereotyped descriptions of their habits and dress. The ideology that Anglo people have created about Native Americans is different from racial ideology. It has its own history and has grown out of unique forms of ethnic relations.

Sports among Native Americans have traditionally combined physical activities with ritual and ceremony (Oxendine, 1988). Although Native Americans have made significant achievements in certain sports over the past century, public acclaim has been limited to those few who have been standout athletes on the football and baseball teams of government-sponsored reservation schools and training schools. For example, when Jim Thorpe and his teammates at the Carlisle School, a segregated government training school, defeated outstanding mainstream college teams in 1911 and 1912, they attracted considerable attention (Oxendine, 1988). Apart from the success of a few teams and a few individual athletes in segregated government schools, Native American participation in most sports has been and continues to be limited. If participation is not made impossible because of poverty, poor health, and lack of equipment and programs, it is discouraged by a combination of prejudice, lack of understanding (see box on pp. 258-260), or fears of being cut off from the cultural roots that are at the heart of personal identity for many Native Americans.

For example, Billy Mills, gold medalist in the 10,000 m at the 1964 Olympics, explained that

Text continued on p. 260.

Although African American athletes are visible in certain high profile sports in the U.S., there are few or no African American student-athletes on many high school and college sport teams. In fact the residential segregation that is common in many American communities is simply reflected in the racial and ethnic make-up of local teams. Many small colleges have no minorities on the vast majority of their teams. (Colorado Springs Gazette Telegraph)

Team Names, Logos, and Mascots:
When Are They Indications of Bigotry?

According to Concerned American Indian Parents, a group dedicated to eliminating the use of Native American stereotypes in advertising and sports, Anglos have been stereotyping Native Americans for so long that they don't even realize they are doing it. The stereotypes are so commonplace that many Anglos have accepted them as valid depictions of native peoples. Anglos say that team names and mascots based on stereotypes are not meant to offend anyone, even though they exploit, trivialize, and demean the history and cultural heritage of Native Americans.

Consider the following story from a statement by the Concerned American Indian Parents:

An American Indian student attended his school's pep rally in preparation for a football game against a rival school. The rival school's mascot was an American Indian. The pep rally included the burning of an Indian in effigy along with posters and banners labeled "Scalp the Indians," "Kill the Indians," and "Let's burn the Indians at the stake." The student, hurt and embarrassed, tore the banners down. His fellow students couldn't understand his hurt and pain.

This incident occurred in 1962, but this student's pain has not prevented hundreds of sport teams at the high school, college, and professional levels from using stereotypical images of Native Americans for team names, logos, and mascots.

The pain continues today. There are still "non-Indians" who dress in war bonnets and war paint and run around brandishing spears and tomahawks or pounding tom-toms. For example, Chief Wahoo, the mascot of the Cleveland Indians, is built on long accepted stereotypes of Native Americans. Sadly, Chief Wahoo is only one of many examples of disrespectful caricatures used by American sport teams. People do not seem to realize that such names and mascots could perpetuate stereotypes that have contributed to the powerlessness, poverty, unemployment, alcoholism, and dependency of many native peoples in the United States. What would people say if the mascot for the San Diego Padres was a fat, self-indulgent missionary who ran around swinging a rosary and waving a crucifix in a menacing or celebratory way? Some Christians would object, and rightly so!

If teachers, administrators, and students in U.S. schools had a deep knowledge of the rich and diverse cultures of Native Americans and realized the discrimination currently faced by native peoples, they would not use names such as Indians, Redskins, Chiefs, Braves, Savages, Tribe, and Redmen for their teams; they would not allow Anglo students to entertain fans by dressing up as caricatures of Native Americans, and they would not allow fans to mimic Native American chants or to act out stereotypes of war whooping, tomahawk-chopping Native Americans.

Schools should not use any Native American name or symbol in connection with sport teams unless they do the following:

1. Sponsor a special curriculum to inform students of the history, cultural heritage, and current living conditions of the native group after which their sport teams are named. Unless 70% of the students can pass annual tests on this information, schools should drop the names they say are used "to honor" native people.

2. The school must send out for publication two press releases per year in which information about the native peoples honored by their team names is described and analyzed; similar materials must be published annually in schools newspapers and yearbooks.

3. Once per year, during homecoming or a major sport event, there must be a special ceremony designed by and for native peoples in the local area; the purpose of the ceremony is to inform students and parents about the people they say they honor with team names.

Continued.

(Martin Williams Advertising, Minneapolis)

REFLECT ON SPORT

Team Names, Logos, and Mascots—cont'd
When Are They Indications of Bigotry?

If schools did these three things, they would be less likely to perpetuate some of the most destructive and vicious stereotypes in American history. Shouldn't schools be careful not to distort history through their own team names, logos, and mascots? Don't schools teach history? Of course they do. But those using names and mascots related to Native Americans often forget history and perpetuate misunderstandings and bigotry in the process. Is that a tradition worth maintaining?

If schools did the three things suggested, their students would think twice before using certain team names. For example, students would know that to many Native Americans "redskin" is as derogatory as "nigger" is for African Americans, or "spic" is for Chicanos. Ironically, the capital city of the government that has broken hundreds of treaties with Native Americans still has a profes-

sional football team named "Redskins." From the cultural perspective of Native Americans this symbolizes continued Anglo ignorance of the heritage and cultures of native peoples. Other names are often similarly offensive to anyone aware of the history of native peoples in North America. Only when native peoples have a representative share of power and resources in this country might the situation be right for using their names and images in association with sport teams. This is why the Irish do not object to Boston's use of the name "Celtics" or Notre Dame's use of the "Fighting Irish."

The poster pictured on p. 259 was developed to make people question dominant ideas about Native Americans and think about how bigotry has become an accepted part of sport culture in the United States. What do you think?

---

becoming immersed in sport programs away from the reservation on which one grew up is:

> . . .like walking death. . . . If you go too far into [Anglo] society, there's a fear of losing your Indian-ness. There's a spiritual factor that comes into play. To become part of white society you give up half your soul (cited in Simpson, 1987).

For the young Native Americans attending schools or watching games between schools with team names such as Indians, Redskins, Redmen, Renegades, and Savages and with mascots who run around and mimic white stereotypes of "Indian" behavior, playing sports involves giving up much more than half their soul. When they

see a distorted or historically inappropriate caricature of a Native American on a gym wall of a school that doesn't even try to increase student awareness of the cultures of local native peoples, it means swallowing cultural pride, repressing anger against insensitive, historically ignorant Anglos, and giving up hope of being understood in terms of their own feelings and cultural heritage. Dimensions of this process were also discussed in Chapter 4.

Hispanics and Sport Participation

The term "Hispanic" is a generic term used by the U.S. government to group together all people whose ethnic roots can be traced to

Spanish-speaking countries. This group encompasses a wide range of different cultures related by language, colonial history, or Catholicism. Chicanos (with cultural roots in Mexico) comprise the largest Hispanic group in the United States, followed by Puerto Ricans, Cubans, other Central and South Americans, and people from Spain. There are about 22 million Hispanics in the United States (in 1993).

Little attention has been given to any Hispanic group in North American sports. For example, at this writing, the *Sociology of Sport Journal* has published only two papers (Foley, 1990; Leonard, 1988) devoted to any Hispanic group since its first issue in March 1984. Other scholarly publications have similar records. A 1982 reference guide to historical materials on American sports lists over 200 pages of summaries and citations of literature, 40 pages of important events in the history of American sports, and 21 pages of information on research centers, special collections, and directories; but there is not a single reference to athletes or sport histories of any Hispanic group in the United States, nor are Latin American athletes in the United States mentioned (Higgs, 1982). Finally, a survey of the first 11 volumes of the proceedings of The Association for the Anthropological Study of Play revealed articles on Eskimos, rural Africans, and Arab Bedouins, among dozens of other groups, but not a single article on any Hispanic group in the United States or Canada. Even though the ancestors of Chicanos have resided in what is now the southwestern United States since before the Pilgrims set foot at Plymouth Rock, their experiences in sports have been largely ignored in the sport sciences.

The experiences of Latin Americans in major league baseball were discussed by anthropologist Alan Klein (1991) in his book, *Sugarball: The American Game, the Dominican Dream.* Although Klein focuses his attention on the Dominican Republic and what happens there in connection with the baseball academies sponsored by major league teams, he also notes that Dominican players who sign contracts and play in the minor or major leagues in North Amer-

ica often confront problems. They not only face significant cultural adjustments and language problems, but they must also deal with behaviors based on ethnic stereotypes and a general lack of understanding of their cultural backgrounds.

Anthropologist Doug Foley gave special attention to Mexicano-Anglo relations in his study of rituals associated with high school football in a small Texas town. He describes the working class Chicano males (vatos) who rejected sport participation but used sport events as occasions for publicly displaying their style (cool pose?) and establishing their social reputations in the community. He describes how Mexicanos* protested a homecoming ceremony that gave center stage to Anglos and marginalized Chicanos, how Mexicano players defied coaches when Anglo players were given high status positions on the team, and how the Mexicano coach resigned in frustration because he could not appease powerful Anglo boosters and school board members and still maintain his ethnic integrity by challenging bigotry. Despite these examples of protest against prevailing Anglo ways of doing things in the town, Foley concludes that the rituals associated with high school football tend to perpetuate the power and privilege of Anglos. As long as Mexicanos saw things and did things the Anglo way, they were accepted. But the protests did nothing to make Anglos see or do things to fit the values and experiences of the Mexicanos.

There is a need for more research along the lines of the studies done by Klein and Foley so we can better understand sport participation in light of patterns of ethnic relations in specific cultural settings.

Asian Americans and Sport Participation

There are about 6.7 million Asian Americans. The diversity of their cultural roots is great. To group them together is the same as grouping all Europeans together and making no

---

*This was the self-descriptive term used by people with a Mexican heritage in Foley's study.

distinctions between Italians and Norwegians. This diversity presents major problems for researchers, and I don't know anyone in the sociology of sport who would claim to be an expert on Asian Americans in sports. This is unfortunate because recent immigrants from Asian countries have had a major influence on the sport programs in certain high schools in California and other parts of the country. Asian students from families that have recently come to the United States are not likely to try out for football teams, but some may be interested in establishing teams in badminton or other sports related to their past experiences. Coaches working with athletes from Asian countries may need to learn about cultural traditions important to the athletes. Language differences may challenge teammates and coaches. These patterns would vary from group to group and they would probably be unrelated to the experiences of Asian Americans born and raised in the United States. We need to know more about these issues.

Anthropologist Mark Grey (1992) has dealt with some of these issues in his study of high school sports and relations between immigrants from southeast Asia and the established residents of Garden City, Kansas. Grey reports that despite beliefs about sports serving democratic functions in schools, sports at Garden City High School were organized so participation could occur only in narrowly defined terms. The immigrant and minority students had to "fit in" with the dominant system of values and game orientations, and this system was grounded in the experiences of Anglo Americans. The school failed to provide these newcomers with sports they wanted to play, and when the immigrant students did not try out for football, basketball, baseball, and softball, they were seen as unwilling to become "true Americans." Over time, their failure to participate in the major high school sports led them to be socially marginalized in the school and community. The belief of the established community residents was that "if *those people* really wanted to become Americans, they would participate in true American sports."

When they didn't participate, new tensions were created and existing tensions were intensified. It is possible that this pattern also exists in other communities, although we don't know enough about it or about alternative patterns.

THE RACIAL DESEGREGATION OF CERTAIN AMERICAN SPORTS

The visibility of black athletes in high profile spectator sports in the United States and other countries raises an interesting sociological question: Why have some sports been desegregated to the point that black male athletes are proportionately overrepresented, relative to the size of the black population in the country as a whole? Three reasons may explain why. *First*, the organization of certain sports provides a unique context for desegregation at the player level. *Second*, built-in financial incentives encourage desegregation of certain sports. *Third*, black Americans have responded to perceived opportunities for success and developed skills in sports in which payoffs depend on an investment of effort rather than money. Each of these reasons requires further explanation.

The Organization of Certain Sports

Unlike many organizations, certain sport teams and leagues are set up to discourage discrimination against blacks or members of any other minority group (Edwards, 1973). Consider the following characteristics of sport teams:

1. An individual player's achievements benefits the other members of the team. This means that whites in sports organizations are more likely to control their prejudices than they would be in other organizations, in which the individual achievements of workers seldom benefit fellow workers.
2. Superior performances by athletes neither lead to promotions in the organizational structure of sport nor do they put a person in control over fellow players. This means that whites in sports will not be as threatened by the achievements of blacks

as they would be in other settings, in which superior performances often lead to power and authority over coworkers.

3. Sport teams do not depend on friendships between teammates to achieve success. This means that interracial relationships need not continue in off-the-field social situations as they must in many work organizations, in which social obligations are an accepted part of the job.

4. The organizational structure of a sport team grants athletes little power or authority. This means that sport involvement does not change the fact that blacks have little formal and legitimate power in the economy or the political world; being an athlete is therefore consistent with the relatively powerless status of blacks in the rest of society, and their involvement in sport is not seen as a threat to the status quo.

When these four organizational characteristics are combined with the fact that individual performances in sport can often be measured precisely and objectively, it is clear why the whites who control sport teams would take advantage of the skills of any minority athletes without feeling threatened by the achievements of those athletes. However, it is difficult to change patterns of exclusion grounded in long-standing race relations. This means that racial desegregation has seldom occurred unless there have been good reasons for whites to open doors and make opportunities available to black athletes. Money and the desire to win have generally been powerful reasons.

Money and Winning: Incentives for Desegregation

Two of the best reasons for changing American sports are money and winning. People generally believe that if revenues can be increased or win-loss records improved, change is worth it—even if the change is inconsistent with patterns of race relations. The history of desegre-

gation in American sport clearly shows that when a winning season is necessary to generate money for a sport team, there is a tendency to recruit and play the best athletes, regardless of skin color. When sport team owners discovered they could make large profits in baseball, football, and basketball, they and their coaches abandoned their traditions of racial exclusion in favor of making money. Although some teams tried to remain competitive without recruiting black players, they dropped their policies when they found that winning can be difficult if you ignore the talents of skilled athletes who are eager and willing to play.

Because money is such a powerful motivator it is not surprising that desegregation first occurred in horse racing and boxing and then in the other major money-making sports. Black jockeys were plentiful before the turn of the century, but because the ability and performance of the horse were the most important factors in winning a purse, a racist press, a white jockeys' union, and laws making segregation mandatory (Jim Crow laws) forced blacks out of the public eye in horse racing and back into the less prestigious and less visible roles of trainer and stable attendant. Because horse owners did not see black jockeys as crucial to making money, they did not resist this form of exclusion. In boxing, however, the individual fighter was responsible for victory. Segregation existed, but there were notable (and newsworthy) exceptions. White promoters and boxing managers saw blacks as potentially big money makers because they were box-office attractions. Given the race logic used by many whites, even the rumor of a fight between a black and a white would sell newspapers, and an actual fight would generate ticket sales bringing handsome profits to white promoters and managers.

Desegregation was also financially motivated in professional and college sports, where money could be made by people other than the athletes themselves. Desegregation started slowly, but as soon as people saw there was money to be made by opening doors for all who could help win games, an increasing number of blacks were recruited as players. This is one of the major reasons why the nonrevenue-producing sports in U.S. colleges and universities seldom have black team members. Ironically, the scholarships received by many white athletes from well-to-do families (in gymnastics, golf, swimming, tennis, soccer, and volleyball) may be subsidized by the revenue-producing teams whose success is often owed to the hard work and efforts of black athletes from lower-income families (Edwards, 1986). This results in welfare for the wealthy in college sports! Even though white scholarship athletes in nonrevenue sports seldom think of their athletic grants in this way, this is one of the reasons why intercollegiate sports opened their doors to black athletes.

If black athletes had not improved winning records and increased profits for the people who controlled sports and sport sponsoring organizations, the policies of exclusion that had restricted black participation for so long would not have changed as rapidly or as completely as they did in certain sports. In sports in which sponsors make little or no money, there has been much less interest in recruiting blacks or in communicating to the black community that opportunities are available. Because blacks have not had opportunities in many other spheres, they have been very sensitive and responsive to opportunities in certain sports.

Perceived Opportunities and the Development of Sport Skills

The people who control sports are not the only ones influenced by financial factors and the desire for success. These things also influence all young people with athletic potential, and blacks are no exception. In fact, blacks are even more likely than whites to emphasize sports as a means of achieving prestige and economic success because they perceive more barriers to achievement in other activities (Harris and Hunt, 1984).

It is also important to note that blacks in the United States have excelled in sports requiring little expensive equipment and training. For example, basketballs are inexpensive and the best coaching is widely available in public school programs. Furthermore, outdoor basketball courts are inexpensive to build and maintain. No grass is needed, and they can be squeezed into confined spaces. This is why basketball has come to be known as "the city game" and why it is the game of choice among many black youths growing up in low-income urban areas where resources are scarce and opportunities to be noticed in other activities are rare (Axthelm, 1970; Telander, 1988).

As black males have become increasingly successful in a few highly visible sports, young blacks focus their attention on developing skills in the same sports. This has not only contributed to the high proportion of blacks in certain sports, but it also accounts for the tendency among many young black males to put all their motivational "eggs" into just a few sport "baskets." Because they haven't had the chance to see payoffs connected with education, they conclude that running and jumping offer the best chances for fame and fortune. Therefore many of them dedicate themselves to being the best runners and jumpers around. Unfortunately, occupational opportunities for runners and jumpers are very limited (see Chapter 11).

Why Haven't All Sports Been Desegregated?

Desegregating any activity or organization is usually a complex process. In sport, desegregation has been influenced by the organizational structure of sport leagues and teams, by the payoffs associated with eliminating policies of exclusion, and by the motivation among blacks to take advantage of opportunities to develop certain sport skills.

In discussions of race relations and sport it is important not to equate desegregation with the elimination of bigoted racial ideologies or with the achievement of true racial integration. Desegregation is simply the opening of doors; actual changes in race relations are marked by unqualified invitations to come through the doors and join *all* the activities going on inside, regard-

African Americans have excelled in sports requiring no expensive equipment or training. Basketballs are cheap, opportunities to play are relatively plentiful, and good coaching is available in public schools. These are some of the reasons why basketball is often described as "the city game." (Colorado Springs Gazette Telegraph)

less of where they are happening or who is involved.

Jackie Robinson (1972) recognized the differences between desegregation and real changes in racial ideology when he once remarked that some of his racist teammates on the Brooklyn Dodgers tolerated him as a fellow athlete only because he "could help fill their wallets." He knew those teammates never fully accepted him as a human being either on or off the field. The door to sport was opened for Robinson, but he knew there were no unqualified invitations to participate in everything going on inside sports or in the rest of life outside of sports.

Many things have changed in the 45 years since Jackie Robinson signed his first major league contract, but bigoted racial ideologies still exist. Just because blacks have been accepted as

athletes in certain sports does not mean that skin color has lost its relevance in all sports or in the rest of society. It's one thing for people to say nice things about black athletes who run around football fields, basketball courts, and Olympic tracks, but it is quite another thing for them to be comfortable with racial integration off the playing field and across a wide range of social situations.

This point is important when explaining why some sports have not become desegregated over the years. Exclusionary policies are least likely to be maintained in sports in which there is little off-the-field social interaction, especially interaction between men and women. However, when sports directly involve informal, personal, and sexually mixed social contact either on the field or off, desegregation has been very slow.

This is one of the reasons why golf, tennis, swimming, bowling, and other sports learned and played in social clubs have been slow to open doors for blacks or other minorities. When sport participation is accompanied by informal social contact between family and friends and by intimate and personal interaction, dominant racial ideology among whites is likely to keep doors closed— or only partially open.

SPORTS AND INTERGROUP RELATIONS

If players and spectators can come together in sports despite racial and ethnic differences, are sports contexts in which personal prejudices can be broken down, dominant racial ideologies challenged, and intergroup relations improved? Research shows that contact between people from different racial and ethnic groups can lead to favorable changes when members of each group:

- Have equal status
- Pursue the same goals
- Depend on one another's cooperation to achieve their goals
- Receive positive encouragement for interacting with one another without discrimination

Even though these conditions exist in many sports, especially when players from different racial or ethnic groups are on the same teams, there are at least three reasons to be cautious before concluding that interaction in sports reduces prejudice:

1. When people use racial and ethnic ideologies to help interpret their worlds they are remarkably resistant to changing those ideologies.
2. Contact between members of different racial and ethnic groups in sports is often so superficial that it fails to break down prejudices, or challenge ideologies, or change people's behaviors, especially off-the-field behaviors.
3. The competition involved within and be-

tween teams may aggravate existing prejudices among players and spectators and lead to the reproduction of hostile and destructive ideologies.

Racial and Ethnic Ideologies Resist Change

When people have sets of ideas they've used for many years to interpret what goes on in the world, they will go to great lengths to defend and preserve those ideas. This is often true with ideas about race and ethnicity. When intergroup contact occurs, prejudiced people generally preserve their racial or ethnic ideology by using any one of the following tactics:

1. Ignore all information contradicting their ideology.
2. Define contradictory information as an exception to the rule of their ideology.
3. Reinterpret the information so it fits with their ideologies.

Each of these tactics can be used within the context of sports. For example, players from one racial or ethnic group may simply ignore players from other groups and selectively tune out information inconsistent with their ideas about race and ethnicity. When forced to interact with players who do not fit their ideologies, people may simply define those players as exceptions— not like other blacks, whites, Hispanics, and so on. This allows them to preserve their ideologies while they play sports with teammates from other groups. When information clearly challenges ideologies, people often reinterpret the information so it fits with and supports their negative ideas about race and ethnicity.

Studies of sport teams that have members from different racial or ethnic groups show that contacts between teammates are usually friendly in connection with practices, games, and other team get-togethers. But this pattern of contact and friendliness does not usually carry over into other situations in which pressures to follow dominant racial ideologies are simply part of the fabric of social relations (Chu and Griffey, 1982; Miracle, 1981). Furthermore, coaches exert considerable influence over what happens in sport-related situations. When coaches organize team relations to emphasize the irrelevance of dominant racial and ethnic ideologies, players are more likely to be friendly and supportive of one another, regardless of race or ethnicity. But when coaches tell racial or ethnic jokes, use racial or ethnic nicknames, and do other things to emphasize dominant racial ideologies, players may adopt similar approaches (Miracle, 1981; Fine, 1987).

Types of Social Contacts in Sports

Despite what many people think, teammates do not have to be friends with one another to win games. In fact, many teams have won championships despite serious interpersonal problems among players. Winning games requires a knowledge of the playing abilities of teammates, but this knowledge can be gained without any close, personal interaction. In other words, people from different racial and ethnic groups do not have to get to know one another just because they are teammates.

During the early days of racial desegregation in U.S. sports, this lack of close relationships forced black athletes to lead lonely lives. They had to cope with the racism and cautious acceptance of spectators, teammates, and coaches (Robinson, 1972). Contacts with teammates off the playing field were rare, and there were few opportunities for blacks and whites to share experiences and feelings (Charnofsky, 1968). As the number of black athletes has increased in some sports, there has been a tendency for blacks to confine their close relationships to black teammates. This has resulted from a combination of factors. Black athletes share an awareness of race-related problems not often possessed by whites, and they are often hesitant to interact with whites, who may think in terms of dominant racial ideologies or simply be ignorant about racial issues. Whites, on the other hand, sometimes avoid black teammates or do not seek them out for social relationships, especially outside of sport settings. The box on p. 268 provides a real life example of intergroup relations and how they can affect young people from minority backgrounds.

Research on this topic tends to suggest that high school athletes are not unique when it comes to various forms of interracial social contact (Chu and Griffey, 1982; Miracle, 1981). High school and college athletes may play on teams with members of other racial and ethnic groups, but they seldom interact across racial and ethnic lines off the field (Miracle, 1981; Thirer and Ross, 1981; Thirer and Wieczorek, 1984). Social life in many American schools involves little social mixing between students from different racial and ethnic groups and sometimes it even involves hostilities and conflicts (Jarvis, 1993). Sharing membership on a high school sport team may override this pattern within the special sphere of the sport team itself, but it doesn't seem to override it in nonsport settings.

Competition Often Subverts Intergroup Cooperation

Sports provide a unique form of intergroup contact. They involve competition, which often destroys the common goals needed for the contact to challenge dominant racial and ethnic ideologies and open the door for supportive intergroup relations. In fact, when athletes from different racial or ethnic groups are opponents, sports often become sites for the reproduction of negative ideas about race and ethnicity. This is the case for spectators as well.

This should not be surprising. Social psychologists have long used competition when they have wanted to create hostility and negative attitudes between groups in their experiments (Sherif, 1976). They realized that competition consistently evoked negative feelings. They also found that when competitors were from different racial or ethnic groups, existing negative feelings were usually intensified in connection with intergroup contact.

These patterns also exist in sports. In fact, sport competition may even intensify emotions and generate hostile intergroup behavior during events. As one black student athlete wrote in a paper on race and sport, ". . . in the heat of sport competition, restraint gives way to raw emotion, and racism takes the place of sportsmanship." He noted that his statement was based on his experiences through years of sport

REFLECT ON SPORT

A Dilemma For Minorities In Sports

Whenever minorities in a society come face to face with prejudice or discrimination they must make difficult choices. They can directly confront the source of prejudice or discrimination, or they can ignore the situation. If they are confrontive, they risk personal rejection; if they ignore the situation, they give passive approval to the prejudices and discrimination that cause problems in inter-group relations.

To illustrate how this dilemma affects minorities, imagine you are a 14-year-old Chicano student in a junior high school where nearly 95% of the students are Anglos. You are standing in the hall between classes with seven Anglo students who you hang around with. Four of them are your teammates on the varsity basketball team. One of your teammates tells a racist joke about "lazy Mexicans who are always late for work," and everyone laughs. What should you do? You can respond in one of four ways: (1) you can laugh with everyone else and be accepted as "a good guy" by your teammates; (2) you can confront the joke teller and let him know he has offended you; (3) you could explain to him he has a misconception about Mexicans; or (4) you could accuse him of bigotry.

If you confront the joke teller or accuse him of ignorance or bigotry, you risk being rejected by peers whose acceptance is crucial to your social survival in junior high school. If you object to the joke, you could be told that you're too uptight, you can't take a joke, or you shouldn't worry about bigotry because "you're not like other Mexicans." Then how would you respond to these comebacks by your naive Anglo friends? To avoid making them defensive, you'd need a detailed understanding of the nature of bigotry and how it affects people and social relationships. However, as a 14-year-old you haven't learned this yet. So you decide it's easier to laugh and passively approve the stereotype used

in the joke.

Then when you're late to basketball practice later in the day, you tell everyone that "I'm just a lazy Mexican operating on 'Mexican time.'" Now everyone laughs and they all think you're really great. Even the Anglo coach laughs and excuses you for being late.

Because you've dealt with the situation by conforming to their stereotypes, your teammates really like you now. You've made them feel comfortable about their cruel and destructive attitudes. But what you don't realize is your tactics have also helped perpetuate bigotry. Then, in the locker room after practice, one of your teammates calls you "beaner," and everyone laughs. Everyone expects you to laugh too, and accept this new nickname. Now what do you do? You begin to wonder if your decision to conform to their stereotypes might already be backfiring. You think about the future and what might happen if you applied for a job in a company controlled by one of your former teammates. Would he give an important, high paying job to someone called "beaner," to someone who referred to himself as a "lazy Mexican" when he made mistakes? You wonder.

This story is true; it was told by a Chicano student. The dilemma he faced is common. It occurs whenever minority group members encounter people who can affect their lives and use stereotypes (racist, sexist, or ageist) as a basis for behavior. It often occurs in sports because many people have stereotypes about the physical and psychological characteristics of minority athletes. This puts pressure on minority athletes: they don't know if they should be confrontive or if they should ignore things. Therefore, there is a need for dominant group members (whites, men, and younger people) to become more aware of how their insensitivity creates problems for others.

Players from different racial or ethnic backgrounds may have special relationships within the context of a sport team, but those relationships seldom carry over into nonsport situations in which certain forms of social segregation are often the rule. (Colorado Springs Gazette Telegraph and Tom Kimmell)

participation. Race relations expert Richard Lapchick (1984), director of the Center for the Study of Sport in Society at Northeastern University, has made a similar observation. He says that when black and white athletes meet in sport they often carry "a great deal of racial baggage . . . [and] prejudices are unlikely to evaporate with the sweat as they play together. . . . Any display of negative behavior is likely to reinforce existing biases. . . ." When this happens, games may be defined in racial terms and become racial battles.

The effects of competition are not always limited to the members of opposing teams. Members of the same team often compete with one another for starting positions and other honors. When players from different racial or ethnic groups compete, their personal rivalries may create race or ethnic relations problems on the team. Many coaches have faced such problems through the years. This is one of the reasons why there is a need for some form of training in intergroup relations in many sports.

Is Change Possible?

People don't give up their ideologies easily, especially racial ideologies. Sports may bring people together, but they do not automatically lead people to question the way they think about race or ethnicity or the way they relate to people from other racial or ethnic groups.

Sadly, sports have often been used to perpetuate destructive racial ideologies and extend practices of racial and ethnic exclusion around the world. For example, the traditional definition of amateurism used in the Olympic Games worked for many years to the disadvantage of all people who were not white men and members of well-to-do social classes in Western societies (Eitzen, 1988). The actual competitive events that make up the Olympic Games have been chosen by people who do not represent people of color around the world. Although many people of color have adjusted to this situation, it still leads us to ask how sport is related to intergroup relations on an international level. When one group gets to choose the events and make up the rules, sports can be used to perpetuate its power and privilege. Research shows that this is true in local communities and on the international level (Foley, 1990 a, b; Grey, 1992; see Ch. 14).

My purpose in this discussion is not to argue that sports are never sites for improving intergroup relations. Whenever racial and ethnic groups mix on relatively good terms, there is at least a chance for them to challenge negative ideas and to find new ways of seeing others and relating to one another. According to both athletes and spectators, there are cases when this *has* happened in sport. This is hopeful. However, these good things do not happen automatically or as frequently as many people think. Although sports bring people together, they do not necessarily create the social experiences that will inspire them to challenge and change negative ideas about racial and ethnic groups. In fact, when competition is defined in racial or ethnic terms, sports can intensify these negative ideas.

For intergroup relations to be improved through sports, those who control sport teams and sport events must make organized, concerted efforts to bring people together in ways that will get them to confront and challenge dominant racial ideologies. This is no easy task, and it is seldom attempted. But if it were attempted—and it did work—it would be significant because sports attract so much public attention. If sports served as sites for regularly challenging dominant racial ideology and improving racial and ethnic relations, it could be used as a model for changes in others spheres of social life.

The symbolic significance of sports has been recognized and used by Richard Lapchick and the Center for the Study of Sport in Society at Northeastern University in Boston. Lapchick and his multiracial, multiethnic staff have developed Project TEAMWORK, a creative program for improving intergroup relations in schools and communities. Before Project TEAMWORK enters a school, information on intergroup relations in the school and the surrounding community is studied and used to guide strategies used in the project plan. Then a trained team consisting of former athletes from diverse racial and ethnic backgrounds goes into the school and conducts training sessions for students. The training sessions emphasize awareness of intergroup relations issues and how to deal with those issues in the school and in the communities in which the students live. The sessions are also designed to promote intergroup tolerance and respect.

Project TEAMWORK spends at least two weeks in a target school. But before the intergroup relations experts leave the school they help form a "Human Rights Squad." The size of this squad varies from school to school, but all of its members are trained and entrusted to monitor intergroup relations in the school and initiate intervention strategies to control intergroup conflict when it does occur. The Human Rights Squad in a school is also responsible for promoting positive intergroup relations in its community by using the strategies it has learned at school. A Project TEAMWORK representative stays in touch with representatives of the Human Rights Squad and may even return to schools when help is needed to deal with issues.

The initial evaluations of Project TEAMWORK have been very positive. Significant numbers of students in all Project TEAMWORK schools have been interested in participating in the training sessions and then joining Human Rights Squads. Students are aware of the real dangers of the destructive racial ideologies that exist in society as a whole. They see the consequences of those ideologies in their own lives and they want to do something to make race and ethnic relations better.

Project TEAMWORK is only one approach to change. Other approaches are desperately needed so people throughout the country can begin to look critically at how ideas about race and ethnicity have turned cities and neighborhoods into dangerous places. We need a new vocabulary to deal with the existence of diversity in social life. We must get away from the notion that skin color signifies some sort of biological essence that shapes character and physical abilities. We must shift our focus from racial and ethnic "difference" to racial and ethnic relations (Birrell, 1989).

In sports, we must realize that when we ask questions about so-called racial performance differences we are merely reproducing a racial ideology that has caused hatred, turmoil, and confusion in much of the world for nearly 400 years. Difference is not the issue; the process of how people think about and deal with other people is the issue. Therefore sport programs in high schools and colleges, and even at the professional level, should sponsor racial and ethnic diversity training sessions. Everyone from team owners and athletic directors to the people in training rooms should attend these sessions. Coaches need these training sessions and so do athletes. Even those who are already sensitive to diversity issues should know that there is a formal commitment in their organizations to acting on those sensitivities.

The training sessions should familiarize everyone in sports with the history and implications of dominant racial ideology in their society. That history must be told from the perspective of racial and ethnic groups as well as from the perspective of whites. Too often, the perspectives of racial and ethnic minorities get lost in efforts to make things better. When this happens, "better" often comes to mean that everyone should do things the same way as those with power and influence do them. Therefore the training sessions should question traditional ways of seeing and doing things and emphasize

that real change depends on seeing the world in new ways.

ARE SKIN COLOR AND CULTURAL HERITAGE IMPORTANT?

Attempts to define race in biological terms have been futile; races are *socially* identified categories of people rather than biologically unique and distinct categories. The concept of race emerged in the eighteenth century and it has been associated with confusion and turmoil since then. The desire to classify all people of the world into distinct categories has been fueled by different factors at different points in history. The colonial expansion of Western societies was associated with the development of a racial ideology that claimed intellectual superiority for light skinned people over dark skinned people. As part of this ideology the physical abilities of dark-skinned peoples were reinterpreted as signs of arrested evolutionary development. Thus people of color were seen as possessing physical prowess but lacking the character, fortitude, intelligence, and spirit possessed by whites. This race logic was used to justify colonization, slavery, and the exploitation of people of color around the world.

Race logic also influenced sport participation patterns and the interpretation of sport performance. Black athletes were thought to be less than human in a number of respects; white athletes were thought to be driven by inborn spirit and determination. However, many whites were uncomfortable with the notion of black physiological superiority and looked for examples to prove that whites could combine physical strength with intelligence to surpass the physical accomplishments of black people. The Tarzan myth and the search for great white athletes were associated with this desire by whites to establish their racial superiority. Racial ideology continues to exist today although it has been revised to fit with historical changes.

Racial and gender ideologies and class relations in American society have led many black males to create "cool pose." Cool pose is a combination of stylized persona and sport skills that makes the black male body a valuable commodity in popular spectator sports. It also enables black male athletes to use the social distance created by dominant race ideology to intimidate fellow athletes, especially white athletes. Race logic is also a factor underlying both racial stacking patterns and the absence of blacks in coaching and administrative positions in sports.

Sport participation patterns among different racial and ethnic groups have been influenced by a combination of ideological, historical, and structural factors. But the sport participation of any minority group usually occurs under terms set by the dominant group in a community or society. Minority groups have seldom been able to use sports to challenge the power and privilege of the dominant group even though some individual minority group members may experience great personal successes in sports. This is probably why minority athletes only become cultural heroes when they present themselves as politically neutral good guys with understated racial or ethnic identities. Engaging smiles also help minority athletes defuse the racial ideology that leads many whites to define minority men, especially black men, as threatening.

Racial desegregation of certain sports in the United States was associated with a combination of factors, including the organizational characteristics of sports, strong financial incentives for recruiting blacks in sports in which money could be made, and the desire of blacks to take advantage of any available opportunity to live the American dream of success. The importance of economic factors cannot be underestimated in the desegregation process. Only when winning has been tied to profits and when blacks have been able to contribute to winning have doors been opened for black athletes in sports.

Just because some sports have histories of racially mixed participation does not mean that racial and ethnic problems have been eliminated in those sports. In fact, intergroup harmony is never automatic in any setting or group and it doesn't last long unless attention is paid to intergroup relations. Sport is unique in the sense that it may even trigger a form of race awareness that makes skin color and certain cultural differences very important to many people. When this happens, race and ethnicity become "identity handles" used to differentiate athletes by potential, character, and physical abilities.

Sports can be also sites for challenging dominant racial ideology and transforming race and ethnic relations. But this happens only if people in sports plan strategies to encourage critical awareness of racial ideology. This awareness then must be directed into efforts to develop new ideas about race and ethnicity and new forms of racial and ethnic relations. This necessarily involves a shift away from a consideration of so-called racial differences to a consideration of how people think about and interact with each other.

SUGGESTED READINGS

Arbena, J.L., ed. 1988. Sport and society in Latin America. Greenwood Press, Westport, Conn. (*the eight papers in this anthology provide a good starting point for looking at sports in Central and South America; neither race nor ethnicity are dealt with directly although some papers can inform analyses of ethnicity in U.S. sports*).

Ashe, Jr., A.R. 1988. A hard road to glory: a history of the African American athlete. Warner Books, New York (*this three-volume work traces the involvement of African Americans in sports from 1619 to the present; it contains a wealth of useful reference data; although it is short on analysis, it is the most comprehensive source of information on black Americans in sports ever compiled*).

Brooks, D., and R. Althouse, eds. 1993. Racism in college athletics: the African American athlete's experience. Fitness Information Technology, Inc., Morgantown, WV (*10 original essays dealing with historical, structural, gender, and intergroup relations issues*).

Cashmore, E. 1982. Black sportsmen. Routledge & Kegan Paul, Boston (*the only available overview on black athletes in England*).

Edwards, H. 1969. The revolt of the black athlete. The Free Press, New York (*the first book written about black athletes by a sociologist*).

George, N. 1992. Elevating the game: black men and basketball. Harper Collins Publishers, Inc., New York (*journalistic overview containing interesting historical and anecdotal information; provides a loose interpretation of how black men have brought a unique style to basketball*).

Hoose, P.M. 1989. Necessities: racial barriers in American sports. Random House, New York (*a response to the 1987 Al Campanis statement on ABC's Nightline; provides an easy-to-read overview of examples of racism in sports in the late 1980s*)

Jarvie, G., ed. 1991. Sport, racism, and ethnicity. The Falmer Press, Bristol, Pa. (*six of the eight papers in this anthology deal with racial and ethnic relations outside North America; papers offer good critical analyses*).

Klein, A.M. 1991. Sugarball: the American game, the Dominican dream. Yale University Press, New Haven, Conn. (*study of intercultural relations as exhibited and informed by baseball; shows how baseball simultaneously generates pride among Dominicans, competition with the United States, and acceptance of North American interests*).

Lapchick, R. 1991. Five minutes to midnight: race and sport in the 1990s. Madison Books, Lanham, Md. (*contains autobiographical and historical material along with insightful analyses of issues related to race and sport; presents useful data from Lapchick's Center for the Study of Sport in Society*).

Mead, C. 1985. Champion Joe Louis: black hero in white America. Charles Scribner's Sons, New York (*review of Louis's career and an overstated analysis of his influence on the overall desegregation of sport in the United States*).

Oxendine, J.B. 1988. American Indian sports heritage. Human Kinetics Publishers, Inc., Champaign, Ill. (*much-needed book on neglected topic; good analysis of events prior to 1940s; weak analysis of what has happened since then*).

Robinson, J. 1972. I never had it made. G.P. Putnam's Sons, New York (*autobiography of the man who broke the color line in major league baseball*).

Ruck, R. 1987. Sandlot seasons: sport in black Pittsburgh. University of Illinois Press, Urbana, Ill. (*a unique study of sport in an urban black community during the twentieth century; excellent historical information*).

Telander, R. 1988. Heaven is a playground. A Fireside book, New York (*first published in 1976, this is a personal account of a summer of playground basketball in Brooklyn; captures the futility of life in a low-income, inner city neighborhood in which basketball offers an temporary alternative to street life*).

Wacquant, L.J.D. 1992. The social logic of boxing in black Chicago: toward a sociology of pugilism. Sociology of Sport Journal 9(3): 221-254 (*read Telander's book first and then read this study—the comparison illustrates the difference between a journalistic account and a sociological analysis; excellent material on boxing, boxers, and the training gym in urban American culture*).

Wagner, E.A., ed. 1989. Sport in Asia and Africa: a comparative handbook. Greenwood Press, Westport, Conn. (*presents papers offering a good starting point for understanding sports and cultural relations in African and Asian countries*).

Wenner, L.A., ed. 1993. Mascots and team names. Journal of Sport and Social Issues 17(1), April (*3 articles in this issue focus on the use of Native American names, mascots, and logos*).

CLASS RELATIONS AND SOCIAL MOBILITY

Is sport participation a path to success?

One of the most widely held beliefs in North America is that family background and social characteristics don't count when it comes to sports. Most people see sports as open to everyone; and they see success in sports as the result of individual abilities and hard work. This view often leads to the conclusion that sports are unique because they provide equal opportunities and enable everyone to gain experiences that ultimately lead to success in occupational careers. This connection between sports and occupational success has been repeatedly emphasized by athletes who say that sports turned their lives around and by rags-to-riches stories about highly paid athletes from low-income backgrounds.

This chapter will focus on three questions about the connection between class relations, social mobility, and sports:

1. Is sport participation truly open and democratic or is it connected with class relations?
2. Do sports and sport organizations offer unique career opportunities?
3. Does sport participation contribute to the overall career success of former athletes?

SPORTS AND CLASS RELATIONS

Throughout history some people have had more material resources, political clout, or social power than others. Because these things are important in social life, they affect how people see themselves and others, and they affect how people interact with one another. The processes through which material resources, political clout, and social power are incorporated into social life are called **class relations**. Because class relations often involve a combination of intergroup tension, conflict, exploitation, and oppression, they attract considerable attention in sociology, including the sociology of sport.

Many people believe that sports and sport participation are open and democratic, that the inequalities existing in other parts of social life don't spill over into the organized games we play

and watch. However, this is not true. In fact, the very existence of sports in any society is connected with class relations. This is because sports consist of formally organized, institutionalized competitive physical activities (see Chapter 1) that could not exist without material resources and without a group of people that has the time, power, and social connections to organize activities and bring people together to play them.

Sports cannot be developed, scheduled, and maintained unless people have free time, money, access to facilities or open spaces, and the ability to organize. The people who possess or control these resources in a society are in the best position to organize games and physical activities. They also have the power to make sure that sports are organized around their own values and interests and that sports emphasize ideas and orientations that fit with how they think social life should work (Bourdieu, 1978; Gruneau, 1983). This has been true throughout history. Elite and powerful groups in society have always had considerable influence over what types of activities will be organized into sports and how sports will be promoted, played, and interpreted (see Chapter 3). Even when the games and physical activities of the general population have become formally organized and developed into sport forms, they have not become widely sponsored and promoted unless they fit the interests of people with resources in the society at large. Sports cannot exist for long without resources, nor are they likely to become popular forms of entertainment without the sponsorship of people with resources.

The Dynamics of Class Relations

Sometimes it is difficult to understand the dynamics of class relations at work in sports. So I will explain the dynamics of age relations in sports and use the explanation as a basis for explaining class relations. Here's an example of the dynamics of age relations in sports and sport participation: Even though children are capable of creating their own games, organized youth sport programs have been developed by adults to reflect the interests and concerns of adults (see Chapter 5). Children organize informal games that emphasize action, personal involvement, stimulating competition, and relationships with their friends. Adults, however, organize youth sport programs that emphasize discipline, obedience, conformity to rules, and learning "correct" orientations, physical techniques, and competitive strategies. Because adults possess the *resources* needed to develop, schedule, and maintain organized youth sports, those sports reflect what adults think children should be doing and learning as they play. This does not mean that children don't have fun in organized sports, but it does mean that fun must occur within a general framework created and sustained by adults.

When the behavior of children in youth sports programs deviates from adult expectations, adults use their power to force compliance or convince children that it's in their best interest to play "the right way." When children play "the right way" and meet adult expectations, the adults say they possess "character" (Fine, 1987). This is why coaches obsessed with maintaining tyrannical control over athletes (such as University of Indiana basketball coach Bobby Knight) are hailed as heroes by many adults in North America (Pyros, 1987). These coaches make sure that sports are played to promote the idea that the world is a better place when adults have full control over young people. This is how sport reproduces a form of age relations in which adult power and privilege is defined not only as good but as a "natural" aspect of social life.

Class relations work in a similar way. People with money and power are able to organize and promote games and physical activities that fit their interests and foster particular ideas about how social life should be organized. For example, they can use their money and power to play sports among themselves in exclusive clubs or in settings inaccessible to others. When this happens, sports become tools for elite groups to call attention to social and economic differences between people and to promote the idea that people with power and influence are special in society.

Another way for elite groups to preserve their power and influence in society is to create and sponsor forms of organized sports that encourage people to adopt an ideology (an integrated set of ideas and beliefs) that reinforces existing economic and political relationships in society. For example, North American sports are organized to emphasize competition and dominance over opponents instead of other qualities such as cooperation and self-expression. This ties sports to an ideology of achievement, stressing that success is grounded in the ability to compete against others and is gained only by working hard to acquire a higher score than everyone else. According to this ideology, economic success (winning) becomes temporary proof of individual worth. People who use this *class logic* to interpret their own lives often set out on an endless quest to acquire as many "things" as they can. Things are used to symbolize a person's identity, status, and worth. Lives then become evaluated by the advice coaches sometimes emphasize in locker room pep talks: "When you're satisfied with your performance, you're finished." Corporate executives and sales managers give similar advice to their workers.

This ideology combined with consumerism drives market economies (such as the United States and Canada) and enables people with power and privilege in those economies to preserve and extend their power and privilege. When people in a society adopt a class logic that says, "You get what you deserve, and you deserve what you get," they will usually view the rich and powerful as "winners." Books written by those boasting the highest economic scores in society will become best-sellers, and television shows may even feature the rich and famous so everyone can look at their lifestyles with curiosity and envy. Most importantly, however, most people will learn to interpret their own lives by the belief that only those who work hard get rewards and those who don't work hard will never be rewarded. This is why the rags-to-riches stories of athletes get so much publicity—they reaffirm a class logic that works to the advantage of those who already have power in sports, the media, and the economy. This is also how sports can be used to promote the idea that existing forms of economic inequality in society are not only good but just and natural.

Because most people who want to participate in sports at elite levels of competition usually depend on the approval and sponsorship of powerful and privileged people in their societies, sports themselves become effective tools for justifying and perpetuating certain forms of economic inequality. In other words, people learn that if they want to play sports, they have to look to the wealthy and powerful to give them opportunities. And, as you might expect, the wealthy and powerful generally fund opportunities that promote their own interests and concerns. Ironically, the widespread mistaken belief is that sports are models of social equality.

Class Relations and Sport Participation Patterns

Who plays, who watches, and who consumes information about sports is clearly connected with class relations in all societies: involvement in and with sports goes hand-in-hand with money, power, and privilege (Miller Lite Report, 1983). People in high-income and high-status occupational groups have the highest rates of active participation, the highest rates of attendance at sport events, and even the highest viewing rates for sports on television. For example, Olympic athletes and officials are more likely to come from more privileged groups in society (Beamish, 1990; Gruneau, 1976; Hall et al, 1990). People from households with annual incomes of over $50,000 are much more likely to watch television broadcasts of tennis, college and pro football, college basketball, and major league baseball than people from households with lower incomes (Stacey, 1987; $27,000 was

the median household income in 1987).

Although the health and fitness movement has often been described as a grass roots phenomenon in the United States and Canada, it primarily involves people who have higher than average incomes and educations and people who work in professional or managerial occupations. People from lower income groups may get exercise in some jobs involving physical labor, but they don't run, cycle, swim, or sign up for triathlons as often as their high-income counterparts do. Nor do they play in as many organized sports on their lunch hours, after work, on weekends, or during their vacations. This pattern holds true throughout the life course, for younger and older age groups.

This participation pattern is best explained by class relations; it is related to a combination of differential resources and life-styles. Because it takes money and time to play in organized sports and attend events, people who don't punch time clocks or watch every dollar they spend have opportunities not enjoyed by others. Furthermore, historical circumstances combined with economic inequality have given rise to connections between certain sports and the life-styles of people with differing amounts of wealth and power. For the most part, these connections reflect patterns of sponsorship and access to opportunities for involvement. Sports sponsored by private clubs and sports that require expensive equipment and facilities gradually become parts of the life-styles of the well-to-do. Sports that by tradition are free and open to the public, that are sponsored by public funds, and that do not require expensive equipment or facilities are more likely to become parts of the life-styles of middle- and low-income groups. However, people from the lowest income groups often spend so much of their time and energy coping with the challenges of everyday life that they have no energy left for sports, even when sports are free and accessible, or they have no interest in playing or watching sports emphasizing an ideology that has nothing positive to do with their lives.

Historical factors combined with social inequality have given rise to connections between certain sports and certain status groups. In this way sport has perpetuated and re-created socioeconomic differences between people. Contrary to what many people think, sport is not the "great equalizer" in societies. (Jay Coakley)

HOMEMAKING, CHILD REARING, AND EARNING A LIVING: WHAT HAPPENS WHEN GENDER RELATIONS AND CLASS RELATIONS OVERLAP? Women in family situations have often been less likely than their male counterparts to be able to negotiate the time and resources needed to maintain sport participation. When a married woman with children decides to join a soccer team that schedules practices late in the afternoon, she may encounter resistance from members of her family. Resistance is certain if she has traditionally served her family as chef, chauffeur, and tutor. "Time off for good behavior" is not a principle that applies to married women with children. On the other hand, married men with children do not often face the same resistance. In fact, when they play softball or handball after work, their spouses may delay family dinners, keep dinners warm for when they arrive home, or even go to the games and watch them play.

Women in middle- and lower-income families most often feel the constraints of homemaking and child rearing. Without resources to pay for child care, domestic help, and sport participation expenses, these women simply don't have many opportunities to play sports. Furthermore, sports are often social activities occurring among friends. So if friends don't have resources enabling them to participate, opportunities and motivation for involvement may decrease even further. Of course, this is also true for men, but women from middle- and lower-income families often lack the network of relationships out of which sport interests and activities emerge (Deem, 1986; Woodman, 1977).

Women from upper-income families often face a different situation. They have resources to pay for child care, house cleaners, carryout dinners, and sport participation. They often participate in sport activities by themselves or with other family members (Unkel, 1981). Furthermore, they have social networks made up of other women who also have the resources to maintain high levels of sport participation. They

have often attended college and played at least some sports while growing up. They do not experience the same constraints as their lower-income counterparts. This is not to say they do not have any problems negotiating time for sport involvement, but their rates of successful negotiations are relatively high. Their opportunities are much greater than those among lower-income women, but they are not quite the same as those among many upper-income men.

The sport participation of young women may also be limited when they are asked to shoulder adult responsibilities at home. For example, in low-income families, especially those with only one parent, teenage daughters are often expected to care for younger siblings after school until after dinner, when their mothers get home from work. According to one girls' team coach in New York City, "It's not at all unusual that on a given day there may be two or three girls who aren't [at practice] because of responsibilities at home" (Dobie, 1987). The coach also explained that child care duties keep many girls from coming out for teams. His solution was to coordinate a cooperative child care program at practices and games so girls from low-income families could meet family expectations *and* play sports. When coaches are not so creative or accommodating, some girls drop out of sports to meet responsibilities at home. Boys and girls from higher income families seldom face similar expectations that would force them to drop out of sports.

BECOMING A MAN AND GETTING RESPECT: WHAT HAPPENS WHEN GENDER RELATIONS AND CLASS RELATIONS OVERLAP? Boys and young men in low-income communities often see sport participation as a special and legitimate means of establishing a masculine identity. Sociologist Mike Messner notes ". . . the more limited a boy's options appear to be, and the more insecure his family situation, the more likely he is to make an early commitment to an athletic career" (1992, p. 40). It seems that the stakes associated with sport participation are different for boys from low-income backgrounds than for boys from higher income backgrounds.

Messner's study of men who were former elite athletes indicated that males from lower class backgrounds often saw sport participation as a means of obtaining "respect." This was not so much the case among males from middle class backgrounds. One former athlete who later became a junior high school coach explained this in the following way:

> For . . . the poorer kids, [sports] is their major measuring stick. . . . They constantly remind each other what they can't do in the sports arena. It's definitely peer-acceptable if they are good at sports—although they maybe can't read, you know—if they are good at sports, they're one of the boys. Now I know the middle- and upper-class boys, they do sports and they do their books . . . But as a whole, [they put] less effort into [sports] (quoted in Messner, pp. 57-58).

This coach was suggesting that because of class relations in society as a whole, young men from lower income backgrounds often have more at stake in sport participation. But what this coach didn't point out is that the development of sport skills often requires material resources that do not exist in low-income families. So unless equipment and training are provided in public school athletic programs, young men from low-income groups stand little chance of competing against upper income peers who can buy equipment and training if they want to develop skills. But young people from upper income backgrounds often have so many opportunities to do different things that they may not focus attention on one sport to the exclusion of other sports and other activities. For someone who has a car, nice clothes, "guaranteed" college tuition, and good career contacts for the future, playing sports may be good for bolstering popularity among peers, but it is not perceived as a necessary foundation for an entire identity (Messner, 1992, p. 59). This often leads young men from middle and upper-income backgrounds to gradually disengage from an exclusive commitment

to playing sports and striving for careers as athletes. When these young men become adolescents, they see many different opportunities in their lives.

The power of class relations and gender relations in producing the motivation to dedicate oneself to sports was explained by Chris Dundee, a boxing promoter, when he pointed out that, "Any man with a good trade isn't about to get himself knocked on his butt to make a dollar" (quoted in Messner, p. 82). What Dundee meant was that upper class males see no reason to have their brain cells destroyed in a quest to get ahead through a sport such as boxing. Of course, this is why boxers always come from the lowest and most economically desperate income groups in society and why boxing gyms are located in low-income neighborhoods (Wacquant, 1992).

CLASS RELATIONS IN ACTION: THE DECLINE OF HIGH SCHOOL SPORTS IN LOW-INCOME AREAS In chapter 5 it was noted that publicly funded youth sports programs are being cut in communities facing government budget crises. The same thing is now occurring with high school sports in school districts with high proportions of low-income families. Varsity sport programs are being cut or dropped in many big city and poor rural schools (Miles, 1991; Swift, 1991). As this continues to happen, fewer young people from low-income backgrounds have opportunities to participate in sports such as baseball and football, each of which requires facilities that are expensive to maintain. Meanwhile, basketball grows in popularity among low-income boys and girls because schools can offer basketball as long as they can maintain a usable gym. Varsity sport programs in middle and upper income areas are also threatened by cuts, but they are usually saved by "participation fees" paid by athletes and their families. These fees, often as expensive as $250 per sport, guarantee that opportunities to participate in varsity programs will continue to go to those from upper income groups.

With funds being cut and coaches being laid off, people in poor neighborhoods realize that bake sales and car washes can no longer keep sports programs going. They are now looking to foundations and large corporations to sponsor high school sports. But corporations tend to sponsor only those sports that promote their images; for example, they may support basketball rather than other sports because basketball's popularity makes it effective in their own marketing and advertising programs. If high school sports are funded by corporations there will be increased emphasis on using sports to generate visibility and revenues through state and national tournaments. High school athletes may then wear Nike or Ford Taurus insignias on their uniforms instead of lions, tigers, and Spartans. This will make the link between sports and class relations even more clearcut.

In summary, sports and sport participation are closely tied to class relations in any society. Because the existence of sports depends on surplus resources, sport programs usually depend on the approval and support of those with power and influence. This creates a tendency for sport programs to be organized in ways that recreate and perpetuate existing forms of class relations in a society. Furthermore, patterns of participation clearly reflect the distribution of resources and opportunities in a society.

OPPORTUNITIES IN SPORTS: MYTH AND REALITY

Do sports provide opportunities for satisfying and rewarding careers? The general answer to this question is yes, but it must be carefully qualified in light of the following factors:

1. The number of career opportunities for athletes is severely limited.
2. Career opportunities for athletes (as opposed to coaches, trainers, etc.) are short-term, seldom lasting more than 5 years.
3. Most career opportunities in sports do not bring fame or fortune.
4. Opportunities for women are limited.

5. Opportunities for African Americans and other minorities are limited.
6. Opportunities for older people and for disabled people are limited.

Each of these qualifications is discussed in the following sections.

Opportunities Are Limited

Young athletes often have visions of receiving scholarships to play sports in college; some even have visions of eventually playing at the professional level. Their parents often have similar visions. Unfortunately, the chances for turning these visions into reality are quite low.

Statements about the chances of becoming a professional athlete vary greatly because they are based on different methods of computation. For example, some computations give the chances of a high school or college athlete in a particular sport becoming a professional; others give the chances for people from a particular racial or ethnic group; and still others give the chances for *anyone* in a particular age group in the whole population of a society.

The information in Table 11-1 summarizes the chances for high school and Division I college football, basketball, and baseball players in the United States to play professionally in their sports.

Table 11-2 provides similar information for black football and basketball players. Table 11-3 provides different computations for five racial and ethnic groups in nine professional sports (Leonard and Reyman, 1988). The data in Table 11-3 were generated by listing the total numbers of athletes in each of the nine men's and women's professional sports in the United States. These numbers were then broken down by how many athletes come from each of the major racial and ethnic groups in the population. The probabilities given in Table 11-3 are then based on the numbers of athletes in each sport compared to all the people in the United States in the same age ranges as the pro athletes in that sport. Here's how you read Table 11-3: 1 out

Table 11-1   Chances of making it to the top in football, basketball, and baseball in the United States*

	Number of players at various career points					Percentage of players who will make it from:			
Sport	High school	College	College senior year	Pro rookie year	Pros	High school to college sport	4th year college athlete to pro rookie	High school to pro sport	College to pro sport
Football	1,000,000	40,000	13,333	150	1,400	4.0%	1.1%†	0.14%	3.5%
Basketball	500,000	11,000	3,667	50	360	2.2	1.0	0.07	3.3
Baseball	400,000	17,000	5,667	80	730	4.2	1.4†	0.18	4.3

*These figures are estimates made on the basis of available data in 1992; they do not represent exact numbers of participants.
†These percentages are inflated; actually the chances are considerably lower than this because the pool of players eligible for the pro draft includes more than just college players. Major league baseball signs players out of high school and junior college, and out of numerous Latin American Leagues.

Table 11-2   Odds against making it to the pros among high school and college football and basketball players.

	All high school players	Number making pros each year	Odds against
Football	947,755	150	6,318 to 1
Basketball	517,271	50	10,345 to 1
Combined	1,465,026	200	7,325 to 1

	*Black high school players	Blacks making pros each year	Odds against
Football	350,699	80	3,897 to 1
Basketball	289,672	38	7,622 to 1
Combined	640,371	128	5,003 to 1

	All college	Number making pros	Odds against
Football	5,500	150	37 to 1
Basketball	1,000	50	20 to 1
Combined	6,500	200	33 to 1

	Black college seniors	Blacks making pros each year	Odds against
Football	2,035	90	23 to 1
Basketball	560	38	15 to 1
Combined	2,595	128	20 to 1

Source: Lapchick, 1991, p. 261.
*Figures for black high school athletes are estimates based on the assumption that proportions of black and white athletes in high school and college are equal and are derived from college statistics.

Table 11-3 Odds of becoming a professional athlete by race/ethnicity and sport

Sport (age range)	Race/ethnicity				
	White	Black	Hispanic	Native American	Asian and Pacific Islander
Football (20-39)	1/62,500	1/47,600	1/2,500,000	1/12,500,000	1/5,000,000
Baseball (18- 39)	1/83,300	1/333,300	1/500,000	—	1/50,000,000
Basketball (20-39)	1/357,100	1/153,800	1/33,300,000	—	—
Hockey (17- 39)	1/66,700	—	—	—	—
Golf					
Men's (20-39)	1/312,500	1/12,500,000	1/33,300,000	—	1/20,000,000
Women's (20-39)	1/526,300	—	1/33,300,000	—	1/3,300,000
Tennis					
Men's (16-34)	1/285,700	1/2,000,000	1/3,300,000	—	—
Women's (15-34)	1/434,800	1/20,000,000	1/20,000,000	—	—
Auto racing*					
Men†	1/1,000,000	—	1/20,000,000	—	—
Women† (16-39)	1/100,000,000	—	—	—	—

Source: Revised version of Table 3 in Leonard and Reyman (1988).

*Auto racers often drive beyond age 39. Unfortunately, it was impossible to obtain ages for all 125 drivers studied, so we used census data only to age 39. If we included the higher ages, the odds against a successful career for any given person increased significantly.

†Technically there is no sex segregation in auto racing. Therefore, male totals have been aggregated to compute the odds.

of 47,600 men between the ages of 20 and 39 is a black football player in the NFL; and 1 out of 434,800 women between the ages of 15 and 34 is a white tennis player on the women's circuit. The odds of making it to professional sports for people in some racial and ethnic groups are so low that they haven't even been computed.

Some of the probabilities in Table 11-3 should be qualified. For example, if minor league players are taken into account in baseball and hockey, the odds get better for people from certain groups, especially whites, but the pay in minor leagues is often quite low. In the case of hockey, the odds in the table are greatly inflated because most of the NHL players come from Canada, not the United States. Similar qualifications are needed for the odds in golf, tennis, auto racing, and baseball—all of which draw athletes from outside the United States. As sports become more global, the computation of odds based on national population figures becomes less relevant.

Even though we can question these computations, one thing is clear, regardless of the computational method used: *opportunities for making it to the top as an athlete are limited.* Of course, this does not mean that young athletes should not try for those opportunities, but it does mean that they should also pursue other, more realistic career alternatives while they play sports. When the goal of becoming a professional athlete interferes with educational achievement, sport participation often becomes linked with personal frustration, disappointment, and unemployment.

Opportunities Are Short-Term

Children, especially boys, often say they want to become professional athletes. But what these children do not realize is that few athletes

SIDELINES

HIS EARNINGS ON THE PRO TOUR HAVE DECLINED DRASTICALLY THIS YEAR!

Not all athletes achieve fame and fortune. Despite highly publicized information on salaries and prize money, many athletes do not earn enough to pay for their own expenses associated with participation. This is especially true of athletes in some individual sports.

have playing careers lasting longer than 3 to 5 years. This leaves *40 additional years* for some other career. Unfortunately, many people—including many athletes, coaches, and parents—ignore this fact.

Ideas about careers in professional sports are often distorted by misinterpretations of media coverage. The media focus on the best athletes in the most popular sports. The best athletes tend to have longer playing careers than others in their sports. In golf we think of the careers of Arnold Palmer, Jack Nicklaus, and Nancy Lopez—all successful players who have participated for their entire adult lives. We never hear about the numerous golfers who play for one or two seasons before being forced to quit because of a lack of funds—even though they far outnumber the success stories. In football we hear about the long careers of popular quarterbacks, but no coverage is given to the numerous players whose 1-year contracts are not renewed after their first seasons.

In professional football, basketball, and baseball the length of an average career ranges from 4 to 7 years. But this average is deceiving because it obscures the fact that the number of people who play for only 1 or 2 years is far greater than those who play for more than 5 to 7 years. Most people do not recognize this reality.

Opportunities Do Not Always Bring Fame and Fortune

When discussing careers in sports, people tend to focus their attention on the active careers of athletes. They generally ignore opportunities in coaching, officiating, sport medicine, athletic training, management and administration, and community sport programs. However, careers in these areas are as attractive as many nonsport occupations even though they do not bring the fame and fortune some athletes receive. The chances of getting jobs in these positions are better than they are for landing player contracts in professional sports.

However, having one of these sport-related careers requires more than just experience as an athlete or a knowledge of sports. It usually calls for a good education, interpersonal skills, indepth knowledge of training strategies, knowledge of how sport is organized and administered, and connections with people who can provide recommendations and job leads. In other words, a career in sport-related jobs calls for the same personal qualifications as careers in other areas.

Opportunities for Women Are Limited

There are few career opportunities for women athletes. Table 11-3 partially illustrates this, but the table does not show that the odds for becoming a professional in some sports are *zero* because there are no women's events, teams, or leagues. Apart from tennis and golf, few women have been able to make sport participation into even short-term careers. The number of professional women skiers, bowlers, jockeys, auto racers, bicyclists, and track athletes is very low. Even women in volleyball and basketball, two popular North American sports, have no opportunities unless they go to Europe, where women's leagues do exist, or unless they are one of the few players on the beach volleyball circuit in the United States.

There was a women's professional basketball league in the United States during the late 1970s, but it folded because it failed to make money. The financial failure was generally blamed on lack of interest among potential spectators. However, there may have been more important reasons. The league was organized just like pro basketball for men. Games were played in large, high-rent facilities. All of the owners and coaches were men. Most of the coaches had annual salaries of $50,000 or more, whereas the players made between $5,000 and $20,000. Marketing strategies emphasized the male coaches rather than the women athletes. Promotions were expensive because they were directed at all people interested in sports rather than those with specific interests in women's basketball. Taken together, all these things may have doomed the women's league to failure because they never tapped into potential spectator interest among people with personal connections to girls' basketball all over the United States. If two or three regional leagues had been organized, if teams had spent less money for coaches, if games had been played in smaller gyms, if marketing had been localized and directed at girls and their families connected with community and interscholastic leagues, the fate of women's professional basketball might have been different. Maybe the next attempt to form a professional league for women will be more successful.

What about opportunities apart from being an athlete? Are there jobs for women in coaching, training, sport medicine, and administration? The answer to this second question is yes, but women have seldom been hired in men's programs, and the majority of jobs in women's programs are held by men (Holmen and Park-

Opportunities for women coaches have not increased as fast as women's sport programs have grown. Women coaches are seldom promoted into administrative positions as is the pattern among men coaches. (University of Colorado and Dan Madden)

house, 1981; Acosta and Carpenter, 1992a, b; Lenskyj, 1988).

For a number of reasons, including sex discrimination, the opportunities for women coaches have not increased as rapidly as women's programs have grown. The same pattern exists in officiating, administration and other job categories, except for secretary in the athletic director's office.

Trends at the high school level have been similar. As girls' programs expanded and became more important in the schools, many of the coaching and administrative jobs have gone to men. A pattern typical in most states is that the percentage of male coaches of girls' teams has gradually increased while the percentage of female coaches has decreased. Similar patterns exist in other sport-related employment settings such as athletic clubs and community programs. Men are in most of the higher-paying jobs even though the number of women participating in sports and physical activities has increased over the past 2 decades. It is expected that this pattern will change, but change will be slow and mobility opportunities for women in sport will remain limited for some time even though we will see a few more women as sports broadcasters, athletic trainers, and administrators. Changes will occur more rapidly in recreation programs, fitness club management, sportswear sales, physical therapy, and public relations and marketing.

It also should be remembered that the "gender logic" underlying sports and sport organizations often creates extra burdens for women with jobs in sports. First Lady Hillary Rodham Clinton has explained why this is so when she answered a question about women in many occupational careers:

> . . . I think that it is an extra burden that we [women] carry to be able to fit into a workplace that is based on values and experiences that we didn't have much role in shaping, but in which we want to make our contribution (quoted in Clift, 1992)

This comment is especially applicable to sports and it partially explains why many women who worked as coaches and administrators in women's sport programs in the past, left their careers when the NCAA took over women's sports in the early 1980s. These women didn't feel comfortable with the overall philosophy that men used, their reasons for working sports became irrelevant, and they became alienated and detached from careers they had once loved. Because they didn't like the prospect of being forced to do things as men did them, many women retired or quit and many others decided not to apply for jobs in women's programs.

Meanwhile, when men took power and control in women's programs they were anxious to hire people who thought as they did, coached as they coached, and saw the world as they did. And who were these people likely to be? Men, of course. But the male administrators who hired these men did so because they were looking for the most "qualified" coaches and administrators. It's just that the deck was stacked in a way that led many women to be automatically defined as "unqualified" because they did not do things as men did them. Those who were most "qualified" were simply those who could be expected to do things as men had done for years. So it is not surprising that men have replaced women in many of the coaching and administration jobs in women's programs, and it is not surprising that many women either have been defined as unqualified or have not bothered to apply for jobs that do not fit with the reasons they chose sport as a career (Hart et al., 1986). Many women also get discouraged because they seldom are paid what men are paid who do the same things they do (see the box on pp. 288-289). This is one way gender logic works in sports and in many other organizations.

To make matters worse for women, it seems that young athletes of both sexes are likely to perceive men as more competent than women in coaching roles, even when the records and credentials of the men and women are basically the same. In the eyes of many people, women have to do more to prove themselves than men have to do in certain jobs, especially those defined as "men's jobs." Therefore it may be more difficult for women to gain the respect they need to feel satisfied as coaches. If satisfaction is low, the turnover rate tends to be relatively high when compared with the rate among men, who are more likely to receive the respect they need to feel satisfied in their jobs (Parkhouse and Williams, 1986). This is another example of gender logic in action.

In summary, barriers to career opportunities for women in sports remain strong despite the growth of women's sports programs. The forces creating gender inequities have been built into the actual structures of many sport programs, and as long as women lack the power to define their own program philosophies and their own roles as coaches and administrators, these inequities will remain.

Opportunities for African Americans Are Limited

"For fifteen years we have had a race problem. We have raped a generation and a half of young black athletes. We have taken kids and sold them on bouncing a ball and running with a football and that being able to do certain things athletically was going to be an end in itself. We cannot afford to do that to another generation."

This statement, made in 1983 by Joe Paterno, the head football coach at Penn State University, does not fit with popular perceptions in North America. The visibility of black athletes in popular U.S. spectator sports often leads to the conclusion that sports provides many career opportunities for African Americans. In fact, according to a nationwide survey done in 1983, 70% of the adults in the United States, both blacks and whites, agreed with the statement, "There are more opportunities in sports than in any other field for the social advancement of blacks and other minorities" (Miller Lite Report, 1983). Nearly half of those questioned in the survey agreed that, "Athletics is one of the best ways for blacks to advance their social status." These beliefs are sometimes strengthened by testimonials from black athletes who claim to owe all their success to sports. However, the extent to which job opportunities for blacks exist in sports has been greatly overstated.

Very little publicity is given to the actual number and proportion of blacks who play professional sports and work in sports in the United States. Instead there are numerous references to *individual* success stories. Of course, these stories are real, but they draw attention away from two very crucial facts. *First*, sports provide almost no career opportunities for black women, who obviously make up half the black population. *Second*, the number and proportion of black males making their livings as athletes in professional sports is so small it is almost insignificant. A review of the professional sport scene shows few blacks in hockey, golf, tennis, bowling, and auto racing—five of the most lucrative sports for athletes. Professional track and field offers a few opportunities to black athletes, but the rewards are generally small, and careers seldom last more than a few years. The same goes for soccer. Even in professional boxing, there are few black fighters able to make comfortable livings. History shows that even the most successful black boxers often were not able to retire in comfort or use their athletic careers as stepping-stones into other careers (Hare, 1971; Weinberg and Arond, 1952).

In light of the small number of blacks making their livings as professional athletes (out of over 30 million African Americans), it is irresponsible to suggest that sports provide blacks significant opportunities for upward social mobility. In fact, if some other business organization tried to encourage all young black males in the United States and Canada to train for a very specific job available to only a mere 3,000 employees, it would be accused of fraud. Yet professional sports have done this for years and have been praised for their supposed "contributions" to the economic success of blacks! To make matters worse, the skills required in sports are worthless in the general job market. Who wants to hire a 22-year-old who has spent the last 15 years learning how to shoot a 30-foot jump shot or how to run the 100-yard dash in 9.5 seconds? Young blacks would be much better off putting away basketballs and track shoes and trying to become president of the United States. Of course, the chances for getting elected would be slim-to-none, but the skills learned in pursuing the goal would be marketable in numerous other careers.

Despite the dismal prospects for success in

Contracts for Two Coaches: Is This Fair?

Most people in North American agree that people should get equal pay for equal work. However, this is not the way it always happens in sports. Women who coach women's teams almost always make much less money than men who coach men's teams in the same sports. A typical example is summarized below. This example comes from the actual contracts for two head basketball coaches of Division I teams in the same university:

CONTRACT COMPARISON

TERMS	MEN'S BASKETBALL COACH	WOMEN'S BASKETBALL COACH
Contract Term:	April 1, 1990 - March 31, 1995	July 1, 1989 - July 1, 1992
Salary:	$85,000 to start, raises to be determined but not to be less than 4% annually ($3,400)	89-90: $43,000 90-91: $47,250 91-92: $53,750
Expense Allowance:	Not less than $10,000	Not less than $1,200
Additional Compensation:	Minimum of $40,000 guaranteed in annual compensation for 1st two years (for endorsements, radio and TV appearances and similar commercial endeavors). Amount to be renegotiated after 2 years.	NONE
Bonuses:	$10,000 if team receives bid and plays in NIT $20,000 for winning Conference Championship or making the first round of the NCAA Tournament An additional $5,000 if team makes it to 2nd round of NCAA Tournament, and $5,000 for each additional round. An additional $10,000 for playing in a championship game.	NONE
Benefits:	Use of one University automobile	Use of one University automobile
Opportunities:	Right to run basketball camp and the university will pay $25,000 for promotion and operation of camp.	Right to run a basketball camp; can engage in additional employment and consulting activities if they do not conflict with efficient conduct of program or duties as head coach.
Cause for Termination:	Demonstrated dishonesty Substantial neglect of assigned duties as head coach	Neglect of duty Insubordination

REFLECT ON | SPORT

	Personal conduct that substantially impairs his fulfillment of assigned duties	Conviction of a felony or any offense involving moral turpitude or following a plea of nolo contendere
	A major infraction of NCAA or conference legislation	Sexual harassment or other conduct that falls below the minimum standards of professional integrity
	Substantial violation of NCAA or conference rule resulting in an imposed penalty that affects ability to carry out duties.	Intentional disregard of any NCAA or conference rule or regulation.
Formal Limitations:	If contract is breached and does not continue as head coach, he pays the university $150,000 if he quits between 4/1/91 and 3/31/91, or $80,000 if he quits between 4/1/91 and 3/31/92.	Cannot seek, negotiate, or accept any full or part-time employment during term of contract without advising the Athletic Director and the university President.

As far as I can tell in 1992, the male coach was making about $92,000, with a $10,000 expense account, a $25,000 cash fund to promote a profit making sports camp, at least $40,000 for media appearances, a car, and up to about $60,000 in incentives if the team played and won games in major tournaments. Meanwhile, the woman coach was making about $54,000, with an expense account of $1200, and a car. Both coaches could be terminated for certain reasons, but the woman coach had a special clause in her contract that said she can be terminated for sexual harassment; the man has no such clause in his contract. The man's contract has built-in penalties if he quits; the woman's contract doesn't. Overall, the man can make about $160,000 more per year than the woman if his team goes to post season tournaments and advances to final rounds. If his team has a lousy season, or even loses every game, he makes about $110,000 more than the woman coaching the women's team, if he runs a successful sport camp. I might add that over the past two years the women's team in this comparison has been ranked in the top 20 in the nation, it has gone to the NCAA tournament twice, and at one time it had the longest winning streak in women's college basketball. The men's team, on the other hand, has an average win-lose record and has gone to no post season tournaments. Neither team generates significant gate receipts relative to their expenses. Both coaches work equally hard in the recruiting process, both coach about the same number of games, and run about the same number of practices.*

Some people claim that this is a classic example of gender inequity in sports, and that universities have no business perpetuating such inequities regardless of the reason. Others say that a men's coach should be paid more because compared to women's basketball, men's basketball is more challenging to coach, more popular in the community, and more likely to bring money into the athletic department. What do you think?

---

*In 1992 the woman coach in this comparison signed a contract extension that paid her $58,000 for the 1992-93 season. However, in May, 1993, two weeks after the athletic department was reviewed by the U.S. Department of Education Office for Civil Rights (in a Title IX compliance case), and one week after another university offered the coach a high paying job, the university announced it would boost the woman coach's salary to $78,000 for the 1993-94 season and then to $95,000 for the 1994-95 season. This shows that a combination of legal threat and a good outside job offer can sometimes lead to equity. Unfortunately, this university is only one of 4 major universities in the U.S. where the coach of the mens' team and the coach of the women's team are paid equal base salaries. But the men's coach still has more perks and additional opportunities to make "extra" maoney.

Career opportunities for blacks in coaching and sport administration do exist, but patterns of discrimination still remain in many sports, even in basketball. (University of Colorado and Eddie Kosmicki)

professional sports, young blacks often set their sights on making it as professional athletes and they are often encouraged by their parents (Braddock, 1980a; Harris and Hunt, 1984; Oliver, 1980; Lapchick, 1991). Research shows that in elementary and junior high school the proportions of blacks and whites who have their sights set on becoming professional athletes are about the same. During senior high school, however, blacks are less likely than whites to shift their sights to other occupational goals. Othello Harris and Larry Hunt (1984), sociologists who have studied race and sports, give the following explanation:

As they near (possible) entry into the job market, young blacks are becoming more aware that the rhetoric that "You can become anything you want to be in America" is, for them, a myth. As the doors for the conventional means of occupational advancement close, many turn to the one industry which has an open door policy with regard to "good, talented" blacks—the entertainment industry. The many rags-to-riches stories, the testimonies of athletes who now own fine cars, furs and homes, and the [visibility] of super heroes ... encourage many young men to abandon dreams of success in traditional arenas for a life of basketball, football, or baseball (Harris and Hunt, 1984).

Harris and Hunt emphasize that the aspirations of these high school students do not reflect socialization into the values of a unique subculture. Instead, young blacks seem to have accepted American achievement values, and as they perceive obstacles to conventional success, they simply try to avoid failure by focusing on other routes to achievement. What they don't realize and haven't been told is that there are nearly 22,000 black lawyers and over 15,000 black physicians in the United States. They need to know there are 12 times as many jobs for blacks in law and medicine as in professional sports as athletes. Meanwhile, 43% of all African American high school students who play on varsity basketball and football teams think they have a chance of making it to the pros (Lapchick, 1992). It appears that even the next generation may be raped in the terms that Joe Paterno described in 1983.

If the desire to become a professional athlete interferes with educational achievement, the time spent on sport decreases the likelihood of future occupational success. If being athletes leads young black men and women to become more concerned with success in school, sport can enhance occupational success, even if few blacks make it to the pros. When sport skills are combined with education, there are career possibilities in coaching, physical education, and recreation (Braddock, 1980a; 1981). Since the mid-1970s an increasing number of blacks have found opportunities in these areas, but significant barriers still remain (see box on pp. 292-293).

In summary, the number of real opportunities for African Americans in sports is quite limited. Although this fact has led some people to discourage sport participation in favor of other pursuits, Harry Edwards (1979) has argued that being an athlete is a legitimate goal, as long as young black aspirants are aware of their chances for success and as long as they keep a balanced perspective on sport participation. But Edwards' argument often competes against the popular belief that sport offers blacks "a way out of the ghetto." This belief is seductive, and many young blacks think they will beat the odds and achieve fame and fortune from careers in sports. They will continue believing this until opportunities in other careers become real in their minds.

Opportunities for Older People and the Physically Challenged Are Limited

Aging athletes have received increased media coverage since the late 1980s. This is because the baby boom generation (people born between 1946 and 1964) in North America is hitting middle age, and large numbers of people are now concerned about the aging process. Some baby boomers use athletes over the age of 35 as models of what is possible in fitness and sport performance. However, few older athletes compete in sports that emphasize physical domination of others. Golf and tennis are the most popular "senior" competitive circuits.

Although we need research on age relations and sports, it is possible that sports could be sites for challenging dominant ideas about aging. In the past, aging was seen as a process involving increasing dependency and incapacity, but the achievements of older athletes seem to contribute to the notion that getting old doesn't automatically mean becoming incapable.

At this point we do not know the extent to which older people maintain careers in sport organizations. Sports have always emphasized youth, so it wouldn't be surprising if older people face certain forms of exclusion in sport organizations. The older people who do work in sport organizations are usually those who have been working in those organizations since they were young adults, but data on these patterns are scarce.

Physically challenged people have always been systematically excluded from sports. Since the late 1970s there have been more sport programs and competitive tournaments for people in wheelchairs and for people who have impaired vision or hearing. But the provision of these opportunities has seldom been a high priority outside of specialized community-based recreation programs. This means that many physically challenged people never have opportunities to develop sport skills or display those skills in competition.

Career opportunities for physically chal-

REFLECT ON SPORT

Opportunities for African Americans in U.S. Sports
Selection and Retention Barriers

When sports were first desegregated in the United States, African Americans were not hired or given scholarships unless they were outstanding athletes with exemplary personal characteristics (Robinson, 1972). Prejudices were strong, so it was assumed that blacks would not be accepted by teammates, coaches, administrators, or spectators unless they could make immediate and valuable contributions to the team when they stepped onto the field or the court. This created a situation in which black athletes had performance statistics far surpassing those of whites. Even though stacking patterns confined blacks to certain positions, they excelled at those positions because entry barriers demanded excellence.

Although entry barriers have declined over the last 40 years, there is evidence that opportunities for blacks are restricted by what might be called retention barriers. Such barriers were identified by Richard Lapchick (1984) in an analysis of data in the National Basketball Association. As of 1982 he found the following:

1. Among all players in the NBA, blacks outnumbered whites three to one.

2. Among players in the league for 5 or more years with scoring averages of *more* than eight points per game, blacks outnumbered whites by 72 to 28.

3. Among players in the league for 5 or more years with scoring averages of *less* than 8 points per game, *whites outnumbered blacks* by 19 to 16(!).

Lapchick's findings indicated that marginal white players had a much better chance than marginal black players to be retained by pro basketball teams. Whites with mediocre records were kept longer than blacks with mediocre records were kept. Retention barriers have not been the subject of other studies, so their full impact on opportunities for black athletes in the 1990s is not known.

RACIAL QUOTAS: AFFIRMATIVE ACTION FOR WHITES

Racial quotas existed in many sports through the 1970s. They were never formal, although it was widely understood that when the percentage of blacks on any team got "too high," there would be changes made to increase the number of white team members (Lapchick, 1984). The existence of quotas in the 1990s is a touchy issue. People will not talk about them, but some owners and administrators may be hesitant to let teams get "too black." Their hesitancy is based on fears that white spectators will lose interest in teams if whites don't play. These fears are probably unfounded in the case of successful winning teams, but the situation may be different for losing teams. This may be why some black athletes feel that white athletes in certain sports, especially basketball, are hot commodities, and are treated more favorably than blacks with the same skills. This may sometimes be the case, but is very difficult to prove.

BARRIERS TO ADVANCEMENT IN COACHING AND MANAGEMENT

The exclusion of blacks from coaching and management jobs in sports has evoked massive media coverage since 1987, when Al Campanis, the longtime director of player personnel for the Los Angeles Dodgers, said that blacks were excluded from these jobs because they "lacked the necessities" to handle them. Campanis later apologized for his remark, but his apology does not change the fact that during the nearly 30 years he was helping shape the coaching and management staff on the Dodgers, they never had a black general manager, a black field manager, a black pitching coach at any level, or a black third base coach (the most influential coach below the head coach on any baseball team).

REFLECT ON | SPORT

The Los Angeles Dodgers have not been alone. For seasons ending in 1992, blacks held 18% of the support staff personnel positions and 7% of the head coaching positions in the NBA, even though 75% of the players were black. In the NFL black held 7% of the staff positions and 7% of the head coach positions, even though 62% of the players were black. And in major league baseball blacks held 9% of the staff positions and 11% of the head coach/manager positions, even though 17% of the players were black (all data from Lapchick and Brown, 1992). Blacks hold almost none of the management jobs in amateur and college sports, even in those with high rates of participation among black athletes. Since 1980 some black coaches have been hired by universities, but the proportion of black coaches is still nowhere close to matching the proportion of black athletes in any sport, especially track and field, football, and basketball.

Why has the desegregation of coaching and management been so difficult? Pete Rozelle, the long-time commissioner of the National Football League, was once asked when the NFL would see its first black head coach. He explained to the reporters that when an owner of an NFL team chooses a coach, it's "like choosing a wife. It's a very personal thing. . . ." His comparison of coaching with marriage was meant to emphasize that desegregation always occurs most slowly in settings characterized by the most interpersonal intimacy.

People in top management must work closely with one another; they like to feel comfortable with each other. This is why they often hire old fraternity brothers or people who graduated from the same college they did. Those who share similar backgrounds are "known quantities." Therefore, if those doing the hiring are white males, it is likely that the job qualifications for top management positions have been consciously or unconsciously defined in ways that automatically cut down the probabilities of defining as qualified a person from a different racial or ethnic background. After all, if people don't have similar histories and experiences, can they be trusted? Are they dependable? Do they think like others in top management? If there are *any* doubts, conscious or unconscious, those doing the hiring will be likely to stick with candidates like themselves and, if they are white males, they may see more of themselves in other white males. It is likely that this process has long been in operation in sports. As long as it continues, there will be few minorities in coaching or top management positions in any sport organizations controlled by whites.

Affirmative action programs have produced results at lower levels of management and in the work force (that is, among staff), but they have not been successful in top management because job descriptions are written in ways that often raise doubts about the qualifications of women and minorities. The problem is that the only "qualified" minorities are those "just like" the whites doing the hiring. When people from one racial or ethnic group make the rules, the rules are likely to favor that group. Change will occur only as the rule makers become more diversified and more sensitive to the advantages of diversity, or when something else forces the rule makers to open their doors to others who aren't "just like" them.

lenged people have been severely limited in sport organizations. As is the case in other types of organizations, sport organizations are not especially good in providing access for people in wheelchairs. This has also been true of sport facilities. Access to stadiums and arenas has been notoriously difficult, but when newer facilities have been designed for wheelchair access, many people in wheelchairs have responded by purchasing tickets and attending sports events. The passage of the Disabilities Act in 1992 will affect opportunities for physically challenged people in the United States, but the extent of that effect in sports and sport organizations is not yet known.

SPORT PARTICIPATION AND OCCUPATIONAL CAREERS AMONG FORMER ATHLETES

What happens in the occupational lives of former athletes? Are their career patterns different from their counterparts who never played competitive sports? These are difficult questions, but at this point, studies have generally shown that former athletes as a group have no more or less career success than others from comparable backgrounds. This does not mean that playing sports has never helped anyone in special ways; it only means that there have been no consistent research findings indicating that former athletes have some systematic advantage over comparable peers when it comes to future occupational careers.

Most of the inconsistent research findings on this issue are probably due to the fact that sport participation experiences vary from one person to the next. When two people play varsity sports in high school or college it does not mean their experiences, or the career implications of those experiences, are the same. This is also true among professional and world-class amateur athletes, and this is why there is a wide range of failures and successes among former athletes.

Research has not examined the precise ways in which the process of sport participation may be connected to processes underlying career de-

velopment. It may be that under certain circumstances, sport participation teaches young people interpersonal skills that could carry over into success in various jobs. Or some former athletes may be defined or labeled by others as good job prospects because of their past participation in sports. Or playing sports may put young people in touch with others, especially adults, who are able to help them get good jobs after they retire from sports.

After reviewing many studies* comparing former high school athletes with their old classmates who didn't play varsity high school sports, I would argue that former athletes are most likely to have advantages when they enter the job market if their sport participation fits the following profile:

1. When sport participation increases opportunities to complete academic degrees, develop job-related skills, and/or extend knowledge about how the world outside of sport is organized and operates.
2. When sport participation leads close friends and family members to provide consistent social, emotional, and material support for *overall* growth and development.
3. When sport participation provides opportunities to make friends and develop social contacts with people connected to activities and organizations apart from sports and sport organizations.
4. When sport participation provides material resources along with the management abilities needed to use those resources to create or nurture career opportunities.

---

*See especially Braddock (1981); Coakley (1983b); DuBois (1978, 1979); Eisen and Turner, 1992; Hanks (1979); Hanks and Eckland (1976); Hare (1971); Howell and Picou (1983); Howell and others (1984); Loy (1969a); McPherson (1980); Melnick and Sabo, 1992; Melnick, Sabo, and Vanfossen, 1992; Nixon (1984); Otto and Alwin (1977); Picou et al (1985); Sabo, Melnick, and Vanfossen, 1993; Sack and Thiel (1979); Semyonov (1984); Spady (1979); Spreitzer, 1992; and Stevenson (1976b).

5. When sport participation has been used to expand personal and social experiences fostering the development of nonsport-related identities and an awareness of abilities having implications apart from sports.

6. When sport participation does not result in serious injuries that restrict physical movement and require extensive and expensive medical treatment.

This is not an earthshaking list of conclusions. It contains no surprises. It simply emphasizes that sports have the potential either to constrict or to expand a young person's overall development. When expansion occurs, participation is likely to enhance career opportunities along with the abilities to take advantage of those opportunities. This can give former athletes an edge over others for career success.

Sport Participation, Class Relations, and Career Success

Because sport participation and class relations are linked, the chances for career success following sport participation vary from sport to sport. Some sports, such as tennis and golf, offer sets of experiences that not only enhance career opportunities but foster the development of abilities to take advantage of opportunities. Other sports, such as boxing, seem to have a lower potential.

Boxing provides a good illustration of this point. Schools do not sponsor boxing. This forces young people to develop their skills apart from formal education. In fact, trainers may encourage promising boxers to drop out of school to concentrate on training; seldom do young men earn college degrees while training to be boxers. Boxers come from the racial and ethnic groups most likely to face occupational discrimination and from families having few material resources to promote overall growth and development. Boxing seldom increases social contacts with people outside the small world of boxing; it seldom leads to financial payoffs or learning

"WELL, I'VE NEVER ACTUALLY SOLD A HOUSE... BUT MY COACH ALWAYS SAID THAT FOOTBALL IS BASICALLY THE ACQUISITION OF REAL ESTATE."

Being a good athlete does not guarantee success after retirement from sport. Athletic skills are usually worthless in the job market.

financial management skills; it does not offer opportunities for identity development apart from the ring and the gym; and it often leaves participants with millions of dead brain cells—not an advantage when starting an occupational career!

The result of this combination of factors is that boxing seldom serves as a springboard into good occupational careers; in fact, it often does the exact opposite. Nathan Hare (1971) vividly described this in a study of retired professional boxers. None of the 48 boxers in Hare's study had been able to save much of the money they earned during their careers. Hare described the reality of life after boxing this way:

> In the gyms, I watched the active fighters working and waiting for the lucky break which, they believed, would take them to the wealth and glory of a championship. In the taverns and pool-rooms, I listened to the former fighters reliving their own fighting careers, boasting to sustain their pride, dissatisfied now with their present lot and trying to call back in conversation the youth and skills that had once been theirs.

In contrast to boxing, a totally different picture emerges when attention is shifted to sports such as golf and tennis. Opportunities after retirement from either intercollegiate or professional competition in these sports are likely to be much more attractive than opportunities for boxers. Whenever people participate in sports that cut them off from experiences and social contacts that might help them prepare for, gain access to, and take advantage of occupational opportunities, they will be at a disadvantage when entering the occupational world.

Highly Paid Professional Athletes and Occupational Success

Conclusions about the connection between sport participation and career success must be qualified in light of the dramatic jump in the annual incomes of some professional athletes over the past 25 years. Before 1970 few athletes made enough money in sports to pave their ways into other careers after they retired. However, some athletes now make enough money in a few years to finance career alternatives after they retire from sports—if they save and invest wisely. For example, Andre Agassi, even without a college degree, will have no trouble supporting himself after he quits the tennis tour; and his financial status will not even depend on the support of family or friends. Michael Jordan, the already legendary basketball player on the Chicago Bulls, has a contract and endorsements that guarantee he will retire from basketball with all the resources anyone would need to move into an attractive nonsport career.

Of course, not all former professional athletes earn enough to retire in style and initiate successful nonsport careers. Many play only for a couple of years before retirement, and most do not earn anything close to the extremely high salaries publicized in the media. These ex-athletes frequently enter occupations in which they receive lower salaries than they received in sports, but this does not mean they should be seen as failures or victims. For example, if former athletes manage a bar or restaurant, return to school, or teach and coach in a high school, they should not be considered career failures. Just because these jobs do not enable

former athletes to drive new cars, travel to exciting places, or read their names in newspapers every week doesn't mean that they've experienced career setbacks due to sport participation (Coakley, 1983b).

Athletic Grants and Occupational Success

Whenever sport participation and career success is discussed in the United States, people raise the topic of athletic scholarships or grants. It is widely believed that if it were not for these grants, many young people would not attend college. This belief raises a number of questions: How many athletic scholarships are actually given? How much are they worth to the students receiving them? Who receives them? Do women receive their fair share? Do blacks and other minorities receive their fair shares? How many scholarship recipients would not attend college without their athletic awards?

Surprisingly, the information needed to answer these questions is difficult to get. Furthermore, the actual number of full athletic grants is often exaggerated by student-athletes. High school students who simply get standard recruiting letters from one or more university coaches often tell people they are anticipating full scholarships. College students receiving tuition waivers or other forms of partial grants often lead people to believe they have full scholarships. Generally, fewer students receive athletic scholarships than is commonly believed.

DISTRIBUTION OF ATHLETIC GRANTS BY GENDER AND RACE According to the best estimates I have been able to make (as of 1993), about 15% to 20% of the varsity athletes at *all* levels of competition in American colleges and universities have full scholarships; another 15% to 25% have some form of partial athletic grant. This means that 55% to 70% of all intercollegiate athletes participate in sports without any sport-related financial assistance. In over 750 NCAA schools, there are approximately 150,000 male intercollegiate athletes and about 80,000 female athletes; women comprise about 52% of all college students, yet they make up

Young blacks are often led to believe that sport offers a road to fame and fortune. The visibility and popularity of black athletes provide them with ready-made role models. Unless black athletes are careful, they can quickly become modern Pied Pipers. (Colorado Springs Gazette Telegraph)

only 35% of intercollegiate athletes and receive about 31% of the athletic scholarship dollars.

Information on Division I NCAA universities (see Chapter 15 for an explanation of NCAA divisions) indicates blacks received 24% of the full and partial athletic scholarships in 1992. However, when scholarship athletes at all schools at all levels of competition are grouped together, blacks probably receive no more than 10% to 15% of the total athletic grant dollars. This is proportionate to the percentage of blacks in the U.S. population. However, many people overestimate the proportion of African Americans receiving athletic grants because 82% of the black men receiving them in Division I universities play football or basketball. These sports receive heavy media coverage, so this makes black athletes especially visible. In fact, 92% of all blacks, both male and female, who receive athletic grants in Division I NCAA schools are involved in three sports: football, basketball, and track. This means African Americans receive almost no scholarships in the 21 other men's sports and the 22 other women's sports in intercollegiate programs. At the Division II level there are fewer black athletes, and a lower proportion of the scholarships are given to blacks.

According to 1992 NCAA data there were 11,827 athletic grants given to all men and women athletes entering Division I schools, and 8556 (72%) of those went to nonminority whites. When men's and women's sports at all levels of competition are grouped together, I estimate that about 85% of all athletic grants go to nonminority whites, and about 70% go to men.

DISTRIBUTION OF ATHLETIC GRANTS BY FAMILY INCOME Do those who receive athletic grants need them? If they did not have them, would they be forced to drop out of school for financial reasons? Again, these are difficult questions to answer because there is little information available. In a study of women intercollegiate athletes Coakley and Pacey (1984) found that nearly 80% of grants were awarded to women coming from families who could afford to pay for their daughters' educations (see Table 11-4). This pattern would not be as strong in the case of men who receive athletic grants, but the majority of those men would be able to attend school without sport-related financial assistance.

It is often forgotten that young people in higher-income families have more opportunities than young people from lower-income families to develop skills in a wide variety of sports. Grants in gymnastics, golf, ice hockey, soccer, swimming, tennis, volleyball, and a number of other sports go to those who have had opportunities to participate in those sports through childhood and adolescence. Resources are needed to take advantage of opportunities. Lower-income people are less likely to have those resources.

In summary, when athletic grants go to financially needy young people who focus their attention on educational attainment, sport participation is very likely to promote career success. But there are fewer athletic grants given by university sport programs than many people believe, and many grants go to young people who could and would attend college without them. This does not mean that the legitimacy of athletic grants should be questioned; it merely means that the link between those grants and career success must be carefully qualified.

Is Retirement from Sport a Problem?

Research suggests that even though retiring from competitive sport participation may cause

Table 11-4 College women with athletic scholarships: what do their fathers do for a living?

Aid received by athletes	Father's occupation				
	Professionals and top executives	Mid-level managers and officials	Skilled/ clerical workers	Minimum wage/semi-skilled workers	Total
Full scholarships	135	170	56	22	383
	(35%)	(44%)	(15%)	(6%)	(100%)
Partial scholarships	242	246	96	32	616
	(39%)	(40%)	(16%)	(5%)	(100%)
No scholarships	444	423	161	65	1,093
	(41%)	(39%)	(14%)	(6%)	(100%)

Adapted from Coakley and Pacey (1984). This table includes information on 2,092 female intercollegiate athletes. Of these athletes, 18% had full scholarships, 30% had partial scholarships, and 52% had no sport-related financial assistance. Approximately 80% of all the athletes had fathers with higher-status occupations. This was true regardless of the form of athletic scholarship received. In other words, very few female intercollegiate athletes came from lower-income families, and very few scholarships were given to women whose families could not possibly afford to help them pay for college.

SIDELINES

Only a small proportion of former athletes make enough to live in comfort for the rest of their lives. The others must make it through their own ingenuity, just like rest of us.

some stress, it does not automatically create problems that disrupt people's lives and interfere with seeking and finding occupational careers (Coakley, 1983b; Eisen and Turner, 1992; Greendorfer and Blinde, 1985; Swain, 1991). Many people assume that retiring from sport careers is a problem because they think of retirement as a life-changing event that happens at a particular point in time, often without warning or preparation. But research on athletes shows that retirement from sports is best described as a process rather than a single event (Swain, 1991). In fact, retirement from sports often occurs in connection with other changes or transitions in a person's life such as high school or college graduation, marriage, the birth of a child, the availability of a long-term career opportunity, or a desire to return to school. This means that retirement is usually anticipated and frequently timed to correspond with developments in a person's overall life course.

Many athletes develop interests outside of sports while they are playing and then use retirement from sports as an opportunity to pursue those interests and grow as a person in the process. Sometimes athletes stay connected with

sports after they stop playing. They may take jobs in sport organizations, coach in youth programs, or become officials. Most athletes don't retire from sports on a moment's notice; instead, they gradually disengage from sports and shift their personal priorities in the process (Blinde and Greendorfer, 1985; Greendorfer and Blinde, 1985). Many may continue sport participation at a less intense level in community sport programs or other settings that offer challenging competition. Others may continue working out in their sports for their own enjoyment, health, and fitness. A few even renew their involvement in sports and seek new competitive challenges at later points in their lives by participating in Masters or Seniors events (Hastings et al, 1989).

Although some athletes are caught off guard by retirement from sports, most anticipate it and begin preparing for what they will do when playing sports is no longer a full-time activity in their lives (Swain, 1991). They may focus on their education, cultivate career options, or actively seek occupational opportunities. Some American universities and amateur sport organizations are beginning to assist athletes in this process by developing career transition programs. These programs are designed to aid athletes as they move out of athletic careers into occupational careers either in or out of sports. They often involve workshops dealing with resumé writing, job search strategies, interviewing skills, and career placement contacts. Of course, many organizations do not see this as a high priority or they do not have the resources to put such a program into operation. But there is a growing belief that after athletes are asked to dedicate full-time energy and attention to playing sports, the organizations that benefit from their dedication have an obligation to help those athletes as they move into other parts of their lives (Thomas and Ermler, 1988).

Although most athletes smoothly disengage from sports, develop other interests, and move into relatively satisfying occupational careers, some encounter adjustment problems. Sometimes these problems can be very serious. For example, when sociologist Mike Messner interviewed former elite athletes he found that many men who had been involved in sports for a long time encountered serious adjustment problems when they retired. One of his quotes from an interview with a former NFL player highlights these problems:

> [When you retire] you find yourself scrambled. You don't know which way to go. Your light . . . has been turned out. . . . Of course you miss the financial deal, but you miss the camaraderie of the other ballplayers. You miss that—to be an elite, to be one of a kind . . . [T]he game itself . . . the beating and all that . . . you don't really miss. You miss the camaraderie of the fellas. There's an empty feeling . . . the one thing that has been the major part of your life is gone . . . [Y]ou don't know how people are going to react to you . . . you wonder and question (1991, pp. 120-121).

Messner's interviews led him to suggest that retiring athletes, especially those who had dedicated themselves to playing sports ever since they were children, face two major challenges: (1) reconstructing their identities in terms of activities, abilities, and relationships unrelated to sport participation, and (2) renegotiating relationships with family members and close friends so they get feedback and support for identities having little or nothing to do with playing sports. Messner also noted that young men from low-income families are more likely to have problems when retiring from sports because they have fewer material resources to aid them in the transition process. Men from middle-class backgrounds, on the other hand, seemed to benefit from the doors opened by sport and the social connections related to sport participation.

Research also suggests that adjustment problems are more likely when an injury forces retirement from sports. Injuries often complicate retirement and tie it to other problems related to self-esteem or health; they disrupt "life plans" by throwing off the timing of retirement (Kleiber et al, 1987; Kleiber and Brock, 1992). This is not surprising, and it raises again the is-

sue of organizational responsibility. Many sport organizations traditionally have cut athletes loose when they experience career-ending injuries. However, it seems to me that these organizations have some ethical responsibility to offer occupational therapy and/or career transition assistance to those athletes.

CONCLUSION:

IS SPORT PARTICIPATION A PATH TO SUCCESS?

Class relations and sports are interwoven. This is because sports cannot exist unless people have time, money, facilities, and organizational experience. Therefore the economic inequalities that exist in society spill over into sports in a variety of ways. People with money and power organize sports that fit their own interests and foster ideas that support economic arrangements that work to their advantage. This is why dominant sport forms in North America promote an ideology of achievement that stresses the notion that "you always get what you deserve, and you always deserve what you get." This type of "class logic" also perpetuates the belief that economic inequality in society is not only good but just and natural.

Sport participation patterns in society reflect the dynamics of class relations. Furthermore, they often combine with gender relations to create conditions that (1) limit sport participation among girls and women from low-income backgrounds and (2) alter the orientations and motivations of boys and men from low-income backgrounds who play sports. Class relations are also significant in the sponsorship and promotion of high school sports. Budget crises in school districts have led to a combination of cuts in varsity sports programs and efforts to seek corporate sponsorships to maintain programs. The implications of these changes are yet to be determined in the United States.

Career opportunities in sports exist, but for athletes they are usually limited and short-term. Other opportunities, including those in coaching, sport medicine, training, and management, do not bring the fame and fortune some athletes receive. Furthermore, they call for qualifications that go beyond the skills learned in sport participation. Opportunities to become professional athletes or enter occupations in sport organizations are very limited for women and minorities. The path to success for women remains partially blocked; many changes are needed to ensure that women have equal career opportunities in sports. For African Americans, the path is open, but it is narrow and not heavily traveled. Few blacks achieve fame and fortune in sports, but because of perceived obstacles to achievement in other careers, many young blacks see sport participation as their best chance for occupational success. Older people and those who are physically challenged also confront constraints in sports, both as participants and when seeking career opportunities.

Research on the connection between sport participation and the process of career development generally indicates that when young people are able to use sport participation to expand their social worlds and their experiences, they have an advantage when they seek occupational careers. However, when sport participation constricts a person's social world and range of personal experiences, it is likely to have a negative effect on occupational success. The existence of these patterns varies by sport although the extremely high incomes of some athletes almost guarantee future career success.

Athletic grants help some student-athletes further their educations and possibly achieve career success. However, receiving an athletic grant does not always change the future career patterns of young people because many grant recipients have the motivation and resources they need to attend college on their own without sport-related financial assistance.

Retirement from athletic careers often creates stress and adjustment challenges, but most athletes move through the retirement process without experiencing excessive trauma or difficulty. Those who do experience difficulties are usually those whose identities and relationships have

been built exclusively on sports. These people may need outside assistance as they move into the rest of their lives and face the challenge of seeking jobs and maintaining satisfying occupational careers.

In conclusion, the idea that sports are paths to success should be accepted only with reservations. It applies to only a limited number of people, and it depends on much more than the display of physical skills on the playing field.

SUGGESTED READINGS

Bartell, T., et al. 1984. Study of freshman eligibility standards. Report submitted to and distributed by the NCAA, Kansas City, Mo. (*an in-depth technical study of the academic achievements of over 16,000 student athletes in 206 Division I schools; the only study of this type in existence*).

Coakley, J. 1983. Leaving competitive sport: retirement or rebirth? Quest 35:1-11 (*a review of the literature on what happens to top-level athletes when they stop participating in competitive sports*).

Hargreaves, J. 1986. Sport, culture and power. St. Martin's Press, New York. (*analysis of ties between sport and power in Britain; first seven chapters focus on class relations as a context for the social construction of sports*).

Howell, F., et al. 1984. Do high school athletics pay? The effects of varsity participation on socioeconomic attainment. Sociology of Sport Journal 1(1):15-25 (*an empirical study of the incomes made by high school athletes after they leave high school*).

Lapchick, R. 1991. Five minutes to midnight: race and sport in the 1990s. Madison Books, Lanham, Md. (*the last third of this book covers a wide range of information about how sports and sport participation are connected to the lives of African Americans*).

McPherson, B. 1986. Sport and aging. Human Kinetics Publishers, Inc., Champaign, Ill. (*interdisciplinary proceedings from 1984 Olympic Scientific Congress; good review of issues related to sport and aging*).

Nixon, H.L. II. 1984. Sport and the American dream. Leisure Press, New York (*this book remains a helpful source of information on sport participation and social mobility*).

Swain, D.A. 1991. Withdrawal form sport and Schlossberg's model of transitions. Sociology of Sport Journal 8(2):152-160 (*an excellent source of information on retirement from sports; the study has a very small sample, but Swain's analysis is insightful*).

CHAPTER 12

SPORTS AND THE ECONOMY

What are the characteristics of commercial sports?

Baseball is not just a sport anymore; we are a business. We are show business. To compete for the entertainment dollar . . . you have to have more than nine guys playing baseball; you've got to have an attraction. And I have tried to do the best job I possibly can to give my fans an "attraction.

George Steinbrenner, Owner, New York Yankees (1983)

What corrupts an athletic performance . . . is . . . the presence of an unappreciative, ignorant audience and the need to divert it with sensations extrinsic to the performance. It is at this point that . . . sports . . . degenerate into spectacle.

Christopher Lasch, Social Critic (1977)

Money is killing our game . . . The motivation for true greatness is gone for most players by the time they are eighteen. They win a couple of matches as juniors and they are millionaires. . . . Now you don't have to win, you just have to have an act.

Philippe Chatrier, President, International Tennis Federation (1990).

Image is everything.

Andre Agassi, Professional tennis player (1992)

Throughout history sports have been used as forms of public entertainment. However, sports have never been so heavily packaged, promoted, presented, and played as commercial products as they are today. Never before have decisions about sports and the social relationships connected with sports been so clearly influenced by economic factors. The bottom line has replaced the goal line for many people, and sports no longer exist simply for the interests of the athletes themselves. Fun and "good games" are now defined in terms of gate receipts, concessions revenues, the sale of media rights, market shares, ratings points, and advertising potential.

In light of the importance of economic factors in sports, this chapter will focus on the following questions:

1. Under what conditions do commercial sports emerge and prosper?
2. How does commercialization influence the way sports are played and organized?
3. Who owns, sponsors, and promotes sports, and what are their interests?
4. How much money do athletes make in sports, and what is their legal status in different sports?

EMERGENCE AND GROWTH OF COMMERCIAL SPORTS
General Conditions

The existence of commercial sports depends on revenues generated from a combination of gate receipts and the sale of broadcasting rights to radio and television. This means they grow and prosper best under certain social and economic conditions. *First*, they grow best in market economies where material rewards are given high priority in the lives of people connected with sports, including athletes and those who own teams or sponsor and promote events.

Second, because they require large concentrations of potential spectators, commercial sports tend to exist in societies with large, densely populated cities. Although it would be possible to maintain simple forms of commercial sports in

rural societies, revenues would not support full-time professional athletes, nor full-time sport promoters.

Third, commercial sports require that people in a society have time, money, and freedom of movement to attend sport events. In this sense, commercial sports are a luxury. They prosper only in societies where the standard of living is high enough that people can afford to spend time and resources playing and watching events that produce nothing tangible. They are more likely to flourish if supported by relatively sophisticated transportation and communication systems. The easier it is to get to sport events and the more widely they can be publicized or presented, the more profitable they will be. Therefore commercial sports are most commonly found in relatively wealthy, urban, industrial or post-industrial societies.

Fourth, commercial sports rely on the availability of *large amounts of capital* to build and maintain stadiums and arenas in which events can be played and watched. Capital funds can be accumulated in either the public or private sector, but in either case, the willingness to invest in sport depends on anticipated payoffs in the form of publicity, profits, or power. Private investment in sports is motivated primarily by expected financial profits; public investment is motivated primarily by a belief by those in power that commercial sports will serve their own interests, the interests of "the public," or a combination of both. This is one way that class relations become linked to commercial sports.

Class Relations and Commercial Sports

Which sports become commercialized in a society? Priority is usually given to those sports followed and watched by people who possess or control economic resources in society. For example, golf does not lend itself to commercial presentation. It is inconvenient to present to a live audience or to televise. Camera placement and media commentary are difficult to arrange, and live spectators see only a small proportion of the action. Golf does not involve head-to-head competition or vigorous action. In fact, if you don't play golf there is little or no reason to watch it.

But those who do play golf include a high proportion of relatively wealthy and powerful people. These people are important because they not only make consumption decisions for themselves and their families but they also make them for businesses. Furthermore, they make investment decisions involving money from a variety of sources and they buy high ticket items that other people can't afford.

This makes golf an attractive sport for advertisers who want to pitch images or products to consumers with money and influence. This is why Cadillac sponsors and advertises on the Senior PGA tour (golf for tournament professionals over the age of 50). This is why major networks televise golf. As long as commercial time for a particular sport can be sold at a high rate per minute, television stations will televise that sport. This usually means that sports attracting low- and middle-income audiences will be ignored by television or only rarely covered.

Class relations in market economies always privilege the interests of those who have power and resources to influence which sports will be selected for promotion and coverage. Unless people with power and resources are interested in playing, sponsoring, or watching a sport, it is not likely to be commercialized. When wealthy and powerful people are interested in a sport, it will be covered, promoted, and presented as if it had cultural significance in society. The sport may even be described as a "national pastime" and come to be associated with the development of personal character, civic unity, community spirit, and political loyalty. It may even be supported with public money so that stadiums and arenas can be built, even if this directly subsidizes and benefits wealthy team owners, sponsors, and promoters.

This portrait of popular commercial sports does not support those who claim that sports promote the overall democratization of a society.

Only when sports promote the interests of powerful and wealthy people are they likely to be commercialized. This is one reason why football has become "America's game." Football celebrates and privileges the values and experiences of people who control and benefit from corporate wealth and power in North America. This is why men get in line to pay hundred's of dollars to buy expensive season tickets to college and professional football games, why male executives spend thousands of dollars to buy "company tickets" to football games, and why male corporation presidents write checks to pay for fancy skyboxes and "spectator suites" for themselves, their friends, and their clients.

The Creation of Spectator Interest in Sports

SUCCESS IDEOLOGY AND SPECTATOR INTEREST Many people watch games or read about them now and then, but spectator involvement is highest among people committed to the dual idea that success in any aspect of life is based on hard work and that hard work always leads to success. These people often use sports as a model of how, in their opinion, the occupational world should operate. When sports are organized to emphasize the idea that success is achieved only through hard work and dedication to efficiency, these people have their beliefs and expectations reaffirmed, and they are willing to pay for that reaffirmation. This is why sport commentators on radio and television often emphasize that athletes and teams make their own breaks and that luck comes to those who work hard.

YOUTH SPORT PROGRAMS AND SPECTATOR INTEREST Spectator interests are often created and nurtured during childhood sport participation. When organized youth sport programs are publicized and made available to many young people in a society, commercial sports have a better chance to grow and prosper. With some exceptions, sport participation during childhood leads to spectator interest during adulthood. When children learn to value sport skills and emphasize competitive success in their sport experiences, they will generally grow up wanting to watch the "experts" compete with each other. For those who continue to actively participate in sports, watching the experts provides models to improve skills and maintain interests in participation. For those who have discontinued active participation, watching the experts provides opportunities to maintain connections with sport and vicariously experience success through the achievements of the athletes with whom they identify. These patterns of spectator interest usually continue long after participation in youth programs has stopped.

MEDIA COVERAGE AND SPECTATOR INTEREST The media are closely associated with the commercialization of sports (see Chapter 13). They provide needed publicity and create and sustain spectator interest among large numbers of people. In the past, newspapers and radio did this job, but today television has the greatest effect on spectator involvement.

Along with increasing spectator access to events and athletes all over the world, television provides a unique "re-presentation" of sports. It lets viewers see close-up camera shots of the action on the field and the athletes and coaches on the sidelines. It replays crucial plays and shows them in slow-motion. It even brings viewers into the locker rooms of championship teams. On-air commentators serve as "fellow spectators" for a viewing or listening audience. But more than that, commentators dramatize and embellish the action in the event; they supply "inside stories," analyze strategies, describe athletes as personalities, and glorify the importance of the event.

Television is especially effective in recruiting new spectators. This is because people need opportunities to learn the rules and strategies of a sport before they will become committed fans. This learning occurs easily through television. No tickets need be purchased, and questions that may sound stupid in front of strangers can be asked without embarrassment in the family living room. In other words, television provides a painless way to become a spectator, and it in-

WHY ARE THEY JUST SITTING THERE? ARE THEY ALLOWED TO DO THAT?

Television provides a relatively painless means of becoming socialized into the role of spectator. It enables people to avoid the embarrassment of asking stupid questions in public.

creases the number of people who will buy tickets, watch televised games, and even become pay-per-view customers in the future.

Economic Motives and the Globalization of Commercial Sports

Commercial sports have now gone global in a big way, for two reasons. *First*, those who control, sponsor, and promote sports are constantly looking for new ways to make more money. *Second*, businesses can use sports as vehicles for introducing products and services all around the world. Recent examples illustrate each of these reasons.

SPORT ORGANIZATIONS LOOK FOR GLOBAL MARKETS Sport organizations, like other businesses, are interested in expanding their markets into as many countries as possible. For example, team and league profits would increase significantly if the NFL, NBA, NHL, and Major League Baseball (MLB) could sell broadcasting rights to television companies in countries around the world and if they could sell licensed products (hats, shirts, jackets, etc.) to people all around the world. This is already being done, but the continued success of these ventures depends on creating spectator interest outside North America, and spectator interest partially depends on a combination of game knowledge and identification with athletes who play the game.

A desire for global expansion was the main reason the NBA was happy to let the so-called "Dream Team" play in the Olympics, even though the players risked injury and fatigue that could have jeopardized their participation in the 1992-93 NBA season. The worldwide coverage of Olympic basketball provided the NBA with publicity worth many millions of dollars. This publicity has helped to market NBA broadcasting rights and "official NBA products" all over the world. High profile NBA players have been introduced to hundreds of millions of people, and many of these people have become more interested in seeing these players in action. Therefore the NBA finals are now televised in over 80 countries every year.

The spirit of global expansion has also led NFL, NBA, NHL, and MLB teams to play games in Japan, England, France, Germany, and a number of other countries. It led the NFL to form the World Football League and even subsidize the formation of a football league in England (Maguire, 1990). Other investors have formed sport organizations to compete for international markets in certain sports. For example, the Global Basketball Association and the World Basketball League tried to gain footholds in international sport markets during the early 1990s.

This spirit of global expansion is not new, nor is it limited to American sport organizations. The International Olympic Committee (IOC) has gradually incorporated National Olympic Committees from nearly 200 nations and has turned the Olympic games into the most successful and lucrative media sports events in history. Similarly, tennis and golf have long been international sports, playing tournaments around the world. FIFA (Federation Internationale de Football Association) has a long history

of global expansion that now includes playing the World Cup in the United States (Tomlinson, 1986). When the 1994 Soccer World Cup was scheduled in the United States, the people in charge of FIFA clearly realized they had much to gain if they could create spectator interest in soccer among Americans.

CORPORATIONS USE SPORTS AS VEHICLES FOR GLOBAL EXPANSION The fact that sports, sporting events, sport teams, and athletes can be used to capture the attention and the emotions of millions of people has not gone unnoticed in the world of business. This is why many large corporations have been eager to sponsor international sports and enlist athletes to endorse products around the world. People who have watched the televised coverage of the Olympics in dozens of countries have seen commercials by Coca-Cola and McDonalds, people who watch tennis know about Volvo, and those who watch international auto racing events know that race cars are high speed billboards, often promoting products such as cigarettes and alcohol that cannot be advertised on television in some countries (see photograph on p. 318).

In an analysis of the growth of American football in England, British sociologist Joe Maguire provides a classic example of how large corporations and sport organizations often team up to promote their mutual interests in global expansion. The executives at Anheuser Busch, the company that makes Budweiser beer, worked with the NFL to introduce American football to England because they thought the association between Budweiser and football would improve the beer's image with British men. The link between beer drinking and masculinity is strong in England, and many British men learn to define dark, heavy, barrel beer ("bitter") as more consistent with a strong, masculine image than light, carbonated, foamy beers ("lagers"). Because lager beers, such as Budweiser, were seen as weak—similar to soft drinks—they were not the beers of choice among British men.

Of course, this was an image that Budweiser

had to shake before it could capture a portion of the beer market in England, or in most of Europe for that matter. And what better way to shake the image of being a weak, "unmanly" beer than to connect Budweiser with a sport emphasizing toughness, the use of force, physical domination, playing with pain, throwing "bombs," "punishing the opposition," and carrying "injured warriors off the field"? When a high profile "warrior" in full football gear praised Budweiser in commercials it was hoped that at least some British men would begin to see that they could drink Budweiser without compromising their "traditional masculinity."

The combined financial interests of Anheuser Busch, the NFL, and a major private television company in England spurred the introduction of American football in England during the early 1980s. In the decade that followed, American football, sponsored by Budweiser, was televised weekly in England, and Budweiser helped fund the formation of the "Budweiser League," initially consisting of 105 football teams, all trying to reach the post-season "Budweiser Bowl." In 1986 Anheuser Busch teamed up with TWA and American Express to sponsor the first "American Bowl" in which two NFL teams played an exhibition game in England; these games continue in the 1990s. Since the mid-1980s the sponsorship of American football in England has become increasingly complicated (Maguire, 1990), but in 1993, Budweiser remained a central sponsor of television coverage and a league of American football teams across England. Young men from middle class backgrounds, especially those in colleges and universities, have become more interested in the American game. As football has become more trendy, more Budweiser is being sold in England, and young men are more likely to see lager as an appropriate beer for men to drink, especially when they watch football.

The Budweiser experience is not unique. Various sporting goods companies have long used similar strategies to promote products around the world. Golf clubs were endorsed by internationally known golfers long before golf became a commercialized television sport. Nike was very aware that if Michael Jordan played in the 1992 Summer Olympic Games and caught the world's attention, their market for sport shoes and clothing could expand dramatically. After all, there are over 2.4 billion feet in China, and Nike would like to see Air Jordans on every one of them. Similar motives led U.S.-based Reebok to enter a sponsorship agreement with the Russian Olympic Committee in 1993. Reebok wanted people from all over Russia to flock to their specialty stores in Moscow.

Summary

Commercial sports grow and prosper best in urban, industrial societies with relatively efficient transportation and communications systems combined with a standard of living that allows people the time and money to play and watch sports. Class relations are usually involved in the process through which sports become commercialized. Spectator interests for sports are often connected with ideologies emphasizing efficiency and hard work, with sport programs that foster childhood involvement in sports, and with television coverage that introduces people to the rules of sports and the athletes who play sports. The economic motives of sport organizations and other businesses has led to the global expansion of certain commercial sports. This expansion will continue into the foreseeable future and it will be more carefully discussed and analyzed in the sociology of sport as it occurs.

COMMERCIALIZATION AND CHANGES IN SPORTS

What happens to sports when they become commercialized? Do they change when they become dependent on gate receipts and the sale of media rights?

We know that whenever any sport is converted into commercial entertainment, its success depends on spectator appeal. Although spectators often have a variety of motives underlying their attachments to sports, their interests in any sport event are usually related to a combination of three factors:

- The uncertainty of an event's outcome ("Is it going to be a close contest?")
- The risk or financial rewards associated with participating in an event ("How much is at stake in the contest?")
- The anticipated display of excellence or heroics by the athletes ("Is anybody good playing, and do they have special reasons for playing well?")

In other words, when spectators refer to a "good game" or an "exciting contest," they are usually talking about one in which the outcome was in doubt until the last minutes or seconds, one in which the stakes were so high that athletes were totally committed to and engrossed in the action, or one in which there were a number of excellent or "heroic" performances. When games or matches contain all three of these factors, they are remembered and discussed for a long time.

If spectators are attracted by uncertainty, high stakes, and heroic performances, commercial sports are likely to emphasize these things to attract large audiences. To understand the changes associated with commercialization, it is necessary to look at three aspects of sports:

1. The format and goals of sports
2. The orientations of athletes, coaches, and sponsors
3. The organizations through which sports are controlled

Format and Goals

Commercialization has not had a dramatic effect on the format and goals of most sports. Terry Furst (1971) reached this conclusion after examining the histories of various sports. He explained that:

> In spite of the influence of spectators, what has occurred historically is that sports have . . . maintained their basic format. Innovations have been made within this framework (e.g., rule changes) rather than completely dismantling the design of a game and starting anew with the entertainment inclination of the spectators as a guide.

This conclusion seems to fit with most of our everyday observations. For example, the commercialization of the Olympic Games has led to minor rule changes in certain events, but the basic structure of each Olympic sport has remained much the same as it was before the days of corporate endorsements and the sale of television rights. In American football, rules have been changed to protect quarterbacks, to encourage the use of passes in offensive strategy, to discourage strategies that emphasize field goals over touchdowns, and to give teams an extra time-out in connection with a 2-minute warning at the end of each half of play. But the basic format and goals of football have undergone little change.

The rule changes associated with commercialization are usually intended to do at least one of four things: (1) speed up the action in an event so fans won't get bored, (2) increase scoring to generate more excitement, (3) balance competition so events will have uncertain outcomes, and (4) provide commercial breaks in the action so sponsors can advertise products (this is most common in the United States, where commercial sponsorship on television is more prevalent than it is in other countries).

A review of rule changes in many sports shows the importance of these four factors. For example, the designated hitter in the American League was designed to increase scoring opportunities and heighten the dramatic action in major league baseball. Soccer rules have been changed to adapt it to indoor facilities so spectators can watch year round without interruptions or discomfort caused by the weather. Tennis scoring has been changed to meet the time requirements of television schedules. Golf tournaments now involve total stroke counts rather than match play so big-name players will not be eliminated in the early rounds of televised events. Free throws have been minimized in basketball to speed up action. Sudden death over-time periods have been added to many sports so spectators can answer the question "who won" without having to assess the quality of play in an event.

Even though many of these changes have been prompted by economic considerations, they have not altered the basic formats and goals of the sports in which they have been made. Furthermore, some changes also reflect the concerns and interests of the players themselves. After all, players often have more fun when there is more action, scoring, and close contests, and many of them become accustomed to commercial breaks and TV time-outs.

The cases in which commercialization has had a dramatic effect on formats and goals are few, but they are noteworthy. Examples include roller derby, American professional wrestling, arena football, indoor soccer, rollerhockey, motorcycle jumping, the made-for-TV gladiators contest, and other events created primarily for entertainment purposes. These examples are the exceptions rather than the rule. At times they may be heavily promoted, but many people view them as forms of "spectacle" rather than sports.

Orientations of Players, Coaches, and Sponsors

Commercialization seems to affect the orientations of sport participants more than it does the format and goals of sports. To make money on a sport, it's necessary to attract a mass audience to buy tickets or watch events on television. Attracting and entertaining a *mass* audience is not easy because it's made up of many people who don't have technical knowledge about the complex athletic skills and strategies used by players and coaches. Without this technical knowledge, people are easily impressed by things extrinsic to the game or match itself; they get taken in by hype. During the event itself they often focus on things they can easily understand. They enjoy situations in which players take risks and face clear physical danger;

they are attracted to players who are masters of dramatic expression or who are willing to go beyond their normal physical limits to the point of endangering their safety and well-being; and they like to see players committed to victory no matter what the personal cost.

For example, when people lack technical knowledge about football, they are more likely to be entertained by a running back's end-zone dance after a touchdown than by the lineman's block that enabled the running back to score the touchdown. Those who lack technical knowledge about basketball are more likely to talk about a single slam dunk than about the consistently flawless defense that enabled a team to win a game. Similarly, those who know little about the technical aspects of ice skating are more entertained by triple and quadruple jumps than by routines carefully choreographed and practiced until they are smooth and flawless. Without dangerous jumps, naive spectators get bored. They like athletes who project exciting or controversial personas, and they often rate performances in terms of dramatic expression leading to dramatic results. They want long touchdown passes, not 9-minute touchdown drives. They want home runs, not sacrifice bunts and hit-and-run plays. They want to see athletes occasionally collapse as they surpass physical limits, not athletes who know their limits so well they can successfully compete for years without going beyond them.

Sports are not the only things affected by commercialization in this way. For example, rock music has been developed as a form of mass entertainment so that style (or the ability to project a distinct and dramatic persona) often supersedes musical ability as a basis for popularity and commercial success. Some popular rock stars are great musicians, others average, and some lousy. When audiences lack technical knowledge about music, significant differences in musical ability can be buried under large amounts of style. It is style that sells; musical ability is often incidental. Elvis Presley became a legend because of his style, not his musical talent (despite what his fans would like to think). Contemporary rock groups sell out concerts because they put on good shows, not because they are accomplished musicians (although some are accomplished musicians who discovered they needed more than musical abilities to attract fans).

When a sport comes to depend on entertaining a mass audience, those involved in the sport often revise their ideas about what is important in sport. This revision usually involves a shift in emphasis from what might be called an *aesthetic orientation* to an *heroic orientation*. Figure 12-1 outlines the implications of this shift. It shows that when there is a need to entertain people who don't have technical knowledge about a sport, the people in sport often revise the criteria they use to evaluate what happens during a game or match. In fact, they may even refer to games or matches as "show-time," and they may refer to themselves as entertainers as well as athletes. This does not mean that aesthetic orientations disappear, but it does mean that they often take a back seat to the heroic actions that en-

tertain spectators who don't know enough to appreciate the strategic and technical aspects of the game or match.

As the need to please naive audiences becomes greater, so does the emphasis on heroic orientations. This is why television commentators for U.S. football games continually talk about danger, injuries, playing with pain, and courage. In fact, long-time Monday Night Football commentator Frank Gifford even wrote a book, *Gifford on Courage* (1977), in which he talks about the dedication of athletes who play with pain and sacrifice their bodies for the sake of victories. Some athletes, however, realize the dangers associated with heroic orientations and try to slow the move away from aesthetic orientations in their sports. For example, some former figure skaters have called for restrictions on the number of triple jumps that can be included in skating programs. These skaters are worried that the commercial success of their sport is coming to rely on the danger of movement rather than the beauty of movement. However, some skaters seem to be willing to adopt heroic

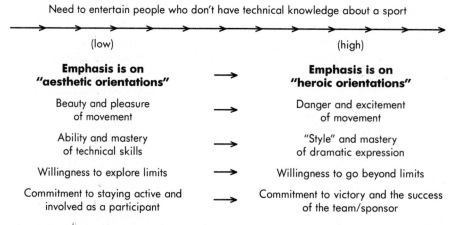

FIGURE 12-1 How orientations change when sports become a form of mass entertainment.

orientations if this is what will please audiences and generate revenues. These athletes usually evaluate themselves and other athletes in terms of the sport ethic (see Chapter 6) and they learn to see heroic actions as signs of true commitment and dedication to their sport.

Sport Organizations

Commercialization also leads to changes in the organizations that control sports. When sports begin to depend on generating revenues, the control of sport organizations usually shifts further and further away from the players. In fact, the players often lose effective control over the conditions of their own sport participation. These conditions come under the control of general managers, team owners, corporate sponsors, advertisers, media personnel, marketing and publicity staff, professional management staff, accountants, and agents.

The organizations that control commercial sports are usually complex, since they are intended to coordinate the interests of all these people, but their primary goal is to maximize revenues. This means that organizational decisions generally reflect the combined economic interests of many people having no direct personal connection with a sport or with the athletes involved. The power to affect these decisions is grounded in a variety of resources, many of which are not even connected with sports. Therefore athletes in many commercial sports find themselves cut out of decision making processes even when decisions affect their health and well-being.

As decision making in sport organizations moves further away from athletes and the interests of athletes become less immediate and less important, there is a tendency to hire employees, develop policies, and negotiate deals that give a low priority to the interests of athletes. These organizational changes have important implications for what happens in sports. They also make it necessary for athletes to seek new tactics for promoting their own interests, financial and otherwise.

As people with commercial interests have become involved in figure skating, more attention has been paid to entertaining spectators who do not know much about the sport. This has led to an increasing emphasis on heroic orientations among skaters. Now the danger and excitement of triple axel jumps and quadruple jumps are the focus of media hype and coverage, and injuries among figure skaters have risen significantly. (Colorado Springs Gazette Telegraph)

OWNERS, SPONSORS, AND PROMOTERS IN COMMERCIAL SPORTS

Professional Sports in North America

On the one hand, team owners, event sponsors, and promoters have been praised for putting teams together, staging impressive events, and bringing professional sports to cities all over North America. On the other hand, they have been criticized for establishing monopolistic and exclusive businesses in the interest of making money, avoiding taxes, manipulating athletes, and turning sports into media spectacles resembling circuses. These contradictory evaluations make it important to understand who these people are and why they do what they do.

Because the cost of a franchise in some sports can be as high as $165 million (the Dallas Cowboys—as of 1993), the owners of professional sport teams are usually individuals, partnerships, or corporations with massive amounts of investment capital (Beamish, 1988). The same is true of the sponsors and promoters of major tournaments and special events—they must have access to large amounts of investment capital. Nevertheless, if all those who owned sport teams and sponsored major sport events were interested only in making money, some would have chosen other investments.

Professional sports are big business and sometimes risky business. For example, many teams, leagues, and events have been financial disasters during the past 30 years. Four football leagues, a hockey league, a number of basketball and soccer teams, a soccer league, a volleyball league, a women's basketball league, and a team tennis league have all gone out of business, leaving many owners, sponsors, and promoters in debt (this is just in the United States alone).

So why invest in sports? According to sociologist Jon Brower (1976) people invest in sports so they can do business and have fun. Owners and sponsors are frequently wealthy superfans. They buy teams and stage events to satisfy lifelong fantasies, build their egos, and vicariously experience the public achievements of athletes. Their investments in sport gain them more prestige than any of their other business ventures. They become instant celebrities in their cities—from the mayor's office and the Chamber of Commerce to neighborhood bars and local elementary schools.

However, those who invest in sports seldom get so carried away with fun and fantasy that they forget business. They do not enjoy losing money. They may look at their athletes as heroes and may even treat them as their children, but they want to control their athletes for the

purpose of securing returns on their investments. When it comes to the business of sports, the wealthy people who own sport teams and sponsor sport events focus on generating revenues and establishing a firm basis for continued financial success. They may not agree with fellow owners and sponsors on all issues, but they all agree on the need to protect their investments and maximize profits.

TEAM OWNERS AND SPORT LEAGUES AS MONOPOLIES The tendency to think alike has been especially strong among the team owners in the major North American sport leagues— the NBA, NFL, NHL, and MLB. In fact, unity among these owners has led to the formation of some of the most influential monopolies in the history of North American business. Even though the 107 individual teams in these leagues are separate businesses, the owners of those teams in each sport have come together to form organizations representing their collective interests. These organizations have traditionally been used to limit the extent to which teams compete against each other for players, fans, and media revenues, and to eliminate competition from others who might try to form teams and leagues in their sport.

For example, each league (NBA, NFL, NHL, and MLB) has developed a system to force new players entering the sport to negotiate contracts only with the team that has drafted them; this enables owners to sign new players to contracts without bidding against other teams who might be willing to pay the players more money. Owners have also agreed to prevent new teams from being added to their leagues without their collective permission, and when permission is given, the new team (franchise) owner is charged a heavy entry fee to become a part of the league. For example, in 1992 the new Denver Rockies had to pay $95 million dollars to the other baseball team owners just for the privilege of becoming a part of Major League Baseball. Furthermore, new owners can locate teams only in cities approved by current owners, and existing owners cannot move their teams to another city unless the other owners collectively approve of the move. These policies prevent new teams from competing with established teams for players, spectator interest, gate receipts, and local broadcasting rights, and they regulate the competition between existing owners. Team owners in each league never allow changes that could threaten their collective interest, their control over their sport, or their ability to generate revenues.

The owners in each sport league have also agreed to sell the broadcasting rights to their games as a group, and then equally share the revenues from national media contracts. This limits the number of games available to the viewing public, but it enables team owners to make huge sums of money in their media contracts. Amazingly, the U.S. Congress has approved this monopolistic method of doing business. In fact, it even passed an amendment to the U.S. Code in which it was stated that "antitrust laws . . . shall not apply to . . . [the] organized professional team sports of football, baseball, basketball, or hockey." This rule has not only guaranteed revenues for team owners in these professional sports but it has given them the power to influence television companies and the commentators working for those companies.

Furthermore, team owners have combined their monopolistic media tactics with exclusive-use clauses in their contracts with the stadiums or arenas they use. This has been an effective tool for preventing other leagues from forming and competing for spectator interest. The World Football League discovered this in 1975 when it went out of business after its second season. The teams in the WFL had been forced to locate in cities that did not have NFL teams because the NFL teams had "exclusive-use" clauses with the big stadiums in their cities. This prevented the stadiums from being rented to any other football team. Also, none of the television networks bought the rights to WFL games for fear they might be frozen out of future negotiations with the NFL. They didn't want to be denied the possibility of televising the games of teams lo-

cated in the largest television markets in North America. Therefore without large gate receipts and without revenues from the sale of television rights, the WFL went broke. In the 1980s the USFL ran into a similar NFL power play even though it scheduled games during the spring rather than the fall. In 1985, after only 2 years of operation, the USFL also went broke. As a cartel, the NFL has been very effective in protecting its own interests. It plans to extend those interests around the world in the form of the World League of American Football that NFL owners hope to have operating in a number of European cities during the 1990s.

Exempting existing professional sport leagues from antitrust laws in the United States has limited the number of professional teams in each sport and has driven up the monetary value of teams. Being part of a legal monopoly has enabled many team owners to make massive sums of money when they sell their teams. This happened often during the late 1970s and throughout the 1980s. For example, Edgar Kaiser, Jr. purchased the Denver Broncos football team for $35 million in 1981 and sold it in early 1984 for $70 million—after Kaiser complained for 2 years that he couldn't make any money because his players' salaries were too high and ticket prices were too low! In another case, Clint Murchison purchased the Dallas Cowboys in 1960 for $500,000 and sold it in 1984 for $80 million (including a $20 million stadium lease). The money made on the sales of these teams does not include the annual profits and tax benefits owners enjoy or the annual salaries, which sometimes amount to millions of dollars per year, that many owners pay to themselves. Similar patterns of profit have existed in MLB, the NBA, and, to a lesser extent, the NHL.

Even though I have grouped the NBA, NFL, NHL, and MLB together in this section, it must be pointed out that each of these leagues differs from one another in many important respects. These differences are complicated and they regularly change as each league encounters new and unique challenges and opportunities. For exam-

"I hope this city takes pity on me. I just can't afford the rent on the new stadium paid for by the taxpayers. Don't they realize that I'm doing the city a favor by keeping my team here?"

ple, contracts with networks and major cable television companies vary from one league to another. The NHL has been the least successful in negotiating big money contracts, whereas the NBA, NFL, and MLB have each been very successful through the mid-1990s. Each league also has different internal agreements regulating the ways teams can negotiate the sale of *local* broadcasting rights to their games. The NFL does not allow teams to sign independent television contracts for local broadcasts of their games, but MLB does allow teams to negotiate and keep the revenues from the sale of local broadcast rights. This means that all NFL teams benefit equally from media contracts whereas MLB teams differ to the extent that they each negotiate separate *local* media contracts. Therefore a team such as the NY Yankees has the potential to generate much more revenue than baseball teams located in smaller media markets. Of course, this is a major issue among people who own baseball teams in Milwaukee, Kansas City, Seattle, Minnesota, and Montreal. They worry about being able to keep up with the Yankees and other teams located in massive media markets.

The biggest differences between the NBA, NFL, NHL, and MLB are related to their contractual agreements with players' associations in each league. Although each league has traditionally tried to give athletes as few rights as possible, athletes have fought for nearly 30 years to gain control over important parts of their careers and to increase their salaries in the process. This will be discussed in the sections on the legal status and salaries of professional athletes (pp. 317-323).

TEAM OWNERS AND FORMS OF PUBLIC ASSISTANCE The belief that all big cities must have professional sport teams and must provide big sport events has led to various forms of public support for sport owners and sport sponsors. The most common form of support is the use of public funds to construct and maintain athletic facilities. Of course, owners and sponsors pay rent to use these facilities, but, in the case of team owners, the rent payments usually cover only a fraction of maintenance and construction costs. This means local taxpayers make up the difference by subsidizing team owners. When information on these subsidies was collected and made available to a federal commission during the late-1970s, a congressperson on the commission said, "A lot of cities would be embarrassed if people knew how much [they] subsidize pro teams." However, these embarrassing patterns still exist in the 1990s.

Political leaders in most cities justify subsidies and other forms of public support for professional sport teams by saying that public expenditures on sports and sports facilities are matched by (1) the publicity gained by the cities, (2) the increases in civic pride created by teams, and (3) the spin-off economic benefits experienced by the cities. However, these consequences are difficult to document (Baade, 1987), and in the case of the spin-off economic benefits, it is certain they are enjoyed primarily by wealthy business people in the cities; others in the community gain little. In fact, many city residents cannot even afford tickets for games in the facilities they subsidize. For example, many families in Louisiana can't afford a guided tour of the Superdome, much less tickets to a New Orleans Saints game. But millions of tax dollars from the people of Louisiana are spent every year to support the Superdome and the New Orleans Saints. Of course, almost everyone loves the Saints, but some people benefit much more than others by having the Saints in town. While the multimillionaire owner of the Saints receives "welfare" in the form of public subsidies, the people of New Orleans, many of whom are poor, pay the highest city sales tax in the United States (9%), send their children to what may be the poorest public schools in North America, and cope with inadequate public transportation and city services (Henry, 1986). In light of this, some people might wonder if the money spent on the Superdome and the Saints might be better spent on city infrastructure, bus systems, schools, jobs programs, or hundreds of other programs that would benefit people who can't afford Saints tickets.

Despite the fact that money for sports might be better spent on other things, the owners of professional sport teams in many cities have threatened to move their franchises to other cities if they didn't get more subsidies in the form of new or improved facilities. For example, the owners of the White Sox, one of Chicago's major league baseball teams, were ready to take their team to Florida unless they were given a new stadium, new practice facilities, and other new support facilities costing about $150 million. Meanwhile, St. Petersburg, Florida, spent millions getting ready to be the new home of the White Sox. Then, in a last-minute action, the state legislature in Illinois passed a resolution providing state funds to satisfy the demands of the owners. Now the people of Illinois subsidize the White Sox. St. Louis and the state of Missouri couldn't generate support for a similar subsidy of the owners of the St. Louis Cardinals in the NFL, so the team moved to Phoenix. This tactic of threatening to move teams unless subsidies are increased is becoming so common that it is now called **sportmail**—a form of blackmail used by sport team owners to coerce public support from cities (Purdy, 1988).

In addition to facility subsidies, team owners

receive other forms of public support. For example, the federal government allows a large portion of the cost of game tickets to be deducted as a business expense on annual tax returns. Therefore a large proportion of season tickets for some teams are purchased by local businesses and large corporations. This means the companies not only save on taxes while their upper level employees use company tickets to attend games but they also help teams sell out their seats. When all seats are sold out, the game can be televised locally. This makes the media rights in the sport leagues more valuable and provides teams with great local publicity. This makes everyone happy and a few people, especially team owners, very wealthy. Meanwhile, other wealthy people sit in luxury skyboxes sometimes built with public money. Of course, the skyboxes are rented, but the rent payments are usually deducted from corporate taxes as business expenses. This lowers tax revenues that could be used for public programs.

In summary, the owners and sponsors of professional sports are successful business people. They invest in sports for a variety of reasons, but they are primarily interested in making money. Although some of them do not make large amounts of money, those who own teams in the NFL, MLB and, for the most part, in the NBA and the NHL, have enjoyed significant financial benefits. Their benefits have been greatly influenced by two factors: (1) owners in each league enjoy monopolistic control over their sports, and (2) owners receive public assistance in the form of permission to ignore antitrust regulations and in the form of subsidies from host cities. However, players are now successfully challenging the monopolistic practices of owners in court, and the voters in many cities are refusing to approve new or extended subsidies for sport teams. The extent to which these developments will change the business of professional sports in North America is difficult to say, but there will be changes.

Amateur Sports

Amateur sports don't have owners, but they do have commercial sponsors and governing bodies that sanction events and control athletes. Generally, the sponsors are large corporations who support amateur sports for advertising purposes; and the governing bodies of amateur sports operate on a nonprofit basis, although they do use revenues from events to maintain their organizations and power over amateur sports.

In most countries around the world, amateur sports are administered by centralized sport authorities working with the governing bodies of individual sports. Together these groups attempt to exercise consistent control over events, athletes, and revenues. In the United States, however, the organization of amateur sport is much less centralized. Amateur sports in the United States are regulated and controlled by many different organizations, each of which develops its own policies and raises its own funds. For example, the major organization in intercollegiate sport is the National Collegiate Athletic Association (NCAA). However, rules for intercollegiate sports and for athletes vary in each of the four major membership divisions in the NCAA. Each member school in the NCAA is also free to develop its own policies to supplement NCAA policies. Schools must finance sport programs on their own; they receive no direct aid from the NCAA. Amateur sports in colleges and universities are also controlled by the National Association for Intercollegiate Athletics (NAIA), the College Football Association (CFA), and, up until 1983, the Association of Intercollegiate Athletics for Women (AIAW). The rules in these organizations have usually differed from the rules in the NCAA.

For amateur sports not directly connected with universities, the major controlling organization is the United States Olympic Committee (USOC). However, within the USOC each of nearly 50 separate national governing bodies (NGBs) regulates and controls a particular amateur sport. NGBs raise most of their own funds through corporate and individual sponsors, and they each set their own policies to supplement the rules and policies of the USOC. The USOC has tried for many years to develop continuity in American amateur sports, but the NGBs and other sport organizations are very protective of their own turf, and they seldom give up power to regulate their sports or athletes. This has led to many political battles between organizations. NGBs are afraid of giving up their power so they fight to maintain control over their rules, revenues, and athletes. As the USOC has been more effective in raising money, it has also been able to use a system of monetary grants to increase its control over various NGBs. This will continue, although most NGBs will strive to maintain their autonomy, independence, and control over the athletes in their sport.

Despite variation and confusion in amateur sports, all amateur sport organizations share an interest in two things: *power*, and *money* generated through sponsorships and revenue-producing sports events. For example, when the popularity of women's sports reached new heights in the early 1980s, the NCAA's interest in maintaining power over all college sports led it to abandon its long-time policy of ignoring women's teams; it started to sponsor championship events for women and quickly forced the Association for Intercollegiate Athletics for Women (AIAW) out of existence, even though the AIAW had controlled women's intercollegiate sports for many years. The NCAA's interest in money has led it to operate as a monopoly in its control of intercollegiate sports. This is especially true in the case of revenue-producing sports through which the NCAA has been able to make considerable money by selling broadcasting rights. However, this monopolistic control was partially eroded in 1984 when a series of court decisions made it possible for individual universities to break away from the NCAA and sell broadcasting rights on their own and then keep the money from the sale. But despite this change, the NCAA remains a powerful organization in amateur sports.

Sponsorship patterns in amateur sports also take many forms. Football bowl games are now funded and partially controlled by large corporations. Intercollegiate sport programs now seek a variety of different forms of corporate support.

The use of sport as a setting for product advertisements is common in most countries. Fees from corporate sponsors in the United States are used to support amateur athletes, events, and the administrative structures of sports organizations.

The NGBs of amateur sports have long depended on corporate sponsorship money, and they continue to seek those sponsorships to pay for athlete training, operating expenses, and the staging of events. Individual athletes now seek corporate sponsorships on their own, hoping to remain free to train and compete without having their lives completely controlled by NGBs. As this model of corporate sponsorship continues to be used more and more around the world, the economics of sports will become increasingly tied to the fortunes and fluctuations of market economies. Will this mean that sports will become highly visible cheerleaders for the interests of international corporate capitalism in the world? I think this is already true, and it will become even more pervasive in the future.

LEGAL STATUS AND INCOMES OF ATHLETES IN COMMERCIAL SPORTS

"I consider myself an entertainer. I don't look at myself as a record-setting athlete." This statement, made by John Riggins when he was a running back for the Washington Redskins, calls attention to the fact that whenever sport is designed to generate revenues, athletes become en-

In the quest for sponsorships, race cars have become fast moving billboards. A similar pattern is appearing in other sports in which athletes' clothing is beginning to resemble the exterior of race cars—numerous sponsor logos now appear on shirts, pants, and hats. (Colorado Springs Gazette Telegraph)

tertainers. This is obvious at the professional level, but it is also true in other commercial sports, such as big-time college football and basketball and elite international sports. When people pay to watch sports, or when television companies pay to broadcast them, athletes become entertainers. Professional athletes get paid for their efforts whereas amateur athletes may or may not get paid. In this section of the chapter I will provide information on the legal status and incomes of professional athletes and athletes in other forms of revenue-producing sports. My primary focus will be on commercial sports in the United States.

Professional Athletes

LEGAL STATUS: TEAM SPORTS The legal status and rights of athletes have traditionally been the most controversial issues in professional team sports in the United States. Until the mid-1970s, professional athletes in team sports had little or no legal power to control their own careers. Within each sport league they could play only for the team drafting them. They could neither pick the team for which they wanted to play nor control when and to whom they might be traded during their careers, even when their contracts expired. To make matters worse, they were obliged to sign standard contracts forcing

them to agree to forfeit rights to control their careers. Basically, they were bought and sold like property, and they were seldom consulted about their own wishes. They were mercenaries at the mercy of team owners and officials hired by team owners.

In each sport, this set of employee restrictions has been referred to as the **reserve system.** Although the precise nature of this system varies from one sport to the next, it has enabled team owners to control the lives of athletes in a variety of ways. For many years the reserve system kept salaries low (compared with what they are now) and prevented players from being free to sell their abilities to the team that would give them the best deal in terms of money and playing conditions. In any other business this system would violate antitrust laws but, until recently, it has been totally legal in professional sports. For example, it would be illegal for all electrical engineering firms to get together and decide among themselves who they each wanted to hire next year. It would also be illegal for them to agree not to hire an engineer who had been "reserved" by another company. This type of "reserve system" would destroy the freedom of electrical engineers to choose where and with whom they wanted to work. Furthermore, if the engineers could not take a job with another company without permission from their current employer, even after their employment contracts expired, and if they were subject to being sold or traded to other companies without being consulted, they would have no real control over their own careers. However, sport teams used such a system for many years with minimal interference from any law enforcement agency. As would be predicted, this system kept athletes' salaries lower than they could have been and it gave team owners an extreme degree of control over the lives of athletes.

Professional athletes have always objected to the reserve system, but they began to challenge it legally only in the 1970s. Then in 1976 the courts ruled that under certain conditions professional athletes had the right to become *free agents*. This right to become free agents was important because it allowed players whose contracts had expired to accept contract offers from other teams. This legal change had a dramatic effect on the salaries of NBA and MLB players during the late 1970s and through the 1980s. Team owners in the NFL and NHL were able to avoid much of the effect of this legal change by negotiating restrictions on free agency with players' associations. But in 1992 these restrictions were challenged in both leagues. The hockey players went on strike during the Stanley Cup playoffs and, after 10 days, signed a short-term contract in which they got slightly more control over their careers. The football players, after challenging the NFL for about 5 years in a series of court cases, won an antitrust suit that forced team owners to agree to let NFL players become free agents after being in the league for 5 years.

It would take many pages to explain the full implications of recent court decisions on legal status and rights of players in each professional team sport. The explanations would change every time a new case is resolved or a new labor agreement is made in a particular league. In part, it was this complexity that kept most players from challenging the restrictions of the reserve system over the years. It was not until the formation of players' associations and unions in the 1970s that they had the support and organization needed to push for changes. The players' associations have been able to use the collective strength of all the players in a specific league to bargain against the collective strength of all the owners in that league. Although the players' associations have often been unpopular with many sport fans and regularly detested by team owners and league officials, they have enabled players to gain more and more control over their salaries and working conditions since the late 1970s. In fact, the labor negotiations and players' strikes in all professional team sports have always focused on issues of control (Eitzen, 1984), even though money has attracted most of the attention in the media coverage.

Although players' organizations and unions have done much to change the legal status of athletes in various professional sports, it has not been easy to keep players organized (Beamish, 1988). Owners have not looked kindly on players who have served as representatives in unions and players' associations. Athletes are often hesitant to join any organization that may ask them to strike for an entire season, especially since their careers seldom last more than about 5 years in team sports. Therefore a season-long strike for the average player means sacrificing 20% of his lifetime income as a professional athlete. Furthermore, a strike is risky because owners may drop veteran players to sign nonunion players just waiting for a chance to be professional athletes. This happened during the 1987 NFL players' strike, when the owners had no trouble finding replacement players. These and other unique problems make it very difficult to keep players organized even though players' associations have brought about significant changes in the past. The short careers of many professional athletes often lead them to have short collective memories of past progress.

LEGAL STATUS: INDIVIDUAL SPORTS Professional athletes in individual sports seldom share a common legal status with their counterparts in team sports. Although the situations in boxing, bowling, golf, tennis, automobile racing, rodeo, horse racing, track and field, skiing, and other sports are all different, a few generalizations are possible.

The legal status of athletes in individual sports largely depends on what athletes must do to train and qualify for competition in their sports. For example, few athletes can afford to pay for all the training needed to develop professional-level skills in a sport. Few athletes are in positions to meet the other requirements associated with official participation in sport competitions, which may include having a recognized agent or manager (as in boxing), being formally recognized by other participants (as in most automobile racing), obtaining membership in a professional organization (as in most bowling, golf, and tennis tournaments), or gaining a special invitation through an official selection group (as in track and field meets). Whenever sponsors are needed to pay for training and whenever contractual arrangements with other persons or groups are required for participation, the legal status of athletes is shaped by their agreements with sponsors and sanctioning groups. This is why the legal status of athletes in individual sports varies so much from one athlete to the next. Let's use boxing as a example of this variation.

Because boxers frequently come from low-income backgrounds, it is nearly impossible for them to develop on their own the skills to become recognized competitors. They need trainers, managers, and someone to sponsor their training. After skills are developed it takes more money and carefully monitored business connections to arrange and promote matches. Each of these relationships — with trainers, managers, and sponsors — comes with conditions attached for the boxers. Sometimes these conditions are spelled out in formal contracts, sometimes they may be informal. But in all cases, they involve boxers giving up control of their lives and a portion of the rewards they may earn in bouts in return for the help needed to become professional. Unless boxers have good legal experience

SIDELINES

©1982 M.T.F.-T.W.S.-Lakewood, CO   Bill Whitehead ©'82

"I MAKE NINE HUNDRED GRAND A YEAR... AND I DON'T FEEL GUILTY!"

Many superstar athletes have no reason to feel guilty about their incomes. As entertainers they usually generate revenues that surpass their salaries. In fact, the creation of superstars is a useful tactic in the staging of successful entertainment events.

or are very skilled, they are likely to have almost no control over their careers. In a sense, they are forced to trade control for the opportunity to continue boxing because they lack the resources needed to gain access to opportunities on their own. This is a classic example of how class relations operate in sports — they provide the context in which athletes in individual sports negotiate their careers and the control they have over their careers.

The legal status of athletes in individual sports may also be defined in the bylaws of professional organizations. Examples of these organizations include the Professional Golf Association (PGA), the Ladies Professional Golf Association (LPGA), the Association of Tennis Professionals (ATP), and the Professional Rodeo Cowboys Association (PRCA), among many others. Because these organizations are often partially controlled by the athletes themselves, their official policies are likely to be supportive of athletes' rights.

INCOME: TEAM SPORTS Despite the publicity given to the supercontracts of some profes-

Table 12-1 Average salaries in the major team sport leagues in the United States

Year	National Basketball Association	Major League Baseball	National Football League	National Hockey League
1967-1968	$ 20,000	$ 19,000	$ 21,000	$ 20,000
1979-1980	185,000	143,000	65,900	100,000
1984-1985	325,000	363,000	178,000	140,000
1988-1989	600,000	485,000	239,000	158,000
1992-1993	1,250,000	1,090,000	496,000	379,000

sional athletes in the NBA, NFL, NHL, and MLB, salaries vary widely between and within different sports. If minor league baseball, indoor and outdoor soccer, and semiprofessional ("semipro") football, basketball, and hockey are considered, it is clear that many professional athletes do not have annual incomes surpassing the incomes of other workers. For example, salaries for the players on 158 minor league baseball teams—nearly seven times as many teams as in the major leagues—range from about $1200 to $3000 per month (in 1993 dollars) depending on the level played. The players do not always get paid 12 months a year; their jobs are seasonal. This pattern is characteristic in many other professional sports including men's and women's basketball, football, hockey, soccer, and volleyball.

Despite the relatively low salaries among many professional athletes, the opinion of most people is that all professional athletes have attractive multiyear contracts enabling them to live comfortably for their entire lives. This is true for some players, but when evaluating player contracts it must be remembered that few athletes have professional careers lasting more than 3 years. In fact, the average in the four major team sports is between 3.5 and 7 years. As former baseball player Willie Mays once said: "The financial careers of most professional athletes can be summed up in these words: short and sweet—but mostly short." Furthermore, it has been only since the late 1970s that salaries

have gotten so big. For example, when Gale Sayers was the number one draft choice of the Chicago Bears in 1965 he signed one of the best ever rookie contracts in the NFL: it was $25,000 per year for 4 years. The average salary for major league baseball players in 1967 was only $19,000 per year. But things are very different today. A few 22-year-old basketball players have signed contracts giving them over a million dollars per year in salaries, and a few established baseball players have signed contracts paying them around $7 million per year beginning in the mid-1990s. Current average salaries in the NBA, NFL, NHL, and MLB now compare very favorably with the incomes of other popular entertainers in television, film, and music, although most top athletes make *less* than top stars in these other entertainment fields.

The growth of player salaries is illustrated in Table 12-1. Salaries for every year in every sport since 1970 show that major changes in salary levels have closely corresponded to court decisions and other events that have either changed the legal status of athletes or given them bargaining power in their contract negotiations with team owners. Baseball is a good case in point. Table 12-2 shows salary data for major league players from 1967 through 1993. Note that increases were gradual until the 1976 season. Then there was a series of dramatic jumps. These jumps were associated with the growing revenues from gate receipts and the sale of television rights, but they were primarily caused by

Table 12-2 Minimum, average, and median salaries of major league baseball players, 1967-1993*

Year	Minimum salary	Average salary	Median salary†
1967	$ 6,000	$ 19,000	$ 17,000
1968	10,000	Not available	Not available
1969	10,000	24,909	19,750
1970	12,000	29,303	21,750
1971	12,750	31,543	24,750
1972	13,500	34,092	27,000
1973	15,000	36,566	28,000
1974	15,000	40,839	30,000
1975	16,000	44,676	34,000‡
1976	19,000§	51,501	40,000
1977	19,000	76,066	58,000
1978	21,000	99,876	68,000
1979	21,000‖	113,558	80,000
1980	30,000	143,756	95,000
1981	32,500	185,651	135,000
1982	33,500	241,497	Not available
1983	35,000	289,194	200,000
1984	40,000	329,408	225,000
1985	60,000	371,000	262,500
1986	60,000	412,000¶	275,000
1987	62,500	402,000¶	254,110
1988	62,500	438,000	250,000
1989	68,000	485,000	300,000
1990	100,000	597,537	350,000
1991	100,000	891,188	425,000
1992	109,000	1,028,667	400,000
1993	109,000	1,089,666	450,000‡

*Data from Major League Baseball Players Association.
†Half the players receive less than the median salary; the other half receive more. Since 1979 the MLBPA has not computed median salary.
‡Estimated.
§The year in which the reentry draft system was first introduced. This system allowed up to 13 of the 26 teams in baseball to bid for players who had played out their option years and become free agents.
‖1979-1985 salary figures have been discounted for salary deferrals without interest at a rate of 9% per year for a period of delayed payments.
¶Salaries held down by illegal collusion on the part of team owners; players collectively lose between $70 million and $90 million.

the changes in the legal status of the players themselves. Because of a favorable court decision prompted by the efforts of their union, baseball players received the right under certain conditions to become free agents and sell their abilities to the highest bidders after the 1976 season. This allowed a number of top players to negotiate lucrative long-term contracts. For example, during the 10 years before free agency, salaries increased 270% from $19,000 to $51,501. In the 13 years since free agency, salaries have increased about 2000%, from $51,501 to nearly $1.1 million. However, not all baseball players have shared equally in the increases since free agency. The *average* or *mean* salary listed for a sport is always pulled up and distorted by players who have the big money contracts. This is why the *median* salary should be consulted if you want to get a more realistic idea of the salaries of all players in a sport. Unfortunately, most data neither refer to median salaries in sports nor mention that 5% to 30% of a player's total contract value is paid to agents who negotiate the contracts.

INCOME: INDIVIDUAL SPORTS As with team sports, publicity is given to the highest-paid athletes in individual sports. However, not everyone in these sports makes enough money from tournament winnings to support themselves comfortably. In fact, a number of golfers, tennis players, bowlers, automobile racers, and rodeo cowboys must carefully watch expenses on their tours so they do not go too far into the red. In commenting on this point, Martina Navratilova (1984) made the following statement about players on the women's tennis tour:

> Yes, the top players make a fortune playing a game they love, myself included. But looking down the ranking list, the payouts are not so generous. The [women] ranked [in] . . . the bottom 50 of the top 100 have a heck of a time earning a living. . . . For some reason, the general public seems to think that the players clear all this money and all the expenses are picked up by someone else. Wrong. The players have to pay their own airfare, hotels, food and ground transportation in the cities that they play.

Navratilova's point is still applicable, although many sports have much more money to spread around in the mid-1990s than they did in the mid-1980s. But when we assess tournament winnings for athletes in individual sports we should also remember than many of these athletes do pay $50,000 per year or more on basic expenses. In sports such as track and field, motorcycle racing, and rodeo, athletes seldom make enough to cover more than their expenses. A few, of course, win big purses and receive media attention, but they are the exception rather than the rule.

In some cases, athletes in individual sports have to share their winnings with investors who sponsor them. The investors cover expenses during the lean years, but then take a percentage of winnings when the athlete wins matches or tournaments. For example, boxers have traditionally received very little of the prize money from their bouts; most goes to promoters, managers, trainers, and sponsors. Only a few boxers have avoided this situation; many others face bankruptcy and poverty soon after their careers are over. However, few athletes in individual sports experience as many negative consequences as boxers. Although arrangements for financial backing have sometimes caused problems for professional bowlers, automobile racers, and rodeo cowboys, the effects of such backing are usually short-term. In some sports, athletes' families cover at least some expenses.

OTHER QUESTIONS ABOUT MONEY

Are athletes overpaid? The answer to this question is yes and no. On the one hand, a number of players are overpaid, and everyone, including the players, knows it. On the other hand, if sport is a profitable form of entertainment, and if athletes do the entertaining, they should be rewarded accordingly. That's the way it works in the rest of show business. For example, if 50,000 people are willing to pay $30 a seat to see Madonna perform, then Madonna should get her fair share of the $1.5 million from gate receipts. Furthermore, the fact that NBA players make an average of $12,000 per game (less agent fees) is not out of line when one con-

siders that other television stars make 10 to 20 times that amount for every weekly show they do. In fact, not even the highest paid athletes can come anywhere close to the $46 million made by Oprah Winfrey in 1992, the $40 million made by Bill Cosby, or the $35 million made by Prince. This is why players' associations are now asking that some proportion (usually between 50% and 67%) of the gross revenues in a sport are dedicated to players' salaries.

Athletes make big money when owners and promoters think they are worth it in terms of gate receipts and other revenues. For example, superstars in the major team sports often "pay" for their own salaries by attracting new revenues for team owners, and this is why the owners pay them as they do. The owner of the Chicago Bulls knows that Michael Jordan attracts enough people to the Bulls games and increases the value of media rights enough to more than pay for his annual contract. Furthermore, spectators are attracted by star performers, and the best way to create *stars* in sport is by signing athletes to big money contracts. The contracts themselves generate massive media coverage, which is useful publicity in itself; and fans often see money as an indicator of excellence, so they will pay to see someone who is making a lot of money even if they do not think the athlete is worth it. This method of attracting audiences is also used in individual sports, for example tennis, golf, boxing, and bowling. Big prize money attracts big-name athletes, and big-name athletes create spectator interest and television coverage. Interest and coverage mean profits for sponsors and promoters.

But big money also raises another issue: some sport fans now claim that they have difficultly identifying with athletes who make so much money. These fans think that money is more important to athletes than sport itself, and this leads them to raise questions about the sincerity and dedication of the athletes. If big money contracts really do cause some fans to stop buying season tickets and tuning in to sports on television, then athletes will probably make less money. Have we reached that point in certain sports? I don't know, but many of us in the sociology of sport are interested in what spectators do in response to athletes' paychecks.

How much do athletes make on endorsements? Athletes can make great amounts of money on endorsements if they have personalities and "images" causing people to recognize and identify with them. Gender, race, and ethnic relations clearly come into play in endorsements. For example, the "advertising value" of women athletes is thought to be low except when they can endorse products purchased by other women. The advertising value of African American athletes depends on how advertisers think white consumers will perceive them. Bruce Jenner, the 1976 Olympic decathlon gold medalist and occasional ABC sports announcer, noted the importance of race when he made the following statement:

> It's unfortunate, but black athletes don't have the same commercial value [as white athletes]. . . . You just have to admit it's tougher for them. . . . Middle America buys products, so advertisers stay away from blacks. That's the system we live in.

Many advertisers claim their decisions to avoid women and blacks are based on sound business sense. However, many women and black athletes wonder where sound business sense ends and sexism and racism begin. If discriminatory actions are based on business sense, are they any less dangerous or unfair than discriminatory actions based on prejudices among advertisers? Unfortunately, this issue is discussed more often in locker rooms than it is in conference rooms at ad agencies.

In summary, endorsement income can be significant—up to millions of dollars per year, but it is limited to those *few* athletes who advertisers think will be influential spokespersons for their products.

Do athletes' salaries affect ticket prices to sports events? Ticket prices and athlete salaries are primarily a function of the public demand for sports. Both ticket prices and salaries go up or down as the entertainment value of a sport goes up or down. This makes it look as if salaries are causing ticket prices to go up, but this is not really the case. For example, the basketball fan is not paying $30 for a ticket because Michael Jordan signs a contract for $5 million; the ticket price is $30 because many fans are willing to pay that much to see Michael Jordan and the Bulls play basketball. The ticket price would be the same even if no player on the Bulls were making over $100,000—*as long as the consumer would pay that much to see a game*. The people who control ticket prices are in the business of making money, and they will charge whatever they can get from spectators. This is why Notre Dame charges as much for tickets as the San Francisco 49ers, even though their athletes are "paid" (in scholarship dollars) about 1/25th of what the 49ers' players make.

The economic reality of sports is that team owners and event promoters would gladly pay athletes less money if they could get away with it, but they will set ticket prices at whatever spectators are willing to pay. Athletes' salaries increase *only* when they have the power to force owners and promoters to give them a greater share of the expected gross revenues in sports.

Do big salaries influence the motivation of athletes? Few people would argue with the idea that money motivates athletes. However, another issue is related to this question. If athletes think they should be making more money than they are, will they become disappointed and lose their motivation? This is a difficult question to answer. Athletes generally take pride in their abilities, but it is possible for their pride to take a back seat to a concern for money. If this happens, their commitment to doing their best is bound to suffer.

Has this occurred in commercial sports? Maybe, but no one knows how common it is. Coaches sometimes complain that today's athletes are too wealthy to give their best throughout the whole season, and fans sometimes complain that highly paid athletes do not play hard

SIDELINES

"THE ONE THING THAT HELPS ME WIN SO MANY TOURNAMENTS? OH THAT'S EASY... GREED!"

SIDELINES

IF WE'RE GOING INTO OVERTIME, DOES THAT MEAN WE GET PAID TIME AND A HALF?

Like the greedy golfer, most people assume that the cash rewards for professional athletes are a source of motivation. However, as the bored basketball players suggest, one of the dangers of commercial sports is that they focus the attention of athletes on external rewards rather than the intrinsic satisfaction of involvement. When this happens, some players may become cynical about their participation.

until the play-offs at the end of the season. But we have no easy way to measure motivation, and even if we did, we have no way of comparing today's athletes with the athletes who played during the times when salaries were low. The only thing we can say at this point is that when the pleasure of playing a sport comes to be defined strictly in terms of money earned, the character of sports will change dramatically. In fact, it might change so much that spectators would not find it as interesting to watch.

Amateur Athletes in Commercial Sports

LEGAL STATUS OF AMATEUR ATHLETES

The primary goal of amateur athletes has always been simple—to train and compete. However, the achievement of that goal has not always been easy because amateur athletes have not had significant control over the conditions of their sport participation. Instead, control has rested in the hands of amateur sports organizations, such as the Amateur Athletic Union (AAU), the NCAA, the IOC, the USOC, and 40-plus International Sport Federations and 40-plus

NGBs within the USOC (for each of the amateur sports in the United States). Each of these organizations sets rules restricting the training and competition of amateur athletes. In many instances these rules have prevented athletes from participating when and where they choose.

Research done by the President's Commission on Olympic Sports (1975 to 1977) indicated that "an amateur athlete who has been denied the right to compete by any of these groups . . . has little chance of judicial rescue. No statute guarantees an amateur athlete the right to compete." To make matters worse for athletes, these groups have been difficult to challenge in court because they are private associations, and private sport associations have traditionally been immune to legal action, especially when they are international organizations that are not subject to the rulings of courts in any one country. This means that amateur athletes often have no legal basis to argue for their rights to train and compete under conditions of their own choosing. This powerlessness has affected them in a variety of ways.

The restrictions amateur athletes face in the United States are much too complex to explain in detail here. However, it is possible to use a hypothetical case to outline some of the everyday implications of those restrictions. Our case will be a talented young man attending an NCAA university on an athletic grant. As an NCAA athlete, he is limited to 4 seasons of eligibility, unless he is a Proposition 48 athlete, in which case he is limited to 3 seasons (see Chapter 15). Those 4 seasons must be completed within 5 years after starting college. If he decides to transfer to another NCAA school for academic reasons or because he and his coach don't get along, there would be a 1-year waiting period before he could resume intercollegiate sport participation. In all likelihood this would mean he would have to attend school during that year without an athletic grant. As an NCAA athlete his athletic grant always depends on whether his coach thinks he is contributing to the success of the team. If the coach says he is not contributing, his athletic grant can be taken away or he might simply be notified during the summer that his grant was not being renewed for the upcoming academic year. In fact, the grant could even be withdrawn because of an injury preventing participation—even if the injury was received while playing on the intercollegiate team. If our hypothetical athlete thinks any of this is unfair, he has no effective means of registering protest. If he wanted to try out for a special traveling basketball team during the summer, permission would have to be obtained from the NCAA. Or if there was an opportunity to participate in a special tournament in another country, permission would again be needed. In fact, if the NCAA did not recognize a team or tournament as legitimate, he could lose a full year of eligibility if he played. If he was lucky enough to make a U.S. national team (for the Pan American Games or the World University Games, for example) the NCAA would approve, but participation would then be governed by the rules of the NGB for basketball.

The point of this hypothetical case is to show that amateur athletes in the United States have little control over the conditions of their sport participation. They are limited in numerous ways by various amateur sport organizations. Concern about these limitations was one factor leading to the formation of the President's Commission on Olympic Sports in 1975. The report of the commission was instrumental in the passage of the Amateur Sports Act of 1978. The Amateur Sports Act did not guarantee amateur athletes any rights, but it did clarify the relationships between various sport organizations so that disagreements and bickering over control issues among organization executives would not interfere as much as before with participation opportunities for athletes. However, disagreements and bickering continue in the 1990s.

The concern for the legal status and rights of intercollegiate athletes led to the formation of the Center for Athletes' Rights and Education (CARE) in 1981. The purpose of CARE was to aggressively advocate the rights of high school and college athletes. However, their 3-year grant from the Fund for the Improvement of Postsecondary Education was cut after 1 year because they pushed too hard for changes in the legal status of athletes. Especially unpopular with powerful people in amateur sports was their attempt to organize intercollegiate athletes into unionlike groups on campuses around the country. The prospect of college athletes engaging in collective bargaining to gain rights and benefits was seen as a threat to the whole structure of big-time college sports. Athletes are often treated as employees by coaches and athletic departments, but many people feared that if athletes were legally defined as employees they would be subject to the same considerations granted to other workers in the United States. This made people in sports nervous and it still does.

In light of the powerlessness of most amateur athletes I think advocacy groups are greatly needed. Athletes need legal support so they are able to control their sport lives and have access to the rewards associated with those lives.

INCOME FOR AMATEUR ATHLETES Amateur athletes who play in revenue-producing sports are in a paradoxical position: they generate money through their performances, but they are restricted from sharing that money with sponsors and sport organizations. In fact, these athletes frequently receive no compensation at all for their involvement in events generating gate receipts and media rights payments.

Intercollegiate athletes playing big-time college football and basketball may generate hundreds of thousands of dollars for their schools, but the rules of the NCAA prohibit them from receiving anything more than renewable 1-year scholarships, and those scholarships can cover nothing more than tuition, room, board, and books. This means that a basketball player from a low-income family can bring fame and fortune to a school for 3 or 4 years and never get a legal penny for college expenses outside the classroom. He gets no money for laundry, dates, transportation around town, or travel to visit family during vacations; no money for non-sport-related medical or dental bills, phone calls home, clothes, typist fees for papers, school supplies, and so on. It is the unfairness of this situation that has led to many of the under-the-table cash payments to college athletes. These payments and other illegal gifts have become so commonplace that many leaders in college sports have suggested that the NCAA revise its policies on compensation for athletes; this will probably happen in the 1990s.

Outside of intercollegiate sports, athletes competing at the amateur level have traditionally been unable to capitalize on their commercial value. However, a few recent court decisions have forced changes in the rules of the IOC, USOC, and various NGBs so athletes now can put income from endorsements, prize money, and appearance fees into trusts administered by the NGBs in their sports. The athletes with money in these trust accounts can withdraw limited amounts every year for a cost-of-living allowance. Further withdrawals require approval from the NGB. The remainder

of the athletes' incomes is available when they retire from amateur competition. This paternalistic system is being challenged and revised as this book is being written. The fact that some professionals can play in "amateur" events such as the Olympics has made many of these rules obsolete and hypocritical.

Most amateur athletes make very little money. In fact, they usually go into debt trying to maintain training schedules from one competition to the next. However, there are a few popular track and field performers who do quite well when they combine money from the track and field circuit with endorsements, appearance fees, and consulting fees. Top performers with high name recognition can make good money from these sources. But the vast majority of amateur athletes *do not* share in the rewards received by their popular, record-setting counterparts.

CONCLUSION:

THE CHARACTERISTICS OF COMMERCIAL SPORTS

Commercial sports have become visible parts of many contemporary societies. This development is associated with urbanization, industrialization, improvements in transportation and communications technology, the availability of capital resources, and class relations. Furthermore, commercial sports have taken on a global character and they will continue to expand globally as economic interests extend across national boundaries and people develop a nonnationalistic viewpoint toward sports and athletes.

Commercialization has influenced the orientations of people involved in sports and the organizations through which sports are controlled, but it has not affected the actual formats and goals of most sports. Those connected with commercial sports tend to emphasize heroic orientations over aesthetic orientations. It seems that style and dramatic expression impress mass audiences, whereas fine distinctions in ability are often overlooked except by those who have an in-depth knowledge about a particular sport.

As control over the conditions of sport participation moves further away from athletes, the prospects for minimizing the negative effects of commercialization on sports become less and less likely. Prospects will improve only when athletes themselves become formally and integrally involved in the governance structures of both professional and amateur sport organizations. With the development of players' associations, this has occurred in professional sports. However, amateur athletes have been unable to form organizations enabling them to have a consistent influence on those who control their careers and the events in which they participate.

Commercial sports are unique businesses. The owners and sponsors of professional sports are successful business people who buy teams and stage events in the hope of making money while having fun and establishing good public images for themselves or for nonsport products. Investments in sport are often risky, but they have paid off very nicely for owners and sponsors who have been able to use monopolistic business practices to keep costs down and revenues up. Profits have also been enhanced by public support and subsidies. It is ironic that North American professional sports are often used as models of competition when, in fact, they have been built through a system of autocratic control and monopolistic organization. As Art Modell, owner of the Cleveland Browns, once said about himself and his fellow team owners in the NFL, "We're 28 Republicans who vote socialist." What he meant was that the NFL owners were all wealthy conservative businessmen who have eliminated competition in their sport businesses and used the socialist goal of "the common good" to increase their wealth and power.

The administration and control of amateur sports rests in the hands of numerous sports organizations. Although these organizations exist to provide support and guidance for amateur athletes, many of the people who run them have become primarily concerned with power and control. Power struggles in amateur sports have usually been won by those with the most money; athletes seldom have the resources needed to promote their own interests in these struggles. Of course, they could boycott events, but such a tactic would be risky because the general public is not aware of anything beyond superficial aspects of sport participation among top-level amateur athletes.

Commercialization also has turned athletes into entertainers; athletes generate revenues through their performances. With this change, issues related to rights and income become important. In professional sports the issue of players' rights has always been a major concern. As rights have increased, so have salaries. Salaries have also gone up with the increased gate receipts and television money in certain sports.

Not all athletes in professional sports make vast sums of money; many outside the NBA, NFL, NHL, and MLB have incomes that are surprisingly low. Income among amateur athletes is limited by the rules set by sport organizations. Intercollegiate athletes in the United States have what amounts to a maximum wage in the form of athletic scholarships. This has led to illegal under-the-table payments to some college athletes, especially to those from low-income backgrounds. In other amateur sports, athletes may receive direct cash payments for performances and endorsements, but there are some limits on how that money may be used.

When discussing commercial sports it is important to remember that the structure and dynamics of those sports vary from country to country. Outside North America commercial sports have not generated the massive amounts of revenues associated with a few North American sports. Profits for owners and sponsors in the United States and Canada have depended on working out supportive arrangements with the media and government. These arrangements have done much to shape the character of all sports in North America, professional and amateur.

It should be noted that the commercial model

of sport is not the only one that might provide athletes and spectators with enjoyable and satisfying experiences. However, because most people are unaware of alternative models, they simply continue to express a desire for what they get, and their desires are based on limited information manipulated by commercial and corporate interests (Sewart, 1986). Therefore changes will occur only when people connected with sports are able to develop visions for what sports could and should look like if they were not so overwhelmingly shaped by economic factors.

SUGGESTED READINGS

Beamish, R. 1988. The political economy of professional sport. In J. Harvey and H. Cantelon, eds. Not just a game. University of Ottawa Press, Ottawa, Ontario (*excellent critical analysis of professional sports in North America; good discussion of hockey*).

The Economist, 1992. A survey of the sports business. Special issue, July (*excellent data from the United States and western Europe; reprints available through The Economist Newspaper Group, Inc., Reprints Department, 111 W. 57th St., New York, NY 10019 or call 212-541-5730*).

Goldlust, J. 1987. Playing for keeps: sport, the media, and society. Longman Cheshire Pty. Limited, Melbourne, Australia. (*excellent historical analysis of the growth of contemporary commercial sport; good information on England, Australia, Canada, and the United States*).

Gruneau, R., and H. Cantelon, 1988. Capitalism, commercialism, and the Olympics. In J.O. Segrave and D. Chu, eds., The Olympic Games (pp. 345-364). Human Kinetics Books, Champaign, Ill. (*analysis of the Los Angeles Games showing that they represent a fully developed expression of how sports have been integrally linked to economic issues and considerations through the twentieth century*).

Hargreaves, J. 1986. Sport, culture and power. St. Martin's Press, New York. (*analysis of ties between sport and power in Britain; first seven chapters focus on class relations as a context for the social construction of sports*).

Klatell, D.A., and N. Marcus, 1988. Sports for sale: television, money, and the fans. Oxford University Press, New York. (*good overview of economic issues from a communication perspective; discussion of economic factors related to television coverage of sport*).

Lasch, C. 1977. The corruption of sports. New York Review of Books 24:24-30 (*insightful analysis of how spectators can change the structure, content, and organization of sports*).

Maguire, J. 1990. More than a sporting touchdown: the making of American football in England 1982-1990. Sociology of Sport Journal 7(3): 213-237 (*as part of a larger analysis, attention is paid to marketing strategies of the NFL, Anheuser Busch, and a British television company as they promote football in England*).

Mandle, J.R., and J.D. Mandle, 1988. Grass roots commitment: basketball and society in Trinidad and Tobago. Caribbean Books, Parkersburg, Ia. (*an economist and sociologist do a qualitative study of how the organization and playing of basketball is tied to social relationships; heavy focus on the commercialization of basketball*).

Purdy, D. 1988. For whom sport tolls: players, owners, and fans. The World & I 3(10):573-587 (*critique of economic issues related to professional sports in North America*).

Sage, G.H. 1990. Power and ideology in American sport. Human Kinetics Books, Champaign, Ill. (*Chs. 5-8 provide a good overview of commercialization and sports*).

Staudohar, P.D. 1986. The sports industry and collective bargaining. ILR Press, Cornell University, Ithaca, New York (*detailed information on the employment practices of professional sports; contracts, drafts, free agency, trades, strikes, and substance abuse*).

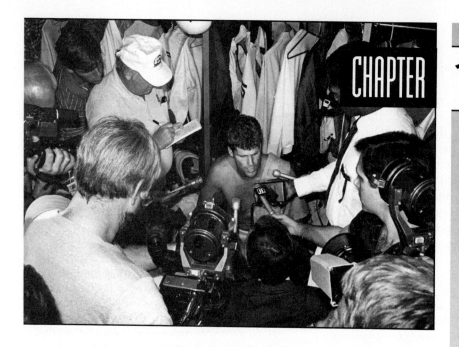

CHAPTER 13

SPORTS AND THE MEDIA

Could they survive without each other?

Media today saturate our daily lives . . . [they serve] as the central nervous system of modern society. . . . Popular media today operate on a scale of inclusiveness unimaginable in earlier generations. . . . [They create] the environment where identities are formed.

Michael Real, SUPER MEDIA (1989, pp. 13-15)

Any sportswriter who thinks the world is no bigger than the outfield fence is not only a bad citizen of the world but also a lousy sportswriter.

Red Smith, Sportswriter (undated)

It's not just games you're watching. It's soap operas, complete with story lines and plots and plot twists. And good guys and villains, heroes and underdogs. And all this gets scripted into cliffhanger morality plays. . . . And you get all caught up in this until you begin to believe it really matters.

Kerry Temple, Editor, Notre Dame Magazine (1992)

Sport has become the shill of television. . . . Instead of harnessing the good of television for the good of sport, sport has been swept up by it. The irony is that the custodians of sport think . . . they have made television pay . . . when actually they have just been bought off.

John Underwood, Sports Illustrated writer (1984)

The media, including newspapers, magazines, books, movies, and television, pervade human culture (Real, 1989). Although people incorporate the media into their lives in different ways, what we read, hear, and see in the media constitute important parts of our experience. Media content structures our experiences and therefore influences how we think about the world, how we evaluate social events, and what we envision for the future; it influences our ideas about everything from personal relationships and consumer products to political candidates and international affairs (Real, 1989). This does not mean we are slaves to the media or that we are passively duped by those who control the media. But our lives and our social worlds are clearly informed by media content, and, if the media didn't exist, out lives would be different than they are today.

Sports and the media have become interconnected parts of our lives. Sports programming has become an important segment of media content, and many sports have become dependent on the media for publicity and revenues. In light of these interconnections, this chapter will consider four general questions:

1. What are the characteristics of the media in today's societies?
2. What are the ways in which sports and the media have become interconnected?
3. What images and messages are emphasized in the media coverage of sports in North America?
4. What are the characteristics of the profession of sports journalism in both the print and broadcast media?

UNIQUE FEATURES OF THE MEDIA

Considered by themselves, the media perform three major functions in society. They (1) inform us about events and people, (2) interpret what is going on in the world, and (3) entertain us in various ways. The media are unique in that they are bridges between us and the rest of the world. As bridges, they connect us with information, experiences, and people that would not usually be a part of our everyday lives. But they also direct our attention to specific items of information, specific types of experiences and people. In general, the media expose us to limited and selected ideas and perspectives.

The reality brought to us through the media—what we read, hear, and see—is always edited and "re-presented" by those who control them—the producers, editors, program directors, technicians, writers, commentators, and sponsors. These people try to provide information, interpretation, and entertainment, but their decisions on how to do this are based on their interests in five things: (1) making profits, (2) shaping values, (3) providing a public service, (4) building their own reputations, and (5) expressing themselves in artistic form. For example, in countries where most of the media are privately owned and operated, the dominant interest is profit making. This is not the only interest, but it is usually the most influential. In countries where the media are controlled and operated by state officials, dominant interests are to shape values and provide a public service.

Although decisions about media content are influenced by one or more of these interests, they are also influenced by power relations in society as a whole. Those who make media content decisions act as "filters" as they select the images and messages to be re-presented through the media. In the filtering process they tend to give preference to images and messages consistent with dominant ideologies in the society as a whole. This is how the media are tied to power relations and why the media often serve the interests of those who have power and influence in society. Of course, there are exceptions to this, but whenever media content challenges dominant ideologies, those responsible for that content may have their credibility and trustworthiness scrutinized. This is not a terrible problem unless it causes financial problems (in the case of privately owned media), or unless it causes the state to further regulate media operations (in the case of state supported media).

Therefore those who control media content usually think carefully about presenting images and messages that challenge the interests of those who have power and influence in society.

This does not mean that we in media audiences are forced to read, hear, and see things we are not interested in nor that those who control the media ignore what we think. But it does mean that we seldom have direct control over the content of what we read, listen to, and see in the media. The media "re-present" to us an edited version of information, interpretation, and entertainment that media people think we want to consume. For example, in the case of sport, those controlling the media not only select which sports and which events will be covered, but they also decide what will be emphasized in the coverage. When they do this, they help construct the overall frameworks that we in media audiences use to define and explain sports in our lives (Clarke and Clarke, 1982).

Those of us who have grown up with radio and television seldom think about media content in this way. For example, we tend to forget that when we watch sports on television the images and messages we see and hear have been carefully designed to heighten the dramatic content of the event and emphasize dominant ideologies in the society as a whole.* The pregame analysis, the camera coverage, the camera angles, the close-ups, the slow-motion shots, the attention given to particular athletes, the announcer's play-by-play descriptions, the color commentary, the quotes from athletes, and the postgame summary and analysis are all presented to entertain the media audience and keep the broadcast sponsors happy. In the United States, for example, the emphasis in media coverage of sports is on action, competition, aggression, individual heroism, teamwork, and the importance of final scores as indicators of success (Kinkema and Harris, 1992). But the emphasis comes in a form that makes it seem as if the "real" game is the one on television, not the one seen in the stadium (Temple, 1992). In other words, television has constructed sports and spectator experiences in important ways. It's happened so smoothly that most people think that when they watch a game on television they are experiencing sports in a "natural" form!

Even though the media coverage of sports is carefully edited and "re-presented" in an entertainment package, most of us believe that when we see a sport event on television we are seeing it "the way it is." We also think that when we hear the commentary, the commentators are "telling it like it is." We don't usually think that what we are seeing and hearing is a series of images and messages chosen for particular reasons and grounded in the social worlds of those producing the event, controlling the images, and making the commentary. Of course, television coverage gives us only one set of *many* possible sets of images and messages related to a sport event; there are a wide array of images and messages that we do *not* get. For example, if we went to the event in person, we would see something quite different than the images "re-presented" on television, and we would come up with our own descriptions and interpretations that might be completely unrelated to those provided by media commentators.

Too often we watch sports on television without thinking about *why* we are seeing what is on our screens or *why* we are hearing certain things said by the commentators. But whether we are aware of it or not, our experiences as television spectators are heavily influenced by the decisions of those who control the media, and their decisions are influenced by social, political, and economic factors—including dominant ideologies related to gender, race, and class (see Chapters 9 to 11). This will be discussed later in the chapter, but first I will examine the relationship between sports and the media, and outline how each has influenced the other. My major frame of reference in the next section will be North America, although examples from other parts of the world will be used whenever possible.

---

*See Bryant et al., 1977; Gruneau, 1989a, 1989b; Hargreaves, 1986; Hesling, 1986; Real, 1989; Wenner, 1989.

SPORTS AND THE MEDIA: A TWO-WAY RELATIONSHIP

The commercialization of sports and the media are closely related topics in the sociology of sport. In fact, the media intensify and extend the process and consequences of commercialization. For this reason, much attention has been given to how sports have been influenced by the media, and little attention has been given to how the media have been influenced by sports. But there is actually a reciprocal relationship between these two important spheres of life: both have influenced each other, and each has grown to depend on the other for its popularity and commercial success.

Do Sports Depend on the Media?

The existence of sports does not depend on the media. However, the success of sports as commercial entertainment does depend on the media. People played sports long before the newspaper sports section and television were around to announce, report, and "re-present" the events. Even now, people participate in a variety of sports receiving no media coverage. When sports exist just for the participants, there is no urgent need to advertise games, publicize results, and interpret what happened. The players already know these things, and they are the only ones who matter. It is only when sports become commercial entertainment that they depend on the media.

Sportswriter Leonard Koppett (1981) describes sports as unique forms of entertainment. Unlike other forms, sports require the media to provide a combination of coverage *and* news. People attend plays, concerts, and movies and engage in many other leisure activities without needing regular up-to-the-minute media coverage to enjoy their attachment to these activities. However, with sports this coverage is very important. When a stage play is over, it's over—except for a review after opening night and the personal conversations of those who attended the play. But when a sports event is over, many people are interested in discussing statistics, important plays, records, standings, the overall performances of players and teams, upcoming games or matches, the importance of the game or match in terms of the season as a whole, the post-season, the next season, and so on. The media are important vehicles for these discussions.

Without media coverage, the popularity of many commercial spectator sports would be seriously limited. Information about events generates interest, and interest generates ticket sales. After games or matches have been played, the scores become news items, and the interpretations of action become entertainment for fans, regardless of whether they attended the event in person or not. This seems to be the case from one culture to another—for bullfights in Mexico, hockey games in Canada, soccer matches Russia, and sumo wrestling bouts in Japan.

Sports promoters and team owners, especially in countries with market economies, are well aware of the need for media coverage for sports. Therefore they often go out of their way to accommodate reporters, commentators, and photographers (Koppett, 1981). Media personnel are often given comfortable seats in press boxes, special access to the fields of play and the players' locker rooms, special summaries of statistics and player information, and special play-by-play information on what is happening during events. Providing these services costs money, but it guarantees media coverage, and it encourages those covering the events to be supportive and sympathetic in what they write and say.

Although all commercial spectator sports depend on the media, some of them have a special dependence on television. For example, in North America, television is different from the other media in that it actually provides a direct source of revenues for certain sports. Unlike other media organizations, the television companies pay considerable amounts of money for broadcasting rights. These "rights fees" paid by television companies provide sports with relatively predictable sources of income. Once contracts are signed, radio and television money can be counted on regardless of bad weather, injuries to key players, and other factors that often interfere with ticket sales.

Television revenues also have a much greater growth potential than revenues from gate receipts. Only so many tickets can be sold to an event, and tickets can cost only so much without turning people off. But television audiences can include literally billions of viewers now that satellite technology can transmit signals to most locations around the globe. This is partly why the value of television rights has increased at phenomenal rates since the early 1970s. Television rights fees have not only made commercial sports more profitable for promoters and team owners but they have increased the attractiveness of sports as vehicles for advertising products nationally and internationally. They have also increased the potential incomes of athletes and turned some athletes into national and international celebrities, who have sometimes been able to use their celebrity status to make money on product endorsements.

There is no question that some sports have become very dependent on television for revenues and publicity. The NFL, for example, brings in over 60% of its revenues from television contracts. But the benefits of television seldom come without strings attached. Accommodating the interests of commercial television has required numerous changes in the ways sports are packaged, scheduled, and presented. Some of these changes include the following:

- The schedules and starting times for many sports events have been altered to fit the programming needs of television.
- Halftime periods in certain sports have been shortened so television audiences will be more likely to stay tuned to events.
- Managers in major league baseball have been restricted in the number of times they can go out to the field to talk strategy with their players.
- Prearranged schedules of time-outs have been added to football, basketball, and

hockey games to make time for commercials.

Many other changes have been associated with television coverage but are not entirely the results of television influence. For example, college football teams added an eleventh game to their schedules, and professional teams extended their seasons and the number of games played. But these changes would have occurred even if television didn't exist. Commercial sports would have added extra games simply to increase gate receipts. Extra games do make television contracts more lucrative, but the economic reasons for adding games include more than just the sale of television rights. The same thing is true for the additions of sudden-death overtime periods in some sports, the tiebreaker scoring method in tennis, and the addition of medal play in golf. Each of these changes is grounded in general commercial interests that exist apart from television coverage alone. But television adds to the urgency and importance of these changes.

Television expands the commercial interests that are already an inherent part of spectator sports in many societies. Although some changes in sports are related to meeting the requirements of television coverage, the real reason for most changes over the past 3 decades has been the desire to produce more marketable entertainment for all spectators and a more attractive commercial package for sponsors and advertisers. Furthermore, these changes have not been made unwillingly in most cases. The trade-offs have usually been attractive for both players and sponsors. In fact, many of the sports not currently receiving television coverage would gladly make changes in the way their events are packaged, scheduled, and presented if they could reap the rewards associated with television contracts.

When sports and the media are discussed, many people wonder if dependence on the media, especially dependence on television, might corrupt sports. Some people argue that this has already happened and that television is the root

"The TV network people said that the public would never watch professional swimming unless we made it more exciting."

of all evil in sports (Rader, 1984). However, this argument fails to take into account the following two things:

1. *Sports are not primarily shaped by the media in general or by television in particular.* The idea that television has by itself somehow transformed sports does not hold up under careful examination (Gruneau, 1989a). Sports are social constructions and, as such, they have been gradually created through interaction among athletes, facility directors, sport team owners, event promoters, media representatives, sponsors, advertisers, agents, and spectators who have diverse interests and backgrounds. The dynamics of these interactions have been grounded in power relations and shaped by the resources held by different people at different times. Of course, not everyone has equal influence over changes occurring in sports, but media interests are not the only factors producing changes in sports or in the relationship between sports and media. It is unrealistic to think that media people have been able to shape sports to fit their interests alone.

2. *The media, including television, do not operate in a political and economic vacuum.* The concerns of those connected with sports and the relationships they have with one another are heavily influenced by the social, political, and economic contexts in which they live. For example, the media in both the United States and Canada have been and continue to be regulated by various government agencies and policies; therefore they must negotiate contracts with teams and leagues under certain legal constraints. Economic factors also constrain the media by setting limits on the value of sponsorships and advertising time, and by shaping the climate in which types of programming, such as pay-per-view sports, might be profitable. Finally, the media are also constrained by social factors that inform people's decisions on whether they will read about, listen to, or watch sports.

These two factors raise serious questions about whether the media corrupts sports. There are certainly important connections between these two spheres of life, but those connections are grounded in complex sets of social relationships. It is those relationships that must be understood if the media's impact on sport is to be understood. In other words, the conclusion that the media corrupt sports is based on an incomplete understanding of how the social world works and how sports are connected with social relations in society.

In summary, noncommercial sports are neither dependent on the media nor likely to be changed or "corrupted" by the media. *Commercial sports,* on the other hand, are dependent on the media for their success as entertainment. For some commercial sports, the dependence on television is especially strong, but media people alone have not determined how sports are planned, packaged, presented, and played. The coverage of media sports emerges from relationships between media representatives and many others connected with sports, and those relationships are formed within a social, political, and economic context influencing the interest and the power of everyone involved.

Do the Media Depend on Sports?

Media content generally encompasses much more than sports. This is certainly true for magazines, books, movies, and radio, although it is less true for newspapers and television. Most magazines devote little or no attention to sports coverage, and there are only a few successful sports magazines. Neither the book publishing nor movie industries depend on sports; in fact, there have been very few successful books or movies about sports. Most radio stations give coverage to sports only in their news segments, although football, baseball, and men's basketball games may be broadcast on a local radio station when local teams are playing. "Talk radio" stations in some communities have sports talk programs. But unlike magazines, books, movies, and radio, some newspapers and television companies at least partially depend on sports for their commercial success. This is especially true in the United States. Let's look at some examples.

NEWSPAPERS Newspaper coverage of sports began around the turn of the century in the United States. In a typical big city paper at that time, the sports page consisted of only a few notices about upcoming activities, a short story or two about races or college games, and possibly some scores involving local teams. By the late 1920s the sports page had grown into the sports section, and it resembled the sports sections of today's newspapers (Lever and Wheeler, 1993).

In a detailed study of the *Chicago Tribune* between 1900 and 1975, Janet Lever and Stan Wheeler (1984) found that sports coverage became an increasingly significant part of the paper during those years (Table 13-1). Sports coverage made up 9% of the total newsprint (minus advertisements) in 1900 and 17% in 1975. But even more significantly, the ratio of sports coverage to general news coverage (excluding special features, comics, and so on) grew from 14%

Table 13-1 The increasing importance of the sports section in *The Chicago Tribune*, 1900-1975

Year	Percentage of newsprint given to sport*	Ratio of sport news to other news†
1900	9%	.14 (or about 1:7)
1925	12%	.28 (or about 2:7)
1950	15%	.32 (or about 1:3)
1975	17%	.52 (or about 1:2)

Data from Lever and Wheeler (1984).
*Excludes advertising space.
†Includes local, national, and international news items: does not include society pages, arts and leisure, photo pages, comics, or business sections.

Big city newspapers in the U.S. depend on sports sections to generate advertising and circulation revenues, but an effort to establish a national daily sports newspaper failed in 1991, after less than 17 months of publication. (Wide World Photos, Inc.)

in 1900 to slightly over 50% in 1975. Similar patterns have existed in other North American newspapers. In *USA Today*, the only national daily newspaper in the United States (apart from the Wall Street Journal), sports coverage accounts for 25% of the entire paper, and about 50% of daily news items.

In most major North American papers more daily coverage is given to sports than any other single topic of interest, including business or politics. The sports section is the most widely read section of the paper, and according to some estimates it accounts for about 30% of the total circulation for big city newspapers (Greendorfer, 1983; Smith and Blackman, 1978). In other words, if the sports section were eliminated, newspaper sales would go down 30%—along with the advertising revenues tied to circulation figures. This means many newspapers depend on sports for advertising revenues as well as general subscriptions and sales.

Additionally, the sports section attracts advertisers who might not put ads in other sections of the paper. Advertisers know that if they want to reach young to middle-aged males with average or above average incomes, they should place their ads in the sports section. This is an attractive prospect for businesses that sell tires, auto-

mobile supplies, new cars, car leases, airline tickets for business travelers, alcoholic beverages, power tools, building supplies, and sporting goods. Ads for these items generate considerable income for newspapers.

TELEVISION COMPANIES Some television companies in North America have also developed a dependence on sports. For example, sports events are a major part of the programming schedules of national network stations and cable stations, and they account for a sizable proportion of the dollars made on the sales of commercial time (over 20% of the advertising revenues sold by the networks). Many cable stations, including ESPN, TNT, TBS, and Prime Sports Channel Networks (an alliance of nearly 30 local and regional sports channels), have used sports programming to attract subscribers from particular segments of the viewing public. Overall, it has gotten to the point that people in North America can watch over 7500 hours of sport programs every year, if they have the time, interest, and cable hook-ups!

An attractive feature of sports programming for the networks (ABC, CBS, NBC), is that it can be scheduled on Saturday and Sunday afternoons—the slowest times of the week for television viewing. This is one of the reasons why many of the new corporate owners of professional sport teams in the United States also own television broadcasting companies; they see the interests of both as being interconnected. Of course, television executives recognize that regular season games do not usually receive high ratings compared to most prime time weeknight shows. But they also know the games are the most popular weekend television programs, especially among viewers who may not watch much television at other times during the week. This means the networks are able to sell advertising time at relatively high rates during what would normally be "dead time" for programming.

The networks also use sports programming to attract particular types of commercial sponsors who might take their business elsewhere if television stations did not cover certain sports. For example, games in the major team sports, especially college and professional football, are ideal for promoting the sales of beer, life insurance, trucks and cars, computers, investment services, credit cards, and air travel. The people in the advertising departments of major corporations realize these games attract male viewers. They also realize that most business travelers are men and that many men make family decisions on the purchases of beer, cars, computers, investments, and life insurance. Finally, they may also be interested in associating their product or service with the culturally positive image of sport. This is especially important for a product such as beer that has a dubious image in a country where some people have strong prohibitionist sentiments.

Golf and tennis are special cases for television programming. These sports attract few viewers and the ratings are exceptionally low. However, the audience for these sports is attractive to certain advertisers. It is made up of people from the highest income groups in American society, including many professionals and business executives. This is why television coverage of golf and tennis is sponsored by companies selling luxury cars and high-priced sports cars, business and personal computers, imported beers, investment opportunities with brokers and consultants, and trips to exclusive vacation areas. This is also the major reason why the networks continue to carry these programs. Few people watch them, but they generate revenues from sponsors with special products to sell to high-income consumers.

Between 1980 and the mid-1990s television companies paid rapidly increasing amounts of money for the rights to televise certain sports. Here are some examples:

- CBS paid $1.06 billion to cover major league baseball from 1990 to 1994; and ESPN paid $400 million to televise certain games not televised on CBS. NBC and ABC will begin in 1994 an advertising revenue sharing deal with major league baseball; the deal involves no guaranteed rights fees, and it is expected to bring major league baseball about half of what it received from CBS through the 1993 season.
- ABC, CBS, and NBC paid the NFL $2.74 billion for the rights to televise games from 1990 through 1994; for the same period the NFL also received $445 million from ESPN and $445 million from TNT.
- NBC, TBS, and TNT paid the NBA $875 million for a 4-year television contract ending in 1995. NBC extended its part of the deal with the NBA by agreeing to pay $750 million for the right to cover NBA games from 1993 through the 1997-1998 season.
- CBS paid $1 billion to televise NCAA men's basketball tournament games over 7 seasons (ending in 1998), ABC paid $210

million to cover college football from 1991 to 1996, and NBC gave the University of Notre Dame $35 million for the right to televise its football games from 1991 through 1995.

- Sports Channel America paid the NHL $51 million for a 4-year deal that ended in 1994.
- NBC paid $401 million for the rights to the Barcelona Olympic Games, CBS paid $300 million for the 1994 Winter Games in Lille-hammer, and the Atlanta Games may attract up to $800 million for European and U.S. broadcasting rights.

These amounts clearly show that television companies want to include sports in their programming lineups and they think sports will make them money. They realize that the Olympics have become the biggest world television event in human history, that over half of the top 30 television programs in history are Super Bowls, that the cost of advertising on the top sport events is generally much higher than it is for other types of programs ($1.8 million per minute in the 1994 Super Bowl), that sports involve minimal production costs, and that sports have a reasonably predictable success rate. However, some of this may be changing as we move through the 1990s. NBC made about $80 million on the 1988 Seoul Olympics, but it lost nearly $170 million on the Barcelona Olympics (partly because of a failed pay-per-view scheme arranged with Cablevision Systems). CBS could lose $300 million on its 4-year baseball contract, and the networks could lose $450 million on their 1990-94 football contract.

It is clear that as the amount of television sports programming has gone up, ratings have gone down. More people are tuning in to sports events, but there are many more events to choose from, and ratings have declined between 20% and 30% for many individual sports programs. This means that as we move toward the end of the century, rights fees may level off—or even decline in some cases—and there will be a gradual move toward pay-per-view (PPV) sports programming. In 1993 only about 20 million homes were equipped to receive PPV programs,

but this number will increase rapidly during the rest of the decade. As it does, so will the number of PPV sports events. Television companies know that PPV sports has the potential to be a big money maker, but they also know it must be introduced cautiously and selectively. But we can count on more sports events being available only through PPV.

Regular sports programming will continue at current levels. Even though it occasionally loses money, it provides opportunities for the networks to promote their other programs and boost ratings during the rest of the week. It also serves a public relations function by enhancing the image of television among people who may watch very few programs other than sports.

Finally, as we think about the dependence of television on sports in the United States, it is important to remember that Americans are not the only people who watch sports on television. In fact, some other countries have a higher proportion of television programming devoted to sports than does United States. This is illustrated in Table 13-2. But remember, the total hours devoted to sports coverage on *all* channels is highest in the United States.

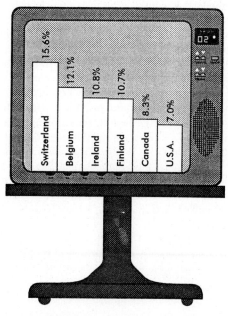

Table 13-2 Percentage of *all* television programs devoted to sports events in six countries. (Source: *USA Today*, 1993)

REFLECT ON SPORT

Television And The Olympic Games
A Marriage of Mutual Interest

The Olympics provide a good example of the interdependence between sports and television. Beginning with the 1972 Olympic Games in Munich, both the International Olympic Committee (IOC) and the television networks in the United States have mutually benefitted from the coverage of the Olympic Games, and the relationship between the IOC and the networks has not led to any significant changes in the games themselves (Lucas and Real, 1984). Let's look at the evidence.

First, *money from the sale of television rights has established the legitimacy and power of the IOC and it has fueled the organization and growth of the Olympic movement around the world.* The IOC receives one third of the total amount paid for television rights to the games. The remaining two thirds go to the Olympic Organizing Committee (OOC) in the host city. The amount received by the IOC is then divided into thirds with one share going to the International Federations for each of the Olympic sports, a second share going to promote unity between the National Olympic Committees (NOC), and a third share being kept by the IOC for its own administration. In 1972 (Munich) the IOC split $6 million into thirds; in 1976 (Montreal) it was $7 million; in 1980 (Moscow) it was $15 million; in 1984 (Los Angeles) it was over $60 million, in 1988 (Seoul) it was about $70 million, in 1992 (Barcelona) it was about $170 million, and in Atlanta, it may be as high as

$250 million. These figures clearly indicate that the IOC depends on television for much of its power and legitimacy (Lucas and Real, 1984).

Second, *television networks in the United States have each benefitted from their coverage of the Olympic Games.* Benefits have come in the form of advertising revenues and programming content. The Summer Olympic Games occur in the summer when TV viewing rates are low; summer reruns don't get good ratings. This means that televising the games can boost a network's ratings and give the network a stage for promoting its new fall lineup of shows. The winter games are also valuable to a network because they are scheduled during the "February sweeps" when crucial Nielsen ratings are compiled and used to compute advertising rates. Therefore even if a network breaks even or loses money on Olympic coverage, there are considerable carryover benefits associated with presenting either the summer or winter games. ABC enjoyed these benefits after its coverage of the 1976 Montreal games. Gross profits went from $17 million in 1975 to $110 million in 1977. This is the major reason why the bidding levels have escalated to such high amounts through the 1980s and 1990s (see p. 339). Network executives know that covering the Olympics can boost profits through the year and even carry over into following years (Lucas and Real, 1984).

REFLECT ON | SPORT

Third, *changes in the Olympic Games themselves have been influenced—but not dictated—by television*. The relationship between the IOC and television networks has not led to *major* changes in the location and dates of the games, the scheduling of events during the games, the rules of Olympic competition, or the Olympic Charter itself. However, minor changes have occurred. For example, in 1978 the IOC made the summer games a 16-day event rather than a 15-day event so there would be an extra prime-time weekend day of competition to generate advertising revenues. The dates for the 1988 winter games in Calgary were shifted so that the host network could benefit from the February Nielsen ratings period. These changes, combined with other factors, have led to dramatic increases in the money paid to televise the Olympics.

Game locations are very important to U.S. television networks. When the Olympics are hosted in places where events can be televised live during prime-time viewing hours in the United States, the potential for advertising revenues goes up. This drives up bids from the networks, and it has probably been a factor contributing to the selection of locations such as Mexico City, Montreal, Lake Placid, Los Angeles, Calgary, and Atlanta through eight Olympiads since 1968. Before television was a source of big money for the Olympics only 2 out of 15 summer games were held in the Western hemisphere (1904 in St. Louis and 1932 in Los Angeles).

The scheduling of events during the games has been influenced occasionally by television interests, but the extent of this influence has not been significant up to now. Also, there have been only minor changes in the rules for events; for example, athletes are required to wear visibly displayed numerals on their uniforms so they can be identified by television commentators.

Finally, the Olympic Charter has undergone only one change to accommodate television: it now states that the IOC can award exclusive broadcast rights to a single television company and that no other companies can show any film coverage of an event until after the end of the broadcast day in which the event occurred.

Overall, it seems that because the Olympic Games are the only international spectacle in the world today, they have been able to resist major changes based on the interests of television. Therefore the relationship between the Olympics and television appears to be a marriage of mutual interests. Television has promoted the growth of the IOC and the Olympic movement, and the IOC has provided television a chance to cover the only truly international event that regularly attracts world attention. The Olympics and television have a symbiotic relationship. But television is a powerful economic force, and what will happen in the future may favor the interests of television over the interests of the Olympic Games. As in all marriages, it is a constant struggle to maintain a true balance of interests over the long run.

Conclusion: A Symbiotic Relationship

When discussing the relationship between sports and the media, there is a tendency to emphasize the impact of the media on sports. There is no question that this impact has been significant in the case of commercial spectator sports, although noncommercial sports continue to exist without dependence on the media. Receiving less attention has been the effect of sports on the media. The media cover much more than sports, but an analysis of newspapers and television in North America shows that they have come to depend on sports nearly as much as sports depend on them.

Newspapers devote considerable space to the coverage of sports, and television uses sport events to fill its programming needs on weekends and holidays. People who read papers and watch television have come to expect this coverage. Furthermore, it attracts those who may not normally buy newspapers or turn on their televisions. Finally, the coverage of sports links both newspapers and television to an increasingly popular sphere of life in contemporary society. This link is a crucial part of their commercial success.

The interdependence of sports and the media has led Sabo and Runfola (1980) to conclude the following:

> A symbiosis has developed between sports and the mass media. Sports are used to promote newspaper sales, to sell advertising space, and to win lucrative contracts for TV and radio time. In turn, the media help to sell spectator sports and attendant sports-related consumer products to the public.

The nature of this symbiosis varies depending on whether the media are publicly or privately owned. But the interdependence and reciprocal influence is strong in all cases (Claeys and Van Pelt, 1986; Greendorfer, 1983). Both sports and the media could live without one another, but they have come to depend on one another for their success and popularity in contemporary society.

IMAGES AND MESSAGES IN MEDIA SPORTS

When sports are "mediated," they are "re-presented" to readers, listeners, and viewers through selected images and messages. These images and messages are grounded in the ideas and ideologies of the people who control the media. This means that sports coverage is produced and constructed to fit media people's ideas about how the world works and what media audiences want to read, hear, and see.

A growing number of sociologists are interested in digging into these images and messages to identify the ideas or themes upon which they are based. As they do their digging, sociologists assume that mediated sports are symbolic constructions, much like Rambo and Rocky films, television soap operas, and Walt Disney cartoons are symbolic constructions (Duncan, 1989). In other words, a telecast of a football game is a representation of certain people's ideas about football, social life, human beings, what is important in the world, and what the viewing audience wants to see and hear. Although sociologists realize that different people interpret media images and messages in different ways, they also realize that many people use mediated sports as reference points as they form, revise, and extend their ideas about sports, social life, and social relations.

Because media sports have become a part of everyday experience in today's societies, it is important to consider the following questions:

1. How are sports constructed in the media?
2. What general ideas or themes underlie the images and messages "re-presented" in media sports?
3. Does reading about, listening to, and viewing sports have an effect on other types of behavior, such as active sport participation, attendance at sport events, and gambling on sports?

The Media Construction of Sports

The media provide selective versions of sports. In societies where media are privately

"Remember, it's not whether we win or lose, but how much money we can get for selling our games to cablevision." (The survival of big-time intercollegiate sports is increasingly dependent on the sale of broadcasting rights to television companies.)

owned and depend on financial profits, sports events are selected for coverage on the basis of their entertainment value. The images and messages emphasized in that coverage are edited so they fit with the perceived interests of both audience and sponsors. Research suggests that sports are re-presented to media audiences in the United States to emphasize action, competition, final scores, statistics, records, elite levels of performance, aggression, heroic action, and athletes' emotions and personalities (Hargreaves, 1986; Kinkema and Harris, 1992).

The sports sections of American newspapers give scores, statistics, descriptions of "big plays" and individual heroics, and behind-the-scenes stories about events and athletes; newspaper photos generally capture action or emotion.

American television coverage focuses on the ball and/or the athlete who is currently winning the game, match, meet, or race. Commentators interpret the event, discuss heroic actions and heroic athletes, and emphasize toughness, aggression, and achievement in the form of records, scores, and wins. Of course, there are some important differences between the print and broadcast media when it comes to sport coverage. Table 13-3 summarizes some of these differences.

The media have also been known to "hype" sports by exaggerating the spectacular, inventing rivalries that don't exist, and manufacturing reasons for why events are important and why they should be read about, listened to, or viewed. The media also emphasize *elite* sport competition. For example, Lever and Wheeler's

Table 13-3 Differences between the print and broadcast media: the case of sports coverage*

Print media	Broadcast media
• Emphasize news, analysis, and special features.	• Emphasize entertainment in the form of action and drama.
• Offer summaries of events that have already occurred.	• Offer play-by-play descriptions and interpretations.
• Provide broad scope of tangible information.	• Provide immediacy in coverage of on-the-spot action.
• Success depends on maintaining credibility.	• Success depends on generating hype.
• Coverage is diversified and aimed at a set of separate and distinctive audiences.	• Coverage is focused and aimed at a large single audience at a particular point in time.
• Content is more likely to provide criticism of sports and sport personalities.	• Content is more likely to provide support for sports and sport personalities.

*This comparison is based on material in Leonard Koppett: *Sports illusion, sports reality* (1981).

Table 13-4 The coverage of elite sports in *The Chicago Tribune*, 1900-1975

| Year | Percentage of stories in each sport devoted to professional athletes | | | |
	Football	Basketball	Baseball	Golf
1900	0.0	0.0	86.8	25.5
1925	5.6	5.7	87.2	30.1
1950	41.2	20.2	89.2	43.3
1975	53.5	61.3	98.4	70.1

From Lever, J., and S. Wheeler, 1984. *The Chicago Tribune* sports page, 1900-1975. Sociology of Sport Journal 1(4):299-313.

study (1984) showed that the *Chicago Tribune* has, over the years, increased its coverage of professional sports and decreased its coverage of amateur sports, including high school and college sports (Table 13-4). This is also the case with other big city newspapers. Television has always focused attention on professional sports, with some coverage given to selected big-time intercollegiate sports for men. This exaggerated coverage of professional sports ultimately emphasizes the importance of winning and heroic actions over other factors associated with sport participation (Gelinas and Theberge, 1986; Goldstein and Bredemeier, 1977). The result is

that media audiences get slanted versions of sports.

Even though mediated sports are slanted, most people do not give much thought to how and why sports are re-presented the way they are. In fact, most people just enjoy what they read, listen to, and view. They don't ask critical questions. This leads sociologists to ask if people's ideas about sport itself are constructed by mediated sports. Do people use media sports to define what sports are, what they should be, how sports should be included in their lives, and how they should evaluate themselves when they participate in sports? These questions need further examination, but there are good reasons to believe that people's ideas about sports are heavily informed by the images and messages represented in mediated sports. Furthermore, the themes underlying these images and messages can also inform our ideas about social relations and social life in general.

Themes Underlying Images and Messages

SUCCESS THEMES The images and messages re-presented in mediated sports emphasize selected themes that identify important issues and particular ways of looking at and interpreting the world. When people read about, listen to, and view sports, these themes may inform their own ideas about the world. For example, television broadcasts of sports in the United States emphasize success through competition, hard work, assertiveness, dominance, and obedience to authority. The idea that success can also be based on empathy, autonomy, personal growth, cooperation, compromise, progressive changes, or the achievement of equality and intrinsic personal satisfaction gets little or no attention (Bindman, 1982; Prisuta, 1979).

The "success theme" underlying images and messages in American media sports was highlighted in Joan Chandler's (1983) comparison of sports commentary in the United States and England. She noted that in American commentaries there was a heavy emphasis on competition, dominance, and final scores. By comparison, the sports commentaries in England downplayed competition, winning, and final scores. In explaining these differences, Chandler said that,

> [In Britain] where mobility is usually achieved by sponsorship, the importance of competition in all facets of public and private life is played down. . . . TV executives working in Britain and the United States thus have to deal with quite different public attitudes towards the importance of competition. I am not suggesting that the British do not want "their side" to win; but winning is by no means "the only thing." I do not know of the British equivalent of the American term "loser"; the nearest is probably "also-ran." Nor does one speak of "winners"; the equivalent term varies according to the context, but in educational activity it would be "high-flyers."
>
> In both soccer and cricket, it is honorable to draw; indeed, to gamble on winning rather than to play for a draw, may be regarded as simple-minded and rash, whatever the outcome (p. 21).

Therefore when you watch sports on television in the United States the emphasis is on winners, losers, and final scores. Commentators talk of "shoot-outs" and sudden-death play-offs instead of ties; success is denoted as dominance over others and "big hits" rather than learning, enjoyment, and competing *with* others. Commentaries don't "tell it like it is" as much as they tell it in a way that fits the interests of people with power and influence in society.

MASCULINITY AND FEMININITY THEMES

The media coverage of sports generally emphasizes that sport participation is more appropriate for boys and men than for girls and women, that males are naturally superior to women when it comes to sports, that women's sports are less important than men's sports, and that women's ideas about sports are neither as important nor interesting as men's ideas about sports.

The evidence supporting these themes is overwhelming. Some of that evidence is summarized in the following list:

- Men's sports receive at least 90% of all media coverage, whether it is in newspapers, sport magazines, radio, or television (Duncan, et al, 1990; Lumpkin and Williams, 1991). Women's sports are now televised more, especially on certain cable stations, but the air time given to women's sports is still less than 10% of total sports air time. Many people never see women's sports on television apart from the Olympics and major tennis and golf tournaments. There is some indication that the coverage of women's sports in big city newspapers even declined through the 1980s (Women's Sports Pages, 1991). This pattern of underrepresentation of women's sports in the media is even greater in England (White, 1991) and Japan (Kimura and Saeki, 1990).
- The women's sports most likely to attract media coverage are those emphasizing grace, balance, and aesthetics—all of which are consistent with traditional images of femininity. This is why Olympic coverage focuses on women gymnasts in the summer games and women figure skaters in the winter games. The men's sports most likely to attract media coverage are those emphasizing bulk, height, physical strength, and the use of force and intimidation to physically dominate opponents—all of which are consistent with traditional images of masculinity.
- Commentaries on women's sports sometimes undervalue or undermine the achievements of

women athletes by emphasizing how they look, their attractiveness to men, their interest in becoming wives and mothers, their domestic interests and skills, and their vulnerabilities and weaknesses (Lumpkin and Williams, 1991; Heinz, 1991). In general, the media "paint a very confused picture of female athletes—strong, but weak; courageous, but vulnerable; powerful, but cute" (Heinz, 1991). Images of strength and weakness are often mixed together in ways that signal ambivalence about women in sports (Duncan and Hasbrook, 1988).

- Television commentators for women's sports often refer to women athletes by first names and as "girls" or "ladies." Commentators for men's sports seldom refer to men athletes by their first names and almost never call them "boys" or "gentlemen" (Duncan et al, 1990). Commentators for women's sports are less likely to give attention to the physicality of women athletes or to the complexity of techniques and strategies used by women's teams; at the same time they often focus on the nonathletic dimensions of women athletes' lives and they often express "concern" or amazement when women athletes are tough and aggressive (Blinde, et al. 1991).

- References to physical strength are much more common in commentaries about men athletes, and references to weaknesses are much more common in commentaries about women athletes (Duncan et al, 1990). References to the character flaws of men athletes emphasize that men are too aggressive, too independent, and too determined to succeed, whereas references to the character flaws of women athletes emphasize that women are too emotional, too dependent, or too unfulfilled in their overall lives (Hilliard, 1984).

- The most widely covered men's sports often use women as media distractions, as seen through "honey shots" picking out women in the crowd, through closeups and weird angle shots of cheerleaders and various cheerleader body parts, and through feminine images used in commercials, including male sexual fantasy beer commercials.

- Men's sports events are often promoted or described as if they had some special historical importance, whereas women's sports events are usually promoted in a lighter, less serious manner (Duncan et al, 1990). Men's events are referred to as *the* events—for example, *the* NCAA Basketball Championship Tournament; whereas women's events are almost always referred to as *women's* events—for example, the NCAA *Women's* Basketball Championship Tournament (Blinde et al, 1991).

- Women's sports events and women athletes almost never get a lead headline in a newspaper sports section (Women's Sports Pages, 1991). The coverage of women's sports in newspapers and magazines is less likely to be accompanied by photographs, and when photographs are included, they are less likely to portray action and more likely to picture athletes in nonsport settings (Boutilier and San Giovanni, 1983). Over the years, men have been featured on about 90% of the covers of *Sports Illustrated* and half of the women featured on *SI* covers have not even been athletes (Reid and Soley, 1979; Women's Sports Foundation, 1987). Even in *Sports Illustrated for Kids* there are subtle but powerful photographic images suggesting that most sports are *mainly* for boys and men, and some sports are *only* for boys and men (Duncan and Sayaovong, 1990).

- The entire system of sports information in the United States, Canada, and most other countries is set up to make it easy to cover men's sports. Even the work schedules of sports reporters have been established so that men's sports get regular coverage, and women's events are covered only when they are identified as special features (Theberge and Cronk, 1986).

- The vast majority of sports media personnel are men. Fewer than 1 in 20 reporters for the sport departments of newspapers or for major sport magazines are women (Thomas, 1990).

The broadcast media coverage of sports is totally dominated by men. A few women work in the news side of the business, reporting scores and doing interviews, but I know of only one case in which a woman has done regular commentary for a men's sport (in tennis). When women reporters cover men's sports, they are often defined as outsiders "invading" men's turf. This is because locker room talk about women generally treats women as nonpersons, sex objects, butts of sexist and homophobic jokes, and victims of male athletes' bedroom conquests (Curry, 1991; Kane and Disch, 1992; Messner, 1991; 1992). When women reporters threaten male power and privilege by entering the locker room, they are likely to encounter harassment by some male athletes.

In light of this "re-presentation" of women's sports in the media, it is easy to see that some people might conclude that sports are "naturally" suited to men rather than women, and that men are better suited than women to be athletes. Some people might even conclude that women's sports are much less important than men's sports and that women were never meant to be sports reporters or commentators because they just don't have the same "feel" for sports that men do. But those people have never asked critical questions about gender ideology or about sports.

RACE THEMES Just as the media coverage of sport can influence ideas about gender and gender relations, it can influence ideas about race and race relations. However, the information on this issue is sketchy (Barnett, 1982; Braddock, 1978a, b; Condor and Anderson, 1984; Pearman, 1978; Wiggins, 1983). Research done in the mid-1970s (Rainville and McCormick, 1977) indicated that television commentators in the past tended to criticize black players more and praise them less than white players in the same positions with similar abilities. Furthermore, the announcers emphasized the physical and cognitive skills of whites and described them as being aggressive and in control of their own ac-

tions. Blacks, on the other hand, were more often described as the targets of aggression and as players whose actions were determined by factors other than their own choices and decisions.

A more recent informal study done by Derek Jackson at the *Boston Globe* analyzed commentary in seven NFL playoff games and five NCAA Men's basketball games during the 1988-89 season (Hoose, 1989; Lapchick, 1991). Jackson found that commentators were more likely to describe or refer to white athletes' character and intelligence, but were more likely to describe or refer to black athletes' physical assets and abilities. White athletes were more often criticized for lacking physical talent, and black athletes were more often criticized for mental errors. Of course, these descriptions and references were not made with any racist intent, nor were they meant to perpetuate destructive and dangerous ideas about race. But racial ideology is so deeply rooted in western societies that racism sometimes exists without awareness or intent; however, it is always destructive.

One of the ways to increase awareness is to hire more reporters, editors, photographers, writers, producers, directors, camera people, and commentators from different racial and ethnic backgrounds. Lip service has been given to this goal, but progress toward achieving the goal has been slow; various racial and ethnic groups are still underrepresented in sports newsrooms, press boxes, broadcast booths, and media executive offices. Another way to increase awareness is to provide personnel with good training workshops on racial ideology and racial relations. Some of these people need to learn that ideology is like B.O.—you seldom smell your own.

Finally, there is a chance that race themes underlying the images and messages of mediated sports also influence the aspirations and choices of African American children, especially boys. If black children watch television and see black athletes excelling in various sports, and if they think it is their personal destiny to achieve great things in sports, these children may dedicate themselves to becoming athletes and give lower priority to pursuing other occupational goals (Bierman, 1990; Gaston, 1986). This possibility needs further examination.

OTHER IDEOLOGICAL THEMES IN MEDIATED SPORTS It is not easy to identify themes underlying the images and messages in mediated sports. Many different theoretical approaches and research methods can be used to guide the search for themes, but each approach and method leads the search in a particular direction (Real, 1989). Analyses grounded in various forms of critical theory have focused on the extent to which images and messages in mediated sports represent dominant ideas about social life and social relations in society as a whole. Studies using critical theory have identified the three themes I have already discussed (success, gender, race), and they have also identified themes related to nationalism, competitive individualism, teamwork, aggression, and consumerism (Hargreaves, 1986; Kinkema and Harris, 1992).

These themes should not surprise anyone who has read about, listened to, and viewed sports in the United States. The images and messages in mediated sports clearly emphasize *nationalism and national unity* grounded in traditional American loyalty and patriotism. In fact, the sports "invented" in the United States—football, basketball, and baseball—are the most widely televised sports in the country. Other sports may get air time, but if they don't fit with traditional ideas about what it means to be an American they won't be emphasized in media coverage. When teams or athletes from the United States are competing against teams or athletes from other countries, the sport events are usually framed in an "us vs. them" format. When American teams or athletes win, media commentary emphasizes that "we won." (This topic will be discussed further in Chapter 14).

Even in team sports, media images and messages emphasize *individual efforts* to achieve competitive victories. NFL games are often promoted by announcing that it is "Steve Young and his 49ers looking for blood against Jim Kelly and his Buffalo Bills," or it is "Michael Jordan vs Charles Barkley as the Bulls face the Suns." This emphasizes the idea that individuals must take responsibility for what happens in their lives and that failures can be traced to individual character flaws. This idea is central to the ideology of American individualism that influences everything from the structure of our welfare system to the use of grading curves in classrooms.

Media images and messages also stress *teamwork* in the form of obedience to authority, group loyalty, and willingness to sacrifice for the good of the group (Kinkema and Harris, 1992). Media coverage clearly identifies coaches as the organizers and controllers of teams; commentators praise athletes for being team players, and praise coaches for their ability to fit players into team roles that lead to victories. This teamwork theme clearly fits with ideology underlying the American market economy and most American business organizations—teamwork means loyalty and productivity.

The importance of *mental and physical aggression* is another theme underlying the images and messages in mediated sports. Rough, aggressive play is described as a sign of commitment and skill. Tackles in football are described as bone-crushing hits, hard fouls in basketball are described as warnings to the opposition, brushback pitches in baseball are said to keep batters on their heels. Even the scores on the late night news are full of violent images—the Bulls *annihilated* the Knicks, the Jets *destroyed* the Dolphins, the Blackhawks *scalped* the Bruins, Seles *blew away* Capriati, and on and on to the point that the scores sound like the results of military operations in a war. The language of mediated sports in the United States is a language of violence and warfare (Jansen and Sabo, 1992). Aggression is celebrated and images of kindness and sensitivity are seldom found. This clearly fits with the ideology many Americans use to determine strategies in interpersonal and international relations; "kicking ass" is a celebrated goal and failing to punish the opposition is a sign of weakness.

Finally, it must be remembered that over 15% of the air time of televised sports is commercial time; newspapers are full of ads placed around sports stories. "TV time outs" are a standard feature of televised football and basketball games, and announcers remind media audiences that "this game is being brought to you by. . . . " Super Bowl commercials are even the subject of special analyses, and media audiences are polled to see which Super Bowl commercial they liked the best. Commercial images and messages promote *consumerism*. The audiences in mediated sports are encouraged to express their connections to teams and athletes by consuming shirts, shoes, jackets, official NFL hats, official NBA sweat pants, and Notre Dame coffee cups. This is clearly consistent with consumer ideology in American society. "You are what you buy" is one of the tenets of a market economy.

Overall, the images and messages in the media coverage of sports in the United States stress themes representing conventional ideology and widespread ideas about how the world does and should work: order, control, and tough discipline are essential; sex and race differences are physical and natural; the primacy of the nation must be preserved; individuals must be accountable and must work with others to be productive and competitive; and consumption is essential to happiness. These themes run through mediated sports. This is why media coverage of sports is heavily sponsored by people and corporations with power and influence in society—they like these themes and they promote images and messages that keep them part of the public consciousness in American society. Of course, similar patterns also exist in other socities.

Media Impact on Sport-Related Behaviors

ACTIVE PARTICIPATION IN SPORTS Does reading about, listening to, and watching sports cause people to be more active sport participants or does it turn them into couch potatoes? This question has generated considerable debate, and in the United States, for example, the media are often blamed for everything from obesity to a perceived shortage of gold medals in the Olympics.

We do know that when children watch sports in highly promoted television broadcasts, some of them will develop participation interests in those sports. Children are great imitators and they have great imaginations, so when they identify with popular and successful Olympic athletes in gymnastics or swimming, they may join a youth sport program to pursue their dream. However, it is not known how long this media-created interest lasts, especially after the young people and their parents discover that noteworthy accomplishments require years of dedication and expense.

We also know that many adults—both men and women—who watch football, basketball, baseball, and ice hockey on television play none of these sports. However, it is not known if these people are less physically active than others in their communities. A series of studies in Norway showed that those who watched the most sports on television also had the highest rates of active participation (Fasting, 1977). But

WHY CAN'T YOU GUYS STAY IN BETTER PHYSICAL CONDITION?

Some people use televised sports as a source of motivation for their own active participation; others use it as an excuse for their own inactivity.

a Finnish study of participation rates before and after televised coverage of the 1976 Olympic Games found that active participation rates declined following the games (Vuolle, 1977). Another study suggests that those who use the media as sources of information tend to be active sport participants, and those who use the media as sources of entertainment tend to be passive and inactive (Famaey-Lamon and Van Loon, 1978). In light of these confusing findings, the only safe conclusion is to say that the media probably have no significant *net* effect one way or the other on active participation.

ATTENDANCE AT SPORT EVENTS Information on game attendance and the mass media is also confusing. On the one hand, the owners of many professional teams enforce a television blackout rule based on the belief that television coverage hurts game attendance and ticket sales. In support of this belief, research shows that up to half of the people interested in a sports event would rather watch it on television than attend it in person (Fasting, 1977). On the other hand, it is clear that the media publicize and promote interests in sports and provide the information people need to identify with athletes and teams and become committed fans.

The most logical conclusion to make at this point is that the media and game attendance are positively related. However, this conclusion must be qualified because the media focus attention on elite sports. This suggests that the media may be positively related to attendance at the top levels of competition, but negatively related to attendance at lower levels of competition. Research is needed to explore this issue in more depth.

GAMBLING ON SPORTS It has been argued that people who listen to and watch mediated sports don't experience the excitement that goes with attending an event in person, so they place bets on sports to regain some of that excitement (Schuetz, 1976). This could be why there are so many "betting pools" at offices and among friends, but there are no systematic data to support this argument. In fact, the only certain link

between gambling and the media is an indirect one. The media, especially newspapers and television, make people aware of *point spreads* and *betting odds* for different events (D'Angelo, 1987; Kaplan, 1983). Point spreads and betting odds are determined by bookies who want to make sure they don't go broke by taking too many bets on a particular outcome in a sport event. When the media publicize point spreads and odds, they make it easier for many forms of gambling to occur.

The publication of spreads and odds has been a matter of concern among newspaper editors and television program directors (Straw, 1983). They realize that when they publish this information, people can use it to figure their own bets or set up betting pools. But they also realize that people who follow sports like to compare their predictions for event outcomes with the predictions of "the experts, " even when they don't place bets on the events.

As long as there are people who want information on point spreads, odds, player injuries, weather conditions, and other bet-related topics, there will be editors and program directors who will oblige them. If there are no rules against it, many media people will communicate any information they think will sell newspapers and magazines or increase radio and television ratings. Their decision will not be seriously questioned as long as gambling on sports is not defined as an important legal or moral issue within society as a whole. At this time, I would argue that the media do not cause gambling, but the information communicated through the media makes it easier for people to arrange and place bets on sport events. But I would also argue that people do not bet on sports simply because mediated sports are less exciting than attending games in person; many people bet on the games they attend in person.

THE PROFESSION OF SPORTS JOURNALISM

Leonard Koppett, a well-known and respected sportswriter, said that one of the goals of sports journalism was "the generation of more and more entertaining material about something that doesn't *really* matter too much." However, sports do matter—not because they produce a tangible product or make an essential contribution to our survival, but because they are constructed and mediated to represent ideas about how the world works and what is important in life. Therefore sports journalists do things that matter very much when it comes to ideas and ideology in the public consciousness.

In addition to constructing the meanings that underlie how people experience sports, journalists also help people enjoy and understand sports. According to a national study in the United States, nearly 80% of those who watch sports on television consistently pay close attention to commentators during sports events; and over half say that commentators add to their enjoyment of sports (Miller Lite Report, 1983). Furthermore, the words of sports journalists often affect the sports they cover and the athletes they write and talk about (Altheide and Snow, 1978).

In this section we will look at how sports journalists do their jobs and how they are connected to the sports and the athletes they cover. Our definition of journalist will include newspaper and magazine writers as well as announcers for radio and television.

Before television: When Sportswriters Created the Images and Messages

It is 1928 and the baseball writers covering the New York Yankees on this rail trip are sitting in the train's club car, playing nickel-ante poker. Suddenly the door to the club car bursts open and Babe Ruth sprints down the aisle, followed closely by an attractive young woman wielding a knife. "I'll kill you, you son of a bitch!" the woman screams as she disappears after Ruth into the next car. The writers observe the action, then turn and look at each other. "That'd make a helluva story," one of them says. The others chuckle and nod, and the poker game resumes. Of course, no one reported the incident. . . .

This true story was used by Rick Telander (1984), staff writer for *Sports Illustrated*, to show

how sports were covered by the press before World War II. He explains that sportswriters in the pretelevision era did things much differently than they're done now:

Those were the days. . . . [Sportswriters] dealt in mythology. They felt that if they told the truth about athletes, readers would revolt and there would be no need for sports sections or sports reporters. The Babe was not real. Few people could see him; almost nobody could hear him; his prowess on the field was all that counted. Thus his bout with gonorrhea in 1926 was passed off as "stomach cramps." A 1919 home run of his rose "into some floating white clouds" while opponents stood "transfixed with the splendor of it."

Radio simply reinforced the images and messages re-presented in the press, and media audiences used those images and messages as they formed ideas about sports and about the connection between sports and the rest of their lives. Since people could not actually see what happened at games, writers and radio broadcasters could make athletes bigger than life; they could make them into heroes. And so they did. Their words constructed images of heroic deeds and dramatic action. Those words did much to contribute to what is now called the *Golden Age of Sports* in the United States.

This process of hero building and the creation of drama was clearly tied to the ways people defined sports in society. Athletes were imagined to be superhuman characters shaped by sport participation; sports were defined as exciting and challenging forms of competition. This did much to intensify the traditional turn-of-the-century idea that sport participation and competition built character in young people, especially boys and young men.

After Television: A New Age for Sports Journalists

In the 1950s things changed. Television created a new situation. Newspapers and magazines had to print something other than scores and descriptions of the action. Since people could now *see* sports at home, sportswriters had to have stories that went beyond the action. They "had to tell readers more about the players as personalities, delve more thoroughly into the reasons for strategies, be more critical of managers and coaches, and report more thoroughly the behind-scenes maneuvering and conflicts" (Ray Sons, quoted in Telander, 1984). This type of coverage created serious tension in player-press relationships in North American sports, and some of that tension still exists today.

When the sportswriters needed to come up with stories going beyond the action in sports, players discovered they had no privacy. No matter what they said or where they said it, their words could end up in print if there was a sportswriter around. This kept most athletes from saying the spontaneous things that made good material for reporters (Koppett, 1981). The reporters, on the other hand, were under constant pressure to get good stories—to dig into the lives of the athletes whom their readers were watching on television.

The tension between players and sportswriters escalated in the 1960s when the "new journalism" was popularized by writer Tom Wolfe (Telander, 1984). Newspapers and magazines started to publish sports stories written in the same style as paperback novels. The stories were full of intrigue, but they often offended athletes and invaded their personal lives. In 1970, Jim Bouton published the book *Ball Four*, and players realized once and for all that even their private conversations with other players could end up in print. The invasion of privacy by the press hit its peak after the Watergate conspiracy in 1972, as Telander (1984) explains:

> Conspiracies and coverups lurked everywhere, and sports could be no exception. At the same time a music writer was going through Bob Dylan's garbage cans looking for relevant material, sports writers were checking out athletes' views on drugs, sex, and politics. . . . Aging sports writers . . . were rapidly being replaced by college-educated, "me generation" reporters—"barking dogs" the players call them—who had no problem thinking they could break big stories by revealing the dirty tricks of sport.

"THE LOSING TEAM HAS MADE IT CLEAR TO ME THAT THEY ARE IN NO MOOD TO BE INTERVIEWED...BACK TO YOU, RON."

Tension between players and media personnel increases when the search for good stories and interesting coverage infringes on the privacy of the athletes and coaches.

Tension was also grounded in growing differences in the salaries and backgrounds of players and sportswriters. Before the 1960s, players did not earn much more than sportswriters, so writers and players could identify with one another. But when players' salaries increased at dramatic rates in the 1980s, the basis for this mutual identification disappeared. Athletes became national superstars instead of local heroes and their incomes far surpassed the incomes of the reporters who wrote about them. The fact that many of the athletes were blacks without college degrees, while the reporters were whites with degrees, also interfered with mutual identification. In the face of these differences, reporters no longer felt compelled to protect or glorify athletes in their stories, and athletes became more protective of their newfound wealth and status. In fact, some professional athletes had personal policies of not talking with sportswriters. The athletes believed they could use television and television commentators to keep their names in front of the public, so they no longer felt obligated to respond to sportswriters.

Table 13-5 Sportwriters and sports announcers: a comparison of roles

Role characteristics	Sportswriters*	Sports announcers†
• Job security	High	Low
• Salary	Low	High
• Popularity/public recognition	Low	High
• Freedom of expression in job	Moderate to high	Low; heavily restricted
• Purpose of role	To give information about sport events	To "sell" sport events
• Role expectations	To be an objective investigator	To be a personable entertainer
• Opportunities to do investigative reporting	Sometimes	Very rare
• On-the-job contacts	Copy desk editors and sub-editors	Broadcast executives, team management, sponsors, advertising people
• Relationships with players	Often tense and antagonistic	Friendly and supportive
• Level of response evoked from public	Low	High

Data from Koppett (1981).
*The primary focus here is on newspaper reporters. Magazine writers have similar jobs, but they are different in some important respects.
†The primary focus here is on television announcers. Radio broadcasters have similar jobs, but they are different in some important respects.

As players became less willing to talk, sports management people became worried. Promoters and team owners realized the importance of the written media in marketing their games, matches, and other products. Some sport team owners even offered players seminars on the importance of newspaper coverage, and others provided training sessions to teach players how to handle interviews without saying things that would sound bad. In some cases, teams even fined players who refused to talk to the press (Telander, 1984). This awareness of the importance of press coverage continues in commercial sports today. But tension between sportswriters and athletes still exists. In some cases it has reached points where players have threatened writers and writers have quit their jobs in search of less stressful occupations (Telander, 1984).

Ethics and Sports Journalism

Questions about ethics apply to all forms of sports journalism, but they are especially important for the print media. The foundation of the written media rests on its reputation as a dependable source of facts. Before television, sportswriters were merely extensions of the teams and players they covered. In some cases, they were even on team payrolls; and if they weren't, they often depended on teams and team owners for travel funds, hotel rooms, transportation to games, meals, and other favors. As radio and television coverage became increasingly popular, announcers and commentators replaced sportswriters as the voices of public relations for sports. In fact, some radio and television commentators are now hired by teams and given guidelines on what to say and what not to say during broadcasts. Most audiences realize this and simply expect the commentators to be personable entertainers. However, with sportswriters, it's different. Writers are expected to dig into sports and report things that cannot simply be shown on television. A detailed illustration of the differences between the role of sportswriter and the role of television commentator is given in Table 13-5.

Sportswriters no longer depend on teams for money or favors. They are seldom bought off as they were in the past (Koppett, 1981). But there are still factors that discourage tough, investigative reporting. According to Koppett (1981), the judgment of many reporters is distorted by very subtle aspects of their jobs. He points out that to get more information for their stories, reporters must get well-acquainted with the people they are assigned to cover. The better acquainted they get, the more likely they are to take on the attitudes of those people (players and sponsors). When this happens, they find it difficult to do critical, investigative reporting.

In discussing this issue, Koppett has noted that writers must strive to be fair in their reporting. But being fair does not mean writing without personal opinion. In fact, personal opinions will always influence what is written. Fairness simply depends on not letting opinions "distort the accuracy of your account, to whatever extent you can be aware of distortion." In other words, being a sportswriter is similar in some respects to being a sport sociologist: both must be aware of the perspectives they use to look at sports, and both must try to use systematic methods and critical thinking to explore the questions they raise.

Another important ethics issue is related to the impact of the media on the people they cover. Journalists, especially those in the print media, must be especially sensitive to this issue. They are called on to be fair, but they must also take care not to jeopardize someone's reputation simply for the sake of entertainment. This does not mean that a journalist should avoid criticism that might hurt someone. But according to Koppett (1981), a journalist should never hurt someone unintentionally. When someone is hurt, it should be done intentionally and with good reason. Without good reasons, the sportswriter is simply engaging in a destructive self-serving form of sensationalism that raises ethical concerns about the invasion of privacy. This issue was widely discussed in 1992 following an editorial decision at *USA Today* to report that Arthur Ashe was HIV-positive. The controversy created by the report led many journalists to rethink issues of ethics and privacy.

Sportswriters and Sports Announcers: A Comparison

Not everyone who covers sports for the media emphasizes the same things in their jobs. In the print media the focus is on information and analysis, and in the broadcast media it's on entertainment. This difference has important implications for writers and commentators. These implications have been discussed in detail in Leonard Koppett's book, *Sports Illusion, Sports Reality*. His discussion is summarized in Table 13-5.

According to Koppett, the main difference between the print and broadcast media is that,

> A newspaper woos the readership with reliability and thoroughness and hires people who strive in that direction. A broadcast tries to dazzle and fascinate the audience enough to keep it glued to the set and hires people who can create that effect (1981).

This is why the best investigative reporting is done by newspaper and magazine writers (especially the latter), and why the most popular media personalities sit in television broadcasting booths.

However, while looking at Table 13-5, remember there are exceptions to these role descriptions. Some writers—especially syndicated columnists—write to entertain. The successful ones have relatively high salaries and a reasonable amount of job security. On the other hand, some television announcers do investigative reporting in which information and analysis take priority over entertainment. However, the major patterns for the roles of sportswriter and sports announcer are closely represented by the information in the table.

The efforts of television companies to provide a combination of expert analysis and entertain-

Radio and television commentators are entertainers. People do not generally expect them to do investigative reporting or to cover games in objective ways. (University of Colorado)

ment is seen in the fact that they hire popular retired athletes and coaches to do commentaries for games. Some people complain that ex-athletes have few skills to make them successful broadcasters, but most television executives realize that media spectators identify with athletes and also with coaches. So they put former athletes or coaches in the broadcast booth for entertainment purposes, even when former athletes and coaches know little about broadcasting.

In summary, sports journalism is important because the images and messages provided by writers and commentators construct people's experiences with sports. In the first half of this century, sportswriters and radio commentators created heroes and heroic deeds—the illusions and images on which much of the attractiveness

of sport has always rested. Television destroyed much of the mystique used in the written media and forced sportswriters to take a different approach to their coverage. The growth of televised sports also changed the relationship between players and press. With sportswriters searching for good stories and athletes trying to protect their privacy, tension has grown between the two groups.

The media coverage of sports also involves ethical issues. The task of writers and commentators is to describe and analyze what happens in sport while avoiding coverage that needlessly hurts the people they write and talk about. To hurt others for the purpose of entertainment is generally thought to violate norms among journalists, although it seems to be happening with increased frequency.

CONCLUSION:

COULD SPORTS AND THE MEDIA LIVE WITHOUT EACH OTHER?

The media, similar to other parts of culture, are social constructions. This means they are created, organized, and controlled by human beings whose ideas are grounded in their experiences and perspectives on the world. Therefore the media don't reflect reality as much as they provide "re-presentations" of selected versions of reality. These selected "re-presentations" are grounded in power relations that exist in society as a whole. This means that the images and messages contained in the media are likely to represent dominant ideas and ideologies in the society and promote the interests of those who benefit the most from those ideas and ideologies.

Sports and the media have grown to depend on each other as both have become more important parts of culture in many contemporary societies. They could survive without each other, but they would both be different than they are now. Commercial forms of sports would not be so widespread and there would be less emphasis on elitist forms of sports, although active participation in sports would not automatically increase. But without exposure to sports through the media, people would probably give lower priority to sports in their everyday lives.

The media could also survive without sports. But they too would be different, especially newspapers and television. Newspaper circulation would probably decrease, and television programming on weekends and holidays would be different and less profitable for television companies.

More important than trying to determine whether sports and the media are interdependent is understanding the ways in which mediated sports are incorporated into the lives of human beings. The strong symbiotic relationship between them guarantees that none of us will live to see organized sports without media coverage or the media without sports programming.

However, history in North America suggests that the relationship between sports and television has been developed within a larger cultural context in which commercial profits and the creation of media events are given a high priority. This relationship did not take shape on its own; it has been and continues to be created through the ever-changing interactions between athletes, agents, coaches, administrators, sport team owners, sponsors, advertisers, media representatives, and a diversified collection of spectators. Each group has tried to exert influence on the relationship between sports and television, and they have had differing amounts of resources to use in the process.

What exists today are what we might call **"vidiated" sports**—that is, sports that are "re-presented" to viewing audiences through video technology used to create dramatic, exciting, and stylized images and messages for the purpose of entertaining viewers and maintaining sponsors.

The influence of mediated sports in our lives depends on how much information about sports we get through the media and how much we get through direct experiences. Direct experiences with sports influence how we interpret and use what we read, listen to, and view in the media. We reinterpret much of what the media "represent" to us, but when we have little direct experience in and with sports, we heavily depend on media images and messages to construct our sport experiences and connect those experiences to other parts of our lives.

Research suggests that dominant ideologies related to success, gender, race, nationalism, competition, individualism, teamwork, violence, and consumerism are perpetuated through the images and messages contained in the media coverage of sports in the U.S. Future research in the sociology of sport needs to focus on the process of re-presentation that occurs through the media, and on how audiences use media images and messages in the construction of their own ideas about sport, about the world, and about their relationships to one another.

SUGGESTED READINGS

Cantelon, H., and R. Gruneau. 1988. The production of sport for television. In J. Harvey and H. Cantelon, eds. Not just a game. University of Ottawa Press, Ottawa, Ontario (*critical analysis of the production and consumption of images and meanings associated with sport on television; focuses on the unique characteristics of television as a medium for the production of culture*).

Chandler, J. 1988. Television and national sport: the United States and Britain. University of Illinois Press, Urbana, Ill. (*good cross-cultural information on differences in the ways sport is defined and perceived and differences in the economics of television in the two countries; focuses on network coverage of live events*).

Claeys, U., and H. Van Pelt, eds. 1986. Sport and mass media. Special double issue of the International Review for the Sociology of Sport 21(2,3) (*12 papers encompassing a range of cross-cultural analyses; excellent information in a number of the papers*).

Clarke, A., and J. Clarke. 1982. Highlights and action replays—ideology, sport and the media. In J. Hargreaves, ed. Sport, culture and ideology. Routledge & Kegan Paul, Ltd., London (*critical analysis of how and why certain media content is selected in British broadcasts of sport; contains good framework for understanding the media-sport-society connection*).

Duncan, M., M.A. Messner, L. Williams, and K. Jensen. 1990. Gender stereotyping in televised sports. Amateur Athletic Foundation, Los Angeles (*this report of two studies funded by the AAF received widespread national publicity because it so clearly documented the extent to which gender ideology permeates television sports*).

Gannett Center Journal. 1987. vol. 1, no. 2. Sports and mass media (*special issue with 13 papers by authors from sport, the media, and social science*).

Goldlust, J. 1987. Playing for keeps: sport, the media and society. Longman Cheshire Pty Limited, Melbourne, Australia (*critical analysis with helpful historical information on the United States, Canada, Britain, and Australia; best book available for a sociological analysis of this topic*).

Kinkema, K., and J. Harris. 1992. Sport and the mass media. Exercise and Sport Science Reviews 20:127-159 (*this excellent review article provides 152 references along with information on the production, content, and audiences of mediated sports*).

Klatell, D.A., and N. Marcus. 1988. Sports for sale: television, money, and the fans. Oxford University Press, New York (*an inside look at bottom-line issues and how they have influenced the relationship between sport and television; interesting predictions; no real sociological analysis*).

Koppett, L. 1981. Sports illusion, sports reality. Houghton Mifflin Co., Boston (*a reporter's view of sports, journalism, and society; excellent discussion of how the members of the media cover sports*).

Lever, J., and S. Wheeler. 1993. Mass media and the experience of sport. Communication Research 20(1):125-143 (*brief, but informative overview of the history of the media-sport relationship*).

Rader, B. 1984. In its own image: how television has transformed sports. The Free Press, New York (*discusses how changes induced by television have altered sports and destroyed sport's potential to serve useful functions*).

Wenner, L. ed., 1989. Media, sports, and society. Sage Publications, Newbury Park, Calif. (*13 articles on mediated sport; focus on production of media sports, content, and audience experiences; very good source*).

CHAPTER 14

SPORTS AND POLITICS

Can they be kept separate?

We now have to face the reality that the Olympics constitute not only an athletic event but a political event.

Peter Ueberroth, Former President of the Los Angeles Olympic Organizing Committee (1984)

The Church approves and encourages sports seeing in it . . . a training for social relations based on respect for others . . . and an element of social cohesion which also fosters friendly relations on the international level.

Pope John Paul II (1979)

I know why we're here. We're here to spread basketball internationally and make more money for somebody. . . . We're going to win the gold medal, but there won't be any life changing decisions made because of it. . . . poor people will still be poor and racism and sexism will still exist . . .

Charles Barkley, USA Olympic Basketball Team (1992)

If the images of shared humanity generated by the [Olympic] Games ignore the structural realities that separate [human beings] from one another . . . then the spectacle has made us victims of the most dangerous illusions.

John MacAloon, Cultural Anthropologist, 1984

358

As we approach the end of the twentieth century, it is clear that organized competitive sports are closely connected to politics and political organizations in important ways. As societies have become more complex and as relationships within societies have become more interdependent, governments have become more involved in many spheres of social life. This includes sports.

The purpose of this chapter is to explore this relationship between sports and government, and the general relationship between sports and politics. We will focus attention on the following questions:

1. Why do governments become involved in the sponsorship and control of sports, and how does this involvement occur in different societies?

2. What are the political consequences of international sports events such as the Olympic Games? Do these events really promote unity and peace?

3. What are the political consequences of the globalization of certain sports and sport forms?

4. Do "politics" occur within sports and sport organizations?

THE SPORTS–GOVERNMENT CONNECTION

As sports grow in popularity in a community or society, government involvement in sports often increases. Sport events and activities require sponsorship, organization, and facilities — all of which depend on resources that frequently go beyond the means of individuals. For example, sport facilities are often so expensive that regional and national governments may be the only organizations with the power and the capital to build and maintain them. For this reason, many people see government involvement in sports as a necessity.

Government involvement is also tied to the belief that sport organizations and the people associated with sports often need to be regulated and controlled by an "outside" organization perceived to represent the interests of all people in a community or society.

The nature and extent of government involvement in sports varies from one community and society to the next, but the reasons for involvement generally fall into the following categories (Johnson and Frey, 1985; Hargreaves, 1986; Harvey and Proulx, 1988; Macintosh et al., 1987; and Shaikin, 1988):

1. To safeguard the public order

2. To maintain and develop fitness and physical abilities among citizens

3. To promote the prestige of a community or nation

4. To promote a sense of identity, belonging, and unity among citizens

5. To emphasize values and orientations consistent with dominant political ideology in a community or society

6. To increase citizen support of individual political leaders and government itself

Explanations and examples of each of these reasons are given in the following sections.

Safeguarding the Public Order

To protect individuals and groups with different interests, governments often make rules about what types of sports are legal or illegal, how sports are organized, who should have opportunities to play sports, and who can use public sports facilities at certain times. For example, a local or national government may officially outlaw sports such as bullfighting or barefisted boxing. In the case of commercial sports, government agencies may regulate the rights and duties of owners, sponsors, promoters, and athletes; government rules may even set official limits on the extent to which sports organizations can legally control the lives of athletes.

Local governments may try to eliminate conflicts between citizens by regulating the use of public facilities and playing fields through reservation or permit systems; and they may pass rules prohibiting certain sports activities in public places so the general public can freely and safely use those places. Likewise, local law enforcement officials may temporarily close streets or parks so that sports events can occur in an orderly manner.

Because *fairness* is often defined as a matter of public order, governments may pass laws or establish policies to make sure that participation in publicly funded sports is open to a range of citizens. Title IX is a classic example of a federal government regulation that defines what is fair when it comes to who should have opportunities to participate in sports programs sponsored by American schools receiving federal funds. Sport Canada, in response to federal antidiscrimination legislation, has gone a step further than the United States by establishing a nationwide policy on women in sport. This policy outlines equity strategies to be used in government sponsored sport programs throughout the country.

Government interests in safeguarding the public order may also lead to the policing of sports events. Local police or even military forces may be called on to control crowds and individuals who threaten the safety and well-being of others. For example, Russian army units are often used to patrol Moscow's Lenin Stadium during major events such as soccer games. After the games hundreds of soldiers form lines to channel the flow of spectators leaving the stadium. The police in England are conspicuously present at most soccer games, and they may even ride the trains that carry spectators from one city to another. The Atlanta Olympic Organizing Committee will work with thousands of law enforcement officials from the federal, state, and local governments to assemble a security force to safeguard the public order during the 1996 Summer Games.

Some governments have attempted to safeguard the public order by sponsoring sports events and programs for special groups of people who have been labeled as potentially disruptive within communities and societies. For example, The Sports Council, an official policy-making agency in the British government, has sponsored sports programs in the hope of providing what they see as "constructive activities" for young people, minorities, and the unemployed. The ultimate goal of these programs is to use sports to control crime rates, vandalism, loneliness, and alienation in British society. However, the failure of these programs to achieve these goals has led critics to argue that sports participation cannot eliminate the deprivation, dislocation, community disintegration, and political powerlessness that often cause social problems in communities and societies. But beliefs about the character-building effects of sport participation still lead people to think that the public order can be safeguarded through government-sponsored sports programs, especially if the programs target people defined as potentially disruptive within communities and societies.

Finally, sports have often been used in military and law enforcement training. For example, military academies in the United States and other countries have traditionally sponsored numerous sports for their cadets. In fact, national sport programs in some countries are even administered through government defense departments. Even the founding of the modern Olympic Games was partially grounded in Baron Pierre de Coubertin's belief that sports could be used to motivate young Frenchmen to safeguard French society by developing the skills needed to be effective leaders and soldiers (Tomlinson, 1984).

Maintaining and Developing Fitness and Physical Abilities

Governments have also become involved in sports to promote fitness among the general population. For example, countries with national health insurance programs often promote and sponsor sports to improve overall health among their citizens and thereby reduce the cost of health services. This was one of the major reasons why the Canadian government promoted and funded fitness and sport programs during the mid-1970s. The government was facing serious financial crises and officials believed that sports participation among Canadians would ultimately increase fitness and cut health care costs (Harvey and Proulx, 1988).

Similar motives have led to government sponsorship and organization of fitness and sports programs in other countries including England, Sweden, Norway, China, and the former Soviet Union. Many people believe that sport participation improves fitness, fitness improves health, and good health reduces medical costs. It should be pointed out that this set of beliefs persists in the face of the following factors (Wagner, 1987):

- Many of the illnesses that increase health care costs are caused by environmental factors and living conditions, and they cannot be changed through any sports or fitness programs.
- Many forms of sport participation do not lead to overall physical fitness or identifiable health benefits.
- The win-at-all-costs orientation that sometimes develops in connection with sports may actually contribute to injuries and increased health care costs (for example, 40,000 knee injuries in American football every year require costly care, surgery, and rehabilitation).
- The demand for health care sometimes increases when people become more concerned with fitness and the physical condition and appearance of their bodies; in other words, under certain conditions, people who participate in sports can become so concerned with their abilities to perform that they become obsessed with physical and health issues to the point that they demand more health care.

If these factors are considered in the formulation of official policies, governments will become increasingly cautious and selective in their sponsorship of sports for the purpose of maintaining fitness.

Government involvement in sports is also grounded in the belief that fitness and physical abilities are related to economic productivity. For example, governments in countries that have socialist or planned economies often promote and sponsor sport participation in the hope that workers will become more fit, more skilled, and more productive. This was the approach used in the former Soviet Union, as illustrated through the following words of sociologist Nikolai Ponomaryov (1981):

> The main way to train people for work activity is to strengthen their health and improve their physical development. . . . Physical culture . . . encourages a more rational use of work resources, since it extends the bounds of actual work capacity beyond (the normal retirement) age, i.e., it prolongs the active life of workers. . . . "Athletic" employees are (also) less prone to sickness and therefore take less time off.

Ponomaryov also argued that when workers had highly developed physical skills they could handle on-the-job stress and respond more quickly to the physical demands of changing production processes. However, the government of the Soviet Union discovered that trying to use sports to control workers was not very effective in the long run. Other governments are in the process of learning the same lesson.

Although many people may be skeptical about the work-related consequences of sport participation, it should be pointed out that many private corporations in the United States, Canada, and other countries with market economies fund their own fitness centers and sport programs for some of the same reasons the former Soviet government intervened in sports and physical culture. These companies are usually discovering the same things that happened in the Soviet Union: productivity and worker satisfaction are related to the overall quality of working conditions and the autonomy of workers, not to employee fitness or opportunities to participate in sports.

Promoting the Prestige of a Group, Community, or Nation

Government intervention in sport is frequently motivated by a quest for prestige. For example, a spokesperson for the South Korean government said that its sponsorship of the 1988 Summer Olympic Games was an announcement to the world of its emergence as a developing nation. This motive also underlies government subsidies for national teams across a wide range of amateur sports, usually those designated as Olympic sports. Government officials believe that when athletes from their country win medals, the image of the entire country is enhanced around the world. This belief is so strong that many governments have also offered their athletes financial rewards for winning medals in the Olympics.

The quest for prestige among nations is also the reason why most governments fund national sport training centers and maintain national teams in a number of sports. For example, in 1958, when Brazil won its first World Cup in soccer, there was a strong feeling among most Brazilians that they could now stand tall in the international arena and that their way of life was equal to or perhaps even better than European ways. They felt that Brazil now had to be recognized and dealt with as an equal in international relations (Humphrey, 1986).

The use of sport to gain prestige also underlies intervention at local government levels. City governments in many countries fund sport clubs and community teams that compete against other communities. And the victors often use the event to promote the advantages of their towns. For example, the competitive success of varsity teams from publicly funded schools in the United States has often prompted city governments to display signs telling people driving into town that they are entering the "home of the state champions" in a particular sport. State governments in the United States may subsidize sport programs at their major colleges and universities for similar reasons: competitive success is believed to bring prestige to the entire state

as well as to the school represented by the athletes and teams.

Although the federal government in the United States does not give financial support to national teams, it has intervened in amateur sports in many other ways. For example, after American athletes had apparently lost their domination of international sports to athletes from East Germany and the Soviet Union, President Gerald Ford issued an executive order in 1975 that established the Commission on Olympic Sports. The investigation and hearings of this commission, funded by the federal government, led Congress to pass the Amateur Athletics Act in 1978. This legislation officially chartered the United States Olympic Committee as the rule-making body for amateur sports in the United States. Even though President Carter prevented American athletes from competing in the 1980 Moscow Games, the Amateur Sports Act prompted many in the United States to think that the USOC would bring future successes in international sports and that such successes would help the country regain its prestige on the world scene. The federal government has also supported the USOC by allowing contributions to the USOC to be considered as tax deductible donations. Also, nine state governments have check-off boxes on their state tax return forms so that taxpayers can contribute money to the USOC in connection with tax refunds or tax payments.

Promoting a Sense of Identity, Belonging, and Unity

Any team or athlete representing a specific group has the potential for bringing people together and creating emotional unity among group members. For example, when a nation's soccer team plays in the World Cup, it seems to unite people in the country regardless of differences in race, religion, language, education, and social class. This unity may also be connected with feelings of attachment to the country as a whole. Although serious sociological questions must be asked about the long-term

People in Ashland, PA (pop. 4235) use this sign to promote the image of their town. Many people believe that the competitive success of local teams brings prestige to the entire community. (Robert N. Kyler)

consequences of this emotional unity and these feelings of attachment (see box on pp. 364-365), there is no doubt that sports can create strong emotional feelings, and this often leads to government involvement and sponsorship.

Local government involvement in sports is also motivated by this factor. Club soccer teams in Europe often receive support from local governments because the teams are major focal points for community attention and involvement. The teams not only reaffirm community identification among local citizens but they also bring large numbers of community people together when games are played. In fact, the games often become important social occasions within towns or regions and provide opportunities for meeting new people, renewing old ac-

quaintances, and maintaining a personal sense of belonging to a group. This is partly why towns and cities in many countries sponsor and support local sports events—they are believed to play an important role in producing community identity.

When the population of a community or society is very diverse, governments are even more likely to intervene in sports. For example, in the 1970s the Canadian government developed sport policies designed to highlight the participation and achievements of groups that did not feel they were a part of Canadian culture (Harvey and Proulx, 1988). It was hoped that sports could be used to create a feeling of unity in the midst of diversity and political alienation. However, little is known about the effectiveness of

Unity For What?
The political consequences of rooting for the home team

Sports differ from other cultural forms in society. Art, literature, drama, and music have the power to bring people together, but sports are unique. In spite of the complex rules in some games, most sports are simple and easy to understand. Events have definite beginnings and endings, and game boundaries are usually clear-cut. Opponents in most sports are identifiable, and they often compete directly with one another. Scores are objective and outcomes are clear-cut. These characteristics make many sports easy to understand.

Sports also provide spectators with a combination of action, drama, and uncertainty that can be entertaining. For this reason, sports often bring people together to cheer for the same athletes or teams despite differences related to social class, gender, race, ethnicity, religion, language, education, and cultural heritage.

Sociologist Janet Lever, in an extended analysis of soccer in Brazil, studied sports' potential for bringing people together. Lever (1983) concluded that soccer brought people together from all over the country, giving them "a set of common symbols and a basis for identity and interaction"—even when they cheered for opposing teams in interregional games. In other words, soccer games showed Brazilians it was possible to forget their exclusive and tightly defined in-groups and join together with others from diverse backgrounds.

What Lever found in Brazil was accurate. In fact, her findings describe how sports operate in many areas all over the world. For example, community-based sport teams, such as high school teams in small towns across the United States, have often been sources of this type of togetherness among townspeople. However, an analysis of sports and social solidarity must do more than simply show that games and teams bring people together. It must also explore the *consequences of togetherness*.

Alan Klein, a social anthropologist from Northeastern University in Boston, emphasized the need to explore the consequences of the unity and togetherness created by sports. In a review of Lever's research, Klein (1984) raised doubts about whether the unity created by soccer has had any effect on the political and economic realities of Brazilian life. He agreed that sports often transcend everyday differences and create emotional unity. But he questioned whether the unity created by soccer in Brazil actually helped people deal with their differences in a manner that would improve their quality of life.

Klein's review implied that any discussion of the unity and togetherness created by sports must address the following questions:

• How large a territory does the unity cover? Does it go beyond the community or regional level? When does this happen? Can it bring a whole country together? How about groups of countries?

• What form does the unity take? How long does it last? Does it go beyond the emotional level?

• Does the unity affect everyone equally? Are some groups able to benefit from it more than others?

• Most important, does the unity affect issues apart from sport? If so, how?

In connection with these questions, Klein noted that in spite of a regular schedule of soccer games that consistently brings people together, social life in Brazil remains plagued with political tension and economic problems. For those who lack economic and political power in Brazil, soccer provides nothing more than momentary relief from the pressures of making a living and supporting a family.

REFLECT ON SPORT

The unity created by soccer does not change the realities of important political and economic relations; for example, it does not address issues of poverty or the need for democratic political involvement. It does create a common emotional focus, and it does show the Brazilians that unity is possible. However, whether the unity goes beyond the emotional level is debatable, and whether it can provide an impetus for dealing with community, regional, or national problems is yet another question.

In summary, sports can create emotional unity among people from different backgrounds. This unity feels good, and it may even be associated with a spirit of possibility. But it usually does more to distract people's attention away from the need for social transformation than it does to give people

creative ways of dealing with their differences. Therefore the unity associated with sports almost never gets converted into collective action that might transform society and make it more democratic and economically fair. The likelihood of social transformation is lowest when people refuse to acknowledge that sports are connected with other parts of social life and social relations. When people assume that sports are detached from the rest of life, the emotional unity created by sports will do nothing to transform social life. It is only when people recognize the political, economic, and social significance of sports that they can begin to identify, initiate, and create ways to link sports to changes that go beyond temporary good feelings of togetherness.

this type of strategy. Usually sports have been used much more effectively to celebrate dominant values rather than cultural diversity or the values of marginalized groups.

Emphasizing Values and Orientations Consistent with Dominant Political Ideology

Governments may also become involved in sports to promote certain values and ideas among citizens. Governments generally have strong vested interests in maintaining the idea that success is based on discipline, loyalty, determination, and the ability to keep working in the face of hardship and bad times. Sports—especially world-class and elite competitive

sports—can be used to promote these values and foster particular interpretations of how social life does and should work. For example, this was a major motive underlying the sponsorship of elite sports in the former Soviet Union:

Physical culture is an important means to educate . . . an active fighter for communism, and it is an effective social factor in the ideological education of the public. . . . When people engage in physical exercise their ideology and moral consciousness are shaped through acquiring information on sports ethics and its manifestation in the activities of Soviet athletes; this is assimilated through the practical mastery of communist standards of behavior during training and competition (Ponomaryov, 1981).

The Soviet government also used sports to emphasize the importance of "teamwork, common aims and interests, . . . collectivism, comradeship, [and] hard work and responsibility for the common cause." These were the values connected with Soviet sport, and the hope was that people would adopt them in their lives as Soviet citizens. However, because the Soviet government lacked legitimacy in the eyes of a majority of Soviet citizens, sports could do little to shape values supportive of that government.

In countries with market economies, sports are also used to promote the connection between success and hard work, but instead of references to collectivism and common causes, there are references to individualism and achieving excellence through competition. Instead of an emphasis on comradeship, the focus is on unique success stories illustrating how individuals have reached personal goals and achieved self-fulfillment. But regardless of whether countries have planned or market economies, sports are usually organized to provide people with words, orientations, and real-life examples that reaffirm and strengthen the dominant political ideology of the country.

One classic example of a government's use of sport to promote its own political ideology was Hitler's use of the Olympics in 1936. Most countries that host the Olympic Games have used the occasion to present themselves favorably to their own citizens and the rest of the world. However, Hitler was especially interested in using the games to promote the Nazi ideology of "Nordic supremacy." His government devoted considerable resources to the training of German athletes, and those athletes won 89 medals—23 more than U.S. athletes won and over four times as many as any other country won during the Berlin Games. This is why the performance of Jesse Owens, an African American, was so important during the games in Berlin. Owens's 4 gold medals and world records challenged Hitler's ideology of Nordic supremacy, although it did not stop Hitler.

Increasing Citizen Support of Individual Political Leaders and Government Itself

"All governments, regardless of . . . type, use sport to generate political support." This is the conclusion made by political scientist Art Johnson (1982) in his analysis of the connection between government and sport. Johnson also indicates that even in political systems that promote a

". . . belief in the separation of sport and government, it is likely that intervention . . . will be needed to ensure that sport serves the purposes of government rather than its opponents. Sport, therefore will become too important to be left alone to excite the fans; it will be needed to service the state" (1982).

These comments suggest that governments use sports not only to increase the legitimacy of their political systems but also to generate support for the ruling parties within those systems.

Johnson also points out that if government officials do not use sports in this way, those who oppose the political system or the ruling party will use sports to generate support for themselves. For example, government investigations of violence in sports in the United States, Great Britain, and Canada were initiated in the hope of making changes before sports became useless as a means of promoting values consistent with political ideologies in these countries. Hitler abolished the Worker's Sports Movements in Germany so that his government could organize sports to serve his fascist ideology and the Nazi party. In other words, governments often sponsor sports so they can prevent others from using sports to challenge their power.

When governments sponsor or promote activities and events that people value and enjoy, they increase their perceived *legitimacy* in the eyes of citizens. Without legitimacy, governments and government officials risk losing their power. This is why many political figures present themselves as friends of sport, even as faithful fans. They may make it a point to at-

Former president Ronald Reagan was very good at using sport to his political advantage. He seldom missed opportunities to be seen or connected with highly visible championship teams during his 8 years in office. As sport has become more visible in many societies, more political figures are using sport to generate political support. (Jeff Morehead)

tend highly publicized sports events and associate themselves with high profile athletes or teams that win major competitions. For example, most recent U.S. presidents have traditionally tried to demonstrate their knowledge of sports, and they have even made calls to the locker rooms of World Series and Super Bowl winners to express their congratulations.

Former President Ronald Reagan was especially adept at using sports to his political advantage. Before the 1984 election, his campaign staff hinted at a connection between Reagan's first 4 years in the White House and the United States' success at the 1984 Olympic Games in Los Angeles. The claim was that Reagan had restored American pride and America's place in the international political arena. Even though U.S. athletes were not directly subsidized by the federal government, Reagan tried to enhance

the legitimacy of his political ideology and the American political system by implying a connection between his presidency and all the gold medals won by U.S. athletes. Following in the footsteps of other recent presidents, Reagan also invited national championship teams in the country's most popular sports to the White House for press conferences and photographs, attracting extensive national media coverage. In 1985 he even shortened his inauguration ceremony so it would not interfere with the telecast of the Super Bowl, and then he scheduled an appearance during the game in front of the largest television audience of the year (Shaikin, 1988). Of course, Reagan and U.S. politicians are not the only ones to do this; there are similar examples from other countries. When taken together, all these examples provide strong support for Johnson's conclusion about the political uses of sport: "All governments . . . use sport to generate political support" (1982).

GOVERNMENT INVOLVEMENT AND "THE COMMON GOOD"

It would be ideal if government involvement worked to the equal advantage of all citizens, but differences between individuals and groups make it impossible for political decisions to reflect equally the interests of everyone. This means that government involvement in sports usually reflects the interests of some people more than others. The individuals and groups who benefit most tend to be those capable of influencing policy makers or those who think and act as policy makers think and act. This does not mean that government policies always reflect the interests of wealthy and powerful people, but it does mean that they reflect political power struggles between various groups within a society.

History shows (Goldlust, 1987; Gruneau, 1983; Hargreaves, 1987; Macintosh et al., 1987; Macintosh and Whitson, 1990; Stoddard, 1986) that when government intervention occurs, priority is usually given to sport programs in which there is an emphasis on

1. Fitness rather than fun
2. Discipline and physical skills rather than expression and overall self-development
3. Elite sport rather than mass participation
4. Records and victories rather than participation and relationships

Priorities exist in any sport program, and priorities are determined in light of limited resources. Choices have to be made that often represent the interests of those who have the most political clout. For example, government support is disproportionately given to the training, development, and sponsorship of top athletes; mass participation programs that are not directly tied to elite competition receive little attention.

Those who represent elite sports are often organized, generally have strong backing from other organized groups, and can base their requests for support on visible accomplishments achieved in the name of the entire country, community, or school. Those who would benefit from mass participation programs are less likely to be politically organized or backed by other organized groups and less able to give precise statements of their goals and the political significance of their programs. This does not mean that mass participation is ignored by government decision makers, but it does mean that it usually has lower priority for funding and support.

Opposition to the priorities used to determine government involvement is often defused by the myth that there is no connection between sports and politics. Those who believe the myth seldom have their interests reflected when government involvement occurs. Those who realize that sports have political implications and that governments are not politically neutral arbitrators of differences within societies are likely to benefit the most when intervention occurs. Sports are connected with power relations in society as a whole; therefore sports and politics cannot be separated.

POLITICAL CONSEQUENCES OF INTERNATIONAL SPORTS
Goals and Realities

According to many, unity and peace are the goals of international sports. This idea that sports should bring nations of the world together has been emphasized ever since Baron Pierre de Coubertin founded the modern Olympic Games in 1896. The potential impact of sports on international relations has been described in many ways over the past century, but it has never been summarized more clearly than in the following statement by Alan Reich (1974), a former U.S. State Department official:

- Sports open doors to societies and key leaders. They pave the way for expanded contact—cultural, economic, and political. . . .
- Sports provide an example of friendly competition and two-way interchange which,

hopefully, will characterize and lead to other types of friendly relationships between nations. . . .

- Sports convey on a person-to-person basis and through the media to the broader public a sense of commonness of interest shared with other peoples across political boundaries. . . .
- Sports enhance understanding of another nation's values and culture, so important but often absent in many forms of international communication.
- Sports thus can help to improve perceptions of other peoples and to close the gap between myth and reality. . . .
- Sports organizations, in administering international sports activities, develop the bases for ongoing communication and cooperation. In this work, [they] travel and communicate across national boundaries . . . further the ideals of freedom . . . [and] also develop leadership, which is needed especially by the developing nations as they struggle to reduce the gap between the "have" and "have not" peoples of the world.

This sums up what many people hope international sports can accomplish. Unfortunately, sports usually fall short of these hopes.

History shows that most nations have used international sport events, especially the Olympic Games, to pursue their own interests rather than the collective goals of international communication, friendship, and peace; this has been true especially since World War II (Heinila, 1985; Hoberman, 1986; Macintosh and Hawes, 1992; Tomlinson and Whannel, 1984; Vinokur, 1988). Statements substantiating this pursuit of national interests over and above the international common good are not difficult to find. The following comments illustrate this point:

[It is] in our national interest that we regain our Olympic superiority—that we once again give the world visible proof of our inner strength and vitality. (Bobby Kennedy, U.S. Attorney General, 1964)

Do we realize how important it is to compete successfully with other nations? Not just the Russians, but many nations are growing and challenging. Being a leader, the United States has an obligation to set high standards. . . . A sports triumph can be [as] uplifting to a nation's spirit as . . . a battlefield victory. (U. S. President Gerald Ford, 1974)

Sport [in East Germany] did its part in obtaining recognition internationally for the German Democratic Republic. Sport led the way in increasing the international prestige of our socialist republic and led to its diplomatic recognition by a majority of states of the world. (Guenther Heinze, Vice President of the German Sport and Gymnastic Federation, 1973)

The increasing number of successes achieved by Soviet sportsmen in sport has particular significance today. Each new victory is a victory for the Soviet form of society and the socialist sports system; it provides irrefutable proof of the superiority of socialist culture over the decaying culture of the capitalist states. (Yuri Kotov and Ivan Yudovich, Political writers, U.S.S.R. 1978)

These statements are all from the post-World War II "cold war era." They illustrate how sports were clearly connected with national and international politics. This connection between sports and politics was so widely recognized that Peter Ueberroth, president of the Los Angeles Olympic Organizing Committee, concluded in 1984 that "we now have to face the reality that the Olympics constitute not only an athletic event but a political event." Ueberroth's statement was not prophetic; it was simply based on an observation of events connected with previous Olympic Games. Nations have seldom put international understanding and the good of the world community ahead of their own interests. The demonstration of superiority through sports has been given a much higher priority than the achievement of understanding (Frey, 1984; Heinila, 1985).

Powerful industrial countries are not the only ones that have used international sports to promote national interests. For example, many nations lacking international political and economic clout have used participation in the Olympics in their overall quest for international recognition and legitimacy. They have used international sports as stages to show that their athletes and teams could stand up to and sometimes even defeat athletes and teams from powerful and economically advantaged nations (James, 1984). For example, when the West Indian cricket team defeated England, the country that had colonized the West Indies, it was seen as an event that contributed greatly to West Indian prestige in the international arena.

Some emerging industrial nations have also realized that hosting the Olympics is a special opportunity to announce to the world their readiness and ability to fully participate in international politics and trade relations. This is why Tokyo spent hundreds of millions of dollars to host the 1964 Summer Games and Seoul spent much more to host the 1988 Summer Games. Overall, the Olympics have been widely used as an international stage on which nations could generate international recognition and display their power and resources.

Worldwide media coverage has intensified and added new dimensions to the connection between sports and politics (Real, 1989). For example, television companies—especially the American networks—have sometimes tried to attract viewers to their Olympic programming by stressing political controversies along with national interests and symbols. The theme underlying their coverage has not been international unity as much as it has been an "us vs. them," "nation vs. nation" theme. The American media have justified this type of coverage by saying that Americans prefer nationalist themes because they see the world with an "us vs. them" attitude and Olympic medals as reaffirmations of the American way of life. Although past coverage has probably encouraged ethnocentrism and a military mentality about international relations, the recent decline of the "Soviet bloc" will discourage western media coverage that defines the Olympics in terms of "us against the communists." American television

coverage of the Olympics may therefore give greater priority to themes that celebrate cultural and human diversity as opposed to nationalist themes.

The boycotts of the Olympics, especially by African countries in 1976, by the United States and its political allies in 1980, and by the Soviet Union and its allies in 1984, are also expressions of the extent to which people have seen international sports as political as well as athletic events. When these examples are combined with dozens of other examples in both the ancient and modern Olympic Games, it is seen that sports and politics are no strangers. In fact, keeping them separate seems to be impossible. Does this mean that international sport events cannot be a positive force on the world political scene? This brings us to the next topic.

Factors That Influence the Political Consequences of International Sports

Do sports contribute to peace or do they create and intensify hostility between people? Do they blur differences between people, lead to the acceptance of differences, or turn differences into reasons for bigotry and animosity? A review of the literature on this topic suggests that sports can do all of these things. Under certain conditions they foster understanding and friendly relationships, and under other conditions they accentuate differences and foster hostility by encouraging people to see differences as negative. These sets of conditions are outlined in Table 14-1.

The conditions listed in Table 14-1 do not inspire optimism about most highly publicized international sport events. These events are usually characterized by the conditions on the right side of the table—the hostility and polarization side. Athletes in these events often emphasize competitive success over and above the process and experience of involvement (at least that is what is emphasized in the press coverage of athletes' orientations). People from different countries (even political leaders) use the events to gauge their nation's prestige and political

Table 14-1   Sports and international relations: factors shaping the political consequences of international events*

Factors likely to create friendly relationships	Factors likely to create hostile relationships
• Players emphasize the process and experience of involvement.	• Players emphasize outcomes and competitive success.
• The event is defined as an opportunity to establish or reaffirm social ties between the competitors.	• The event is defined as an opportunity to establish dominance over competitors.
• The existing relationship between the competitors is already friendly.	• The existing relationship between the competitors is hostile and polarized.
• Athletes identify themselves in terms of athletic skills.	• Athletes identify themselves in terms of nationalism or national identities.
• Media and spectators focus on athletes as individuals.	• Media and spectators focus on athletes as representatives of nations.
• Symbols related to the event emphasize unity between opponents.	• Symbols related to the event emphasize differences between opponents.
• Public expectations focus mainly on athletic excellence.	• Public expectations focus mainly on who wins medals.
• Victories are attributed to athletes.	• Victories are attributed to sponsoring nations.

*The factors listed in this table can be applied to any pair of opponents. This would include competitors from work groups, schools, communities, states, and regions, as well as nations.

strength. Heavy emphasis is placed on nationalistic symbols such as flags and anthems; athletes are defined as representatives of nations; medal counts are scored by country; and victories are often attributed to the nations in which athletes were born or trained. This method of organizing and staging an international event may serve the interests of some of the participating nations, especially those whose athletes win many medals, but it does little to bring nations together in a spirit of peace and understanding.

Whenever international events are organized in line with the conditions on the right-hand side of Table 14-1, there is a tendency for people from countries winning disproportionate shares of medals to be swept up in waves of nationalistic fervor. There is also a tendency for them to define their intense feelings of patriotism and nationalism as good. However, the expressions of patriotism and nationalism by the people of one country may not be received well by people from other countries. This is because displays of nationalism often express feelings of su-

periority that are not consistent with international peace and harmony. Waving flags and chanting "we're number one" may make people in one country feel good, but people in other countries will often see them as symbols grounded in a lack of international understanding rather than a commitment to sharing an international experience.

The point here is not that patriotism is bad. Instead, the point is that the official reason for the existence of international sport events, especially the Olympic Games, is to further the *common* international cause of friendship, peace, and mutual understanding between nations. When patriotism or nationalism among the people of any country interferes with or distract people's attention from this goal, the very legitimacy of international sport is called into question. Olympic history has clearly shown that when there is no attempt to control and regulate political expression in sports, sports will be controlled and regulated by politicians and political interests.

Is it possible to organize sports in ways that lead to understanding and friendly relationships? It is, but it isn't easy; it must be planned, because it almost never happens by accident. For example, the diplomats interested in establishing closer ties between the United States and mainland China during the early 1970s initiated contact between the two nations in the form of a series of table tennis matches, a tactic that was later described as "Ping-Pong diplomacy." However, the matches were designed to emphasize the process and experience of involvement rather than the competitive success of one nation over another. They were organized for the sole purpose of bringing the countries together, not for the purpose of establishing superiority or reaffirming national prestige in the eyes of the international political community or the people of either country. The symbols associated with the event, the media coverage, and the attention of the spectators were all focused on unity between the opponents and the skills of individual athletes; the victories in the matches were attributed to the athletes themselves rather than to the nations in which they were born or trained. The result was that the table tennis matches themselves provided occasions for contact and understanding, and these occasions were used by people from both countries who were interested in establishing closer political and economic connections.

The Goodwill Games were founded after the boycotts of the 1980 and 1984 Olympic Games in an attempt to bring the best athletes in the world together in a forum that emphasized unity through sports. They were designed by Ted Turner of TBS to defuse the growing hostilities between the sport communities of the United States and the former Soviet Union. The Goodwill Games have in the past been accompanied by art festivals, conferences, and friendship initiatives that bring people from many different countries together to discuss world issues. The Goodwill Games were held in Moscow in 1986, in Seattle in 1990, and they are scheduled to be held in St. Petersburg, Russia in 1994 and New York City in 1998. Although we have no information about the impact of these events on political attitudes or trends, they have been promoted and covered in ways that downplay political differences and nationalism.

The Institute for International Sport at the University of Rhode Island has sponsored a Sports Corps program that sends both athletes and coaches to other countries in an attempt to establish transnational relationships through sports. When representatives of the Sport Corps organize sport programs in other countries there is an explicit emphasis on peace, improving relationships among nations, and developing leaders committed to international understanding.

Each of these examples shows that sports can be used to emphasize friendship and mutual understanding. But this does not occur without careful planning.

The Olympic Games: Suggestions for Reform

According to many people, including IOC president Juan Antonio Samaranch, the future success of the Olympic Games requires changes in the way the games are defined, promoted, staged, and played. Of course, it would be naive to think politics could ever be eliminated from the Olympic Games, but it may be possible to restructure the Games so they are less likely to be used by politicians and more likely to foster friendly relationships among participating nations.

There have been many recommendations for making changes in the organization of the Olympic Games, but these recommendations have seldom been taken seriously by those who control Olympic sports around the world. Representatives from National Olympic Committees and International Sport Federations around the globe have traditionally given lip service to the notion that the Olympic Games involve athletes striving to achieve excellence as they compete *with* others. But at the same time they have promoted the idea that the Olympics are entertainment spectacles involving "war without weapons," nations competing against nations, and athletes representing national political ideologies and economic systems.

The end of the cold war era now provides an excellent opportunity to take action and make changes. Of course, there is little agreement about the nature and extent of changes needed. But there is a need to start somewhere. My suggestion would be to use Table 14-1 as a guide for recommendations. To bring the Olympic Games in line with the points listed on the left side of the table, I suggest the following:

1. *Do away with national uniforms for athletes.* To focus attention on athletes and human achievement, and to discourage nationalism, it is necessary to eliminate political symbols that lead people to perceive athletes as representatives of nations. Therefore a range of clothing with approved styles and colors should be made available to qualifying athletes before they come to the Olympic site. Specific clothing choices should be made by the athletes themselves. Identification numbers would be visible on the uniforms so individual athletes could be identified.

2. *Revise the opening ceremonies so athletes enter the arena with other athletes in their events.* If athletes were grouped by event rather than citizenship, spectators would be less likely to see the Olympics and the athletes in political terms. Flags for each event could be developed to maintain the pageantry and the color of the ceremony. Artists from around the world would be commissioned to design the flags for different sports. National flags could be displayed in the middle of the field during the ceremonies, but they would not be associated with any particular group of athletes. An Olympic flag and a "peace and unity flag" should be flown above the national flags to symbolize international peace and unity above national identities and interests. The emphasis in the opening ceremonies would be on unity and fellowship among athletes, not on the political and economic systems in which the athletes were born through no choice of their own.

3. *Eliminate national anthems and the display of national flags during the award ceremonies.* These forms of nationalism may bring tears to the eyes of patriots, but they emphasize athletes as political symbols rather than as individuals who have met standards of excellence in their respective events. Award ceremonies should involve the display of the Olympic flag, the peace and unity flag, and a special flag representing the athletic event. The music played during the award ceremony could be an Olympic anthem, an anthem composed by an artist in the host country, or an anthem composed specifically for the event in which the athletes participated (such as a swimming anthem, or a figure skating anthem, and so on). This would renew the notion that the Olympics exist to celebrate cultural achievements and expressions that go beyond competitive sports. The emphasis in the awards ceremonies would be on athletes as representatives of all humanity rather than a single nation. This emphasis could be extended by grouping award ceremonies and awarding medals to athletes across a range of sports at the same time (see Lucas, 1992). This could be done daily in a special ceremony in the main stadium.

4. *Eliminate medal counts associated with countries.* National medal counts have always been contrary to the spirit of the Olympic Movement. They do nothing but foster chauvinism and fan the fires of existing political differences between countries. Furthermore, they distract attention away from the achievements of athletes and focus attention on nationalist sympathies and animosities. We all know that Olympic medals depend on talent pools, resources, and access to training, so medal winners will consistently come from the larger and wealthier countries of the world. Current medal counts are unfair and they tell us nothing about the athletes themselves. Therefore they should be eliminated, or they should be officially calculated by the IOC through a formula that would weight the medal count for each country in light of the country's population size and per capita income. Even this alternative would

defuse some of the nationalism associated with current medal counts.

5. *Eliminate or revise team sports.* Team sports, as they are now structured, automatically focus attention on national affiliations. They encourage players and spectators to define games in terms of national honor and pride. This may boost television ratings in some cases, but it does not provide a climate for fostering friendly relationships and a spirit of internationalism. Team sports could be eliminated, since there are only a few of them, and they could be played in World Cup formats apart from the Olympic Games—similar to the way international soccer is now organized. If team sports are not eliminated, then there should be some method of choosing teams so players from different countries could be on the same teams, and players from any one nation would play on different teams. Having teams from various combinations of countries would cut down on nationalism. And the combinations could be switched every 4 years. Then our "Dream Teams" would emphasize international unity rather than a nationalistic, militaristic approach to sports.

6. *Eliminate sports associated with the lifestyles of the wealthy.* This suggestion was made by historian John Lucas in his book on *The Future of the Olympic Games* (1992). Lucas argues that some sports are inconsistent with the democratic spirit of the Olympics because their exclusiveness precludes participation in most countries around the world. He notes that the differences between "have" and "have not" countries should not be accentuated in the Olympics if the Games are to foster understanding instead of feelings of superiority or inferiority.

7. *Revise the Olympic motto of "Citius, Altius, Fortius."* This is another suggestion made by Lucas (1992, p. 213). I think it is good for at least two reasons. First, as Lucas says, it provides an opportunity to establish a new motto emphasizing the process of participation rather than the product of performance. And second, it officially discourages forms of positive deviance among athletes (see Chapter 6). Emphasizing the

process of involvement over the goal of "faster, higher, stronger" would at least bring an important symbol of the Games more in line with the spirit of fair play and international cooperation among athletes.

8. *Use multiple sites for each Olympic Games.* Holding the Olympic Games at a single site not only creates bad feelings in countries whose bids for the games were rejected, but it puts pressure on the selected host nation to spend huge amounts of money in planning and construction. This pressure could be reduced and the political implications of hosting the games could be defused by selecting four sites for each Summer Games and two sites for each Winter Games. Events would be split so that fewer events would be held at any one site. This would make it possible for additional countries, especially some who lack massive economic resources, to submit bids. Hosting only a portion of the events would be more affordable and it would not raise many of the political issues created in countries when billions of dollars have to be spent on sport instead of on other things such as housing, food production, and infrastructure. More countries could experience the economic benefits of hosting the Olympics, and media spectators would see more countries while still seeing all the events traditionally included in the games. Security requirements would also be scaled down.

These suggestions may be resisted by certain sponsors and the television companies that make money by promoting the games as nationalistic spectacles. They may also be resisted by people concerned with using the Olympics to foster nationalistic interests rather than international unity. But I would argue that each suggestion serves to focus attention on athletes rather than sponsoring nations, and on athletic excellence rather than national superiority. Spokespersons for national Olympic committees have often said that politicians have ignored athletes and the true spirit of Olympism. These changes would allow those spokespersons to prove they really have the interests of athletes and Olympism at

nations *share* information and develop *mutual* cultural understanding. But true 50/50 sharing and mutual understanding is rare when two nations have unequal power and resources. This means that sports often become "cultural exports" shipped from wealthy nations and incorporated into the everyday lives of people in poorer nations. Although there is a chance that sports will be revised and reshaped to fit the values and lifestyles of people in poorer nations, it is more likely that their values and lifestyles will gradually change so that they will become new consumers of other goods, services, and ideas from wealthy nations.

SPORTS AND WORLD POLITICS Recent changes around the world have led some people to think that "superpower politics" involving economic and military relationships between sovereign nations will decline in importance in the future (Macintosh and Hawes, 1992). As this happens, we will see an increase in what might be called transnational relations. Transnational relations involve the interaction of various nongovernmental and governmental actors dealing with a wide range of global issues unrelated to the interests of any single nation.

Because the IOC and other sport organizations, both amateur and professional, are transnational organizations, they could become important global political players in the future. These sport organizations now have agendas unrelated to any specific nation and they can use their power to influence both the domestic and foreign policies of sovereign nations (Macintosh and Hawes, 1992). For example, the IOC could pressure certain nations to recognize the legitimacy or sovereignty of new nations formed as a result of conflicts challenging old national boundaries (such as in the former Czechoslovakia and Yugoslavia). Or the IOC could exclude a nation from participation in the Olympic Games as it did in response to South Africa's policy of racial apartheid. I think this will be one of the most interesting aspects of the relationships between sports and politics in the future.

SPORTS AND POLITICAL CHANGE Can sports be used to bring about real political transformation around the world? This is not likely to happen very often, and the impact of sports-based change strategies is usually very limited in scope. However, the long-term boycott of sports competitions involving South African teams did make an important contribution to the overall effort to break down apartheid policies in that country (Lapchick, 1978). Racial apartheid in South Africa was established in 1948, and efforts to isolate South African teams date back to the late 1950s. These efforts became increasingly organized to the point that there was an effective global boycott beginning in the 1960s. The boycott was associated with bitter conflicts in a number of nations (Archer and Bouillon, 1982; Jarvie, 1991; Kidd, 1988; Lapchick, 1975, 1991; Ramsamy, 1982, 1984). However, the boycott gradually took on symbolic significance around the world, and it continually reminded people around the world of the racial oppression in South Africa. It also put continuing pressure on white South Africans to reconsider their government's formal policy of racial separation and discrimination.

In the early 1990s racial barriers started to be removed and the African National Congress, under the leadership of Nelson Mandela, made sports the first area of everyday life where it would lift sanctions and work for racial integration. Changes in sports became a symbol of the need for changes in other parts of South African social life (Lapchick, 1992). Then in 1991, Richard Lapchick from the Center for the Study of Sport in Society at Northeastern University (in Boston) began working with black sport leaders in South Africa to adapt Project TEAMWORK, a special race relations program (see Chapter 10), to South African schools and communities. According to Kunle Raji (1992, p. 5), the goal of TEAMWORK South Africa is to

. . . help South Africans, especially the young people, deal constructively with the social challenges and transformations in the post-apartheid South African life. The program is designed to use sports to make young people more sensitive to human rights, racial and ethnic issues, and to teach them how the principles of teamwork can help them develop greater respect and harmony in these areas. Initially, this will be accomplished by the expansion of sports opportunities for young people coupled with incentives to have them act in a socially responsible way.

The success of TEAMWORK South Africa will depend on hard work and carefully planned strategies. But if the project can be a catalyst in the social transformation of race relations in South Africa, it could provide a model for building positive racial and ethnic relations in other settings as well.

Lapchick and his South African colleagues are experienced political change agents, so they realize that sports are seldom effective tools for promoting democracy and social transformation. However, they also realize that sports have great symbolic significance in many parts of the world, and this makes them a potential vehicle for change. Just because sports have usually led to the reproduction of ideologies and social relations characterized by inequality does not mean they cannot be used to question inequality and transform social relations that are characterized by domination and exploitation.

THE GLOBALIZATION OF SPORTS

Recent changes in the organization of sports and the composition of sport teams indicate that national identity is becoming increasingly blurred in many sports. Corporate sponsorships frequently cross national boundaries, professional sport teams in many nations now recruit players from around the world, and sport organizations are rapidly expanding into a number of nations to take advantage of new "spectator markets."

At this time it is very difficult to describe what might happen in connection with this globalization of sports. On the one hand, it could provide a basis for breaking down destructive feelings of nationalism and chauvinism. On the other hand, it could foster the expansion of global capitalism that would focus on corporate profits made by shaping global consumer behavior.

Transnational and multinational corporations may do some commendable things around the world, but their main purpose is to make profits. This, of course, raises questions about their long-term impact on social relations and living conditions around the world. For example, Coca Cola may sponsor the Olympics because it wants to "teach the world to sing," but it is primarily interested in selling the world a Coke—in fact, they want to sell the world billions of dollars worth of Cokes (Farhi, 1992). But what are the long-term political and health implications of using sports to teach the world to want Cokes?

Sut Jhally from the University of Massachusetts notes that when corporate sponsorships of sports cross national lines, large corporations tend to become "global cultural commissars." Jhally says that if you listen closely and critically to the advertisements of these sponsors you'll discover that they are selling much more than their products: "What they are selling [is] a way of life predicated on consumption" (quoted in Farhi, 1992).

The global expansion of certain sports and sport organizations also raises interesting political issues. For example, Joe Maguire (1991), a British sociologist, notes that we may soon see national sports teams replaced by multinational teams owned by large transnational corporations. Instead of political ideology and national interests being associated with sports there will be a shift to economic ideology and corporate interests. National governments will no longer control sports; instead, sports will be controlled by corporate boards and executive officers of multinational companies whose main goal is to create a world in which profits can be made.

Sport leagues within many countries now recruit athletes from around the world. Major League Baseball teams have an increasing number of players from nearly a dozen different Central and South American countries. Teams in the Italian basketball league have players from the United States, Lithuania, Croatia, Germany, and other countries. Teams in the new

Like many sports stores located in Japan, this one sells a wide range of products from the NBA, NFL, NHL, and Major League Baseball. The globalization of sports is not just limited to watching events; product consumption is also part of globalization. (Jay Coakley)

Japanese professional soccer league have players from the United States and a number of South American and European countries. Amateur athletes from former socialist nations such as the Soviet Union are no longer supported by their governments, so they are seeking corporate sponsors from all around the world. The IOC funds an Olympic Solidarity Program to help "have not" nations in the world join the "have" nations in international sports competitions. And American football, basketball, and baseball are expanding to dozens of nations.

Are these forms of sport globalization a sign that we are recognizing cultural diversity and moving toward more mutual understanding in the world, or are they simply clever means for introducing billions of people to Euro-American style consumerism driven by global capitalist interests? Sports provide seductive forms of science and technology that are controlled and dis-

tributed by a handful of powerful nations. When science and technology come packaged in sports, few people question their political implications. Studying these implications will be an important part of the sociology of sport in the future.

POLITICS IN SPORTS

The term "politics" is usually associated with affairs of the state. However, politics also encompasses any process of governing people and administering policies at any level of organization. Therefore politics are an inherent part of sport organizations. This is especially apparent because we refer to many sport organizations at the local, national, and international levels as "governing bodies." This means they are political bodies.

Sport organizations exist for a variety of reasons. But most are concerned with providing and regulating sport participation opportunities, establishing and enforcing policies, controlling and standardizing competitions, and acknowledging the accomplishments of athletes. This sounds like a straightforward set of tasks. However, seldom are these tasks done without some form of opposition, debate, and compromise. Members of sport organizations may agree on many things, but they do not all have the same interests or orientations. In fact, conflicts of interest often arise over (a) participation eligibility, (b) rules governing games and matches, (c) methods of investigating and punishing rule violators, (d) organizing and officiating competitive events, and (e) methods of distributing rewards to athletes and other organizational members.

Because many people mistakenly assume that sports make up a special part of life, separate from politics and other "real world" processes, they are sometimes surprised and shocked when they hear about "politics in sports." But just as sports are connected with the politics of the state, sport organizations have politics of their own. These politics affect everyone from athletes, coaches, and administrators in sport organizations to promoters and sponsors. Let's look at a few examples.

Participation Eligibility

Who plays and who doesn't play is often a contested issue in sports. Even when children play informal games they discuss and occasionally argue over who will play and who will sit out. In sport organizations these discussions and arguments are formalized. People in authority positions in sport organizations—whether they are volunteers, elected representatives, or appointed—make determinations about participation eligibility. They may use factors such as gender, age, weight, height, ability, place of residence, educational affiliation, social status, income, or even race and ethnicity to determine participation eligibility. Although eligibility policies are often presented as if they are somehow based on unchanging truths about human

beings and sports, they are grounded in arbitrary standards debated and agreed upon by groups of officials.

The arbitrariness of eligibility rules has often been contested. For example, American college athletes have challenged NCAA rules that prohibit them from transferring schools and immediately playing sports at their new schools. Similar challenges have been made by high school students when they or their families move from one school district to another. Even in youth sports there are frequent debates about age and weight rules often used to determine eligibility.

These debates about eligibility become particularly heated when there is much at stake for the athletes and officials involved. This was the case when the IOC banned South African athletes from participating in the Olympics (from 1963-1991) because of their country's formal policy of racial apartheid. Because the South Africa National Olympic Committee (SANROC) formally used race to determine eligibility on their national teams, the IOC decided that their athletes were no longer eligible to participate in the Olympics. However, it should be noted that IOC policy on this matter was hotly contested, and IOC officials were threatened by massive boycotts of the Olympic Games if they did not withdraw their recognition of SANROC. Similar pressures and threats were associated with the "eligibility politics" associated with women's participation in the marathon and other distance events that the men in the IOC thought were too strenuous for what they defined as "the weaker sex." The same eligibility politics now keep women out of wrestling, boxing, and many other events.

There are literally hundreds of other noteworthy cases of "eligibility politics" in sports at amateur and professional levels of participation. The "no pass, no play" rules in American high school sports have been the subject of political debates all over the United States. In amateur sports there have long been debates over the meaning of "amateur" and qualifications for "amateur status." Because these meanings are arbitrary and socially determined, they change over time. This will always be the case; and this is one of the many reasons why politics will always be a part of sports.

Rules for Games and Matches

Sports are social constructions. This means that they consist of games and challenges that have been "invented" by human beings as they interact with each other. The rules that govern sports are also social constructions and, as such, they are determined through political processes. Why should first base be 90 feet from home plate in Major League Baseball? Why should a basketball rim be 10 feet above the ground? Why should a women's basketball be slightly smaller and lighter than the ball used by adult men? Why should 6-year-olds hit a baseball off a tee instead of hitting a pitched ball? Why should the top of a volleyball net be 88⅛ inches off the ground in international women's volleyball? Why can't pole vaulters use any type of pole they want? Why can't golfers use any type of golf club or golf ball they want? This list of questions could go on for dozens of pages. But the point is that the rules of sport are arbitrary and this makes them political.

Many people fail to realize that whenever there are formal rules governing what people can and can't do, there will always be political processes. And sports have more rules than most human activities. This makes sports more political than most things we participate in during our lives.

Rule Enforcement

When rules exist, there are bound to be rule violations. This sounds simple, but anyone who has ever refereed or officiated a game or match will tell you that rule violations are seldom clearcut, that identifying violations is difficult, and that not everyone sees violations the same way. This is true not only during games and matches, but it is also true of alleged off-the-field rule violations.

The process of investigating rule violations, determining innocence or guilt, and punishing rule violators is a process full of arbitrary determinations of what is good and bad for sports, for sport organizations, and for various people in sport organizations. These determinations may be grounded in ideas about fairness, moral principles, economic interests, personal reputations, organizational prestige, or other factors. How these factors are defined and which ones will prevail in the rule enforcement process is a matter for discussion, debate, and compromise. The belief that "justice is blind" may be necessary to keep order in a group, but a close examination of the process of justice in sports shows that it is seldom blind.

The sociology of sport has few studies of the "politics of rule enforcement" in sports. This is partly because data are usually difficult to gather on this topic; data are often protected by privacy considerations and by organizations whose credibility and prestige could be threatened if people really knew how they enforced rules. For example, how does the NCAA deal with alleged rule violations in American college sports? Are all schools treated equally? Getting information to answer these questions is difficult because the NCAA does not want people highlighting the political processes that underlie their enforcement procedures.

Organizing and Overseeing Events

Apart from making up and enforcing eligibility rules and rules for games and matches, sport organizations also organize and oversee formal competitive events. How these events are organized is arbitrary and political. Where they are located, how they are scheduled, who will be given press passes to cover them for the media, what television company will have the rights to broadcast the events, who will sponsor the events, how much tickets will cost, and so on are all questions that call for political answers.

Certainly the selection of Olympic sites is a political process, as anyone who has been involved in putting together an Olympic site bid will emphasize. The selection of Atlanta for the

1996 Summer Games was part of an overall political process during which IOC officials were wined and dined and possibly even pressured by people who reminded them of everything from television rights fees coming from American television companies to the location of a major corporate Olympic sponsor in Atlanta. In fact, some people outside the United States are convinced that Atlanta was chosen to host the Games because it is also the home of the international headquarters of Coca Cola, one of the largest corporate sponsors of the Olympics in the world; and they are concerned that the 1996 Games might become the "Coca Colympics," and that corporate sponsors might begin to have more influence over how the Olympic Games are organized and presented to the world. This will clearly be part of the "future politics" of sports.

Overseeing events also involves political processes. For example, even though people have tried to devise organized standards for evaluating and judging performances in sports such as figure skating, diving, and gymnastics, "statistical evidence suggests that political loyalties have played a role in judges' voting preferences." This was the conclusion made by Seltzer and Glass (1991) in their 20-year study (1968-1988) of "all figure and dance skating events in the Winter Olympics." They found that judges gave higher scores to athletes from their own countries, and scoring patterns were often linked to "cold war" political blocs. Of course, this is disheartening to athletes, but no more disheartening than knowing that "cuteness," "hair styles," "body build," or "eye color" can influence judges when it comes to women athletes in certain events. This is why some athletes spend thousands of dollars on everything from braces for their teeth to plastic surgery for their jaws and noses. Politics comes in many forms!

Distributing Rewards

As sports have been increasingly organized as entertainment, there have been longstanding, heated debates about how entertainment revenues should be distributed. These revenues could be given to sport organizations, organization officials, owners and promoters, athletes, and others connected with sports; or they could be split among these groups in some way. As we have already seen in Chapter 12, the political processes associated with the distribution of revenues is complex and never-ending. Of course, these processes take different forms and come to different resolutions in different countries and in different sports. The debates even involve different people depending on whether they occur in a country with a market (capitalist) economy or a country with a planned (socialist) economy.

Why should intercollegiate athletes who risk health and personal well-being while they generate millions of dollars of revenue (such as a University of Miami football player) be limited to receiving an athletic grant-in-aid that is not much more than minimum wage? Why should professional sport team owners make up to five times more than some star players on their teams? Why should an amateur track athlete receive only a token appearance fee for competing in international events when the International Amateur Athletic Federation receives millions of dollars for selling broadcast rights to those events and then spends some of those dollars to pay for lavish "meetings" they attend in vacation resorts? Why should professional athletes who participate in the Olympics not be allowed to wear warm-up suits made by the companies who pay them endorsement fees? These and hundreds of similar questions show that the "politics of rewards" is an integral part of sports.

Sometimes rewards involve status or prestige rather than money. For example, in 1992 there was considerable debate in Japan over whether Akebono (aka Chad Rowan), an American sumo wrestler from Hawaii, would be voted into the rank of yokozuna, or grand champion, by the Yokozuna Promotion Council. Many Japanese people informed the council that such a prized status should be reserved for native Japanese or else Japan might lose control of a celebrated part of their own culture. However, the council voted to name Akebono as the 64th yokozuna in over 300 years of sumo wrestling.

Similar political decisions over status occur in connection with the selection of American professional athletes into Halls of Fame and All-Star games. Even Little League teams have a "politics of status" connected with who is the "most improved player of the year," "the most valuable player," "the most dedicated player," and so on. When people agree on who should receive these awards and special statuses, they tend to forget that the selection process was political. The only time they remember that selection processes are political is when they don't agree with the selection.

CAN SPORTS AND POLITICS BE KEPT SEPARATE?

The idea that sports and politics can be kept separate is naive. Sports do not exist in cultural vacuums. They are integral parts of the social world. As parts of that world, they are influenced by social, political, and economic forces. Sports do not exist apart from the people who create, organize, and play them. The lives of those people and their relationships with one another are at least partially connected to issues of power and control. Therefore politics becomes a part of sports just because politics is a part of people's lives. It is unavoidable.

Actual government intervention in sports is related to the need for sponsorship, organization, and facilities. The fact that sports are important parts of people's lives and that sports can be the scene for problems often leads to government regulations and controls. The form of government involvement in sports varies by society, but when it occurs its purposes are (1) to protect people and maintain order, (2) to develop physical abilities and fitness, (3) to promote the prestige of a group, (4) to establish a sense of social solidarity among group members, (5) to re-

affirm political ideology within a group, and (6) to increase the legitimacy of the political system and the people in power.

Government involvement that occurs in state-controlled societies with planned economies is especially clear. Sponsorship of sports is direct; facilities are owned and operated by the state; and the state determines rules and policies about sport and the conditions under which it is played. Government involvement in countries with market economies is less direct but usually quite extensive. Sport programs and facilities are often supported by city, state, provincial, or federal funds. Various government officials and agencies regulate who may participate in what sport activities under what circumstances, and they often regulate the circumstances under which commercial sports are sponsored and played.

The rules, policies, and funding priorities set by government officials and agencies reflect the political struggles between groups within any society. This does not mean that the same people will always benefit when government involvement occurs, but it does mean that involvement will seldom result in everyone receiving equal benefits. For example, when funds are given to elite sport programs and the development and training of elite athletes, fewer funds are available for general-participation programs. Of course, funding priorities could favor mass participation instead of elite sports, but the point is that the priorities themselves are subject to debate and negotiation. This political process is an inevitable part of sports.

History shows that groups with the most resources, organization, and outside support and with goals that most closely fit with the interests of decision makers are most likely to be favored when government involvement in sports occurs. The groups least likely to be favored are those that fail to understand the connection between sports and politics or who do not have the resources to effectively influence political processes. As long as people believe the myth that sports and politics are unrelated, they remain at a disadvantage when rules and policies are made and funds are allocated.

The connection between sports and international relations is dependent on how sports are promoted, organized, and played. When there is a heavy emphasis on competitive success, the national affiliations of athletes, and medal counts by country, there is little chance for the development of friendly international relationships. If relationships between nations are already unfriendly, such events may increase hostilities. The Olympic Games are a good case in point. The major emphasis among many of those who promote and watch the Olympics is on outcomes rather than the experiences of athletes. Medal counts and national prestige are often primary concerns.

The future of the Olympic Games may depend on changes in the way they are defined and staged. Opening ceremonies and medal award ceremonies may have to be revised to recognize individual achievements while emphasizing international unity among athletes. It may also be necessary to discard national uniforms, flags, and anthems and to change how medal counts are calculated. Team sports should be revised, sports that demand wealth for participation should be dropped, and the Olympic motto should be revised to emphasize the process of participation and a commitment to fair play. It may also be necessary to use multiple sites rather than a single host country for Olympic Games. These changes will not eliminate politics from the Olympics, but they will enable the games to be played in the spirit described in the Olympic Charter.

The impact of sports on foreign policy deliberations seems to be primarily symbolic and ideological. Sports have been used in the realm of public diplomacy, but it is difficult to measure how effective they are in producing changes in the way particular nations are viewed by others throughout the world. However, sports may also be a means for economically and militarily powerful nations to exercise subtle influence over social life and political events in less powerful nations around the world. Under certain conditions, this constitutes a form of **cultural imperialism,** that is, a process through which powerful countries extend their economic or political influence in other countries by controlling or appropriating various forms of popular culture associated with particular ideologies and consumption patterns. Research on this topic suggests that the role of sports in the relationships between powerful nations and developing nations is very complex (James, 1984; Klein, 1989; Mandle and Mandle, 1988, 1989).

As international sports organizations become increasingly powerful they may become important political players in transnational relations and world politics. The likelihood that sports will be used to promote social transformation is small, but sports have been used in that way in connection with challenging racial apartheid in South Africa. The globalization of sports raises important questions about whether people are sharing their cultures and developing mutual understanding, or whether corporate capitalism is simply using sports to spread a Euro-American form of consumer ideology around the world. Although the sociology of sport has given little attention to issues of transnational relations, world politics, and globalization in the past, these topics will attract increasing attention in the future.

Politics is also part of the very structure and organization of sports. Political processes exist whenever people in sport organizations make determinations about eligibility, game rules, rule enforcement, organizing and overseeing events, and distributing rewards associated with sports. This is why many sport organizations are described as "governing bodies"—they are the context for political decision making that affects everyone connected with sports.

Looking at sports from the inside or looking at their connections with social relations in local, national, and international contexts clearly shows that they are inseparable from politics.

SUGGESTED READINGS

Cantalon, H., and R. Gruneau, eds. 1982. Sport, culture and the modern state. University of Toronto Press, Toronto, Ontario (*contains 11 articles in which the relationship between sport and the state is given a thorough theoretical treatment*).

Eichberg, H. 1984. Olympic sport—neocolonialization and alternatives. International Review for the Sociology of Sport 19(1):97-106 (*discussion of how powerful nations have used international sport to make less powerful nations dependent on them*).

Hoberman, J.M. 1984. Sport and political ideology. University of Texas Press, Austin (*a high-level, detailed analysis of sports and politics*).

Hoberman, J. 1986. The Olympic crisis: sport, politics and the moral order. Aristide D. Caratzas, New Rochelle, N.Y. (*an in-depth critique of the modern games and why they have failed to promote internationalism*).

James, C.L.R. 1984. Beyond a boundary. Pantheon Books, New York (*classic analysis of cricket and British colonialism in the West Indies; first published in 1963*).

Jarvie, G. 1991. Highland Games: The making of the myth. Edinburgh University Press, Edinburgh (*critical historical and sociological analysis of the emergence of contemporary forms of Highland Games in Scotland; focuses on the role of sports in shaping cultural identity*).

Johnson, A., and J. H. Frey, eds. 1985. Government and sport. Rowman & Allanheld, Totowa, N.J. (*14 papers on sports and public policy issues in the United States*).

Lucas, J.A. 1992. The future of the Olympic Games. Human Kinetics Books, Champaign, Ill. (*an "insider's look" into Olympism and the Olympic movement; uncritical but informative description and analysis of recent IOC policies, programs, and prospects for the future*).

Macintosh, D., with T. Bedecki and C.E.S. Franks. 1987. Sport and politics in Canada: Federal government involvement since 1961. McGill-Queen's University Press, Montreal & Kingston (*analysis showing how organized sports in Canada became institu-tionalized, rationalized, and elitist as government used sports to promote national unity*).

Macintosh, D., and D. Whitson. 1990. The game planners: Transforming Canada's sport system. McGill-Queen's University Press, Montreal & Kingston (*informative study of national sport organizations and how their policy-making processes are influenced by government funding and philosophy; lists recommendations for limiting and directing government involvement in sports*).

Mandle, J.R., and J.D. Mandle. 1988. Grass roots commitment: Basketball and society in Trinidad and Tobago. Caribbean Books, Parkersburg, Iowa (*ethnographic analysis of what happened in one case in which a sport from an economically powerful country became part of popular culture in a less advantaged country; looks at basketball in light of class, gender, racial and ethnic divisions in communities in Trinidad and Tobago*).

Olympika, 1992- (journal published by The Center for Olympic Studies and co-edited by R.K. Barney and K.V. Meier at the University of Western Ontario; *articles emphasize sociocultural research on the Olympic Games and the Olympic Movement, including connections between sports and politics*).

Peace and understanding through sport: a monograph. 1989. vol. 2, no. 1 (Winter) (*20 papers on the problems and prospects of influencing international relations through the use of sports; authors include social scientists, amateur sport officials, media and government representatives; published by The Institute for International Sport at the University of Rhode Island in Kingston, RI*).

Segrave, J., and D. Chu, eds. 1988. The Olympic Games in transition. Human Kinetics Publishers, Champaign, Ill. (*contains 28 articles on the Olympics*).

Shaikin, B. 1988. Sport and politics. Praeger, New York (*a journalist looks at the political intrigue surrounding the Olympics and the 1984 Los Angeles Games*).

Vinokur, M.B. 1988. More than a game: sports and politics. Greenwood Press, New York (*a functionalist analysis of international sport; special attention given to sport in Romania and the German Democratic Republic*).

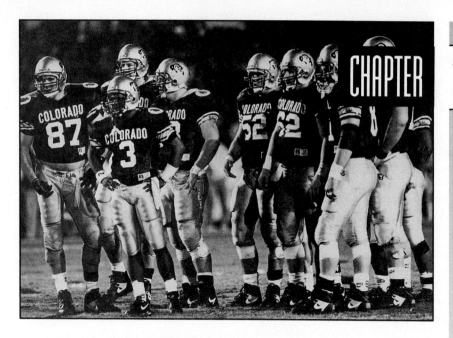

SPORTS IN HIGH SCHOOL AND COLLEGE

Do varsity sports programs contribute to education?

Athletics, band, drill team, cheerleading—all . . . contribute to the total growth of a young person, providing these activities are conducted from a balanced educational perspective. Athletics is only one slice of the educational pie. . . . Yet it is an integral part of the pie.

Raj B. Chopra, Superintendent of Schools, Shawnee Mission, Kansas (1983)

The overall message being drilled into our kids is clear and dangerous. . . . Superstars sign 5-year contracts for $20 million. Teachers sign 1-year contracts for $20,000. In those circumstances, to whom will you listen, your teacher or your coach? Where will you spend your time, in the library or the gym?

Tom McMillen, former NBA player and member of U.S. Congress

. . . intercollegiate athletics has become . . . a huge commercial entertainment conglomerate, with operating methods and objectives totally separate from, and mainly opposed to, the educational aims of the schools that house its franchises.

Murray Sperber, Author, College Sports, Inc. (1990)

Our expectations are to play for and win the national championship every year . . . Second, third, fourth, and fifth don't do you any good in this business.

Dennis Erickson, Head Football Coach, University of Miami (1993)

Interscholastic sports do not exist in every country. In fact, few schools outside North America and Japan sponsor and fund varsity sport programs. Organized sports for adolescents and young adults in most countries are tied to community-based athletic clubs funded by the state or a combination of public and private sources. However, interscholastic sports have become an accepted and important part of U.S. high schools and colleges, and they are becoming increasingly important in Canadian and Japanese schools.

This chapter focuses on whether interscholastic sports have an effect on the achievement of the overall educational mission of high schools and colleges. In exploring this issue I will consider five questions:

1. What are the arguments for and against varsity sports?
2. Is varsity sport participation related to academic achievement and overall social development among student-athletes?
3. How are interscholastic sports programs related to the lives of all students in high schools or colleges?
4. Do high schools and colleges experience organizational benefits from interscholastic programs?
5. What are the major problems associated with interscholastic programs, and how might they be solved?

ARGUMENTS FOR AND AGAINST INTERSCHOLASTIC SPORTS

Most Americans take interscholastic sport programs for granted. However, recent budget cutbacks and highly publicized problems in certain high school and college sports programs have raised questions about how sports are related to educational goals and the overall development of young people. Similar questions are being raised about interscholastic sports in Canadian schools. Responses to these questions are varied. Program supporters claim interscholastic sports are supportive of the educational mission of schools; critics claim they interfere with that mission. Both arguments on this issue are summarized in Table 15-1.

Although interscholastic sport programs have been the objects of many studies, the debate about their educational relevance continues today. When people enter this debate they often exaggerate the benefits or the problems associated with varsity sport programs. Supporters emphasize glowing success stories, and critics emphasize shocking cases of excess and abuse, but the most accurate descriptions probably lie somewhere in between. Nonetheless, both the supporters and the critics call attention to many of the important issues in the relationship between sports and education. This chapter will focus on some of those issues.

INTERSCHOLASTIC SPORTS AND THE EXPERIENCES OF HIGH SCHOOL STUDENTS

Do varsity sport programs affect the educational and developmental experiences of high school students? This question is difficult to answer. Education and development occur in connection with many activities and relationships. Even though varsity sport programs are very important in some schools and for some students, they are only one of many sources of potentially influential experiences. Research on this issue has primarily focused on the characteristics of student-athletes, although some social scientists have tried to study how sports are connected with the overall school culture that exists among high school students.

High School Student-Athletes

Studies have consistently shown that when compared with students who do not play varsity sports, high school athletes, *as a group*, generally have better grade point averages, more positive attitudes towards school, more interest in continuing their education after graduation, and a slightly better educational achievement rate. These differences have usually been modest, and it has been difficult for researchers to

Table 15-1 Popular arguments for and against interscholastic sports

Arguments for	Arguments against
1. Involve students in school activities and increases interest in academic activities	1. Distract the attention of students away from academic activities
2. Build the responsibility, achievement orientation, and teamwork skills required for adult participation in society	2. Perpetuate dependence and immaturity and focus the attention of students on a set of "macho" values no longer appropriate in industrial society
3. Provide fitness training and stimulate interest in physical activities among all students in the school	3. Relegate most students to the role of spectator and cause too many serious injuries to active participants
4. Generate the spirit and unity necessary to maintain the school as a viable organization	4. Create a superficial, transitory spirit subverting the educational goals of the school
5. Promote parental, alumni, and community support for all school programs	5. Deprive educational programs of resources, facilities, staff, and community support
6. Give students opportunities to develop and display skills in activities valued in the society at large	6. Apply excessive pressure on student-athletes and lead some adults to educate young people for their athletic skills rather than other human qualities

separate the effects of sport participation from the effects of family backgrounds, support from friends, and other factors related to educational attitudes and performance. However, membership on a varsity team is a valued status in most U.S. schools, and it seems regularly to go hand-in-hand with positive educational experiences. The problem is that we don't know if sport participation actually *causes* those positive experiences.

Of course, the most logical explanation for differences between varsity athletes and other students is that interscholastic sports, like other co-curricular activities, attract students who already have characteristics associated with academic and social success in high school. Most studies have not been able to test this explanation because they don't actually follow students throughout their high school careers and keep track of how and why changes occur in their lives. Usually, the studies simply report information collected from students at one point in time. This makes it impossible for researchers to say whether playing varsity sports really

changes people, or whether students who try out for varsity teams, get selected for teams, and continue as team members are simply different from other students before they become varsity athletes. Even when researchers think that playing varsity sports does change people, they are unable to say anything about the specific aspects of sport participation that account for the changes.

Just because young people grow and develop during the same years they play on varsity teams does not mean that sport participation *causes* the growth and development. After all, 14- to 18-year-olds grow and develop in many ways whether they play varsity sports or do other things. Most studies do not distinguish between all the different things that might explain growth and development.

Fortunately, there are a few studies that have been designed to follow students over time and measure changes that occur in their lives. For example, Elmer Spreitzer, a sociologist from Bowling Green State University, did a study in which he analyzed data from a national probability sample of 12,000 young men and women from 1100 public and private schools around the United States. Information had been collected from high school sophomores and seniors in 1980, and then follow-up information was collected from the same students in 1982, 1984, and 1986. This enabled Spreitzer to track students who played on varsity sport teams, and compare them with other students as they got older. Spreitzer found that compared with other students, young people who played on varsity sport teams were more likely to come from *economically privileged* backgrounds, and have *above average* cognitive abilities and self-esteem and academic performance records (grades and test scores). In other words, students who tried out for teams, made teams, and stayed on them were different in certain ways from other students before they became high school athletes.

Spreitzer found that this type of "selection" pattern was common to nearly all co-curricular activities, not just varsity sports. In other words, students who choose to participate in school sponsored activities tend to be slightly different from other students. These differences are the greatest in activities in which student self-selection is combined with formal try-outs during which teachers or coaches select students for participation. In the case of varsity sports, this selection process is especially powerful because it begins in youth sports and continues through junior high school.

Spreitzer also found that young men and women who started playing varsity sports as sophomores and continued through their senior years were different from those who were cut from teams or who voluntarily quit teams. Students who discontinued varsity sport participation were more likely to come from *less advantaged* economic backgrounds; they were more likely to have *lower* cognitive abilities, lower self-esteem, and lower grade point averages; and they were less likely to take college preparation courses. Furthermore, young women were twice as likely as young men to discontinue participation. These findings suggest that in addi-

tion to a selection process, there is a complex, but nonrandom *filtering* process that occurs in varsity sports.

One of the difficulties Spreitzer faced when he analyzed the data was that many young people who played varsity sports also participated in other co-curricular activities. Therefore he could not say whether changes in the lives of these young people were due to playing sports or participating in other activities, such as working on the yearbook, participating in a student club or student government, or doing community service.

In the last part of his analysis, Spreitzer tracked changes during the 6-year period after students left high school. He found that those who played varsity sports as seniors were no different on a number of traits from those who did not play. The traits included psychological adjustment, patterns of alcohol use, level of self-esteem, age at marriage, and age at birth of first child. There was a slight difference in educational achievement, but playing varsity sports was not nearly as important as other factors affecting college attendance and degree completion. Furthermore, playing varsity sports seemed to be important only for white males, not for females or African Americans.

Other studies that track students over time have reported findings very similar to those of Spreitzer's (Hauser and Leuptow, 1978; Melnick, Vanfossen, and Sabo, 1988; Rees, Howell, and Miracle, 1990). So what does this research tell us about interscholastic sports?

- *First*, it tells us that we should be very careful when generalizing about the educational value of interscholastic sports. Playing varsity sports does not automatically change high school students in positive ways or in any ways that make them significantly different from other high school students. Usually those who try out for teams, get selected by coaches, and stay on teams for more than one year are somewhat different from other students to begin with. Therefore simple statistical comparisons between them don't prove anything about the value of sport participation itself.

- *Second,* the research suggests that if we want to learn more about the effect of interscholastic sports in the lives of high school students we must do long term studies that allow us to look at the overall lives of students, not just their sport lives. Growth and development occur in connection with many different experiences—some outside the school and some inside the school. Unless we know something about young people's lives in general we can't claim that varsity sport participation is more influential than working in a part-time job, joining the debate team, writing for the school newspaper, or caring for younger brothers and sisters.

- *Third,* the research also suggests that we should study the effect of varsity sports on the larger student culture that exists in high schools. It may be that the social importance of sports rests in how they are connected with gender, class, and race and ethnic relations in an entire school. Studying this possibility would seem to be a higher priority than focusing only on the students who try out for and make teams.

"Student Culture" in High Schools

Sociologists have long recognized that varsity sports are among the most important social activities sponsored by high schools. Being a varsity athlete brings a student prestige among peers, formal rewards in the school, and recognition from teachers, administrators, and even people in the local community. Athletes, especially males in high-profile sports, are usually accorded recognition that guarantees popularity in the student culture. Certain sport events have traditionally been scheduled and promoted as major social occasions on the school calendar. These social occasions have often become important for students because they provide opportunities for social interaction—especially

male-female interaction—outside the classroom (Eder and Parker, 1987). Furthermore, going to a high school sport event is usually defined by parents (even strict, controlling parents) as an approved social activity for their sons and daughters.

From a sociological perspective it is important to ask what varsity sports contribute to student culture in a high school. Because being an athlete on certain teams is socially significant and because certain sports events are important in the social lives of many students, interscholastic sports have the potential to influence values and behaviors among students. For example, do they influence how students evaluate one another or how they think about social life and social relations?

SPORTS AND POPULARITY For many years, sociologists studied student culture simply by studying the criteria high school students used to determine popularity (Coleman, 1961a, b; Eitzen, 1975; Thirer and Wright, 1985). Usually it was found that when male students were given the choice of how they wished they could be remembered after graduation they chose "athletic star" over "brilliant student" or "most popular." Female students, on the other hand, were more likely to choose "brilliant student" and "most popular" over "athletic star" (Thirer and Wright, 1985). More recent research indicates that many young men in high school prefer to be known as "scholar-athletes" whereas young women generally prefer to be known as "scholars" and "members of the leading social group" (Chandler and Goldberg, 1990). Therefore the link between being popular and being an athlete is stronger for male students than female students. When it comes to popularity for high school women, being in the "in-group" is crucial and being an athlete does not by itself put a female student in the in-group (Chandler and Goldberg, 1990).

What do these research findings mean? Are young men more concerned with being athletes than with being scholars? Are young women unconcerned about sport? The answer to both

"These guys on the Honor Roll may be able to get good grades, but they don't really do anything for the school."

these questions is *no*. In fact, most high school students *are* concerned with academic achievement. They are aware of the importance of finishing high school and going on to college or a trade school, and their parents usually remind them regularly of how important school should be in their lives. However, *outside* the classroom high school students are concerned with social acceptance, personal autonomy, sexual identities, and "growing up" into adults. They want to be popular enough to fit in with their peers, to have opportunities to control their own lives, to feel secure about their own sexual development, and to show others they are "grown up." This means that a wide range of things are important in the *social* lives of adolescents. Because males and females in North America are still treated and evaluated in different ways, adoles-

cents use different strategies for seeking acceptance, autonomy, sexual development, and recognition as young adults. As things are now, sport participation for males is an important basis for popularity, as long as the young men don't neglect school. Sport participation is also important for young women, but being an athlete must usually be combined with other things for young women to be popular within the student cultures of most high schools. Young women don't have to conform to traditional definitions of femininity, but to be popular they usually need to show they are something other than just tough and competitive in sports.

SPORTS AND IDEOLOGY Interscholastic sport programs do more than simply affect the status structures of high school students. This was clearly illustrated in H.G. Bissinger's book,

Friday Night Lights (1990). Bissinger, a noted Pulitzer Prize winning author, wrote about a football team in a Texas high school known for its emphasis on football. His account was deliberately dramatic, and he made the case that in Odessa, Texas, as in many other American towns:

> Football stood at the very core of what the town was about. . . . It had nothing to do with entertainment and everything to do with how people felt about themselves (p. 237).

As Bissinger described events through the football season he noted that football was important because it celebrated a male cult of toughness and sacrifice and a female cult of nurturance and servitude. When the team lost, people accused the coaches of not being tough enough and the players of being undisciplined. Women stayed on the sidelines and faithfully tried to support and please the men who battled in behalf of the school and town. Students and townspeople could go to football games and have their ideas about "natural differences" between men and women reaffirmed. Young men who couldn't hit hard, physically intimidate opponents, or play with pain were described as "pussies." "Gay bashing" was considered an approved weekend social activity by the athletes. A player's willingness to sacrifice his body for the team was taken as a sign of commitment and character.

Bissinger also noted that high school sports were closely tied to a long history of racism in the town, and football itself was organized and played in ways that reaffirmed traditional racial ideology among whites and produced racial resentment among African Americans. Many Anglo townspeople in 1988 still referred to blacks as "niggers" and they blamed blacks and Mexicans for most of the town's problems. But they had accepted desegregation in 1980 because it could be used to strengthen the football team. This irony associated with blacks working hard in behalf of whites was noted by a local black minister when he observed that "Today, instead of the cotton field, it's the sports arena" (p. 109).

When a white coach was asked what the star halfback would be without football, he quickly answered, "a big ol' dumb nigger" (p. 67). Meanwhile, white people generally used physical explanations based on traditional racist ideology to explain the abilities or lack of abilities among black players.

Unfortunately, Bissinger did not write about the students who didn't participate in sports or those who didn't agree with the values and experiences glorified through football. His account provides only a partial picture of sports and student culture. But another study, done by anthropologist Doug Foley (1991), provides a much more complete picture of student culture. Foley studied a small Texas town and focused much of his attention on students in the local high school. He paid special attention to the school's football team and how the team and its games were incorporated into the overall social life of the school and the local community. He also studied social and academic activities among a wide range of different students, including those who ignored or deliberately avoided sports.

Foley's findings revealed that student culture in a high school cannot be summarized simply by studying the football team. In fact, Foley emphasized that student culture "was varied, changing, and inherently full of contradictions" (p. 100). Football and other sports provided important social occasions for getting together with friends, flirting, and defusing the anxiety associated with tests and over-controlling teachers, but sports were only one small part of the lives of adolescents at the school. Being an athlete was used by students in their "identity performances" with other students and with adults, but identity for most students was grounded more in gender, class, and ethnicity than in sport participation. Foley concluded that sports were important to the extent that they presented students with a language or vocabulary they could use to identify important values and experiences. For example, most sports came with a vocabulary that extolled and naturalized individualism, competition, and differences related to gender, race, ethnicity, and social class.

We need more qualitative research on student culture, but the projects that have been done seem to suggest that the most important social consequences of interscholastic sports may be more related to ideas about social relations than to grade point averages, attitudes toward school, or student popularity (see also Rees, Howell, and Miracle, 1990).

Additional Consequences of High School Sports

One of the themes running through this book is that sports are social constructions. This means they can be organized and played in many different ways and their consequences can be creatively manipulated to meet a variety of goals. However, most people associated with interscholastic sports have simply assumed that sports and sport participation automatically produce positive results, so they have not taken the time to critically examine sports in student culture as a whole.

Research on interscholastic sports has led me to conclude that sports in and of themselves are not educational. However, if sports are organized and played in certain ways, they can be used in the educational process. For example, when varsity sports are organized so young people are taken seriously as human beings and valued by those who are important in their lives, they can be educationally useful. But if varsity sports are organized in ways that lead young people to think that adults are simply treating them as "athletes to be developed," interscholastic programs will turn into developmental dead-ends and students will not even be excited about playing on school teams. Adolescents need to be an integral part of their schools, they need opportunities to develop and display their competence in contexts where they get noticed and rewarded, and they need chances to prove they are on their way to becoming valued adults in their communities. If interscholastic sports can be organized to do these things, they make valuable contributions to education and development.

Interscholastic sports can also be valuable if they are intentionally organized to provide young people opportunities to connect with adults who can serve them as advocates. This is especially important in schools located in low-income and impoverished areas, where young people are most in need of advocates. Sports can give them a chance to be noticed for something good rather than for how "bad" they are in the school hallways or on the streets.

Finally, sports could also be valuable educationally if teachers and coaches took them more seriously as learning experiences. For example, Jomills Braddock and his colleagues (1991) have studied the importance of sports to young African American males and argued that sports in middle schools could be used to rekindle a commitment to education among young people who are ready to give up on classroom learning by the time they are 7th or 8th graders. They suggest the following:

> . . . both players and nonplayers . . . could write or contribute to sport columns in school or local newspapers, thereby enhancing student writing and language skills. Students could collect and generate team and player statistics for a variety of school and local sport activities, utilizing . . . crucial . . . mathematical skills. . . . [Students] could organize the sport sections of school yearbooks, participate on a sports debate team, or perhaps start a sports enthusiast club (p. 129).

The point of these suggestions is to use sports as part of a larger process of giving students responsibility, including them into activities that will help them develop skills, rewarding them for their competence, and connecting them with adults who can exert positive influence in their lives.

This notion of deliberately designing sports to give students responsibility has been emphasized in applied research on moral development (cf., Bredemeier and Shields, 1993) and prosocial behavior (Hellison, 1983, 1985, 1993; Hellison et al, 1990). This research also suggests that unless care is taken, sport participation can actually subvert moral development and self-responsibility among young people. But it does not have to be that way if teachers, coaches, and others work together to make sports into learning experiences.

INTERCOLLEGIATE SPORTS AND THE EXPERIENCES OF COLLEGE STUDENTS

Does varsity sport participation affect the educational and developmental experiences of college athletes? This became a hot question in the mid-1980s and it has gotten even hotter since then. Stories about the academic failures of college athletes, and the failures of colleges and universities to take the education of student-athletes seriously have appeared in newspapers, magazines, books, and television specials. Research on this issue has become more common over the past decade.

Knowing how to assess media and research reports is difficult unless you have an overall picture of intercollegiate sports. Part of this picture is described in the box on pp. 396-397. It is important to realize that not all intercollegiate programs are the same. However, most people focus attention on *big-time, entertainment-oriented* intercollegiate sports; these are the ones that get heavy media publicity, and have most of the problems. Unfortunately, most people forget that many college athletes participate in programs similar to high school programs. Athletes in these *lower profile* programs often do not have scholarships; they participate on a voluntary basis just as they would in any co-curricular activity. Being on a varsity team may be a source of prestige in some schools with *lower profile* programs, but it is not likely to have much effect on how students evaluate one another. In many of these programs, coaches may even go out of their way to set up practices and game schedules that don't interfere with students' coursework. Studies of *lower profile* programs show that the academic performance of their athletes is very similar to other college students (Eitzen,

1987b; McTeer, 1987; Meyer, 1990; Sack, 1987). *Lower profile* programs generally include many women's teams, most teams in NCAA Division III and Canadian university programs, and teams in many nonrevenue-producing sports.

Student-Athletes in *Big-Time* Programs

Being an athlete in a *big-time* intercollegiate program is not always compatible with being a good student; this is especially true for those who play on *entertainment-oriented* sport teams. Athletes in big-time programs often have some form of scholarship aid, and they are expected to commit time and energy to their sports. When commitments to sports interfere with academic work and having a social life, student-athletes have to make choices.

There isn't much information on how student-athletes handle these choices. However, there is reason to believe that male athletes in *big-time, entertainment-oriented* sports often rank their athletic and social lives ahead of their academic lives (Adler and Adler, 1991). Not all student-athletes do this, but putting academic work ahead of sports and social life is not an easy choice, and even after it's made, the task of taking a full load of courses while playing sports is very challenging. Those with poor academic preparation usually have to limit their course loads so they can handle coursework and still honor commitments to sports; many others have to arrange course schedules around their sports, and then catch up on coursework during summers and the off-season. The dynamics underlying these choices are explained in the box on pp. 398-400.

Interestingly, women intercollegiate athletes, even those in big-time programs, are much more likely than their male counterparts to sacrifice their social lives to make the most of educational opportunities. It seems that the atmosphere on most women's teams is quite supportive of educational achievement and intellectual development, whereas the atmosphere on many men's teams is clearly anti-intellectual (Meyer, 1988, 1990). But this may change in the future if certain women's sports become entertainment-oriented in the same way certain men's sports are. This is also discussed in the box on pp. 398-400.

The fact that so many student-athletes in big-time, entertainment-oriented sports have chosen to focus on their athletic lives and ignore their academic lives has raised serious questions about the educational relevance of intercollegiate sports. These questions have embarrassed many colleges and universities because their athletic departments were organized to not only encourage student-athletes to give low priority to their academic lives but to actually require it. The fact that university presidents, academic administrators, and faculty allowed this to occur was also embarrassing.

Throughout the 1980s there was a growing concern about the extent to which big-time, entertainment-oriented athletic departments were systematically ignoring the educational mission of the schools of which they were a part. Information about how some athletic departments recruited, used, and cut loose young men in their quest to win games and increase revenues became so widespread that many Americans questioned the integrity of the universities that sponsored the programs. Many people thought that big-time sports were subverting education rather than enhancing it, and that young people were simply being used to make money and generate publicity without taking them seriously as students or as human beings. Slowly, universities have responded to this challenge to their integrity, and they have begun to make serious attempts to change intercollegiate sports so the experiences of student-athletes are more compatible with the achievement of educational goals.

Understanding the connection between intercollegiate sport participation and academic performance is important when discussing sports and education. The next section outlines some of what we know about the academic lives of student athletes.

Grades and Graduation Rates: How Do Athletes Compare with Other College Students?

Unlike athletes in high schools and small colleges, athletes in big-time university programs often differ from other students on campuses. Although their characteristics vary from one sport to another, they tend to come from more diversified socioeconomic backgrounds than other students and they often choose different courses and majors. This makes it difficult to compare the academic achievements of varsity athletes with the achievements of other students at schools with big-time programs. Grade point averages (GPAs) have different meanings from one university to another and from department to department within universities. For similar reasons it is also difficult to use graduation rates as indicators of academic experiences.

Research findings on grades and graduation rates are confusing. Some studies show athletes earning higher grades than students who do not play on varsity teams; other studies show the exact opposite. Some studies show athletes attending graduate school more often than nonathletes, and others show athletes taking an abundance of courses requiring little or no intellectual effort (Case et al., 1987). A study done by the American Association of Collegiate Registrars/Admissions Officers (1984) reports that the grades received by 2,000 freshman athletes in 57 schools with big-time sport programs were as good as those received by freshman nonathletes from comparable academic backgrounds. Unfortunately, the study did not control for differences in the types of classes taken by each of the two groups of freshmen. Nor were the grades bro-

Text continued on p. 401.

Intercollegiate Sports Are Not All The Same*

The amount of money spent every year on intercollegiate sports varies from less than $50,000 at some small colleges to over $20 million at some large universities. Large universities may sponsor 10 to 18 different varsity sports for men and a similar number for women. In small colleges, coaches are often members of the teaching faculty and one person may coach two or more teams. Larger universities may have up to 10 coaches for football alone, and these coaches are not likely to have faculty appointments.

Because intercollegiate sports are so diversified, it is difficult to discuss them without grouping them into categories. One way of doing this is to simply identify the athletic associations with which schools are affiliated. Schools with intercollegiate sports can be affiliated with two major national associations: the National Collegiate Athletic Association (NCAA), or the National Association of Intercollegiate Athletics (NAIA). A third group, the College Football Association (CFA), was formed by NCAA schools with big-time football programs.

The NCAA, with 895 member institutions and about 200 affiliated conferences and professional organizations, is the largest intercollegiate athletic association. Member institutions are divided into four major divisions reflecting program size and level of competition. *Division I* includes schools that have what might be described as big-time programs; about 301 institutions are classified in this category. Division I is broken down into two subgroups—schools with big-time football teams (106) and schools without football teams. *Division II* and *Division III* contain 247 and 347 schools, respectively; these schools have smaller programs and compete at less than a big-time level.

So-called *big-time programs* usually emphasize either football or men's basketball, because these sports are seen by most people as the best potential money makers.

Football has the best potential to make money, although large losses are also possible and common. Men's basketball seldom generates the money that football does, but it is cheaper to sponsor and usually does not incur risk of such large losses. Although hockey makes money in a handful of schools, no other sports make enough money to pay their own expenses.

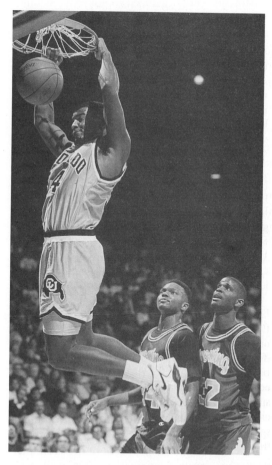

Big-time intercollegiate sports are major forms of entertainment; their reasons for existence have little to do with educational goals. (University of Colorado and Brian Lewis)

*Throughout this chapter, attention will be focused on 4-year institutions. Junior colleges and 2-year community colleges will not be covered in our discussion.

The general level of athletic talent is higher in NCAA Division I schools than in Divisions II or III or the NAIA. Athletes in Division I schools are more likely to have scholarships and access to academic support programs sponsored by athletic departments. Additionally, the amount of team travel in Division I schools is greater, the national and regional media coverage is more extensive, and the consequences of winning and losing are usually greater.

Not all schools maintain membership in the NCAA. Some choose to affiliate with the NAIA. NAIA schools also sponsor teams in a variety of sports; scholarships may or may not be given, and most of their teams are not considered big-time. The NAIA lists 425 colleges and universities as members (in 1993), some of which also maintain membership in the NCAA. However, the 1993 budget of the NAIA was less than $4 million, whereas the NCAA had an annual budget of around $175 million.

Even though the majority of intercollegiate programs are not considered big-time, people often assume that the typical program is represented by the universities whose teams play in televised games. The University of Notre Dame, Ohio State University, the University of Alabama, UCLA, Indiana University, and similar schools are the exceptions rather than the rule in intercollegiate sports.

The idea that all colleges and universities have big-time programs is also encouraged by the fact that some smaller colleges and universities give priority emphasis to one or two sports. The NCAA does not allow Division II or III schools to have big-time football teams, but it does allow them to compete at a big-time level in one or two other sports. Because some Division II and III schools choose to do this, many people assume that all their sports are played at a big-time level. But this is not true. Big-time teams capture 99% of the media attention and spectator interest, but most sports at most schools are not played at a big-time level. When attention is restricted only to big-time sports, we get a distorted picture of intercollegiate programs.

LOWER PROFILE PROGRAMS

Many intercollegiate programs operate much like larger high school programs. The major difference is that because college athletes are free to choose their schools, college coaches actively recruit for their teams. Depending on their skills, athletes may receive some form of financial assistance. The most valued form of direct assistance is a scholarship covering all expenses for room, board, tuition, fees, and books. However, most schools with lower profile programs cannot afford to give full scholarships. They usually limit their direct financial assistance to tuition waivers, free meal tickets, or similar benefits. Indirect forms of financial assistance include providing student-athletes with jobs or finding them housing at reduced rates.

Unfortunately, we know little about student-athletes in schools with lower profile intercollegiate programs. No data exist on how these programs influence on-campus social life, the way students view the world around them, and the educational achievements of the athletes themselves.

BIG-TIME PROGRAMS

Big-time programs have little in common with high school programs. Athletic departments in large universities often operate as separate organizations, and much of their funding may come from outside sources such as gate receipts, contributions from boosters, media rights, and sponsorships. Athletes in big-time programs often receive grants or scholarships, and some enjoy adulation from others on campus.

Most research on intercollegiate sports and most data on athletes focus on Division I programs and on the revenue generating sports in those programs. Some of this research and data are discussed in this chapter. It is important to know about these programs, but it is also important to remember that few sports and sport teams on college campuses resemble big-time football and men's basketball teams. Most intercollegiate sports, even in large universities, do not get much publicity, and athletes in these sports are not as likely as football and men's basketball players to receive special attention or adulation.

Making Choices: The Experiences Of Athletes In Big-Time Programs

Intercollegiate athletes are often described with statistical profiles, but we know little about what goes on in their everyday lives and how they make choices related to sports, school, and social life. Fortunately, two studies provide a glimpse of this choice-making process. One was done by Peter and Patricia Adler (1991), who observed and interviewed members of a major college men's basketball program during a 9-year period. The other, by Barbara Meyer (1988, 1990), involved a series of in-depth interviews with members of women's volleyball and basketball teams at a major university.

The Adlers' study led them to conclude that playing in a big-time basketball program and being seriously involved in academics seldom went hand-in-hand. The young men they studied usually began their first year of coursework in college with optimism and idealism; they expected their academic experiences to contribute to their future occupational success. However, after one or two semesters they discovered that the demands of playing basketball, the social isolation that went along with being an athlete, and the powerful influence of their peers in the athletic subculture drew them further and further away from academic life.

Even though coaches often told them to focus on their courses, the athletes discovered it was necessary to select easy courses and the least challenging majors if they were to meet the coaches' expectations on the basketball court. Fatigue, the pressures of games, and limited time kept the players from becoming seriously involved in academic life. Furthermore, nobody ever asked these athletes about their studies. Attention was always focused on basketball, and few people really expected the athletes to identify themselves as students or to give priority to their academic lives.

When these young men received positive feedback, it was for athletic, not academic, performances. Difficulties in their courses often led the athletes to view academic life with pragmatic detachment—in other words, they became very "practical" in the way they chose classes and arranged their course schedules. They knew what they had to do to stay eligible, and coaches would make sure course schedules were arranged so their time and energy could be devoted to basketball. After taking a series of easy but uninteresting courses, and having a tough time in other courses, the student-athletes gradually detached themselves and withdrew from academic life on their campus.

This entire process of academic withdrawal was encouraged by the peer subculture that developed among the athletes. These young men were with one another constantly—in the dorms, at meals, at practices, on trips to away games, in the weight room, and on nights when there were no games. During these times they would seldom talk about academic or intellectual topics. If they did talk about the courses they were taking, it was in negative terms. They encouraged cutting classes rather than regular attendance, and they joked about each other's bad tests and failing papers. They provided each other with needed social support, but it was support for their athletic identities rather than academic identities. Therefore many came to see themselves as athletes, not as *student*-athletes.

Not all the athletes studied by the Adlers underwent this change in their academic lives. Some managed to strike a balance between their athletic and academic lives. This was most likely among those who entered college with realistic ideas about academic demands and those who had family members actively supporting their academic achievements. But striking this balance was never easy. It required solid high school preparation combined with ability or luck in developing relationships with faculty and other students.

REFLECT ON SPORT

These relationships with people outside of sports were important because they emphasized academic achievement and provided day-to-day support for academic identities. Therefore even though all the basketball players faced pressures to give first priority to their athletic lives, there were some who were able to balance athletics and academics.

The most important thing the Adlers found was that the entire structure of big-time intercollegiate sports works against maintaining a balance between athletics and academics. For example, when the basketball players they studied did have time to catch up on schoolwork, they often chose to ignore schoolwork and catch up on their social lives instead. As high profile people on campus, they had numerous social opportunities, and it was difficult for them to pass up the social opportunities for the sake of their coursework.

The Adlers suggested that this structure would never be changed unless athletes in big-time programs could be protected from the seductive attention and publicity that comes with a high-profile status. As part of this protection process, they suggested that freshman eligibility be banned so student-athletes could be more fully integrated into the social and academic life of the university when they first arrive on campus. Other suggestions were that athlete dorms should be abolished and that academic advisors, not coaches, should assist student-athletes in scheduling their courses and choosing their majors. Finally, athletes should also have faculty sponsors who encourage them to view their academic experiences from a different perspective than the one used by the athletic department.

Barbara Meyer's study was much less involved than the Adlers' study, but it is important because it focused on the experiences of women athletes. As in the Adlers' study, Meyer found that the basketball and volleyball players she studied entered college with positive attitudes about school and about the value of a college education. They wanted to earn degrees, and they weren't too concerned about issues of athletic eligibility. They said that playing their sports was very time-consuming and much more worklike than sports had been in high school. Their roommates often were athletes and they generally spent much of their time with other athletes, who usually became their best friends. All this was similar to the experiences of the men.

But Meyer also found a big difference between the women in her study and the men in the Adlers' study. Unlike the men, the women gradually became *more* interested in and concerned with their courses and academic lives. Unlike the men, they did not expect special treatment in their classes; rather than depending on coaches for academic advice they talked with academic advisers and friends about their course selections and majors. They also received support for academic achievement from their parents and their teammates; they thought their classes were interesting and useful; and they saw participation in sport as having an overall positive effect on academic achievement. Furthermore, the atmosphere on their teams was clearly supportive of academic and intellectual development.

The women athletes wanted to have good seasons, but they were less concerned with winning games than they had been in high school. Even though they were good athletes, other people treated them as students and reaffirmed their academic identities instead of their athletic identities. And none of the women had dedicated their lives to playing professional sports as some of the men had done. When the women had time away from their sports to catch up on coursework or their social lives, they often sacrificed their social lives in favor of academic work.

Continued.

REFLECT ON SPORT

Making Choices: The Experiences of Athletes in Big-Time Programs—cont'd

In summary, the men and the women student-athletes began college with similar attitudes and orientations. However, the sport subculture among

Research suggests that the academic implications of sport participation may be different for women than it is for men. The atmosphere on women's teams is generally supportive of academic achievement, whereas the atmosphere on men's teams, especially in big-time programs, is more supportive of athletic identities than of academic identities. (Tim Morse)

the men emphasized different priorities than did the sport subculture among the women. The men gradually withdrew from academic life whereas the women gradually became more involved in it. The reasons for this difference probably include one or more of the following:

• The women may have come from different social and educational backgrounds that encouraged them to give priority to academic choices.

• The women's programs probably did not receive the attention the men's program received, which made it easier for the women to develop and maintain academic identities and make different choices in their everyday lives.

• The women may not have received the same kind of encouragement as the men to focus on sport because their friends and parents did not see sport as a possible career option after college graduation.

• The women may not have received the same kind of encouragement to reaffirm their athletic image in social relationships and social activities on campus. Because women's sports are not publicized or defined by most students in the same way as high-profile men's sports, women may not be seen by other students as heroes or sought out to lend prestige to campus social activities and events.

Regardless of the possible reasons for the differences in the experiences between the men and women athletes in these two studies, both studies emphasize that student-athletes face choices during their college lives, and the decisions they make depend on the context in which they play, study, and interact with others.

ken down for athletes in different sports. These two factors are important for the following reasons:

1. Athletes in certain sports are often over-represented in specific courses and majors. This phenomenon is known as *clustering* (Case et al., 1987), and it seems to happen frequently on teams emphasizing eligibility over academic achievement and intellectual development. This means that all intercollegiate athletes should not be lumped together when discussing grades and graduation rates. Their experiences from sport to sport vary according to many factors.

2. Athletes in entertainment-oriented sports often come to college with lower high school GPAs and lower ACT and SAT scores than other students, including other athletes. Sometimes their academic goals are quite different from the goals of other students. All these things affect grades.

Studies of graduation rates are also confusing, partly because rates can be computed in many different ways. Some computations are based on the proportion of seniors on a particular team who graduate in a given year; others are based on the proportion of graduates among those who used all their years of athletic eligibility at the school. Some computations give the proportions of student-athletes in a particular class who graduate 4 years after they started as freshmen, and others are based on those who graduate after 5 or 6 years. Still others take into account those who transfer to other schools and graduate, or who leave school in good standing. During one year in the mid-1980s the graduation rate for the University of Nebraska football team was reported to be 48%, 60%, 69%, 70%, and 92%, depending on the computation method used (see Eitzen, 1987b). Each of these different rates was "true," but none of them gave a complete picture of what really went on in the football program.

SIDELINES

"YOUR LECTURE ON THE IMPORTANCE OF A STRONG BENCH REALLY INSPIRED ME, COACH!"

Although some athletes fit the "dumb athlete" stereotype, many have been able to combine participation in sport with academic pursuits in a constructive manner.

It is not surprising that reported graduation rates for athletes vary by conference, school, and sport. In the past, the rates in big-time sports programs at many universities were shameful. This was especially the case in entertainment-oriented sports such as football and men's basketball (Edwards, 1983, 1985; Eitzen, 1987b; Lapchick, 1984, 1987; Sack, 1987; Shapiro, 1984). The pressure to win and make money led many coaches and athletes to focus attention on eligibility rather than learning and graduation.

The best statistical information about the academic performance of student-athletes in big-time intercollegiate programs comes from a *USA Today* study and an NCAA study, both done in 1991. *USA Today* surveyed 276 schools with Division I men's and women's basketball teams and asked for graduation data on all students and all basketball players who began school between the 1980-81 and the 1984-85 academic years. Seventy-six percent of the schools responded. The goal of the study was to find what proportions of students and basketball players had graduated from those schools five years after they started. Here's a summary of what was found (Brady, 1991):

- 46% of the basketball players graduated within 5 years, compared to a 48% rate for all students. However, basketball players went to school full-time whereas other students may not have attended school full-time. During the 1980s about 75% of college students who went full-time graduated in less than 5 years.
- 36% of minority basketball players graduated in 5 years, compared to rates of 31% for blacks and 33% for Hispanics in the student body as a whole. However, over one-third of the schools had graduation rates of less than 25% for minority male players. (Most minority players on basketball teams are blacks).
- The basketball teams that went to NCAA post-season tournaments had lower graduation rates than teams at other schools.
- Women basketball players graduated at a 60% rate, although the rate has declined as women's teams have become more entertainment-oriented.

The NCAA study was done differently. It reported the 5-year graduation rates for 3,288 recruited student-athletes in all sports who entered 85 Division I universities in 1984 and 1985. Here's what was found (Wieberg, 1991, 1992):

- 46% of all student-athletes graduated in 5 years, 29% left school in good standing, and 25% left not in good standing. Only 25% of all student-athletes graduate in 4 years.
- 52% of white student-athletes graduated in 5 years, compared to 27% of black student-athletes; 20% of the white student-athletes and 43% of the black student-athletes left school not in good standing.
- Female student-athletes graduated at a 54% rate, whereas male student-athletes graduated at a 42% rate.

- Overall graduation rates are lowest in big-time men's basketball, and the rates for black basketball players are the lowest for any sport.

What do these rates mean? To whom should athletes be compared when determining the academic integrity of big-time sports? On the one hand, student-athletes might best be compared to regular full-time students who work 30 or more hours per week because athletes often devote at least that many hours to their sports. On the other hand, student-athletes might be best compared to other students with full scholarships, or those who enter college with similar ACT or SAT test scores and high school grades, or those who enter college with similar academic goals. My conclusion is that there is no single ideal comparison; many need to be done to get a comprehensive and fair idea of whether sport teams, athletic departments, and universities are living up to the spirit of higher education.

Finally, it should be noted that even though graduation is an important educational goal, it should not be the only criterion used to judge academic success. Degrees are important, but they may not mean much unless those who receive them have learned something while in college. Unfortunately, it is difficult to measure "learning" in a survey of student-athletes, but it is possible to go into universities and see if their athletic departments are being run in academically responsible ways. Until there is a system for doing this, we will have to depend on grades and graduation rates to show us what is going on. However, statistics don't tell the whole story. They alert us to possible problems and the need for action, but they don't tell us what all the problems are or what needs to be done to correct them.

Recent Changes in Big-Time Intercollegiate Sports

Before the late 1980s it was clear that the spirit of higher education was *not* being honored by big-time intercollegiate sports; education was irrelevant in many athletic programs, and academic courses were viewed only in terms of eligibility issues. Between 1988 and 1993 things started to change. In fact, there were increased efforts to correct abuses and bring intercollegiate sports closer in line with the spirit of higher education. Progress was made during that time but problems remain.

Big-time sport programs—especially entertainment-oriented programs—are *very* difficult to change. Teams in those programs are tied to many interests having nothing to do with education. Some athletes on those teams may be in school only to get the coaching needed to stay competitive in amateur Olympic sports (such as in swimming, track and field, volleyball, wrestling, rowing, etc.) or to become draft prospects in professional sports (such as baseball, basketball, football, and hockey). Coaches for those teams may view sports as businesses, and they may be hired and fired on the basis of how much revenue they can attract to the athletic program. Even academic administrators, including college presidents, may use the programs for public relations or fund raising tools instead of focusing on them as programs that should be educational in themselves.

Now there are major corporations who sponsor media coverage of intercollegiate sports and support teams for advertising purposes. These corporations have little or no interest in the academic development of athletes. When a shoe company pays a coach or school to put athletes' feet in their shoes, or when a soft-drink company buys an expensive gym scoreboard with their logo on it, they don't care if student-athletes are learning in their classes as long as they are attracting attention to the companies' products. Similarly, the local businesses that make money when the home team attracts fans are not concerned about whether the athletes scoring touchdowns and doing slam dunks have 1.6 grade points averages or are on the honor role; they just want them to be eligible to pack spectators into the stadium or arena.

Despite the influence of these noneducational interests, universities have begun to take more seriously the idea of academic reform in their athletic programs The passage of Proposition 48 and university responses to the Knight Foundation Commission on Intercollegiate Athletics are two examples that signal reform in intercollegiate sports.

PROPOSITION 48. In 1983 the NCAA passed a rule setting minimum standards for a first year athlete to be eligible to play on Division I college teams. This rule, known as Proposition 48 or Bylaw 5-1(j), stated that first year students were not eligible to participate in sports unless they entered college with a 2.0 GPA in 11 core subjects in high school *and* a score of 700 on the Scholastic Aptitude Test (SAT) or 15 on the American College Test (ACT). This rule went into effect in 1986. It permitted students who met only one of the requirements (SAT/ACT score *or* the 2.0 GPA in core courses) to be accepted at college and given athletic aid *if* they had graduated from high school with a 2.0 GPA in *all* their courses. However, these partial qualifiers, or "Prop 48 athletes," as they have been called, were not permitted to work out with their teams during their first year, and they had to forfeit 1 year of athletic eligibility, which meant they could play for only 3 years instead of the normal 4 years.

The purpose of Proposition 48 was threefold: (1) to send a message to high schools and high school athletes that a commitment to academic achievement was a prerequisite for playing big-time college sports, (2) to set new guidelines for colleges and universities that regularly recruited athletes who had no reasonable chance to be academically successful or graduate from college after 5 years, and (3) to give first year student-athletes who needed to catch up in their academic work a year to focus exclusive attention on school rather than sports.

Since Proposition 48 has gone into effect, some people have tried to supplement it with even tougher standards, and others have tried to make it more flexible. The proponents of tougher standards point out that many high schools and high school athletes have successfully risen to the challenge of meeting higher academic standards and that they ought to be challenged even further. Others who want tougher standards are simply interested in keeping what they define as "academic riffraff" out of the university. The proponents of more flexibility argue that Proposition 48 discriminates against young people from low-income backgrounds who have not had quality educational opportunities in high school and were not financially able to take SAT and ACT tests over and over or take high-priced preparation courses to improve their test scores. They also argue that Proposition 48 disproportionately hurts black student-athletes because SAT and ACT tests have built in cultural biases.

However, Proposition 48 seems to have done more good than harm (Lapchick, 1987, 1988). Since 1986, about 75% to 80% of all Proposition 48 athletes have become students in good standing in their universities. Having one "catch-up year" seems to have helped many young people who needed one more chance to turn their academic lives around. Proposition 48 also led many universities to be more careful about who their coaches were recruiting as student-athletes, and it alerted them to the need to establish academic support services for student-athletes. In some universities with big-time sport programs these support services are very impressive (and very expensive.)

The apparent success of Proposition 48 led NCAA members in 1993 to boost qualifying criteria to a 2.5 high school GPA in 13 (not 11) core courses, effective in 1995. Qualifying criteria get even more strict in 1996. Efforts to restore the 4th year of athletic eligibility to Proposition 48 student-athletes who have turned their academic lives around have not been successful (as of 1993). Proposition 48 students can no longer receive athletic grants during their first year, although they can get institutional financial aid from approved nonathletics sources (this has been another hotly contested issue).

THE KNIGHT FOUNDATION COMMISSION ON INTERCOLLEGIATE ATHLETICS. The report of this commission, released in 1991, proposed "A New Model For Intercollegiate Athletics." This model emphasized that university presidents must control big-time sports, and that intercollegiate programs must have academic and financial integrity. Commission recommendations were criticized for being too general, and the Commission itself was said to be ineffective because it had no power to enforce its recommendations. However, the Commission Report was, by chance, released when many others were critically investigating big-time college sports; even the U.S. Congress had just passed a law in 1990 that forced all colleges to make public their athlete graduation rates starting in 1991. Therefore the report served to focus a spotlight on the reform of intercollegiate sports.

This spotlight produced immediate results. Since 1991, university presidents have taken a much closer interest in the integrity of intercollegiate sports and the NCAA has passed rules to emphasize the "student" in student-athlete. For example, athletic dormitories must be eliminated by 1996; training table has been limited to one meal a day; there are new limits on the hours teams can practice during a week and new limits on the length of seasons; there are new official definitions of "academic progress" that must be used to determine student-athlete eligibility on a year-to-year basis; and all athletic departments must conduct annual exit interviews with student-athletes as part of a team-by-team self-assessment process.

There have also been attempts to contain spiraling costs in intercollegiate programs, but these have not led to significant reforms. The idea of imposing cost limits on certain big-time programs has been discussed, but resistance to serious cost containment measures is very strong. Some athletic departments have developed sophisticated and successful fund raising programs that they do not want to limit. However, these programs are often based on models that have little to do with the emerging spirit of academic and fiscal integrity called for in the Knight Foundation Commission Report.

Big-time, entertainment-oriented intercollegiate sport programs will be forced to deal with the need for reform through the 1990s. They will have to come to terms with whether they are part of the world of education or part of the world of entertainment. If they decide that they are entertainment, then what are they doing in the university, and if they are part of education, then what are they doing acting as if they were professional sport team franchises (while paying players only a minimum wage)? These are some of the questions that will be hotly debated in the future.

DO SCHOOLS BENEFIT FROM VARSITY SPORTS PROGRAMS?

The influence of high school and college varsity sport programs extends well beyond the athletes who play on varsity teams. In this section we will look at the effect of those programs on school spirit and school budgets.

School Spirit

Anyone who has attended a well-staged student pep rally or watched the student cheering section at a well-attended high school or college game realizes that sports have the potential to generate impressive displays of energy and spirit. Of course, this does not happen in connection with all sport teams in a school, nor does it happen in all schools. Teams in low-profile sports usually play games without student spectators, and teams with long histories of losing records seldom create a spirited response among more than a handful of students. However, in many cases, high school and college games do provide the basis for spirited social occasions. And students frequently use those occasions to express their feelings about themselves, their teams, and their schools.

The supporters of varsity sports say that displays of school spirit at sport events strengthen student identification with their schools and create the feelings of togetherness needed to achieve educational goals. The critics of varsity sports say the spirit created by sports is temporary, superficial, and unrelated to the achievement of educational goals. Unfortunately, we lack reliable research on this issue. There have been no studies on the conditions under which sports create spirit among students, the nature of the spirit created by sports, or the effects of this spirit on schools themselves or the achievement of educational goals.

Being a part of any group or organization is more fun when there are feelings of togetherness. In the United States—and to an increasing extent in Canada and Japan—sports are one of the ways these feelings of togetherness are created in schools (Miracle, 1978, 1980). But there is nothing magic about sports. Schools in other countries have used other methods of bringing students together and providing them with fun and educational experiences. This point has been made by Anita White (1981), a sport sociologist from England. She observes that:

> The American system of interschool sports is unique, and other formal educational systems function perfectly well without it. Though school spirit in England is not expressed as overtly and strikingly as in the cheering crowd at a high school game in America, there are other equally effective mechanisms for generating and maintaining a corporate identity, for example, community aid programs and group fundraising activities for school projects or charitable causes. Any activity in which individuals from a school corporately engage, representing the school as a unit, which is recognized as worthwhile by significant others inside and outside the school, can fulfil this integrative function. Sport is not the only integrating force, and other activities which involve more genuine participation [than cheering a sport team] may be equally if not more worthwhile.

White's point is well-made; schools *could* offer satisfying experiences to students without sponsoring interscholastic sport teams. In fact, there are North American high schools and colleges that provide a variety of worthwhile social and educational experiences for their students apart from varsity teams. Varsity sports are not necessary for education, and other activities could be used to make young people feel valued and rewarded in their schools and communities.

Some sports are associated with loud and expressive displays of spirit. However, little is known about the actual affects of this spirit on the achievement of educational goals in the schools. (Colorado Springs Gazette Telegraph and Mary Kelley)

Some coaches say sports are needed to "keep kids off the streets," but maybe there should be programs to enable kids to make the streets better places to be, then we wouldn't have to worry about kids being on the streets. Or maybe sports could be reformed to assist in this process.

In conclusion, it can be said that varsity sports often create school spirit. However, for that spirit to take on educational significance, it must be part of an overall school program in which students are treated as valued participants and given a sense of ownership in the school and its programs. Without being a real part of what happens every day at school, cheering at weekly games is simply a superficial display of youthful energy having nothing much to do with education.

School Budgets

HIGH SCHOOLS What are the financial consequences of interscholastic sports programs? At the secondary level, nearly all programs are funded through school district appropriations. Seldom does the money spent directly on varsity teams exceed 3% of the budget for any school. In fact, in most cases, expenditures for interscholastic sports account for less than 1% of school budgets. When certain sports enjoy big budgets, much of the money is likely to come from gate receipts and private sources such as donations from booster clubs. This sometimes happens in football- or basketball-crazy communities where there are large stadiums or arenas, and where local residents and business people take it upon themselves to build big-time high school teams.

It is generally safe to say that interscholastic sports do not cut into the resources used for basic educational programs. Nor do sports add to those resources. However, when classroom teachers try to do their jobs without adequate funds for educational supplies, varsity sports programs will often be asked to make cuts regardless of how little money they are using. In the face of recent budget problems, this continues to happen in many schools and districts. This has given rise to sport participation fees that leads to an even greater overrepresentation of students from upper-middle-income families in many sports.

COLLEGES AND UNIVERSITIES The relationship between varsity sports and school budgets is much more complex on the college level. Intercollegiate sports at small colleges are usually low-budget activities funded through a combination of student fees and student support money. At larger schools with big-time programs, vast sums of money are spent on intercollegiate sport programs. This money comes from student fees, boosters, gate receipts, the sale of media rights, concessions, logo license fees, and general university funds. But the big question is: how much do expenditures on intercollegiate sports cut into school budgets for academic programs?

Big-time athletic departments are now run like businesses. They try to be self-supporting, if not profit-making. However, all but about 45 universities in the United States lose money every year on intercollegiate sports (Wieberg and Witosky, 1991). In some cases, the loses are $1 million to $4 million. Even most big-time football programs lose money every year. When profits are made by a few successful entertainment-oriented teams, they are kept in the athletic department and used to support other sports or to expand team budgets. There have been only a few cases when money made by sport teams has been used to support academic programs.

When big-time sports programs lose large amounts of money, why do universities continue to support them? The answer is that many people believe the programs have *indirect* financial benefits. They say that big-time sports attract tuition-paying students and influence others—including alumni, granting agencies, and state legislators—to give greater financial support to the schools. Data documenting these indirect benefits are hard to come by. Do students really choose a college to attend on the basis of the records of its sport teams? How many students do this? What kind of students are they? Do they leave school if teams lose? Are team records more important than such things as academic programs, tuition costs, housing arrangements, parents' wishes, the enrollment decisions of close friends, and the location of the school? These questions have never been answered systematically, even though schools spend millions of dollars on the untested assumption that sports do matter.

The idea that big-time sports inspire increased donations to the general educational funds of colleges and universities is also difficult to test. Winning teams do generate money for sports-related things—such as new artificial turf, a stadium addition, or a new building to showcase sport trophies and house offices for coaches and athletic department staff. But studies suggest there is *no direct link between the success of a school's sport programs and the money given to support education and research programs* (Business Week, August 28, 1971; Frey, 1985; Lederman, 1988).

Even though there have been a few exceptions to this conclusion, most university development officers agree that successful fundraising is seldom shaped by the wins and losses of a school's sport teams. For example, the assistant vice-president for university relations at the University of Notre Dame claims, "There isn't any correlation between giving at Notre Dame and athletic success." The vice-president for development at the University of Southern California says, "The bulk of our fund-raising

"I told you we sent our daughter to a top-notch school—her basketball team just beat Duke University." (Do people equate academic quality with the success of athletic teams? Some may, but it is not known if the number is large enough to affect the public relations image of a school.)

would be intact with or without athletics" (both cited in Lederman, 1988). In fact, sometimes fund-raising improves after schools drop sport programs. The year after Tulane University dropped basketball, donations increased by $5 million, and Wichita State's donations doubled the year after its financially strapped football team was dropped (Lederman, 1988).

These examples are *not* given to suggest that sport programs cannot be used in fund-raising efforts. University presidents and development officers often use sport events as social occasions to bring wealthy and influential people to their campuses, but they know these people will not donate new buildings simply because the football team gets invited to a bowl game. They also know that pouring money into expensive sport teams is not the way to solve money problems at their schools. But this does not stop them from using the publicity created by varsity sport teams to call attention to the academic reputation and potential of their universities.

When sport is used in connection with fund-raising, care must be taken not to create an image of the school as a "sports factory." This can

cause prospective donors to question the quality of academic programs, and it can backfire if athletic programs are perceived as lacking integrity and honesty. Unfortunately, no one has studied the effect of sport scandals and NCAA punishments. It is not known whether fund-raising suffers at the many schools that have been found guilty of NCAA violations.

In conclusion, when sports have long been used to create a university's public relations image, varsity teams cannot be suddenly dropped without causing problems. But if there are good reasons for dropping sports programs, most alumni and other donors respect the decision to do so. Furthermore, many schools have not used sports to create public relations images, and some of these schools have been very successful with fund-raising. They highlight academic and research programs rather than coaches and quarterbacks. When their programs are good, donations are as high as at schools with publicized sport programs. Winning games and championships may receive good press coverage, but it will not consistently increase donations unless the school has a good academic reputation (Lederman, 1988).

School-Community Relations

Interscholastic sport programs have always done two things in the realm of school-community relations: they have attracted attention, and they have provided entertainment. In other words, they help make the school a part of community life, and they help bridge the gap between "town and gown" that exists in some communities. For those who do not have school-aged children, one of the only times they hear about the local high school or college is when there are news stories about sport teams. Even for some of the parents of students, the fates of varsity teams may be of more noticeable concern than the fates of academic programs. Sports are an easy connecting point for people in the community. Through sports, people can maintain an interest in their local school high school or college without having to know about all the complex dimensions of academic life.

It is easy to see that sports can connect communities to schools, but it is not known if these connections benefit academic programs or achievement of educational goals. Benefits are most likely in small towns where local attachments to high schools are strongly reinforced by school teams. The dynamics of this process have been described by journalists (Wolff, 1983) but not by sport sociologists. In the case of larger high schools in metropolitan areas and universities with big-time sport programs, people may attend games and read team scores in the paper, but their attachments to the schools themselves seldom go beyond occasional attendance at games (Frey, 1985; Lederman, 1988).

Some people have even argued that universities have an obligation to provide community entertainment through sports (Michener, 1976). However, this argument is difficult to make when sports take forms that distort the entire image of higher education. Another problem with this argument is that when varsity sports are entertainment-oriented, the needs of student-athletes often become secondary to the need to put on a good show. This has happened in a few high school and more than a few intercollegiate programs around the United States.

VARSITY HIGH SCHOOL SPORTS: PROBLEMS AND RECOMMENDATIONS

Existing interscholastic programs enjoy widespread support, and many people have vested interests in keeping them the way they are. However, many are in need of reform. Some high school programs have not only lost direct connections with education but they have subverted the educational process for some students. Problems vary from one high school program to the next. But the most serious problems include the following: (1) an overemphasis on "sports development" and "big-time" program models, (2) limited participation access for students, and (3) too many coaches who emphasize conformity and obedience rather than responsibility and autonomy.

Overemphasis on "Sports Development" and "Big-Time" Program Models

Some high school administrators, athletic directors, and coaches seem to think that the best way to organize high school sports is to model them after big-time intercollegiate programs. When this happens, people involved with varsity sports become overconcerned with winning records and presenting a tightly organized, high profile program to the community at large. In the process of trying to build high profile sports programs they often overlook the educational needs of all students in their schools. Their goal is to be "ranked" rather than to respond to the needs of students, although they will sometimes say that when they are "ranked" the needs of students are truly being served.

"Sports development" people give regular lip service to the idea that sports must be kept in "proper perspective," but they often forget their own words when it comes to the programs at their schools. In fact, they may even encourage students to specialize in a single sport 12 months a year instead of encouraging them to develop a wide range of different skills in different sports. They set up sport camps or identify camps that they strongly encourage "their athletes" to attend during summer break. They sometimes forbid "their athletes" to play other sports and then recommend that they join community clubs where they can continue playing one sport through the "off-season." And they continually tell students that they must sacrifice to get better at some point in the future. This, of course, turns off many students who want to have fun with a sport right now, and who want to enjoy participation even if they do not intend on being an all-American athlete in the future.

People who adhere to a big-time sports model sometimes hire and fire coaches on the basis of win-loss records rather than teaching abilities. They may even describe coaches as good teachers when teams have winning records, or as bad teachers when teams lose. Their goal is to build a "winning tradition" without ever critically examining how such a tradition is connected to the education of students; they just assume that "winning" is educational. Although this orientation exists in different types of schools, there are some private schools now recruiting 7th and 8th grade athletes in certain sports to build big-time, nationally ranked teams. They want to use the public relations generated by sports to increase their visibility and recruit more tuition-paying students. These big-time sports programs have created an atmosphere in which many high school students now mistakenly believe that athletics are a better route to rewards and college scholarships than are academics. This is just one of the ways that big-time high school varsity sports can subvert the achievement of educational goals.

RECOMMENDATIONS Varsity sport programs ought to be subjected to regular educational assessments. Coaches should be provided with opportunities to learn more about the ways sports can be made into educationally relevant activities. Coaches should also be given access to coaching education programs and other pro-

fessional development opportunities that emphasize "student development" rather than "sports development."

The educational value of state and national rankings should be assessed. Is there a need to crown national high school champion teams? How about state championship teams? Are there alternative ways to define and seek excellence other than through such a system? Why not have more boy/girl teams in sports such as long distance running, doubles tennis and badminton, bowling, golf, cycling and tandem cycling, soccer, hacky-sack, wall climbing, archery and shooting, volleyball, swimming, racquetball and billiards? If high school is a time for social development, there should be combined boy/girl teams in many sports. Scoring and handicap systems could be designed to accommodate certain skill differences. Why are interscholastic sports so gender-segregated when learning how to handle male-female relationships is an important developmental goal?

Limited Participation Access

The major advantage of interscholastic sports is that they provide students opportunities to develop and test skills, especially physical skills, outside the classroom. But many programs are organized to discourage participation by certain students or in ways that fail to provide true gender equity. In recent years, participation fees have become the biggest threat to open participation in varsity sports.

RECOMMENDATIONS Not everyone is physically able or motivationally inclined to participate in interscholastic sports. However, most programs do little to encourage the involvement of those who do not measure up to their bigger, faster, taller, and stronger counterparts. There is no reason why only one team should represent a school in varsity competition. Why not have two teams? Why not have a football league with players under 140 pounds, or a basketball league with all players under 5'8" tall, or track meets with height and weight breakdowns for certain events? In places where this has been

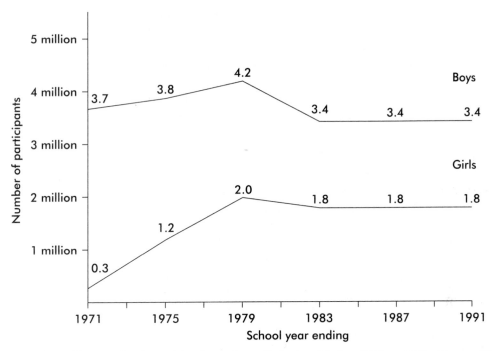

FIG. 15-1 Number of boys and girls participating in interscholastic athletics, 1972 to 1992. (Source: National Federation of State High School Associations [1993].)

tried it has been successful.

There should be efforts to develop new interscholastic sports in which size and strength are not crucial for success. Too often the focus is on football and basketball rather than a variety of sports suited for a variety of participants. Why not have Frisbee teams, racquetball teams, flag football teams, softball teams, weight lifting teams, or teams in any sport where there is enough interest to get people to try out? With a little guidance, the students themselves could administer and coach these teams and coordinate meets and games with their counterparts at other schools. If responsibility builds autonomy and decision-making skills, why not let students direct their own teams so more of them would have opportunities to participate? This has been successfully done in many countries.

Disabled students have been almost totally ignored by varsity sports programs. The Minnesota High School League became the first in the United States to organize interscholastic

sports for students with disabilities. Although the Minnesota program must be evaluated, strategies must also be developed for including disabled student-athletes on existing high school teams. Of course, this would not work in all sports, but there are certain sports in which disabled competitors could be included in meets, matches, and games.

Girls' sports still do not have the support that boys' sports enjoy. Of course, this problem has a history that goes far beyond the high school. But the result is that girls still participate at rates below those for boys (Figure 15-1). In some areas there is still an emphasis on boys' teams with the expectation that girls in pep clubs, cheerleading squads, and drill teams will support the boys rather than play on teams of their own. As long as the atmosphere in high schools encourages this orientation rather than one in which girls see themselves as capable athletes, unequal participation rates will continue to exist. Gender equity in varsity programs could be handled through more gender-mixed sports (see previous section), or by using combined scoring methods in certain sports. For example, when the basketball teams of School A and School B play each other, the final outcome of the game would be determined by combining the scores of the girls' team with the scores of the boys' teams for each school. This could lead boys to take girls more seriously as basketball players and even get them to attend the girls' games. After all, their place in league standings would depend on the girls' performance and vice versa.

An increasing number of schools are using participation fees to save interscholastic sports from being completely cut. This is a serious problem because fees, even when they are waived for students from low income families, tend to limit participation. The need for fees is related to a general unwillingness to support public education in many states and communities, but it is also related to the fact that faculty and administration in many school districts have not done enough to make varsity sports into educational experiences for young people. This must be done before others can be expected to support taxes that would fund varsity sports.

Emphasis on Conformity and Obedience Rather Than Responsibility and Autonomy

When high school coaches exert excessive control over the lives of their athletes, sport loses its educational relevance. Although coaches need authority, they should use their authority to support the personal and social development of students on interscholastic teams. Verbally or physically abusing adolescent athletes has no educational value. Although most coaches do not use abusive methods, there are some who seem to think that young people need to be cut down to grow up. They think that obedience is the same as self-discipline and that a singular dedication to sport is a sign of maturity. These coaches may create loyalty on high school teams and they may win games because of their rigid systems of control, but they are not providing

athletes opportunities to become independent and responsible adults.

In fact, the educational benefits of sport involvement are greatest when athletes themselves make decisions affecting the nature of their sport participation. This does not mean that athletes do not need guidance. They do. But they also need chances to become independent, autonomous young adults. Autocratic coaches reduce these chances and perpetuate immaturity and dependence—in spite of the fact that they may win games with their methods.

RECOMMENDATIONS In most high schools, student-athletes should be more involved in decision-making for their teams. This can be done in a variety of ways. In fact, sports are ideal settings for students to learn responsibility through decision-making. For example, team rules and punishments for rule violations should be determined by team members. Elected team representatives should be responsible, with adult guidance, for applying punishments when someone violates the rules. Team strategies, plays, and game plans should frequently be developed by athletes with the guidance of a coach. Players should have opportunities to voice their thoughts during games, meets, and matches. Why should adult coaches make all the decisions on student sport teams? Ideally, the goal should be to prepare the team to be self-coached. In fact, some leagues should require that for the last two or three games of the season, coaches must sit in the stands and watch while the players coach themselves. This would be real leadership training. Athletes should also be involved in the evaluation of coaches and sports programs. Internship programs should be organized to enable senior athletes to serve as assistant coaches, or as coaches for junior varsity and junior high school teams. This would give them opportunities to handle many different tasks and get management and interpersonal experiences in the process.

Varsity sports should be based on the principle that responsibility grows out of making decisions and living with the consequences of those decisions. Responsibility is learned, not implanted in a young person's character by the commands and warnings of adults in positions of authority. Unfortunately, many varsity sports are organized to teach conformity and obedience instead of responsibility and independence. This should be changed.

INTERCOLLEGIATE SPORTS: PROBLEMS AND RECOMMENDATIONS

Problems are not new to intercollegiate sports. Even in the late nineteenth century, college teams were accused of being too commercial and professional. In 1905 there were 18 student-athlete deaths in intercollegiate football and President Theodore Roosevelt warned educators of the negative consequences of ethically corrupt, big-time intercollegiate sports. Things did not improve, and in the mid-1920s the Carnegie Corporation commissioned a detailed 3-year study of college sports. The study clearly documented the continued existence of commercialism, professionalization, and the neglect of educational issues in intercollegiate programs (Savage, 1929).

A continuing absence of regulation during the 1930s and 1940s led the American Council on Education to commission yet another study of intercollegiate sports in 1951. The study findings and recommendations were generally the same as those Savage noted in 1929, but, as before, few of the recommendations were put into policy. Problems continued to grow along with the size, popularity, and scope of intercollegiate sports. Television created new sources of revenue and attracted new fans. Then, in the light of the women's movement, the programs were revealed to be sexist and discriminatory. These and other issues, such as recruiting abuses and economic problems, led the American Council on Education to sponsor another investigation in 1973. It was not surprising that the study discovered the same kinds of problems found in the past (Hanford, 1974, 1979).

Now in 1991 we have the Report of the

"I LIKE YOUR NEW RECRUIT, COACH... AN EXCELLENT EXAMPLE OF HIGHER EDUCATION!"

In big-time intercollegiate sports, the meaning of higher education sometimes gets distorted.

Knight Foundation Commission on Intercollegiate Athletics noting that big-time intercollegiate sports are in drastic need of reform. The major problems requiring immediate attention are (1) commercialism and "corporatization," (2) lack of athletes' rights, (3) gender inequities, and (4) distorted priorities related to race relations and education.

Commercialism and "Corporatization"

Big-time, entertainment-oriented intercollegiate sports are big businesses. Of course, there is nothing wrong with big business—except when financial concerns take priority over the education and development of student-athletes. The likelihood of this happening increases as the stakes for intercollegiate sports get higher. When media rights to games are sold, the academic progress of the college players often becomes less important than television ratings and network profits. Corporate sponsors are not concerned with educational issues. Too much money is involved to consider education. This problem is intensified by the fact that many decisions affecting intercollegiate sports are made by people having nothing to do with higher education. Instead, they are experts in marketing, accounting, business management, and the media. I call this "corporatization," and I see it as a major problem in intercollegiate sports.

RECOMMENDATIONS   Serious cost containment measures should be implemented in big-time intercollegiate sports. Revenues from media contracts should be shared by all NCAA members, and limits should be set on the amount of money spent by teams in different sports at different levels of NCAA membership. Unless limits are set, student-athletes will be subjected to pressures to be entertainers rather than students. As the Knight Report suggests, university presidents should have ultimate control over athletic department budgets, and no athletic departments or coaches should be able to enter contracts that involve the manipulation of student-athletes for financial gain. Furthermore, cutting scholarships and other benefits for athletes should be *last* on the list of cost containment strategies.

Along with cost containment measures, coaches should have some form of job security to encourage them to concentrate on developing a commitment to academics among athletes on their teams. Coaches should be evaluated as educators rather than fund raisers.

Lack of Athletes' Rights

Student-athletes in big-time intercollegiate programs are rewarded with prestige and financial support, but their lives are pretty much under the control of others. This is not a problem until others act in ways athletes think are unfair. Then what happens? According to Stanley Eitzen (1992), a sociologist from Colorado State University, student-athletes are out of luck. He notes that,

> Athletes do not have free speech or the right to a fair trial [within the context of athletic programs]. If they challenge the athletic power structure, they will lose their scholarship and eligibility. Athletes who have a grievance are on their own. They have no union, no arbitration board, and rarely do they have representation on campus athletic committees.

Eitzen also notes that some athletes generate millions for schools, but are limited in what they can receive from schools; athletes must make 4-year commitments to schools, but the schools make only year-to-year scholarship commitments to athletes; athletes' privacy can be routinely invaded by coaches and representatives of the athletic department; athletes' must accept all rules imposed by coaches and athletic departments, regardless of whether the rules would be considered fair by anyone but the coach; and athletes seldom have any means for formally objecting to coaches' abusive and oppressive actions.

RECOMMENDATIONS   Student-athletes must be represented on university advisory committees to athletic departments. There should also be formal appeals systems put in place so athletes can register complaints and have complaints investigated in ways that do not jeopardize their scholarships or playing time on teams. Athletes should be formally involved in the evaluation of coaches, and all coaches should be required to have a student-athlete advisory/ disciplinary committee that handles team issues. Furthermore, every university should have an independent ombudsperson (an appointed official who investigates situations where the rights of individuals may have been violated) to whom student-athletes can go when they need an advocate to help them deal with the athletic department, team, or coach about issues related to their rights.

Other recommendations for the treatment of athletes include the following:

- Scholarship athletes should have need-based financial aid packages that enable them to receive university bookstore vouchers so they can purchase supplies needed for courses; vouchers should also enable athletes to get term papers typed. It seems strange to provide athletic equipment to student-athletes and then not provide them with essential academic equipment.

- Need-based financial aid packages would also allow certain student-athletes to receive cash stipends not exceeding $200 per month. Under certain circumstances athletes should be able to apply for need-based travel grants enabling them to go home for one vacation per year and in the case of family emergencies.
- If athletes are unable to afford their own insurance, or are not covered on parents' policies, they should receive full medical coverage for eye exams, eyewear, dental care, and other medical care while they are playing. This coverage should be extended for 5 years after their last season of participation for any condition indirectly related to their sport participation.

Gender Inequities

Men and women go to college in about equal numbers; they all pay student fees, and these fees are often used to help pay for intercollegiate sports. This has been the case for dozens of years, even before there were full-fledged women's teams at many universities. For many years, women's fees subsidized men's teams. Now there are still over twice as many male athletes as female athletes, male scholarship recipients outnumber female recipients 2-to-1, over 75% of the athletic department operating funds go to men's teams, and men's teams use over 80% of all recruiting funds (Lederman, 1992a). This is illustrated in Figure 15-2.

Gender inequities are so blatant that Christine Grant, director of women's athletics at the

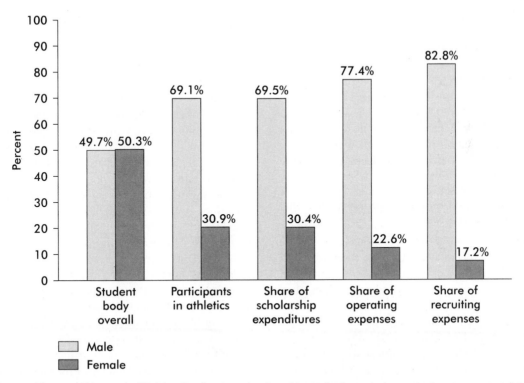

FIG. 15-2 Men and Women in Division I colleges and universities: a look at gender equity in percentages, 1990-1991. (Source: Chronicle of Higher Education survey of 203 NCAA Division I colleges and universities [see Lederman, 1992a].)

University of Iowa, calls the situation "pathetic." Donna Lopiano, Director of the Women's Sport Foundation notes that intercollegiate sports are so far from equity that it is "laughable." Richard Schultz, the former Executive Director of the NCAA says that gender inequity "is more than a financial issue. It's a moral issue as well" (in Lederman, 1992a, p. A45).

RECOMMENDATIONS Many equity recommendations have been made since 1972 when Title IX became law. Getting athletic departments to follow them has been the problem. Now women need to get lawyers and sue athletic departments. Athletic departments claim that equity is not possible unless there are major changes in the way football is organized and played, and changes could jeopardize revenues. This is a serious dilemma, and I see no way around it. My recommendation would be to heavily cut football expenses, cut the size of football teams, and build some women's sports into revenue producers. After all, it took 75 years to build football into something that could make money for a few schools. Shouldn't women get 75 years to build their programs? Or should we reconsider entertainment-oriented sports altogether? We will know that gender equity has been achieved when men would not complain if men's programs and women's programs were forced to trade places and walk in the shoes of the other.

Distorted Priorities Related to Race Relations and Education

A 1992 survey by the National Collegiate Athletic Association showed that whereas blacks made up only 6% of the full-time students at 245 NCAA Division I colleges and universities, they held about 22% of all athletic scholarships, 43% of football scholarships, and 60% of basketball scholarships (Lederman, 1992b). Overall, nearly 15% of all black male students on those 245 campuses were scholarship athletes, whereas only 2.3% of white males were scholarship athletes. Figure 15-3 highlights these data. Harry Edwards, a sociologist at the University of Califor-

nia at Berkeley, says that this situation not only reinforces dangerous racial stereotypes but it demoralizes thousands of black students struggling to use education rather than sports in their pursuit of the American Dream (in Lederman, 1992b). Arthur Ashe responded to the data by saying that "The message is clear: The colleges are interested in us primarily as athletes" (cited in Lederman, 1992b).

Of course, many young black men and a few black women benefit from athletic scholarships. This is not the problem. According to Andrew Hacker, a political scientist from Queens College in New York City, the problem is that universities have cynically capitalized on the fact that blacks have historically been led to believe that sports are their way to get ahead (in Lederman, 1992b). In other words, universities have used the results of racist history to their advantage while they have not tried hard enough to make changes in race relations in the student body as a whole.

Meanwhile, many black athletes feel isolated on campuses where there are few African American students, faculty, or administrators. The isolation is especially intense if black student-athletes come from working class or low income backgrounds and the white students on campus come from upper-middle income backgrounds. Ironically, many black athletes play on teams that generate revenues to pay for athletic scholarships awarded to white student-athletes from wealthier backgrounds. If those white athletes ever act in a manner that black athletes define as superior or racist, feelings of isolation among black student-athletes increase even further.

RECOMMENDATIONS Universities must be more aggressive in the way they recruit and support minority students in general. It is not fair to bring black male athletes to a campus where they have little social support and little they can identify with as students. Furthermore, white students must be made aware of the fact that not all blacks play sports or are even interested in sports. If universities would make more concerted efforts to incorporate racial and cultural diversity into all spheres of campus life, recruit-

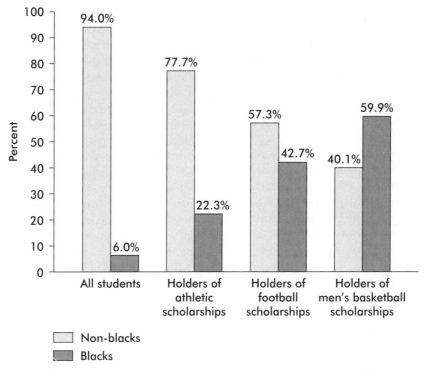

FIG. 15-3 Percentage of non-blacks and blacks in various college student categories, 1990-1991. (Source: NCAA survey of 245 Division I colleges and universities [see Lederman, 1992b].)

ing black athletes would not be defined as part of a distorted set of priorities.

CONCLUSION:

ARE VARSITY SPORTS EDUCATIONAL?

It is difficult to make generalizations about all varsity sports programs. They differ from one another in numerous ways. However, varsity sports have no place in high schools or colleges unless they are legitimate parts of educational programs and unless they receive their direction from educational purpose. In other words, if the programs do not educationally benefit student-athletes, they cannot be justified as school-sponsored activities.

At this time there is no consistent evidence that high school sports produce negative conse-

quences for those who participate in them. Of course, there are some schools, some parents, and some young people who lose sight of educational goals in their pursuit of winning records and championships. Sports can be seductive, and people connected with high school teams sometimes require guidance to keep their programs in balance with what is going on in the rest of the school. It is up to school superintendents and principals to oversee what happens in their districts and schools. Parents should also be sensitive to the possibility of sports subverting educational goals. When sport participation interferes with educational achievement, steps must be taken to restore sports to their proper place.

The possibility that sport participation might interfere with the educational progress of student-athletes is greatest in big-time intercollegiate programs. The attractiveness of being an athlete in a big-time program is often enough to distract students from academic work. In fact, it can make coursework nearly irrelevant in the lives of impressionable young people, especially young men.

Interscholastic sport programs usually create school spirit. But it is not known if that spirit contributes to the achievement of educational goals. It is certain that other school activities could be used to bring students together, but sports provide students unique social activities making schools more interesting places to be. Although they occupy the everyday attention of a considerable number of students, it is not known if they actually distract attention away from academic matters.

It is doubtful that high school sport programs seriously cut into budgets for academic programs. The money they require is well spent if they provide students opportunities to explore their physical selves and meet challenges outside the classroom. On the intercollegiate level, the funding situation is complex and confusing. However, it is clear that most programs are not self-supporting, and that they do not generate revenues for their schools' general funds. What is not clear is the extent to which the athletic programs cut into the budgets for academic programs.

Interscholastic sport programs often bridge the gap between schools and the communities in which they are located. However, when those programs are controlled by people not connected with the schools, there is a tendency for educational goals to be overlooked. Some schools may be able to use their sport teams as vehicles to create community support for educational programs, but this goal is very rarely achieved.

When high school programs overemphasize "sports development," limit access to participation, and focus on controlling students rather than enabling them to become responsible, they subvert the achievement of educational goals. Similarly, when intercollegiate programs are characterized by commercialism, lack of rights for athletes, a lack of gender equity, and distorted priorities related to race relations and education, they are counterproductive to the reputation and mission of higher education. If these problems are allowed to exist by high schools and colleges, there is no educationally sound reason for those schools to continue sponsoring interscholastic programs.

Interscholastic programs will never be perfect. There will always be a need for reform, just as there is in any part of the curriculum. This means that the educational relevance of those programs depends on constant evaluation and assessment. A critical approach is the only approach that will keep them meaningful activities in the everyday lives of students and in the social organization of the schools themselves.

SUGGESTED READINGS

Adler, P.A., and P. Adler. 1991. Backboards & blackboards: College athletes and role engulfment. Columbia University Press, New York (*an excellent sociological study of college athletes; authors focus on male basketball players in a big-time program and deal with the sport experiences from the perspective of the athletes themselves*).

Bissinger, H.G. 1990. Friday night lights. Addison-Wesley Publishing Company, inc., Reading, MA (*dramatic journalistic account of Texas high school football team during the 1988 season deals with issues of race and gender relations, education and the connection between a varsity sport and the local community*).

Chu, D., J.O. Segrave, and B.J. Becker, eds. 1985. Sport and higher education. Human Kinetics Publishers, Inc., Champaign, Ill. (*a comprehensive anthology on American intercollegiate sports; 31 articles by leading researchers; articles focus on history, athletes' rights, controversies, and recommendations for reform*).

Foley, D.E. 1990. Learning capitalist culture. University of Pennsylvania Press, Philadelphia, Pa. (*author pays special attention to high school sports in this excellent ethnography of a small Texas town; focuses on youth, community rituals, and the reproduction of class, ethnic, and gender inequalities*).

Knight Foundation Commission Report on Intercollegiate Athletics. 1991. Keeping faith with the student-athlete: a new model for Intercollegiate athletics. Knight Foundation, Charlotte, N.C. (*this report and a follow-up published in 1992 inspired numerous discussions and national publicity focused on the need to reform intercollegiate sports; the report itself was not a critical document, but it incited much critical discussion*).

Ladd, W.M. and A. Lumpkin, eds. 1979. Sport in American education: history and perspective. American Alliance for Health, Physical Education, Recreation and Dance, Reston, Va. (*12 articles about the historical roots of interscholastic and intercollegiate sports in the United States; clearly illustrates that the past cannot be described as the good old days*).

Lapchick, R. (with Malekoff, R.) 1987. On the mark: putting the student back in student-athlete. St. Martin's Press, New York (*a guide for high school athletes about the dangers of drugs, the importance of education, and the ways athletes can control their own intercollegiate sport experiences*).

Lawrence, P. 1987. Unsportsmanlike conduct: the National Collegiate Athletic Association and the business of college football. Praeger, New York (*comprehensive study of how the NCAA has come to control intercollegiate sports and how it turned them into a big business and created an environment in which there are very strong pressures to violate the spirit of sportsmanship*).

Purdy, D., ed. 1987. Sport and the student athlete. ARENA Review 11(2) (*12 papers discussing issues related to the experiences of intercollegiate athletes; includes two papers on intercollegiate sport in Canada*).

Smith, R.A. 1988. Sports and freedom: The rise of big-time college athletics. Oxford University Press. New York (*insightful social history providing useful background on how intercollegiate sports have become what they are today*).

Sperber, M. 1990. College Sports, Inc.: The Athletic Department vs The University. Henry Hold and Company, New York (*this book was published just before the Knight Foundation Commission Report was released; it was widely read because it dug into and criticized intercollegiate sports in a way that the Commission did not. This book did much to inspire response to the Commission Report*).

Telander, R. 1989. The hundred yard lie: The corruption of college football and what we can do to stop it. Simon and Schuster, New York (*author has covered college football for Sports Illustrated for many years; this journalistic critique provides an insider look at the problems of big-time college football during the 1970s and 1980s*).

Wheeler, S., ed. 1987. Special issue on intercollegiate sports. Journal of Sport and Social Issues 11(1, 2) (*9 papers commissioned by the Amateur Athletic Foundation of Los Angeles to help prepare recommendations for the Presidents' Commission of the NCAA; together, the papers summarize much of what is known about intercollegiate athletes and they call attention to what should be studied in the future*).

CHAPTER 16

SPORTS AND RELIGION

Is it a promising combination?

To have religion, you need to have heroic forms to try to live up to. . . . You need to have a pattern of symbols and myths that a person can grow old with. . . . You need to have a way to exhilarate the human body, and desire, and will, and the sense of beauty. . . . All these things you have in sports.

Michael Novak, Philosopher and Theologian (1976)

Our Father, we don't want to be mediocre, we don't want to fail. We want to honor You by winning.

Jerry Falwell, Chancellor, Liberty University (1986)

If somebody comes into my territory, my zone, I want to hit him hard. I don't ever want to take a cheap shot, but I'll hit him with all the love of Jesus I can muster.

Gill Byrd, Pro Football player on San Diego Chargers (1991)

. . . God is not going to provide any leadership on this basketball team. . . . He is not going to parachute through the roof . . . and score when we need points. . . . God does not give a damn what goes on in athletics. Nor should He.

Bobby Knight, Basketball Coach, Indiana University (1985)

Through history, sports and religion have had a changing relationship. During some periods sport activities have either been sponsored in connection with religious ceremonies and festivals or they have been endorsed by church authorities as worthwhile pursuits. But during other periods they have either been ignored or defined as indulgent and sinful. Since the late nineteenth century, there has been a tendency in some Western societies for Christian churches to sponsor sport activities and for some individuals to combine religious beliefs (mostly Christian beliefs) with their sport participation.

The purpose of this chapter is to explore how religion and religious systems of meaning inform the way sports are defined, organized, and played among different groups of people. As you read this chapter it is important to remember that similar religious systems of meaning can be applied to sports and sport participation in different ways, depending on the experiences, relationships, and interests of individuals and groups. The questions discussed in this chapter are:

1. How is religion defined, and why do sociologists study it?
2. What are the similarities and differences between sports and religion?
3. Why have sports and Christian organizations and beliefs been combined?
4. What are the consequences of combining Christianity and sports?

In discussing this last question, special attention will be given to whether the combination of religion and sports offers any promise for eliminating racism, sexism, deviance, violence, or other problems in sports.

HOW DO SOCIOLOGISTS DEFINE AND STUDY RELIGION?

Sociological discussions of religion have sometimes created controversy in sociology of sport classrooms. This is because when people think about religion they often use only their personal religious beliefs and practices as a point of reference; thus they have strong feelings about and vested interests in how religion is discussed. Religion is powerful because it gives rise to general systems of meaning related to ultimate issues and questions. These systems of meaning affect the way people think about the world, about social life and social relationships, and even about sports.

A sociological discussion of religion and sports requires that we dismiss preconceived ideas about what religion should be and should do. Although there are many definitions of religion, most sociologists agree that *religion* is a socially shared set of beliefs and rituals focused on ultimate concerns of human existence—birth, life, suffering, illness, tragedy, injustice, and death. Religious beliefs and rituals form the foundation of systems of meaning and cultural practices that are special because people believe them to be linked to a sacred and supernatural realm. Objects, symbols, and ceremonies are *sacred* when they are identified with the supernatural or with forces that go beyond the here and now world. Religious beliefs and rituals also make distinctions between the sacred and the *profane*. The profane consists of all things that are a part of common, everyday, worldly experiences. Sacred things inspire awe, mystery, and reverence; profane things may be impressive but they seldom inspire thoughts going beyond everyday issues and concerns among believers.

Distinctions between the sacred and profane can be illustrated through examples from our experience. As you know, Christians define certain types of crosses as sacred by connecting them with their God. Therefore these special crosses (crucifixes) have been given symbolic meaning that can be understood only by their connection to the supernatural; they are part of the sacred. On the other hand, the letter jackets worn by some American high school student-athletes have no connection with the sacred or supernatural within a Christian religious belief system; letter jackets are understandable in terms of everyday meanings and experiences. These jackets and what they represent may be important to high school students, but they and their meanings belong to the world of the profane. Religion is defined as beliefs and rituals that a group of people have agreed are associated with the sacred and supernatural.

It is important to remember that human beings have dealt with ultimate questions and the meaning of ultimate and inescapable problems of existence in many different ways. In fact, they have developed literally thousands of rich and widely varied religions (Ferrante, 1992). Sociologists are not concerned with the truth or falsity of any particular religious system of meaning; instead, they assume that all religions are true in their own ways because they enable believers to deal with ultimate questions and issues. This makes religion important sociologically because it informs the way people think about who they are and how they are connected to the world and to other human beings.

Sociologists also study religion because it has unique social dynamics and social consequences. For example, religion and religious systems of meaning usually connect power, authority, and wisdom with a God, gods, or other supernatural forces. This connection can lead people to resist negotiation and compromise on any issue they see as tied to their religious beliefs. People avoid negotiating or compromising the word of their God or gods because they often fear that compromises would undermine the ultimate power, authority, and wisdom they use to make sense of their worlds and their lives. This helps to explain why people responded the way they did in late 1992 when Irish rock singer Sinead O'Conner intentionally tore up a picture of Pope John Paul II on an American television program. O'Connor was subsequently booed off the stage at a multi-star rock concert, and a coalition of ethnic people outraged by her treatment of "the sacred" burned her recordings in protest on a New York street. Although many people who questioned O'Connor's action were neither Catholic nor very religious, they saw her as challenging authority connected with dominant conceptions of the sacred and supernatural in the

United States. Popular responses would have been different and less dramatic if O'Connor had torn a photo of basketball player Michael Jordan. Even though Jordan is widely known and respected, he is associated with this world—with the here and now, not with the eternal, not with what many people define as ultimate power, authority, and wisdom.

Religious systems of meaning are also socially significant because they set believers apart from others and then ground that separation in otherworldly terms. This process of identification and separation can lead to combinations of the following social consequences:

- The creation of powerful forms of group unity and social integration
- Group conflict and violent warfare
- A basis for believers to evaluate the moral worth of ideas and people, including themselves
- Encourage believers to accept or rebel against social norms and civil authority in a community or society
- Encourage believers to maintain or challenge systems of power that underlie social relations among men and women, racial and ethnic groups, social classes, homosexuals and heterosexuals, the able and disabled, and other groups

This is why religion is important in sociology: it informs social relations by distributing moral power in the cultural world.

WHAT ARE THE SIMILARITIES AND DIFFERENCES BETWEEN SPORTS AND RELIGION?

Discussions about sports and religion are often confusing because different people see them as connected in different ways. Some people argue that sports are actually a new form of religion or at least a "quasi-religion." Others argue that there are *essential* differences between what they define as the "nature of sport" and "the nature of religion." Still others argue that sports and religions are simply two distinct forms of cultural practices that sometimes overlap as people devise ways to live with each other and struggle to make their lives satisfying and meaningful. The purpose of this section is to explain and clarify each of these three positions.

Sports As a Form of Religion

The most extreme position to take when discussing this issue is to say that sports are actually a form of religion. Although this position is difficult to defend, Charles Prebish (1984), a religious studies professor, has made the following case:

> If sport can bring its advocates to an experience of the ultimate, and this . . . experience is expressed through a formal series of public and private rituals requiring a symbolic language and space deemed sacred by its worshippers, then it is both proper and necessary to call sport itself a religion. It is also reasonable to consider sport the newest and fastest-growing religion, far outdistancing whatever is in second place.

Others stop short of the position taken by Prebish. For example, sociologist Harry Edwards (1973), describes sport as a "secular, quasi-religious institution" because sports share with religion certain characteristics and social functions. Theologian Michael Novak (1976) claims that sports are a form of "natural" religion because both are shaped by what he sees as "an impulse for freedom, respect for ritual limits, a zest for symbolic meaning, and a longing for perfection." Novak even refers to sports as types of godliness because they emerge out of the same quest for perfection in body, mind, and spirit that leads people to form their conceptions of god—conceptions that always embody the ideals of a particular group or society. Sociologist James Mathisen (1992) describes sports as forms of "folk religion" because they combine values, beliefs, myths, and cultic observances into a social form that has continuity and tradition for masses of people in the United States. Religious studies professor Joseph Price says that sports are a form of "civil religion" because they create

metaphors that promote patriotism and commitment to what he sees as American values.

These and other comparisons of religion and sports have highlighted the following similarities between sports and Judeo-Christian religious systems of meaning (cf., Hoffman, 1992, Parts 1 and 2):

- Both have places and buildings for communal gatherings and special events; sports have stadiums and arenas decorated with pictures of athletes and championship trophies; some religions have churches and temples decorated with statues of saints and/or stained-glass windows depicting great achievements.
- Both have procedures and dramas linked to personal betterment; sports have playbooks, practices, and overtime periods; religions have sacred books, prayers, and retreats.
- Both are controlled through structured organizations and hierarchical systems of authority made up of commissioners and bishops, athletic directors and pastors, coaches and priests.
- Both have events scheduled to celebrate values in the context of festival and festive occasions and both capture considerable attention on the sabbath.
- Both set aside certain times as special— such as Super Bowl Sunday and Easter Sunday, the NBA play-offs and Lent, Sunday morning worship and Monday Night Football.
- Both have rituals before, during, and after major events—such as initiations and baptisms, the national anthem and opening hymns, half-time pep talks and Sunday sermons, hand-slapping and the joining of hands, band parades and choir processions, shaking hands after a game and greeting the minister after the services.
- Both have heroes and legends about their accomplishments; sport heroes are elected to "halls of fame" and their stories are re-

peatedly told by sports journalists and fans; religious heroes are christened saints and their stories are repeatedly told by religious writers, ministers, and Sunday school teachers.

- Both are used to celebrate and reproduce the values of particular groups in society.
- Both can evoke intense excitement and emotional commitment from individuals and groups.
- Both can give deep personal meaning to people's lives and to activities that occur in a variety of circumstances.
- Both can be sources of existential experiences involving the temporary suspension of boundaries between self and the rest of the world; in other words, both can be sites for the transcendence of self, for flow, for peak experiences, or for a euphoric emotional "high."
- Both emphasize asceticism in that they stress discipline, self-denial, repetition, and the development of character—the notion of "no pain, no gain" is promoted by coaches and ministers alike.

In summary, it is easy to see why many people talk about sports as "religionlike." There are many similarities. Participation in sports, as a player or spectator, is characterized by many of the same trappings that characterize involvement in religion. In fact, the parallels are so apparent that it is often easy to get carried away with the similarities and ignore the differences between these two spheres of life.

"Essential" Differences Between Sport and Religion

Some people believe that religion and sport each have a unique but separate "essence" that is grounded in divine inspiration and/or nature itself.* They talk about religion and sport revealing different parts of a basic, unchanging

---

*These people refer to "sport" in the singular because they assume that all sport forms express the same essence.

"human nature" regardless of history, culture, or social circumstances. In other words, they assume that religion and sport each have an essence that transcends time and space, and that human beings "live out" that essence when they participate in religion or sport. In sociology these people are referred to as "essentialists." These essentialists are concerned with discovering "nature" and then outlining the ways that human beings and human behavior are "natural." When they turn their attention to religion and sport, essentialists argue that the fundamental character of religion is different from the fundamental character of sport. For example, they would highlight the following differences:

- Religious beliefs, meanings, rituals, and events are grounded in the sacred and supernatural realm whereas sport beliefs, meanings, rituals, and events are grounded in the profane and material realm.
- The purpose of religion is to transcend the circumstances and conditions of material life in the pursuit of spiritual goals whereas the purpose of sport is to focus on material issues in the pursuit of here-and-now pleasure, fame, or fortune.
- Religion is fundamentally rooted in faith whereas sport is fundamentally rooted in social relationships.
- Religion is fundamentally noncompetitive whereas sport is fundamentally competitive.
- Religion emphasizes a spirit of service and love whereas sport emphasizes a spirit of personal achievement and self-promotion.
- Religious rituals are essentially expressive and process-oriented whereas sport rituals are essentially instrumental and goal-oriented.
- Religion is fundamentally mystical and pure whereas sport is fundamentally clear-cut and crude.

As you might guess, essentialists would say there are important differences between the nature of the meanings attached to Super Bowl

Sunday by sports fans and the meanings attached to Easter Sunday by Christians, despite the fact that both are defined as important days. Similarly, they would highlight fundamental differences between the meanings underlying a hockey team's initiation ceremony and a baptism, between a seventh inning stretch and silent prayer during a religious service. They would see the meanings connected with St. Patrick's Cathedral as different from those connected with Yankee Stadium, even though both are important structures in New York city.

Some essentialists are religious people who simply would say that religion and sport are fundamentally different because religion is divinely inspired and sport is not. I've never encountered religious essentialists who argue that both the Ten Commandments and the rules of football were given to humans by God. Instead, they would say that when religion and sport come together, the essential character of religion often becomes corrupted by sport (Hoffman, 1992, pp. 275-285).

In summary, essentialists would not say that sport is never "religionlike," or that the social and psychological consequences of sport are always different from the consequences of religion. They would recognize overlap, but they would also stick to their position that sport and religion are fundamentally and essentially different.

Religions and Sports As Cultural Practices

A growing number of sociologists see both religions and sports as two forms of cultural practices created by groups of people as they devise ways to live with each other and struggle to make their lives satisfying and meaningful. These sociologists are sometimes called "social constructionists" because they do not assume that either religion or sport has an essential character. Instead, they see all religions and sports as "social constructions" or "social formations" with social dynamics and social consequences that may overlap or differ depending on social relations in particular social situations.

Social constructionists generally use some form of critical theory to guide their work. This leads them to focus on issues of power and social relations when they study religions or sports. For example, they would want to know why both sports and religions are male-dominated spheres of life, why men occupy all the important positions of power in both religious and sport organizations, why beliefs and rituals in both sports and religions generally privilege men over women, and why events in both sports and religions focus on men as the major participants. They would be interested in patterns of racial and ethnic participation in both sports and religions, and how those patterns are a part of general intergroup relations in the society as a whole.

Social constructionists also assume that both religious and sport systems of meaning do undergo change. They point out that religious beliefs and rituals vary from one social and cultural group to another and that beliefs and rituals change with new revelations and visions, new prophets and prophecies, new interpretations of sacred writings, new teachers and teachings. They see these variations and changes as examples of how the social acceptance of religious belief systems depends on the extent to which the belief systems are expressions of the cultural contexts in which they exist. They point out that when monotheistic people describe their God it is usually with characteristics that are highly valued and privileged in their culture (for example, as a white, male, adult). They are interested in the fact that when religious beliefs contradict or conflict with dominant cultural ideologies and practices, believers are often persecuted or marginalized to the point that they practice their beliefs in sects or cults.*

---

*A sect is a group organized around religious beliefs that differ in emphasis and priorities from dominant cultural beliefs in a community or society. A cult is generally a small, loosely organized group developed around a charismatic leader who promotes religious beliefs that are new, unconventional, and often in conflict with dominant cultural beliefs.

Social constructionists are also interested in the many examples in religious history that show that revelations, new teachings, and revisions in rules and beliefs nearly always arise in association with cultural changes. For example, Christian churches and denominations in some countries affected by women's movements have even approved the ordination of women as priests and ministers—a radical change for many of them. Other revisions of religious rules on everything from birth control to burial rituals are also associated with changes in social relations and cultural conditions.

Similarly, social constructionists would highlight changes in sports and differences in the way sports are defined, organized, and played from one society and culture to another. For example, they would explore how changes in sports are connected to power relations in society as a whole, how sports celebrate particular definitions of masculinity and femininity, and how sports may encourage the marginalization of people who do not fit those definitions. Generally, they would be interested in sports as social arenas in which existing social relations are reaffirmed and reproduced or challenged and changed.

In summary, social constructionists emphasize that religions and sports, just as other cultural practices, change as people struggle over how to live with each other and what their lives mean.

Evaluation and Summary

Each of these conceptual approaches to religions and sports offer food for thought. I use a constructionist approach because it enables me to ask questions about religions and sports that deal directly with people's experiences and social relations. It also alerts me to the different meanings that religions and sports have for different people, meanings that affect how people see the world, themselves, and their connections to other people.

In Sendai, Japan, youth baseball games are played on a field with a massive statue of Buddha in the background. However, little is known about the ways in which religious beliefs may be connected with sport participation outside of North America. (Jay Coakley)

One of the shortcomings with analyses using any of these approaches is that they draw almost exclusively on the American experience, and they refer almost exclusively to popular spectator sports played by men and promoted heavily by the media. Furthermore, none of these approaches has generated much work that might help us understand the connection between sports and religious systems of meaning other than those grounded in Christianity (see the box on p. 427). The sociology of sport has much work to do to understand the connection between sports and religions. The rest of the chapter provides an overview of what we know and what has been done.

Sports and Religions Around the World

Most of what we know about sports and religion focuses on various forms of Christianity, especially Christian fundamentalism. Little has been written about the connections between sports and Buddhism, Confucianism, Hinduism, Islam, Judaism, Shinto, Taoism, and the hundreds of variations of these and other religions. The systems of meaning associated with each of these religions do have implications for the ways people view physical activities, define their bodies, and relate to each other through human movement. However, those systems of meaning do not seem to be compatible with participation in formally organized competitive sports in the same way that various forms of Christianity have been made to be compatible.

Unfortunately, my knowledge of these issues is very limited. In fact, I know more about how some North American athletes have converted Zen Buddhist beliefs into strategies that will improve their golf scores and marathon times than I do about how Buddhism is related to sports and sport participation among the 307 million Buddhists around the world. (I am realizing more and more how my knowledge is grounded in a combination of Eurocentric science and limited personal experiences!) However, I am very interested in the fact that Buddhism and philosophical Hinduism, two systems of religious meanings that emphasize physical and spiritual discipline, do *not* seem to inspire believers with concerns for winning Olympic medals or physically outperforming or dominating other human beings in organized competitive sports. Instead, Buddhism and Hinduism seem to focus the attention of believers on transcending the self and all earthly matters. Their emphasis on transcendence does *not* seem to support interests in becoming elite athletes. It is only elite athletes from Christian, capitalist countries who want to know how the practices and meditation rituals from these religions can be used to improve sport performances and give meaning to lives that revolve around competitive sports.

The sociology of sport would greatly benefit from in-depth studies of how people holding various religious beliefs view the body, physical activity, human movement, and organized competitive sports. These studies would help us understand the lives of billions of people who *do not* grow up learning to compete in formally organized physical activities, who *do not* use physical and mental discipline to extend sport skills, who *do not* use competitive physical activities to give religious witness, and who *do not* use religious beliefs and organizations to promote and even glorify sports.

In-depth studies of the everyday experiences of people around the globe would also help us understand how various religions inform gender relations in ways that privilege some people and marginalize others when it comes to sport participation. For example, Muslim and Hindu beliefs have been used to legitimize extreme forms of patriarchy* and definitions of men's and women's bodies that discourage if not deny girls and women access to sport participation. Physical activities among Muslims and Hindus are nearly always sex segregated; men are not allowed to look at women in certain settings, and women must cover their bodies in certain ways even as they exercise. Norms such as these are especially strong among fundamentalists in each religion. This is why the national Olympic teams from many Muslim and Hindu countries have seldom had women athletes or women's teams.

Studies of religions and sports in diverse cultural settings would not only increase our understanding of other cultures but they would also increase our abilities to reflect on our own experiences and ask critical questions that enable us to see more clearly the ways in which the cultural practices of religions and sports are integrated into our own lives.

---

*Patriarchy is a form of gender relations that privileges men over women, especially in regard to legal status and access to political power and economic resources.

SPORTS AND CHRISTIAN ORGANIZATIONS AND BELIEFS

Sports and various Christian religions have had what might be described as a symbiotic relationship since the mid-nineteenth century. Despite differences, sports and religions have overlapped and been combined in mutually supportive ways over the past 150 years. People associated with certain religions and religious organizations have used sports as a means of achieving their personal and organizational goals, and people associated with sports have used various forms of religion to achieve their goals. This has been done frequently enough in recent years to make the combination of sports and Christian organizations and beliefs very popular in some Western countries, especially the United States and Canada.

The growing popularity of these combinations raises interesting questions for the sociology of sport. Why have Christian organizations and beliefs been combined with sports? How have religious organizations used sports and how have sports used religion and religious beliefs? What are the social consequences of these combinations? These are the topics covered in the remainder of the chapter.

The Protestant Ethic and the Spirit of Sports

In the late nineteenth century German sociologist-economist Max Weber did a classic study, *The Protestant Ethic and the Spirit of Capitalism*, in which he outlined the connection between the reformist religious ideas of Martin Luther and John Calvin and the growth of capitalist economic systems. His conclusion was that Protestant religious beliefs and the growth of capitalism went hand in hand, reinforcing and shaping each other in the process. Weber provided examples of how Protestantism promoted deep moral suspicions about erotic pleasure, physical desire, and all forms of idleness ("idle hands are the devil's workshop"). He also documented a connection between Protestantism and an emphasis on a rationally controlled lifestyle

in which emotions and moods were suppressed in a quest for worldly success and eternal salvation. This orientation involved defining work (people's jobs in the economy) as "a calling" (from God) through which a person's spiritual worth could be displayed and expressed.

Shaped over the last 250 years by the application of religious principles to economic and political life, the Protestant Ethic emphasizes rationality, organization, discipline, hard work, success in one's occupational calling, and a willingness to sacrifice and endure pain in the process of honoring that calling. This emphasis has been socially significant because it encouraged the public expression of spiritual beliefs through physical action, especially *work*.

What does the Protestant Ethic have to do with sports? I would hypothesize that automation, the use of technology, and the loss of power among workers in Western capitalist countries has so alienated many people from work that work no longer serves as an important means of expressing personal worth. Furthermore, the emphasis on rationality and efficiency that have traditionally driven production do not clearly fit with the narcissistic emphasis on the self and the social emphasis on egalitarianism that drives material consumption. Sport, however, brings the emphasis on rationality and the narcissistic emphasis on the self together in highly rational efforts to mold bodies to fit the image of a hard, efficient, performance machine. Over time, fitting this image has also become a way for people to prove they are worthy, responsible, and even sensuous or attractive.

Therefore it may not be a coincidence that the importance of the body in production and consumption closely fits with changes in the way the body has been defined in Christian systems of meaning. Dominant Christian beliefs before the twentieth century emphasized that the body was the root of all evil; the pleasures of the flesh were to be avoided, or enjoyed only if they conformed with God's word. However, organized sports focused acceptable attention on the body because organized sports could celebrate the body's productive potential, which could be achieved through discipline, sacrifice, denial, and even the endurance of pain. Because organized, competitive, sports were about bodily performance rather than bodily pleasure, the body could be defined as a worthy spiritual tool, as a means of expressing spiritual worth in the very same terms emphasized in the Protestant Ethic. This may be one reason why sports have been defined more and more often by Christians as a site for the expression of spiritual worth.

In summary, sports have been increasingly incorporated into Christian organizations and beliefs because they emphasize a rationally controlled lifestyle characterized by discipline, hard work, sacrifice, and the endurance of pain in the pursuit of success. When sports are constructed in this way Christian athletes can even define being the best athlete they can be as their calling (from God). This is how playing sports comes to be defined as a form of giving witness among some Christian athletes.

How Have Christians and Christian Organizations Used Sports?

TO PROMOTE SPIRITUAL GROWTH Around the middle of the nineteenth century, influential Christian men, described as "muscular Christians" in England and New England, promoted the idea that the physical condition of one's body had religious significance. They believed the body was the instrument of good works and that meeting the physical demands of godly behavior required good health and physical conditioning. Although most religious people at the time did not agree with the ideas of the muscular Christians, there was a growing recognition of the possibility that there might be a connection between the physical and spiritual dimensions of human beings—that there might be important links between body and spirit (Guttmann, 1988).

These new ideas that the body had moral significance and that moral character was associated with physical conditioning encouraged many religious organizations to use sports in their programs. For example, the YMCA and the YWCA grew rapidly between 1880 and 1920; they built athletic facilities in numerous communities, and they sponsored teams in numerous sports. In fact, James Naismith invented basketball in 1891 while he was a student at the Springfield, Massachusetts YMCA (see Chapter 1), and William Morgan invented volleyball in 1895 while he was the physical activities director at a YMCA in Holyoke, Massachusetts.

Sport programs were also sponsored by numerous Protestant churches and congregations, Catholic dioceses and parishes, Mormon wards, the B'nai B'rith, and a few Jewish synagogues. These organizations sponsored sports and sport programs because their leaders believed that sport participation was linked to the development of moral character. Pope John Paul II has said that:

> Sport, because of the wholesome elements it gives value to and exalts, may become more and more a vital instrument for the moral and spiritual elevation of the human person and therefore contribute to the construction of an orderly, peaceful, and hard-working society (quoted in Kerrigan, 1992, p. 256).

Evangelist Billy Graham, an outspoken promoter of sports as a builder of moral character, summarizes the spirit in which many religious organizations have used sports. Back in 1971 Graham declared,

> The Bible says leisure and lying around are morally dangerous for us. Sports keeps us busy; athletes, you notice, don't take drugs. There are probably more committed Christians in sports, both collegiate and professional, than in any other occupation in America.

In light of publicized cases of drug use by many athletes Graham's statement may sound naive in the 1990s. But it illustrates that people associated with Christianity have for many years been committed to using sports to symbolize and promote moral development—especially among boys and young men. This continues in the 1990s.

TO RECRUIT NEW MEMBERS AND PROMOTE RELIGIOUS BELIEFS AND ORGANIZATIONS American religious leaders at the turn of the century became concerned that their churches and programs were not attracting the participation of boys and young men. In fact, the vast majority of Protestant congregations consisted of mostly girls and women (Rader, 1983). This encouraged many of these leaders to shift their emphasis from what they saw as "feminized" values (meekness, humility, and submissiveness) to a new set of "manly values." Their purpose was to attract young males and shape them into "manly youth." Sport teams and sport programs were used as recruiting tools because sports could be constructed to emphasize what the religious leaders defined as "Christian manliness."

According to historian Benjamin Rader (1983), a manly youth around 1900 was described in this way:

> The manly youth . . . practiced sexual continence and resisted the "secret vice" [of masturbation—which was believed to deplete] the body of vital energy and [result] in a host of other dire consequences. . . . The manly youth cultivated self-command and absolute candor; he abhorred display, pretension, sentimentality, and capitulation to pain. He insisted on justice and was quick to defend honor with physical prowess; he was physically active, striving to develop the utmost robustness, animal energy, and personal courage. His spirit found its truest expression in the out-of-doors, in the refreshing vigor of the countryside, and on the athletic field.

This idea that a "manly man is a Godly man" has become increasingly popular in recent years, especially among Christian fundamentalists. According to scholar and journalist Carol Flake (1992, p. 165), the incorporation of the image of the tough athlete into the character portrait of the "Christian man" has allowed men to rescue "the Bible from women and overly refined preachers." For example, in 1991 Bill McCart-

ney, the football coach at the University of Colorado, formed a Christian fundamentalist men's movement called *The Promise Keepers*. The goal of the movement is to get men to assume leadership of today's families and communities. McCartney says that "a Godly man is a manly man," and that society today is in a state of moral decline because men have not used the ultimate, unchanging truth found in the Bible to guide their lives. McCartney's *Third Men's Conference of The Promise Keepers* attracted over 42,000 men to the football stadium at the University of Colorado in Boulder for 2 days of presentations on Christian manhood (in July, 1993). The success of this organization is at least partly due to its association with the image of a "manly man" as embodied by men associated with sports, especially sports involving the use of strength and power. For these people, Jesus is "the Master Coach" with answers to all questions.

American colleges and universities have frequently used sports as a recruiting tool. For example, in 1965, when Oral Roberts founded his university in Tulsa, Oklahoma, he emphasized the importance of its sports programs in the following statement:

> Athletics is part of our Christian witness. . . . Nearly every man in America reads the sports pages, and a Christian school cannot ignore these people. . . . Sports are becoming the No. 1 interest of people in America. For us to be relevant, we had to gain the attention of millions of people in a way that they could understand.

More recently, Jerry Falwell, the noted television evangelist, explained,

> To me, athletics are a way of making a statement. And I believe you have a better Christian witness to the youth of the world when you competitively, head-to-head, prove yourself their equal on the playing field (cited in Capouya, 1986).

Falwell was talking about the importance of sports at Liberty University, the school he founded in connection with Jerry Falwell Ministries.

Other colleges and universities have used sports in a similar but less overt way. Catholic schools—including the University of Notre Dame, Boston College, and Georgetown University—have traditionally used their football and/or basketball programs to build their prestige as church-affiliated institutions. Brigham Young University, affiliated with the Mormons, has also done this. Smaller Christian colleges even formed the National Christian Collegiate Athletic Association (NCCAA) in the mid-1960s to sponsor championships and recruit student-athletes, especially men, to their academic programs (Mathisen, 1990) .

In some cases, religious organizations have developed solely around sports in an effort to attract more people to Christian beliefs and provide support for athletes who already hold Christian beliefs. Examples of this practice are found in organizations such as the Fellowship of Christian Athletes (FCA), Athletes in Action (AIA), Pro Athletes Outreach (PAO), and a number of smaller groups (see box on page 440). These "sport ministries" use a variety of approaches to spread fundamentalist Christian beliefs and, along with other Christian organizations, they now even target certain sport events as opportunities to spread those beliefs to athletes and spectators. For example, thousands of volunteers were in Barcelona at the 1992 Olympic Games to distribute copies of *Winning for Life*, a 36-page booklet published by the Colorado Springs-based Bible Society. Over 18,000 booklets were given to athletes and Olympic officials, and an attempt was made to contact each of the 500,000 households in Barcelona. A spokesperson for the Bible Society explained that:

> The Olympics serve as an opportunity to piggy-back on the respect athletes have and communicate Christianity to those who would not normally be interested (quoted in Rabey, 1992).

According to plans being made by some of the 60 national and international religious groups headquartered in Colorado Springs, the 1996

Teams sponsored by Athletes in Action travel all over the world to share their religious beliefs with members of opposing teams and the spectators attracted to games played with local teams. According to the AIA, sports provide a ready-made platform for delivering their message. (Jay Coakley)

Olympic Games in Atlanta will attract a massive effort to use sports to recruit new people to Christian organizations and beliefs. Such efforts are not new, but they are increasingly organized and coordinated (Mathisen, 1990). Since 1986 the major sport ministries have been linked together through the International Sports Coalition, an umbrella organization designed "to promote unity and cooperation . . . so that together we might follow God's leading in worldwide evangelism" (organizational statement quoted in Mathisen, 1990, p. 246).

Finally, various religious groups and organizations have used athletes themselves to attract new believers and group members. Extreme examples include *Karate for Christ* and *John Jacobs Power Team*, a group of "born-again Christian" musclemen who travel around putting on displays of strength by breaking bricks and concrete slabs with blows from their forearms and breaking loose from chains and handcuffs—all in the name of Jesus to show young people, especially young men—that "God never told His people to be weak." While wearing shirts with "God Made You to Win" printed on them, they define their displays of strength as religious expression. These and other groups try to capitalize on the extent to which young people in North America identify with athletic heroes and use them as sources of information about sports and about life in general. This method of marketing fundamentalist beliefs has made elite athletes important "messengers" for religious organizations (Norton and Wilkerson, 1975).

TO PROMOTE CHRISTIAN FUNDAMENTALIST BELIEF SYSTEMS Most of the religious groups and organizations previously mentioned are nondenominational, but they clearly promote a specific form of Christianity—one based on a conservative theology and a fundamentalist orientation toward life.

Religious fundamentalism is a complex social phenomenon (Ferrante, 1992). Even though it may not appeal to the majority of people in a particular society or religious group it can capture the interest and involvement of a wide array of people from different social and economic backgrounds. This is true of Islamic fundamentalism in Iran and of Christian fundamentalism in the United States and Canada. Regardless of their religion, fundamentalists share the belief that there is a need for people to return to what they define as their culture's religious roots and that this return can occur only if individuals develop personal relationships with the supernatural source of truth (God, Allah, Christ, "the universe," the spirit world, etc.). Fundamentalists see the supernatural realm as the source of absolute, unchanging truths offering answers to personal and social problems. These answers are

revealed through sacred writings or the verbal teachings of divinely inspired prophets.

Fundamentalist movements arise when people perceive moral threats or crises that involve what they see as corruption of an entire way of life that was once ideal because it was believed to be based on pure religious principles. Therefore fundamentalists emphasize tradition; they usually are interested in returning to past ways of doing things shaped by a one-and-only truth, and separating themselves from people who refuse to apply that truth to their lives.

It is within the fundamentalist Christian movements in the United States, Canada, England, and Australia that sports have often been used to promote religious beliefs. Although individual athletes apply their Christian beliefs to their sport lives in many different ways, as we will discuss later in this chapter, the beliefs themselves tend to emphasize traditional and conservative values based strictly on a literal reading of the Bible.

How Have Sports Used Religion?

People often use religious beliefs and rituals to provide them with psychological support in the face of uncertainty. Religions provide systems of meanings that can be used to make sense out of one's life. Because religious beliefs and rituals are shared they can provide a basis for group integration and unity, and because they are related to the sacred and supernatural they can be used as a powerful basis for social control on both the individual and group levels. It is partly because religions can do these things that religious beliefs have become used in certain sport contexts. For example, athletes and coaches may use their religion as a source of psychological support as they cope with the challenge and uncertainty of competition, and as they try to find special meaning for their sport lives. Coaches may also use various forms of religion and religious beliefs to produce team unity and establish a basis for social control over their athletes. Each of these possibilities needs further explanation.

TO COPE WITH UNCERTAINTY Through history people have used various combinations of religion, magic, and superstition to cope with uncertainties in their lives.

Religion and uncertainty. Judeo-Christian religions have a sequence of rituals that are performed at points in the life cycle characterized by challenges and uncertainty. As the uncertainty of life begins there is baptism; when moral responsibility is faced there is the eucharist; and when moral adulthood begins there is confirmation. The rituals of matrimony and holy orders exist to enable adults to face the challenge and uncertainty associated with difficult lifetime decisions and commitments. Dying people are given the last rites to cope with the spiritual and intellectual uncertainties associated with death. Using religious rituals to cope with uncertainty is a characteristic practice throughout the world.

Because uncertainty is a part of competition, it is not surprising that some forms of religion are used in conjunction with competitive sports. Religious beliefs and rituals can provide athletes with physical and spiritual reinforcement, relieve anxiety, help them concentrate and face competition with confidence, and supply reasons for practicing and developing physical skills (Prebish, 1984). This is why Christian athletes and coaches sometimes use pre-game prayers; as with sport psychology, religion helps eliminate anxieties so athletes can focus attention on their own performance. For example, Willye White, a former gold medalist in the women's long jump, explained her success in the Olympic Games this way:

> I was nervous, so I read the New Testament. I read the verse about have no fear, and I felt relaxed. Then I jumped farther than I ever jumped before in my life (quoted in *Life*, 1984).

Some teams in North America now use spiritual counselors to help athletes cope with uncertainty before games. Of course, not all religious athletes use their beliefs in this manner, but there is a tendency for some to call on their religion to help them successfully face challenges and uncertainty.

Magic and uncertainty. Magic consists of rituals explicitly designed to produce immediate and practical results in the material world. These rituals are like recipes because they precisely specify what materials to use and how to use them to produce results. Magic is used in many societies when individuals or groups face threats or uncertainty. Because traditions of magic have faded from popular experience in many industrial societies, some people have used religious symbols and rituals in an effort to produce magical results. For example, some people may pray to achieve material goals such as winning games, staying healthy, minimizing injuries, getting a hit, making a free throw, making a first down, scoring a goal, and so on. Interestingly, athletes who pray before games or at anxiety-provoking points during games seldom pray before practices, and few athletes make the sign of the cross during batting practice or when they shoot free throws during practice. Why not? I think it is because games create anxiety and uncertainty while practices do not.

Some coaches and athletes have raised questions about the use of magic in sports. Whitey Herzog, a long-time manager in baseball, once said that ". . . when I tell a player to hustle and he says to me that God will take care of his slump, I tell him God . . . don't know nothing about hitting." Bobby Knight, the basketball coach at Indiana University expressed similar sentiments in the quote on the opening page of this chapter. In another example, an athlete who played for a Catholic high school indicated that whenever an opponent crossed himself before attempting a free throw, he would lean into the free throw lane and also cross himself while facing the free throw shooter. This was to let his opponent know that if a religious gesture was going to be used as a form of magic, it was going to be used by both teams.

Sometimes it is easier to recognize magic when it is used by people from other cultures. Author Larry Merchant (1971) once observed a Kenyan soccer team that spent thousands of dollars enlisting the help of witch doctors during

According to Bobby Knight, Indiana University basketball coach, God "is not going to score when we need points . . . God does not give a damn what goes on in athletics." However, the uncertainty that comes with sport participation sometimes leads athletes to turn to the supernatural for support and inspiration related to performance. (Jay Coakley)

its season. The players on the team would paint their bodies with pig fat to ward off the evil spirits who might impede their success during games. In turning his attention to the United States, Merchant noted with some sarcasm that American teams "are much too sophisticated to travel with witch doctors and wear pig fat. [Instead, they] travel with clergymen and wear medals."

Superstition and uncertainty. Athletes are generally superstitious. They often believe that their sport lives are determined by external forces over which they have no control, and they have been known to do many strange things to control those forces.* Like magic and some re-

*See Becker, 1975; Buhrmann and Zaugg, 1981; Gmelch, 1979; Gregory and Petrie, 1975; Neil, 1975, 1982; Neil et al, 1981; Womack, 1979; and Zimmer, 1984.

ligious rituals, superstitions are associated with uncertainty and the stakes associated with an event. As uncertainty increases in an important event, so does the frequency of superstitions, the use of rituals, and the existence of taboos and fetishes (Gmelch, 1979). This is especially true at elite levels of sport competition where the outcomes of events determine important personal and team rewards (Neil et al., 1981). A good summary of how rituals are used in sports has been given by anthropologist Mari Womack. Her summary is in the box on p. 435.

TO GIVE SPECIAL MEANING TO SPORT PARTICIPATION Sport participation emphasizes personal achievement and self-promotion; it does not produce any essential goods or services, nor does it make the world a better place for people to live in; in many ways, it is a self-indulgent

REFLECT ON SPORT

Why Rituals Are Widely Used in Sports

According to anthropologist Mari Womack (1992), when people face uncertainty in competition or intense challenges, they frequently use rituals to make them feel as if they have some control over what happens to them. These rituals may be grounded in religion, magic, or personal habits.

After examining the use of rituals in sports, Womack concluded that athletes, coaches, spectators (and maybe even umpires and referees) turn to rituals for the following reasons*:

1. Ritual helps the player focus his (or her) attention on the task at hand. It can be used by the player to prevent anxiety or excessive environmental stimuli—such as the chanting of fans—from interrupting his (or her) concentration.

*From "Why athletes need ritual: a study of magic among professional athletes" by M. Womack. In *Sport and Religion* (pp 200) by S.J. Hoffman (Ed), 1992. Champaign, IL: Human Kinetics. Copyright 1992 by Shirl J. Hoffman. Reprinted by permission.

2. Ritual can signal intent to the other team. Specifically, ritual can be used to "threaten" the other team.
3. Ritual provides a means of coping with a high-risk, high-stress situation.
4. Ritual helps establish a rank order among team members and promotes intragroup communication.
5. Ritual helps in dealing with ambiguity in interpersonal relationships, with other team members, and with people on the periphery of the team, such as management and the public.
6. Ritual is a "harmless" means of self-expression. It can be used to reinforce a sense of individual worth under pressure for group conformity, without endangering the unity of the group.
7. Ritual directs individual motivations and needs toward achieving group goals.

The uncertainty that exists in highly competitive sports is so great that many athletes use rituals. In fact, the use of rituals among athletes has become so widespread that it has been described by journalists and noted by many spectators.

activity despite the sacrifice and pain often involved in training. This can be discouraging for athletes who have made the sacrifices, endured the pain, and dedicated their lives to developing physical skills. How do these athletes justify the expenditure of so much time and energy on sports? How do they explain giving up the relationships and experiences that their peers enjoy as a part of growing up? How do they explain why their families have been disrupted or why so many family resources have been spent on their participation? How do they deal with the need to outperform and even dominate oth-

ers if they want to continue playing or move to higher levels of competition?

One way of justifying and dealing with all these things is to define participation and achievement in sports as spiritual offerings, as acts of worship, and as ways of giving witness (Hoffman, 1992). Thus a commitment to a sport becomes "sanctified" because it is done for "the glory of God."

An increasing number of athletes have seemingly used Christian religious beliefs to give this type of meaning to their sport participation, even though there may be conflict and tension between Christian beliefs and certain types of behavior in sports. This conflict and tension is discussed on pp. 437-441.

TO CREATE COHESION AND MAINTAIN SO-CIAL CONTROL Religious beliefs and rituals can be powerful tools. They can create strong bonds of attachment between people, and they can be used to sanctify norms and rules by connecting them with the sacred and supernatural. When religious beliefs and rituals are combined with sport participation, they can link athletes together in ways that transcend the everyday lives of teammates. When this happens, team cohesion and team morale can be significantly heightened. This benefit has been noted by some coaches who have used their own Christian beliefs as rallying points for their teams. Their desire to promote their Christian beliefs and create a collective focus for team members encourage them to combine religion and sport. For example, George Allen, a widely respected American football coach, once said that he supported religious worship and team prayers among his athletes because they "foster togetherness and mutual respect like nothing I have found in 21 years of coaching" (cited in Hoffman, 1982).

Objections to this practice, especially when it involves the use of pregame prayers in public schools, has led some U.S. students and their parents to file lawsuits to ban religious expression in connection with sport events. But coaches continue to insist that prayers bring team members together in positive ways. According to a survey done in 1988, these coaches are supported by 59% of U.S. adults, who think "it's good for sporting events at public high schools to begin with a public prayer" (*USA Today*, Feb. 4, 1988). However, these people are assuming that the prayer will not be an Islamic, Hindu, or Buddhist prayer. Their support assumes that the public prayer will support their own beliefs about the sacred and supernatural.

Religion can also be used to connect the moral worth of athletes with the quality of their play and their conformity to team rules and the commands of coaches. For example, Wes Neal, the president of the Institute for Athletic Perfection, a Christian sport organization, explains that performance in sport is a means of revealing an athlete's love for God (Neal, 1981). This means that performances in sports are somehow connected to the moral worth of athletes. This connection not only encourages athletes to become committed to improvement and excellence, but it also encourages them to become willing followers of their coaches and trainers.

In his *Handbook of Athletic Perfection*, Wes Neal (1981) explains that the "complete Christian athlete" has a will "bound to the command of his coach." In discussing his own success in sports, Neal reveals that he always wants his actions "to be the instant and complete response" to his coach's desire for him. He believes that "by being obedient to my coach, I [am] also being obedient to God." He explains that "You may not agree with [your coach] on every point, but your role [as a Christian athlete] is to carry out his assignments. The attitude you have as you carry out each assignment will determine if you are a winner in God's sight" (1981, p. 193). When the rules and assignments of coaches are tied in this way to the religious beliefs of athletes, the athletes are much more likely to obey them without question. In this way, religion can be used by coaches, either intentionally or unintentionally, as a means of controlling the behavior of athletes.

Neal also explains that a Christian athlete's goal is to achieve what he calls a "Total Release Performance" (T-R-P). This goal can be achieved only when athletes accept the sacrifice and pain involved in training, give a total effort at all times, and dedicate what they do to Jesus Christ. This may sound like a worthy set of goals to Christians, but pursuing them makes athletes easily controlled by coaches. According to Neal, this is desirable. In fact, he says that when an athlete becomes a true bond-servant of Christ, his "will is bound to the command of his coach, [so] if his coach yells 'jump!' the [true Christian athlete] doesn't waste time asking 'why?' He puts everything into the jump *immediately!*"(Neal, 1981, p. 194). From a sociological perspective, it is not difficult to see why coaches would see such an orientation as valuable and why they might encourage athletes to focus on "Total Release Performance."

This connection between religion and social control is important because many coaches are very concerned with issues of authority and control on their teams. They see obedience among players as necessary for team success. For example, in a book on how athletes can be good Christians (*The Game Plan*), Dan Stavely (1975), a former college football coach and an active supporter of the FCA, writes that "the good coach demands obedience" and that "God expects you and me to be obedient." In his explanation of God's expectations, he reminds athletes that the Bible is full of stories in which people were punished for failing to obey the "Master Coach" (God), and that when athletes do not obey their team coaches, they create problems and get into trouble. This approach may contain some valuable spiritual lessons, but it also tends to turn the words of coaches into commandments that must be followed by athletes who use their sport participation as a form of Christian witness. When this happens, the control coaches have over athletes becomes extensive, and potentially dangerous.

THE CONSEQUENCES OF COMBINING SPORTS AND RELIGIOUS BELIEFS

Organized competitive sports and Christian beliefs and rituals are cultural practices that have different histories, traditions, and goals; they have been socially constructed in different ways. This means that when certain sports and Christianity are combined, conflicts may occur in the lives of Christian athletes and Christian sport organizations.

Conflicts for Christian Athletes

The sources of this conflict for Christian athletes have been clearly identified by Shirl Hoffman, a physical educator and editor of an informative anthology entitled *Sport and Religion*

(1992). I've tried to summarize my reading of Hoffman's ideas in the model outlined in Figure 16-1. The model shows that Hoffman raises questions about whether any and all sport behavior can be used by Christian athletes as spiritual offerings or worship. Hoffman thinks that the form and consequences of behavior are important to consider if they are to be used as religious expressions.

Hoffman's model suggests that a conflict might exist when a Christian boxer uses his performance in the ring as a spiritual offering even though he punches another human being senseless while he does his sport. The model suggests that similar conflicts might exist for football players whose behavior regularly injures others. Of course most football players don't intend to injure others, but benign intent does little to heal the cartilage and bones of fellow players in traction or on crutches as a result of "loving hits" from a Christian opponent. Can these "hits" be used as spiritual offerings and acts of worship? What about Christian pitchers who throw brush-back pitches to intimidate batters, or Christian baserunners who slide into second with their spikes up to break up a double play? What about Christian basketball players who use their elbows to keep opponents away from rebounds? Hoffman asks questions such as these and then outlines what he thinks happens when Christian athletes ask similar questions.

Hoffman suggests that when Christian athletes ask these questions, they develop doubts about the value of sports as spiritual offerings or forms of worship. These doubts may be intensified if coaches and/or teammates think that a player's Christianness jeopardizes his willingness to do what it takes to win. To ease these doubts Christian athletes might choose one of the two following strategies. The strategy most often chosen involves becoming obsessed with the ascetic aspects of sport. In other words, athletes get caught up with discipline and self-denial in sport participation. This leads them to romanticize the importance of sacrifice and pain as signs of moral worth, to emphasize total dedication to perfection, and to accept the idea that

There are three aspects of dominant forms of sport that clearly raise questions about whether sport participation can be used as a spiritual offering or act of worship. Questions exist because sport often involves the following:

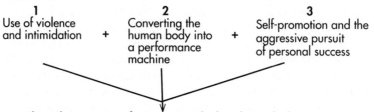

| **1** | | **2** | | **3** |
| Use of violence and intimidation | + | Converting the human body into a performance machine | + | Self-promotion and the aggressive pursuit of personal success |

These three aspects of sport create doubts about whether sport
(A) contains any intrinsic worth as a symbolic religious offering
and
(B) can be used by athletes to engage in an authentic spiritual encounter with the divine

These doubts can be eased or eliminated in two ways:

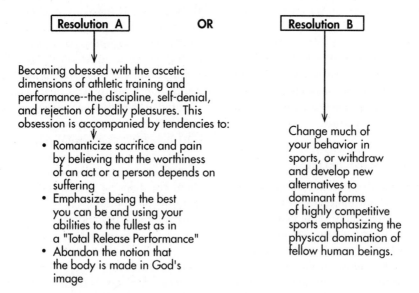

| Resolution A | OR | Resolution B |

Becoming obsessed with the ascetic dimensions of athletic training and performance--the discipline, self-denial, and rejection of bodily pleasures. This obsession is accompanied by tendencies to:

- Romanticize sacrifice and pain by believing that the worthiness of an act or a person depends on suffering
- Emphasize being the best you can be and using your abilities to the fullest as in a "Total Release Performance"
- Abandon the notion that the body is made in God's image

Change much of your behavior in sports, or withdraw and develop new alternatives to dominant forms of highly competitive sports emphasizing the physical domination of fellow human beings.

FIGURE 16-1 Christian religious beliefs and sport participation: a model of conflict, doubt, and resolution. (Adapted from ideas in Hoffmann, 1992.)

the body is a performance machine and nothing more. A second strategy for easing or eliminating doubts about the spiritual value of sports is for Christian athletes to change their behavior in sports so it conforms to dominant Christian beliefs or withdraw from traditional sports participation and develop new alternatives to dominant forms of organized, competitive sports. The new alternatives, according to Hoffman, would consist primarily of informal games that did not involve any heavy physical contact or any emphasis on physical domination.

Although Hoffman's model has never been tested in research, there are at least two studies that examine what happens or might happen when professed Christians participate in organized competitive sports. Chris Stevenson (1991a, b) conducted in-depth interviews with 31 "current and former college and professional athletes associated with the Athletes-in-Action (AIA) organization in Western Canada"(p. 362) and found that Christian athletes do not apply their religious beliefs to sport participation uniformly. He found that some athletes avoided conflict between religious beliefs and sport participation simply by compartmentalizing these two aspects of their lives and not thinking about how they might be incompatible. However, most athletes in the study were aware of potential conflicts and avoided them by emphasizing the importance of obeying game rules and playing sports with "the right attitude." However, these athletes also tended to accept the legitimacy of any sport behaviors that were within the rules even though they might involve intimidation or cause injury; they mostly used religion to deal with emotional or personal problems and to justify their sport behaviors. Finally, there were a few athletes who gave priority to their Christian role identities when they played sports, and a few of those had even withdrawn from elite competitive sports because of the conflicts between their Christian beliefs and what they were expected to do as elite athletes. Stevenson's findings support at least parts of Hoffman's model.

In another study Kelley, Hoffman, and Gill (1990) surveyed 308 students from small liberal arts colleges and found that professing to be a Christian did not seem to influence what the students defined as important when they participated in sports. However, the data did suggest that Christian student-athletes who valued religion for its practical usefulness tended to emphasize the importance of winning in sports, whereas those who valued religion for its own sake tended to emphasize personal goals and the enjoyment of competition in sports. Overall, the study did not find that Christian beliefs led students to raise questions about the legitimacy of dominant behaviors in sports. This study provides only indirect support for part of Hoffman's model.

Anecdotal data often highlight cases in which athletes who profess Christian beliefs seem to have no problem conforming to what they are expected to do as athletes. For example, a Liberty University baseball player once indicated that to demonstrate his Christian manliness to opposing pitchers, he always walked up to bat and looked "the pitcher right in the eye to let him know a Christian can still have aggression" (cited in Capouya, 1986). When Rick Saul, a former player on the Los Angeles Rams football team, told his Christian opponents what they could expect from him on the playing field, he said, "I'm going to hit you guys with all the love I have in me" (cited in Hoffman, 1982). When boxer Floyd Patterson gave Archie Moore a sound beating in a championship boxing match, he summed up his efforts in the following manner:

> I could see his eyes go glassy as he fell back, and I somehow knew if he got up again, it wouldn't do him any good. I just hit him again, and the Lord did the rest. (cited in Hoffman, 1982)

But as Hoffman suggests in his model, professed Christian athletes regularly have trouble reconciling the fact that material success, self-promotion, and lack of concern for opponents are emphasized in competitive sports, whereas the Bible emphasizes humility, "turning the other cheek," and a sincere concern for the welfare of others. For example, Doug Plank, a former defensive player for the Chicago Bears, once said that "As a Christian I learn to love, but when the whistle blows, I have to be tough—you're always walking a tightrope" (cited in Hoffman, 1982). My guess is that many Christian athletes walk the tightrope or they simply don't think much about the implications of their Christian beliefs once the competition begins.

Conflicts for Christian Sport Organizations

On an organizational level the combination of Christianity and many sports would seem to make people aware of issues and problems in sports and inspire them to call for reforms. However, this has not happened. Instead of calling for changes in sports, Christian sport groups have simply used sports to recruit new members and promote certain religious beliefs. These groups have not tried to identify problems and push for reforms in the ways sports are defined, organized, and played.

The policy position in most Christian sport organizations is that changes in sports will occur only *after* there have been changes in the individuals who participate in sports. Therefore the racism, sexism, violence, cheating, and exploitation that now exist will not disappear until all athletes, coaches, and spectators have developed a personal faith in Christ. This position is not very popular among those interested in immediate social reforms. For example, when Frank Deford (1976a) did a special story on sports and Christianity for *Sports Illustrated*, he found that:

> No one in the movement—much less in any organization—speaks out against dirty play, no

REFLECT ON SPORT

Christian Sport Organizations that Have Sport Ministries*

COORDINATING UMBRELLA ORGANIZATIONS

International Sports Coalition (ISA)
Sports Outreach America

MAJOR ORGANIZATIONS

Athletes in Action (AIA)
Fellowship of Christian Athletes (FCA)
Pro Athletes Outreach (PAO)
Sports Ambassadors

OTHER ORGANIZATIONS

Athletes for Kids
Baseball Chapel
Beyond Victory Ministries

OTHER ORGANIZATIONS—cont'd

Champions for Christ
Christian Bowhunters Association
Christian Surfers Australia
Epistle Sport Ministries
Fellowship of Christian Anglers
Golf Fellowship
Hockey Ministries International
Motorsports Ministries
New Life in Sports
Pro Athletes for Christ
Professional Skiers Fellowship
Sports Association for Jesus
Team Jesus-Cycle Crusade
The Tennis Ministry

*Partially adapted from a list compiled by Rabey (1991)

one attacks the evils of recruiting, racism or any of the many other well-known excesses and abuses. Sport owns Sunday now, and religion is content to lease a few minutes before the big games.

Deford's comments are strong, but in the 1990s they still describe the major policy thrust of most Christian organizations with sport ministries. However, it should be noted that some individuals in these organizations have recognized the need for changes in sports and are aware of how religious beliefs have been used to divert attention away from dealing with problems (Warner, 1979). But the official policies in the organizations themselves, especially organizations in North America, seldom reflect the concerns of those calling for reforms.

Overall Consequences of Combining Religious Beliefs and Sports

Because religions and sports are both cultural practices that have been socially constructed as people work out ways for living together it is not surprising that they change as people's interests change and as power is gained or lost by various groups in communities and societies. I think it is interesting that when Christian religious beliefs are combined with sport participation, the cultural practices of sports change very little. Instead, it seems that religious beliefs and rituals are simply called into the service of sports or modified to fit with the way sports are generally defined, organized, and played.

Overall it seems that Christian religious beliefs have more often been used to transform winning, obedience to coaches, and commitment to improving sport skills into moral virtues than they have been used to call attention to what might be defined as social problems within sports. In other words, the use of Christian beliefs and rituals has reaffirmed and intensified existing characteristics of sport experiences and sport organizations in North America. It is also likely that the combination of Christianity and sports has supported dominant forms of gender relations in both the United States and Canada.

Most of the Christian sport organizations have few women members and their ministries are disproportionately directed at male athletes, especially young, white males.

IS IT A PROMISING COMBINATION?

Religion, unlike other social institutions, has beliefs and rituals that people have connected to the supernatural. This makes the systems of meaning associated with religion a unique part of cultural life. Because these systems of meaning affect the way believers think about the world, themselves, and their connections to other people, they have an effect on social life in groups, communities, and society as a whole. This makes religion an important phenomenon for sociologists to study.

Discussions about sports and religions have often focused on how these two spheres of cultural life are similar or different. Certainly they are socially similar because they often create strong collective emotions and celebrate selected group values through rituals and public events. Furthermore, both have heroes, legends, special buildings for communal gatherings, and institutionalized organizational structures. On the other hand, those who assume that sport and religion each have a fundamental essence that is somehow "fixed in nature" argue that the inherent differences between these spheres of life are more important than any similarities. Most sociologists, however, recognize that sports and religions consist of socially constructed sets of cultural practices and meanings that sometimes overlap and sometimes differ depending on social relations among fans and believers within communities and society as a whole. Therefore sociologists see the beliefs and rituals of sports and religions as subject to change as people struggle over how to live with each other and about what their lives mean.

Unfortunately, we in the sociology of sport know little about the relationship between sports and major world religions apart from particular forms of Christianity. It seems that certain dimensions of Christian beliefs and meanings can be constructed in ways that fit well with the beliefs and meanings underlying participation and success in organized competitive sports. In fact, it may be that organized, competitive sports offer a combination of experiences and meanings that are uniquely compatible with the rationality and asceticism that form at least part of what has been described as the Protestant Ethic.

Sports and certain forms of religion have been combined for a number of reasons. Some Christians have promoted sports because they believed that sport participation naturally fosters spiritual growth along with the development of strong character. Christian groups and organizations have used sports to promote their belief systems and attract new members, especially young males who view themselves as possessing "manly virtues." Athletes, because of their visibility and popularity in society, have often been seen by religious groups as effective spokespersons for their messages.

People in sports, especially athletes and coaches, have used religious beliefs and rituals to cope with the uncertainty of competition, to sanctify athletic involvement and achievement, to foster cohesion on teams, and to reaffirm the authority and control of coaches. The individuals and groups most likely to incorporate sports into their religious lives usually profess some form of Christian fundamentalism.

Although there has been little research done on the social consequences of combining sports and religious beliefs, it seems that this combination seldom encourages people to question the way sports are played and organized. In fact, there are many anecdotal examples of how religion has been used to simply reaffirm and intensify orientations that lead to success in competitive sports. However, this does not occur automatically, nor does it occur without creating conflict and doubts for many individual athletes.

Physical educator Shirl Hoffman (1992) has hypothesized that combining certain sports and Christian beliefs can lead to personal conflicts and doubts about whether many sport behaviors are appropriate to use as spiritual offerings and forms of worship. According to Hoffman, these doubts can be resolved in one way by emphasizing dimensions of training and sport participation that fit well with the certain aspects of the Protestant Ethic. This strategy involves focusing on sacrifice and pain as indicators of moral worth, striving to achieve "total release performance," and abandoning the notion that the human body is sacred. Another resolution strategy is to change how one behaves in sports or to withdraw from certain competitive sports and develop new forms of physical activities that eliminate any emphasis on intimidation, the domination of others, and competitive success. Research *suggests* that both these strategies are used in some form or other, but it also suggests that athletes professing Christian beliefs have many creative ways of ignoring, defusing, or reconciling the tension created when their behavior in sports does not fit with some of their beliefs as Christians.

On an organizational level, this tension either does not exist or, if it does, it creates few efforts to resolve conflicts between Christian beliefs and what goes on in sports. In fact, Christian organizations with sport ministries have paid little attention to what might be identified as moral and ethical problems in sports. Instead, they have focused their resources on spreading beliefs—usually fundamentalist beliefs—in connection with sport events and sport involvement. Their emphasis has been on playing hard for the glory of God, using athletic performances as indicators of moral worth and as tools for giving Christian witness, uniting teammates into cohesive organizational units, and being obedient to the rules and recommendations of coaches.

In conclusion, the combination of sports and religious beliefs offers little promise for changing dominant forms of sport. In fact, in some cases, it may actually obscure an awareness of the need for reforms and social transformation. Of course, individual athletes may alter their sport-related behaviors when they combine sport and religion in their own lives, but at this time such changes have had no observable effect on what occurs in most sports.

SUGGESTED READINGS

British Journal of Sports History. 1984. Sport and religion. Special issue, 1(2) (*five papers on the historical dimensions of the combination of sports and religions; special reference to British experiences*).

Deford, F. 1976. Religion in sport. Sports Illustrated, Part I, 44(16):90-100; Part II, 44(17):55-69; Part III, 44(18):43-60 (*journalistic investigation of religious/sports organizations in the United States*).

Harvey, J. 1988. Sport and the Quebec clergy, 1930-1960. In J. Harvey and H. Cantelon, eds. Not just a game: essays in Canadian sport sociology. University of Ottawa Press, Ottawa, Ontario (*excellent critical analysis of how the Roman Catholic clergy in Quebec recognized the significance of sports in popular culture and used it as a tool in the French-Canadian resistance to the spread of Anglo-Saxon culture and Protestant religious beliefs*).

Hoffman, S.J. 1992. Sport and religion. Human Kinetics Publishers, Champaign, IL (*this is the best available collection of work done on religions and sports in the United States. Twenty-five papers are organized into four sets devoted to sport as religion; sport as religious experience; religion in sport; and sport, religion, and ethics. Hoffman's introductions to each set of papers are very informative and thought provoking*).

Mathisen, J. 1990. Reviving "Muscular Christianity": Gil Dodds and the institutionalization of sport evangelism. Sociological Focus 23(3):233-249 (*this article clearly outlines the historical roots of contemporary sport evangelism; it also shows how the meaning of "muscular Christianity" has changed from the use of sports as a tool for promoting religious beliefs to the use of religion to sanctify sports*).

Neal, W. 1981. Handbook of athletic perfection. Mott Media, Milford, Michigan (*written by director of the Institute for Athletic Perfection, a religious/sport organization; describes recommended applications of Christianity in sport*).

Neil, G. 1982. Demystifying sport superstition. International Review of Sport Sociology 17:99-124 (*review of the literature and analysis of data on how athletes use superstition in connection with sport performance*).

Sage, G.H. 1981. Sport and religion. In G. Luschen and G.H. Sage, eds. Handbook of social science of sport. Stipes, Champaign, Ill. (*a general overview of the relationship between sports and religions from a sociological perspective*).

Stevenson, C. 1991. The Christian-athlete: an interactionist-developmental analysis. Sociology of Sport Journal 8(4):362-379 (*one of the few studies that looks at the way religion is combined with sport participation among athletes who profess Christian beliefs*).

CHAPTER 17

SPORTS IN THE TWENTY-FIRST CENTURY

What can we expect?

> *It may be that sport . . . is incapable of the profound changes necessary to successfully meet the challenges of modern life. . . . If this be the case, then the collapse of traditional sport appears inevitable . . . and perhaps a new sports order will then emerge.*
>
> **Harry Edwards, Sociologist and Social Activist (1976)**

> *Americans must win back the natural birthright of their bodies, a birthright which has been distorted and manipulated by the political and commercial forces which have used sports . . . for purposes that often negate [its] potential for individual and community progress.*
>
> **Robert Lipsyte, Author and Journalist (1982)**

> *It is genetic engineering . . . that promises to bring about the most profound biological transformations of the human being, and it is likely that this technology will be used to develop athletes . . .*
>
> **John Hoberman, Author of** Mortal Engines (1992)

> *Whatever else you learn in school, I would like you to master at least two "life sports," those you can play long after you are out of school . . . Sports can teach you so much about yourself . . . Never think of yourself as being above sports.*
>
> **Arthur Ashe,** My Dear Camera (in Days of Grace, 1993)

Discussions of the future are often full of exaggerations. Predicting that tomorrow will bring dramatic changes is always more exciting than predicting that tomorrow will look much like today. Therefore people tend to describe the future in science fiction terms and emphasize extreme hopes and fears. These types of predictions are fun. They spark our interest and sometimes leave us temporarily awestruck. But, in most cases, they are neither accurate nor realistic accounts of what is likely to happen.

For better or worse, the future seldom unfolds as rapidly or dramatically as many forecasters would have us believe. Instead, changes are usually tied to a combination of existing social conditions and the efforts of people to shape those conditions to fit their visions of what life should be like. Of course, some people have more power and resources to promote their visions of what life should be like, and those people seldom want revolutionary changes because their privileged positions depend on keeping things under control and pretty much the same. This tends to slow the rate of change in societies.

As I discuss sports in the twenty-first century, it is important to understand that the future is not determined by fate, computer forecasts, supernatural forces, or sociologists. Instead, it is produced through the collective actions of human beings. This means that the future of sports will not just happen according to predictions in a sociology of sport book. Much more important than a sociologist's predictions are the visions people have for the future and the choices they make in connection with sports in their lives. Therefore the primary goal of this chapter is to describe and evaluate different models of sports that people might use as they envision the future and make choices in their own lives.

MODELS OF SPORTS FOR THE 21ST CENTURY

The major theme running through this book is that sports are social constructions—that sports are parts of culture invented and played by people as they interact with each other and try to shape social life to fit their ideas of what it should be. Therefore dominant sports in any culture tend to reflect the interests and ideas of those who have power in that culture, and they usually celebrate the values and experiences of powerful people. However, dominant sports are not always accepted by everyone in a group or society. In fact, it is possible for people to modify dominant sports or develop alternative forms that challenge current systems of power relations and promote the interests and ideas of people who lack power and resources.

History shows that dominant sports in Western societies, including the United States and Canada, have traditionally been grounded in the values and experiences of men concerned with military conquest, political control, and economic expansion. These sports fit what might be called a **Power and Performance Model.**

Although the Power and Performance Model has been used by many people as the "standard" for determining what sports are about, it has not been accepted by everyone. In fact, some people have maintained or developed other sports grounded in values and experiences related to their connections with each other and their desire to express those connections through playful and enjoyable physical activities. These sports fit what might be called a **Pleasure and Participation Model.**

These two models certainly do not encompass all the different ways that sports might be defined and played. However, they are consistent with two important sets of values in Western societies and, for that reason, they can be used as a starting point for thinking about what sports might be like in the future.

The Power and Performance Model

As we enter the 21st Century, dominant sports continue to resemble the characteristics that comprise the Power and Performance Model. This model is based on "the sport ethic" (as it was described in Chapter 6) and it empha-

Dominant sport forms in many countries are based on a *Power and Performance Model*. This model emphasizes the use of strength, speed, and power to dominate opponents in the quest of competitive victories. (Colorado Springs Gazette Telegraph and Bob Jackson)

sizes the use of strength, speed, and power to push human limits and aggressively dominate opponents in the quest of victories and championships.

Although the Power and Performance Model encompasses a range of forms, it generally emphasizes the idea that excellence is proved through competitive success and achieved through intense dedication and hard work combined with making sacrifices and risking one's personal well-being. It also emphasizes the importance of setting records, pushing human limits, using the body as a machine, and using technology to supplement the body. According to

the Power and Performance Model, the body is to be trained, controlled, and constantly monitored so it will respond to the challenges and demands of sports efficiently and forcefully. This is necessary because sports are defined as battles in which the opposition should be intimidated, punished, and defeated.

Sports based on the Power and Performance Model tend to be exclusive. Participants are selected for their physical skills and abilities to dominate others; those who lack these skills and abilities are cut or put in "developmental" programs. According to this model, sport organizations and sport teams consist of hierarchical authority structures in which athletes are subordinate to coaches and coaches are subordinate to owners and administrators. In coach-athlete relationships it is generally accepted that coaches can humiliate, shame, and derogate athletes to push them to be the best they can be. Athletes are expected to respond to humiliation by being tougher competitors willing to give even more of themselves in their quest for excellence.

The sponsorship of sports based on the Power and Performance Model is generally motivated by the idea that it is important to be associated with "winners." This association can be used to make money or to establish a favorable public relations profile. It is assumed that winners are special and that the person, organization, or corporation that sponsors those winners is also special. Therefore sponsorships based on the Power and Performance Model often shift and change as winners come and go.

The Pleasure and Participation Model

As we enter the 21st Century, an increasing number of people will begin to realize two things: (1) that there are many different ways to do sports, and (2) that dominant sport forms are often inconsistent with their personal values and experiences. This dual realization will lead to the creation of alternative sports, many of which will be based on a Pleasure and Participation Model. In line with this model, these alternative sports will emphasize active participation

Although sports based on a *Pleasure and Participation Model* may involve competition, the emphasis is on connections between people and personal expression through participation. (Suzanne Tregarthen/Educational Photo Stock)

and a combination of different types of connections—connections between people, between mind and body, and between physical activity and the environment.

Although the Pleasure and Participation Model also encompasses a variety of sports, it generally emphasizes an ethic of personal expression, enjoyment, growth, good health, and mutual concern and support for teammates and opponents. It focuses on empowerment (not power) in connection with participation, and it stresses that the body is to be experienced and enjoyed (not trained and used as a tool). People who use this model as a basis for developing sports are likely to see their bodies as gardens that must be cultivated to continue growing; they do not see their bodies as machines to be used as tools and repaired when they break.

Sports based on a Pleasure and Participation Model are characterized by inclusiveness. Playing, not winning, is the most important thing. Differences in physical skills among participants are accommodated informally, or formally through the use of handicap systems, so players can enjoy competition *with* each other even when they have unequal skills. Sport organizations and sport teams based on this model have democratic decision-making structures characterized by cooperation, the sharing of power, and give-and-take relationships between coaches and athletes. Humiliation, shame, and derogation are inconsistent with the spirit underlying the model.

The sponsorship of sports based on a Pleasure and Participation Model is generally motivated by the idea that it is socially useful to promote widespread participation in a wide range of physical activities and sports, and that overall participation, health, and enjoyment are more important than the achievement of performance excellence. Unfortunately, most people and corporations with money are more interested in sponsoring sports that emphasize power and performance than sports that emphasize pleasure and participation. But not everyone thinks that way.

Sports in the Future

CONTINUED DOMINANCE OF THE POWER AND PERFORMANCE MODEL The Power and Performance Model will continue to serve as the basis for dominant sports as we move into the next century. This does not mean that everyone will automatically accept these sports without question, or that alternative sports won't become increasingly popular. But vested interests in this model are very strong and those who benefit from sports based on it have considerable power and influence.

The Power and Performance Model will remain dominant for another reason: sports based on the model have consistently attracted corporate sponsors. American football, the classic embodiment of the model, not only continues to attract billions of dollars in television rights fees and other revenues but it is expanding to a number of European countries. In fact, an economic attraction of American football is that it is so combative and brutal that few people want to actually play it. This means that when people identify with football players and teams they can be encouraged to express their identification through the consumption of official NFL and college football products rather than playing the game itself. When sports can be used to create idols, they become important tools for stimulating consumption in market economies.

Because sports based on the Power and Performance Model emphasize pushing human limits they are especially alluring to many people. Attempts to break barriers or do what no one else has done before can be seductive. Sports emphasizing attempts to break barriers are relatively easy to market and sell. Throughout this century we have seen the development of what some people have called "technosport," a sport form in which technology and human beings are combined to push limits and dominate opponents (Johnson, 1974). Widespread fascination with technosport forms is clearly illustrated by parents willing to have synthetic Human Growth Hormone given to their children in the hope of "creating" world class athletes (Hober-man, 1992). It is also illustrated through numerous examples of athletes searching for technological aids to get bigger, stronger, and faster.

After examining how athletes and sport scientists have used technology in connection with sports based on the Power and Performance Model, social scientist John Hoberman predicted that we might see some form of genetic engineering in the sports of the 21st century. He noted that the Human Genome Project has already developed information that could in the future guide "gene grafting techniques that would permit the crossing of men and beasts" and other efforts that would lead to the creation of genetically engineered "designer athletes" (Hoberman, 1992). In addition to genetic engineering there may also be attempts to push human limits by regulating human brains. For example, a noted German sport physician told fellow sport scientists during the late 1980s that, "Every adaptation to training occurs in the brain, in the nervous system." He went on to declare that, "It is [in the brain], through the hormonal regulation of the body, that we must do our regulating" to boost athletic performance (cited in Hoberman, 1992, p. 285).

Although these changes, informed by the spirit underlying the Power and Performance Model, will raise many bioethical issues, they will be accepted by many people who use the model to set their standards for judging what sports are about. For example, many young people today have grown up with rapidly changing mediated images that blur the boundaries between human and nonhuman. The notion of bionic parts has long been a dream of people who need artificial organs or who could benefit from the use of synthetic bones, tendons, and ligaments. Therefore it won't be shocking when superstrong synthetic ligaments are used to repair damage from athletic injuries. It may not even be shocking when mechanical body parts are used to replace injured limbs and to improve performance in sports.

However, questions will be raised about the use of technology in sports. Dominant sports will not simply be the result of what is technologically possible. In its extreme form, technosport eliminates the "human" element in sport—the errors, the oversights, the mistakes, the letdowns—in order to perfect athletic performances and achieve competitive success. It is based on the idea that humans reach their potential only when they become machinelike. This approach to sports subverts creativity, freedom, spontaneity, and expression among athletes and it turns sports into programmed spectacles involving dramatically presented physical actions. Both athletes and spectators will have problems with this set of possibilities. Athletes may resist becoming pawns in such activities, and spectators may not watch them because it will be difficult to identify with robotlike athletes playing games lacking human spontaneity and expression. Unless athletes *feel pressure, emotionally respond* to victory and defeat, *make mistakes, work hard* for success, and have their *good and bad days*, spectators may have trouble identifying with them. If this happens, dominant sports would lose much of their commercial value. Because the success of spectator sports depends on fan identification with athletes, that success may be jeopardized if technology is used to make athletes too unlike the spectators who pay to watch them.

Finally, the popularity of sports based on the Power and Performance Model is also tied to dominant forms of gender relations. When attention is focused on pushing physical limits, men will often be the center of attention, especially when limits are related to strength, power, and speed. Women may outperform men in ultraendurance events and a few other sports in the future, but efforts to push human limits will usually celebrate not only the differences between men and women but the superiority of men over women. This in itself will preserve the dominance of sports based on the Power and Performance Model for many years to come.

INCREASED EMPHASIS ON THE PLEASURE AND PARTICIPATION MODEL The future will certainly bring a diversity of sports, and many of these sport forms will embody at least some characteristics from the Pleasure and Participation Model. Reasons for this include growing concerns about health and fitness, participation preferences among older people, women bringing new values and experiences to sports, and groups seeking alternative sports. Each of these reasons are discussed in more detail in the following sections.

Growing concerns about health and fitness. As the U.S. federal government develops a health care policy and some form of national health insurance, people will become more sensitive to health and fitness issues. In connection with this they may avoid sports based on the Power and Performance Model. People will also become more aware of the value of certain types of exercise in the maintenance of health, and they will use the Pleasure and Participation Model to organize alternative sports that involve these exercises. Health and fitness concerns will also be promoted through changes in physical education curriculum. Physical educators will continue to move away from teaching students sports based on the Power and Performance Model, and more toward teaching a range of alternative sports involving lifetime skills, noncompetitive challenges, inclusive participation philosophies, respect and support for other participants, and concerns for health—all characteristics related to the Pleasure and Participation Model.

Participation preferences among older people. As the median age of the population in many societies gets older, and as more people live longer, there will be a search for sports that do not involve intimidation, the use of physical force, domination of opponents, and the risk of serious injuries. As people age they are less likely to risk physical well-being to establish a reputation in sports, they are more likely to see sports as social activities, and they are more interested in making sports inclusive rather than exclusive. Older people also realize that they have but one body, and it can be enjoyed only if it is cultivated as though it were a garden rather than driven as if it were a machine.

Sport forms preferred by older people will not be based on the Power and Performance Model. Instead, they will be noncompetitive physical activities and altered versions of competitive activities. There will be new "senior" sport leagues in which rules are changed to emphasize the pleasure of movement, connections between people, and the challenge of controlled competition. But there will also be an emphasis on walking, hiking, weight lifting and other activities that will be taken seriously but done in settings in which health and social connections are the focus, not setting records or dominating opponents.

The rising popularity of golf is indicative of general trends we will see as we move into the next century. Golf involves healthy exercise, it's nonviolent, it doesn't involve "punishing" the opposition, and there is a handicap system so people with different skills can play as equals in competitive events. Importantly, men and women and parents and children can play golf together. Although golf has traditions of exclusiveness, and it is too expensive for many people to play, there will be similar but less expensive sports based on the Pleasure and Participation Model that older people will develop as they seek to be physically active.

Women bringing new values and experiences to sports. As women continue to gain more power and resources, some of them will more assertively seek to develop sports based on their rejection of the Power and Performance Model. Although many women will seek equity in sports based on this model, others will try to change sports to correspond with the spirit underlying the Pleasure and Participation Model. The example of "feminist softball" described in Chapter 2 provides a good illustration of how sports might be transformed by women interested in playing a sport but not interested in playing it the way most men do (Birrell and Richter, 1987). There are a growing number of other examples in which women have trans-

formed both the rules and the spirit of a sport to fit the characteristics of the Pleasure and Participation Model (Hargreaves, in press; Zipter, 1988). Even when women play sports such as rugby and soccer there are indications that they often emphasize inclusiveness and support for teammates and opponents in explicit ways that are seldom present in the men's versions of these sports (Hargreaves, in press). Women sometimes encounter difficulties when trying to get sponsors for alternative sports. Because the sports differ from men's sports, they are often seen as second rate or not serious enough to attract the attention sponsors seek. Because people have for so long seen sports as involving elitist displays of strength, speed, and power many do not take alternative sports seriously. For example, when a sport involves the use of balance, coordination, flexibility, artistry, creativity, or timing, it is not seen as demanding or as dramatic as sports based on the Power and Performance Model. But this conclusion continues to be challenged.

Groups seeking alternative sports. Groups rejecting at least parts of sports based on the Power and Performance Model will continue to exist and, in some cases, increase in numbers. Some high school students will continue to form their own sport groups and play games on their own rather than put up with the constraints of playing on varsity teams whose coaches often try to control their lives and where the emphasis on competition and win-loss records is given priority over enjoyment and the experience of outside the school for alternatives to dominant sports largely depends on how schools organize their sport programs in the future.

Disabled and physically challenged people have sought to develop alternative sports as well as to adapt dominant sports to fit their needs and to mainstream disabled people into dominant sports in which they compete with the able-bodied. However, some programs for the disabled, especially those based on versions of the Power and Performance Model, focus on the interests of men and neglect to recruit or provide equal opportunities for women (Hargreaves, in press). But the programs have generally emphasized care and support for teammates and opponents as well as inclusiveness related to physical abilities. Such support and inclusiveness have also been characteristic in the Special Olympics (see Chapter 4).

The Gay Games also represent an example of an alternative sport form emphasizing participation, support, inclusiveness, and the enjoyment of physical movement (Messner, 1992; Pronger, 1990). The 1992 Games held in Vancouver, Canada involved over 7000 athletes from 27 countries, and the 1994 Games in New York City are expected to draw 10,000 athletes from 35 countries. Although the Gay Games resemble dominant sports in some ways, they explicitly challenge the notions of heterosexual masculinity and femininity and the homophobia that underlie those sport forms. Gay and lesbian athletes will continue to form sport groups and teams to provide enjoyable experiences in their social lives. As one lesbian explains:

> I use sports . . . to meet people—I rarely go to bars for that purpose. . . . Team sports are the main social outlets in my life. I depend on them for emotional support, physical activity, a sense of belonging, a comfortable atmosphere, and an outlet for my competitive nature (quoted in Zipter, 1988, p. 82).

Similar feelings were expressed by a gay man in Brian Pronger's study of sports and homosexuality:

> The nice thing about playing gay sports is . . . to interact with gay people in other than a bar environment. And it's also really nice to do sports . . . [where you] don't have to be on guard. You can joke around, you can play. That's a good feeling. It's also the sense of community that comes from it. . . . It's not that I didn't fit in [when I played volleyball at work, but it] is probably more relaxed in gay sports (Pronger, 1990, p. 238).

In summary, we will continue to see various alternatives to dominant sports in the future.

They will frequently embody at least some of the characteristics associated with the Pleasure and Participation Model. One of the challenges to be faced in the future is how to maintain alternative sports as sport participation rates increase. This challenge is discussed in the box on pp. 452-453.

CONTINUING TRENDS AND EXPECTED CHANGES IN SPORTS
Professional Sports

Professional sports in North America will recruit more athletes from other parts of the world, and they will develop new teams or subsidiary leagues in Europe and Asia. Transportation and communication technology will enable professional sport leagues to expand internationally. Before long we will see the Chicago Bulls heading to Europe to play games against new NBA teams like the London Slammers, the Madrid Conquistadors, the Rome Gladiators, and the Munich Bavarians. People on different continents will see television broadcasts of the games. The political implications of this expansion will be significant because a North American model of professional and commercial sports will be taken all over the world and presented as the "right" way to organize, play, and sponsor sports.

After the United States hosts the 1994 Soccer World Cup, there will be increased efforts to develop soccer at all levels of competition in North America. A professional league will be developed, and television contracts will be awarded to the new league and even to some college teams. Cities will bid for pro soccer team franchises, and international matches will be scheduled between North American teams and teams from Europe and South America.

If the academic requirements for participation in intercollegiate sports continue to increase, the NFL and the NBA will subsidize the development of minor leagues in football and basketball. New and existing minor leagues will be used to replace intercollegiate programs,

What Will Happen If More People Play Sports?

Most research shows that less than 20% of the population in the United States accounts for over 80% of the sports participation. Even the fitness boom that began in the 1970s has not involved 60% of adult Americans. So what would happen if the 60-80% of "inactive" adults in the country began to regularly participate in physical activities and sports? Would this lead to changes in the way sports are organized and defined by most people? Would the *Pleasure and Participation Model* replace the *Power and Performance Model* as the basis for dominant sport forms? These questions are difficult to answer, but we can get an idea of what increased sports participation might bring if we extend current trends into the future (Coakley, 1979). Here's a step-by-step description of what we might expect:

- *First*, higher participation rates will increase demands on existing spaces and facilities where people do sports. And it is likely that demands will be especially high on specialized physical settings that are expensive to construct and maintain. In many communities, the participants in tennis, racquetball, bowling, softball, soccer, golf, volleyball, ice hockey, and many other sport activities are already very aware of the shortage of spaces and facilities.
- *Second*, when existing spaces and facilities cannot handle increased demands for usage, conflict among groups of participants is very likely (Devall and Harry, 1981; Gramann and Burdge, 1981; Jackson and Wong, 1982). Overt conflict has already occurred on softball and soccer/football fields, in gyms, and on tennis courts. Walkers, joggers, runners, bicyclists, and skaters (in-line and 4-wheel) in many cities have debated and fought over who should have access priority to precious sidewalk and street space; and young skateboarders have been banned from many public spaces and forced to use private facilities—an expensive alternative to sidewalks. Additional conflicts between surfers and swimmers, water skiers and fishing enthusiasts, snowmobile drivers and cross country skiers, and others have created management crises in both urban and wil-

derness areas in North America. Future conflicts are most likely to occur in large cities where the scarcity of spaces and facilities required for sport involvement is highest.

- *Third*, when scarcity leads to conflicts, most people call for more spaces and facilities along with closer regulation of existing spaces and facilities. The continuing financial crises in most cities and communities will prevent new construction and may even interfere with the maintenance of existing spaces. In fact, as far back as the 1970s, park and recreation officials in Los Angeles were instructed to "stop encouraging certain sports because competition for playing space between organized and unorganized factions [had] reached a point that [was] . . . sometimes too violent" (Stingley, 1972). This policy is extreme, but it illustrates that scarcity and conflict will lead to more comprehensive and tighter systems of administrative control over existing spaces and facilities.
- *Fourth*, when the use of spaces and facilities is regulated by public or private organizations, participation generally requires some combination of planned schedules, permits, memberships, user fees, reservations, and political influence. In meeting demands from different user groups, priorities will usually be given to *organized* groups of participants, especially those representing traditionally popular, highly structured programs. Beyond favoring individuals and teams in organized programs there will be a tendency to give highest access priority to the most skilled groups of users, to top-level athletes and teams, and to programs that base their sports on the *Power and Performance Model*. For example, interscholastic teams, especially those playing sports that attract spectators, will continue to receive priority usage of school facilities. The best teams in community leagues will get priority usage of public fields and gyms through invitations to participate in preseason, midseason, and postseason tournaments as well as playoffs and championship games. All-star teams and other elite sport groups will be given priority for their practices so they can be

Mass participation in some sports leads to conflict over spaces and facilities. Conflict leads to regulation of spaces and facilities, with access priority often being given to those with the most organized programs or the most money. If children's participation in sport increases, we can anticipate more conflict over the use of spaces and facilities in the future. (The Denver Post and Karl Gehring)

"respectable representatives" of their sponsors. Finally, there will be a tendency for people with money for membership dues and user fees to have high access priority, especially in the private sector where the expenses associated with certain forms of participation are and will continue to be extremely high.

The primary outcome of this four-stage process is that there will be continued priority given to athletes and teams playing sports based on the *Power and Performance Model*. Since these sports are grounded in the values and experiences of men, sport participation will continue to celebrate traditional definitions of masculinity. A related outcome is that dominant sport forms will continue to emphasize competition, rationalization, bureaucratization, specialization, quantification, and setting records. In connection with these sport forms, girls and women will continue to be defined as "naturally" inferior because they are not as big, strong, and fast as men.

Another outcome will be an intensification of the connection between money and sport participation. User fees associated with public spaces and the dependence on private clubs and facilities to play certain sports guarantee that class relations will remain central in the social organization of American sports. Low income people will continue to be underrepresented in most sports, even if more people participate in sports.

In summary, more people may participate in sports at the turn of the century, but they will be playing, spectating, and defining their experiences in much the same way people do today. The *Pleasure and Participation Model* may be increasingly attractive as a basis for organizing sports, but finding the spaces and facilities for playing sports based on this model will not be easy, nor will it be cheap.

Of course, this set of predictions should *not* be taken as what will automatically happen in connection with increased sport participation. For those interested in other types of outcomes, there is a need to intervene in the process outlined above. The challenge is finding strategies for accommodating sport participation increases without reproducing elitist sport forms. These strategies will vary from one community to another, and their effectiveness will vary with the creativity and political sensitivities of the people who put them into action.

which have always provided professional teams with free on-the-job training for their future employees. As this happens, more communities will make bids for minor league franchises, and more voters will be asked to pass bond issues and tax increases to fund the building of arenas and stadiums. As minor league teams come into mid-sized cities, attendance at local high school games will be jeopardized, and revenues for high school sports and some college sports will decline.

Professional athletes will gain more autonomy and power in the future, but they will not use their power to make any major changes in the structure of commercial sports; their primary goal will be to increase control over their careers and guarantee their own financial security.

Intercollegiate Sports

Intercollegiate sports will continue to exist, despite all the investigations, exposes, and doomsday predictions. Gender equity will be the central issue in many intercollegiate programs, and new pressures will be put on athletic departments to achieve equity in terms of participation opportunities and resource allocation. Dealing with the gender equity issue will cause discussions about the place of football in intercollegiate programs. However, most big-time football programs will continue to exist.

In the face of budget crises, colleges and universities will continue to cut the number of varsity sports they offer. There will also be a continuation of efforts to make intercollegiate sport programs academically accountable. In some cases, athletic programs will be evaluated in connection with academic accreditation processes.

The NCAA will change its rules so college athletes in revenue producing sports can be legally paid money in addition to their athletic grants. However, student-athletes will continue to lack autonomy and power. This will lead to the development of advocacy groups and some student-athletes will try to organize teammates to protest unfair or coercive tactics used by coaches. The success of these groups and organizational efforts will be mixed.

High School Sports

Playoffs, league championships, and state titles will continue to be important in high school sports, although funding shortages will force many schools to question the necessity of elitist sports programs in the schools. While these questions are being raised, some American high school teams will strive to be included in new national ranking systems, and cable television stations will begin to cover high profile high school games in certain sports.

These developments will continue to encourage high schools to maintain sport programs along the lines of big-time college programs, if they can afford to do so. Standout athletes in elementary schools will be heavily recruited by high schools seeking national reputations, and high school game schedules will take these young players all over the country. Private high schools will recruit most heavily because their student bodies are not restricted by geographic boundaries, as in public school systems. Private schools will use the reputations of their sport teams to market their academic programs and increase tuition revenues. This trend will lead to national tournaments and national championships in certain high school sports.

Along with this trend toward sports elitism in some high schools, an increasing number of schools will continue to experience serious financial problems that will force them to cut back or eliminate varsity sports. As this happens, some schools and coaches will seek corporate sponsors for programs and teams, or they will develop new alliances with local agencies and groups to maintain certain programs. Even if outside funding and support is acquired, some high schools will cut most of their varsity sports. The sports least likely to be cut will be boys' football and basketball, and girls' basketball and volleyball. Outside of these sports, high school students will increasingly play in programs sponsored by community clubs. In the varsity sports that continue to exist, the participation of girls will be encouraged, but their programs and teams will be modeled after boys' programs and teams. One of the major functions of varsity programs for both boys and girls will continue

In response to the highly structured character of many organized youth sport programs, many young people in the future will look for alternative activities allowing them to make up their own rules and develop skills without adult interference and adult control. (Colorado Springs Gazette Telegraph and Raleigh Savitt)

to be the development of players who have the abilities to be "fed into" programs at higher levels of competition.

Youth Sports

Organized youth sports will become increasingly privatized in most American communities. Publicly funded programs will be cut back or eliminated, and park and recreation departments will increasingly become brokers of public spaces and facilities. Youth programs in middle-income and wealthy communities will be organized and funded through participation fees, and children in these communities will be encouraged by parents to join teams.

Coaching education programs will become more popular because of an effort to certify youth coaches as experts. This will be done to satisfy parents' demands for more professional approaches to youth sports and to minimize legal liability. Youth programs will emphasize "sports development" rather than recreation, and parents will become increasingly concerned about how their children's participation may pay off in the future—in scholarships and social acceptance. In response to the structured character of youth programs, many young people will seek out alternative sports such as skateboarding and various informal games in which they can make up their own rules and develop skills without being under the control of adults.

Spectators and Spectator Sports

In the immediate future, *spectator sports* will continue to be popular despite some shifts in interests among sports. For example, an increasing number of people may watch soccer in the future while fewer may watch ice hockey, but they will still devote considerable time to spectating. The media will encourage this trend with increased sport programming. At the same time there will be more attempts to sell pay-per-view broadcasts of sport events.

Some spectators will form ad hoc organizations to represent their interests when it comes to setting prices for tickets and concessions, controlling the location of team franchises, and guaranteeing fan safety at events. Ad hoc spectator organizations will not become very influential because they will not attract many younger fans who are more likely than older fans to accept commercialized sports, expensive ticket prices, and high salaries for athletes (Heistand, 1991).

Spectators will continue to gamble on sports, and in the United States there will be attempts to make sport gambling legal throughout the country. At the same time, many states will use lotteries to generate funds to pay for sports and sport teams in their cities or schools.

Organization and Rationalization

At elite levels of competitive sports, athletes and teams will continue to enlist specialists to help them improve their performances. Therapists and sport psychologists, fitness advisers and drug advisers, aerobics instructors, nutritionists, cooks, biomechanists, and exercise physiologists will make up an expanding corps of "sports advisors" expected to help athletes hit their performance peaks when they compete in important events.

An expanding emphasis on the "constructive" use of leisure time will lead to an increasing number of highly organized leisure and sports programs. Participation in the activities sponsored through these programs will be associated with achieving rationally chosen "participation goals" and the consumption of clothing and equipment that will facilitate the achievement of those goals. There will continue to be many "sport experts" to whom eager new sport participants can go for lessons on how to play "correctly." Wealthier people will join athletic clubs

in increasing numbers. Their social lives and friendships will be more heavily connected with their patterns of participation in sport activities; their children will learn how to swim, bowl, kick soccer balls, hit backhands, ski, sail, and to do a variety of other things under trained sport tutors who will also teach them that having fun depends on doing physical activities and playing sports the "right" way, by the "right" rules, and with the "right" equipment, and wearing the "right" clothes and shoes.

Like sport fans and athletes of today, people in the 21st Century will be interested in scores and records. They will continue to value rationality, hard work, the pursuit of excellence, and the achievement of goals through well-planned efforts and specialized skills. Sport participation will continue to be linked to character-building, although its connection with nationalism will decline in importance.

Consumerism

As we enter the next century sports will continue to be grounded in commercial interests and sponsored as a form of entertainment to generate profits or political payoffs. The ideology and organization of sports will continue to reflect the distribution of resources in society. The people with economic and political power will have the most effect on decisions about who will watch and participate in sports and under what circumstances they will do so. As in the past, these people will play a major role in shaping the way sports are presented to and defined by the masses of people in their societies.

Sports equipment manufacturers will continue to sell the idea that involvement in sports requires warm-up suits, numerous combinations of attire for different sports, the best equipment money can buy, and a spare set of everything in case of an emergency. For wealthier people, sports will offer a context in which their identities can be announced through appearance and visual display as much as through their physical abilities.

CONCLUSION:

THE CHALLENGE OF MAKING THE FUTURE

For those interested in changes, the predictions in this chapter serve as a challenge: *changes will occur only if the people who want them actually make them*. We are not locked into what is written in this chapter or in any other set of predictions. It is possible for sports and the meanings of sport experiences to be altered on both the individual and societal levels. It is also possible to create new goals for sport involvement and new organizations to promote those goals so that sports become more democratic and more compatible with a wider range of values and experiences.

The growing importance of sports in contemporary society will lead more people to take a closer and more critical look at how sports have been defined, organized, and played. As this oc-

curs, some of these people will call for changes in dominant forms of sports, or reject those forms and call for the development of alternative sports. But this process should not be expected to lead to widespread, revolutionary changes in sports. The process of social transformation is always tedious and difficult; it requires long-term efforts and carefully planned strategies. Transformation does not occur overnight.

Three Approaches to Change

Change means different things to different people. Efforts to make change generally fall into three categories: *conservative*, *reformist*, and *radical*.

A *conservative approach* is based on the assumption that changes in sports, as well as in the rest of society, should consist of raising more money, developing more effective marketing

"I can't understand it; I thought things were going to be different for our kids."

strategies, and generally strengthening traditional values, definitions, experiences, and organizational structures. Conservatives believe that problems are best solved by strengthening what already exists rather than by making changes in social relations or social structures.

A *reformist approach* focuses primarily on eliminating problems and making sports more socially useful and responsive. Reformists are concerned with issues such as discrimination against women and minorities, violence, the exploitation of athletes, cheating, unfair business practices, the use of drugs, extreme nationalism, and excessive concerns with winning and making money. In other words, they focus their attention on equity issues, safety, fairness, and the expansion of sports programs so that more people will have opportunities to play and enjoy sports.

A *radical approach* to change focuses primarily on changing how people think about sports, changing the way sports are defined, organized, and played, and using sports as sites for transforming the structure and dynamics of gender, race, and class relations so that power is equally distributed in social life. Radicals want to create new models for sport experiences and build new sport organizations for the purpose of making changes in social life as a whole.

When people talk about changes in sports they are most likely to take a conservative approach. They see change as expansion and growth, not transformation. They are interested in "management" issues and strategies for keeping things organized and profitable, not making real changes in the way sports are organized and played. In fact, when you listen closely to people using conservative approaches you will detect an underlying concern with using sports as tools for social control, for teaching other people lessons on how to behave in conformity with traditional values and expectations for how people ought to be.

A reformist approach overlaps with conservative approaches to the extent that both are interested in expanding participation opportunities. However, the reformist is also interested in making sure that those opportunities are characterized by fairness and a lack of preferential treatment. Reformists are committed to democratic participation and deal with issues related to fairness and equality of opportunity in sports.

A radical approach to change overlaps with a reformist approach in that both are concerned with inequities and democratic participation. But the radical believes that democracy ultimately depends on equality, empowerment, and the elimination of all forms of oppression and exploitation (Marable, 1993). Therefore the radical is concerned with the redistribution of power in society and the reorganization of social relations so that people can equally pursue their interests in connection with others. Radicals make many people nervous because they take sides with socially marginalized groups and call for changes that challenge the structures and ideologies that have led certain groups to be ignored or pushed aside. This can be threatening to those who have learned to live their lives comfortably within the context of those structures and ideologies. Privileged people don't like radicals.

Each of these approaches to change can be found in connection with sports in society. However, conservative approaches are dominant in sports because sports are seen by conservatives as important in their overall world view. Radical approaches are rare in sports because most radicals are more concerned with issues such as poverty, homelessness, universal health care, quality education for children, the availability of public transportation, full employment, and guaranteed minimum standards of living (Marable, 1993). These issues are difficult to focus on in connection with sports. However, radicals concerned with ideological issues are now starting to see sports as sites for challenging dominant definitions of masculinity and femininity, for raising questions about the meaning of race, and for getting people to think critically about the antidemocratic features of hierarchical relationships.

Four Vantage Points for Making Changes

In the book, *Sport in Canadian Society* (1991), Ann Hall and her colleagues from the University of Alberta argue that there are four vantage points from which to make changes related to sports and social life. They are:

- *Work within the system of sports.* This means that people can make changes by becoming involved in sports and sport organizations and then using their position or power in sports. Change agents with an "insider" vantage point can be very effective. However, becoming an insider often involves making serious compromises as one seeks a position of power and influence. Furthermore, there are "very real dangers of becoming absorbed into the very system one sets out to change" (Hall et al, 1991, p. 248). Sometimes people become involved in sports with many ideas about needed changes, but by the time they are in positions to make those changes they themselves have a vested interest in keeping things as they are. This is not inevitable, but it does happen.

- *Become involved in "oppositional" groups.* This means that people can make change by forming and joining political groups that challenge problematic sport policies and put pressure on sport organizations that have antidemocratic programs. For example, such groups could lobby for the building of a community sport center in a low-income neighborhood or they could lobby against building a stadium that would primarily serve the interests of already privileged people in a community. Or they could apply pressure so that hosting a major sport event such as the Olympics would also involve building low-cost housing for low-income community residents.

- *Create alternative sports.* This means that people can reject or ignore dominant sports and the organizations that sponsor them, and develop new sports grounded in the values and experiences of a wide array of different groups of people. This is often difficult to do because resources are seldom available to people who choose this vantage point for making change.

This was discovered by those who developed New Games in the United States, Cooperative Games in Canada (see Orlick, 1978), and TROPS in Japan (see Kageyama, 1992). But this vantage point can also be effective, even when it doesn't lead to concrete institutionalized changes, because it provides clear cut examples of new ways to look at and play sports, and new ways to look at and interact with other people. These examples may then inspire other people to envision how they can create alternative sports in their own lives and communities.

- *Focus on culture and social relations.* This means that people could ignore sports and try to produce changes in social relations that would indirectly raise questions about the organization and structure of sports in society. For example, as people learn to question dominant gender ideology and the cultural practices associated with that ideology, they can also be expected to raise questions and call for changes in dominant sports. They will do this because they realize that dominant sports reproduce a set of ideas about masculinity and femininity that are destructive in the lives of many women and men.

Regardless of the vantage point used to make change, any significant social transformation requires two things: (1) a vision of what sports and social life *could* and *should* be like, and (2) the power and resources to enter the political arena and deal with the reality of putting visions into actions. The future of sports will be created out of this combination of visions and actions.

SUGGESTED READINGS

Aburdene, P., and J. Naisbitt. 1992. Megatrends for women. Villard Books, New York. (*Chapter 2, "The sporting life," contains a basic overview of trends related to women's sport participation and women's achievements in sports*).

Coakley, J. 1979. Participation trends in physical activity and sport: implications for the sociology of sport. Review of Sport and Leisure 4(2):30-47 (*detailed hypotheses on how an increase in sport participa-*

tion could affect the organization of sports and the sociology of sport).

Dyer, K. ed., 1989. Sportswomen towards 2000: a celebration. Hyde Park Press, Richmond, South Australia (*40 papers from an Australian conference on women in sports; topics include politics, law, medicine, coaching and training, but there is also an emphasis on what women's sports will be like at the end of this century*).

Edwards, H. 1976. Change and crisis in modern sport. The Black Scholar 8(2):60-65 (*assesses the prospects for radical change in sport throughout the world*).

Johnson, W.O. 1974. From here to 2000. Sports Illustrated 41(26):73-83 (*journalist puts together two scenarios of the future*).

Lucas, J. 1992. Future of the Olympic Games. Human Kinetics Publishers, Champaign, Ill. (*this book is more about the past than the future, but the final chapter on "The 21st-Century Olympic Games . . . " offers a brief look at what could and should happen in the future*).

Macintosh, D., and D. Whitson. 1990. The game planners: transforming Canada's sport system. McGill-Queen's University Press, Montreal and Kingston (*this critique of sport policy in Canada offers strategies for changing sports in the future; it raises questions about the merits of funding priorities that favor high performance sports rather than recreational sports emphasizing participation*).

Scott, J. 1973. Sport and the radical ethic. Quest 19:71-77 (*critique of sports and recommendations for what sports could be like in the future*).

BIBLIOGRAPHY

Acker, J. 1992. Gendered institutions. Contemporary Sociology 21(5):565-569.

Acker, J., K. Barry, and J. Esseveld. 1983. Objectivity and truth: problems in doing feminist research. Women's Studies International Forum 6:423-435.

Acosta, R.V., and L.J. Carpenter. 1985. A. Women in athletics: a status report. B. Status of women in athletics: changes and causes. JOPERD 56(6):30-37.

Acosta, R.V., and L.J. Carpenter. 1992a. Women in intercollegiate sport: A longitudinal study—fifteen year update. Unpublished paper.

Acosta, R.V., and L.J. Carpenter. 1992b. As the years go by—Coaching opportunities in the 1990s. JOPERD 63(3):36-41.

Adler, P.A., and P. Adler. 1991. Backboards & blackboards: College athletes and role engulfment. Columbia University Press, New York.

Adler, P.A., S.J. Kless, and P. Adler. 1992. Socialization to gender roles: popularity among elementary school boys and girls. Sociology of Education 65(July):169-187.

Allison, M.T. 1979. On the ethnicity of ethnic minorities in sport. Quest 31(1):50-56.

Allison, M.T., and G. Luschen. 1979. A comparative analysis of Navajo Indian and Anglo basketball sport systems. Int. Rev. Sport Soc. 3-4(14):75-85.

Althiede, D.L., and R.P. Snow. 1978. Sports versus the mass media. Urban Life 7(2):189-204.

Anderson, C.H., and J.R. Gibson. 1978. Toward a new sociology. The Dorsey Press, Homewood, Ill.

Archer, R. and A. Bouillon. 1982. The South African game: Sport and racism. Zed Press, London.

Ardrey, R. 1961. African genesis. Dell Publishing Co., Inc., New York.

Ardrey, R. 1966. The territorial imperative. Atheneum Publishers, New York.

Ash, M.J. 1978. The role of research in children's competitive athletics. In R.A. Magill, et al., eds. Children in sport: a contemporary anthology. Human Kinetics Publishers, Inc., Champaign, Ill.

Ashe, A. 1992. Can blacks beat the old-boy network? Newsweek, Jan. 27:40

Axthelm, P. 1970. The city game. Harper & Row, Publishers, New York.

Bain, L. 1978. Differences in values implicit in teaching and coaching behaviors. Res. Q. 49(1):5-11.

Baker, W.J. 1982. Sports in the western world. Rowman & Littlefield, Totowa, N.J.

Ball, D.W. 1975. A note on method in the sociology of sport. In D.W. Ball and J.W. Loy, eds. Sport and social order. Addison-Wesley Publishing Co., Inc., Reading, Mass.

Ballanger, L. 1981. Editorial. In Your Face: America's Bluecollar Sport Letter 1(4):1.

Barkley, C., 1992. Petty issues won't change the world. USA Today, Aug. 5:7E.

Barnett, C.R. 1982. The reaction of the popular press to the first two black National Football League players, 1932-1934. Paper presented at the meetings of the North American Society for Sport History, Manhattan, Kans.

Barr, S. 1987. Women, nutrition, and exercise: a review of athletes' intakes and a discussion of energy balance in active women. Progress in Food and Nutrition Science 11:307-361.

Beamish, R. 1988. The political economy of professional sport. In J. Harvey and H. Cantelon, eds. Not just a game. University of Ottawa Press, Ottawa.

Beamish, R. 1990. The persistence of inequality: An analysis of participation patterns among Canada's high performance athletes. International Review for the Sociology of Sport 25(2):143-153.

Becker, J. 1975. Superstition in sport. Int. J. Sports Psychol. 6(3):148-152.

Bender, D.L., ed. 1988. What should be done about the drug problem in sports? Greenhaven Press, Inc., St. Paul, Minn.

Benedict, R. 1961. Patterns of culture. Houghton Mifflin Co., Boston.

Berkowitz, L. 1969. Roots of aggression: a reexamination of the frustration-aggression hypothesis. Atherton Press, New York.

Berkowitz, L. 1972a. Sports, competition, and aggression. In Proceedings: 4th Canadian Psycho-Motor Learning and Sport Symposium, Department of National Health and Welfare, Ottawa.

Berlage, G.I. 1982. Children's sports and the family. ARENA Review 6(1):43-47.

Berryman, J. 1982. The rise of highly organized sports for preadolescent boys. In R.A. Magill, et al., eds. Children in sport. Human Kinetics Publishers, Inc., Champaign, Ill.

Best, C. 1987. Experience and career length in professional football: the effect of positional segregation. Sociology of Sport Journal 4(4):410-420.

Bierman, J.A. 1990. The effects of television sports media on black male youth. Sociological Inquiry 60(4):413-427.

Bindman, S. 1982. The role of the media in sport. In J.T. Partington, et al., eds. Sport in perspective. Coaching Association of Canada, Ottawa.

Birke, L.I.A., and G. Vines. 1987. A sporting chance: The anatomy of destiny? Women's Studies International Forum 10(4):337-347.

Birrell, S. 1983. The psychological dimensions of female athletic participation. In M.A. Boutilier and L. SanGiovanni. The sporting woman. Human Kinetics Publishers, Inc., Champaign, Ill.

Birrell, S. 1984. Separatism as an issue in women's sport. ARENA Review 8(2):21-29.

Birrell, S. 1988. Discourses on the gender/sport relationship: from women in sport to gender relations. Exercise and Sport Science Review 16:459-501.

Birrell, S. 1989. Race relations theories and sport: Suggestions for a more critical analysis. Sociology of Sport Journal 6(3):212-227.

Birrell, S., and D.M. Richter. 1987. Is a diamond forever? Feminist transformations of sport. Women's Studies International Forum 10(4):395-409.

Bissinger, H.G. 1990. Friday night lights. Addison-Wesley Publishing Co., Reading, Mass.

Blair, S. 1985. Professionalization of attitude toward play in children and adults. Research Quarterly for Exercise and Sport 56(1):82-83.

Blinde, E.M., and S.L. Greendorfer. 1985. A reconceptualization of the process of leaving the role of competitive athlete. International Review for the Sociology of Sport 20(1/2):87-94.

Blinde, E.M., D.E. Taub, and L. Han. 1992a. Homophobia and women's sport: The disempowerment of athletes. Paper presented at the annual conference of the American Sociological Association, Pittsburgh (August).

Blinde, E.M., and D.E. Taub. 1992b. Women athletes as falsely accused deviants: managing the lesbian stigma. The Sociological Quarterly 33(4):521-533.

Blinde, E,M., and D.E. Taub. 1993. Sport participation and women's personal empowerment: Experiences of the college athlete. Journal of Sport and Social Issues 17(1):47-60.

Blinde, E.M., S.L. Greendorfer, and R.J. Shanker. 1991. Differential media coverage of men's and women's intercollegiate basketball: Reflection of gender ideology. Journal of Sport and Social Issues 15(2):98-114.

Bloom, M. 1976. Street ball: where foul is fair and fair is foul. New York Times, section 5, p. 2, June 27.

Bock, H. 1986. Martin's act draws fire from all corners. Colorado Springs Gazette Telegraph, section C, p. 12, November 30.

Bolin, A. 1992. Vandalized vanity: Feminine physiques betrayed and portrayed. In F. Mascia-Lees and P. Sharpe (eds.), Tatoo, torture, mutilation, and adornment: the denaturalization of the body in culture and text. SUNY Press, Albany, NY.

Bolin, A. 1992b. Beauty or the beast: The subversive soma. In A. Bolin and J. Granskog (eds.), Athletic intruders: women, culture, and exercise (under review).

Bourdieu, P. 1978. Sport and social class. Social Science Information 17:819-840.

Boutilier, M.A., and L. SanGiovanni. 1983. The sporting woman. Human Kinetics Publishers, Inc., Champaign, Ill.

Braddock, J. 1978a. The sports pages: in black and white. ARENA Review 2(2):17-25.

Braddock, J. 1978b. Television and college football: in black and white. J. Black Studies 8(3):369-380.

Braddock, J. 1980. Race, sports and social mobility: a critical review. Sociol. Symp. 30(Spring):18-38.

Braddock, J. 1981. Race and leadership in professional sports: a study of institutional discrimination in the National Football League, ARENA Review 5(2):16-25.

Braddock, J. et al. 1991. Bouncing back: Sports and academic resilience among African-American males. Education and Urban Society 24(1):113-131.

Brady, E. 1991. Players: 46% earn degrees in five years. USA Today, June 17 (cover story).

Bredemeier, B. 1982. Gender, justice and nonviolence in sport. Perspectives 5:106-114.

Bredemeier, B. 1983. Athletic aggression: a moral concern. In J.H. Goldstein, ed. Sports violence. Springer-Verlag, New York.

Bredemeier, B. 1984. Sport, gender and moral growth. In J. Silva and R. Weinberg, eds. Psychological foundations of sport and exercise (pp. 400-414). Human Kinetics Publishers, Inc., Champaign, Ill.

Bredemeier, B. 1985. Moral reasoning and the perceived legitimacy of intentionally injurious sport acts. Journal of Sport Psychology 7(2):110-124.

Bredemeier, B. 1987. The moral of the youth sport story. In E. Brown and C. Banta (eds.), Competitive sports for children and youth (pp. 285-296). Human Kinetics Publishers, Inc., Champaign, Ill.

Bredemeier, B., and D. Shields. 1983. Body and balance: developing moral structures through physical education. Paper presented at the meetings of the American Alliance for Health, Physical Education, Recreation and Dance, Minneapolis.

Bredemeier, B., and D. Shields. 1984a. The utility of moral stage analysis in the investigation of athletic aggression. Sociol. Sport J. 1(2):138-149.

Bredemeier, B., and D. Shields. 1984b. Divergence in moral reasoning about sport and everyday life. Sociol. Sport J. 1(4):348-357.

Bredemeier, B.J., and D.L. Shields. 1985. Values and violence in sports today. Psychology Today 19(10):22-25, 28-32.

Bredemeier, B.J., and D.L. Shields. 1986. Moral growth among athletes and nonathletes: A comparative analysis. Journal of Genetic Psychology 147:7-18.

Bredemeier, B.J., and D.L. Shields. 1988. Athletic aggression: an issue of contextual morality. Sociology of Sport Journal 3(1):15-28.

Bredemeier, B.J.L., and D.L.L.

Shields. 1993. Moral psychology in the context of sport. In R.N. Singer, M. Murphey, & L.K. Tennant (eds.), Handbook of research on sport psychology (pp. 587-599). Macmillan Publishing Company, New York.

Brohm, J-M. 1978. Sport: a prison of measured time. Ink Links, Ltd., London (translated by Ian Fraser).

Brower, J. 1976. Professional sport team ownership: fun, profit and ideology of the power elite. J. Sport Soc. Issues 1(1):16-51.

Brown, B. 1985. Factors influencing the process of withdrawal by female adolescents from the role of competitive age group swimmer. Sociol. Sport J. 2(2):111-129.

Brown, J.M., and N. Davies. 1978. Attitude toward violence among college athletes. J. Sport Behav. 1(2):61-70.

Brown, E.Y., J.R. Morrow, Jr., and S.M. Livingston. 1982. Self concept changes in women as a result of training. J. Sport Psychol. 4(4):354-363.

Brownell, K., J. Rodin, and J. Wilmore. 1988. Eat, drink and be worried. Runners World 23(8):28-34.

Bryant, J., P. Comisky, and D. Zillmann. 1977. Drama in sports commentary. Journal of Communication 27(3):140-149.

Bryson, L. 1987. Sport and the maintenance of masculine hegemony. Women's Studies International Forum 10:349-360.

Bryson, L. 1990. Challenges to male hegemony in sport. In M.A. Messner and D.F Sabo (eds.), Sport, men, and the gender order (pp. 173-184). Human Kinetics Books, Champaign, Ill.

Buhrmann, H.G. 1977. Athletics and deviancy: an examination of the relationship between athletic participation and deviant behavior of high school girls. Review of Sport and Leisure 2:17-25.

Buhrmann, H.G., and M.K. Zaugg. 1983. Religion and superstition in the sport of basketball. J. Sport Behav. 6(3):146-157.

Burridge, K.O.L. 1957. Disputing in Tangu. Am. Anthropologist 59:763-780.

Butkus, D. 1972. Stop-action. E.P. Dutton & Co., Inc., New York.

Butt, D.S. 1976. Psychology of sport. Van Nostrand Reinhold Co., New York.

Cantor, D.W., and T. Bernay (with J. Stoess). 1992. Women in power: the secrets of leadership. Houghton Mifflin, Boston.

Caplan, P.J. 1981. Barriers between women. Spectrum Publications, Inc., Jamaica, N.Y.

Capouya, J. 1986. Jerry Falwell's team. Sport 77(9):72-81.

Carlston, D. 1986. An environmental explanation for race differences in basketball performance. In R. Lapchick, ed. Fractured focus. Lexington Books, Lexington, Mass.

Carrington, B., T. Chivers, and T. Williams. 1987. Gender, leisure and sport: A case-study of young people of South Asian descent. Leisure Studies 6:265-279.

Carroll, J. 1986. Sport: Virtue and grace. Theory and Society 3(1):91-98.

Carron, A.V. 1978. Role behavior and the coach-athlete interaction. Int. Rev. Sport Sociol. 13(2):51-65.

Case, B., H.S. Green, and J. Brown. 1987. Academic clustering in athletics: myth or reality? ARENA Review 11(2):48-56.

Cavallo, D. 1981. Muscles and morals. University of Pennsylvania Press, Philadelphia.

Chafetz, J.S. 1978. Masculine, feminine or human? F.E. Peacock Publishers, Inc., Itasca, Ill.

Chandler, J. 1983. Televised sport: Britain and the United States. ARENA Review 7(2):20-27.

Chandler, J. 1988. Television and national sport. University of Illinois Press, Urbana, Ill.

Chandler, T.J.L., and A.D. Goldberg. 1990. The academic all-American as vaunted adolescent role-identity. Sociology of Sport Journal 7(3):287-293.

Charnofsky, H. 1968. The major league professional baseball player: self-conception versus the popular image. Int. Rev. Sport Sociol. 3:39-53.

Chase, M.A., and G.M. Drummer. 1992. The role of sports as a social status determinant for children. Research Quarterly for Exercise and Sport 63(4):418-424.

Chu, D. 1981. Origins of teacher/coach role conflict: a reaction to Massengale's paper. In S.L. Greendorfer and A. Yiannakis, eds. Sociology of sport: diverse perspectives. Leisure Press, West Point, N.Y.

Chu, D., and D. Griffey. 1982. Sport and racial integration: the relationship of personal contact, attitudes and behavior. In A.O. Dunleavy, A. Miracle, and R. Rees, eds. Studies in the sociology of sport. Texas Christian University Press, Fort Worth, Tex.

Claeys, U., and H. Van Pelt, eds. 1986. Sport and mass media. International Review for the Sociology of Sport 21(2,3):95-102 (special issue).

Clark, N. 1988. The new breed of bulimics: compulsive eaters-exercisers. Shape 7(12):91-93.

Clark, N., M. Nelson, and W. Evans. 1988. Nutrition education for elite female runners. The Physician & Sportsmedicine 16(2):124-134.

Clarke, A., and J. Clarke. 1982. "Highlights and action replays"—ideology, sport and the media. In J. Hargreaves, ed. Sport, culture and ideology. Routledge & Kegan Paul, Boston.

Clift, E. 1992. Interview (with Hillary Clinton): "I try to be who I am." Newsweek, December 28:24-25.

Coakley, J. 1979. Participation trends in physical activity and sport: implications for the sociology of sport. Rev. Sport and Leisure 4(2):30-47.

Coakley, J. 1980. Play, games and sport: developmental implications for young people. J. Sport Behav. 3(3):99-118.

Coakley, J. 1982. Sport in society: issues and controversies. ed. 2, Mosby, St. Louis.

Coakley, J. 1983a. Play, games and sports: developmental implications for young people. In J.C. Harris and R.J. Park, eds. Play, games and sports in cultural contexts. Human

Kinetics Publishers, Inc., Champaign, Ill.

Coakley, J. 1983b. Leaving competitive sport: retirement or rebirth? Quest 35(1):1-11.

Coakley, J. 1984. Mead's theory on the development of the self: implications for organized youth sport programs. Paper presented at the Olympic Scientific Congress, Eugene, Ore.

Coakley, 1985a. Socialization and youth sports. In A. Miracle and R. Rees (eds.), Sport and sociological theory. Human Kinetics Publishers, Inc., Champaign, Ill.

Coakley, J. 1985b. When should children begin competing? In D. Gould and M.R. Weiss, eds. Sport for children and youths. Human Kinetics Publishers, Inc., Champaign, Ill.

Coakley, J. 1987. Sociology of sport in the United States. International Review for the Sociology of Sport 22(1):63-79.

Coakley, J. 1989. Media coverage of sports and violent behavior: an elusive connection. Current Psychology: Research and Reviews 7(4):322-330.

Coakley, J. 1992. Burnout among adolescent athletes: A personal failure or social problem? Sociology of Sport Journal 9(3):271-285.

Coakley, J. 1993a. Socialization and sport. In R.N. Singer, M. Murphey, & L.K. Tennant (eds.), Handbook of research on sport psychology (pp. 571-586). Macmillan Publishing Company, New York.

Coakley, J. 1993b. Sport and socialization. Exercise and Sport Science Reviews 21:169-200.

Coakley, J. In press. Socialization through sports. In O. Bar-Or (ed.), Child and adolescent athlete, Encyclopedia of Sports Medicine. Blackwell, London.

Coakley, J., and P. Pacey. 1984. The distribution of athletic scholarships among women in intercollegiate sport. In N. Theberge and P. Donnelly, eds. Sport and the sociological imagination. Texas Christian University Press, Fort Worth, Tex.

Coakley, J., and M. Westkott. 1984. Opening doors for women in sport: an alternative to old strategies. In

D.S. Eitzen, ed. Sport in contemporary society. St. Martin's Press, New York.

Coakley, J., and A. White. 1992. Making decisions: Gender and sport participation among British adolescents. Sociology of Sport Journal 9(1):20-35.

Cole, C.L. 1991. The politics of cultural representatiuon: Visions of fields/fields of vision. International Review for the Sociology of Sport 26(1):37-52.

Cole, C.L. 1993. Resisting the canon: Feminist cultural studies and sport. J. Sport Social Issues 17(2):77-97.

Cole, C.L., H. Denny, and J. Coakley. 1993. AIDS, surveillance, and sports. Paper presented at the meetings of the Society for the Interdisciplinary Study of Social Imagery, Denver (March).

Coleman, J. 1961a. The adolescent society. The Free Press, New York.

Coleman, J. 1961b. Athletics in high schools. Ann. Am. Acad. Pol. Sci. 338(November):33-43.

Collins, B. 1984. Playing singles again. Family Weekly, pp. 4-6, May 6.

Condor, R., and D.F. Anderson. 1984. Longitudinal analysis of coverage accorded black and white athletes in feature articles of Sports Illustrated, 1960-1980. J. Sport Behav. 7(1):39-43.

Connell, R.W. 1987a. Gender and power. Allen & Unwin, Sydney, Australia.

Connell, R.W. 1987b. Gender and power: Society, the person and sexual politics. Stanford University Press, Stanford, Calif.

Coser, R. 1986. Cognitive structure and the use of social space. Sociological Forum 1(1):1-26.

Courson, S. 1988. Steroids: another view. Sports Illustrated 69(21):106.

Cousy, B. 1975. The killer instinct. Random House, Inc., New York.

Critcher, C. 1986. Radical theorists of sport: the state of play. Sociology of Sport Journal 3(4):333-343.

Csikszentmihalyi, M. 1990. Flow: the psychology of optimal experience. Harper Perennial, New York.

Curry, T.J. 1991. Fraternal bonding in the locker room: A profeminist anal-

ysis of talk about competition and women. Sociology of Sport Journal 8(2):119-135.

Curry, T.J. 1992. A little pain never hurt anyone: athletic career socialization and the normalization of sport injury. Paper presented at the Gregory Stone Symposium, Las Vegas (February).

Curry, T., and R. Jiobu. 1984. Sports: a social perspective. Prentice-Hall, Inc., Englewood Cliffs, N.J.

Curtis, J., and J. Loy. 1978a. Positional segregation in professional baseball: replications, trend data and critical observation. Int. Rev. Sport Sociol. 4(13):5-21.

Curtis, J., and J. Loy. 1978b. Race/ethnicity and relative centrality of playing positions in team sport. Exerc. Sport Sci. Rev. 6:285-313.

D'Angelo, R. 1987. Sports gambling and the media. ARENA Review 11(1):1-4.

Davis, L. 1988. A postmodern paradox? Cheerleaders at women's sporting events. Paper presented at the annual conference of the North American Society for the Sociology of Sport, Cincinnati (November).

Deem, R. 1986. All work and no play: the sociology of women and leisure. Open University Press, Philadelphia.

Deem, R. 1988. "Together we stand, divided we fall"; social criticism and the sociology of sport and leisure. Sociology of Sport Journal 5(4):341-354.

Deford, F. 1976. Religion in sport. Sports Illustrated 44(16):88-100.

Devall, B., and J. Harry. 1981. Who hates whom in the great outdoors: the impact of recreational specialization and technologies of play. Leisure Sciences 4(4):399-418.

Devereux, E.C. 1976. Backyard versus little league baseball: the impoverishment of children's games. In D.M. Landers, ed. Social problems in athletics. University of Illinois Press, Urbana, Ill.

DiPasquale, M.G. 1992a. Editorial: Why athletes use drugs. Drugs in Sports 1(1):2-3.

DiPasquale, M.G. 1992b. Publications

by Mile High Publishing. Drugs in Sports 1(3):13-14.

DiPasquale, M.G. 1992c. Beating drug tests. Drugs in Sports 1(2):3-6.

DiPasquale, M.G. 1992d. Beating drug tests: Part II. Drugs in Sports 1(3):6-12.

Dobie, M. 1987. Facing a brave new world. New York Newsday, November 8.

Domi, T. 1992. Tough tradition of hockey fights should be preserved. USA Today, October 27.

Donnelly, P. 1988. Sport as a site for "popular" resistance. In R. Gruneau, ed. Popular cultures and political practices. Garamond Press, Toronto.

Donnelly, P. (with E. Casperson, L. Sargeant, and B. Steenhof) 1993. Problems associated with youth involvement in high-performance sport. In B.R. Cahill and A. Pearl (eds.), (pp. 95-126). Human Kinetics, Intensive participation in children's sports, Champaign, IL.

Donnelly, P., and K. Young. 1985. Reproduction and transformation of cultural forms in sport: a contextual analysis of rugby. International Review for the Sociology of Sport 20(1,2):19-38.

Donnelly, P., and K. Young. 1988. The construction and confirmation of identity in sport subcultures. Sociology of Sport Journal 5(3):223-240.

Donohoe, T., and N. Johnson. 1986. Foul play: drug abuse in sports. Basil Blackwell, Inc., New York.

Dubois, P.E. 1978. Participation in sports and occupational attainment: a comparative study. Res. Q. 49(1):28-37.

Dubois, P.E. 1979. Participation in sport and occupational attainment: an investigation of selected athlete categories, J. Sport Behav. 2(2):103-114.

Dubois, P.E. 1982. The behavior of youth football coaches. In A.O. Dunleavy, et al., eds. Studies in the sociology of sport. Texas Christian University Press, Fort Worth, Tex.

Duda, J.L. 1981. Achievement motivation in sport: minority consider-

ations for the coach. J. Sport Behav. 4(1):24-31.

Duncan, M.C. 1989. Television portrayals of children's play and sport. Play & Culture 2(3):235-252.

Duncan, M.C., M.A. Massner, L. Williams, and K. Jensen. 1990. Gender stereotyping in televised sports. Amateur Athletic Foundation, Los Angeles, Calif.

Duncan, M.C., and A. Sayaovong. 1990. Photographic images and gender in Sports Illustrated for Kids. Play & Culture 3(2):91-116.

Duquin, M. 1984. Power and authority: Moral consensus and conformity in sport. International Review for Sociology of Sport 19(4):295-304.

Eder, D., and S. Parker. 1987. The cultural production and reproduction of gender: The effect of extracurricular activities on peer group culture. Sociology of Education 60:200-213.

Edwards, H. 1973. Sociology of sport. Dorsey Press, Homewood, Ill.

Edwards, H. 1979. Sport within the veil: the triumphs, tragedies, and challenges of Afro-American involvement. Ann. Am. Acad. Pol. Sci. 445(September):116-127.

Edwards, H. 1983. Educating black athletes. The Atlantic Monthly 252(2):31-38.

Edwards, H. 1986. Speech on race and sport. Conference on Sports, Culture and Society, Stanford University.

Edwards, H., and V. Rackages. 1977. The dynamics of violence in American sport: some promising structural and social considerations, J. Sport Soc. Issues 7(2):3-31.

Eichberg, H. 1984. Olympic sport: neocolonialization and alternatives. International Review for the Sociology of Sport 19(1):97-106.

Eisen, G., and D. Turner. 1992. Myth & reality: Social mobility of the American Olympic athletes. International Review for the Sociology of Sport 27(2):165-176.

Eitzen, D.S. 1975. Athletics in the status system of male adolescents: a replication of Coleman's The Adolescent Society. Adolescence 10(38):268-276.

Eitzen, D.S. 1979. Sport in contemporary society. St. Martin's Press, New York.

Eitzen, D.S. 1987. The educational experiences of intercollegiate student-athletes. Journal of Sport and Social Issues 11(1,2):15-30.

Eitzen, D.S. 1988. The myth and reality of elite amateur sport. The World & I 3(10):549-559.

Eitzen, D.S. 1992. Treatment of athletes is the problem with college sports. The Coloradoan, Sunday, November 29, p. E3.

Eitzen, D.S., and D. Furst. 1988. Racial bias in women's collegiate sports. Paper presented at the North American Society for the Sociology of Sport Conference, Cincinnati.

Eitzen, D.S., and S.R. Pratt. 1989. Gender differences in coaching philosophy: The case of female basketball teams. Research Quarterly for Exercise and Sport 60(2):152-158.

Eitzen, D.S., and M.B. Zinn. 1989. The de-athleticization of women: the naming and gender marking of collegiate sport teams. Sociol. Sport J. 6(4):362-370.

Elias, N. 1986. An essay on sport and violence. In N. Elias and E. Dunning (eds.), Quest for excitement (pp. 150-174). Basil Blackwell, New York.

Elias, N., and E. Dunning. 1986. Quest for excitement. Basil Blackwell, New York.

Evans, J.R. 1988. Team selection in children's games. The Social Sciences Journal 25(1):93-104.

Ewald, K., and R.M. Jiobu. 1985. Explaining positive deviance: Becker's model and the case of runners and bodybuilders. Sociology of Sport Journal 2(2):144-156.

Famaey-Lamon, A., and F. Van Loon. 1978. Mass media and sports practice. Int. Rev. Sport Sociol. 13(4):37-43.

Farhi, P. 1992. I'd like to sell the world a coke. The Washington Post National Weekly Edition, June 22-28.

Fasting, K. 1977. A description of sports programs on television as seen in relation to personal engagement in sports and social and geographic conditions. Norwegian Confederation of Sports, Oslo, Norway.

Faulkner, R.R. 1979a. Coming of age in organizations: a comparative study of career contingencies and adult socialization. Sociol. Work Occupations 2(2):131-173.

Faulkner, R.R. 1979b. Making violence by doing work: selves, situations and the world of professional hockey. Sociol. Work Occupations 2(3):288-312.

Felshin, J. 1974. The social view. In E. Gerber, et al., eds. The American woman in sport. Addison-Wesley Publishing Co., Inc., Reading, Mass.

Ferrante, J. 1992. Sociology: A global perspective. Wadsworth Publishing Company, Belmont, Calif.

Fine, G.A. 1987. With the boys: little league baseball and preadolescent culture. University of Chicago Press, Chicago.

Fisher, A.C. 1976. Psychology of sport. Mayfield Publishing Co., Palo Alto, Calif.

Flake, C. 1992. The spirit of winning: Sports and the total man. In S. Hoffman (ed.), Sport and religion (pp. 161-176). Human Kinetics Books, Champaign, Ill.

Foley, D. 1990a. Learning capitalist culture. University of Pennsylvania Press, Philadelphia.

Foley, D. 1990b. The great American football ritual: Reproducing race, class, and gender inequality. Sociology of Sport Journal 7(2):111-135.

Ford, G.R. (with J. Underwood). 1974. In defense of the competitive urge. Sports Illustrated 41(2):16-23.

Frey, J.H. 1984. The U.S. vs. Great Britain responses to the 1980 boycott of the Olympic Games. Comp. Phys. Ed. Sport 6(3):4-13.

Frey, J. 1985. The winning team myth. Currents: Journal of the Council for Advancement and Support of Education 11(1):32-35.

Frey, J.H., and D.S. Eitzen. 1991. Sport and society. Annual Review of Sociology 17:503-522.

Friedenberg, E. 1974. R.D. Laing. Viking, New York.

Fuller, J.R., and E.A. Manning. 1987. Violence and sexism in college mascots and symbols: a typology. Free Inquiry in Creative Sociology 15(1):61-64.

Furst, T. 1971. Social change and the commercialization of professional sports. Int. Rev. Sport Sociol. 6:153-170.

Garrity, J. 1989. A clash of cultures on the Hopi reservation. Sports Illustrated 71(21):10-17.

Gaston, J.C. 1986. The destruction of the young black male: The impact of popular culture and organized sports. Journal of Black Studies 16:369-384.

Gelinas, M., and N. Theberge. 1986. A content analysis of the coverage of physical activity in two Canadian newspapers. International Review for the Sociology of Sport 21(2,3): 141-152.

George, N. 1992. Elevating the game: Black men and basketball. Harper Collins, New York.

Gilbert, B. 1988. Competition: Is it what life's all about? Sports Illustrated 68(20):88-100.

Gilbert, B., and L. Twyman. 1983. Violence: out of hand in the stands. Sports Illustrated 58(4):62-74.

Gmelch, G. 1979. Baseball magic. In D.S. Eitzen, ed. Sport in contemporary society. St. Martin's Press, New York.

Goffman, E. 1959. The presentation of self in everyday life. Anchor Books, Garden City, N.J.

Goldlust, J. 1987. Playing for keeps: sport, the media and society. Longman Cheshire Pty., Ltd., Melbourne, Australia.

Goldman, B. 1984. Death in the locker room. Icarus, South Bend, Ind.

Goldman, B. (with P. Bush and R. Klatz). 1992. Death in the locker room II. Elite Sports Medicine Publications, Inc. Chicago, IL.

Goldstein, J. 1983. Sports violence. Springer-Verlag, New York.

Goldstein, J., ed. 1989. Violence in sports. Current Psychology: Research and Reviews 7(4) (special issue).

Goldstein, J., and B. Bredemeier. 1977. Socialization: some basic issues. J. Communication 27(3):154-159.

Goode, E. 1989. Drugs in American society. Alfred A. Knopf, New York.

Goodman, C. 1979. Choosing sides. Schocken Books, New York.

Gould, D. 1982. Sport psychology in the 1980s: status, direction, and challenge in youth sports research. J. Sport Psychol. 4(3):203-218.

Gould, D. 1987. Understanding attrition in children's sport. In D. Gould and M.R. Weiss (eds.), Advances in pediatric sport sciences (Volume two, Behavioral issues) (pp. 61-86). Human Kinetics Publishers, Inc., Champaign, Ill.

Gould, D., and R. Martens. 1979. Attitudes of volunteer coaches toward significant youth sport issues. Res. Q. 50(3):369-380.

Gould, D., et al. 1982. Reasons for attrition in competitive youth swimming. J. Sport Behav. 5(3):155-165.

Gouldner, A. 1970. The coming crisis of western sociology. Basic Books, New York.

Gramann, J.H., and R.J. Burdge. 1981. The effects of recreation goals on conflict perception: the case of water skiers and fishermen. J. Leisure Res. 13(1):15-27.

Greendorfer, S. 1983. Sport and the mass media: general overview. ARENA Review 7(2):1-6.

Greendorfer, S.L., and E.M. Blinde. 1985. "Retirement" from intercollegiate sport: Theoretical and empirical considerations. Sociology of Sport Journal 2(2):101-110.

Greendorfer, S., E. Blinde, and A.M. Pelligrini. 1986. Gender differences in Brazilian children's socialization into sport. International Review for the Sociology of Sport 21(1):51-62.

Greer, D.L., and M.J. Stewart. 1989. Children's attitudes toward play: an investigation of their context specificity and relationship to organized sport. J. of Sport and Exercise Psychology 11(3): 336-342.

Gregory, J.C., and B. Petrie. 1975. Superstitions of Canadian intercollegiate athletes: an inter-sport comparison. Int. Rev. Sport Sociol. 10(2): 59-68.

Grey, M. 1992. Sports and immigrant, minority and Anglo relations in Garden City (Kansas) High School. Sociology of Sport Journal 9(3):255-270.

Griffin, P. 1992. Silence encourages fear, discrimination. USA Today,

Gruneau, R. 1976. Class or mass: Notes on the democratization of Canadian amateur sport. In R. Gruneau and J.G. Albinson (eds.), Canadian sport: Sociological perspectives (pp. 108-140). Addison-Wesley, Don Mills, Ontario.

Gruneau, R. 1983. Class, sports, and social development. University of Massachusetts Press, Amherst, Mass.

Gruneau, R. 1988. Modernization or hegemony: Two views of sports and social development. In J. Harvey and H. Cantelon (eds.), Not just a game (pp. 9-32). University of Ottawa Press, Ottawa.

Gruneau, R. 1989a. Television, the Olympics, and the question of ideology. In R. Jackson (ed.), The Olympic Movement and the mass media (pp. 7/23-7/34). Hurford Enterprises, Calgary, Alberta.

Gruneau, R. 1989b. Making spectacle: A case study in television sports production. In L.A. Wenner (ed.), Media, sports, and society (pp. 134-154). Sage Publication, Newbury Park, Calif.

Guttmann, A. 1978. From ritual to record: the nature of modern sports. Columbia University Press, New York.

Guttmann, A. 1986. Sport spectators. Columbia University Press, New York.

Guttmann, A. 1988. A whole new ball game: An interpretation of American sports. University of North Carolina Press, Chapel Hill, N.C.

Hall, A., T. Slack, G. Smith, and D. Whitson. 1991. Sport in Canadian society. McClelland & Stewart Inc., Toronto.

Hall, M.A. 1990. How should we theorize gender in the context of sport? In M.A. Messner and D.F Sabo (eds.), Sport, men, and the gender order: Critical feminist perspectives. Human Kinetics Publishers, Inc. Champaign, Ill.

Hall, S. 1985. Signification, represen-tation, ideology: Althusser and the post-structuralist debates. Critical Studies in Mass Communication 2(2):91-114.

Hallinan, C. 1991. Aborigines and positional segregation in Australian Rugby League. Int. Rev. for the Sociology of Sport 26(2):69-78.

Hanford, G. 1974. An inquiry into the need for and the feasibility of a national study of intercollegiate athletics. American Council on Education, Washington, D.C.

Hanford, G. 1979. Controversies in college sports. Ann. Am. Acad. Pol. Sci. 445:66-79.

Hanks, M., and B.K. Eckland. 1976. Athletics and social participation in the educational attainment process. Sociol. Ed. 49(4):271-294.

Hare, N. 1971. A study of the black fighter. Black Scholar 3(3):2-9.

Hargreaves, John. 1982. Sport, culture and ideology. In Jennifer Hargreaves, ed. Sport, culture and ideology. Routledge & Kegan Paul, Boston.

Hargreaves, John. 1986. Sport, power and culture. St. Martin's Press, New York.

Hargreaves, John. 1987. The body, sport and power relations. In J. Horne, et al., eds. Sport, leisure and social relations. Routledge & Kegan Paul, New York (Sociological Review Monograph 33).

Hargreaves, Jennifer. 1993. Sporting females: Critical issues in the history and sociology of women's sport. Routledge, London.

Harris, J.C. 1980. Play: a definition and implied relationships with culture and sport. J. Sport Psychol. 2(1):46-61.

Harris, O., and L. Hunt. 1984. Race and sports involvement: some implications of sports for black and white youth. Paper presented at the AAHPERD Conference, Anaheim, CA.

Hart, B.A., C.A. Hasbrook, and S.A. Mathes. 1986. An examination of the reduction in the number of female interscholastic coaches. Research Quarterly for Exercise and Sport 57(1):68-77.

Harvey, J., and R. Proulx. 1988. Sport and the state in Canada. In J. Harvey and H. Cantelon, eds. Not just a game. University of Ottawa Press, Ottawa.

Hastings, D.W., S.B. Kurth, and J. Meyer. 1989. Competitive swimming careers through the life cycle. Sociology of Sport Journal 6(3):278-284.

Hauser, W.J., and L.B. Lueptow. 1978. Participation in athletics and academic achievement: a replication and extension. Sociological Quarterly 19:304-309.

Heinila, K. 1985. Sport and international understanding: a contradiction in terms? Sociol. Sport J. 2(3):240-248.

Heinz, M. 1991. Women's sports in the media. CBC radio, *Inside Track* (Spring).

Heller, S. 1991. The human body and changing cultural conceptions of it draw attention of humanities and social-science scholars. The Chronicle of Higher Education, June 12, pp. A4, A8.

Hellison, D. 1985. Goals and Strategies for teaching physical education. Human Kinetics Publishers, Inc. Champaign, Ill.

Hellison, D. 1990. Physical Education for disadvantaged youth—A Chicago story. JOPERD 61(6):36-45 (5 article section).

Hellison, D. 1993. The coaching club: teaching responsibility to inner-city students. JOPERD 64(5):66-71.

Henry, C.P. 1986. A piece of the pie? The Crisis 93(5):20-26, 40-41.

Henschen, K., and D. Fry. 1984. An archival study of the relationship of intercollegiate athletic participation and graduation. Sociology of Sport Journal 1(1):52-56.

Hesling, W. 1986. The pictorial representation of sports on television. International Review for the Sociology of Sport 21(2/3):173-194.

Hiestand, M. 1991. Study finds good market in under-30 age group. USA Today, December 10, Section C.

Higgs, R.J. 1982. Sports: a reference guide. Greenwood Press, Westport, Conn.

Hilliard, D. 1984. Media images of male and female professional athletes: an interpretive analysis of magazine articles. Sociol. Sport J. 1(3):251-262.

Hilliard, D. and J.M. Hilliard. 1990. Positive deviance and participant sport. Paper rpesented at the annual meetings of The Association for the Study of Play, Las Vegas (April).

Ho, L., and J.E. Walker. 1982. Female athletes and nonathletes: similarities and differences in self-perception. J. Sport Behav. 5(1):12-27.

Hoberman, J. 1986. The Olympic crisis: Sport, politics and the moral order. Aristide D. Caratzas, New Rochelle, N.Y.

Hoberman, J. 1992. Mortal engines: The science of performance and the dehumanization of sports. The Free Press, New York.

Hoffman, S. 1982. God, guts and glory: evangelicalism in American sports. Paper presented at the meetings of the American Alliance for Health, Physical Education, Recreation and Dance, Detroit.

Hoffman, S. 1992a. Sport and religion. Human Kinetics Publishers, Inc. Champaign, Ill. (note: 1992a references often refer to Hoffman's section introductions in this book).

Hoffman, S. 1992b. Evangelicalism and the revitalization of religious ritual in sport. In S. Hoffman (ed.), Sport and religion (pp. 111-125). Human Kinetics Publishers, Inc. Champaign, Ill.

Hoffman, S. 1992c. Recovering a sense of the sacred in sport. In S. Hoffman (ed.), Sport and religion (pp. 153-160). Human Kinetics Publishers, Inc. Champaign, Ill.

Hoffman, S. 1992d. Nimrod, Nephilim, and the Athletae Dei. In S. Hoffman (ed.), Sport and religion (pp. 275-286). Human Kinetics Publishers, Inc. Champaign, Ill.

Holmen, M.G., and B.L. Parkhouse. 1981. Trends in the selection of coaches for female athletes: a demographic inquiry. Res. Q. Exerc. Sport 52(1):9-18.

hooks, bell. 1992. Theory as liberatory practice. Yale Journal of Law and Feminism 4(1):1-12.

Hoose, P.M. 1989. Necessities: Racial barriers in American sports. Random House, New York, N.Y.

Horrow, R. 1980. Sports violence. Carrollton Press, Inc., Arlington, Va.

House, T. 1989. The jock's itch. Contemporary Books, Chicago, Ill.

Howell, F., A. Miracle, and R. Rees. 1984. Do high school athletics pay? The effects of varsity participation on socioeconomic attainment. Sociol. Sport J. 1(1):15-25.

Hughes, R., and J. Coakley. 1991. Positive deviance among athletes: The implications of overconformity to the sport ethic. Sociology of Sport Journal 8(4):307-325.

Humphrey, J. 1986. No holding Brazil: football, nationalism and politics. In A. Tomlinson and G. Whannel, eds. Off the ball. Pluto Press, London.

Jackson, E.L., and R.A.G. Wong. 1982. Perceived conflict between urban cross country skiers and snowmobilers in Alberta. J. Leisure Res. 14(1):47-62.

James, C.L.R. 1984. Beyond a boundary. Pantheon Books, New York (American edition).

Jansen, S.C., and D.F. Sabo. 1992. Sportspeak and the Persian Gulf War: Gender, sport, and the New World Order. Paper presented at the annual conference of the American Sociological Association, Pittsburgh (August).

Jarvie, G. 1991a. Highland games: The making of the myth. Edinburgh University Press, Edinburgh.

Jarvie, G. 1991b. Sport, popular struggle and South African culture. In G. Jarvie (ed.), Sport, racism and ethnicity (pp. 175-189). The Falmer Press, London.

Jarvis, B. 1993. Against the great divide. Newsweek, May 3:14.

Johns, D. 1992. Starving for gold: A case study in overconformity in high performance sport. Paper presented at the annual conference of the North American Society for the Sociology of Sport, Toledo (November).

Johnson, A. 1982. Government, opposition and sport: the role of domestic sports policy in generating politi-cal support. Journal of Sport and Social Issues 6(2):22-34.

Johnson, A., and J. Frey, eds. 1985. Government and sport. Rowman and Allenheld, Publishers, Totowa, N.J.

Johnson, D.W., R.T. Johnson, and M.L. Krotee. 1987. The relation between social interdependence and psychological health on the 1980 U.S. Olympic ice hockey team. J. Psychol. 120(3):279-291.

Johnson, D.W., and R.T. Johnson. 1983. The socialization and achievement crisis: Are cooperative learning experiences the solution? In L. Bickman (ed.), Applied social psychology annual 4. Sage Publications, Beverly Hills, Calif.

Johnson, W.O. 1974. From here to 2000. Sports Illustrated 41(26):73-83.

Kageyama, K. 1988. A sociological consideration on sports in Japan. Paper presented at the International Workshop of Sport Sociology in Japan (Sport and Humanism), Gotenba, Shizuoka (September).

Kane, M.J., and L.J. Disch. 1992. Sexual violence and the reproduction of male power in the locker room: A case study of the Lisa Olson "incident." Paper presented at the annual conference of the North American Society for the Sociology of Sport, Toledo (November).

Kaplan, H.R. 1983. Sport, gambling and television: the emerging alliance. ARENA Review 7(1):1-11.

Keating, J.W. 1964. Sportsmanship as a moral category. Ethics 75(1):25-35.

Keefer, R., J.H. Goldstein, and D. Kasiarz. 1983. Olympic games participation and warfare. In J.H. Goldstein, ed. Sports violence. Springer-Verlag, New York.

Kelley, B.C., S.J. Hoffman, & D.L. Gill. 1990. The relationship between competitive orientation and religious orientation. J. of Sport Behavior 13(3):145-156.

Kennedy, R. 1975. Wanted: an end to mayhem. Sports Illustrated 43(20):17-21.

Kerrigan, 1992. Sports and the Christian life: Reflections on Pope John Paul II's theology of sports. In S.

Hoffman (ed.), Sport and religion (pp. 253-260). Human Kinetics Publishers, Inc, Champaign, Ill.

Kidd, B. 1984. The myth of the ancient games. In A. Tomlinson and G. Whannel, eds. Five-ring circus. Pluto Press, London.

Kidd, B. 1987. Sports and masculinity. In M. Kaufman (ed.), Beyond patriarchy: Essays by men on pleasure, power, and change (pp. 250-265). Oxford University Press, New York, NY.

Kidd, B. 1988. The campaign against sport in South Africa. International Journal 43:643-664.

Kidd, B. 1991. From quarantine to cure: The new phase of the struggle against apartheid sport. Sociology of Sport Journal 8(1):33-46.

Kidd, T.R. 1979. Social-psychological characteristics of physical educators and coaches. Rev. Sport and Leisure 4(1):29-39.

Kidd, T.R., and W.F. Woodman. 1975. Sex and orientations toward winning in sport. Res. Q. 46(4):476-483.

Kimura, M., and T. Saeki. 1990. A study on the mechanism of the sexism strategies in the discourse of media reports on women's sports in Japan. Paper presented at the International Congress for the Sociology of Sport, Madrid (June).

Kinkema, K.M., and J.C. Harris. 1992. Sport and the mass media. Exercise and Sport Science Reviews 20:127-159.

Kjeldsen, E. 1980. Centrality and leadership recruitment: a study of their linkage. Paper presented at the meetings of the North American Society for the Sociology of Sport, Denver.

Kleiber, D. 1980. The meaning of power in sport. Int. J. Sport Psychol. 11(1):34-41.

Kleiber, D.A., and S.C. Brock. 1992. The effect of career-ending injuries on the subsequent well-being of elite college athletes. Sociology of Sport Journal 9(1):70-75.

Kleiber, D., S. Greendorfer, E. Blinde, and S. Samdahl. 1987. Quality of exit from university sports and life satisfaction in early

adulthood. Sociology of Sport Journal 4(1):28-36.

Kleiber, D., and J.D. Hemmer. 1981. Sex differences in the relationship of locus of control and recreational sport participation. Sex Roles 7(8):801-810.

Kleiber, D., and G. Roberts. 1983. The relationship between game and sport involvement in later childhood: a preliminary investigation. Res. Q. Exerc. Sport 54(2):200-203.

Klein, A. 1984. Review of Soccer Madness (Lever, 1983). Sociol. Sport J. 1(2):195-197.

Klein, A. 1989. Baseball as underdevelopment: the political-economy of sport in the Dominican Republic. Sociology of Sport Journal 6(2):95-112.

Klein, A. 1991. Sugarball: The American game, the Dominican dream. Yale University Press, New Haven, CT.

Knight Foundation. 1991. Report of the Knight Foundation Commission on Intercollegiate Athletics (available through NCAA).

Knoppers, A. 1985. Professionalization of attitudes: a review and critique. Quest 37(1):92-102.

Knoppers, A. 1988. Equity for excellence in physical education. JOPERD 59(6):54-58.

Knoppers, A., M. Zuidema, and B. Meyer. 1989. Playing to win or playing to play? Sociol. Sport J. 6(1):70-76.

Kohn, A. 1986. No contest: the case against competition. Houghton Mifflin Co., Boston.

Koppett, L. 1981. Sports illusion, sports reality. Houghton Mifflin Co., Boston.

Kotov, Y., and I. Yudovich. 1978. Soviet sport and Soviet foreign policy. In B. Lowe, et al., eds. Sports and international relations. Stipes Publishing Co., Champaign, Ill.

Landers, D.M., and D.M. Landers. 1978. Socialization via interscholastic athletics: its effects on delinquency. Sociology of Education 51(4):299-303.

Langlois, J.H., and A.C. Downs. 1980. Mothers, fathers, and peers as socialization agents of sex-typed play

behaviors in young children. Child Dev. 51:1237-1247.

Lapchick, R. 1979. South Africa: sport and apartheid politics. Ann. Am. Acad. Pol. Sci. 445:155-165.

Lapchick, R. 1984. Broken promises: racism in American sports. St. Martin's/Marek, New York.

Lapchick, R. (with R. Malekoff). 1987. On the mark. St. Martin's Press, New York.

Lapchick, R. 1987. The high school athlete as the future college student-athlete. Journal of Sport and Social Issues 11(1,2):104-124.

Lapchick, R. 1988a. Blacks and baseball. The CSSS Digest 1(1):4-12.

Lapchick, R. 1988b. The high school student-athlete as the future college student-athlete. Paper prepared for the National School Board Association.

Lapchick, R. 1989. Blacks in the NBA and NFL. The CSSS Digest 1(2):1, 4-5.

Lapchick, R. 1991. Five minutes to midnight: Race and sport in the 1990s. Madison Books, Lanham, M.D.

Lapchick, R. 1992. The battle for a brave new world has just begun: A 'New' South Africa rises from the dust. CSSS Digest 4(3):1, 4

Lapchick, R. (with J.P. Brown) 1992. 1992 Racial report card: Do professional sports provide equal opportunities for all races? CSSS Digest 4(2):1, 4-8.

Laqueur, T. 1990. Making sex. Harvard University Press, Cambridge, Mass.

Lasch, C. 1977. The corruption of sports. New York Review of Books 24(7):24-30.

Lavoie, M. 1989. Stacking, performance differentials, and salary discrimination in professional ice hockey: a survey of the evidence. Sociology of Sport Journal 6(1):17-35.

Lederman, D. 1988. Do winning teams spur contributions? The Chronicle of Higher Education 34(18):1, 32-34.

Lederman, D. 1992a. Men get 70% of money available for athletic scholarships at colleges that play big-time sport, new study finds. The Chronicle for Higher Education 38(28):1, A45-46.

Lederman, D. 1992b. Blacks make up large proportion of scholarship athletes, yet their overall enrollment lags at Division I colleges. The Chronicle for Higher Education 38(41):1, A30-34.

Lee, M.J. 1986. Moral and social growth through sport: The coach's role. In G. Gleeson (ed.), The growing child in competitive sport (pp. 248-255). London: Hodder & Stoughton.

Lenskyj, H. 1986. Out of bounds: women, sport and sexuality. Women's Press, Toronto.

Lenskyj, H. 1988. Women, sport and physical activity: research and bibliography. Minister of State, Fitness and Amateur Sports, Ottawa.

Lenskyj, H. 1991. Combating homophobia in sport and physical education. Sociology of Sport Journal 8(1):61-69.

Lenskyj, H.J. 1992a. I am but you can't tell: Homophobia and the marginalization of women in sport. Paper presented at the annual conference of the North American Society for the Sociology of Sport, Toledo (November).

Lenskyj, H.J. 1992b. Feminism, resistance and the remaking of sport: Theories, methodologies and practices. Paper presented at the annual conference of the North American Society for the Sociology of Sport, Toledo (November).

Lenskyj, H. 1992c. Unsafe at home base: Women's experiences of sexual harrassment in university sport and physical education. Women's Sport and Physical Activity Journal 1(1): 19-33.

Leonard, G.B. 1973. Winning isn't everything, it's nothing. Intell. Dig. 4(2):45-46.

Leonard, W.M. 1977a. An extension of the black, Latin, white report. Int. Rev. Sport Sociol. 3(12):86-95.

Leonard, W.M. 1977b. Stacking and performance differentials of whites, blacks and Latins in professional baseball. Rev. Sport and Leisure 2:77-106.

Leonard, W.M. 1987. Stacking in college basketball: a neglected analysis. Sociology of Sport Journal 4(4):403-409.

Leonard, W.M. 1988. Salaries and race in professional baseball: the Hispanic component. Sociology of Sport Journal 5(3):278-284.

Leonard, W.M., and J.E. Reyman. 1988. The odds of attaining professional athlete status: refining the computations. Sociology of Sport Journal 5(2):162-169.

Lever, J. 1976. Sex differences in the games children play. Soc. Prob. 23:478-487.

Lever, J. 1978. Sex differences in the complexity of children's play. Am. Sociol. Rev. 43(4):471-483.

Lever, J. 1980. Multiple methods of data collection: a note on divergence. Urban Life 10(2):199-214.

Lever, J. 1983. Soccer madness. University of Chicago Press, Chicago, Ill.

Lever, J., and S. Wheeler, 1984. The Chicago Tribune sports page, 1900-1975. Sociol. Sport J. 1(4):299-313.

Lever, J., and S. Wheeler. 1993. Mass media and the experience of sport. Communication Research 20(1):125-143.

Lewis, J.M. 1982. Fan violence: an American social problem. Res. Soc. Prob. Pub. Policy 2:175-206.

Lewis, M. 1972a. Sex differences in play behavior of the very young. J. Phy. Ed. Rec. 43(6):38-39.

Lewis, M. 1972b. Culture and gender roles: there is no unisex in the nursery. Psychol. Today 5(12):54-57.

Locke, L. 1962. Performance of administration oriented educators on selected psychological tests. Res. Q. 33(3):418-429.

Lombardo, B.J. 1982. The behavior of youth sport coaches: crises on the bench. ARENA Review 6(1):48-55.

Lopiano, D. 1984. A political analysis of the possibility of impact alternatives for the accomplishment of feminist objectives within American intercollegiate sport. ARENA Review 8(2):49-61.

Lopiano, D. 1991. Presentation at the Coaching America's Coaches Conference, United States Olympic Training Center, Colorado Springs, C.O.

Lopiano, D. 1992. The stars are lining up in support of gender equity in sport. GWS News 19(3):3-4, 15-16.

Lorenz, K. 1966. On aggression. Harcourt Brace Jovanovich, Inc., New York.

Loy, J. 1968. The nature of sport: a definitional effort. Quest 10:1-15.

Loy, J. 1969a. The study of sport and social mobility. In G. Kenyon, ed. Sociology of sport. The Athletic Institute, North Palm Beach, Fla.

Loy, J. 1969b. Social psychological characteristics of innovators. Am. Sociol. Rev. 34:73-82.

Loy, J. 1992. The dark side of agon: Men in tribal groups and the phenomenon of gang rape. Paper presented at the annual conference of the North American Society for the Sociology of Sport, Toledo (November).

Loy, J.W., J.E. Curtis, and G.H. Sage. 1978. Relative centrality of playing position and leadership recruitment in team sports. Exercise and Sport Science Reviews 6:257-284.

Loy, J., and J.R. McElvogue. 1970. Racial discrimination in American sport. Int. Rev. Sport Sociol. 5:5-23.

Loy, J., and G.H. Sage. 1973. Organizational prestige and coaching career patterns. Paper presented at the meetings of the Southern Sociological Society, Atlanta.

Lucas, J. 1992. Future of the Olympic Games. Human Kinetics Publishers, Inc. Champaign, Ill.

Lucas, J., and M. Real. 1984. Olympic television: a descriptive history of the interdependence of media and sports in the Summer Olympic Games, 1956-1984. Paper presented at the AAHPERD Conference, Anaheim, CA.

Lumpkin, A., and L.D. Williams. 1991. An analysis of Sports Illustrated feature articles, 1954-1987. Sociology of Sport Journal 8(1):16-32.

Macintosh, D. (with T. Bedecki and C.E.S. Franks). 1987. Sport and politics in Canada. McGill-Queens University Press, Kingston, Ontario.

Macintosh, D., and M. Hawes. 1992. The IOC and the world of interdependence. Olympika 1:29-45.

Macintosh, D., and D. Whitson. 1990. The game planners: Transforming Canada's sport system. McGill-Queens University Press, Kingston, Ontario.

MacNeill, M. 1988. Active women, media representations, and ideology. In J. Harvey and H. Cantelon, eds. Not just a game. University of Ottawa Press, Ottawa.

Maguire, J. 1986. The emergence of football spectating as a social problem, 1880-1985: a figurational and developmental perspective. Sociology of Sport Journal 3(3):217-244.

Maguire, J. 1988. Race and position assignment in English soccer: a preliminary analysis of ethnicity and sport in Britain. Sociology of Sport Journal 5(3):257-269.

Maguire, J. 1990. More than a sporting touchdown: The making of American football in England, 1982-1990. Sociology of Sport Journal 7(3):213-237.

Maguire, J. 1991a. Sport, racism and British society: A sociological study of England's elite male Afro/Caribbean soccer and Rugby Union players. In G. Jarvie (ed.), Sport, racism and ethnicity (pp. 94-123). The Falmer Press, London.

Maguire, J. 1991b. The media-sport production complex: The case of American football in Western European societies. European Journal of Communication 6(4):315-335.

Majors, R. 1986. Cool pose: The proud signature of black survival. Changing Men: Issues in Gender, Sex and Politics 17(winter):184-185.

Majors, R. 1991. Cool pose: Black masculinity and sports. In M.A. Messner, and D.F. Sabo (eds.). Sport, men, and the gender order (Pp. 109-114). Human Kinetics Publishers, Inc. Champaign, Ill.

Malcolmson, R.W. 1984. Sports in society: a historical perspective. Br. J. Sports Hist. 1(1):60-72.

Mandle, J.R., and J.D. Mandle. 1988. Grass roots commitment: basketball and society in Trinidad and Tobago. Caribbean Books, Parkersburg, IA.

Mandle, J.R., and J.D. Mandle. 1989. Volunteerism and commercialization in basketball: the case of Trinidad and Tobago. Sociol. Sport J. 6(2):113-124.

Mantel, R.C., and L. Vander Velden. 1974. The relationship between the professionalization of attitude toward play of preadolescent boys and participation in organized sport. In G.H. Sage, ed. Sport and American society. Addison-Wesley Publishing Co., Inc., Reading, Mass.

Marable, M. 1993. A new American socialism. The Progressive 57(2):20-25.

Mark, M.M., et al. 1983. Perceived injustice and sports violence. In J. Goldstein, ed. Sports violence. Springer-Verlag, New York.

Marsh, P. 1978. Aggro: The illusion of violence. Dent & Sons, London.

Marsh, P. 1982. Social order on the British soccer terraces. Int. Soc. Sci. J. 34(2):247-256.

Massengale, J. 1974. Coaching as an occupational subculture. Phi Delta Kappan 56(2):140-142.

Massengale, J. 1975. Occupational role conflict and the teacher/coach. Paper presented at the meetings of the Western Social Science Association, Denver.

Massengale, J. 1981. Role conflict and the teacher/coach: some occupational causes and considerations for the sport sociologist. In S. Greendorfer and A. Yiannakis, eds. Sociology of sport: diverse perspectives. Leisure Press, West Point, N.Y.

Mathes, S.A. 1982. Women coaches: endangered species? Paper presented at the meetings of the American Alliance for Health, Physical Education, Recreation and Dance, Houston.

Mathisen, J. 1990. Reviving "Muscular Christianity": Gil Dodds and the institutionalization of sport evangelism. Sociological Focus 23(3):233-249.

Mathisen, J. 1992. From civil religion to folk religion: The case of American sport. In S. Hoffman (ed.), Sport and religion (pp. 17-34). Human Kinetics Publishers, Inc. Champaign, Ill.

May, R. 1972. Power and innocence: a search for the sources of violence. W.W. Norton Co., Inc., New York.

McCall, M.M., and H.S. Becker. 1990. Introduction. In H.S. Becker and M.M. McCall (eds.), Symbolic interaction and cultural studies (pp. 1-15). University of Chicago Press, Chicago, Ill.

McCallum, J. 1988. The NBA will be going global—and soon. Sports Illustrated 69(20):58-63.

McClendon, M.J., and D.S. Eitzen. 1975. Interracial contact on collegiate basketball teams: a test of Sherif's theory of superordinate goals. Soc. Sci. Q. 55(4):926-938.

McCormack, J.B., and L. Chalip. 1988. Sport as socialization: a critique of methodological premises. The Social Science Journal 25(1):83-92.

McDermott, B. 1982. The glitter has gone. Sports Illustrated 57(20):82-96.

McDonald, M. (1992). Rethinking resistance: The Olympic Games and alternative models. Paper presented the annual conference of the North American Society for the Sociology of Sport, Toledo (November).

McGuire, R.T., Jr., and D.L. Cook. 1983. The influence of others and the decision to participate in youth sports. J. Sport Behav. 6(1):9-16.

McKay, J. 1990. The 'moral panic' of drugs in sport. Paper presented at the Australian Sociology Association Conference, Queensland (December).

McPherson, B. 1980. Retirement from professional sport: the process and problems of occupational and psychological adjustment. Sociol. Symp. 30:126-143.

McPherson, B. 1984. Sport participation across the life cycle: a review of the literature and suggestions for future research. Sociol. Sport J. 1(3):213-230.

McPherson, B. 1985. Socialization: toward a "new wave" of scholarly inquiry in a sport context. In A. Miracle and C.R. Rees, eds. Sport and sociological theory. Human Kinetics Publishers, Inc., Champaign, Ill.

McTeer, W. 1987. Intercollegiate athletes and student life: two studies in the Canadian case. ARENA Review 11(2):94-100.

Mead, C. 1985. Champion Joe Louis: black hero in white America. Charles Scribner's Sons, New York.

Mead, G.H. 1934. Mind, self, and society. University of Chicago Press, Chicago.

Medrich, E.A., et al. 1982. The serious business of growing up. University of California Press, Berkeley, Calif.

Meier, K. 1981. On the inadequacies of sociological definitions of sport. Int. Rev. Sport Sociol. 16(2):79-100.

Melnick, M. 1988. Racial segregation by playing position in the English football league: some preliminary observations. J. Sport Soc. Iss. 12(2):122-130.

Melnick, M. 1992. Male athletes and sexual assault. JOPERD 63(5):32-35.

Melnick, M.J., and D. Sabo. 1992. Sport and social mobility among African-American and Hispanic athletes. Unpublished manuscript.

Melnick, M.J., D. Sabo, and B. Vanfossen. 1992. Effects of interscholastic athletic participation on the social, educational, and career mobility of Hispanic girls and boys. International Review for the Sociology of Sport 27(1):57-75.

Melnick, M.J., B. Vanfossen, and D. Sabo. 1988. Developmental effects of athletic participation among high school girls. Sociology of Sport Journal 5(1):22-36.

Merchant, L. 1971. And every day you take another bite. Doubleday Publishing Co., New York.

Messing, M. 1978. The personality of the physical education teacher from the pupil's point of view. Paper presented at the International Scientific Congress on the Personality of the Physical Education Teacher, Olomouc, CSSR.

Messner, M. 1984. Review of Class, sports, and social development (Gruneau, 1983) and Sport, culture, and ideology (Hargreaves, ed., 1982). J. Sport Soc. Issues 8(1):49-51.

Messner, M. 1991. Women in the men's locker room. Changing Men: Issues in Gender, Sex and Politics 23 (Fall/Winter):56-58.

Messner, M.A. 1992. Power at play. Beacon Press, Boston.

Messner, M.A., and D.F. Sabo (eds.), 1992. Sport, men, and the gender order. Human Kinetics Publishers, Inc. Champaign, Ill.

Meyer, B.B. 1988. The college experience: female athletes and nonathletes. Paper presented at the North American Society for the Sociology of Sport Conference, Cincinnati.

Meyer, B.B. 1990. From idealism to actualization: the academic performance of female collegiate athletes. Sociol. Sport J. 7(1):(in press).

Michener, J. 1976. Sports in America. Random House, Inc., New York.

Miles, G. 1991. Prep sports could lose budget race. USA Today, July 30, Section C (Cover Story).

Miller Lite Report on American Attitudes Toward Sports. 1983. Miller Brewing Co., Milwaukee.

Miracle, A. 1978. Functions of school athletics: boundary maintenance and system integration. In M.A. Salter, ed. Play: anthropological perspectives. Leisure Press, West Point, N.Y.

Miracle, A. 1980. School spirit as a ritual by-product: views from applied anthropology. In H.B. Schwartzman, ed. Play and culture. Leisure Press, West Point, N.Y.

Miracle, A. 1981. Factors affecting interracial cooperation: A case study of a high school football team. Human Organization 40(2):150-154.

Moore, 1990. Sons of the wind. Sports Illustrated 72(8):72-84.

Morgan, W.P. 1984. Physical activity and mental health. In H.M. Eckert and H.J. Montoye, eds. Exercise and health (The American Academy of Physical Education Papers). Human Kinetics Publishers, Champaign, Ill.

Morris, D. 1967. The naked ape. Jonathon Cape, Ltd., London.

Morris, D. 1981. The soccer tribe. Chatto, Bodley Head & Jonathon Cape, Ltd., London.

Mrozek, D.J. 1983. Sport and American mentality, 1880-1920. University of Tennessee Press, Knoxville.

Murphy, P., J. Williams, and E. Dunning. 1990. Football on trial: Spectator violence and development in the world of football. Routledge, London.

Muscatine, A. 1991. The status of women's sports. Women's Sports Pages 3(4):12-13, 18.

Nack, W., and L. Munson. 1992. Blood money. Sports Illustrated 77(21):18-30.

Nash, H.L. 1987. Do compulsive runners and anorectic patients share common bonds? The Physician and Sportsmedicine 15(12):162-167.

Navratilova, M. 1984. Now, you can quote me. World Tennis 31(12):43.

Neal, W. 1981. The handbook on athletic perfection. Mott Media, Milford, Mich.

Neil, G.I. 1975. 1981. Superstitious behavior among ice hockey players and coaches: an explanation. The Physical Educator 32:26-27.

Neil, G.I. 1982. Demystifying sport superstition. Int. Rev. Sport Sociol. 17:99-124.

Neil, G.I., B. Anderson, & W. Sheppard. Superstitions among male and female athletes of various levels of involvement. Journal of Sport Behavior 4(3):137-148.

Nelson, M.B. 1991. Are we winning yet? Random House, New York.

Nelson, L.L., and S. Kagan. 1972. Competition: The star spangled scramble. Psychology Today 6(4):53-56, 90-91.

Nixon, H. 1984. Sport and the American Dream. Leisure Press, New York.

Nixon, H.L., II. 1991. Accepting the risks and pain of sports injuries: Understanding the nature of "consent" to play. Paper presented at the annual conference of the North American Society for the Sociology of Sport, Milwaukee (November).

Nixon, H.L., II. 1993. A social network analysis of influences on athletes to play with pain and injuries. J. of Sport and Social Issues 16(2):127-135.

Norton, K., and M. Wilkerson. 1975. Christianity's super-salesman: the athlete. Paper presented at the meetings of the Southwestern Sociological Association, San Antonio, Tex.

Nosanchuk, T.A. 1981. The way of

the warrior: the effects of traditional martial arts training on aggressiveness. Human Relations 34(6):435-444.

Novak, M. 1976. The joy of sports. Basic Books, Inc., Publishers, New York.

Ogilvie, B., and T. Tutko. 1966. Problem athletes and how to handle them. Pelham Books, Ltd., London.

Ogilvie, B., and T. Tutko. 1971. Sport: if you want to build character, try something else. Psychology Today 5(5):61-63.

Oliver, M. 1980. Race, class and the family's orientation to mobility through sport. Sociol. Symp. 30:62-86.

Opie, I., and P. Opie. 1969. Children's games in street and playground. Oxford University Press, Fair Lawn, N.J.

Orlick, T. 1978. The cooperative sports and games book. Writers and Readers Publishing Cooperative, London.

Orlick, T., and C. Botterill. 1975. Every kid can win. Nelson-Hall Co., Chicago.

Otto, L., and D. Alwin. 1977. Athletics, aspirations and attainments. Sociol. Education 42:102-113.

Oxendine, J.B. 1988. American Indian sports heritage. Human Kinetics Publishers, Inc., Champaign, Ill.

Parkhouse, B.L., and J.M. Williams. 1986. Differential effects of sex and status on evaluation of coaching ability. Research Quarterly for Exercise and Sport 57(1):53-59.

Passer, M.W. 1982. Children in sport: participation motives and psychological stress. Quest 33(2):231-244.

Pastore, D.L., and M.R. Judd. 1992. Burnout in coaches of women's team sports. JOPERD 63(5):74-79.

Patrick, D. 1991. Star decathlete defies easy lables. USA Today, Dec. 16 (Special issue: Race & Sports—Myth & Reality).

Pearman, W.A. 1978. Race on the sports page. Rev. Sport and Leisure 3(2):54-68.

Pepitone, E. 1980. Children in cooperation and competition. Lexington Books, Lexington, Mass.

Phillips, D.P. 1983. The impact of

mass media violence on U.S. homicides. American Sociological Review 48(4):560-568.

Picou, S., V. McCarter, and F. Howell. 1985. Do high school athletics pay? some further evidence. Sociol. Sport J. 2(1):72-76.

Pilz, G. 1979. Attitudes toward different forms of violent and aggressive behavior in competitive sports: two empirical studies. J. Sport Behav. 2(1):3-26.

Podilchak, W. 1982. Youth sport involvement: impact on informal game participation. In A.O. Dunleavy, A. Miracle, and R. Rees, eds. Studies in the sociology of sport. Texas Christian University Press, Fort Worth, Tex.

Ponomaryov, N.I. 1981. Sport and society. Moscow, Progress Publishers (and Imported Publications, Inc., Chicago, Ill.) (translated by J. Riordan).

Pope, H.G., and D.L. Katz. 1988. Affective and psychotic symptoms associated with anabolic steroid use. Am. J. Psychiatry 145(4):487-490.

Prebish, C.S. 1984. "Heavenly Father, Divine Goalie," sport and religion. Antioch Rev 42(3):306-318.

Prisuta, R.A. 1979. Televised sports and political values. J. Communication 29(1):95-102.

Pritchard, T. 1984. The Dean and his students. Family Weekly, March 11:13-17.

Pronger, B. 1990. The arena of masculinity: Sports, homosexuality, and the meaning of sex. St. Martin's Press, New York.

Purdy, D. 1988. For whom sport tolls: players, owners, and fans. The World & I 3(10):573-587.

Pyros, J. 1987. Review of J. Feinstein (1986), A season on the brink. Arete: A Journal of Sport Literature 5(1):204-205.

Rabey, S. 1992. Competing for souls in Barcelona. Colorado Springs Gazette Telegraph, August 8.

Rader, B.G. 1983. American sports. Prentice-Hall, Inc., Englewood Cliffs, N.J.

Rader, B. 1984. In its own image: how television has transformed sports. Free Press, New York.

Rainville, R.E., and E. McCormick. 1977. Extent of covert racial prejudice in pro football announcers' speech. Journalism Q. 54(1):20-26.

Raji, K. 1992. The battle for a brave new world has just begun: TEAMWORK South Africa—hope for positive change. CSSS Digest 4(3):1, 5.

Ralbovsky, M. 1974. Destiny's darlings. Hawthorn Books, Inc., New York.

Ramsamy, S. 1984. Apartheid, boycotts and the Games. In A. Tomlinson and G. Whannel (eds.), Five ring circus: Money, power and politics at the olympic Games (pp. 44-52). Pluto Press, London.

Rankin, J.H. 1980. School factors and delinquency: interactions by age and sex. Sociology and Social Research 64(3):420-434.

Real, M.R. 1989. Super media: A cultural studies approach. Sage Publications, Newbury Park, Calif.

Rees, C.R., F.M. Howell, and A.W. Miracle. 1990. Do high school sports build character? Journal of Social Science 27(3):303-315.

Reich, A.A. 1974. International understanding through sports. U.S. Department of State Bull. 70:460-465.

Rejeski, W., et al. 1979. Pygmalion in youth sport: a field study. J. Sport Psychol. 1(4):311-319.

Retton, M.L. 1992. Family a big matter for every Olympian. USA Today, August 5:6E.

Richmond, P. 1986. Weighing the odds. Colorado Springs Gazette Telegraph, January 19:F1-F4.

Riordan, J. 1985. Some comparisons of women's sport in East and West. International Review for the Sociology of Sport 20(1,2):117-126.

Roberts, G. 1983. Understanding the motivation of children in competitive sport: the problem of dropping out. Paper presented at the National Recreation and Parks Association Fourth National Forum on Youth Sports, Chicago.

Roberts, G., et al. 1981. An analysis of motivation in children's sport: the role of perceived competence in participation. J. Sport Psychol. 3(3): 206-216.

Robinson, J. 1972. I never had it made. G.P. Putnam's Sons, New York.

Robinson, T.T., and A.V. Carron. 1982. Personal and situational factors associated with dropping out versus maintaining participation in competitive sport. J. Sport Psychol. 4(4):364-378.

Rosen, L.W., et al. 1986. Pathogenic weight-control behavior in female athletes. The Physician and Sportsmedicine 14(1):79-84.

Ross, J., and R.R. Pate. 1987. A summary of findings (for the National Children and Youth Fitness Study II). JOPERD 58(9):51-56.

Ruck, R. 1987. Sandlot seasons: Sport in Black Pittsburgh. University of Illinois Press, Urbana, Ill.

Russell, G.W. 1983. Psychological issues in sports aggression. In J. Goldstein, ed. Sport violence. Springer-Verlag, New York.

Sabo, D. 1986. Pigskin, patriarchy and male identity. Changing Men: Issues in Gender, Sex and Politics 16 (summer):24-25.

Sabo, D. 1988. Title IX and athletics: sex equity in schools. Updating School Board Policies 19(10):1-3.

Sabo, D., M.J. Melnick, and B. Vanfossen. 1993. The influence of high school athletic participation on postsecondary and occupational mobility: A focus on race and gender. Sociology of Sport Journal 10(1):44-56.

Sabo, D.F., and R. Runfola. 1980. Jock: sports and male identity. Prentice-Hall, Inc., Englewood Cliffs, N.J.

Sabock, R.J. 1979. The coach. W.B. Saunders, Philadelphia.

Sack, A. 1987. College sport and the student-athlete. Journal of Sport and Social Issues 11(1,2):31-48.

Sack, A., and R. Thiel. 1979. College football and social mobility: a case study of Notre Dame football players. Sociol. Ed. 52(1):60-66.

Sack, A., and R. Thiel. 1985. College basketball and role conflict: a national study. Sociol. Sport J. 2(3):195-209.

Sadler, W.A. 1977. Alienated youth and creative sports experiences. J. of the Philosophy of Sport 4:83-95.

Sage, G.H. 1974a. Machiavellianism among college and high school coaches. In G.H. Sage, ed. Sport and American society. Addison-Wesley Publishing Co., Inc., Reading, Mass.

Sage, G.H. 1974b. Value orientations of American college coaches compared to male college students and businessmen. In G.H. Sage, ed. Sport and American society. Addison-Wesley Publishing Co., Reading, Mass.

Sage, G.H. 1975a. Socialization of coaches: antecedents to coaches' beliefs and behaviors. In 78th Proceedings of the National Collegiate Physical Education Association for Men, Washington, D.C.

Sage, G.H. 1975b. An occupational analysis of the college coach. In D.W. Ball and J. Loy, eds. Sport and social order. Addison-Wesley Publishing Co., Inc., Reading, Mass.

Sage, G.H. 1980. Sociology of physical educator/coaches: the personal attributes controversy. Res. Q. Exerc. Sport 51(1):110-121.

Sage, G.H. 1987. The social world of high school coaches: multiple role demands and their consequences. Sociology of Sport Journal 4(3):213-228.

Sage, G.H. 1988. Sports participation as a builder of character? The World & I 3(10):629-641.

Sage, G.H. 1990. Power and ideology in American sport: A critical perspective. Human Kinetics Books, Champaign, Ill.

Savage, H., ed. 1929. American college athletics (Bulletin No. 23). Carnegie Foundation, New York.

Sawyer, Tom (ed.) 1992. Coaching education in North America. Special feature in JOPERD 63(7), 34-64.

Scanlon, T.K., and M.W. Passer. 1978. Factors related to competitive stress among male youth sport participants. Med. Sci. Sports 10(2):103-108.

Scanlon, T.K., and M.W. Passer. 1979. Sources of competitive stress in young female athletes. J. Sport Psychol. 1(2):151-159.

Schaap, D. 1982. The man who would not fight. Parade Magazine, pp. 4-7, May 9.

Schafer, W.E. 1969. Some social sources and consequences of interscholastic athletics: the case of participation and delinquency. In G. Kenyon, ed. Aspects of contemporary sport sociology. The Athletic Institute, Chicago.

Schuetz, R. 1976. Sports, technology and gambling. In W.R. Eadington, ed. Gambling and society. Charles C Thomas, Springfield, Ill.

Scott, J. 1971. The athletic revolution. Macmillan, Inc., New York.

Scraton, S. 1987. "Boys muscle in where angels fear to tread"—girls' subcultures and physical activities. In J. Horne, et al., eds. Sport, leisure and social relations. Routledge & Kegan Paul, New York (Sociological Review Monograph 33).

Segrave, J. 1986. Do organized sports programs deter delinquency? JOPERD 57(1):16-17.

Segrave, J., and D. Chu. 1978. Athletics and juvenile delinquency. Review of Sport and Leisure 3(2):1-24.

Segrave, J., and D.N. Hastad. 1982. Delinquent behavior and interscholastic athletic participation. Journal of Sport Behavior 5(2):96-111.

Segrave, J., C. Moreau, and D.N. Hastad. 1985. An investigation into the relationship between ice hockey participation and delinquency. Sociology of Sport Journal 2(4):281-298.

Selman, R.L. 1971. Taking another's perspective: role taking development in early childhood. Child Dev. 42:1721-1734.

Selman, R.L. 1976. Social-cognitive understanding: a guide to educational and clinical practice. In T. Lickona, ed. Moral development and behavior. Holt, Rinehart & Winston, New York.

Seltzer, R., and W. Glass. 1991. International politics and judging in Olympic skating events: 1968-1988. Journal of Sport Behavior 14(3):189-200.

Semyonov, M. 1984. Sport and beyond: ethnic inequalities in attainment. Sociology of Sport Journal 1(4):358-365.

Seppanen, P. 1984. The Olympics: a sociological perspective. International Review for the Sociology of Sport 19(2):113-128.

Sewart, J. 1987. The commodification of sport. International Review for the Sociology of Sport 22(3):171-192.

Shaiken, B. 1988. Sport and politics. Praeger, New York.

Shapiro, B.J. 1984. Intercollegiate athletic participation and academic achievement: a case study of Michigan State University student-athletes, 1950-1980. Sociol. Sport J. 1(1):46-51.

Sherif, C.W. 1976. The social context of competition. In D. Landers, ed. Social problems in athletics. University of Illinois Press, Urbana, Ill.

Sherif, C., and G.D. Rattray. 1976. Psychosocial development and activity in middle childhood (5-12 years). In J.G. Albinson, and G.M. Andrews, eds. Child in sport and physical activity. University Park Press, Baltimore.

Silva, J. 1983. The perceived legitimacy of rule violating behavior in sport. J. Sport Psychol. 5(4):438-448.

Sipes, R.G. 1975. War, combative sports, and aggression: a preliminary causal model of cultural patterning. In Nettleship, M.A., et al., eds. War: its causes and correlates. Mouton, The Hague.

Sipes, R.G. 1976. Sports as a control for aggression. In T.T. Craig, ed. Humanistic and mental health aspects of sports, exercise, and recreation. American Medical Association, Chicago.

Smith, G.T., and C. Blackman. 1978. Sport in the mass media. CAPHER, Vanier City, Ottawa.

Smith, M. 1974. Significant others influence on the assaultive behavior of young hockey players. Int. Rev. Sport Sociol. 9(3-4):45-56.

Smith, M. 1983. Violence and sport. Butterworths, Toronto.

Smith, N.J. 1980. Excessive weight loss and food aversion in athletes simulating anorexia nervosa. Pediatrics 66 (1):139-142.

Snyder, E.E. 1972. High school athletes and their coaches: educational plans and advice. Sociol. Ed. 45:313-325.

Snyder, E.E., and D. Purdy. 1982.

Socialization into sport: parent and child reverse and reciprocal effects. Res. Q. Exerc. Sport 53(3):263-266.

Snyder, E.E., and E. Spreitzer, 1983. Social aspects of sport. Prentice-Hall, Inc. Englewood Cliffs, NJ.

Solomon, A. 1991. Passing game: How lesbians are being purged from women's college hoops. Women's Sports Pages, March:8, 13.

Spady, W.G. 1970. Lament for the letterman: effects of peer status and extracurricular activities on goals and achievement. Am. J. Sociol. 75:680-702.

Sperber, M. 1990. College Sports, Inc.: The athletic department vs the university. Henry Holt and Company, New York.

Spreitzer, E. 1992. Does participation in interscholastic athletics affect adult development: A longitudinal analysis of an 18-24 age cohort. Paper presented at the annual conference of the American Sociological Association, Pittsburgh (August).

Stacey, J. 1987. Most watched sports on TV. USA Today, January 23, Section C.

State of Michigan. 1978. Joint legislative study on youth sport programs (phase II: agency sponsored sports), Ann Arbor, Mich.

Stavely, D. 1975. The game plan. FCA Devotional, Denver.

Steinbrecher, W.L., et al. 1978. Students' perception of the coaches' role in athletics. Phys. Ed. 35(1):11-14.

Stevenson, C. 1975. Socialization effects of participation in sport: a critical review of the literature. Res. Q. 46(3):287-301.

Stevenson, C. 1976. Institutional socialization and college sport. Res. Q. 47(1):1-8.

Stevenson, C. 1985. College athletics and "character": the decline and fall of socialization research. In D. Chu, et al., eds. Sport and higher education. Human Kinetics Publishers, Inc., Champaign, Ill.

Stevenson, C. 1990a. The athletic career: Some contingencies of sport specialization. Journal of Sport Behavior 13(2):103-113.

Stevenson, C.L. 1990b. The early careers of international athletes. Soci-

ology of Sport Journal 7(3); 238-253.

Stevenson, C. 1991a. The Christian-athlete: An interactionist-developmental analysis. Sociology of Sport J. 8(4):362-379.

Stevenson, C. 1991b. Christianity as a hegemonic and counter-hegemonic device in elite sport. Paper presented at Conference of the North American Society for the Sociology of Sport, Milwaukee (November).

Stewart, C.C., & L. Sweet. 1992. Professional preparation of high school coaches: The problem continues. JOPERD 63(6):75-79.

Stillwell, J.L. 1979. Why P.E. majors want to coach. JOPERD 50(9):80.

Stingley, J. 1972. Recreation boom threatens to bust the city's seams. Los Angeles Times, Aug. 20.

Stoddard, B. 1986. Saturday afternoon fever. Angus and Robertson Publishers, North Ryde, NSW, Australia.

Stone, G. 1955. American sports: play and display. Chicago Rev. 9:83-100.

Surface, B. 1977. Get the rook! New York Times Magazine, section 6, pp. 14-15, Jan. 9.

Swain, D.A. 1991. Withdrawal from sport and Schlossberg's model of transitions. Sociology of Sport Journal 8(2):152-160.

Swift, E.M. 1986. Hockey? Call it sockey. Sports Illustrated 64(7):12-17.

Swift, E.M. 1991. Why Johnny can't play. Sports Illustrated 75(13):60-72.

Tatum, J. (with B. Kushner) 1979. They call me assassin. Everest House, New York.

Taub, D.E. and E. Blinde. 1993. Sport participation and women's personal empowerment: Experiences of the college athlete. Journal of Sport and Social Issues (forthcoming)

Taylor, I. 1982. On the sports violence question: soccer hooliganism revisited. In J. Hargreaves, ed. Sport, culture and ideology. Routledge & Kegan Paul, London.

Taylor, I. 1987. Putting the boot into a working class sport: British soccer after Bradford and Brussels. Sociology of Sport Journal 4(2):171-191.

Telander, R. 1984. The written word:

player-press relationships in American sports. Sociol. Sport J. 1(1):3-14.

Telander, R. 1988. Heaven is a playground. A Fireside Book, New York.

Telander, R. 1989. The hundred yard lie. Simon and Schuster, New York.

Temple, K. 1992. Brought to you by.... Notre Dame Magazine 21(2):29.

The Economist, 1992. Special Issue on Money in Sports. Vol. 324, No. 7769 (July 25-31).

Theberge, N. 1980. A critique of critiques: radical and feminist writings on sport. Social Forces 60(2):341-353.

Theberge, N. 1984. Joining social theory to social action: some Marxist principles. ARENA Review 8(2):21-30.

Theberge, N. 1987. Sports and women's empowerment. Women's Studies International Forum 10(4): 387-393.

Theberge, N. 1989. A feminist analysis of responses to sports violence: media coverage of the 1987 World Junior Hockey Championship. Sociology of Sport Journal 6(3):247-256.

Theberge, N. 1990. Gender, work, and power: the case of women in coaching. Canadian J. of Social. 15(1):59-75.

Theberge, N. 1993. The construction of gender in sport: Women, coaching, and the naturalization of difference. Social Problems 40(3):401-413.

Theberge, N., and A. Cronk. 1986. Work routines in newspaper sports departments and the coverage of women's sports. Sociology of Sport Journal 3(3):195-203.

Thirer, J. 1978. The effect of observing filmed violence on the aggressive attitudes of female athletes and nonathletes. J. Sport Behav. 1(1):28-36.

Thirer, J., and H. Ross. 1981. Examining the degree of on and off field social interaction between black and white male intercollegiate athletes. Paper presented at the meetings of the North American Society for the Sociology of Sport, Fort Worth, Tex.

Thirer, J., and P.J. Wieczorek. 1984. On and off field social interaction patterns of black and white high school athletes. J. Sport Behav. 7(3):105-114.

Thirer, J., and S.D. Wright. 1985. Sport and social status for adolescent males and females. Sociol. Sport J. 2(2):164-171.

Thomas, C.E., and K.L. Ermler. 1988. Institutional obligations in the athletic retirement process. Quest 40(2):137-150.

Thomas, R.M. 1990. 500 are female writers. New York Times, 10/3:B9, B11.

Thorlindsson, T. 1989. Sport participation, smoking, and drug and alcohol abuse among Icelandic youth. Sociology of Sport Journal 6(2):136-143.

Todd, T. 1983. The steroid predicament. Sports Illustrated 59(5):62-78.

Todd, T. 1987. Anabolic steroids: the gremlins of sport. Journal of Sport History 14(1):87-107.

Tolbert, C.M., II. 1975. The black athlete in the Southwest Conference: a study of institutional racism. Doctoral dissertation, Baylor University, Waco, Tex.

Tomlinson, A. 1984. De Cubertin and the modern Olympics. In A. Tomlinson and G. Whannel (eds.), Five ring circus: Money, power and politics at the Olympic Games (pp. 84-97). Pluto Press, London.

Tomlinson, A., and G. Whannel (eds.) 1984. Five ring circus: Money, power and politics at the Olympic Games. Pluto Press, London.

Tomlinson, A. 1986. Going global: the FIFA story. In A. Tomlinson and G. Whannel (eds.), Off the ball (pp. 83-98). Pluto Press, London.

Trujillo, C.M. 1983. The effect of weight training and running exercise intervention programs on the self-esteem of college women. Int. J. Sport Psychol. 14:162-173.

Trulson, M.E. 1986. Martial arts training: a novel "cure" for juvenile delinquency. Human Relations 39(12): 1131-1140.

United States Olympic Committee.

1992. USOC Drug Education and Doping Control Program: Guide to Banned Medications. USOC, Colorado Springs, Colo.

Unkel, M.B. 1981. Physical recreation participation of females and males during the adult life cycle. Leisure Sciences 4(1):1-27.

Vanderzwaag, H.J. 1972. Toward a philosophy of sport. Addison-Wesley Publishing Co., Inc., Reading, Mass.

Vaz, E.W. 1982. The professionalization of young hockey players, University of Nebraska Press, Lincoln.

Veblen, T. 1899. The theory of the leisure class. Macmillan Co., New York (*see also 1953 paperback edition, A Mentor Book, New York*).

Vertinsky, P.A. 1987. Exercise, physical capability, and the eternally wounded woman in late nineteenth century North America. Journal of Sport History 14(1):7-27.

Vertinsky, P.A. 1992. Reclaiming space, revisioning the body: The quest for gender-sensitive physical education. Quest 44(3):373-396.

Vinokur, M.B. 1988. More than a game: Sports and politics. Greenwood Press, Westport, Conn.

Voy, R. 1991. Drugs, sport, and politics. Leisure Press, Champaign, IL.

Vuolle, P. 1977. Influence of mass media on people's sport behavior in Finland. 7th International Seminar on Sports and Leisure, Warsaw.

Wacquant, L.J.D. 1992. The social logic of boxing in Black Chicago: Toward a sociology of pugilism. Sociology of Sport Journal 9(3):221-254.

Wadler, G.I., and B. Hainline. 1989. Drugs and the athlete. F.A. Davis Company, Philadelphia.

Wagner, G.G. 1987. Sport as a means for reducing the cost of illness—some theoretical, statistical, and empirical remarks. International Review for the Sociology of Sport 22(3):217-227.

Walsh, J.M., and A.V. Carron. 1977. Attributes of volunteer coaches. Paper presented at the meetings of the Canadian Association of Sport Sciences, Winnipeg.

Walter, T.L., et al. 1987. Predicting the academic success of college athletes. Research Quarterly for Exercise and Sport 58(2):273-279.

Warner, G. 1979. Clobber thy neighbor. Eternity 30(3):17-19, 33-39.

Wasielewski, P.L. 1991. Not quite normal, but not really deviant: Some notes on the comparison of elite athletes and women political activists. Deviant Behavior: An Interdisciplinary Journal 12:81-95.

Watson, G.G., and R. Collis. 1982. Adolescent values in sport: a case of conflicting interest. Int. Rev. Sport Sociol. 3:73-89.

Webb, B.L. 1973. The basketball man: James Naismith. The Regents Press of Kansas, Lawrence.

Webb, H. 1969. Professionalization of attitudes toward play among adolescents. In G. Kenyon, ed. Aspects of contemporary sport sociology. The Athletic Institute, North Palm Beach, Fla.

Weinberg, S.K., and H. Arond. 1952. The occupational culture of the boxer. Am. J. Sociol. 57:460-469.

Weiss, M.R., and B.L. Sisley. 1984. Where have all the coaches gone? Sociology of Sport Journal 1(4):332-347.

Wenner, L.A. 1989. The Super Bowl Pregame Show: Cultural fantasies and political subtext. In L.A. Wenner (ed.), Media, sports, and society (pp. 157-179). Sage Publications, Newbury Park, CA.

White, A. 1981. Sport in England and America: a cross cultural perspective. Unpublished paper.

White, A. 1982. Soccer hooliganism in Britain. Quest 34(2):154-164.

White, A., et al. 1992. Women and sport: A consultation document. The Sports Council, London.

White, A., and C. Brackenridge. 1985. Who rules sport? Gender divisions in the power structure of British

sports organizations from 1960. International Review for the Sociology of Sport 20(1,2):95-108.

Whitson, D. 1991. Sport in the social construction of masculinity. In M.A. Messner and D.F. Sabo (eds.), Sport, men, and the gender order (Pp. 19-30). Human Kinetics Publishers, Inc. Champaign, Ill.

Whitson, D., and D. Macintosh. 1989. Gender & power: Explanations of gender inequalities in Canadian national sport organizations. International Review for the Sociology of Sport 24(2):137-149.

Weiberg, S. 1991. Graduation rates: a closer look. USA Today, July 3:9D.

Wieberg, S. 1992. Study reveals nagging problems. USA Today, July 6:8C.

Wieberg, S., and T. Witosky. 1991. Most college sports lose money game. USA Today, Oct. 14 (Cover story, Section C).

Wiggins, D.K. 1983. The 1936 Olympic Games in Berlin: the response of America's black press. Res. Q. Exerc. Sport 54(3):278-292.

Williams, J., E. Dunning, and P. Murphy. 1984. Hooligans abroad. Routledge & Kegan Paul, Boston.

Williams, R.L., and Z.I. Youssef. 1972. Consistency in football coaches in stereotyping the personality of each position's player. Int. J. Sport Psychol. 3(1):3-11.

Williams, R.L., and Z.I. Youssef. 1975. Division of labor in college football along racial lines. Int. J. Sport Psychol. 6(1):3-13.

Williams, R.L., and Z.I. Youssef. 1979. Race and position assignment in high school, college and professional football. Int. J. Sport Psychol. 10(4):252-258.

Williamson, K.M., and N. Georgiadis. 1992. Teaching an inner-city after-school program. JOPERD 63(8):14-18.

Willis, P.E. 1981. Learning to labor: how working class kids get working class jobs. Teachers College Press, New York.

Wohl, A. 1970. Competitive sport and its social functions. Int. Rev. Sport Sociol. 5:117-124.

Wohl, A. 1979. Sport and social development. Int. Rev. Sport Sociol. 14(3-4):5-18.

Womack, M. 1992. Why athletes need ritual: A study of magic among professional athletes. In S. Hoffman (ed.), Sport and religion (pp. 191-202). Human Kinetics Publishers, Inc. Champaign, Ill.

Women's Sports Pages. 1991. Yet another study shows women receive less coverage. Vol. 3, No. 4.

Woodman, W.F. 1977. An adapted model of the sport participation choice process. Res. Q. 48(2):452-460.

Woodward, S. 1991. Zmeskal the lion' coach Karolyi never had. USA Today, September 9.

Yablonsky, L., and J. Brower. 1979. The little league game. Times Books, New York.

Yeager, R.C. 1979. Seasons of shame. McGraw-Hill Book Co., New York.

Yetman, N., and D.S. Eitzen. 1984. Racial dynamics in American sport: continuity and change. In D.S. Eitzen, ed. Sport in contemporary society, 2nd ed. St. Martin's Press, New York.

Zillmann, D., et al. 1974. Provoked and unprovoked aggression in athletes. J. Res. Pers. 8(2):139-152.

Zimmer, J. 1984. Courting the gods of sport. Psychology Today 18(7):36-39.

Zipter, Y. 1988. Diamonds are a dyke's best friend. Firebrand Books, Ithaca, N.Y.

NAME INDEX

A

Aburdene, P., 459
Acker, J., 37, 38
Acosta, R.V., 217, 218, 285
Adler, Patricia, 51, 126, 394, 398, 399, 418
Adler, Peter, 51, 126, 394, 398, 399, 418
Agassi, A., 302
Akebano, 282, 283
Albinson, J.G., 132
Allen, G., 386
Allison, M., 91, 103
Althiede, D., 351
Althouse, R., 272
Alwin, D.F., 294
Anderson, C., 41
Anderson, D., 347
Andrews, G.M., 132
Arbena, J., 272
Archer, R. 377
Ardrey, R., 164
Arond, H., 287
Ash, M., 116, 133
Ashe, A., 239, 255, 272, 274, 354, 416, 444
Axthelm, P., 264

B

Baade, R., 315
Bain, L., 191
Baker, W., 52, 56-60, 75
Ball, D., 7
Ballinger, L., 248
Barkley, C. 77, 242, 350
Barnett, C., 347
Barney, R.K., 385
Barr, S., 213
Bartell, T., 301
Beamish, R., 277, 312, 319, 329
Becker, B., 418
Becker, H., 45, 47
Becker, J., 434
Bedecki, T., 385
Bellmon, H., 208

Bender, D., 156, 157
Benedict, J.R., 251
Benedict, R., 90, 91
Berghorn, F., 250
Berkowitz, L., 171, 181
Berlage, G., 116
Bernay, T., 224
Berryman, J., 105
Best, C., 250
Bigger, C., 80, 192
Bindman, S., 345
Birke, L.I., 227, 231
Birrell, S., 34, 41, 42, 51, 83, 223, 224, 236, 237, 248, 271, 450
Bissinger, H. G., 391, 392, 418
Blackman, C., 337
Blair, S. 119
Blanchard, K., 75
Blinde, E., 223, 231, 299, 346
Bloom, M., 120, 121
Bock, H., 174, 248
Bolin, A., 228, 229
Botterill, C., 94, 127, 133
Bouillon, A., 377
Bourdieu, P. 275
Boutilier, M., 216, 237, 346
Bouton, J., 352
Brackenridge, C., 218
Braddock, J., 290, 291, 294, 347, 393
Brady, E., 402
Brecker, B., 232
Bredemeier, B., 97, 98, 145, 172, 176, 177, 187, 344, 393
Brock, S.C., 300
Brohm, J-M., 32, 50
Brooks, D., 272
Brower, J., 116, 133, 312
Brown, B., 122
Brown, J.N., 177
Brown, P., 197
Brownell, K., 213
Bruns, W., 103, 133
Bryant, J., 109, 332
Bryson, L., 38, 176, 223, 224
Buhrmann, H., 146, 434
Burdge, R., 452

Burridge, K., 90
Burroughs, E.R., 244
Bush, P., 150, 161
Butkus, D., 173
Butt, S.D., 97
Byrd, G., 420

C

Callois, R., 23
Calvin, J., 428
Campanis, A., 239, 292
Campbell, T., 107, 159, 224
Cantelon, H., 51, 329, 357, 384
Cantor, D.W., 224
Caplan, P., 113
Capouya, J., 439
Carlston, D., 108
Carnera, P., 243
Carpenter, L., 217, 218, 285
Carroll, J., 178
Carron, A., 122, 191, 197, 206
Case, B., 395, 401
Cashmore, E., 272
Cavallo, D., 68, 75
Cembalisty, J., 180
Chafetz, J., 112
Chaiken, T.,
Chalip, L., 93, 132, 133
Chandler, J., 345, 357, 390
Charles I., 61
Charnofsky, H., 267
Chase, M., 126
Chatrier, P., 302
Cheska, A., 75
Chopra, R., 386
Chu, D., 199, 266, 267, 385, 418
Claeys, U., 342, 357
Clark, N., 213
Clarke, A., 332, 357
Clarke, J., 332, 357
Clift, E., 286
Clinton, H.R., 286
Coakley, J., 41, 44, 45, 51, 89, 93, 103, 106, 116, 118, 119, 122-124, 132, 140, 156, 161, 173, 181, 224,

230, 235, 278, 294, 296, 298, 299, 301, 379, 426, 431, 434, 442, 459
Cole, C., 8, 51, 156, 213, 223, 237
Coleman, J., 390
Collins, B., 97
Collins, N., 220
Collis, R., 122
Condor, R., 347
Connell, R.W., 176
Connelly, H., 151
Cook, D., 94, 122
Cosby, B., 328
Courson, S., 156
Cousy, B., 101
Critcher, C., 43
Cronk, A., 346
Csikszentmihalyi, M., 22
Curry, T., 46, 140, 146, 227, 347
Curtis, J., 250

D

D'Angelo, R., 350
Darwin, C., 243
Davies, N., 177
Davis, L. 220
DeCoubertin, P., 360
Deem, R., 224, 279
Deford, F., 440, 443
DeKoven, B., 132
Denny, H., 156
Devall, B., 452
Devereux, E., 118
DiPasquale, M.G., 134, 154, 156, 157, 161
Disch, L.J., 347
Ditka, M., 164
Dobie, M., 279
Domi, T., 178
Donnelly, P., 34, 40, 45, 51, 140, 145
Donohoe, T., 150, 155, 161
Downs, A., 113
Drummer, G.M., 126
Dubois, P., 98, 204, 294
Duda, J., 91
Duncan, M.C., 342, 345, 346,
Dundee, C., 280
Dunivan, K., 400
Dunning, E., 51, 75, 102, 144, 187, 188
Duguin, M., 177
Dyer, K., 237, 460

E

Easley., K., 152
Eckland, B., 294
Eder, D., 390

Edwards, H., 23, 182, 194, 262, 264, 272, 291, 401, 416, 423, 444, 460
Eichberg, H., 376, 385
Eisen, G., 294, 299
Eitzen, D.S., 65, 93, 103, 128, 161, 191, 214, 250, 252, 270, 319, 390, 394, 401, 414
Elias, N., 51, 55, 75, 102, 144
Elliott, T., 134
Erickson, D., 386
Ermler, K.L., 299
Euripides, 52
Evans, J., 107
Evert-Mill, C., 97, 215
Ewald, K., 139, 161
Ewing, P., 242

F

Falwell, J., 420, 430
Famaey-Lamon, A., 350
Farhi, P., 378
Fasting, K., 349, 350
Faulkner, R., 145, 174
Ferrante, J., 422, 432
Fine, G.A., 45, 113, 125, 130, 132, 267, 276
Flake, C., 430
Foley, D., 25, 43, 51, 261, 270, 392, 418
Ford, G., 362, 369
Franks, C.E.S., 385
Freud, S., 163, 164
Frey, J., 93, 359, 369, 375, 385, 407
Friedenberg, E., 83
Fuller, J., 214
Furst, D., 252
Furst, T., 308

G

Gallico, P., 243
Garrity, J., 91
Gehring, K., 453
Gelinas, M., 344
George, N., 249, 272
Georgiadis, N., 98
Gifford, F., 310
Gilbert, B., 103, 182
Gill, D., 439
Glassner, 47, 51
Gmelch, G., 434
Goffman, E., 229
Goldberg, A.D., 390
Goldlust, J., 329, 357, 368
Goldman, B., 150, 161
Goldstein, J., 173, 182, 187, 344
Goode, E., 152
Goodman, C., 50, 75, 118

Gould, D., 119, 122, 132, 133, 191
Gouldner, A., 30
Graham, B., 429
Graham, G., 274
Gramann, J., 452
Grant, C., 212, 415
Green, T., 237
Greendorfer, S., 211, 299, 337, 342
Greer, D., 119
Gregory, J., 344
Grey, M., 262, 270
Griffey, D., 266, 267
Griffin, P., 231
Gruneau, R., 51, 53, 61, 75, 275, 277, 329, 332, 335, 357, 368, 384
Guttmann, A., 23, 50, 55, 56, 59, 66, 67, 75, 180, 182-184, 187, 429

H

Hacker, A., 416
Hall, M.A., 223, 277, 459
Hall, S., 88
Hallinan, C., 250, 253, 254
Han, L., 223
Hanford, G., 413
Hanks, M., 294
Hare, N., 287, 294, 295
Hargreaves, Jennifer, 450
Hargreaves, John, 51, 301, 329, 332, 343, 348, 359, 368
Harris, J., 21, 106, 332, 343, 348, 357
Harris, O., 264, 290
Harry, J., 452
Hart, B., 286
Hart, M., 70
Hart-Nibbrig, N.,
Harvey, J., 51, 361, 363, 443
Hasbrook, C., 346
Hastad, D.N., 146
Hastings, D., 207
Hauser, W.J., 389
Hawes, M., 377
Heinila, K., 369
Heinemann, K., 23
Heinz, M., 346
Heinze, G., 369
Heller, S., 8
Hellison, D., 98, 393
Henry, C., 315
Herkimer, L., 222
Hesling, W., 332
Hiestand, M., 456
Higgs, R., 75, 261
Hilliard, D., 140, 346
Hilliard, J.M., 140
Hitler, A., 366

Ho, L., 224
Hoberman, J., 150-153, 157, 243, 244, 369, 375, 385, 444, 448
Hoch, P., 50
Hoffman, S., 423, 425, 435-440, 442, 443
Hollman, W., 152
Holmen, M., 285
hooks, b., 26
Hoose, P.M., 273, 347
Horrow, R., 173, 187
House, T., 77
Howell, F., 294, 301, 389, 393
Howell, R., 75
Hughes, R., 140, 161
Huizinga, J., 23
Humphrey, J., 362
Hunt, L., 264, 290

J

Jackson, B., 83, 446
Jackson, D., 347
Jackson, E., 379, 452
James, C.L.R., 370, 384, 385
James I., 51
Janis, L., 237
Jansen, S.C., 232
Jarvie, G., 273, 279, 385
Jarvis, B., 267
Jenner, B., 324
Jensen, K., 348, 357
Jhally, S., 378
Jiobu, R., 139, 161
John Paul II., 25, 358, 422, 429
Johns, D., 140
Johnson, A., 359, 366, 385
Johnson, D.W., 81, 101
Johnson, E., 242
Johnson, N., 150, 155, 161
Johnson, R.T., 81
Johnson, W., 448, 460
Jones, 250
Jordan, M., 77, 242, 296, 307, 323, 422
Judd, M.R., 192, 207

K

Kagen, S., 90
Kageyama, K., 92, 459
Kaiser, E., 313
Kane, M.J., 347
Kaplan, H., 350
Karolyi, B., 104
Kazancigil, A., 50
Keating, J., 16
Keefer, R., 165
Kelley, B.C., 439

Kelley, M., 406
Kelley, S., 239
Kennedy, Ray, 174
Kennedy, Robert, 369
Kenyon, G., 24
Kidd, B., 55, 56, 225-227, 236, 377
Kidd, T.R., 119, 191
Kimmell, T., 214
Kimura, M., 345
Kinkema, K.M., 332, 343, 348, 357
Kjeldsen, E., 255
Klatell, D., 329, 357
Klatz, R., 150, 161
Kleiber, D., 98, 100, 224, 300
Klein, A., 261, 273, 364, 384
Kless, S.J., 126
Knight, B., 276, 433
Knoppers, A., 119, 211
Kohn, A., 81, 89, 90, 93, 99, 103
Koppett, L., 25, 104, 333, 344, 352-354, 357
Kotov, Y., 369
Kyler, R.N., 363

L

Ladd, W., 419
Laird, D., 52
Landers, Dan, 146
Landers, Donna, 146
Langlois, J., 113
Lapchick, R., 250, 251, 269, 270, 273, 282, 290-292, 301, 377, 401, 404, 419
Laqueur, T., 8
Lasch, C., 25, 302, 329
Lavoie, M., 250, 252, 254
Lawrence, P., 419
Le Clair, J., 103
Lederman, D., 407-409, 415-417
Lee, M.J., 98
Lengyel, P., 50
Lenskyj, H., 37, 71, 146, 178, 210, 231, 234, 238, 285
Leonard, G., 90
Leonard, W., 51, 250, 261, 281, 283
Lever, J., 50, 112, 118, 234, 336, 337, 344, 357, 364
Lewis, B., 396
Lewis, J., 182, 244
Lewis, M., 113
Leyba, J., 185
Liessen, H., 153
Lindros, E., 162
Lipsyte, R., 444
Locke, L., 191, 207
Locke, T., 134
Lombardi, V., 164

Lombardo, B., 204
Longino, H., 103
Lopez, N., 284
Lopiano, D., 218, 219, 223, 224, 416
Lorenz, K., 164
Loy, J., 17, 24, 146, 176, 191, 201, 250, 255, 294
Lucas, J., 76, 340, 373, 374, 385, 460
Lueptow, L., 389
Lumpkin, A., 345, 346, 419
Lundquist, V., 208
Luschen, G., 50, 91, 103
Luther, M., 428
Lusko, C., 229

M

MacAloon, J., 358
Macintosh, D., 218, 223, 359, 368, 377, 385, 460
MacNeill, M., 213
Madden, D., 285
Madonna, 323
Magill, R.A., 133
Maguire, J., 144, 182, 250, 252, 254, 306, 307, 329, 378
Maietta, M., 98
Majors, R., 248, 249
Malcolmson, R., 60
Malekoff, R. 419
Mandle, J.D., 329, 384, 385
Mandle, J.R., 329, 384, 385
Manning, E., 214
Mantel, R., 119
Marable, M., 458
Mark, M., 171, 182, 185
Marcus, N., 329, 357
Marsh, P., 164, 187
Martens, R., 132, 191
Marx, K., 31
Massengale, J., 197, 199, 201, 207
Mathes, S., 200
Mathison, J., 423, 431, 443
May, R., 184
Mays, W., 321
McCall, M.M., 45, 47
McCartney, B., 430
McCormack, J., 93, 132, 133
McCormick, E., 347
McDermott, B., 124
McDonald, M., 83
McEnroe, J., 152
McGuire, R., 51, 94, 122
McIntosh, P., 161
McKay, J., 1513, 160
McMillen, T., 386
McPherson, B.D., 24, 93, 122, 294, 301

McTeer, W., 394
Mead, C., 243, 244, 273
Mead, G.H., 116
Medrich, E., 94
Meggyesy, D., 162
Meier, K., 16, 24, 161, 385
Melnick, M., 146, 252, 254, 294
Merchant, L., 433
Messing, M., 204
Messner, M., 38, 42, 43, 51, 96, 102, 116, 117, 125, 146, 161, 176, 178, 223, 225, 238, 248, 279, 280, 300, 347, 357, 451
Meyer, B., 394, 395, 399
Michener, J., 1, 20, 82, 95, 409
Mihevic, P., 166
Miles, G., 280
Miller, C., 123
Mills, B., 256
Miner, V., 103
Miracle, A., 266, 267, 389, 393, 405
Modell, A., 328
Moore, A., 439
Moore, K., 146, 248
Morgan, W., 429
Morgan, William J., 24, 161
Morgan, William P., 166
Morris, D., 164
Morris, G.S.D., 133
Mrozek, D., 68, 76, 190
Munson, L., 150
Murchison, C., 313
Murphy, P., 182, 183, 187, 188
Muscatine, A., 212

N

Nack, W., 150
Naisbitt, J., 459
Naismith, J., 17, 18, 429
Nash, H., 140
Navratilova, M., 322, 323
Neal, W., 436, 437, 443
Neidel, C., 98, 99
Neil, G., 434, 443
Nelson, M. B., 74, 168, 169, 177, 178, 208, 224, 231, 234, 238
Nelson, 90
Nicklaus, J., 284
Nixon, H., 140, 294, 301
Norton, K., 432
Nosanchuk, T., 167
Novak, M., 420, 423

O

O'Brien, 242
O'Conner, S., 422
Ogilvie, B., 92, 192

Oliver, M., 290
Olsen, M., 97
Opie, I., 118
Opie, P., 118
Orlick, T., 94, 103, 127, 133, 459
Orwell, G., 162
Otto, L., 294
Owens, J., 366
Oxendine, J., 52, 62, 63, 256, 273

P

Pacey, P., 298
Palmer, A., 284
Parker, S., 390
Parkhouse, B., 285, 286
Parseghian, A., 194
Passer, M., 119
Pastore, D.L., 192, 207
Pate, R., 113, 211, 233
Paterno, J., 104, 189, 197, 287
Patriksson, G., 122
Patterson, F., 439
Pearman, W., 347
Pearton, R.E., 51
Pepitone, E., 90, 103
Petrie, B., 434
Phelps, R. "Digger," 274
Phillips, D., 165
Picou, J., 294
Pilz, G., 174, 176
Pippen, S., 242
Plank, D., 440
Podilchak, W., 119
Ponomaryov, N., 50, 361, 365
Pratt, S.I., 191
Prebish, C., 423, 433
Presley, E., 309
Price, J., 423
Prisuta, R., 345
Pritchard, T., 82
Pronger, B., 227, 238, 451
Proulx, R., 361, 363
Purdy, D., 116, 329, 419
Pyros, J., 276

R

Rabey, S., 431, 440
Rackages, V., 182
Rader, B., 176, 335, 357, 430
Rainville, R., 347
Raji, K., 377
Ralbovsky, M., 99, 133, 207
Ramsamy, S., 377
Rattray, G., 118
Reagan, R., 367
Real, M., 330, 331, 332, 340, 348, 370

Rees, C.R., 389, 392
Reich, A., 368
Reis, M., 147
Reiss, S., 76
Rejeski, W., 191
Retton, M.L., 135
Reyman, J., 281, 283
Reynolds, B., 157
Rice, G., 243
Richmond, P., 224
Richter, D., 34, 41, 42, 83, 236, 450
Rigauer, B., 50
Riggins, J., 317
Roberts, G., 94, 98, 116, 122
Roberts, O., 430
Robinson, J., 265, 267, 273, 292
Robinson, T., 122
Rojek, C., 51
Rosen, L., 140, 213
Ross, H., 267
Ross, J., 113, 211, 233
Rozelle, P., 293
Ruck, R., 73, 76, 273
Runfola, R., 342
Russell, G., 170
Russell, J., 177
Ruth, B., 351
Sabo, D., 51, 146, 176, 210, 232, 238, 294, 342, 348, 389
Sabock, R., 200, 207
Sack, A., 294, 394, 401
Sadler, W.A., 102
Saeki, T., 345
Sage, G., 51, 93, 103, 191, 192, 197, 199, 200, 201, 207, 329, 443
Samaranch, J.A., 372
Sanders, D., 249
SanGiovanni, L., 216, 237, 346
Sargent, D., 189
Saul, R., 439
Savage, H., 413
Sawyer, T., 204, 207
Sayaovong, A., 346
Sayers, G., 321
Scanlon, T., 199
Schaap, D., 174
Schafer, W., 146
Schmidt, R.L., 51
Schuetz, R., 350
Schultz, R., 416
Scott, J., 195, 460
Scraton, S., 126
Segrave, J., 146, 385, 418
Selman, R., 116
Semyonov, M., 294
Seppanen, P., 375
Sewart, J., 329

Shaiken, B., 357, 385
Shapiro, B., 401
Sheard, K., 75
Sherif, C., 103, 118
Sherif, M., 267
Shields, D., 98, 145, 172, 176, 187, 393
Silva, J., 172, 176
Sipes, R., 165, 187
Sisley, B., 204, 207
Slaney, M.D., 97
Smith, D., 82
Smith, G., 337
Smith, M., 144, 173-175, 177, 181
Smith, N., 213
Smith, R.A., 76, 419
Smith, Red, 230
Smoll, F., 133
Snow, K., 351
Snyder, E., 116, 204, 224
Snyder, J., 246
Sons, R., 352
Spady, N., 294
Spears, B., 76
Sperber, M., 386, 419
Spock, B., 77
Spradling, T., 99, 131
Spreitzer, E., 224, 294, 388, 389
Stacey, J., 277
Staudohar, P., 329
Stavely, D., 437
Steinbrecker, W., 204
Steinbrenner, G., 302
Stevenson, C., 51, 294, 349, 443
Stewart, C.C., 119, 204, 205, 207
Stillwell, J., 191, 204
Stingley, D., 173
Stingley, J., 452
Stoddard, B., 368
Stone, G., 16, 19, 21
Straw, P., 350
Strossen, R., 211
Stuck, M., 161
Sundlum, T., 97
Surface, B., 145
Swain, D.A., 299, 301
Swanson, R., 76
Sweet, L., 204, 205, 207
Swift, E., 172, 174, 175, 280
Sylvester, J., 155

T

Tarzan, 244, 248
Tatum, J., 173

Taub, D.E., 223, 231
Taylor, I., 182, 183
Telander, R., 188, 264, 273, 351-353, 419
Temple, K., 330, 332
TenEyck, J., 190
Theberge, N., 218, 224, 344, 346
Thiel, R., 294
Thirer, J., 167, 267, 390
Thomas, C.E., 299
Thomas, R.M., 346
Thorlindsson, T., 146
Thorpe, J., 256
Todd, T., 150, 151, 155, 157, 161
Tomlinson, A., 306, 360, 369
Tregarthen, S., 48, 104, 447
Trujillo, C., 224
Trulson, M., 143, 161, 170
Turner, G., 294
Turner, T., 372
Tutko, T., 92, 103, 133, 192
Twyman, L., 182

U

Ueberroth, P., 358, 369
Underwood, J., 330
Unkel, M., 279

V

Valentine, J., 101
Van Loon, F., 350
Van Pelt, H., 342, 357
Vander Velden, L., 119
Vanderzwaag, H., 17
Vanfossen, B., 294, 389
Vaz, E., 174
Veblen, T., 68
Vertinsky, P.A., 37, 71, 231
Vines, G., 227, 231
Vinokur, M., 385
Voy, R., 150, 161
Vuolle, P., 350

W

Wacquant, L., 239, 273, 280
Wagner, E., 273, 361
Walker, J., 224
Walsh, J., 191
Warner, G., 441
Wasielewski, P.L., 140
Watson, G., 122
Webb, B., 17

Webb, H., 119
Weber, M., 428
Weinberg, R.,
Weinberg, S., 287
Weiss, M., 132, 133, 204, 207
Wenner, L., 273, 357
Westkott, M., 118, 224, 235
Whannel, G., 369
Wheeler, S., 336, 337, 343, 344, 357, 419
White, A., 51, 122, 124, 182, 218, 224, 230, 345, 405
White, W., 433
Whitson, D., 218, 223, 368, 385, 460
Wieberg, S., 402, 407
Wieczorek, P., 267
Wiggins, D., 347
Wilkerson, M., 342
Wilkins, D., 242
Wilkins, L., 242
Williams, J., 182, 183, 187, 188, 286
Williams, L.D., 345, 346, 357
Williams, R., 250
Williamson, K.M., 98
Willis, K., 109
Willis, P., 34
Winfrey, O., 323
Witosky, T. 407
Wohl, A., 50, 118
Wolff, C., 409
Womack, M., 434, 435
Wong, R., 452
Woodman, W., 118, 279
Woodward, S., 154
Wright, S., 390

Y

Yablonsky, L., 116, 133
Yeager, R., 194
Yetman, N., 250
Young, K., 45, 145
Youssef, Z., 250
Yudovich, I., 369

Z

Zaugg, M., 434
Zillmann, D., 167, 180
Zimmer, J., 434
Zinn, M., 214
Zipter, Y., 450
Zmeskal, K., 154

INDEX

A

AAU; *see* Amateur Athletic Union
Abstract thinking, organized sports and, 115
Abuse
  in high school sports, 412
  spouse, attitudes about gender and, 178
Accountability, coach's, pressure to win and, 194
Achievement
  academic, college athletes and, 398-400
  competition and, 80-81
  participation in sports and motivation for, 30
ACT; *see* American College Test
Action
  informal and formal games and, 106-107
  informal games characterized by, 111
  media coverage of sports and emphasis on, 332, 343
  need for increase of, in children's games, 126-127
Addiction, deviance in sports as form of, 140
Administration
  high school, opportunities for women in, 286
  opportunities for women in, 218
  race logic and availability of jobs in, 255
  sports
    career opportunities in, 284
    opportunities for women in, 285
  underrepresentation of women in, reasons for, 218-219
Adolescence, 11
Advertising
  amateur sports and, 316
  growth of professional golf and, 304

Affiliation, importance of, in play activities, 113
Affirmative action, African Americans as coaches and, 292, 293
African Americans
  aspirations of, to be professional athletes, 287
  career opportunities in sports for, 281, 287-291
    barriers to, 292-293
  explanations of athletic success of, 246
  friendships with teammates and, 267
  high school, participation in sports and, 393
  media coverage of sports and, 347
  participation of, in sports, 255-256
  recruitment of, intercollegiate sports and, 416-417
Age relations, dynamics of, 275-276
Agents, role of, commercialization of sport and, 311
Aggression
  emphasis on, in professional sports, 72
  frustration and, 166-167
  gender equity and, 225
  gender in sports and, 38
  human instincts and, 163-167
  martial arts and control of, 170
  media coverage of sports and emphasis on, 332, 343
  in society, 162-188
  in sports, critical theory and explanation of, 36
  sports as cause of, 170-179
  sports as cure for, 163-170
  as strategy in sports, 172-178
Aggressiveness, emphasis on competitive sports for increase in, 93
AIA; *see* Athletes in Action

Akebono, 382-383
Alcohol
  athlete's use of, 150
  spectator violence and consumption of, 182, 185
Alcoholism, stereotyping of minority groups associated with, 258
Alienation
  causes of, in African American athlete, 249
  sports for control of, 360
Amateur
  definition of, in early twentieth century, 65
  qualifications of, 380
Amateur Athletic Union, 325
Amenorrhea, weight control and, 213
American Alliance for Health, Physical Education, Recreation and Dance, 10
American Association of Collegiate Registrars/Admissions Officers, 395
American Coaching Effectiveness Program, 204
American College Test
  intercollegiate athletes and, 401
  Proposition 48 and, 403
American Council on Education, 413
Amphetamine drugs, athlete's use of, 150, 151
Anger
  aggressive behavior related to, 171
  causes of, in African American athlete, 249
  in fans, 172
Animosity, international sports as cause of, 370-371
Antisemitism, major league baseball and, 248
Applied sport science, changes in youth sports and, 131

Archery
  boy/girl teams in high school for,
    410
  games in ancient Greece and, 55
Asian Americans, participation of, in
    sports, 261-262
Assault
  aggression in contact sports and,
    165
  attitudes about gender and, 178
  felony, sports activities as, 135
  participation in physical sports
    associated with, 147
  sexual
    alternative definition of
      masculinity and, 232
    participation in physical sports
      associated with, 147
Association of Intercollegiate
    Athletics for Women, 316, 317
Association of Tennis Professionals,
    legal status of athlete and, 320
Athlete; *see also* Hearing-impaired
    athlete; Vision-impaired
    athlete; Wheelchair athlete
  aging, opportunities for, 291
  amateur 325-327
  black, segregation in sports and, 73
  career opportunities for, 281
  character of, competition and, 93
  Christian, conflicts for, 437-440
  coach as role model for, 202-204
  coach evaluated by, 414
  coach's relationship with, Power
    and Performance Model of
    sports and, 446
  in commercial sports, legal status
    of, 317-327
  designer, 448
  development of, symbolic
    interactionism and, 45
  deviant behavior by, research on,
    144-150
  as entertainer, 318
  fan identification with, future of
    sports and, 449
  female
    college academic performance
      and, 399-400
    equitable support for, 216-218
    inequitable awarding of
      scholarships for, 415
    intercollegiate, 394-395
    media coverage of, 211

Athlete — cont'd
  female — cont'd
    opportunities in sports careers
      for, 284-287
    television coverage of, 211
    violence in contact sports and,
      176-179
  gay male, 227, 230
  health of, drug testing and, 157
  high school
    aspirations of, to be professional
      athletes, 287
    deviance and, 146
    popularity of, 390-391
    professional opportunities for,
      281, 282t
  immaturity of, sports as
    contributor to, 97
  intercollegiate
    academic performance and,
      398-400
    deviance and, 146
    eligibility of, 147
    in high-profile sports programs,
      398-400
    payment for, 327
    professional opportunities for,
      282t
    recommendations for
      empowerment of, 414-415
  lack of rights of, 414
  male, violence and contact sports
    and, 172-176
  mistreatment of, by coach, 193
  moral worth of, 436
  off-the-field deviance and, 146
  orientation of, commercialization
    and, 309-311
  performance-enhancing drugs used
    by, 150-159
    history of, 150-152
  professional, 318-325
  relationship of, with media, 352
  retiring, challenges for, 299
  as role model, 95
  scholarship, need for changes for,
    414-415
  special bonds between, 143
  sport ethic as motivation of,
    140-144
  student as
    in high school, 387-390
    in major college programs,
      394-395

Athlete — cont'd
  superiority complex in, 143
  use of religion by, 432
  as victim, deviance in sports and,
    138
  women, endorsement opportunities
    for, 324
Athletes for Kids, 440
Athletes in Action, 431, 439, 440
Athletic director
  deviance education for, 158
  high school, problems in high
    school sports and, 409
ATP; *see* Association of Tennis
    Professionals
Attitude
  negative, competition as cause of,
    267
  psychology and focus on, 3
  of teachers and coaches, 195
Authority, religion and, 422
Auto racing
  classification of, as sport, 13
  legal status of professional athlete
    in, 319-320
  opportunities for women in, 284
  professional, salary levels in, 322
Automation, alienation caused by,
    428
Autonomy, interest in, child's interest
    in sport and, 123

B

Badminton, 410
Balance
  as complex physical skill, 14
  state of, sport and, 27
Baseball
  creation and marketing of, 72
  decline of, in low-income area high
    schools, 280
  intercollegiate, athletes goals in,
    403
  legal status of professional athlete
    in, 319
  major league
    antisemitism and bigotry in,
      248
    experiences of Latin Americans
      in, 261
  percentage of athletes becoming
    professional in, 282t
  popularity of, in early twentieth
    century, 65

Baseball—cont'd
    professional
        average length of career in, 284
        percentage of black, white, and
            other players in, 251*t*
        problems in, 73
    racial stacking patterns in, 253
    televised coverage of, 338
    youth, family relationships and,
        116
Baseball Chapel, 440
Basketball; *see also* National Basketball
    Association
    creation and marketing of, 72
    graduation rates of intercollegiate
        athletes in, 401-402
    growth of, in low-income area high
        schools, 280
    high school, future of, 454
    intercollegiate
        athlete's goals in, 403
        revenue generated from, 396
    legal status of professional athlete
        in, 319
    minor leagues for, 451
    opportunities for women in, 285
    perceived opportunities in, for
        black athletes, 264
    percentage of collegiate women
        coaches in, 217*t*
    percentage of professional athletes
        in, by race and ethnicity, 283*t*
    professional
        average length of career in, 284
        percentage of black, white, and
            other players in, 251*t*
    rule changes in, commercialization
        as cause of, 308
    stacking patterns in, 250
    success of African Americans in,
        247
Bearbaiting, in ancient Rome, 57
Behavior
    aggressive, 163
        contact sports and, 172-176
        sports for control of, 167-170
    of coaches, 193-198
    destructive, alternative definition of
        masculinity and, 233
    deviant, sports as cure for, 148-149
    sports participation and, 69
    violent, among sports spectators,
        179-186
    weight-control, 213

Beyond Victory Ministries, 440
Bicyclist, drug use by, 150
Bigotry in sport, 266-267, 268
Binge eating, women's use of, in
    conjunction with training, 213
Bioethics, genetic engineering and,
    448
Biomechanist, athlete's use of, 456
Blood boosting, athlete's use of,
    control of, 158
Blood sample, drug testing and, 156
B'nai B'rith, sports sponsored by, 429
Bodybuilding
    drug use associated with, 151
    women and, 228-230
Bowling
    behavior of spectators of, 180
    desegregation of, 266
    legal status of professional athlete
        in, 319-320
    opportunities for women in, 284
    professional, salary levels in, 322
Boxing
    desegregration in, 263
    games in ancient Greece and, 55
    income level of participants in, 280
    legal status of professional athlete
        in, 319-320
    opportunities for career hindered
        by participation in, 295
    professional, opportunities for black
        athletes in, 247, 287
Boys
    behavior of, in organized sports,
        125
    different treatment of, in families,
        233
    experiences of, in organized sports,
        124-126
    involvement of father in play of,
        124
    play activities of, 112-113
British Journal of Sociology, 11
Broadcasting rights
    commercial sports and, 303
    control of, by NCAA, 317
    globalization of sports and, 305
    monopoly status of professional
        sports leagues and, 313
    revenue from, 333
Buddhism, sports and, 427
Budget, sports
    gender inequity in provision of,
        217

Budget, sports—cont'd
    women's participation in sports
        and, 211-212
Bullbaiting in ancient Rome, 57
Bureaucratization
    competitive sports characterized
        by, 67
    Power and Performance Model of
        sports and emphasis on, 453
Burnout
    changes in youth sports affected
        by, 130
    organized sports and, 122-124

C

Caffeine, athlete's use of, 150
Canada
    Christian organizations and sports
        in, 428
    Industrial Revolution in, 64
    national policy on women in sports
        in, 212-213
    opportunities for women in
        coaching in, 218
    professionalization of sports in, 65
    religion promoted by sports in, 432
    sport and education in, 5-6
    sport and politics in, 6
*Canadian Journal of Applied Sport
    Sciences*, 11
Canadians, stacking patterns in ice
    hockey and, 252, 254
Capitalism
    growth of competitive sports and,
        69
    reward structures in sports and, 89
Career, sports participation and,
    281-294
Carnegie Corporation, college sports
    studied by, 413
Catharsis
    definition of, 163
    sports as outlet for aggression and,
        165
Catholic Church; *see* Roman Catholic
    Church
Cause-effect relationship, sociology
    and, 26
Center for Athletes' Right and
    Education, 326
Center for the Study of Sport in
    Society, 377
Certification, of coaches, 205
Champions for Christ, 440

Change, critical theory and
    explanation of, 41
Character
    commercial sports and development
        of, 304
    competition and, 92-98
    development of
        sports as hindrance to, 97-98
        sports participation and, 29, 65,
            69-70
    lack of, deviance in sports and,
        137, 139
Chariot racing, 55, 57
Cheerleading, 220-222
    support for, 411
Chicanos, participation of, in sports,
    261
Child
    organized sports for, 104-133
        negative effects of, 120
    relationship of parent with,
        organized sports and, 116
Child abuse, attitudes about gender
    and, 178
Childbirth, problems in, women's
    sports participation and, 231
Childhood, sport participation
    during, 304
China
    government sponsorship of fitness
        in, 361
    reward structures in sports in,
        88-89
Christian Bowhunters Association,
    440
Christian manliness, sports and, 430
Christian Surfers Australia, 440
Christianity
    fundamentalist
        sports and, 431
        sports for promotion of, 432
    sports and, 427
    use of sports by, 429
Christians, ancient Roman spectacles
    and, 57
Civic pride, commercial sports and
    development of, 304
Civil religion, sports as, 423
Civil Rights Restoration Act, 210
Class relations
    boxing sponsorship and, 320
    commercial sports and, 303-304
    conflict theory and, 34
    definition of, 275
    dynamics of, 275-278

Class relations—cont'd
    gender relations and, 279
    social mobility and, 274-301
    sports and, 275-281
    sports participation and career
        success and, 295-296
    sports participation patterns and,
        277-281
    transformation of, 458
Clustering, intercollegiate athletes
    and, 401
Coach
    African American, in professional
        sports, 255t
    athlete's relationship with, Power
        and Performance Model of
        sports and, 446
    autocratic, athlete's character
        development hindered by, 98
    behavior of, 193-198
    certification of, 205
    control of deviance in sports and,
        143
    coping with pressure by, 196-198
    deviance education for, 158
    deviant behavior of, 147, 150
    education for, changes in youth
        sports created by, 130-131
    expectations of, organized youth
        sports and, 114-116
    female
        decline in number of, 213
        personality traits of, 191
        role conflicts for, 200
    formal games controlled by, 109
    high school
        changes in approach of, 412
        emphasis on education by, 393
        problems in high school sports
            and, 409
    impact of, on children, 130
    intercollegiate
        goals of, 403
        job security of, 414
    need for education programs for,
        204-206
    orientation of, commercialization
        and, 309-311
    personal characteristics of, 191-192
    racial and ethnic diversity training
        programs for, 271
    racial ideology of, 267
    role conflicts for, control of,
        200-201
    role of, 193-198

Coach—cont'd
    role strain and, 194-196
    as significant other, 202-206
    specialized role of, history of,
        190-191
    sport experience and, 189-207
    student athlete's evaluation of, 414
    teacher compared to, 195
    training programs for, 129
    use of religion by, 432, 436
    volunteer, qualifications of, 205
Coaching
    barriers to African Americans in,
        292-293
    career opportunities in, 284
    certification programs in, 130
    description of, 189-207
    discouragement of change in, 201
    education for, changes in youth
        sports created by, 130-131
    education programs for, 455
    effects of gender relations in, 202
    emergence of, as specialized
        profession, 73
    equality in, for men and women,
        288-289
    gender inequity in provision of,
        217
    high school, opportunities for
        women in, 286
    history of, 190-191
    need for education programs in,
        204-206
    opportunities for women in, 218,
        285
    opportunities in, for African
        Americans, 291
    organizational settings and, 194
    physical education compared to,
        190
    pressure and role strain in, coping
        with, 196-198
    race logic and availability of jobs
        in, 255
    role conflicts in, control of, 200-201
    as subculture, 201-202
    underrepresentation of women in,
        reasons for, 218-219
Cocaine, athlete's use of, 150
Coercion
    alternative definition of masculinity
        and, 232
    critical theory and, 36
Cognition, psychology and focus on,
    3

College Football Association, 316, 396

Commentator, television, spectator interest increased by, 305

Commercialism
intercollegiate sports and, 413-414
of sport and society, 33

Commercialization
intercollegiate sports hurt by, 413
pressure to win created by, 144

Commission on Olympic Sports, 362

Commonwealth Games, drug testing at, 155

Communication, psychology and focus on, 3

Community
identity of, sports and, 363
participation in sports and, 29
sports and prestige of, 362

Community-school relations, varsity sports and, 409

Competition
achievement and, 80-81
character and, 92-98
child's view of, 116
concept of, 78-81
controlled, in Special Olympics, 86-87
cooperation subverted by, 267-269
drug use and fairness of, 157
emphasis on
in professional sports, 72
in sports in United States, 82
individual orientation and, 80-81
lack of emphasis on, in selected sports, 70
media coverage of sports and emphasis on, 332, 343, 356
popular beliefs about, 88
Power and Performance Model of sports and emphasis on, 453
sport and, 16
in sports, 77-103

Competitive orientation, definition of, 80

Compromise, critical theory and, 36

Concerned American Indian Parents, 258

Conflict, 31-35, 48-49
functionalist theory and, 31
religion and, 422

Conformity, emphasis on, in high school sports, 412-413

Confucianism, sports and, 427

Consumerism
future emphasis on, in sports, 456
media coverage of sports and emphasis on, 356
organization of sports and, 276
sports media's promotion of, 349

Cool pose, 249, 272

Cooperation
competition and, 267-269
reward structure and, 80

Cooperative Games, 459

Cooperative orientation, 80

Coordination, as complex physical skill, 14

Corporations
amateur sports sponsored by, 316
globalization of sports and, 378
high school sports sponsored by, 281
intercollegiate sports sponsored by, 403
sports used for global expansion of, 306-307

Corporatization, intercollegiate sports and, 413-414

Cost containment, intercollegiate sports and, 404, 414

deCoubertin, Baron Pierre, founding of Olympic Games and, 368

Cricket, 58, 61, 64

Crime
sports activities as, 135
sports for control of, 360

Critical approach, sport sociology and, 10

Critical theory
alternative forms of sport and, 41-42
emphasis on change in, 48-49
limitations of, 43, 49
research in, 41-43
social constructionist and, 425
sport analyzed with, 35-43
summary of, 28t

Croquet, participation of women in, during Renaissance, 60

Cross country, percentage of collegiate women coaches in, 217t

Crowd control, violence prevented through, 182, 183

Cubans, participation of, in sports, 261

Cultural ideology, 88
normalcy and sickness defined through, 92

Cultural ideology—cont'd
sport and, 7

Cultural studies, critical theory and, 37

D

Death instinct, 163, 164

Decision-making
commercialization of sports and, 311
in informal games 107
racist beliefs about, racial stacking patterns and, 253

Delinquency
sports participation and, 145-146
sports participation and treatment of, 148
Tae Kwon Do and, 170

Democracy

Desegregation, racial, of American sports, 262-266

Deviance
absolutist approach to, 136-138
"law and order" approach to, 137
negative, 139
in sports, 136
off-the-field, 145-147
on-the-field, 144-145
positive, 139
control of, 143-144
in sports, 136
relativist approach to, 138-139
in sports, 134-161
control of, 139, 143-144
research on, 144-150
sport ethic and, 140-144
sports participation as cure for, 148-149

Deviance education, drug use in sports and, 158

Diet pills, women's use of, in conjunction with training, 213

Diets, women's use of, in conjunction with training, 213

Dis-play 16, 19

Disabilities Act, 294

Disability
change in sport and, 36
conflict theory and, 34
sociology and focus on, 3
sports participation and, 71-72

Discipline
Christian athlete and, 437
emphasis on, in Protestant ethic, 428

Discipline—cont'd
    sports organized by adults characterized by, 276
Diuretics, women's use of, in conjunction with training, 213
DNA sample, drug testing and, 156
Domestic violence, aggression in contact sports and, 165
Domination
    alternative definition of masculinity and, 232
    emphasis on, in professional sports, 72
    gender equity and, 225
Donations, intercollegiate sports funded with, 407
Doping, definition of, 152
Drill team, support for, 411
Dropout, from organized sports, causes of, 121-124
Drug education programs, control of drug use in sports and, 158
Drug(s)
    antiinflammatory, athlete's use of, 46
    control of use of, in sports, 157-159
    overconformity in sports and, 136
    performance-enhancing, 150-159
        banning of, 153-154
        definition of, 152-154
        history of use of, 150-152
        pressure to win and, 144
        sport ethic and, 143
        victimization of athletes and, 138
    in sports, banning of, 152-154
    testing for, 154-156
        mistakes in, 157
    use in society of, 154
Dysfunction, functionalist theory and definition of, 29

E

Economic background, participation in high school sports and, 389
Economics
    attitude toward sports and, 65
    conflict theory and, 32
    growth of competitive sports and, 69
    sport participation and, 65
    sports and, 6, 302-329
Education
    attitude toward sports and, 65
    change in sport and developments in, 36

Education—cont'd
    sport and, 5-6
    sports participation as form of, 69
Empowerment
    leadership positions for women and, 224
    participation in sports and, 223-224
    Pleasure and Participation Model of sports and emphasis on, 447
    radical approach to, 458
Endorsements, athletes income from, 324
Enforcers, contact sports and, 174
Enjoyment, Pleasure and Participation Model of sports and emphasis on, 447
Enlightenment period, games in, 60-61
Entertainment
    mass, ancient Roman games and, 74
    media "re-presentation" of, 332
    media role to provide, 331
    sports as, 310
        broadcast media and, 354
        media coverage and, 343
Epistle Sport Ministries, 440
Epitestosterone, testing for, 155
Equal pay for equal work, coaching contracts for men and women and, 288-289
Equality
    competitive sports characterized by, 66
    radical approach to, 458
Equipment, sports, gender inequity in provision of, 217
Equity
    critical theory and, 35
    gender; see Gender equity
    participation in sport and, 209-225
    Title IX and, 210
ESPN network, sports programming on, 337
Essentialist, definition of, 424, 425
Ethnic group, definition of, 240
Ethnicity
    change in sport and, 36
    conflict theory and, 34
    definition of, 240
    endorsement opportunities affected by, 324
    identity of high school student related to, 392-393
    importance of, in sports, 239-273

Ethnicity—cont'd
    negative ideas about, 266
    percentage of athletes becoming professional by, 283t
    popular beliefs about, 240
    social inequality and, 55
    sociology and focus on, 3
Ethnology, aggressive behavior explained by, 164
Ethyl ether, athlete's use of, 150
Exclusivity, Power and Performance Model of sports and emphasis on, 446
Exercise
    depression and, 166
    emphasis on, in nineteenth century, 65
Exercise and Sport Science Reviews, 11
Exercise physiologist, athlete's use of, 456
Exploitation, elimination of, radical approach to, 458

F

Facilities, sports
    demand on, 452
    gender inequity in provision of, 217
Family
    attitude toward sports and, 65
    change in sport and developments in, 36
    of coaches, conflicts in, 199-200
    coach's, role conflicts and, 199-200
    differences in treatment of boys and girls in, 233
    income of, athletic scholarships and, 298
    participation of, in organized sports activities, 116
    sport and, 5
    sport development compared with, 40
Fans, sports; see Spectators
Fatigue, burnout from organized sports caused by, 123
FCA; see Fellowship of Christian Athletes
Federation Internationale de Football Association, 306
Fellowship of Christian Anglers, 440
Fellowship of Christian Athletes, 431, 440
Feminity
    alternative definitions of, 233-234

Feminity—cont'd
  bodybuilding by women and, 228
  change in sport and, 36
  contact sport and, 177
  gender inequities in sports and, 214
  media coverage of sports and, 345-347
  trivialization of women's sports and, 214
Feminism
  critical, masculinity in sports and, 42
  critical theory and, 37
  sociological theory affected by, 50
  sociology and, 27
  sports and gender explained with, 37-39
Feminity, organized sports and, 70-71
FIFA; see Federation Internationale de Football Association
Fitness
  cosmetic, emphasis on, 213
  emphasis on, in nineteenth century, 65
  Pleasure and Participation Model of sports and emphasis on, 447, 449
  sports associated with, 149
  sports for promotion of, 360-361
Fitness adviser, 456
Fitness and Amateur Sport Women's Program, 210
Fitness movement
  equity in sports and, 210-211
  girls in organized sports and, 105
  income level of participants of, 277
Folk religion, sports as, 423
Football; see also National Football League
  corporate sponsorship of, 448
  creation and marketing of, 72
  decline of, in low-income area high schools, 280
  graduation rates of intercollegiate athletes in, 401-402
  high school, 392, 454
  intercollegiate 73, 403, 454
  intimidation and violence in, 172
  percentage of athletes becoming professional in, 282t
  professional 251t, 284
  racial stacking patterns in, 253
  stacking patterns in, 250
  stimulus cues for violence in, 171

Football—cont'd
  success of African Americans in, 247
  violence in, victimization of athletes and, 138
Free agency, salary levels of athletes and, 322
Free agent, professional athlete as, 319
Freud, Sigmund, aggressive behavior explained by, 163
Friendship
  affirmation of, in informal games, 129
  informal games and, 106
Frustration
  aggression and, 166-167
  causes of, in African American athlete, 249
  sports as cause of, 171-172
Functionalist theory 27-31, 47, 49
Fund-raising, intercollegiate sports budgets and, 407-408
Fundamentalism, religious, 432
Funding, women's participation in sports and, 212

G

Gambling, media coverage of sports and, 350
Games
  in ancient Greece, 55-56
  ball, in Middle Ages, 58
  in colonial America, 61
  during Enlightenment period, 61
  folk
    as alternative to competitive sports, 92
    during Renaissance, 60
  formal versus informal, 106-114
  historical comparison of, t
  immorality of, 64
  informal, creation and maintenance of, 117-121
  in Middle Ages, 58-60
  Native American, 62-63
  organized, early forms of, 55
  organized by children, 276
  racial considerations and, 269
  in Restoration England, 61
  rules for, politics and, 381
  war, in Middle Ages, 59
Gang rape
  attitudes about gender and, 178

Gang rape—cont'd
  participation in physical sports associated with, 147
Gay Games, 230, 451
Gender
  athletic scholarships and, 296-298
  Christianity and sports and, 441
  class relations and, 279
  coaching and, 202
  conflict theory and, 34
  endorsement opportunities affected by, 324
  identity of high school student related to, 392-393
  importance of, in play activities, 112-113
  inequities in intercollegiate sports related to, 415-416
  logic of, in sports, 225-231
  media coverage of sports affected by, 347, 356
  physical self-concept and, 124
  Power and Performance Model of sports and, 449
  race logic and, 248-249
  social inequality and, 55
  sociology and focus on, 3
  sports and, 208-238
    feminism and explanation of, 37-39
    feminist perspective on, 38-39
    sports as character builder and, 96-97
  violence in sports and, 178-179
Gender equity
  future of, 450, 454
  high school sports and, 411-412
  need for, 219-224
  organization of sports and, 234-235
  participation in sports and, 223-224
  sport and, 208-238
  strategies for promotion of, 223
Gender logic
  limited opportunities for women in coaching and, 286
  sports inequity linked to, 225-226
Gender relations, transformation of, 458
Genetic engineering
  athletes and, 448
  drug use in sports and, 153
Girls
  behavior of, in organized sports, 125

Girls—cont'd
   different treatment of, in families, 233
   experiences of, in organized sports, 124-126
   high school, support for sports for, 411-412
   involvement of father in play of, 124
   organized sports for, importance of, 120
   participation in organized sports and, 105
   participation in sports and personal empowerment of, 223
   participation patterns of, in sports, 209-214
   play activities of, 112-113
   violence in sports and, 178
Gladiators, ancient Rome and, 57-58
Gladiators contests, rule changes in, commercialization as cause of, 309
Global Basketball Association, 306
Globalization
   economics of, sports and, 305-307
   of professional sports, 451
   of sports, 305-307, 378-379
Goal achievement, competitive games associated with, 92
Goals, in sports, critical theory and explanation of, 36
Golf
   athletic scholarships for, 298
   behavior of spectators of, 180
   boy/girl teams in high school for, 410
   commercialization of, 303-304
   desegregation of, 266
   lack of black athletes in, 256, 287
   legal status of professional athlete in, 319-320
   opportunities for aging athlete in, 291
   opportunities for career enhanced by participation in, 295-296
   opportunities for women in, 214, 284
   percentage of collegiate women coaches in, 217t
   percentage of professional athletes in, by race and ethnicity, 283t
   Pleasure and Participation Model of sports and, 449
   professional, salary levels in, 322

Golf—cont'd
   rule changes in, commercialization as cause of, 308
   scholarships for, economic need and, 264
   television and, 277, 334, 338
Golf Fellowship, 440
Goodwill Games, 372
Goons, contact sports and, 174
Government
   change in sport and developments in, 36
   college sports subsidies by, 362
   sports and, 359-368
Grades
   classroom, reward structure of, 78-79
   college athletes and, 395, 401-402
Graduation rate, college athletes and, 395, 401-402
Greece, ancient
   drug use in, 150
   games and contests in, 67t
   games and sports in, 74
   games in, 55-56
Group development, participation in sports and, 29
Grove City v. Bell, equity in sports and, 210
Gymnastics
   athletic scholarships for, 298
   behavior of spectators of, 180
   emphasis on female participation in, 70
   lack of black athletes in, 256
   opportunities for participation in, for women, 214
   politics in judging of, 382
   scholarships for, economic need and, 264

H

Hate, motivation in sports and, 135
Health
   emphasis on, in Christian organizations, 429
   Pleasure and Participation Model of sports and emphasis on, 447, 449
   sports for promotion of, 360-361
Health care, costs of, government sponsorship of fitness programs and, 361
Health movement
   equity in sports and, 210-211

Health movement—cont'd
   income level of participants of, 277
Hearing-impaired athlete, opportunities for, 291
Heraean Games, 56
Hero, athlete as, 94
Heroin, athlete's use of, 150
Heroism, media coverage of sports and emphasis on, 332, 343
Heterosexuality, sports participation and, 227
HGH; see Human Growth Hormone
High school; see also School
   alternative sports in, 450
   athletes in, rights of, 326
   budgets of, varsity sports and, 406-407
   cheerleading in, 220-222
   coaches in, role conflicts for, 199
   inequitable support for female athletes in, 216
   in low-income area, decline of sports in, 280-281
   "no pass, no play" rule in, 380
   opportunities for women in coaching and administration at, 285
   private, future of sports in, 454
   racial and ethnic diversity programs in, 271
   sports and unity in, 364
   sports eligibility rules in, 380
   sports in, 386-419
   support for girls' sports in, 411-412
   training of coaches for, 205
   varsity sports in 409-413
Hiking, Pleasure and Participation Model of sports and, 449
Hinduism, sports and, 427
Hispanic Americans, participation of, in sports, 260-261
History of sport, 52-76
Hit men, contact sports and, 174
Hockey; see Field hockey; Ice hockey
Hockey league, commercial, failure of, 312
Hockey Ministries International, 440
Homocide, aggression in contact sports and, 164
Homophobia
   organized youth sports and, 125
   participation of women in sports and, 231
   presence of, in sports, 227
   in sports, 42

Homophobia—cont'd
  violence in sports and, 178-179
  women's sports and, 213-214
Hooliganism
  soccer, in England, 184
  soccer fans and, 164
Hormones
  synthetic, athlete's use of, 151
  use of, sport ethic and, 143
Horse racing
  desegregration in, 263
  opportunities for women in, 284
Hostility
  competition as cause of, 267
  international sports as cause of,
    370-371
Human Genome Project, 153, 448
Human Growth Hormone, 448
  testing for, 155, 156
Human instincts, aggression and,
  163-167
Human Rights Squad, intergroup
  conflict resolved by, 270
Husband-wife relationship, coaching
  and role conflicts in, 200

I

Ice dancing, opportunities for
  participation in, for women,
  214
Ice hockey; see also National Hockey
  League
  athletic scholarships for, 298
  fighting in, 181
  intercollegiate 396, 403
  intimidation and violence in, 172
  legal status of professional athlete
    in, 319
  limited number of black athletes in,
    256, 287
  percentage of professional athletes
    in, by race and ethnicity, 283t
  professional, racial stacking in, 252,
    254
  violence in, 171, 178
ICSS; see International Committee for
  Sociology of Sport
ICSS Bulletin, 10
Identity, in sport, symbolic
  interactionism and, 43-47
Ideology
  cultural 376-377
  economic, corporate sponsorship of
    sports and, 378

Ideology—cont'd
  gender logic of sports and, 225-236
  high school sports and, 391-393
  media coverage of sports affected
    by, 356
  political, government involvement
    in sports to promote, 365-366
  racial
    change in, 269-271
    sports and, 242-255
Idioculture, 125
  symbolic interactionism and, 45-46
  youth sports and, 125
Inclusiveness, Pleasure and
    Participation Model of sports
    and emphasis on, 447
Income, sports attendance and, 277
Indians; see Native Americans
Individualism, media coverage of
    sports and, 348, 356
Individualized orientation, definition
    of, 80
Industrial Revolution and emergence
    of sport, 61-74
Inequality
  American society and, sports
    affected by, 88
  economic, sports as tools to
    maintain, 277
  social, sport and, 55
Infant, play activities of, 112-113
Information
  media "re-presentation" of, 332
  media role to provide, 331
Injury
  acceptance of, in athlete, 46
  avoidance of, need for rules
    changes for, 236
  burnout from organized sports
    caused by, 123
  emphasis on, by television sports
    commentators, 310
  games in ancient Greece and, 55
  retirement from sports caused by,
    300
Inspiration, sports and, 27, 30
Instinct
  human, aggression and, 163-167
  racist beliefs about, racial stacking
    patterns and, 253
Instinct theory, aggressive behavior
    explained with, 164-165
Institute for Athletic Perfection, 436
Institute for International Sport, 372

Intelligence, racist beliefs about,
    racial stacking patterns and,
    253
International Amateur Athletic
    Federation, 382
International Committee for
    Sociology of Sport, 10
International Journal of the History of
    Sport, 11
International Olympic Committee
    amateur sport controlled by, 325
    drug testing and, 152, 154-155
International Review for the Sociology of
    Sport, 10, 11
International Sports Coalition, 431,
    440
Internationalism, reform of Olympic
    Games and, 375
IOC; see International Olympic
    Committee

J

Japan
  expansion of American sports to,
    306
  media coverage of women's sports
    in, 345
Javelin, games in ancient Greece and,
    55
Jim Crow laws, 263
Jockey, black, desegregation of horse
    racing and, 263
John Jacobs Power Team, 432
Journalism, sports, 350-355
Judaism, sports and, 427,429

K

Karate, aggression controlled with
    training in, 167
Killer instinct
  emphasis on, 83
Knight Foundation Commission on
    Intercollegiate Athletics,
    404-405, 413

L

Labor unions, emergence of, in
    organized sports, 74
Ladies Professional Golf Association,
    320
Latin Americans, participation of, in
    sports, 261
Laxatives, women's use of, in
    conjunction with training, 213

Laziness, burnout from organized sports caused by, 123
Leadership
  competitive games associated with, 92
  psychology and focus on, 3
  racist beliefs about, racial stacking patterns and, 253
  training for, high school sports and, 412
Legislation
  participation of women in sports and, 209-210
  resistance to, women's participation in sports and, 212-213
Legitimacy, political, involvement in sports and, 366
Leisure
  for children, organized sports and, 120
  patterns of, competitive sports and, 68-69
Leisure Studies, 11
Lesbian, "tomboys" labeled as, 230
Little League baseball, 45-46, 145
Logo, sports, bigotry associated with, 258-260
Long jumping, 55
Louis, Joe, 243, 244
LPGA; *see* Ladies Professional Golf Association

M

Major League Baseball
  free agency in, 319
  monopoly status of, 312
  percentage of black, white, and other players in, 251*t*
  percentages of black athletes and coaches in, 255*t*
  salary levels in, 321, 322
Male bonding, rape and, 147
Male superiority, violence in sports and, 178
Manager, 143, 158
Mandela, Nelson, 377
Martial arts, 170
Marx, Karl, conflict theory and, 32
Mascot
  sports, bigotry associated with, 258-260
  team, trivialization of women's sports and, 214
Masculinity
  alternative definitions of, 232

Masculinity—cont'd
  class relations and, 279-280
  media coverage of sports and emphasis on, 345-347
  organized sports and, 70-71
  violence in sports and, 176
Mass media, sports coverage in, 5
Media
  broadcasting rights for, intercollegiate sports funded with, 407
  coverage of women's sports by, 211, 217
  impact of, on violence in sports, 181
  public perception of athletes conveyed through, 95
  role of, commercialization of sport and, 311
  sports and, 330-357
  sports dependence on, 333-336
Medical services, sports, gender inequity in provision of, 217
Men
  aggressive behavior in, 165
  focus on, by social constructionists, 425
  married, sports participation of, 279
  military model for sports participation used by, 169
Meritocracy, emphasis on competitive reward structure in, 102
Militarism
  reward structures in sports and, 88
  sport and, 33
Military model
  acceptance of, by women, 178
  aggression in sports and, 168-169
  gender equity in sports and, 223
MIlitary training, contact sports and, 38
Misogyny, 42
Money
  amateur sports organizations and, 317
  desegregation in sports and, 263-264
  future growth of sports participation and, 453
  games and sports organized to promote, 276
Monopoly, sports leagues as, 312-315
Morgan, William, 429
Motorsports Ministries, 440

Mythology, games in ancient Greece and, 55, 74

N

Naismith, James, 17, 429
National Association for Intercollegiate Athletics, 316
National Association for Sport and Physical Education, 10
National Association of Intercollegiate Athletics, colleges affiliated with, 396, 397
National Basketball Association
  free agency in, 319
  future of, 451
  globalization of basketball and, 305-306
  monopoly status of, 312
  percentage of black, white, and other players in, 251*t*
  percentages of black athletes and coaches in, 255*t*
  profit patterns in, 313
  salary levels in, 321
  television and, 338
  television contracts negotiated by, 314
National Basketball League, history of basketball and, 18
National Cheerleaders Association, 222
National Christian Collegiate Athletic Association, 431
National Collegiate Athletic Association
  amateur sport controlled by, 325
  athletic scholarships from schools of, 297
  colleges in, 396, 397
    percentages of black athletes and coaches in, 255*t*
  control of amateur sports by, 316, 317
  gender inequity in college sports and, 217-218
  policy on payment to athletes of, 327
  politics and enforcement policies of, 381
  sports of, television and, 338-339
National Football League
  free agency in, 319
  future of, 451

National Football League—cont'd
  globalization of football and, 305-306
  monopoly status of, 312
  percentage of black, white, and other players in, 251*t*
  percentages of black athletes and coaches in, 255*t*
  profit patterns in, 313
  salary levels in, 321
  television and, 338
  television contracts negotiated by, 314
National health insurance, 360
National Hockey League
  free agency in, 319
  globalization of hockey and, 305-306
  monopoly status of, 312
  profit patterns in, 313
  salary levels in, 321
  television and, 339
  television contracts negotiated by, 314
National Olympic Committee, global expansion of sports and, 306
National sports training centers, 362
National unity, media coverage of sports and, 348
Nationalism
  international sports and, 371
  media coverage of sports and, 348, 356
  sport and, 33
  television coverage of Olympic Games affected by, 370
Native Americans
  cooperative relationships and, 90-91
  participation of, in sports, 256-260
  ritual and ceremony in sports and games of, 256
  sports and, distorted views of, 62-63
NCAA; *see* National Collegiate Athletic Association
Neo-Nazi organizations, spectator violence and, 184
"New Games" movement, 92, 459
New Life in Sports, 440
Newborn, play activities of, 112-113
Newspapers
  coverage of women's sports in, 217, 346
  dependence of, on sports, 336-337
  sports coverage in, 5, 336, 344

Nickname
  sports, bigotry associated with, 258-260
  team, trivialization of women's sports and, 214
Nike, globalization of sports and, 307
Nitroglycerine, athlete's use of, 150
Normalcy, definition of, cultural ideology and, 92
North American Society for the Sociology of Sport, 10
Nutritionist, sports, 456

O

Officials, competence of, spectator violence and, 182, 185
Officiating, career opportunities in, 284
Older adult, sports participation and, 71-72
Olympic Games
  amateurism in, racial considerations of, 269
  in ancient Greece, 55
  apartheid and, 377
  boycott of, 370, 375
  commercialization of, 308
  drug testing at, 154-155
  founding of, 360, 368
  future of, 384
  gender inequity in, 215, 216*t*
  income level of athletes at, 277
  political power and, 53-54
  reform of, 372-375
  sites of, politics and, 381-382
  television and, 339, 340-341
Olympic Solidarity Program, 379
Ombudsperson, intercollegiate athlete and, 414
Overconformity
  deviance in sports caused by, 136, 139, 142
  drug use by athlete's and, 151, 58
Overtime, sudden-death, television contracts and use of, 334
Overtraining, deviance in sports associated with, 140
Owens, Jesse, 366
Owner; *see* Team owner

P

Pain
  acceptance of, 46, 141, 168
  drugs for control of, 158

Pain—cont'd
  overconformity to sport ethic and, 142
Pan American Games, drug testing at, 155
PAO; *see* Pro Athletes Outreach
Parent
  behavior of, at organized youth sport events, 129
  coach as, role conflicts and, 199-200
  expectations of, organized youth sports and, 114-116
  involvement of, in child's play, 124
  relationship of child with, organized sports and, 116
Parks, development of, in United States, 69
Participant, orientation of, definition of sport and, 16-21
Partnership model, aggression in sports and, 168-169
Patriotism, 72, 371
Pay-per-view, sports and, 339, 456
Peace, international sports for promotion of, 368-372
Pep club, support for, 411
Perception, psychology and focus on, 3
Perfection, drive for, in athlete, 141
Performance theory, sport and, 36, 43
Personal growth, participation in sports and, 30
PGA; *see* Professional Golf Association
Philosophy, attitude toward sports and, 65
Physical ability, change in sport and, 36
Physical conditioning, emphasis on, in Christian organizations, 429
Physical education
  coaching compared to, 190
  intellectual tradition in, 9-10
  opportunities in, for African Americans, 291
  Pleasure and Participation Model of sports and, 449
Physical Education Review, 11
Play
  comparison of boys and girls regarding, 112-113
  definition of sport and, 16
  formal games and, 111

Play—cont'd
of newborn infant, 113
self-organized, organized sports
and, 120
sport distinguished from, 19
Play and Culture, 11
Play spirit, definition of sport and, 16
Players' associations, 314-315, 319
Playgrounds, development of, in
United States, 69
Pleasure and Participation Model
future of, 449-451
sports described with, 446-447
Point spread, media coverage of
sports and, 350
Poise, emphasis on, in "grace and
beauty" sports, 70
Political loyalty, commercial sports
and development of, 304
Politics
attitude toward sports and, 65
change in, sports and, 377-378
equity for women in sports and,
222
future of professional sports and,
451
international, Olympic Games and,
368-370
sports and, 6, 358-385
Power
amateur sports organizations and,
317
deviance in sports and, 138
economic, future of sports related
to, 456
focus on, by social constructionists,
425
games and sports organized to
promote, 276
growth of commercial sport and,
304
growth of competitive sports and,
68-69
inequality and lack of, 88
loss of, alienation caused by, 428
between men and women, sports
and, 38
Power and Performance Model,
445-449
PRCA; *see* Professional Rodeo
Cowboys Association
President's Commission on Olympic
Sports, 326
Privacy
athlete's, sportswriters and, 352

Privacy—cont'd
lack of, for student athletes, 414
Private leagues, formation of, 129-130
Pro Athletes for Christ, 440
Pro Athletes Outreach, 431, 440
Problem solving, play activities and,
113
Production, sports participation and,
70
Productivity
competitive games associated with,
92
reward structures and, 81
Professional Golf Association
legal status of athlete and, 320
race and, 248
Professional Rodeo Cowboys
Association, 320
Professional Skiers Fellowship, 440
Professionalization, of sport, 65
Profit
emphasis on, in professional sports,
72
media need for, 331
television network, intercollegiate
sports and, 413
Project TEAMWORK, 270, 377-378
The Promise Keepers, 430
Promoter, role of, in commercial
sports, 311-317
Proposition 48, National Collegiate
Athletic Association and,
403-404
Protestant church, sports sponsored
by, 429
Protestant Ethic, sports and, 428, 442
Psychologist, sports, 456
Public funds, athletic facilities
supported with, 315-316
Public order, safeguarding of, sports
and, 359-360
Public service, state-controlled media
and provision of, 331

Q

Quest, 11
Quotas, racial, in sports, 292

R

Race
athletic scholarships and, 296-298
change in sport and, 36
culture and, 240-242
endorsement opportunities affected
by, 324

Race—cont'd
ideology of
change in, 269-271
sports and, 242-255
importance of, in sports, 239-273
media coverage of sports and,
347-348, 356
negative ideas about, 266
problems in intercollegiate sports
related to, 416-417
social inequality and, 55
violence in sports and, 176
Race logic
acceptance of, in society, 253
coaching and administrative jobs
and, 255
gender and, 248-249
Race relations
changes in, sports and, 264
transformation of, 458
Racial desegregation; *see*
Desegregation, racial
Racial stacking, team sports and,
249-255
Rape
attitudes about gender and, 178
participation in physical sports
associated with, 147
Recognition, participation in high
school sports and, 390
Record setting, emphasis on, in
professional sports, 72
Recordkeeping
competitive sports characterized
by, 67
importance of, in organized sports,
73
Recreation activities, development of,
in United States, 69
Recruitment, religion's use of sports
for, 430
Reebok, globalization of sports and,
307
Referee
formal games controlled by, 109
spectator violence and, 182
Religion
attitude toward sports and, 65
conflict theory and, 34
as cultural practice, 425-426
gender inequity in international
sports and, 216
Judeo-Christian, rituals of, 433
Native American games and, 62-63
sport and, 6-7, 420-443

Religion—cont'd
  sport as form of, 423-424
  sport differentiated from, 424-425
Research Quarterly for Exercise and Sport, 11
Reserve system, professional sports and, 318
Responsibility
Retirement
  career transition programs for, 299
  from professional sports, 299-300
Revenue
  distribution of, politics and, 382-383
  maximization of, in commercial sports, 311
  from media contracts, sharing of, 414
Right to privacy, drug testing and, 156
Risk
  acceptance of, by athletes, 141
  assumption of, sports participation and, 135
  Power and Performance Model of sports and emphasis on, 446
  sport ethic and, 143
Ritual
  religion defined by use of, 421
  sports and, 423, 435
Rodeo, 256, 322
Role conflict, coaching and, 198-201
Role model
  athlete as, 95
  coach as, 202-204
Role strain, coaching and, 194-196
Rome, ancient
  drug use in, 150
  games and contests in, 67t
  sport in, 57-58, 74
Rowan, Chad, 382-383
Rowing, 403
Royal Commission on the Status of Women, 210
Rugby
  Australian, racial stacking in, 252-253, 254
  intimidation and violence in, 172
Running, distance, self-injurious overtraining and, 140

S

Sabbath, game playing on, 60
Sacrifice
  Christian athlete and, 437

Sacrifice—cont'd
  emphasis on, in Protestant Ethic, 428
  sport ethic and, 141, 143
Safety
  physical, participation in sports by women and girls and, 224
  promotion of, 236
SAT; *see* Scholastic Aptitude Test
Schedules, sports, gender inequity in provision of, 217
Scholar-athlete, 60
Scholarship
  athletic, 296-298, 414-415
  black athlete and, 416
  gender inequity in awarding of, 415
  gender inequity in provision of, 217
  racial patterns in distribution of, 264
  for women, background on fathers' occupations and, 298t
Scholastic Aptitude Test
  intercollegiate athletes and, 401
  Proposition 48 and, 403
School; *see also* High school
School-community relations, varsity sports and, 409
School spirit, varsity sports and, 405-406
Science, attitude toward sports and, 65
Scores, media coverage of sports and emphasis on, 332, 343
Segregation, sports and, in early twentieth century, 73
Self-confidence
  competitive sports associated with, 94
  psychology and focus on, 3
Self-discovery, reward structures to increase, 81
Self-esteem
  participation in high school sports and, 389
  psychology and focus on, 3
Self-respect, sports associated with, 149
Sexism
  high school football and, 392
  sport and, conflict theory and, 34
Sexual assault, participation in physical sports associated with, 147

Sexual orientation
  change in sport and, 36
  conflict theory and, 34
  sports participation and, 227
Shinto, sports and, 427
Skiing, 256, 284, 320
Soccer
  aggressive fan behavior and, 164
  athletic scholarships for, 298
  British, racial stacking in, 252, 254
  future of, 451
Soccer league, commercial, failure of, 312
Soccer players, drug use by, 150
Social construction 41, 42-43, 425-426
Social contact, desegregation related to, 265-266
Social control, religious beliefs and rituals for, 436-437
Social institutions, sport connected to, 5-7
Social mobility, class relations and, 274-301
Social relations
  focus on, by social constructionists, 425
  sport and, 7-8
Social theory, use of, 25-51
Socialism, reward structures in sports and, 88-89
Socialization
  participation in sports and, 29
  sociology and focus on, 3
Society
  aggression in, 162-188
  defense of, participation in sport and, 30
  deviance in sports related to, 139
  inequality in, sport and, 55
  participation in sports and, 29
  sports as cause of aggression in, 170-179
  theories about, 27-31
Sociology, 11
Sociology of Education, 11
Sociology of Sport Journal, 10,11
Sociology Review, 11
Softball, 256, 271t
South Africa, boycott of Olympic Games and, 377
South Africa National Olympic Committee, 380
Special Olympics, 451
  controlled competition in, 86-87

Special Olympics—cont'd
cooperative and individualized
reward structures emphasized
in, 84
Spectators
aggression among, 179-186
aggressive behavior of, 164, 172
behavior of, at organized youth
sport events, 129
media coverage and, 305
success ideology and, 304
violent behavior of
control of, 184-186
social, economic, and political
issues and, 185-186
Speedball (drug), athlete's use of, 150
Sport
adults as organizers of, 276
aesthetic orientation of, 310
age and, 71-72
aggression in society caused by,
170-179
aggressive behavior controlled with,
167-170
alternative, 41-42, 450-451
amateur
administration and control of,
328
commercialization of, 316-317
in ancient Greece, 55-56
in ancient Rome, 57-58
asceticism of, 437
attendance at
income level and, 277
media coverage and, 350
bigotry in, 266-267
change in
approaches to, 457-458
commercialization and, 307-311
character development and, 65,
69-70, 95, 97-98
Christian organizations and,
428-437
class relations and, 275-281
commercial
characteristics of, 327-329
class relations and, 303-304
emergence and growth of,
303-307
globalization of, 305-307
government regulation of, 359
investment in, 312, 328
legal status of athlete in, 317-327
commercialism of, conflict theory
and, 33

Sport—cont'd
commercialization of, media and,
333-342
competition in, 77-103
reward structures and, 81-93
competitive
characteristics of, 66-67
growth of, 68-74
power and wealth associated
with, 88
conflict theory and, 31-35
contact
aggressive behavior and, 165
violent behavior and, 172-176
corruption of, sport ethic and, 143
creation of spectator interest in,
304-305
as cultural export, 377
cultural ideology and, 7
as cultural practice, 425-426
as cure for aggression, 163-170
as cure for deviant behavior,
148-149
decline of, in low-income area high
schools, 280-281
dependence of
on media, 333-336
on television, 334
dependence of media on, 336-341
dependence of television on,
337-339
description of, 12-21
desegregation of, 262-266
deviance in, 134-161
control of, 139, 143-144
overconformity as cause of, 136
problems in studying, 135-136
research on, 144-150
diplomacy and, 375
drug testing in, 154-157
drug use in, control of, 157-159
economic inequality and, 277
economy and, 6, 302-329
education and, 5-6
emergence of, during Industrial
Revolution, 61-74
ethic of; see Sport ethic
ethnicity and, 239-273
facilities for, government funding
for, 359
family and, 5
feminism and, 37-39
as form of religion, 423-424
frustration relieved through, 166
functionalist theory and, 29-31

Sport—cont'd
future of, 444-460
gambling on, media coverage and,
350
gender inequity in, 214-219
gender issues in, 208-238
gender logic of, 225-231
globalization of, 378-379
government and, 359-368
government involvement in,
promotion of political ideology
by, 365-366
heroic orientation of, 310
high performance, self-injurious
overtraining and, 140
high school, 386-419
future of, 454-455
ideology of, 391-393
historical comparison of, 67t
history of, 52-76
identity in, symbolic interactionism
and, 43-47
ideological changes in, gender
equity and, 236
immorality of, 64
impact of, on international
relations, 375-378
intercollegiate, 386-419
black coaches in, 255
changes in, 402-404
cost-containment of, 414
creation and marketing of, 72-74
desegregation of, 263-264
entertainment-oriented, 394-395
future of, 454-455
gender inequities in, 415-416
high profile programs in, 397
low profile programs in, 397
problems in, 73, 413-417
problems related to race in,
416-417
student experiences and, 394-405
intergroup relations and, 266-271
international
gender inequity in, 215
politics and, 6, 368-378
international relations and, 371t
interscholastic, arguments for and
against, 387
meaning in, symbolic
interactionism and, 43-47
media and, 330-357
media as corrupting influence on,
336
media construction of, 342-344

Sport—cont'd
  media coverage of, race and, 347-348
  in Middle Ages, 58-60
  militarism and, 33
  minority groups in, 268
  models of, for 21st Century, 445-451
  national loyalty and, 65
  nationalism and, 33
  need for changes in rules of, to promote gender equity, 236
  noncontact
    aggressive behavior and, 172
    behavior of spectators of, 180
  opportunities afforded by, 281-294
  opportunities for girls and women in, 209
  organization of
    effect of commercialization on, 311
    gender equity and, 234-235
    racial desegration and, 262-263
  organized
    for children, 104-133
    dropouts from, 121-124
    functionalist approach to, 129
    need for change in, 126-132
    society affected by, 9
  participation in
    African Americans and, 255-256
    character development and, 29
    class relations and, 277-281
    class relations and career success and, 295-296
    eligibility concerns and, 380-381
    fees for, 407
    high-income groups and, 277
    higher rates of, 452
    of married men and women, 279
    media coverage and, 349-350
    occupation patterns following, 294-300
    respect gained from, 280
    special meaning for, 434-436
    work-related consequences of, 361
  participation of minority groups in, 255-262
  perceived opportunities and skills in, 264
  performance-enhancing drugs used in, 150-159
  performance theory and, 43
  play distinguished from, 19

Sport—cont'd
  political support generated by, 366-368
  politics and, 6, 358-385
  popularity in high school and, 390-391
  as preparation for life, 98-102
  professional
    black coaches in, 255
    creation and marketing of, 72-74
    desegregation of, 263-264
    future of, 451-454
    globalization of, 451
    income levels of, 320-323
    legal status of athletes in, 318-320
    in North America, 311-316
    racial and ethnic diversity programs in, 271
    retirement from, 298-300
  professionalization of, 65
  promotion of sense of indentity and unity through, 362-365
  promotion of violence in, 181-182
  Protestant Ethic and, 428
  psychology of, sociology differentiated from, 3-4
  public order and, 359-360
  as quasi-religion, 422-423
  race and, 239-273
  race logic in, 248
  racial ideology and, 242-255
  racial segregation in, in early twentieth century, 73
  racism in, 34
  religion and, 6-7, 420-443
    consequences of, 437-441
  religion differentiated from, 424-425
  ritual in, social life and, 43, 435
  rule changes in, commercialization as cause of, 308
  sexism in, 34
  social construction and, 41
  social contacts in, 267
  social institutions and, 5-7
  social organization of, 9
  sociology of
    controversies in, 4-5
    current status of, 9-10
    disagreements within, 10-12
    human body and, 8
    professional organizations for, 10
    publication sources for, 11
    theories about, 27-35

Sport—cont'd
  spectator
    creation and marketing of, 72-74
    future of, 455-456
  spectators of, violent behavior among, 179-186
  stacking patterns in, 249-255
  team
    abolition of, reform of Olympic Games and, 374
    income levels of, 320-322
    player positions and race logic in, 250
  use of religion by, 432-433
  use of technology in, 448-449
  variation in, over time and place, 54-55
  varsity
    benefits to schools of, 405-409
    educational value of, 417-418
  women's
    media coverage of, 345-347
    trivialization of, 213-214
  world peace and, 368
  world politics and, 377
Sport activities, description of, 13-14
Sport camps, high school athletes and, 410
Sport Canada, public good and, 360
Sport ethic
  deviance in sports and, 140-144
  drug use in sports and, 158
  overconformity to, 142
    drug use and, 151
  Power and Performance Model of sports and, 445
Sport medicine, career opportunities in, 284
Sport ministry
  examples of, 431
  organizations having, 440
Sport Sociology Academy, 10
Sportmail, 315
Sports Ambassadors, 440
Sports America, 375-376
Sports Association for Jesus, 440
Sports Channel America, 339
Sports Corps, 372
Sports Council, sports provided by, 360
Sports events, policing of, 360
Sports medicine, opportunities for women in, 285
Sports Outreach America, 440

Sportsmanship, competitive success and, 82-83
Stacking patterns, race logic and, 249-255
Stadium
    description of, as cultural center for men, 227
    exclusive-use contracts of professional sports teams and, 313
    growth of commercial sports and, 303
    as quasi-religious facility, 423
Standardization, competitive reward structure and, 81
State of balance, sport and, 27
Statistics
    importance of, in organized sports, 73
    media coverage of sports and emphasis on, 343
Status quo, challenges to, 12
Stereotype, sports nicknames and mascots and, 258
Steroid drugs, 150, 151, 153, 155
Stimulus cue, aggression behavior related to, 171
Strategy, sports organized by adults characterized by, 276
Street ball, rules in, 118-119
Strength
    as complex physical skill, 14
    physical
        development of, in women, 211
        gender in sports and, 38
        participation in sports by women and girls and, 224
    Power and Performance Model of sports and emphasis on, 446
Stress management, role conflicts controlled with, 201
Strychnine, athlete's use of, 150
Student culture, high school and, 390-393
Student fees, intercollegiate sports funded with, 407
Success phobia, 92
Suicide, aggressive instincts and, 165
Sumo wrestling, 383
Super Bowl, televised coverage of, 339
Superiority complex, athletes and, 143
Superstition, uncertainty and, 434

Supreme Court; see United States Supreme Court
Survival skills, participation in sports and, 30
Swimming
    athletic scholarships for, 298
    behavior of spectators of, 180
    desegregation of, 266
    intercollegiate, athletes goals in, 403
    lack of black athletes in, 256
    opportunities for participation in, for women, 214
    percentage of collegiate women coaches in, 217t
    scholarships for, economic need and, 264
Symbolic interactionism, 43-47
    sport explained through, 43-47
Systems model, sport explained with, 27

T

T/E ratio, drug testing and, 155, 156
Tae Kwon Do
    juvenile delinquency and, 170
    philosophy of life in, 148-149
Taketak, description of, 90
Taoism, sports and, 427
Teacher
    coach compared to, 195
    high school sports and, 393
    of Native American children, attempts to change cultural ideology by, 90
Teacher-coach, role conflicts and, 199
Team Jesus-Cycle Crusade, 440
Team management, role conflicts controlled with, 201
Team owner
    public assistance for, 315-316
    role of, in commercial sports, 311-317
    sports leagues monopoly status and, 312-315
Teamwork
    media coverage of sports and, 348
    media coverage of sports and emphasis on, 332, 356
    sports participation and, 70
TEAMWORK South Africa, 378
Technology
    attitude toward sports and, 65
    use of, in sports, 448-449
Technosport, 448-449

Television
    blackouts by, sports attendance and, 350
    broadcasting rights to, commercial sports and, 303
    commercialization of intercollegiate sports and, 413
    coverage of baseball on, 338
    coverage of Olympic Games by, politics and, 370
    coverage of women's sports by, 211, 217
    dependence of, on sports, 337-339
    economics of sport and, 6
    effects of watching sports on, 181
    emphasis on success in sports coverage by, 345
    growth of professional golf and, 304
    income level and viewing of, 277
    media interpretation of sports events on, 332
    Olympic Games and, 339, 340-341
    problems in intercollegiate sports related to, 413
    revenue from, for sports, 333, 334
    spectator interest and, 305
    sports coverage in, 5
    sports dependence on, 334
    World Football League and, 313
Tennis
    athletic scholarships for, 298
    behavior of spectators of, 180
    bigotry in, 248
    desegregation of, 266
    lack of black athletes in, 256, 287
    legal status of professional athlete in, 319-320
    opportunities for women in, 214, 284
    percentage of collegiate women coaches in, 217t
    percentage of professional athletes in, by race and ethnicity, 283t
    professional, salary levels in, 322
    rule changes in, commercialization as cause of, 308
    scholarships for, economic need and, 264
    television broadcasts of, 277, 338
Tennis league, commercial, failure of, 312
Tennis Ministry, 440
Testosterone
    athlete's use of, 151, 153

Testosterone—cont'd
testing for, 155, 156
The British Journal of Sport History, 11
Theory, Culture, and Society, 11
Therapist, sports, 456
Thinness, emphasis on, in women's
fitness movement, 213
Time management, role conflicts
controlled with, 201
Title IX
fairness and, 360
gender inequity in college sports
and, 217-218
girls in organized sports and, 105
opportunities for women in sports
and, 210
women's equality in sports and,
150
"Tomboys," definition of masculinity
and, 227-231
Total release performance,
description of, 436-437
Toughness, emphasis on competitive
sports for improvement of, 93
Track and field
behavior of spectators of, 180
intercollegiate, athletes goals in,
403
opportunities for women in, 284
percentage of collegiate women
coaches in, 217*t*
professional, opportunities for black
athletes in, 287
success of African Americans in,
247
Training
athletic, career opportunities in,
284
as form of addiction, 140
gender inequity in provision of,
217
opportunities for women in, 285
sponsors for professional athletes
in, 320
sports, gender inequity in provision
of, 217
Triathlete, self-injurious overtraining
and, 140
TROPS, 92, 459

U

Umpires, spectator violence and, 182
Uniform, abolition of, reform of
Olympic Games and, 373

Unions; *see* Labor unions
United States Football League, 313
United States Information Agency,
375
United States Olympic Committee,
316, 317
amateur sport controlled by, 325
charter of, 362
drug testing and, 155
Unites States, growth of competitive
sports in, 68-74
Unity
group, religion and, 422
international sports and, 368
University; *see* College
Urine sample, drug testing and, 156
USA Today, sports coverage in, 337
USFL; *see* United States Football
League
USOC; *see* United States Olympic
Committee
Uterus, damage to, women's sports
participation and, 231

V

Values
functionalist theory and, 29, 47
state-controlled media and shaping,
331
Vandalism, sports for control of, 360
Violence
alternative definition of masculinity
and, 232
in contact sports, 165, 172-174
crowd dynamics and, 181-183
domestic, aggression in contact
sports and, 165
in ice hockey, 171
media coverage of sports and
emphasis on, 356
need for rules changes to eliminate,
236
promotion of, in sports, 181-182
spectator, 181
sport ethic and, 143
victimization of athletes as cause of,
138
Vision-impaired athlete, opportunities
for, 291
Volleyball
athletic scholarships for, 298
intercollegiate
athletes goals in, 403
racial stacking in, 250

Volleyball—cont'd
men's, lack of black athletes in, 256
opportunities for women in, 285
percentage of collegiate women
coaches in, 217*t*
racial stacking patterns in, 253
scholarships for, economic need
and, 264
Volleyball league, commercial, failure
of, 312
Vomiting, women's use of, in
conjunction with training, 213

W

Walking, Pleasure and Participation
Model of sports and, 449
Warfare
aggression in contact sports and,
165
language of, sports media's use of,
348
religion and, 422
Wealth
competitive reward structures
related to, 84
growth of commercial sport and,
304
growth of competitive sports and,
68-69
inequality and lack of, 88
social inequality and, 55
Weight, control of, emphasis on, 213
Weight control, self-injurious
overtraining and, 140
Weight lifting, Pleasure and
Participation Model of sports
and, 449
Well-being, psychological,
participation in sports by
women and girls and, 224
Wheelchair athlete, opportunities for,
291
Wilderness area, future demand for,
452
Winning
coaching and, 190
desegregation in sports and,
263-264
deviance in sports associated with,
135
emphasis on
in high school sports, 409, 410
in professional sports, 72
in sports in United States, 82-83

Winning—cont'd
in informal and formal games, 128
as moral virtue, 441
organized sports emphasis on, 121
Power and Performance Model of
sports and emphasis on, 446
Women
African American, opportunities
for sports careers for, 287
aggressive instincts of, 165
athletic scholarships for, 298
black, lack of sports participation
of, 256
as bodybuilders, 228-230
career opportunities in sports for,
281
character development of,
competitive sports and, 96-97
as coaches, personality traits of,
191
degradation of, gender order of
sports and, 147
discrimination against, in ancient
Greece, 56
equality in coaching for, 288-289
exclusion of, from ancient Greek
games, 55-56
focus on, by social constructionists,
425
intercollegiate sports for, low
profile of, 394
married, sports participation of,
279

Women—cont'd
media coverage of sports for,
345-347
myths about physiology of, 226
"natural inferiority" of, to men,
225
opportunities in sports careers for,
284-287
participation in Olympic marathon
and, 380
participation in organized sports of,
70-71
participation in sports and personal
empowerment of, 223
participation patterns of, in sports,
209-214
partnership model used by, 169
recruitment of, into coaching, 205
sexual harassment of, by coaches,
147
sports programs for, Title IX and,
150
trivialization of sports for, 213-214
underrepresentation of, in coaching
and administration, 218-219
values of, sports and, 450
violence in sports and, 178
Women in Sport: A Sport Canada Policy,
210
Women's movement
equity in sports and, 210
girls in organized sports and, 105
Women's Sports Foundation, 218

Worker's Sports Movement, 366
World Cup, 362
future of, 451
global expansion of soccer and, 306
World Federation of Sports Medicine,
152
World Football League, 313
World League of American Football,
313
Worship, sports participation as, 435
Wrestling
intercollegiate, athletes goals in,
403
rule changes in, commercialization
as cause of, 309

Y

YMCA
growth of, 429
history of basketball and, 17-18
Yokozuma Promotion Council, 382
Youth & Society, 11
Youth, sports programs for
future of, 455
spectator interest in, 304-305
YWCA, growth of, 429

Z

Zen Buddhism, sports and, 427
Zeus, ancient Olympic Games and,
55
Zuni Indians, cooperative reward
structures and, 90